MARCEL DUCHAMP AND THE ART OF LIFE

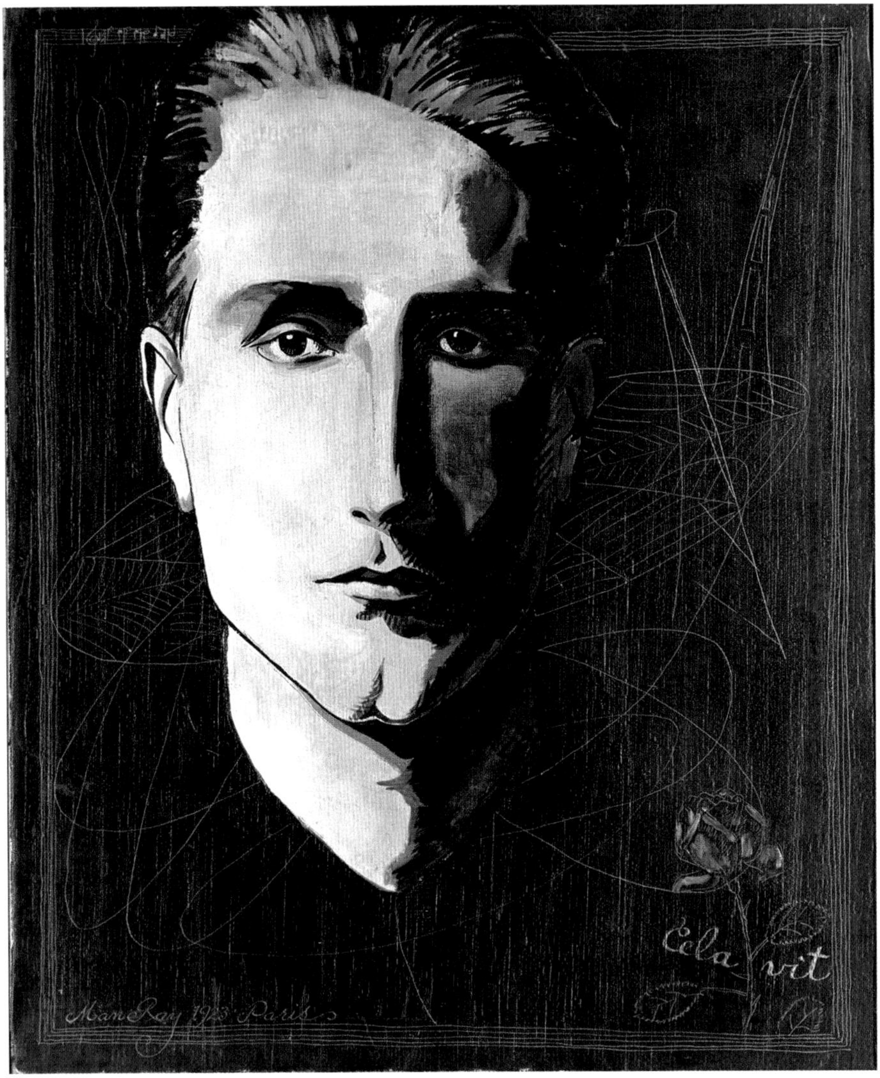

Man Ray
Marcel Duchamp (painting *Rose Cela Vit*), 1923

MARCEL DUCHAMP AND THE ART OF LIFE

JACQUELYNN BAAS

THE MIT PRESS

CAMBRIDGE, MASSACHUSETTS
LONDON, ENGLAND

This book was set in Arnhem Pro by The MIT Press. Printed and bound in The United States of America.

Library of Congress Cataloging-in-Publication Data

Names: Baas, Jacquelynn, 1948- author.
Title: Marcel Duchamp and the art of life / Jacquelynn Baas.
Description: Cambridge, MA : The MIT Press, [2019] | Includes bibliographical references and index.
Identifiers: LCCN 2018054267 | ISBN 9780262042741 (hardcover : alk. paper)
Subjects: LCSH: Duchamp, Marcel, 1887-1968--Criticism and interpretation. | Duchamp, Marcel, 1887-1968--Knowledge--Mysticism. | Mysticism and art. | Mysticism.
Classification: LCC N6853.D8 B33 2019 | DDC 709.2--dc23 LC record available at https://lccn.loc.gov/2018054267

10 9 8 7 6 5 4 3 2 1

TAO CALLED TAO IS NOT TAO.

—Lao Tzu

GOD IS IN THE VAGINA!

—Ramakrishna

I AM MY OWN READYMADE.

—Marcel Duchamp

CONTENTS

PREFACE AND ACKNOWLEDGMENTS

This book belongs to a tradition of speculative scholarship within Marcel Duchamp studies that brings an array of data to bear on a single aspect of this complex artist. *Marcel Duchamp and the Art of Life* applies information about tantric yoga and other Asian perspectives to the interpretation of work by an artist who consistently refused to align himself with any particular set of beliefs. An example from another realm—Linda Dalrymple Henderson's *Duchamp in Context: Science and Technology in the Large Glass*—deals with science, a topic more easily comprehended by the materialistic Western mind. Duchamp's own attitude toward science was recorded by the author Denis de Rougemont, who in his journal entry for August 8, 1945 wrote: "New atomic bomb, day before yesterday on Hiroshima. ... Duchamp consented to interrupt himself in a chess problem to note that the bomb confirmed his point of view that science is only a mythology, its laws and its material itself are pure myths, and have neither more nor less reality than the conventions of any game."[1]

Duchamp was not a tantrist any more than he was a scientist; he was an artist, and artists are notorious plunderers in the service of their art. I hope to demonstrate how a fuller knowledge of the culture in which Duchamp developed can enrich interpretations of his work. Like Henderson, I frequently resort to the subjunctive as I speculate about correlations between Asian philosophies and practices, and Duchamp's thinking and art practices. What may or may not be deduced from comparisons and parallels? In the absence of documents or direct statements, parallels and correlations (similarities and mutual connections between two or more things) may be called into service as evidence. Correlation is coincidence if there is no relationship. Patterns, however, suggest something more. As statistician Edward Tufte observed, "Correlation is not causation but it sure is a hint."[2] Repeated parallels and correlations between Duchamp's artworks and statements with elements of Asian philosophies and practices may not *prove* his work was informed by Asian perspectives, but their sheer quantity constitutes a pattern—cumulative evidence that would seem conclusively to rule out mere coincidence.

As with most things associated with sexuality, tantra in the West has been considered *occult*, "hidden" knowledge, and thus suspect. According to historian of Western esotericism Wouter J. Hanegraaff, "topics associated with 'the occult' have tended to be perceived by most academics as a 'no go area' unworthy of serious study. ... This has resulted in a very serious lack of expertise among academics about what are in fact large and important dimensions of the Western heritage."[3] In art history as in other academic disciplines, explanations that conflict with academic biases, disciplinary insecurities, or scholars' preconceptions tend to be met with repression and denial. Nevertheless, complex cultural developments call for explanations. This book offers readers interested in the relationship between Asian thought and modern art a point of access. The approach taken here is intended to generate new insight into the life and work of modernism's central figure, Marcel Duchamp, as well as members of his circle.

While I have practiced a variety of mind-training techniques myself, I am agnostic regarding the various "-isms" that crop up in this book.[4] Surely this was also the case with Duchamp, who researched the natural history of consciousness *as an artist*. He was not alone in these explorations, as we shall see, but the fact that seemingly clear connections and parallels with Asian perspectives have been largely overlooked attests both to the persistence of the rational, materialistic attitude toward the life of the mind, and to Duchamp's own belief that "the true artist, true art, is always esoteric, [while] the modern approach to art is based on competition, on making art exoteric."[5] Secretive he may have been, but Duchamp's life demonstrates his passionate and very human commitment to art as exploration of reality.

Duchamp and the Art of Life is not a critique, comparison, or survey of research on Duchamp.[6] It presents a set of historical facts, and speculations derived from those facts, intended to complement the work of my predecessors. That doesn't mean this book is not based on scholarship; it just means that I don't dutifully recap and assess previous studies before offering my own observations, and that I try to present this difficult artist in language relevant to art as it is actually practiced and life as it might be lived.

For Marcel Duchamp, art-making was part of an esoteric continuum grounded in eros, a process of making available to the initiated viewer an attitude toward creativity not talked about and unmarketable, but which he believed constitutes "the basis of everything."[7] By focusing on the Asian philosophical strands in Duchamp's art, I risk losing sight of its complexity. But understanding Duchamp requires not so much knowledge as a certain attitude of mind. His art asks us to unlearn what we think we know, both about art and about life, in order to be open to experience. I hope this book will make his remarkable attitude of mind more available to his fellow artists, and to the artist of life in everyone.

••

This book is written for artists, whether students, art professionals, or art participants—Duchamp regarded all as equally creative. There are people without whom this book would not have happened. *Buddha Mind in Contemporary Art*, a book that I coedited, included a groundbreaking essay by the Taiwanese art historian Tosi Lee entitled "Fire Down Below and Watering, That's Life: A Buddhist Reader's Response to Marcel Duchamp"—a distillation of Lee's 1993 doctoral dissertation at the University of Illinois. Editing the first sparked my thinking, and reading the second nourished it, in ways I cannot begin to analyze here. I owe a great deal to Tosi Lee's research and his informed perspective. Both *Buddha Mind* and my book *Smile of the Buddha: Eastern Philosophy and Western Art from Monet to Today* emerged from a five-year consortium project, "Awake: Art, Buddhism, and the Dimensions of Consciousness," co-organized with Mary Jane Jacob, now at the School of the Art Institute of Chicago. The present book would not be what it is—in fact it would not *be*—without the stimulation provided by our partnership.

Also part of "Awake," and sources of inspiration since then, have been artists Laurie Anderson, Sanford Biggers, Kimsooja, Hirokazu Kosaka, Suzanne Lacy, Meredith Monk, and Ernesto Pujol, film producer and director

Gaetano Maida, East Bay Center for the Performing Arts Director Jordan Simmons, arts consultant Melanie Beene, art critic and author Kay Larson, and Soto Zen priest Yvonne Rand. Publications by Duchamp scholars Paul B. Franklin, Linda Dalrymple Henderson, and Michael R. Taylor have served as particularly valuable resources. Conversations with late philosopher Arthur C. Danto, art historian Moira Roth, scholar of Taoism Livia Kohn, and Bataille scholar Stuart Kendall all helped nourish my thinking. Antoine Monnier of the Association Marcel Duchamp and artist Jean-Jacques Lebel have been generous sources of critical information, while curator Geneviève Monnier has provided support in the form of friendly provocation.

I am grateful for critical readings and suggestions for improvement from art historians Joel Isaacson and Marjorie Harth, and from artist-friends Nina Zurier, Keith Wilson, and David Slee. Insight into the artistic process was generously shared by Ai Weiwei, Mari Andrews, Varujan Boghosian, Topher Delaney, Ken Friedman, Lanier Graham, Ronald Jones, Taikkun Li, Moon Kyungwon and Jeon Joonho, Dean Smith, Barbara Stauffacher Solomon, Canan Tolon, Darren Waterston, and John Zurier. Nina Zurier helped with the illustration program, which was deftly managed by Kathy Borgogno. Copy-editor Gillian Beaumont brought welcome consistency and clarity to the manuscript, while production editor Matthew Abbate managed the process of shepherding the book through the press.

These artists, editors, and scholars have, each in their own way, been my mentors in the art of life. Principal thanks, however, are due to the brilliant Victoria Nelson, who took my draft manuscript in hand and whipped both it and me into shape, and to the inimitable Roger Conover, who with characteristic insight and enthusiasm gave it life. Finally, I extend warmest thanks to my husband, Rob Elder, editor extraordinaire and my most faithful reader and critic.

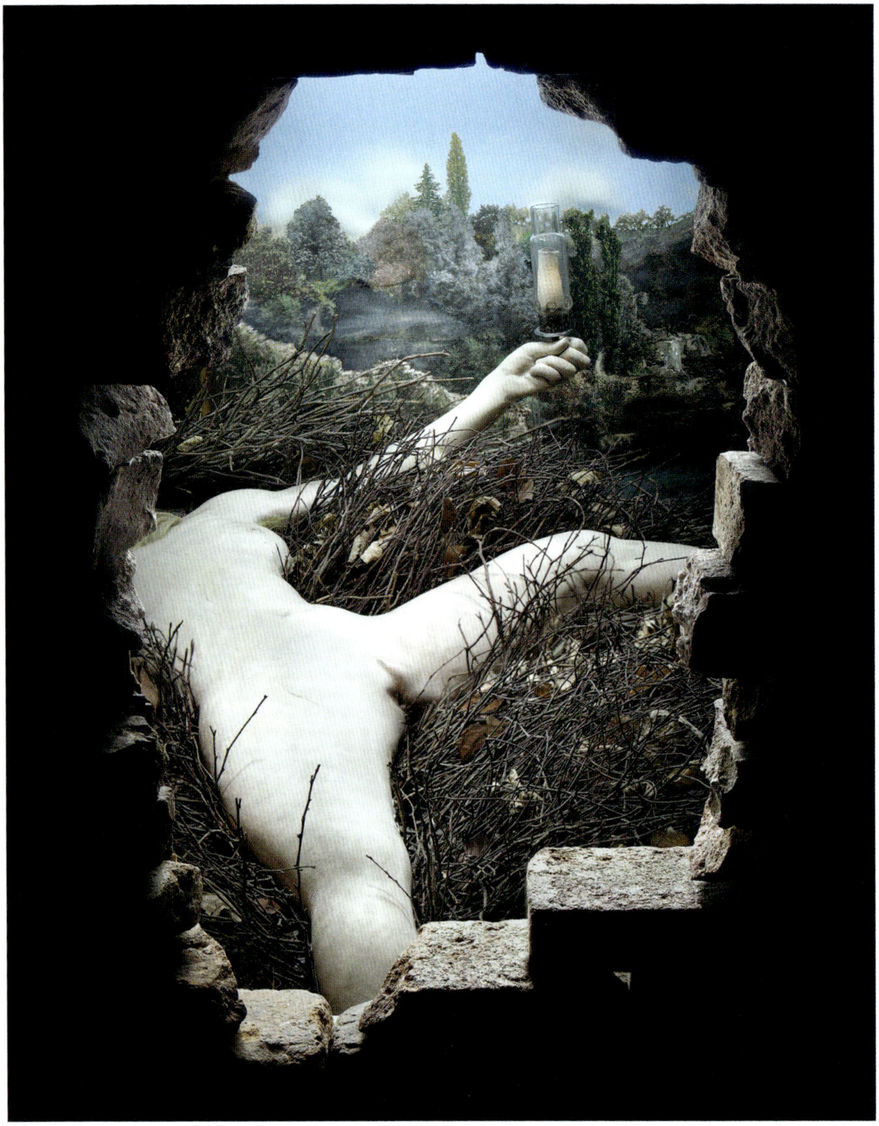

FIGURE 0.1

Marcel Duchamp
Étant donnés: 1° la chute d'eau, 2° le gaz d'éclairage … / Given: 1. The Waterfall, 2. The Illuminating Gas …, 1946–1966
Mixed media, 242.6 × 177.8 cm
Philadelphia Museum of Art, Philadelphia, PA, Gift of the Cassandra Foundation, 1969 / Bridgeman Images

INTRODUCTION
EACH BREATH IS A WORK INSCRIBED NOWHERE

The rationalists claimed to have discovered the most fundamental premises of all—basic truths which could not be denied, but which, because they were basic, could not be proved. Knowledge which satisfies that description is said to be "given."

–J. W. Dunne, 1934[1]

I. DUCHAMP AND THE ART OF BREATHING

At the age of 59, long after he was believed to have given up art for the game of chess, Marcel Duchamp began his most ambitious work. Twenty-three years later, *Étant donnés: 1° la chute d'eau, 2° le gaz d'éclairage*—in English, *Given: 1. The Waterfall, 2. The Illuminating Gas* (1946–1966, figure 0.1)—was posthumously placed on exhibition at the Philadelphia Museum of Art, where Duchamp had previously installed his *Large Glass* (1915–1923, figure 0.2) as part of the Arensberg Collection. *Given* offers its hyperreal contents to anyone curious enough to make the trek through a small, dark gallery to a rugged wooden door with two peepholes at eye level. What participants get out of this experience depends partly on how willing they are to recognize and dismiss their own preconceptions and prejudices. It also helps to know something about Duchamp and his multidimensional view of reality.

The most potentially disturbing features of *Given* are the awkward, splayed-leg pose of Duchamp's prone nude, and the strangely shaped cleft between her legs. Her head, right shoulder and arm, and most of her right leg, are cut off from view; her left leg is raised, exposing an oddly vacant vulva. In her left hand, the figure holds aloft a glowing lamp. The

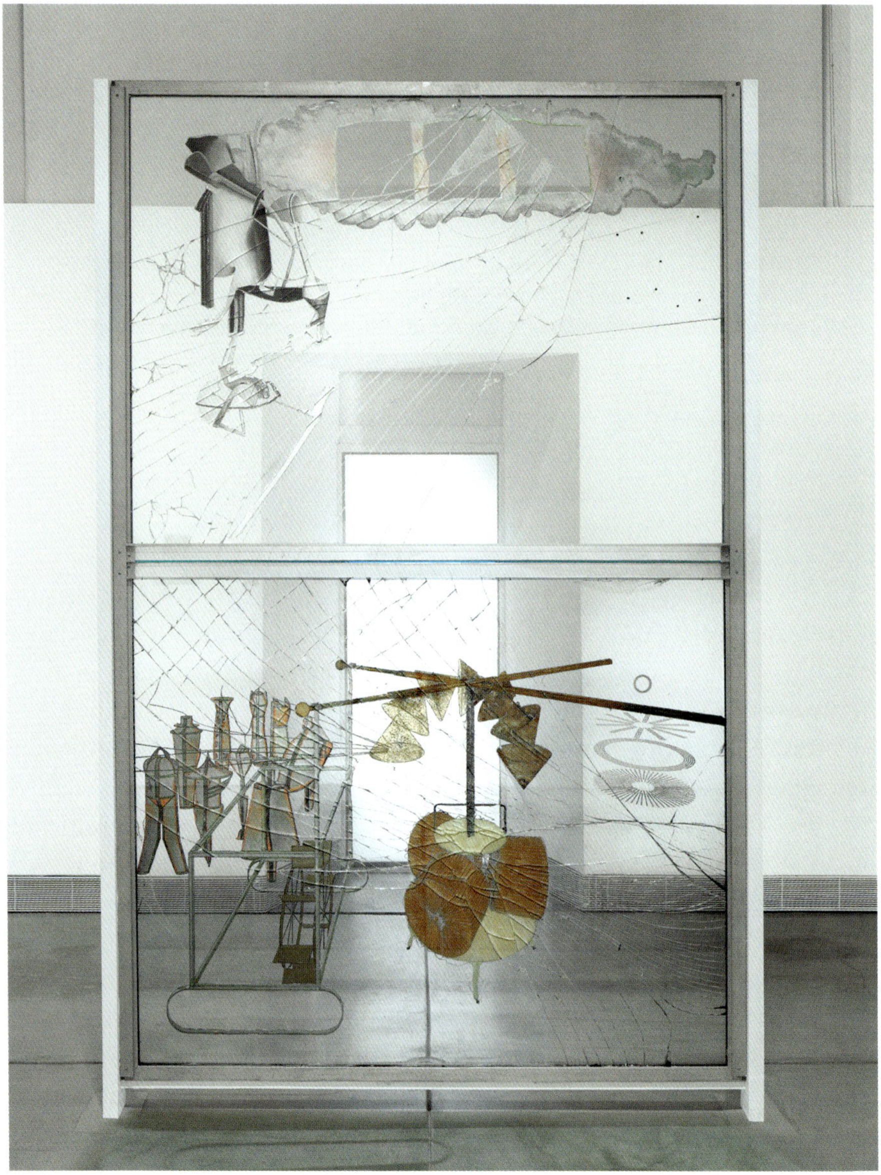

FIGURE 0.2

Marcel Duchamp
La Mariée mise à nu par ses célibataires, même / The Bride Stripped Bare by Her Bachelors, Even (The Large Glass), 1915–1923
Oil, varnish, lead foil, lead wire, and dust on two glass panels, 277.5 × 175.9 cm
Philadelphia Museum of Art, Philadelphia, PA, Bequest of Katherine S. Dreier, 1952 / Art Resource, NY

background—a kitschy version of the mountain landscape in Leonardo's *Mona Lisa*—features a misty lake and an illuminated, moving waterfall, like one of those plug-in paintings that used to be sold at five-and-dimes. An innocent blue sky with puffy white clouds completes the scene, which managed to presage both David Lynch and Thomas Kinkade.

Then and now, *Given* was compared, almost always unfavorably, with Duchamp's odd and mysterious but somehow majestic earlier work, *The Large Glass* (figure 0.2). For the art world, the shocker was not only *Given*'s sexual explicitness, but also the fact that this last major work by the father of conceptual art was so eerily realistic. Czech art historian Jindřich Chalupecký perhaps put it best when he wrote: "the visual resources of *Given* have been reduced to a simplicity that borders on banality, and the viewer can accept the work in a different way only by reading its symbolic meaning, which … is addressed to the spectator with unsuspected force." And: "this work manages to escape entirely from the context of art; even in the middle of modern art, which has so many aspects and facets, it remains entirely unique and alone. It has turned so far away from our civilization that it has turned away even from what that civilization calls art, or even anti-art."[2] *Given* might be a message from another planet; in a way, it is.

Marcel Duchamp's friends testified to his mysterious power. Musician and writer Gabrielle Buffet-Picabia described his "occult prescience of men and things," which "gave him an extraordinary influence on all the innovating artists of his generation." Duchamp's writer-friend Henri-Pierre Roché described him as "a young prophet who wrote scarcely a line, but whose words would be repeated from mouth to mouth and from whose daily life anecdotes and miracles would be construed." Artist and writer Georges Ribemont-Dessaignes concurred, affirming that the young Marcel Duchamp enabled him "to achieve complete liberation." Dadaist turned Surrealist André Breton called him "truly indefinable." Duchamp's friend and biographer Robert Lebel recalled that in the years after he first met Duchamp, in 1936, "his clarity of mind, his composure, his frugality, his supreme manner of mastering any circumstance filled me with wonder beyond words."[3]

Lebel believed that Duchamp's art emerged from a realm of metaphysical experience accessed through focused mental effort that was in no way intellectual: "Duchamp had mastered two separate realities, and he was equally at ease in both. ... Through the disturbance of all senses once recommended by Rimbaud, he reached a state of super-awareness, which raised him to the level of the great visionaries of all time. ... Behind [Duchamp's] works, another world *really* exists. ... His access to a separate reality [was accomplished] without the use of psychotropics, by an unwavering effort of will, courage, and imagination."[4] Lebel agreed with Buffet-Picabia's characterization of Duchamp's insight as "occult," while noting that not all his secrets were secret, even among his close circle of artist-friends: "We who had the privilege of approaching him often have to admit, even if it is hard for us, that people other than ourselves, unknowns uninitiated into our secret society, may have associated with and been inspired by him from afar as much as we, who were close to him. ... He accommodated with equal indifference both secrecy and the disclosure of secrecy."[5]

Despite his apparent indifference, Marcel Duchamp seemed possessed of a kind of missionary spirit when it came to art and its relationship with life. In 1945, his New York gallerists Harriet and Sidney Janis relayed what Duchamp had told them regarding his *modus operandi*: "He identifies the means of working, the creative enterprise, with life itself, considers it to be as necessary to life as breathing, synonymous with the process of living. ... Merging the impulse of procreation with that of artistic creation, there apparently accrues for Duchamp a sense of universal reality which interpenetrates the daily routine of living."[6] Duchamp's concept of the art of life thus had two aspects, according to the Janises: first, identification of the creative impulse with the erotic impulse and, second, a resulting vivid awareness of absolute reality hidden within everyday reality.

One of the things that distinguish Asian from modern Western spirituality is an understanding of eros as transformative energy capable of unveiling absolute reality—in Duchampian terms, stripping reality bare. The Indian Kaula School of tantra, for example, understands the cosmos as ongoing expression of blissful erotic activity. Kaula practice replicates this process in the human body and mind, where it produces an experience of continuum in which every moment of life is an occasion for touching the source of ecstasy that constantly generates the universe.[7] *Marcel Duchamp and the Art of Life* presents evidence that Duchamp's version of artistic realization was grounded in a Western interpretation of Asian body energetics accessed in the context of his Parisian milieu. But the intellectual Duchamp would not have stopped there. After a period of experimentation, he appears to have set out to understand his experience through personal research into both Asian philosophy and Western science, and to devise ways to communicate what he was discovering through his art.

What I shall call "tantra yoga"[8] was a Western version of Indian tantric yoga, a uniquely Asian conception of the union of (male) consciousness activated by (female) creative energy. Although there may be a physical component if two people are involved, this is a mostly mental practice designed to achieve realization of nondual reality (often accompanied by a sensation of intense light) through channeling, uniting, and transforming powerful, purposeful "male" and dynamic, creative "female" energies present in both men and women. Written descriptions of such practices are "veiled" in terms of their sexual aspects. Tantra yoga is therefore not something one studies, as one might study philosophy or science; it is, rather, an esoteric *practice* that requires initial instruction from a guru, or teacher. What the Janises described as Duchamp's merging of the impulse of procreation with that of artistic creation yielded, according to them, a sense of universal reality that interpenetrated every moment of his life, and pervaded his mysterious art.

In his *Box of 1914* Duchamp published a note suggesting just how early he may have arrived at this two-part concept. His note reads: "arrhe is to art as shitte is to shit"—a formulation that is also given as an equation.[9] Duchamp's original "arrhe / art" pairing was likely inspired by the heading "ARR ... ART" on page 64 of *Petit Larousse illustré*—favorite reading for Duchamp, as witnessed by a note in *The Green Box*: "take a Larousse dictionary and copy all the so called 'abstract' words ..."[10] The Larousse definition for the abstract word "art" reads: "Application of knowledge to the realization of a conception"—a definition Duchamp clearly took to heart.[11] "Shitte"—*merdre* in Duchamp's original French—references the emphatic "Merdre!" King Ubu proclaims to the audience at the beginning of Alfred Jarry's infamous play *Ubu Roi* (1896), revealing Ubu's "basic (baser) nature," his absolute reality.[12]

Duchamp added to his formulation a clarifying sentence that emphasizes the sexual aspect of his equation: "*grammatically*: the arrhe of painting is feminine in gender." Duchamp thus proposes "arrhe" as the irrational feminine energizer to the static, male intellectual conception, "art." His ratio generates the equation, art = shit—a classic tantric situation, as defined by historian of religions Christian Wedemeyer: "the enlightened state of nondual gnosis ... in which the deluded perception of things as having an intrinsic nature (pure or polluting, good or evil) is transcended."[13] For Duchamp, shit, like art, was something made by the artist; in terms of absolute reality, there is no difference.

Duchamp's "inexplicable attitude" toward "the *raison d'être* of the arts," wrote Gabrielle Buffet-Picabia, "sprang quite naturally from the imperatives of an imperious reason, from a logic sustained and carried through to its ultimate consequences and which at their furthest horizons could well, at some point, have encountered those of the most rigorous mysticism." One result was "the principle of the readymade." According to Buffet-Picabia, the act of selecting a readymade is "one of strict elimination. There are highly complex reasons for this extremist theory which exalts the transcendent personality and denies it a visual materialization. Above all, here we can find an ironic rationale for the masterpiece conceived from inspiration and divination, for an art which is trance-like and mysterious."[14] Buffet-Picabia observed that Duchamp created the readymade by rigorously accessing some deep form of knowledge. She drew an implicit parallel between Duchamp's disciplined approach to artistic expression and disciplined meditation practice.

Breathing—the foundation of meditation practice in every Asian tradition[15]—is the literal meaning of "inspiration," a word Buffet-Picabia deliberately paired with "divination" to account for Duchamp's trancelike process of creation. Duchamp made a similar comparison when he told an interviewer: "If you wish, my art would be that of living: each second, each breath is a work which is inscribed nowhere, which is neither visual nor cerebral. It's a sort of constant euphoria."[16] Breathing and sexual polarity are of course universal, and need not imply a specific cultural influence. But the evocative comments of Buffet-Picabia and others suggest it is worth exploring the various meditation traditions and their potential relationship with Duchamp's art of life.

Information about Duchamp's early research into various mind-body practices and the role they may have played in the development of his art is scanty. Whatever the relationship, it was not *visual* influence, as Buffet-Picabia makes clear. The search for meaning in Duchamp thus becomes a kind of game, not unlike copying "all the so called 'abstract' words" in Larousse. For the most part, what we have to go on are parallels like art = shit with tantra; and "inspiration" with both breathing, which Duchamp liked to cite as his true art form, and infusion by a power that is at once transcendent and immanent.

The course Marcel Duchamp set for himself as a young artist entailed research into alternative theories of mind involving experiential testing and intuitive analysis, which he integrated into his work. "Religiously attend to your work for yourself alone" was the last of Duchamp's "new commandments," according to his close friend Henri-Pierre Roché.[17] For the greater part of Duchamp's career, promulgation of his very personal discoveries was not of much interest to him. To the contrary: in keeping with their esoteric nature, Duchamp tended to be secretive about what he was up to. He did, however, share certain aspects of his practice with a few close friends, especially his women friends. He also carefully preserved and published many of the personal notes he made in the course of his research, and he made sure that his artworks ended up in the public domain in coherent groupings, most notably at the Philadelphia Museum of Art.

During the 1940s there was a shift. Whether due to his experiences surrounding the Second World War, including his intense love affair with the Brazilian sculptor Maria Martins, or the surrealists' interest in alternative spiritual practices, or the self-assurance that comes with maturity, Duchamp began talking more publicly about his views and practices—though still in veiled language. The best evidence we have for the trajectory of Duchamp's personal practice are his notes and the statements he made, the writings and artworks of his friends, and, most important, his own work—all considered within the context of the culture surrounding him during his long life.

Italian artist Gianfranco Baruchello was born in 1924, and first met Marcel Duchamp in 1962. Baruchello was remarkably perceptive regarding Duchamp's answer to a question about what he did first thing each morning: "He said 'I breathe.' It may be a quip, but it also opens up onto everything that's yoga in Duchamp, just as *eau et gaz* was his way of talking about *prana* [life force, cosmic energy], a whole idea of a science of the body. ... I can't help seeing that there are any number of parallels between Duchamp and certain kinds of Oriental wisdom."[18] Artists in general tend to be Duchamp's best interpreters. Considering Baruchello's remark about "Oriental wisdom," it should not be surprising that artists in this category are often Asian, and thus already culturally grounded in a worldview Duchamp had to work to achieve. Anish Kapoor, Ai Weiwei, and the Korean artist-duo Moon Kyungwon and Jeon Joonhoo are only a few of those who have found in Duchamp an artistic resource for their own worldviews. In 2013 a major exhibition in Beijing featured works by Duchamp and more than twenty contemporary Chinese artists who acknowledge his influence. Artist Huang Tong Ping was quoted in the catalogue: "Marcel Duchamp comes closer to Laozi's concept of 'hiding one's brilliance, appearing dull,' and to his contemplation and wisdom of life, than any modern Asian."[19]

An alert, aware mind without preconceptions is essential to creativity in any realm, but the process of achieving this mind-state is a programmatic teaching of Buddhism, and is fundamental to philosophical Taoism and nondual Hindu Advaita Vedanta. The influence of Asia on the West has been broadly cultural, extending well beyond artistic styles to philosophical perspectives and life views. South Asian, Himalayan, and East Asian philosophical views and psychosomatic practices were important resources for European and American artists both before and during Duchamp's lifetime.[20] Western artists have been attracted to Asian philosophies of mind since at least the eighteenth century. It is now known, for example, that the artist and poet William Blake (1757–1827) incorporated Vedanta into his idiosyncratic political/spiritual ideology, and perhaps practiced a form of tantra or was at least inspired by Indian tantric ideas and images.[21] Baruchello's emphasis on breathing practice alerts us to Duchamp's integration of yogic and tantric body energetics—"a whole idea of a science of the body"—into his artistic process.

II. THE ASIAN MATRIX

The art-historical game of sources has no beginning and no end: it can be argued that Western art has been influencing Asian art for as long as Asian culture has been influencing culture in the West. The most commonly cited example of West-to-East influence is Gandhara art: stylistic elements from Greek art adapted to Indian Buddhist iconography in visual art produced between the first century BCE and the seventh century CE in what is now northwestern Pakistan and eastern Afghanistan.

Early philosophical influence seems to have gone in the other direction. Elements from early forms of Buddhism originating in Northwestern India and Central Asia infiltrated the teachings of the Greek philosopher Pyrrho (360–270 BCE), and also influenced the development of Hinduism.[22] Buddhism was affected in turn by ascetic Hindu practices.[23] After Buddhist missionaries reached China in the first century CE, Taoism developed hybrid practices that incorporated Buddhist elements, while Chinese Buddhism gradually incorporated Taoist concepts such as meditational "sitting in oblivion."[24] One result was Ch'an Buddhism, which in Japan developed as Zen.

Thanks to these hybrid characteristics and the abstract, experiential nature of the various practices, Asian philosophies as resources for Western artists are harder to detect than stylistic influences. The problem is made more difficult by the fact that artists tend to resist identifying their sources, whether stylistic or spiritual. When it comes to philosophical perspectives, which are not only personal but also in constant development, artists can be even more resistant. This is partly for reasons of privacy, but also because artists want viewers to see their work through eyes unclouded by preconceptions.

There is another, more pernicious reason why the influence of Asian philosophies within Western art has been elusive: all too often, Western authors characterize Asian and Asian-influenced artistic expression as "mystical" or "spiritual"—words carelessly associated with religion and Theosophical or New Age adaptions of complex Asian philosophies and practices. It is not hard to understand why rationalist authors interpret mysticism in this way. Nevertheless, developments such as these had historical impacts within Asia as well as in the West. Duchamp, in contrast, appears to have regarded Asian philosophies and practices not as mysticism in this impoverished sense, but as ready-made resources and techniques to be mastered and integrated into his ever-expanding creative process.

There is little documentation to prove that Duchamp knowingly incorporated Asian perspectives into his artistic practice, transforming his art into a rigorous art of life. There is, however, ample *evidence*, offered in narrative form in the chapters that follow. Required to interpret this evidence is a basic knowledge of the interactive nature of Asian religious traditions. Every Asian "-ism" needs to be understood as a temporal construct encompassing wide-ranging geographical and historical practices that both affected and were affected by culture—including, during the colonial era, European culture. The following—necessarily summary—descriptions are offered as a framework for what is to come.

Buddhism exists in many forms; there are dozens of major branches and hundreds of minor branches. Early on, Buddhism was described in terms of four "noble truths" attributed to the first discourse of the Buddha—Siddhartha Gautama, who lived in India sometime between the sixth and fourth century BCE. These might be summarized as, first, recognition of suffering; second, the origin of suffering in attraction and aversion; third, the potential to dispel suffering; and fourth, realizing that potential by living in accordance with the noble eightfold path. ("Noble" because it is associated with self-sovereignty.) Buddhism's eightfold path is both descriptive and prescriptive regarding how one lives and behaves if one is "awake" (*buddha* means: "one who is awake"). Its elements are: right view, which is cultivated through right thought, right speech, and right conduct, which in turn constitute right living, pursued with right effort and right mindfulness generated by right contemplation. These are eight interrelated attitudes and behaviors, just as the four noble truths imply four interconnected mental events capable of generating liberation of mind: *nirvana*, freedom from suffering.[25]

In Buddhist meditation the mind is trained to dismantle habitual patterns of thought until the self is experienced as continuous with the world and thus empty of inherent (self) existence. The Buddha's realization of the interdependent nature of existence emerged as an insight that was complete, but hardly sudden. His "middle way" between austerity and indulgence was preceded by years of rigorous mental and physical discipline. It was an insight so simple that it seemed to him obvious, though not easy to convey in words. The Buddha's teachings were conveyed orally for generations and did not begin systematically to be written down until the fifth century CE, in texts that were translated into European languages only fourteen centuries later.

Over the centuries Buddhism has evolved from Siddhartha Gautama's hard-earned awakening into various systematized sets of observations and behaviors, an evolution that is still going on. Mahayana Buddhism, which developed around the turn of the first millennium, teaches that enlightenment can be attained in a single lifetime, even by laypersons. It spread from India to other South, East, and Southeast Asian countries including Tibet, where esoteric teachings were incorporated into the Mahayana tradition. In the places where it has developed, including India, Buddhism took forms that incorporated preexisting beliefs and practices. Its manifestations thus range from the visual and aural complexity of Tibetan Buddhism to the austerity of Japanese Zen Buddhism.

In the West, Buddhism spread through texts,[26] teachings, travel, and immigration, including by artists. Its various forms adapted themselves to local cultural and spiritual phenomena ranging from Judeo-Christian traditions to psychology. Artists contemporary with Duchamp influenced by Buddhism include Odilon Redon, whose large painting *Buddha in His Youth* was a highlight of the Redon retrospective at the Salon d'Automne in 1904, the year Duchamp arrived in Paris to study art.[27] The Czech artist František Kupka, who lived next door to Duchamp's artist-brothers in Puteaux, created works with themes like *Soul of the Lotus* (1898), while Duchamp's close friend Constantin Brancusi was influenced by Tibetan Buddhism, encountered at the Musée Guimet.[28]

Taoism, the primary indigenous religion of China, is a mostly esoteric complex of traditions that developed over several millennia.[29] In the Taoist worldview, when the Universe began there was only the Tao, the "One"—a void pregnant with possibility. Tao generated swirling patterns of cloudlike *chi* energy that evolved into two complementary aspects: yin, which is dark, heavy, and "feminine," and yang, which is light, airy, and "masculine." Yin energy sank to form the earth, yang energy rose to form the heavens, and when their energies harmonized, human beings developed. The human body thus contains energies from both earth and heaven that can be gathered, circulated, nourished, refined, and ultimately transformed through the process of *nei-tan*: internal alchemy.

Taoism's primary text is the *Tao Te Ching*, a collection of verses traditionally attributed to Lao Tzu. While the legendary Lao Tzu is said to have lived around the sixth century BCE, the actual Lao Tzu probably lived during the tumultuous Warring States period of the fifth or fourth century BCE. One of the world's great poems, *Tao Te Ching* translates literally as "The Classic of the Way's Virtues." A more interpretive translation—"The Classic of This Focus and Its Field"—emphasizes the holographic nature of reality experienced by recognizing the unifying chi energy that flows to us from the world and back into it. Once realized, this skill is put into service for humanity in an effective yet inconspicuous manner, in keeping with the Taoist principles of simplicity, spontaneity, and action through nonaction.[30]

In contrast with the poetic *Tao Te Ching*, the more humorous and irreverent writings of Chuang Tzu (fourth century BCE) and his followers are laced with emphatic anti-authoritarianism.[31] Chuang Tzu's anecdotes came to stand for the opposite of Confucianism's ethos of self-sacrifice: specifically, for escape from societal pressure to an individual path of freedom, often through the liberating power of humor. Taoist attitudes toward change and the importance of humor appealed strongly to Western artists like Duchamp, Picabia, and their fellow Dada artists around the time of the First World War,[32] and surfaced again after the Second World War in surrealist circles.

Vedanta, one of six orthodox schools of Hindu philosophy, is the aspect of Hinduism best known in the West. "Vedanta" is often code for Advaita Vedanta, but there are many schools, including Dvaita Vedanta or dualism. The nondual forms of Vedanta are based on the philosophy contained in the *Upanishads*, the final collection of teachings within the Vedic canon. The Vedic Creation Hymn (*Nasadiya Sukta*, from *ná ásat*, or "not the non-existent") has creation originating in "neither non-existence nor existence." Then, for no discernible reason, "that one breathed, windless, by its own impulse." From within darkness hidden by darkness, "all this was water. The life force that was covered with emptiness, that one arose through the power of heat. Desire came upon that one in the beginning; that was the first seed of mind. Poets seeking in their heart with wisdom found the bond of existence in non-existence. Their cord was extended across. ... Whence is this creation? The gods came afterwards, with the creation of this universe. Who then knows whence it has arisen? ... perhaps it formed itself, or perhaps it did not."[33] The passage evokes not only Duchamp's insistence on the primacy of breath and the creative nature of desire, but also specific works such as *Mile of String* and his ambiguously authored readymades.

Veda means "knowledge"; *anta*, "end." Vedanta comprises the end of knowledge in terms of both the goal of knowledge and its transcendence. The concepts Brahman (Absolute Reality) and Atman (Soul, Self) are central ideas in the *Upanishads*, whose thematic focus is Atman and Brahman as one and the same: the absolute *is* the self, and vice versa. A core text of Vedanta is the *Bhagavad Gita*, part of the Hindu epic *Mahabharata* (fifth to second century BCE). *Bhagavad Gita* was the first Asian religious text to be translated into English, in 1785, and it has influenced Western artists from William Blake to today.[34] Vedantic cosmology and meditation practices are described in a number of texts, including the *Bhagavad Gita*, the *Yoga Sūtras of Patañjali*, and more modern texts such as Swami Vivekananda's *Raja-Yoga: Conquering the Internal Nature* (1896, and many later editions). A popular speaker in both Europe and the United States, Vivekananda (1863–1902) established the Vedanta Society in New York in 1894.

Alfred Jarry, a turn-of-the-twentieth-century writer and artist important to Duchamp and others, took a passage from the *Brihadaranyaka Upanishad* for the epigraph to his novel *Exploits and Opinions of Doctor Faustroll, Pataphysician*, published posthumously in 1911. A foundational text of Vedanta, the *Brihadaranyaka Upanishad*'s theme is the Self. Also incorporating perspectives from Vedanta into their work were European artists such as Kupka, and those in Duchamp's American cohort in the Arensberg circle and Alfred Stieglitz's stable of artists, including Marsden Hartley, Joseph Stella, and Mina Loy.

Yoga derives from the Sanskrit root, *yuj*, which means to yoke, join, or connect—in this case, microcosm and macrocosm. Influenced by early Buddhist breath meditation,[35] yoga emerged in India between the fifth and third century BCE as a range of physical and psychological practices conducive to mentally integrating the Hindu basics of existence: the consequences of one's acts (karma) on the cyclical transmigration of the Self (samsara), and the potential for escape from cyclical existence (moksha).[36] Yoga was exported along with Buddhism from India to China, where it influenced the development of Taoist internal alchemy (nei-tan). Chinese internal alchemy in turn affected Indian alchemy, and with it the development of tantra within Hinduism, Buddhism, and Jainism.[37]

With the emergence of tantra in India around the fifth or sixth century CE, yoga came to be used as a term that encompassed tantric processes as well, ranging from energy yogas through which practitioners manipulate respiration and body functions, to transformational dreaming, to sexual yoga with actual or visualized partners. At the end of the nineteenth century, Swami Vivekananda taught a Western-influenced, Neo-Vedantic form of yoga in the United States, England, and Europe, followed after the turn of the century by Pierre Bernard's hatha yoga and, after World War II, B. K. S. Iyengar's postural yoga. Samkhya-Yoga philosophy as propounded by Patanjali was a source for T. S. Eliot, and appears to have been a resource for Duchamp's theory of the creative act as the interaction, stimulated by the work of art, between maker and viewer-participant.

Tantra can refer to a Hindu, Buddhist, or Jain text,[38] or to the practices derived from them. Indian tantra may have begun as a populist practice derived from shamanistic traditions as old as the Vedas but not recorded until well into the Common Era. "Tantra" is Sanskrit for "system" or "weave," as in a textile or a text. "Tantra is the loom whereon the threads are 'spread out' or 'extended.' It also signified the pattern or design that emerged out of this spreading or extension."[39] Tantra thus refers to "that which is woven," but in many contexts it is used as something like a philosophical system. Tantra's suffix, *-tra*, indicates a mechanism for activating the verbal root, *tan*, "extend." In this sense, *tantra* is a mechanism for extension and connection.[40]

Like the body energetics of Taoist internal alchemy, tantric practices aim to transform erotic energy into mental and spiritual liberation through acute awareness of correlation and integration within a system of micro- and macrocosmic relationships. The cosmos is understood as the product of engagement between two opposites: a dynamic, creative "female" principle, identified with energy; and a powerful, purposeful "male" principle, identified with consciousness. From their union and ongoing bliss, the universe is constantly generated. In tantra, the body and its activities are regarded as divine, and sex is celebrated as emblematic of the process by which the universe manifests from absolute reality.[41]

Tantric practices are said to be mentally and emotionally harmful if performed without full awareness. Specific practices are described in heavily coded language and require direct transmission from a teacher to be effective.[42] The Muslim conquest of north India during the twelfth and thirteenth centuries produced breaks in guru-disciple tantric lineages. Post-conquest versions of tantra include the goddess-focused Shakti tradition popular in Bengal, with Kali and Tara the best-known forms of the goddess; and the Kundalini chakra system popularized in the West around the turn of the twentieth century.[43]

Buddhist tantras developed within Mahayana Buddhist contexts. In Buddhist tantric practice—also known as deity-yoga—enlightenment is achieved through identification with a deity or deities. These are not worshiped or "believed in," as in Judeo-Christian traditions, but are manifestations of qualities to be realized that are intrinsic to the tantric practitioner's own nature. Deity-yoga aids the practitioner in merging his or her own masculine and feminine energies to achieve the bliss of union and the mental radiance that arises from the experienced continuous nature of subject and object.

Hindu tantra as practiced in India, and Buddhist tantra as practiced in the greater Himalayan region, evolved into countless forms and ritual practices that include mantras (vocalization or chanting), mudras (body or hand gestures), and mental visualizations ranging from individual Sanskrit letters to colorful abstractions to multidimensional cosmic mandalas. Buddhist tantra migrated to Japan via China early in the ninth century, manifesting as the spectacularly visual Shingon and Tendai esoteric traditions. Himalayan and Japanese Esoteric Buddhist art depicts in colorful and explicit detail the mandalas and deities of the various Tantric systems as aids to practice.

By the end of the ninth century, physical sexual rituals like those of the Kashmiri Kaula lineage[44] of tantric Shaivism in which the absolute is personified by Shiva, whose power or *Shakti* is feminine, had undergone a hermeneutical transformation. In addition to physical practices, sexual rituals were interpreted by educated practitioners as psychosomatic exercises intended to dissolve ego and remove the veil of otherness from manifest reality, revealing the inherently *aesthetic* nature of lived experience. Duchamp's understanding of the aesthetic as disinterested delight in the interconnection of the senses and the mind was presaged by India's great aesthetician, the tenth/eleventh-century philosopher and Kaula practitioner Abhinavagupta.[45]

The motivating force in tantra is eroticism, the energy of attraction. In the scientifically oriented West, the most prevalent comparisons were with gravity and magnetism. Psychoerotic practices from India first infiltrated Western culture as a result of missionary activity, manifesting in Europe during the eighteenth century in the context of religious movements such as Swedenborgianism and Moravianism.[46] Colonization and increasing travel to Asia during the nineteenth and early twentieth centuries nourished secular sexual mysticisms in England, Europe, and the United States. The Polish-Jewish occultist Max Théon, American obstetrician Alice Bunker Stockham, and English poet Edward Carpenter were among the Westerners who traveled to India and became proponents of erotic mental practices that they promoted in the West in the cause of personal happiness and social improvement.[47] A later, more heterogeneous manifestation of this same impulse was Georges Bataille's secret society, Acéphale.

Women artists closely connected with Marcel Duchamp, including his sister Suzanne, Beatrice Wood, Isabelle Waldberg, and Maria Martins, all displayed tantric elements in their art, as did Duchamp's male artist-friends František Kupka, Constantin Brancusi, Francis Picabia, Suzanne's husband Jean Crotti, and Man Ray, who photographed Duchamp's artistic alter ego, Rrose Sélavy (figure 0.3), paralleling Shiva in his manifestation as Shakti.

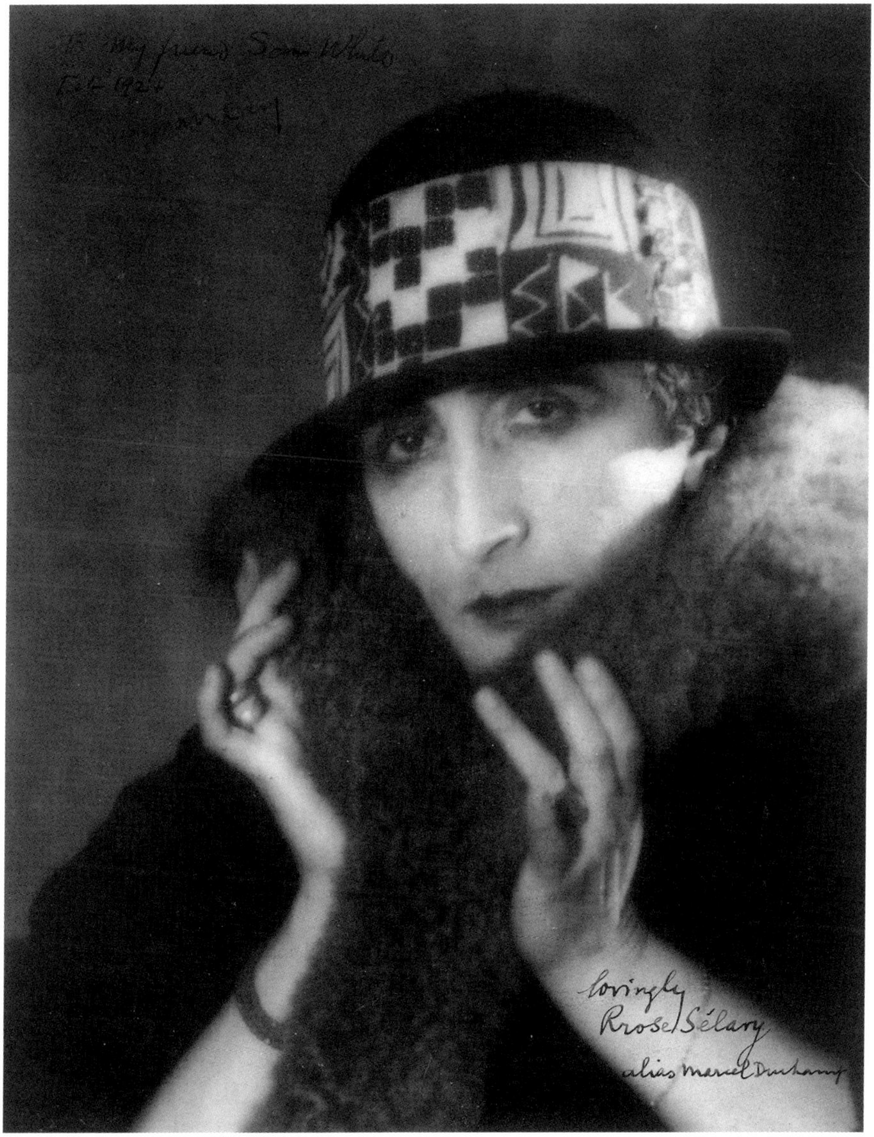

FIGURE 0.3

Man Ray
Marcel Duchamp as Rrose Sélavy, c. 1920–1921
Gelatin silver print, 21.6 × 17.3 cm
Philadelphia Museum of Art, Philadelphia, PA, The Samuel S. White 3rd and Vera White Collection, 1957 / Art Resource, NY

Evidence that Duchamp shared with close friends information regarding his personal practice is contained in a letter to Pierre Roché following Duchamp's prostate surgery in 1954: "even sex exercises are completely normal," he wrote Roché reassuringly.[48] A hint as to the nature of these "sex exercises" was provided five years later in the "Succinct Lexicon of Eroticism" in the catalogue to Duchamp and Breton's 1959 *L'Exposition inteRnatiOnale du Surréalisme*: "TANTRISM. Body of cosmological and mystical doctrines of Hindu origin. In tantric yoga, awareness of sexual energy (Shakti) as a modality of cosmic energy allowed ascetic reintegration of the primordial Unity."[49] The mention of Shakti and emphasis on *ascetic* (a homophone of aesthetic) reintegration suggests that Duchamp and Breton's referent was nondual tantric Shaivism, a philosophy just beginning to be understood in the West when Duchamp was conducting his research for *The Large Glass* in 1912–1915.[50]

Tantra treats sexuality and spirituality not as identical, but as having the same origin. The universe is regarded as an expression of blissful erotic activity: perfect freedom of consciousness energized by creative power. Kaula tantric practice replicates this process in the human body and mind, where it generates an experience of continuum—an important concept for Duchamp, as we shall see. Every moment of life becomes an occasion for touching the source of ecstasy that underlies the whole of creation. "With this changed vision," William Barnard wrote in his preface to J. C. Chatterji's *Kashmir Shaivism*, practitioners "can sense the interconnections that link everything in the world, and can directly experience that each action they perform resonates throughout the entire universe. ... The world is a mirror through which a person can gain self-knowledge in their interaction with others. They continually discover their own face in the world and find their own meaning in life reflected back to them."[51] The implications of this perspective for Duchamp's revolutionary art practice will be explored in the chapters that follow.

Alchemy probably originated in China—a major source of mercury, one of its key ingredients. In addition to a material laboratory practice, from very early on alchemy seems also to have been a psychosomatic practice. The first historical references to alchemy in China, according to J. J. Clarke, "date from the second century BCE, but its origins can be traced back beyond that to the long-established arts of metalworking, to traditional herbal medicine, and to ancient shamanistic and magical practices."[52] From China, alchemy spread to India, the Middle East, Egypt, and Hellenistic Greece.

Western alchemy emerged during the late Hellenistic era as a material practice concerned with the transmutation of substances. According to Wouter J. Hanegraaff, "already at an early stage ... technical descriptions of laboratory procedures were combined with vivid accounts of visions or dreams about initiatory processes of death-and-rebirth grounded in alchemical symbolism suggesting that human beings could escape from gross materiality by being transmuted into spiritual beings."[53] Western alchemy thus has two aspects: historical laboratory practice, and an open-ended experiential realm of inner transformation. The empirical laboratory phase gradually morphed into modern science, leaving Jung and the surrealists to appropriate and reframe experiential alchemy as a metaphysical system featuring arcane numinous symbolic language.

Dada and especially surrealist artists recognized in alchemy a symbolic system capable of expressing the integration of a multifaceted, ever-changing self within the larger universe. Western alchemy has received the lion's share of attention from Duchamp scholars, particularly the reunion of male and female elements symbolized by the androgyne.[54] But Duchamp's nuanced answer to a question posed by art historian Lanier Graham suggests that he was more interested in related experiential erotic practices originating in Asia. In a 1968 interview Graham identified the androgyne as a symbol of "true male-female balance," a "dynamic harmony ... said to be the key to Enlightenment."[55] "May we call your perspective Alchemical?" Graham asked Duchamp. "We may," Duchamp responded, hastening to clarify that the label was allegorical: "It is an alchemical understanding. But don't stop there! If we do, some will think I'll be trying to turn lead into gold back in the kitchen [laughing]. Alchemy is a kind of philosophy, a kind of thinking that leads to a way of understanding. We may also call this perspective Tantric (as Brancusi would say), or (as you like to say) Perennial. The Androgyne is not limited to any one religion or philosophy. The symbol is universal. The Androgyne is above philosophy. If one has become the Androgyne one no longer has a need for philosophy."[56]

Even in this interview in the last year of his life, Duchamp refused to be specific. But he came closer than he ever had to describing his system, which was not a philosophy, much less a belief, but might more accurately be characterized as a practice, even a science, in the sense of systematic study of the structure and behavior of the natural world through observation and experiment. Duchamp had similarly emphasized the experiential nature of his practice a decade earlier, when he assured art educator Serge Stauffer that he had never read a single treatise on alchemy, since "one cannot 'do alchemy' as one can, with an appropriate language, 'do law or medicine'."[57]

What Graham called androgyny was for Duchamp a "perspective" or "kind of thinking." He cited two examples: "Tantric as Brancusi would say, or as you like to say, Perennial [philosophy]." Linking tantra with a close friend from his youth, the Romanian sculptor Constantin Brancusi, was a classic esoteric diversionary tactic on Duchamp's part, intended to deflect attention from himself. Although Graham knew about tantra, he would not have been aware that Brancusi had been interested in it, as Brancusi's interest in Buddhist tantra was not widely known until 1993.[58] Duchamp added a comparison he knew Graham *would* understand: perennialism, the view that all religions can be traced back to a universal nondual experience of reality.

Perennialism is a Western syncretic philosophy that views each of the world's religious traditions as stemming from the same underlying metaphysical given. Rooted in Renaissance Neoplatonism and its idea of The One from which all existence emanates,[59] the concept was popularized in the early nineteenth century by the Transcendentalists and adopted in the last quarter of the nineteenth century by the Theosophical Society, which published Asian as well as Theosophical texts. Aldous Huxley further popularized it in his 1945 book *The Perennial Philosophy*.[60] Under the banner of Max Théon's "Cosmic Philosophy," this concept of a common source underlying all religious and philosophical traditions influenced the Parisian guru Mirra Alfassa, a key player in the esoteric Parisian milieu that helped form the young Duchamp.

It is important to keep in mind that, aside from any textual translations he may have read, the variations of Asian philosophy and practice

Duchamp absorbed would not for the most part have been the so-called classical Asian traditions (if indeed such ideal entities ever existed), but the results of exchanges between Asian tradition and Western modernity. The Indian perspectives available around 1910, the year Vivekananda's *Raja Yoga* was published in French, would have been a nineteenth-century Neo-Vedantic blend of Hinduism with Enlightenment, Unitarian, and Western esoteric principles.[61] The Theosophical movement promoted Buddhism, but published texts spanning a range of Asian religious traditions.[62] Paul Carus's turn-of-the-century Open Court Press in La Salle, Illinois introduced Asian traditions and ideas to the West in texts exploring the relationships between science and religion.

In other words, whatever syncretic practice Duchamp may have developed would have drawn on sources that were already more or less syncretic. Whenever possible, the sources cited in the chapters that follow are translators and commentators contemporary with Duchamp such as Swami Vivekananda, Jagadish Chandra Chatterji, Arthur Avalon, and Alexandra David-Néel, whose publications Duchamp and those in his circle could have accessed.

••

Duchamp's explicit reference to tantra in his interview with Lanier Graham indicates that he viewed the androgyne not just as inner harmony, but as a true merging of male and female energies—a state achieved fleetingly and often superficially in ordinary sex, but which in disciplined tantric practice, alone or with a partner, is intended to generate a new being who "no longer has a need for philosophy." Given his evasive response to Graham, it should not be surprising that when asked by another interviewer what "personal meaning" eroticism held for him, Duchamp responded in esoteric terms: "I don't give it a personal meaning, but finally it is really the way to try and uncover things that are constantly hidden—and that aren't necessarily erotic—because of the Catholic religion, because of social rules. To be able to take the liberty of revealing them and willingly place them at everyone's disposal. I think this is important because it's the basis of everything and no one talks about it."[63] Duchamp here underscores Christianity's conflation of the erotic and the esoteric by emphasizing that his interest in eroticism was not just personal but was intended to make public what previously had been hidden. What Duchamp seemed to be saying is that eroticism was for him a way to uncover important things that he tried through his art to "place at everyone's disposal." Why? Because these things, this process, which "no one talks about," are in fact "the basis of everything."

For Marcel Duchamp, creativity was essentially erotic, and thus inherently esoteric. Esotericism is a nineteenth-century Western term, which makes the concept of *Asian* esotericism problematic.[64] Regarding sexual and other "forbidden" practices in South Indian tantra, Indologist David Gordon White points out that the supposed esoteric secrets of tantric practices were not secrets at all, but were openly disseminated through both writing and teaching. They are thus more like strategies of dissimulation, a "*cult* of secrecy": "In the Tantric context what has perhaps been essential is not keeping a secret itself, but rather maintaining a cult of secrecy, ... maintaining a secret identity in a society where keeping secrets is a near impossibility. ... In other words, dissimulation or role-playing by the Tantric practitioners ... was ... a means by which householders could maintain an acceptable public persona."[65] This is reminiscent of Duchamp's own cult of secrecy—his dissimulation and role-playing intended not so much to maintain an acceptable public persona as to create an aura of mystery like that surrounding esoteric Buddhist art in Japan as described by art historian Cynthea Bogel: "Maintaining an aura of secrecy around Mikkyō icons diverts attention from their magical efficacy at the same time it intensifies it."[66] Duchamp chose to be esoteric less to intensify interest in what he was doing (though it had that effect) than because his art is consistently about the fundamentally erotic nature of existence.

In traditional Christianity eroticism is forbidden knowledge, which helps explain Duchamp's lifelong interest in the theme of the Fall (figures 1.10, 4.8, 9.7). In contrast, eroticism is foundational to the Asian religious traditions of Taoism, Hinduism, and Mahayana Buddhism and their interrelated mind-body practices of internal alchemy, yoga, and tantra. Duchamp's friend Robert Lebel observed that his peculiar radiance resulted from a technological understanding of human sexuality transformed into dazzling ecstasy through a form of autoerotic practice:

> Starting from his conception of the human being, including himself, as a machine, he had blended man and woman in a single machine, though separated into two parts, and put it to work for his own use. The sheer idea, let alone its materialization in the *Large Glass*, was an astounding and revolutionary masterpiece of mock psychology, mock technology, mock sociology, and mock economics. ... Its "production" ... is essentially an autoerotic pleasure that can result in a new birth, a dazzling ecstasy. As far as Duchamp's machine is concerned this description seems rewarding enough, and it accounts for the glittering radiance evident to everyone who encountered him.[67]

During an interview with the writer and curator Pierre Cabanne in 1966, Duchamp commented: "Eroticism was a theme, even an 'ism' which was the basis of everything I was doing at the time of *The Large Glass*. It kept me from being obligated to return to already existing theories, aesthetic or otherwise."[68]

What did Duchamp mean by Eroticism as an "ism": Eroticism with a capital E? Writing about tantra, historian of religion Jeffrey J. Kripal defined the Erotic as "a dimension of human experience that is simultaneously related both to the physical and emotional experience of sexuality and to the deepest ontological levels of religious experience." Eroticism as an "ism" would be a good description of Tantrism: "awareness of sexual energy as a modality of cosmic energy,"[69] a "passage into the oneness of pure Consciousness, when the cognitive energy converts into pure Self-Awareness."[70] What I mean when I use the word "enlightenment" in connection with Duchamp is this "preeminent sense of amazement at one's self" that is neither intellectual nor emotional, but is capable of completely changing one's relationship with the world.[71]

Familiarity with Asian philosophies and practices, and the perspectives they were designed to generate, allows Duchamp's comments, notes, and artworks to make more sense than they might otherwise. For example, his startling assertion: "I want to grasp things with the mind the way the penis is grasped by the vagina."[72] It may be helpful to know that this metaphor is fundamental to the yogachara school of Mahayana Buddhist philosophy, where a sensory object experienced as integral to the mind is described as the "grasped," while its perception is the "grasper."[73] Then there is that vivid remark in a letter from Duchamp to his brother-in-law Jean Crotti:

"To my mind, there is salvation only in esotericism. Yet for 60 years we've been witnessing public displays of our balls and erections."[74] He had written something similar almost forty years earlier, when his sister and Crotti asked him to send something to show at Tristan Tzara's Dada Salon in Paris. Duchamp responded via telegram with just two words, "PODE BAL," "balls to you."[75] These might seem rude remarks to make to one's sister and brother-in-law, unless the plentiful balls and erections featured in Indo-Tibetan tantric images had been the subject of previous discussion among the three of them. Such images are created for personal visualization practice, not for public exhibition. In this light, Duchamp's pithy telegram was more than a vulgar, Dadaesque "no." Both "PODE BAL" and Duchamp's disdain for "public displays of our balls and erections" would have been effective shorthand between likeminded people regarding the incompatibility of creative activity and social display.

Duchamp's writings, his artworks, his statements, along with the artworks and commentary of his friends, offer compelling reasons for thinking that he was interested enough in Asian perspectives on reality to use them as resources in both his life and his art. His stepson Paul Matisse hinted as much in his description of Duchamp's worldview: "I think that his work and his understanding made him apprehend the world in a quite 'authentic' way. … Let us take the word Buddha, which means *the awakened one*, the one who is awake, whose eyes are not troubled by ideas relating to the ego, for example. Marcel was *awake* in this profound way." When asked whether there was some secret to Duchamp's uncommon perception, Matisse replied that what it took was research and discipline: "No, it was not unique from that point of view. With a certain discipline, one can arrive there. This requires an internal force that no longer needs external support. There is no secret here. Marcel conducted his own research and, when he reached the stage where the opposites were able to live together, he held himself there."[76] The tantra yoga techniques I propose Duchamp adopted and then adapted early in his career enabled him to defy the law of gravity, and balance the conflicting polarities of intellect and emotion. As he asserted, quoting T. S. Eliot, "The more perfect the artist, the more completely separate in him will be the man who suffers and the mind which creates; the more perfectly will the mind digest and transmute the passions which are its material."[77]

Despite Duchamp's self-declared interest in Eroticism, theories of mind associated with Asian esoteric eroticism have yet to be fully explored as inspirations for his art. *Marcel Duchamp and the Art of Life* presents evidence that the "hidden" practice, the erotic "ism" that informed much of Duchamp's work from his early paintings of nudes engaged in mysterious activities to his chess-player series to *The Large Glass* to *Given*, was a personal amalgam of Asian philosophical perspectives and mental energy practices derived from Western esoteric versions of Indo-Tibetan tantra and Taoist internal alchemy—practices designed to transform erotic energy into mental and spiritual liberation.[78] These were hardly his only sources. But when everything is taken into consideration, I believe it is fair to conclude that Marcel Duchamp drew on a range of resources to develop a meditative and energetic spiritual practice fueled by erotic desire, a practice that in turn fueled his creativity.

"Duchamp, because of what he calls his 'delay in glass'," Robert Lebel wrote, "seems to have had in mind the anonymity of future archaeological excavations, after the final collapse of our own civilization."[79] Western civilization hasn't quite collapsed yet, but I am hopeful it may finally be ready for the version of Duchamp presented here.

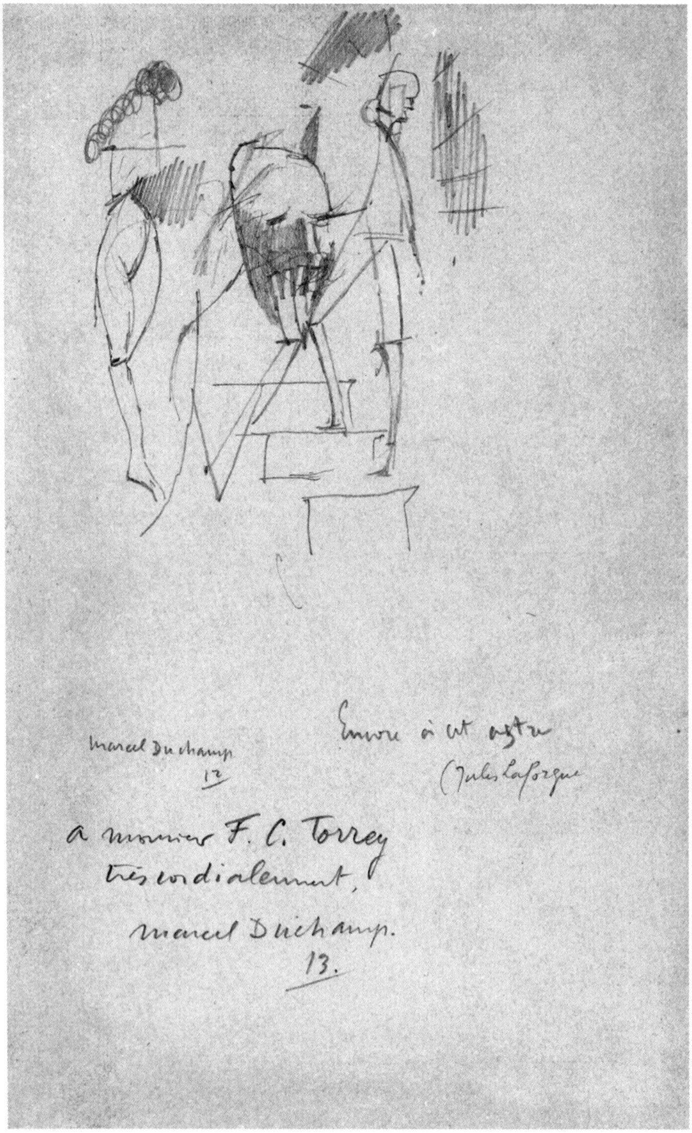

FIGURE 1.1

Marcel Duchamp
Encore à cet astre / Once More to This Star, 1911
Graphite on paper, 25.1 × 16.4 cm
Philadelphia Museum of Art, Philadelphia, PA, The Louise and Walter Arensberg Collection, 1950 / Bridgeman Images

1 ONCE MORE TO THIS STAR

Henri-Robert-Marcel Duchamp was born in 1887 in a village ten miles from Rouen, third in a family of six children—three boys followed by three girls.[1] The four eldest children would all become artists. There was an age gap of eleven years between Marcel and his two older brothers. He came along just six months after a three-year-old sister, Madeleine, died of croup. To replace her lost girl, his mother got another boy, perhaps a factor in Marcel's remarkably fluid sexuality. His sister Suzanne was born in 1889; and the two youngest girls, Yvonne and Magdeleine, in 1895 and 1898. The oldest brother, Gaston, born in 1875, trained as a lawyer and would become the painter and printmaker Jacques Villon. Raymond, one year younger than Gaston, trained as a doctor and would become the talented sculptor Raymond Duchamp-Villon.

Marcel remained at home with his younger sisters until he was almost seventeen. Closest in age to him was Suzanne, a painter who in 1919 would marry Duchamp's artist-friend Jean Crotti. Their amiable father, a notary who became mayor of their little town in 1895, supported his four eldest children in their careers as artists. The only shadow on this otherwise close family was their mother, Lucie, who by the time Marcel was born had become deaf and may have suffered from depression.[2] Marcel later described her with some bitterness as "indifferent" except to the two youngest girls, her favorites.[3] Lucie Duchamp was an artist by avocation, like her father, but her reviews in that realm by her son were as dismal as for her vocation as mother. When, late in Duchamp's life, interviewer Pierre Cabanne asked him about his mother's "still lifes," Duchamp responded: "She wanted to cook them too, but in all her seventy years she never got around to it."[4] Such scorn at his mother's inability to complete artistic projects is telling in light of Duchamp's characterization of his own major early work, *The Large Glass* (figure 0.2), as "definitively unfinished."

An important influence on the young Marcel seems to have come from a woman quite different from his mother. According to Duchamp's first wife, Lydie Fischer Sarazin-Levassor (in whom he confided, though their marriage did not last), his brothers were influenced in their choice of professional names by Marcel's godmother, Julia Bertrand (*née* Pillore, 1868–1960). First trained in medicine, Bertrand was a writer, intellectual, and feminist who at the ripe age of 32 married the artist Paulin Bertrand. Only 19 years old when Marcel was born, she took an active educational interest in the Duchamp children. Having equipped herself with a degree in philosophy, Bertrand taught them that "the first step towards acquiring wisdom ... is to do away with the old self and seek one's true self in what is pure and Absolute."[5]

When Gaston Duchamp decided to become an artist, Bertrand encouraged him to adopt a new identity. He settled on the name of vagabond fifteenth-century poet François Villon. Raymond, in a show of solidarity with both his family and his brother, retained "Duchamp" while adding "Villon." Marcel did not follow their lead, but Villon's poetry—ironic, erotic, and written in jargon—may well have left its imprint on his future work. Duchamp's fondness for double entendres could be a Villon legacy, reinforced by contemporary writers like Alfred Jarry and Raymond Roussel.[6] Another legacy from his young godmother was surely Duchamp's lifelong fondness for lively, intellectual women.

In 1904 Duchamp joined his brothers in Paris, where he attended a private art school, the Académie Julian. He told his biographer Calvin Tomkins that he quickly realized "how different I was even from my brother [Villon]. He aimed at fame. I *had* no aim. I just wanted to be left alone to do what I liked."[7] In spring 1905 the young Duchamp was temporarily derailed by a new law requiring a mandatory two years of military service, with exceptions for professions considered essential to society. One of the exempted professions was that of engraver-printer—the specialty of Duchamp's maternal grandfather, the Rouen painter and printmaker Émile Frédéric Nicolle (1830–1894). In May 1905 Duchamp left Paris for Rouen to learn etching, engraving, typesetting, and printing, becoming a certified "art worker." He got his military service reduced to one year, and gained a mastery of reproductive techniques that would serve him well in the future direction of his art.

By fall 1906 Duchamp was back in Paris. His brothers had moved to the rural western suburb of Puteaux, where they shared a garden with the Czech artist František Kupka. Duchamp visited them regularly, but chose to live in Montmartre, a hotbed of artistic activity in this heyday of fauvism and early cubism. He tried to sell his humorous, risqué drawings to newspapers, and occasionally succeeded. He began painting again, producing competent, colorful still lifes and landscapes.

In 1908 Duchamp moved to Neuilly, at the western edge of Paris, near Puteaux. That fall, three of his paintings were accepted into the Salon d'Automne. Except for trips to Germany in the summer of 1912 and to Herne Bay, England, in the summer of 1913, Duchamp lived and worked in Neuilly from 1908 to 1913. He often spent Sundays in Puteaux, where artists including Jean Metzinger, Fernand Léger, Georges Ribemont-Dessaignes, and the writer Guillaume Apollinaire would gather at his brothers' studios. Marcel painted in the garden of his brother Jacques Villon and his wife Gaby. Besides Kupka, he became friends during this time with the painter Francis Picabia; with Picabia's wife, the musician Gabrielle Buffet-Picabia; and with the eccentric Romanian sculptor Constantin Brancusi.

Paris in 1908 was the birthplace of cubism, and Puteaux of the more ingratiating "Puteaux cubism." Cubism has been portrayed as a radical break with past artistic practice. But the interest of these artists in the fourth dimension—understood, pre-Einstein, as a dimension coexistent with visible reality but unavailable to the senses—suggests that cubism is better understood as a continuation of late-nineteenth-century scientific, psychic, and artistic investigations of reality. Art historian Linda Dalrymple Henderson made this case in her groundbreaking books and in the exhibition catalogue *The Spiritual in Art: Abstract Painting 1890–1985*: "Although interest in a fourth dimension of space was an outgrowth of the development of n-dimensional geometries during the first half of the nineteenth century, the notion of a fourth dimension had become highly popularized by the turn of the century. By that time the term had accumulated a variety of non-mathematical associations, the primary one being an idealist philosophical interpretation of it as a higher reality beyond three-dimensional, visual perception. In fact, the concept enjoyed a symbiotic relationship with the mystical tradition."[8]

In her writings on Duchamp, Henderson focused less on the mystical tradition than on late-nineteenth- and early-twentieth-century developments in science and technology such as X-rays. She perceived no conflict, however, between scientific and "occult" artistic investigations during a period when alternative religions like Theosophy promoted themselves as scientific.[9] Henderson treated Duchamp's scientific interests as primary and his occult interests as secondary. They were no doubt intertwined, but it does seem clear that the cool precision of technical and scientific illustration offered Duchamp a visual language for depicting metaphysical experience very different from the evocative forms deployed by the preceding Symbolist generation, and by Duchamp in his early years.

Henderson emphasized the importance to Duchamp of his brothers' neighbor Kupka, who was sixteen years older than Duchamp and seems to have served as a mentor. Kupka conceived of artistic creation as an empirical synthesis based on interconnectedness. He was acutely aware of his sense impressions, and was an adherent of coenaesthesis: the feeling of existence arising from bodily sensations and emotions. He explored mythology, Swedenborgianism, Theosophy, and the natural sciences, and was interested in the fourth dimension and the relationship between time and space as recorded by high-speed and chronophotography.[10] That Duchamp shared many of Kupka's interests is evident in paintings from the second half of 1911 such as *Yvonne and Magdeleine Torn in Tatters* (figure 1.2), which shows his two youngest sisters in multiple profiles with the passage of time collapsed; and *Sad Young Man on a Train* (figure 1.3), a more overtly cubist composition in which agitated, sticklike forms evoking both motion and emotion appear to emerge from and disappear into darkness.

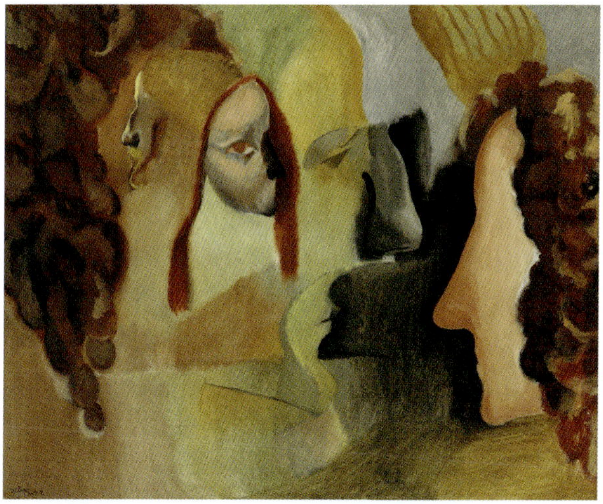

FIGURE 1.2

Marcel Duchamp
Yvonne et Magdeleine déchiquetées / Yvonne and Magdeleine Torn in Tatters, 1911
Oil on canvas, 60.3 × 73.3 cm
Philadelphia Museum of Art, Philadelphia, PA, The Louise and Walter Arensberg Collection, 1950 / Bridgeman Images

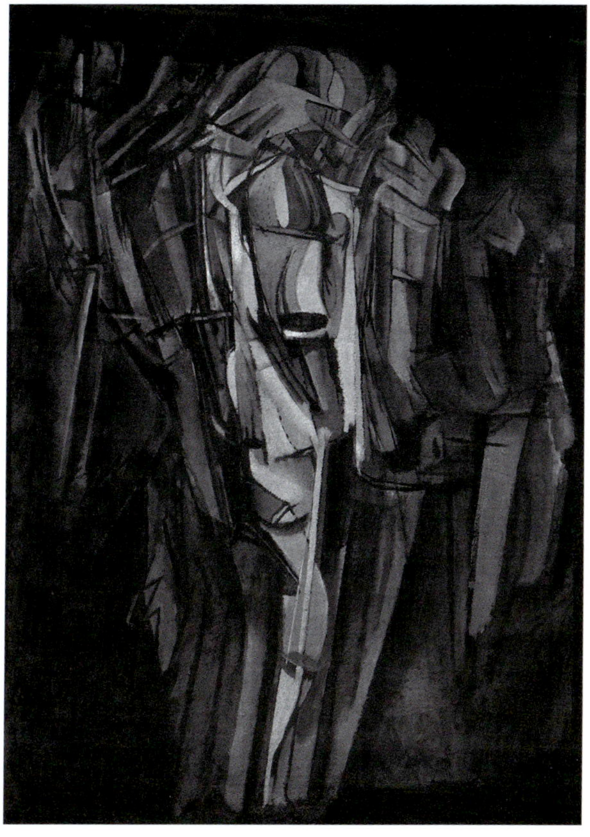

FIGURE 1.3

Marcel Duchamp
Jeune homme triste dans un train / Nude (Study), Sad Young Man on a Train, 1911–1912
Oil on cardboard, mounted on Masonite 100 × 73 cm
The Solomon R. Guggenheim Foundation, Peggy Guggenheim Collection, Venice, 1976, 76.2553.9

The scientific and technological inspirations evident in these and other works by Duchamp have been amply documented by Henderson and others. In contrast, Duchamp's explorations of alternative mind-body concepts (Henderson's "mystical tradition") are murkier, with little or no documentation due to their esoteric nature and Duchamp's elusiveness regarding his sources.[11] From the visual evidence, these explorations predated his scientific interests. Duchamp evinced an affinity for mysticism's connection with eroticism as early as 1907–1909, when during a family holiday on the Normandy coast he painted his sister Yvonne seated, her skirt pushed up to show her thigh, her crotch in shadow (figure 1.4), and a stark, emotive painting of a nude male pierced in the heart with an arrow inspired by a sculpture of Saint Sebastian in the local church (figure 1.5).

More overtly mystical-erotic works would follow over the next three years, works that have never adequately been accounted for in the ample scholarship on Marcel Duchamp. The paintings and drawings he produced in 1910–1912 provide visual evidence that during this time he was intensely engaged with "evaluation of his own thought mechanisms," as Lydie Fischer Sarazin-Levassor described Duchamp's explorations of consciousness.[12] In 1910, for example, he began haloing his depictions of nudes with what Arturo Schwarz described as "a strange white aura."[13] In April of that year he painted a *Portrait of Dr. Dumouchel* in which his medical student friend is surrounded by a reddish-pink aura strongly focused on the hand (figure 1.6). When Louise and Walter Arensberg bought this painting in 1951, Duchamp wrote them: "It is a definite 1910 painting in technique; yet the 'halo' around the hand which is <u>not</u> expressly motivated by Dumouchel's hand is a sign of my subconscious preoccupations toward a metarealism. It has no definite meaning or explanation except the satisfaction of a need for the 'miraculous' that preceded the cubist period."[14] Duchamp studiously avoided the word "aura," which had a very specific meaning associated with Theosophy; even "halo" he surrounded with quotation marks. His neutral term "metarealism" foregrounds the heterogeneous nature of his explorations and his determination not to get pigeonholed into any particular belief system.

According to Henderson, the auras in *Portrait of Dr. Dumouchel* refer to "the practice of Magnetism (i.e., hypnotism by the supposed manipulation

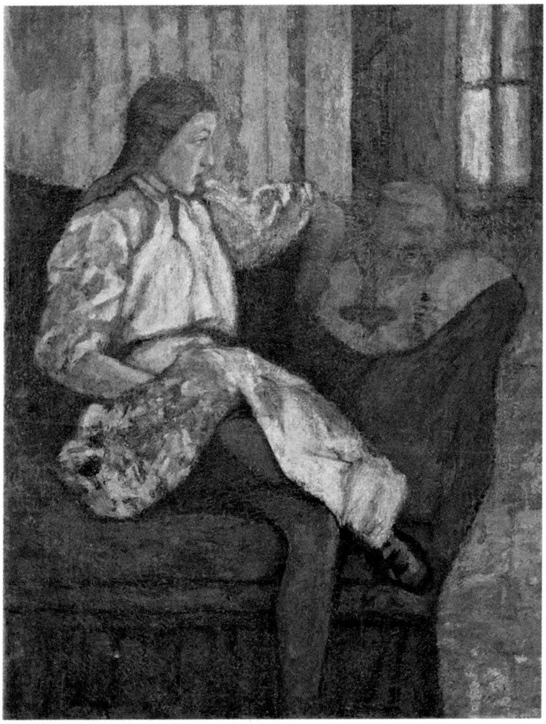

FIGURE 1.4

Marcel Duchamp
Portrait of Yvonne Duchamp, 1907 or 1909
Oil on canvas, 87 × 67.4 cm
The Museum of Modern Art, New York, NY, Mary Sisler Bequest / Digital Image © The Museum of Modern Art/Licensed by SCALA / Art Resource, NY

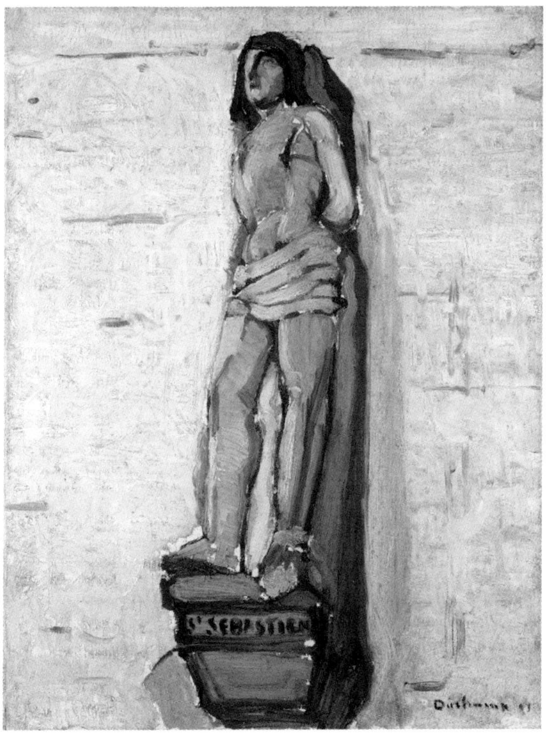

FIGURE 1.5

Marcel Duchamp
Saint Sebastien, 1909
Oil on canvas, 61.3 × 46.4 cm
Gift of Mary Sisler Foundation, 1979, Collection of the John and Mable Ringling Museum of Art the State Art Museum of Florida, Florida State University, MF79.1.5

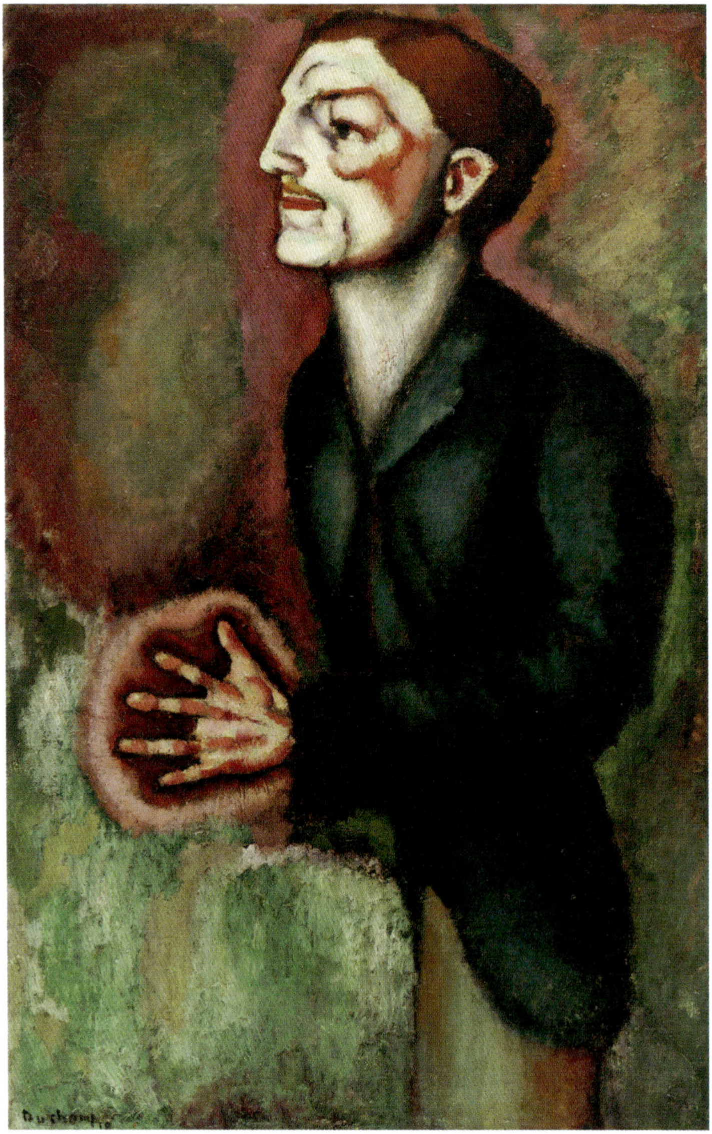

FIGURE 1.6

Marcel Duchamp
Portrait of Dr. Dumouchel, 1910
Oil on canvas, 100.3 × 65.7 cm
Philadelphia Museum of Art, Philadelphia, PA, The Louise and Walter Arensberg Collection, 1950 / Bridgeman Images

of magnetic fluids)," which she believes would have been of interest to Duchamp's doctor friends, Dumouchel and Ferdinand Tribout.[15] Henderson refers to the writings of parapsychologist Albert de Rochas on the subject of so-called animal magnetism. Rochas translated into French the mid-century writings of German chemist Karl von Reichenbach, who had observed a visible "force" emanating from various objects and body parts. "In the context of the physics of electromagnetism in the 1890s," Henderson writes, "Reichenbach's magnetic 'vital force' experienced a revival. Rochas ... included discussions of [vital] force in his own writings on the states of hypnosis (a process he and other Magnetizers still linked to the action of magnetic fluid) and on the exteriorization of sensibility (*sensibilité*) and motor activity (*motricité*) by mediums or other sensitive subjects."[16] Henderson notes that Rochas's work was treated in a book Duchamp is documented as having read,[17] and she reproduces a line drawing of flamelike "magnetic emanations" observed by hypnotized patients of one Dr. Luys published in another book by Rochas.[18]

Vital force or energy was also a focus of Advaita Vedanta proponent Swami Vivekananda's *Râja-yoga (ou Conquête de la nature intérieure)*, published in Paris in 1910 and read enthusiastically within Parisian esoteric circles as soon as it appeared. In Vivekananda's disquisition on *Prana*—breath as vital force—magnetism and electricity are more than metaphors: "Out of this Prana is evolved everything that we call energy, everything that we call force. It is the Prana that is manifesting as motion; it is the Prana that is manifesting as gravitation, as magnetism. It is the Prana that is manifesting as the actions of the body, as the nerve currents, as thought force."[19]

Another source was the Polish-Jewish Kabbalist and occultist Max Théon (Louis-Maximilian Bimstein, 1848–1927). According to scholar of Western esotericism Christian Chanel, "Max Théon stands at the crossroads of Eastern and Western spirituality as one of the most attractive figures of the movement devoted to the 'disoccultation of the occult' (i.e., initiation by and through daily life rather than submission to the techniques of occult initiations ...) which he tried to pioneer." Théon's ideas were "thoroughly modern: the primacy of love and liberty, the quest for progress and individual development, ... mistrust of political and religious ideologies."[20] Théon's *Revue Cosmique*, a journal begun in 1902 at the instigation of his wife and primary inspiration,

Alma (born Mary Chrystine Woodroffe Ware, 1843–1908), was "consecrated to the restitution of original tradition, common source of religious and philosophical traditions"[21]—in other words, perennialism, which posits spiritual traditions as sharing a single metaphysical origin.

The Théons, who commuted regularly to Paris from their base in Tlemcen, Algeria, were prime examples of that melding of Asian and Western spiritual practices going on pretty much everywhere around the turn of the twentieth century. In addition to his Western esoteric interests, Théon read Sanskrit, was familiar with the Vedas, and had received "oriental initiations" in India that were presumably tantric in nature.[22] From his writings and from the teachings of his follower Mirra Alfassa (discussed in chapter 2), Théon's practice would appear to have been influenced by a form of Kaula, nondualist Shaiva (Shiva-based) Tantra from Kashmir.[23]

It was not uncommon around the turn of the twentieth century for Westerners to be initiated into Indian tantra; Sir John Woodroffe—who published as Arthur Avalon—is the best-known example, but he was not the only one. American yoga entrepreneur and "Tantrik" Pierre Bernard claimed to have traveled to Kashmir and Bengal before founding the Tantrik Order of America in 1905. Bernard did have a Bengali guru: Sylvais Hamati, an *émigré* from Calcutta whom he met in 1889, and who remained his teacher and then business partner for a number of years.[24] Around 1900 Bernard placed a classified advertisement in a San Francisco newspaper for a "KAULA rite, Chakra Ring, or Full Initiation, with 7 M's begins midnight October 8th; Siva festival following."[25]

What Max Théon and his wife taught seems to have been a form of Indian psychosomatic practice designed to channel, unite, and transform dynamic, creative "female" energy and powerful, purposeful "male" consciousness present in both women and men to achieve an experience of nondual reality. Théon's term for erotic love as a cosmic force was *Pathétisme*—a word that is difficult to translate, but which amounted to what Jeffrey J. Kripal defined as a "dimension of human experience that is simultaneously related both to the physical and emotional experience of sexuality and to the deepest ontological levels of religious experience."[26] Théon described *union pathétique* as a "duality of being" (*dualité d'être*) intended to generate in both partners a state of "dynamic balance" or equilibrium.[27]

Western tantra yoga was an esoteric practice, requiring direct transmission from teachers like the Théons. With regard to the sexual aspect, Théon's written descriptions were far from explicit. He described *Pathétisme* in an article entitled "How to Consider Magnetism," published in Paris in the *Journal du Magnétisme et de la Psychologie* in 1899. I translate from it here at length because, although Théon's description is euphemistic, it is nevertheless helpful in understanding magnetism as an esoteric phenomenon that provides a cultural context for Duchamp's *Portrait of Dr. Dumouchel*, as well as *The Large Glass*:

> Magnetism (called in ancient times *pathotism*) is a natural force because it is subject to the law of Duality—this cosmic law extending from the great unknown to the first material forms and thence to the most insignificant stationary and non-stationary organisms [i.e., plants and animals]. ... We must be careful not to confuse magnetism with hypnotism. Hypnotism or numbing oneself is an abnormal, undesirable pursuit and can be even considered dangerous. ...
>
> Magnetism in its highest sense is the infusion of the psychic active being into the psychic passive being, and the consequent development of the passive sensitive to the highest perfection of which it is capable in all states of being. It is necessary above all to penetrate this truth before Magnetism can be comprehended as sublime and sacred; it is the first step leading to the temple of Truth where the lamp of eternal light shines.
>
> The magnetizer must understand that he cannot without profanity climb even the first step of this temple without having removed his sandals—i.e., to be stripped of any thoughts of selfishness, or lasciviousness. This place is holy land, and each degree leading to it must be jealously guarded by the psychic man, just as in ancient temples no feet trod unless they were bare. ...
>
> A high sensitive—intellectual and refined (remember there is royalty and nobility in terms of talent as well as birth and wealth)—can be compared to a finely tuned instrument of such delicacy that, roughly treated, its harmony could be destroyed. But if entrusted to an individual who by his nature and his own knowledge is able to develop her sensitivity, through her he will be able to communicate with higher intelligences, acquire knowledge of the secrets of life and death, read the cosmic book of the universe whose pages are open to him, and dominate the forces of nature—not to mention other things that have not been touched upon. ...
>
> Finally, purity of intention and pathetic power are not sufficient. For anyone who wants to take responsibility for such a sensitive, it is necessary to add deep knowledge of the highest aspects of psychology, and especially understanding of the nature of the sensitive he wants to develop.[28]

Théon states that the "psychic active being" attains secret knowledge and power through his female partner. In Kaula, the highest form of initiation is by a woman, either a woman initiate willing to act as a master for him, or a yogini who appears to the adept in a dream or while in meditative absorption.[29]

Théon's comparison of "Magnetism"—his pseudo-scientific euphemism for tantric practice—with climbing stairs invites analogy both with Duchamp's drawing *Once More to This Star* (1911, figure 1.1), and with the painting *Nude Descending a Staircase* (1912, figure 1.16). His insistence that the practitioner needs "to be stripped of any thoughts of selfishness, or lasciviousness ... just as in ancient temples no feet trod unless they were bare" suggests that what Duchamp's *Bride Stripped Bare* (figure 0.2) is being stripped of are limitations of emotional attachment and lasciviousness. Limitations of attachment, time, space, and action are described as "Sheaths, cloaks or swaddling clothes of the Spirit" in J. C. Chatterji's *Kashmir Shaivism*, published in 1914.[30] A corollary in Kaula is described by French scholar Lilian Silburn: "A *vira* [victor] or a *siddha* [possessor of spiritual power] is one who, controlling his senses and his mind, has overcome doubts and limitations. Endowed with a pure heart, having renounced everything, without the slightest attachment to his partner, to desire or enjoyment, he is fully dedicated to inner life. ... He proves able to withdraw in a single instant his thought and senses from the source of excitation; oblivious of pleasure at the very climax of enjoyment, he is engulfed in a bliss known as the bliss of *brahman*."[31]

Duchamp's assertion that *Portrait of Dr. Dumouchel* is a 1910 painting in technique, while its content demonstrates "subconscious preoccupations toward a metarealism," suggests that these preoccupations originated before 1910 and were not a passing phase. Far from it: his late etching *The Bride Stripped Bare ...* (1968, figure 1.7) shows a naked girl kneeling on a prayer bench enveloped by a white nimbus. The title connects this etching with *The Large Glass*, which Duchamp worked on between 1912 and 1923. On a sketch with instructions for printing the second state of the etching, Duchamp inscribed: *Encore une mariée mise à nu!*—"Finally a bride stripped bare!"[32]—suggesting that the bride's piety generated her stripping. Also relevant here is Duchamp's emphatic statement that the halo around the hand in *Portrait of Dr. Dumouchel* was expressly *not* motivated by the hand of Dumouchel. By what, then?

••

Spring 1910 through spring 1912 was a key period in Duchamp's life marking an apparent psychological crisis, having to do with sexuality and his identity as an artist, that generated a number of works depicting male and

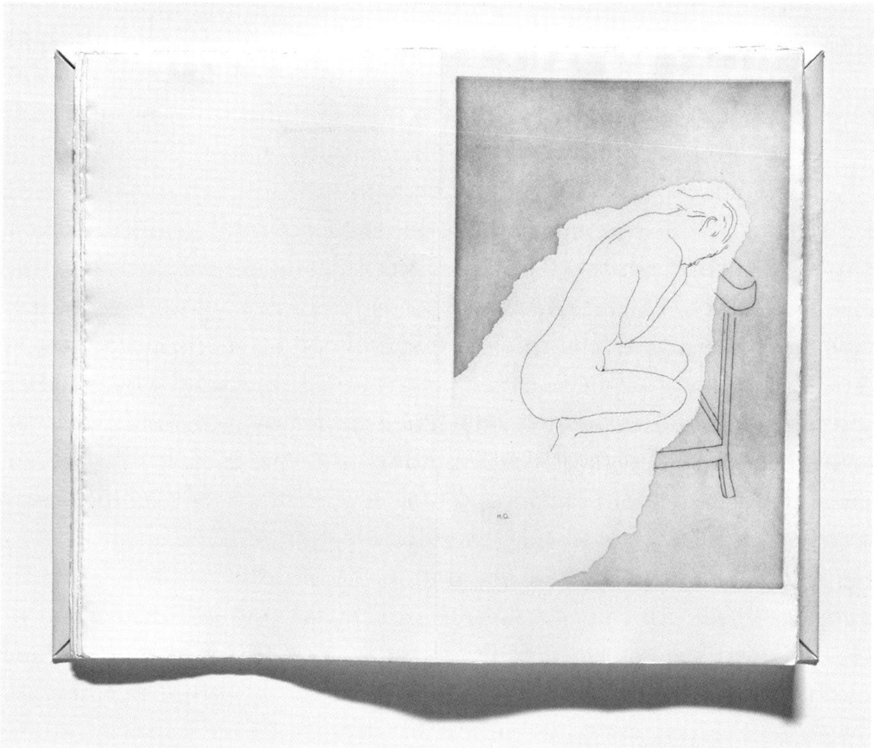

FIGURE 1.7

Marcel Duchamp
The Bride Stripped Bare ... (La Mariée mise à nu ...), from *The Large Glass and Related Works*, volume II, 1968, prints executed 1967–1968
Illustrated book with nine etchings (seven with aquatint), and line block reproduction, page: 41 × 25.2 cm.
Publisher: Schwarz Galleria d'Arte, Milan. Printer: Giorgio Upiglio, Milan. Edition: 135
The Museum of Modern Art, New York, NY, John B. Turner Fund

especially female nudes engaged in mysterious, ritualistic activities evoking initiation, "a procedure whereby the power of one is transmitted to the other."[33] One example, created in late 1910 or early 1911, shows a dark-skinned woman with her hand placed on the head of a lighter-skinned, kneeling woman, both surrounded by a blue-green, womblike aura (figure 1.8). The model for the kneeling woman was Duchamp's lover Jeanne Serre, who would have been pregnant with Duchamp's child at the time.[34] Duchamp called the work *Le Buisson* ("The Bush"), later commenting: "The presence of a non-descriptive title is shown here for the first time. In fact, from then on, I always gave an important role to the title, which I added and treated like an invisible color."[35] For Duchamp, titles became a way of enriching the theme of a work, "an invisible color" that bypasses the senses but appears in the mind, like an intuition.

Duchamp also tended to go for the nondescriptive option when translating his French titles into English, so it is sometimes helpful to take a closer look at the original French. *Buisson* translates not only as "bush," but also as "thicket," calling to mind that "labyrinth beyond time and space" from which Duchamp later said the "mediumistic" artist "seeks his way to a clearing."[36] The main action in *Le Buisson* would appear to be taking place in the minds of the two women, who look neither at each other nor at the viewer, but inward, perhaps toward the "clearing" of their own womblike aura. Or maybe, as with the portrait of Dumouchel, this enveloping, generative form was a sign of Duchamp's preoccupation with metarealism.

Along these lines, it is worth noting that *buisson* is a homonym for *boisson*, "drink." Duchamp labeled a similar painting from this same period *Baptême*[37]—*Baptism* (1911, figure 1.9)—a title that evokes the title of Duchamp's last major work, *Given: 1. The Waterfall, 2. The Illuminating Gas*. Baptism is a form of initiation in which water, sometimes sprinkled on the head, symbolizes cleansing the mind of self-centered desire preparatory to transformative rebirth.[38] Both *Le Buisson* and *Baptism* suggest falling water, and depict a female nude being initiated by a darker-skinned female nude. The fact that Duchamp gave *Le Buisson* to Raymond Dumouchel and *Baptism* to a former Rouen classmate of theirs, Ferdinand Tribout, suggests that together these three friends explored the esoteric milieu of Paris during 1910–1911.

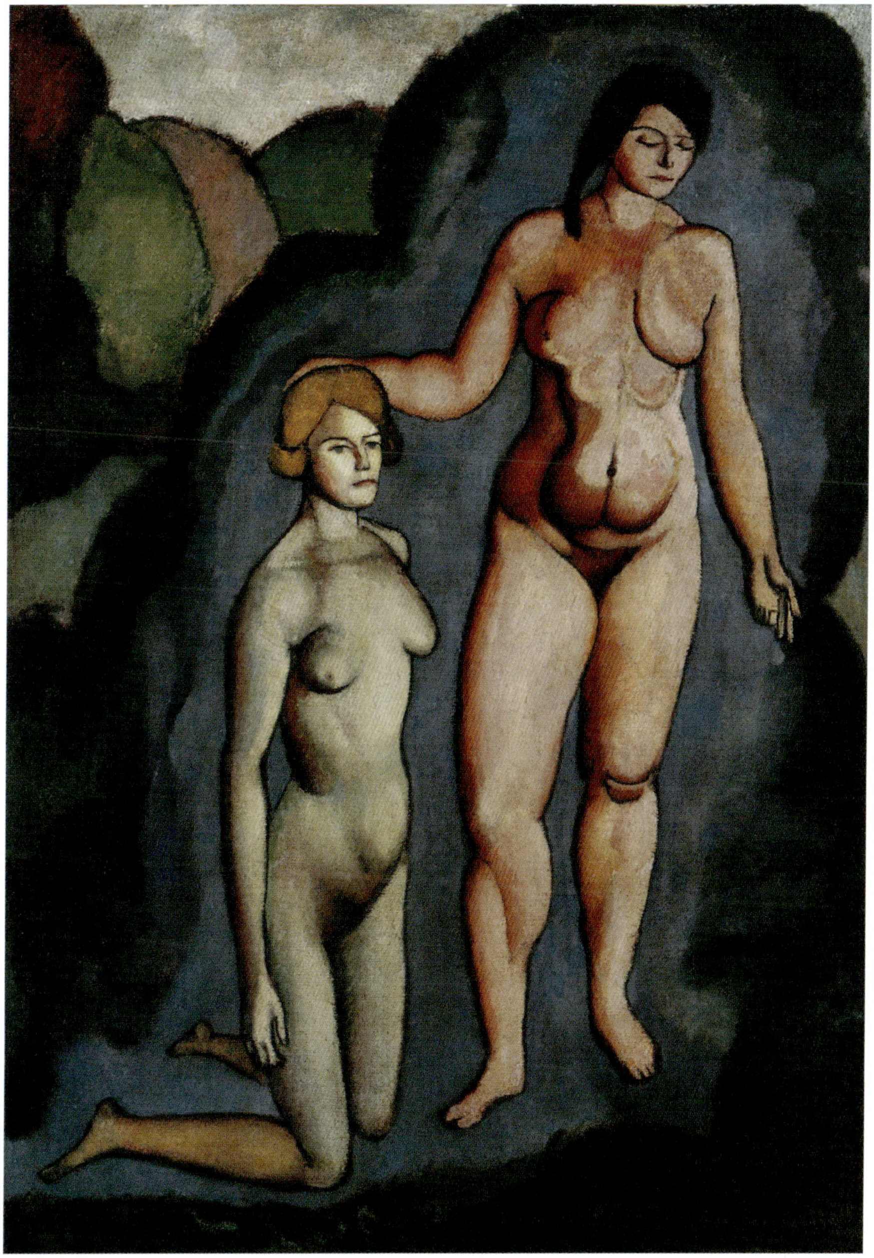

FIGURE 1.8

Marcel Duchamp
Le Buisson / The Bush, 1910–1911
Oil on canvas, 127.3 × 91.9 cm
Philadelphia Museum of Art, Philadelphia, PA, The Louise and Walter Arensberg Collection, 1950 / Bridgeman Images

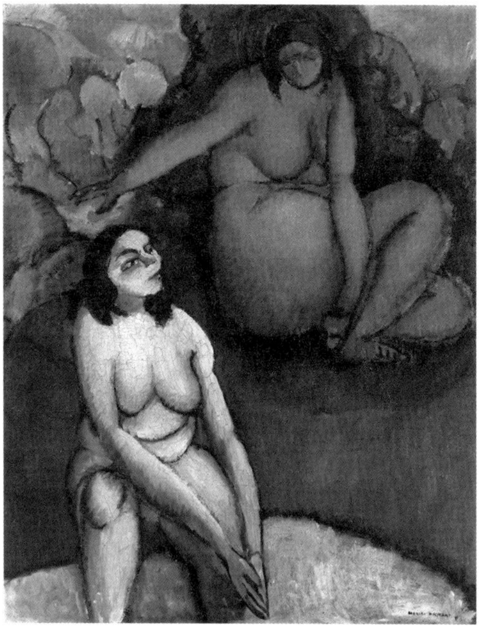

FIGURE 1.9

Marcel Duchamp
Baptême / Baptism, 1911
Oil on canvas, 91.4 × 65.1 cm
Philadelphia Museum of Art, Philadelphia, PA, The Louise and Walter Arensberg Collection, 1950 / Bridgeman Images

Duchamp kept for himself a third painting, *Paradise* (1910–1911, figure 1.10), which shows a nude, dark-skinned woman, seated with knees spread, facing a naked Dumouchel. He covers his genitals with his hands while standing stalwartly in front of her; the expression on his face appears to be one of intense inner concentration. On the reverse of *Paradise* Duchamp would later paint *The King and Queen Surrounded by Swift Nudes*, May 1912, figure 1.17). This layering of Duchamp's chess-player paintings onto earlier, "metarealist" canvases was something of a pattern, as we shall see—a pattern not of erasure, but of connection, continuity, and dimensionality.

The most overtly "metarealist" work Duchamp produced during this period is *Courant d'air sur le pommier du Japon* (*Draft on the Japanese Apple Tree*, figure 1.11), painted in the Puteaux garden of his brother Jacques Villon and his wife, Gabrielle, in spring 1911. *Courant d'air* translates literally as "current of air," like breath. As discussed in the Introduction, breath is a common focus of meditation practices. In the *Bhagavad Gita*, moving air is a metaphor for the mind: "the mind is restless, turbulent, obstinate and

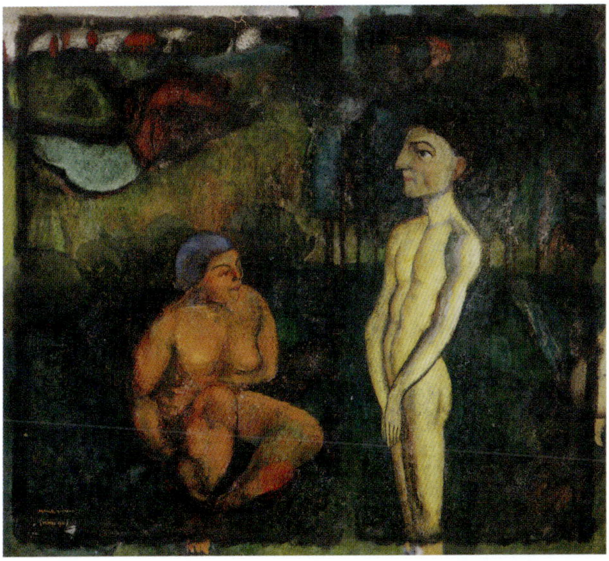

FIGURE 1.10

Marcel Duchamp
Paradis / Paradise (Adam and Eve), 1910–1911
Oil on canvas, 114.6 × 128.9 cm
Philadelphia Museum of Art, Philadelphia, PA, The Louise and Walter Arensberg Collection, 1950 / Bridgeman Images

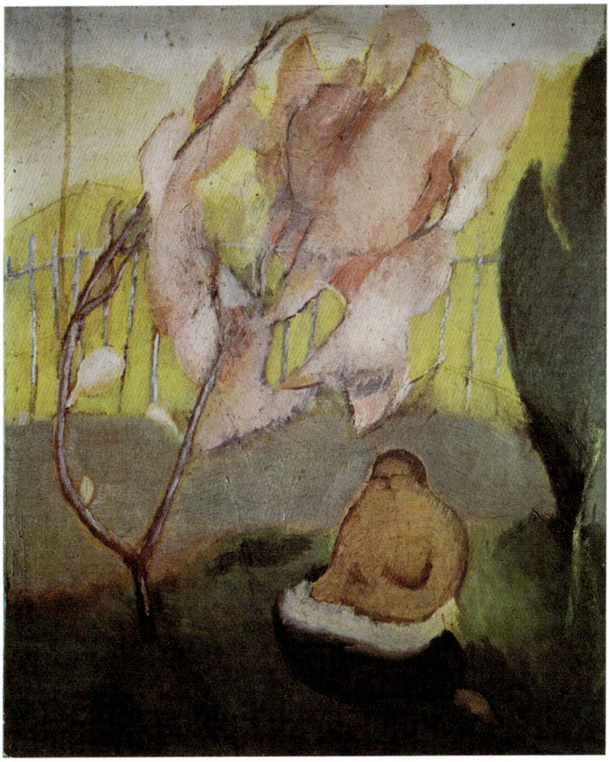

FIGURE 1.11

Marcel Duchamp
Courant d'air sur le pommier du Japon / Draft on the Japanese Apple Tree, Spring 1911
Oil on canvas, 61 × 50 cm
Private collection

very strong, O Krishna, and to subdue it ... is more difficult than controlling the wind."[39] The tree in Duchamp's painting resembles a Japanese plum more than an apple tree, but the "apple" in his title surely references the Garden of Eden and its themes of sexual desire and the Fall. The seated figure beneath the tree has suggested to several commentators "a Buddha-like state of enlightened meditation."[40] "La Japonaise" was a Japanese woman who modeled for Kupka and other artists living in Puteaux at this time. She may have been Buddhist and may, in fact, have been meditating. All of this would seem to indicate that the subject of *Draft on the Japanese Apple Tree* is the transmutation of desire through meditative practice.

Duchamp's paintings and drawings from August 1910 to May 1912 on the theme of chess players exemplify a transition from his painterly, cloisonnist-influenced style of 1910 to his futurist-influenced cubism of spring 1912.[41] At the same time, the imagery in these works became more abstract, even esoteric. Like tantra, chess is about the reconciliation of opposites. (*Opposition and Sister Squares Are Reconciled* was the title of a book on chess Duchamp coauthored with endgame specialist Vitaly Halberstadt in 1932.) As Robert Lebel's son, the artist Jean-Jacques Lebel, observed: "At the end of a chess game, the two players are no longer adversaries, but rather they become of one mind, each knowing what the other is going to do in advance. ... That's what chess is all about."[42] While the subject of Duchamp's chess-player series is nominally the game of chess, and their visual language was drawn increasingly from the realm of science and technology,[43] their content can profitably be read as tantric.

The earliest painting in the series, *The Chess Game* (figure 1.12) from August 1910, depicts a lush, green garden in which Duchamp's two brothers focus intently on a game of chess while their inwardly engaged wives loll in the foreground near a table set for tea. Duchamp here contrasts "active" male consciousness with "passive" female intuition, as the contemplative women complement the intellectually focused men.

The Chess Players (figure 1.13), painted in late fall 1911, is a luminous jumble of a painting in which two chess players engage one another. The right-hand figure is clearly male. The figure on the left is ambiguous but easily read as female, due to what appears to be a breast and a shock of long hair. Her right hand could be gripping a chess piece, but it could also

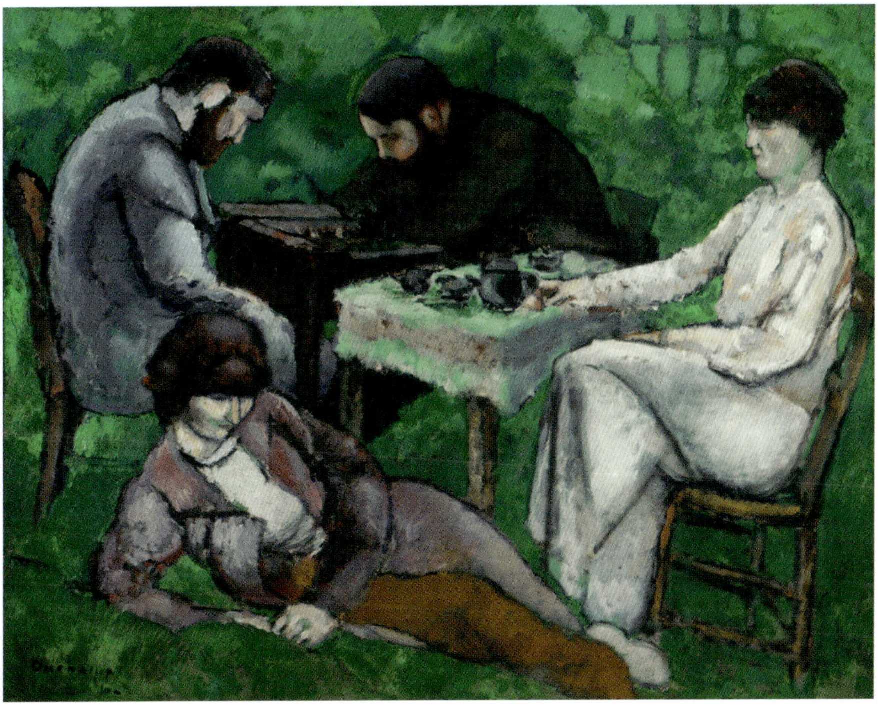

FIGURE 1.12

Marcel Duchamp

La Partie d'échecs / The Chess Game, 1910

Oil on canvas, 114 × 146.5 cm

Philadelphia Museum of Art, Philadelphia, PA, The Louise and Walter Arensberg Collection, 1950 / Bridgeman Images

be placed over the heart of her partner, who rests his chin on his hand in a meditative pose. The most puzzling feature of this painting is a horizontal golden nude whose crotch coincides with the laps of the two players. Duchamp apparently painted this work on top of an old canvas, as he had done previously with *Nu sur nu (Nu aux cheveux verts)* (*Nude on Nude [Nude with Green Hair]*, 1910–1911).[44] *Nude on Nude* looks unfinished, but the same cannot be said of *Chess Players*, as the colors of its female nude—gold and rose—are picked up elsewhere in the painting.

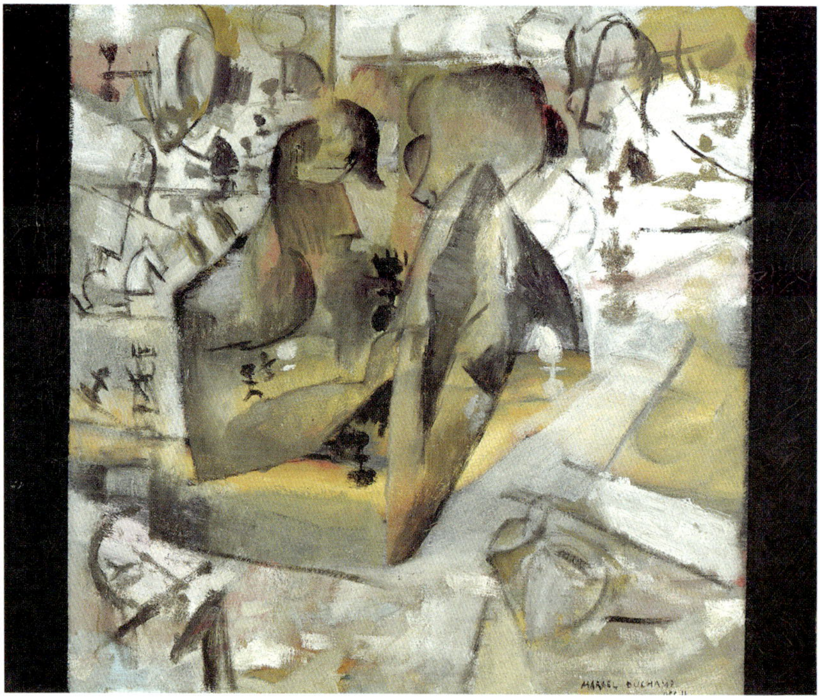

FIGURE 1.13
Marcel Duchamp
Joueurs d'échecs / The Chess Players, 1911
Oil on canvas, 50 × 61 cm
Musée National d'Art Moderne, Centre Pompidou, Paris, France / Bridgeman Images

It has been said that chess was invented in India to channel energies that would otherwise be expressed in warfare. By foregrounding the engagement or "mating" of male and female, *Chess Players* portrays a détente fueled by erotic energy. Duchamp's practice of playing chess with nude women underlines this transformation of aggressive sexual energy into collaborative mental energy. The best-known instance was during his retrospective at the Pasadena Museum in 1963 (figure 1.14), but there was at least one earlier occasion, when the young scholar Michel Sanouillet visited Duchamp in his New York studio in 1951 and observed him playing chess with a naked woman.[45]

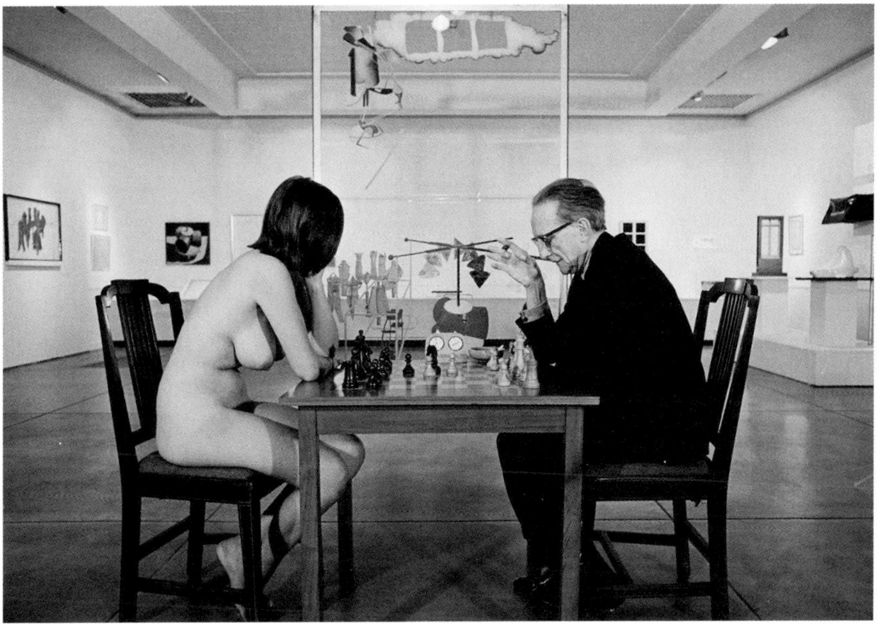

FIGURE 1.14
Julian Wasser
Marcel Duchamp at the Pasadena Art Museum, 1963

In December 1911, Duchamp painted *Portrait of Chess Players* (figure 1.15), the subject of his comments to Pierre Cabanne:

DUCHAMP: "Portrait of Chess Players" ... was painted by gaslight. It was a tempting experiment. You know, that gaslight from the old Auer jet is green; I wanted to see what the changing of colors would do ...

CABANNE: It's one of the rare times when you were preoccupied with problems of light.

DUCHAMP: Yes, but it isn't even really the light. It's the light that enlightened me.[46]

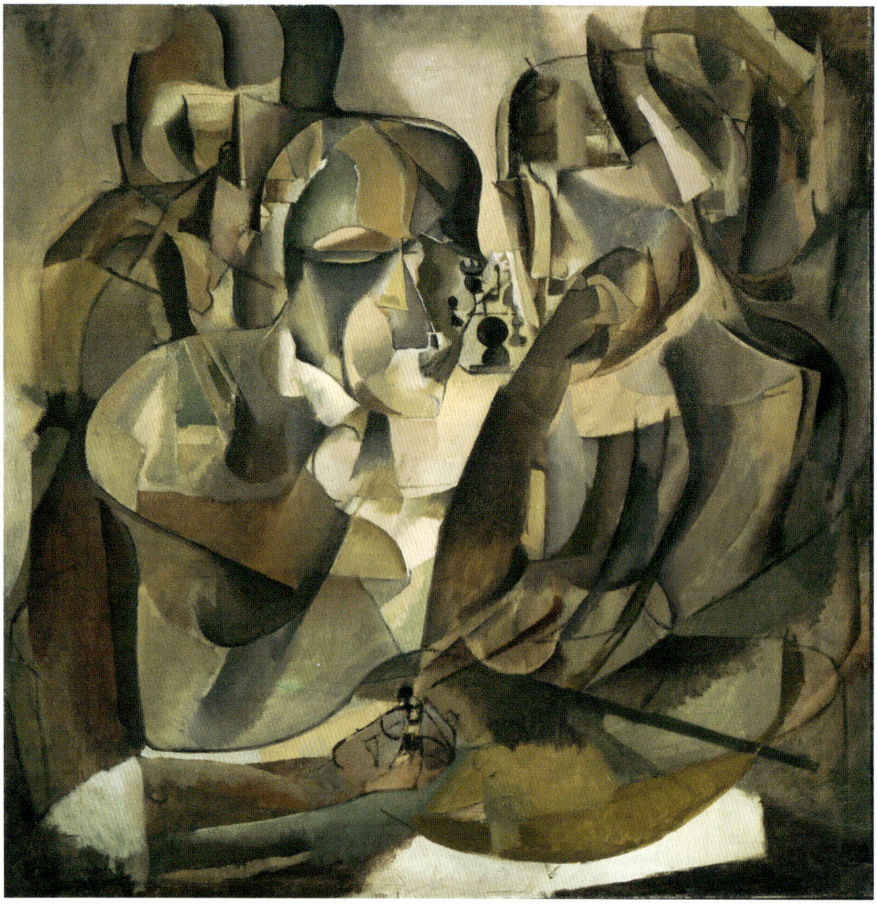

FIGURE 1.15

Marcel Duchamp
Portrait de joueurs d'échecs / Portrait of Chess Players, 1911
Oil on canvas, 100.6 × 100.5 cm
Philadelphia Museum of Art, Philadelphia, PA, The Louise and Walter Arensberg Collection, 1950 / Bridgeman Images

FIGURE 1.16

Marcel Duchamp
Nu descendant un escalier, no. 2 / Nude Descending a Staircase, No. 2, 1912
Oil on canvas, 147 × 89.2 cm
Philadelphia Museum of Art, Philadelphia, PA, The Louise and Walter Arensberg Collection, 1950 / Bridgeman Images

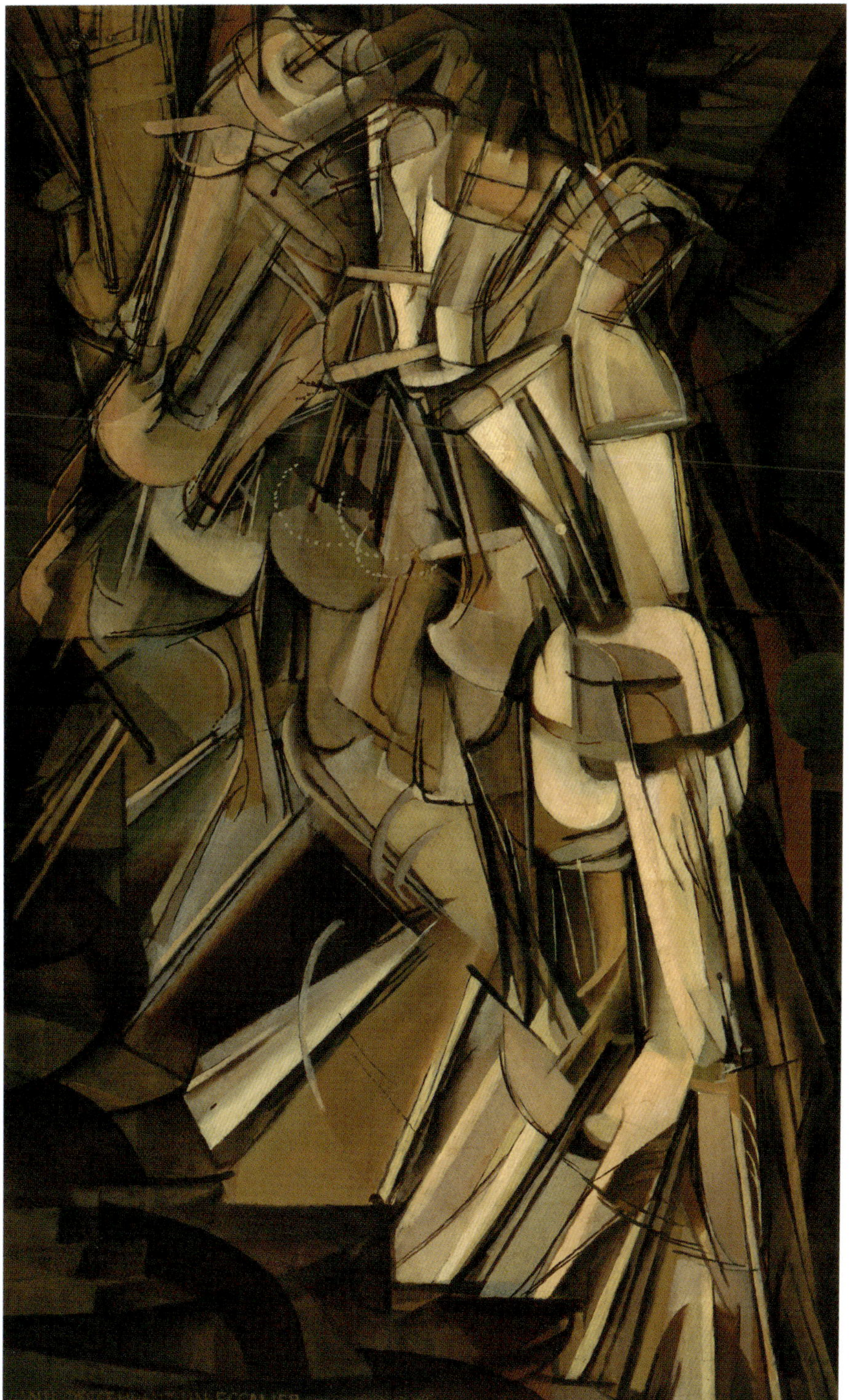
NU
UN ESCALIER

Duchamp said that in *Portrait of Chess Players* he used "the technique of demultiplication in my interpretation of the cubist theory." He also cited his "method of demultiplication of the movement" in his description of *Nude Descending a Staircase* (figure 1.16).[47] Duchamp's technique or method of "demultiplication," which I take to be a term for unification of male consciousness with female energy, as well as a form of rebellion against the biblical injunction to Adam and Eve to "be fruitful and multiply," seems to have provided access to the fourth dimension: a space of mental freedom. The left-hand figure in *Portrait of Chess Players* holds a chess piece in a way that suggests a little winged figure about to take flight—implying liberation, the outcome of enlightenment. It appears here in the same position as the golden nude in the earlier *Chess Players*: at the point of connection between the two players' lower bodies.

The culminating work in the chess-player series was, according to Duchamp, done immediately after the *Nude Descending a Staircase* in the spring of 1912. *The King and Queen Surrounded by Swift Nudes* (May 1912, figure 1.17) marks a dramatic shift in Duchamp's style. It was painted on the obverse of *Paradise* (figure 1.10), four months after *Nude Descending a Staircase, No. 2* (figure 1.16), just before Duchamp left for Munich. What characterizes *King and Queen* above all is a sense of unifying energy. According to Duchamp, "The players of 1911 have been eliminated and replaced by the chess figures of the king and queen. The swift nudes are a flight of imagination introduced to satisfy my preoccupation [with] movement still present in this painting. ... It is a theme of motion in a frame of static entities."[48] The static (ecstatic) entities of the king and queen are two poles charged with positive and negative sexual energies surrounded by "swift nudes"—the infinite mobility through space and time generated by their connection. If *Paradise* on the verso of *King and Queen* can be taken as evidence, their union is psycho-energetic rather than physical. Almost forty years later, Duchamp would summarize this form of engagement in a diagrammatic depiction of the Fall (figure 9.7).

The King and Queen Surrounded by Swift Nudes brings closure to a series begun in August 1910 with the static entities of the intellectual male chess players and their introspective female companions. Consciousness and cosmos are finally united in a dialectical reality that is at once static

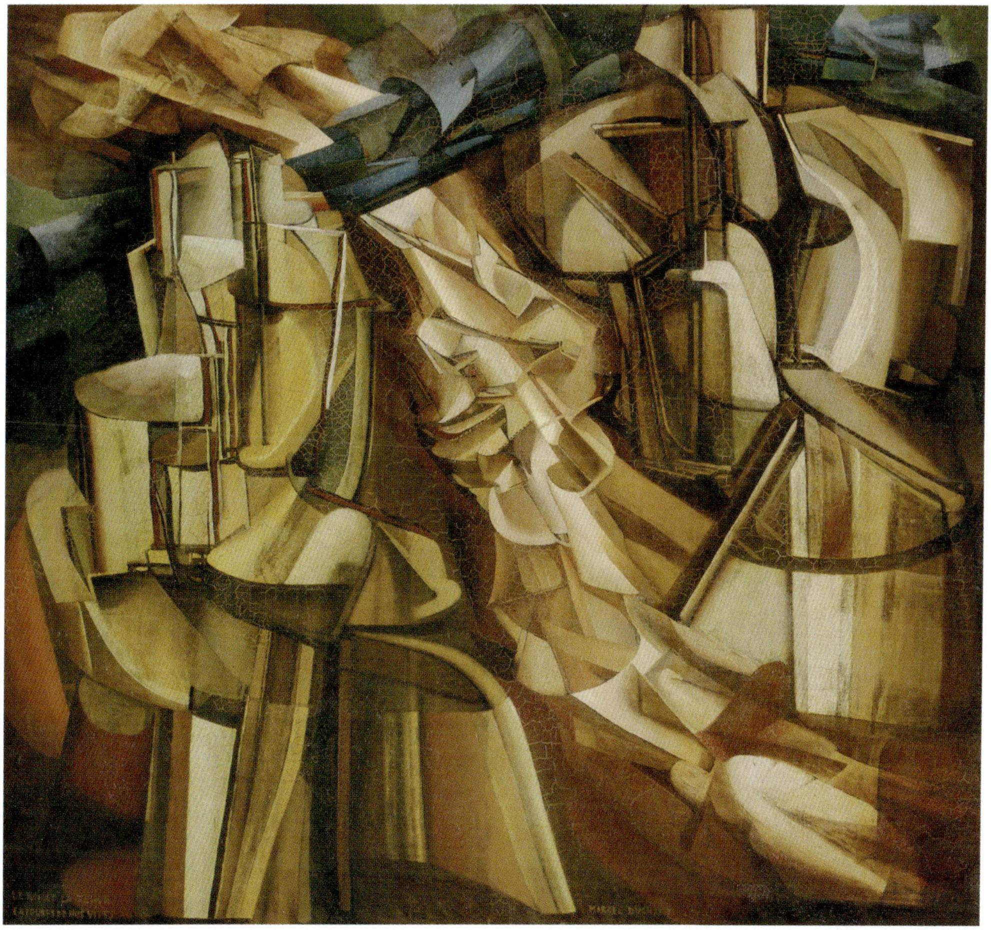

FIGURE 1.17

Marcel Duchamp
Le Roi et la Reine entourés de nus vites / The King and Queen Surrounded by Swift Nudes, 1912
Oil on canvas, 114.6 × 128.9 cm
Philadelphia Museum of Art, Philadelphia, PA, The Louise and Walter Arensberg Collection, 1950 / Bridgeman Images

and dynamic, transcendent and immanent, intellectual and erotic. By May 1912, the king and queen had become aspects of the player him/herself, complementary tendencies unified by erotic energy strategically deployed.

••

Six months earlier, in November or December of 1911, Duchamp integrated into his otherwise painterly *Coffee Mill* (figure 1.18) a diagram-like indication of movement in the form of a curved dotted line and directional arrow, very much like the curved dotted line in the frankly sexual "Jubilation of Père Ubu"—the central image of Alfred Jarry and Pierre Bonnard's *Alphabet*

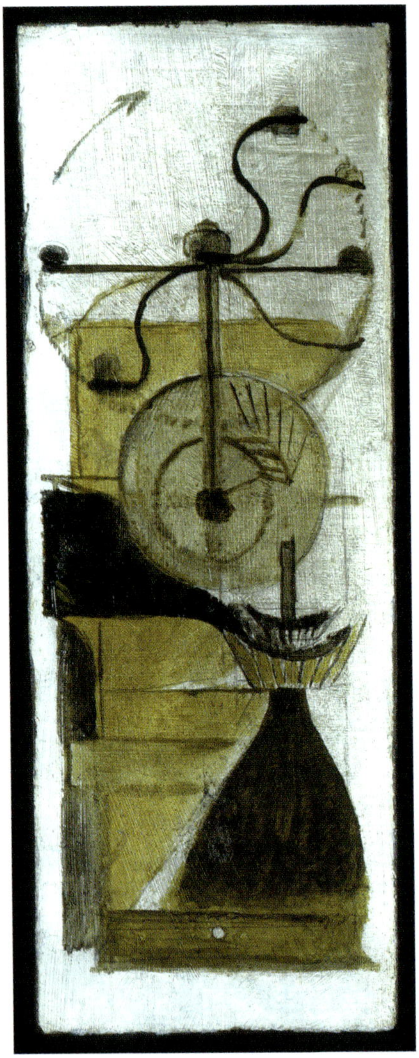

FIGURE 1.18

Marcel Duchamp
Moulin à Café / Coffee Mill, 1911
Oil paint and graphite on board, 33 × 12.7 cm
Tate Gallery, London, Great Britain, Acquisition Purchased 1981 / Art Resource, NY

du Père Ubu (1901, figure 1.19).[49] In *Coffee Mill*, a circular dotted line and arrow traces the path of the rotating handle. A repeated sideways "V" indicates the circular motion of the flywheel, while a rod with a bulb at its tip transfers the manually driven rotation of the handle to the flywheel, which propels the processing of coffee beans into useable form.

Coffee beans, like cocoa beans, resemble female exterior genitals; ground into a powder, both can be transformed into stimulating substances. Duchamp later described *Coffee Mill* in erotic terms, as something that "I made to explode. ... Without knowing it, I had opened a window onto something else."[50] *Coffee Mill* "unveils" the action of a machine that,

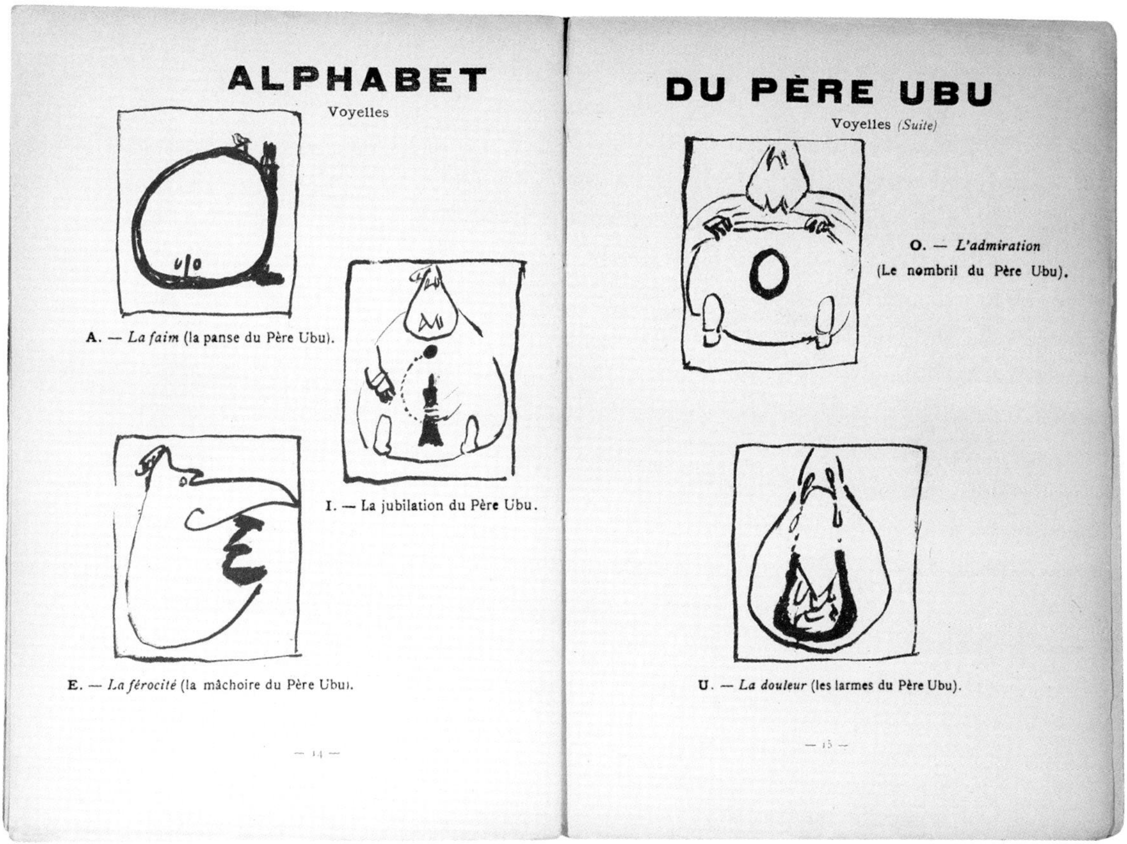

FIGURE 1.19

Pierre Bonnard
Alphabet du Père Ubu / Alphabet of Père Ubu, 1901
Color lithograph, 29.7 × 40 cm
Bibliotheque des Arts Decoratifs, Paris, France. Archives Charmet / Bridgeman Images

through rotational movement, transforms individual coffee beans into a form that produces an awakening liquid via the addition of water and heat—a brilliant metaphor for the mental process of transforming and transmuting erotic passion.

Pressed about whether *Coffee Mill* had any symbolic significance, Duchamp replied: "None at all," adding: "It was a sort of escape hatch. You know, I've always felt this need to escape myself."[51] *Coffee Mill*'s "escape hatch" seems to have served Duchamp not as a symbol, but as an avenue of liberation from his habits of perception. In this way, *Coffee Mill* was a kind of mandala, a device for expanding consciousness. There are Western mandalas—rose windows and labyrinths like the ones at Chartres—but the word itself comes from the Sanskrit for "circle," betraying the Asian source for this "window" to a dimension where small "s" self and large "S" Self, or cosmos, are experienced as a unified whole.

Robert Lebel made this connection in his monograph on Duchamp where, directly adjacent to the upper portion of *Coffee Mill*, Lebel reproduced what he considered to be "an astonishingly similar figure, taken from Dr. Jean Vinchon's study of the Mandala" (figure 1.20).[52] A Jungian neuropsychiatrist who had been friends with Apollinaire, Vinchon published this study, *The Magic of Drawing*, in 1959, the same year Lebel published his book on Duchamp.[53] In Vinchon's book, several similar drawings illustrate a long section on the use of the mandala as a therapeutic device. The drawing Lebel reproduces does not appear there, but it is probably by the same patient—one Henri, a 35-year-old neurotic whose mandala-like drawings demonstrate, according to Vinchon, the gradual "amelioration" of his mental condition. From one of Henri's drawings—an "imperfect" mandala around a "mystic symbol"—Vinchon diagnosed a religious crisis.[54]

Lebel seized on the resemblance between the mandala drawing he chose to reproduce and Duchamp's somewhat sketchy painting of a coffee mill to follow a similar line of therapeutic interpretation:

> We know that Jung sees the Mandala as a representation, common both to Indo-Tibetan mystics and to neurotics, of a struggle against psychic dissociation and of an effort toward unification in the attempt to organize forms around a common center. In the two drawings reproduced [Duchamp's and "Henri's"], the rotation

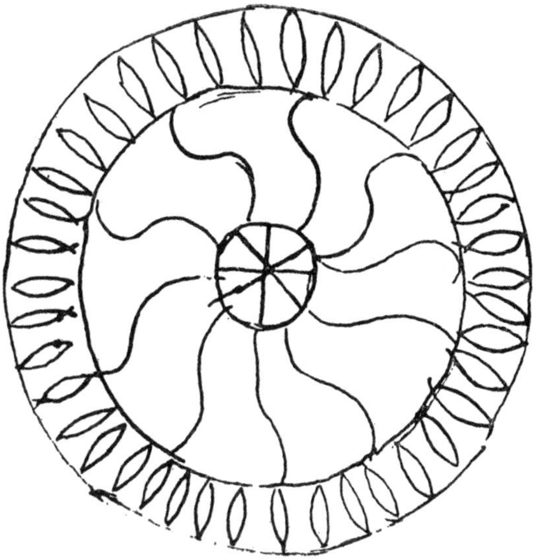

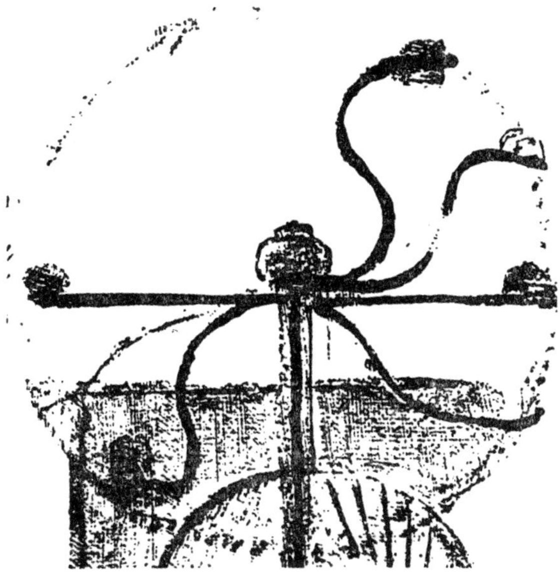

FIGURE 1.20

The upper portion of *Coffee Mill* with "an astonishingly similar figure, taken from Dr. Jean Vinchon's study of the Mandala"
From Robert Lebel, *Marcel Duchamp* (New York: Grove Press, 1959), page 74

> **has only been summarily indicated without reaching completion. It is thus not unimportant that the *Coffee Mill* should have appeared at a time when we believe we have detected in Duchamp the beginning of a crisis, manifested in a moral break with his environment.[55]**

Whatever its moral or psychological source (Lebel suggests schizoid tendencies), Duchamp's impending crisis in late 1911, when *Coffee Mill* was painted, was strongly linked with his identity as an artist. The following summer, this crisis would lead to his break with the Parisian art world and travel to Munich. At this point, however, Duchamp appears to have been still earnestly trying to figure out how to integrate his esoteric explorations of life into his art.

Around this same time, in late 1911, Duchamp created three drawings bearing the names of poems by the symbolist poet Jules Laforgue (1860–1887). He described one of them, *Once More to This Star* (figure 1.1), as a study for *Nude Descending a Staircase*, the first version of which he painted in December 1911.[56] *Once More to This Star* shows the head and upper torso of a man in a meditative pose. His eyes are closed, and his hand supports his chin, as in *The Chess Players* and *Portrait of Chess Players*. It is a shadowy scene, with vertical lines of shading behind the man's head that connect like an energized umbilical cord with the midsection of a naked woman. Or perhaps the shading represents some kind of force emerging from her toward him. Or both. A third figure emanating rays of light ascends three steps. It is hard to make out details of the upper portion of this figure; he could be starting to turn for a descent. The head contains a vertical rectangular shape, like a door or window, foreshadowing the three window-like "Draft Pistons" in the upper portion of *The Large Glass*. Inscribed beneath the sketch are the words *Encore à cet astre* with, in parentheses, "Jules Laforgue."

"Once More to This Star" is indeed the title of a poem by Laforgue. But the poem (about the sun and uncomprehending humankind) would seem to have little to do with what we see going on in Duchamp's drawing, which shows a man visualizing a naked woman linked by a dark, mysterious force with a shining figure ascending an internal stair. The title tells us that the ascent "to this star" is not the first, suggesting that what is being depicted—a yogini materialized within a state of meditative absorption—is an established mental practice.

Once More to This Star is preliminary to *Nude Descending a Staircase* (figure 1.16) in two ways: it was created before the painting, and it depicts a stage previous to the event shown there. The head of the meditating man in the drawing is flanked by two figures: a female nude, and a male ascending an internal stair. In *Nude Descending a Staircase*, a nude of indeterminate sex *descends* what is presumably the same stair. The "nude" in Duchamp's inscription on the front of the painting is the neutral *NU* ("nude figure"), not the feminine *NUE*. Duchamp told a reporter that the descending figure in *Nude Descending a Staircase, No. 2* is neither a woman nor a man.[57] About the drawing, he said to Cabanne: "There was also a

'Nude Ascending a Staircase,' from which came the idea for the painting I did a few months after. ... In the painting, I represented the 'Nude' in the process of descending—it was more pictorial, more majestic."[58] Duchamp's descending Nude is androgynous, uniting male and female, and endowed with majesty—both king and queen.

••

Duchamp's paintings and drawings from 1910 to 1912 reveal an exploration of the relationship between intellect, emotion, and sexuality that echoes the poetry of Jules Laforgue, who died at the age of 27 in 1887, the year Duchamp was born. "I liked Laforgue very much," Duchamp told Cabanne, adding: "I wasn't very, very literary at the time."[59] The American poet and essayist T. S. Eliot described Laforgue as "a young man of ardent feelings, of an active intellect fascinated by abstractions, and with a remarkable gift for metaphysical emotion." Eliot continues in terms that could as easily describe the young Marcel Duchamp: "He had a passionate craving for order: that is, that every feeling should have its intellectual equivalent, its philosophical justification, and that every idea should have its emotional equivalent, its sentimental justification. ... Life was consciously divided into thought and feeling; but his feelings were such as required an intellectual completion, a *beatitude*, and the philosophical systems which he embraced were so much *felt* as to require a sensuous completion."[60] The philosophical systems embraced by Laforgue requiring completion in sensuous form were, as Eliot knew, Buddhism and Advaita Vedanta.[61]

Marcel Duchamp and T. S. Eliot moved in the same Parisian circles during 1910–1911, years that were key for Duchamp's development. Similarities in their thinking at the time are worth looking at, particularly since Duchamp would quote Eliot later in his life, to the puzzlement of art historians. Beginning in October 1910 Eliot spent a postgraduate year in Paris, where, like Duchamp, his closest friend was a medical student.[62] Also like Duchamp, Eliot was fascinated by the links between mystic states and sexual ecstasy.[63] In early summer 1911 he traveled to Munich, precisely one year before Duchamp unexpectedly did the same. Eliot's biographer Robert Crawford suggests that one of Munich's main attractions was its "erotically-supercharged artistic atmosphere,"[64] a factor that would have been equally attractive to Duchamp. They both found lodgings within a block and a half of the Alte Pinakothek, Munich's repository of old master paintings; and in Munich both achieved their first real artistic breakthroughs, with Eliot completing "The Love Song of J. Alfred Prufrock," while Duchamp "abandoned" painting to begin work on his masterpiece, *The Large Glass*.

Following their sojourns in Munich, the young poet and the young artist each took up academic study of ancient languages and texts. Eliot, who returned to Harvard as a graduate student in Philosophy, engaged in an intense course of study of Sanskrit and Asian philosophy.[65] In November 1912 Duchamp began taking courses at École des Chartes, the distinguished French school of paleography where the great Sanskrit scholar Eugène Burnouf had studied.[66] Duchamp told Cabanne that his studies at the École des Chartes were "a kind of intellectual stand against the manual servitude of the artist; at the same time, I was doing my calculations for 'The Large Glass'."[67]

Eliot had first been attracted to the poetry of Jules Laforgue in 1908, while still an undergraduate at Harvard;[68] Laforgue may have been one of the reasons he chose Paris. By the time Eliot arrived in October 1910, Duchamp would already have been exploring Asian philosophical systems capable of evoking (to quote Eliot) "a sensuous completion." After returning to Harvard from Paris and Munich in the fall of 1911, Eliot began seriously studying Patanjali's *Yoga Sutras*, which he came to regard as his guide to life; and the *Bhagavad Gita*, "the next greatest philosophical poem to the *Divine Comedy*."[69]

At precisely this same time—fall 1911—Duchamp "illustrated" three poems by Laforgue: *Mediocrity*, *Eternal Siesta*, and *Once More to This Star*.[70] It seems within the realm of possibility that Duchamp, who described himself as not "very, very literary at the time," had been introduced to Laforgue's poetry by T. S. Eliot. Whether Eliot passed his enthusiasm for Laforgue to Duchamp in 1910–1911, or whether Laforgue happened to be a shared interest; whether Duchamp conveyed his understanding of Laforgue's sources of inspiration to Eliot, or whether Eliot already knew them—the sequence of events suggests contact, or at least a shared intellectual environment, between T. S. Eliot and Marcel Duchamp during a pivotal year for both young artists.

Hindu, Buddhist, and tantric symbolism would come to play unmistakable roles in Eliot's poetic language. From the third of *Four Quartets*, "The Dry Salvages":

> Men's curiosity searches past and future
> And clings to that dimension. But to apprehend
> The point of intersection of the timeless
> With time, is an occupation for the saint—
> No occupation either, but something given
> And taken, in a lifetime's death in love,
> Ardor and selflessness and self-surrender.[71]

Another example, from "Burnt Norton," is the "box circle" mandala of the rose garden with at its center a light-generated lotus that, according to P. S. Sri, "marks the transformation of earthly desire into divine love." Sri notes, however, that in Eliot's poetry the "moment of ecstasy is short lived," and the poet is almost invariably "once again caught up in time."[72]

A lotus within a rose garden implies a merging of East and West, but Eliot was no perennialist. He confessed that, in the end, his assiduous study of Asian metaphysics generated in him only "a state of enlightened mystification." While asserting that the subtleties of Indian philosophy "make most of the great European philosophers look like schoolboys," he also admitted that "study of European philosophy was hardly better than an obstacle," and concluded that his "only hope of really penetrating to the heart of that mystery would lie in forgetting how to think and feel as an American or a European: which, for practical as well as sentimental reasons, I did not wish to do."[73] The more adventurous Duchamp, who would name his artistic alter ego Rose, did not share Eliot's problem. Forgetting how to think and feel as a Westerner seemed to enhance rather than threaten Duchamp's artistic sense of self. As he told Dore Ashton regarding his description of the true artist as a mediumistic being, "I had to reject Cartesianism, in a way. I don't say that you can't be both. Perhaps I am."[74]

So far as I know Eliot never mentioned Duchamp in his writings, but Duchamp referred to Eliot more than once. In his humorous *Le Mémento Universel Da Costa* (1949), Duchamp advertised Eliot as a poet offering "fire to go. Sell wholesale and retail. Fast home delivery."[75] Eight years later,

Duchamp quoted Eliot directly in his pivotal essay "The Creative Act": "The more perfect the artist, the more completely separate in him will be the man who suffers and the mind which creates; the more perfectly will the mind digest and transmute the passions which are its material."[76]

The careers of Marcel Duchamp and T. S. Eliot were so dissimilar that it has been difficult for scholars to understand Duchamp's apparent admiration for his American contemporary. Rosalind Krauss, for example, confessed that "Eliot's conception of tradition, his idea of high culture, his notion that art is redemptive, seems … so far from my understanding of Duchamp. I just don't know where to look in Duchamp to find anything that would connect to this."[77] Where to look is Paris in 1910–1911, a pivotal year for two young artists, still at the beginnings of their careers, with a shared interest in the power of mind to "digest and transmute the passions" and to convey the result through art. What Duchamp experienced in Paris during those years opened him to a boundless realm of eroticism in which he was male and female, lover and loved, knower and known. The result of this union would be *Dulcinea*—Rrose Sélavy in embryo.

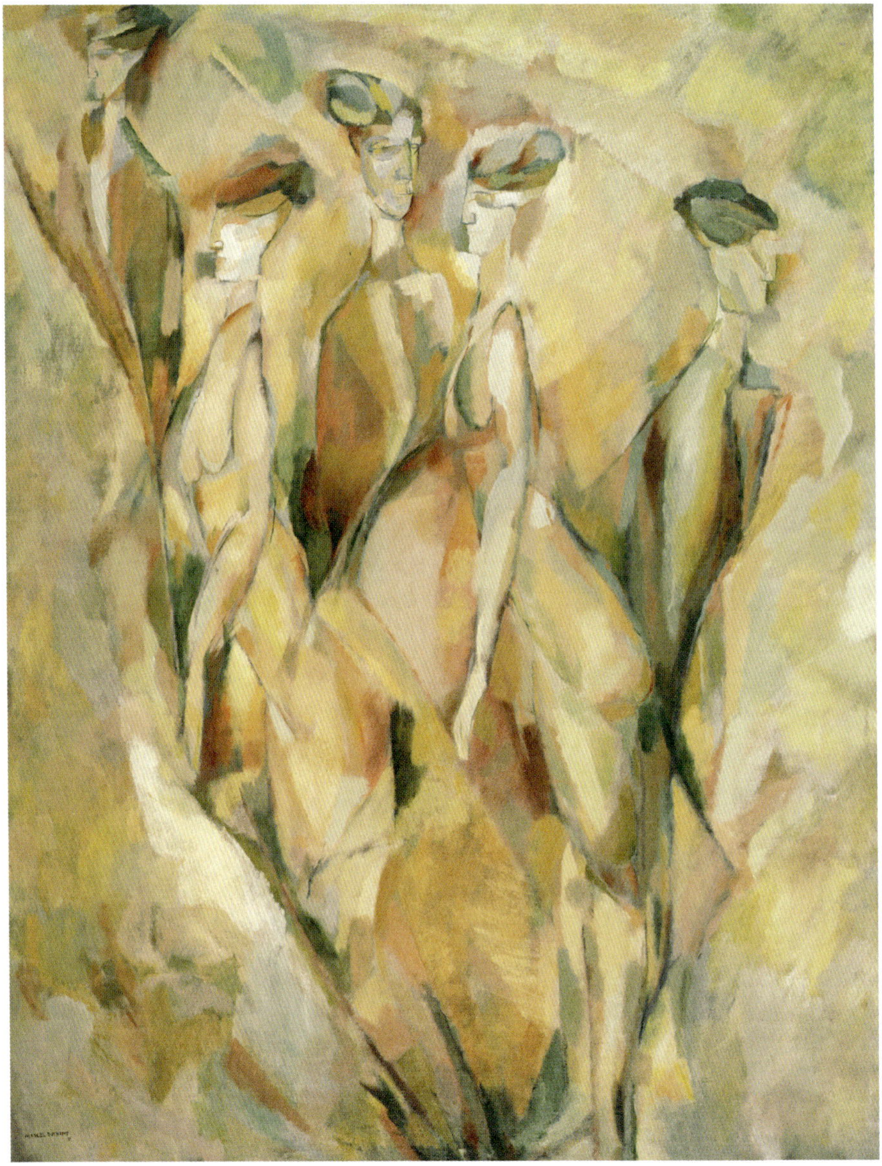

FIGURE 2.1

Marcel Duchamp
Portrait (Dulcinée) / Portrait (Dulcinea), 1911
Oil on canvas, 146.4 × 114 cm
Philadelphia Museum of Art, Philadelphia, PA, The Louise and Walter Arensberg Collection, 1950 / Bridgeman Images

2 DULCINEA

It was as though my existence split into two distinct registers, ... with one focus fathoming the inexpressible, while through the other the real never disappeared from my field of vision.

—Robert Lebel, *La double vue*[1]

In early fall 1911 Marcel Duchamp painted *Portrait*, or *Dulcinea* (figure 2.1), which he described to Pierre Cabanne as "the repetition of the same person four or five times, nude, dressed, and in the shape of a bouquet."[2] *Dulcinea* is a large painting, approximately 58 by 45 inches, larger even than *Nude Descending a Staircase, No. 2* from a few months later (1912, figure 1.16). It depicts, from five points of view, a figure in the process of transformation or transmutation. As a portrait, *Dulcinea* is distinctly unflattering. The clothing, droopy breasts, and suggestion of pregnancy (in the central figure) identify her as female, but her face resembles Duchamp's. In this way, *Dulcinea* is similar to *Yvonne and Magdeleine Torn in Tatters*, also painted in fall 1911 (figure 1.2), where the profiles of Duchamp's two youngest sisters appear mingled with his own in a confetti of family identities.

Duchamp seems to have been conflicted about *Dulcinea*'s title—an obvious reference to the love interest of Don Quixote, who saw his Dulcinea only fleetingly, though she inspired his every quest. He tentatively titled the painting *Dulcinea* only in 1936 while preparing reproductions for his 1941 *Box in a Valise*, labeling the reproduction of this work *Dulcinée* before striking out the name and replacing it with *Portrait*.[3] In Robert Lebel's 1959 catalogue raisonné, the painting was published as "*Portrait*, or *Dulcinea*:

Five silhouettes of a woman on different planes." Lebel described her as "a woman whom Duchamp had seen passing by and whom he loved, he says, without ever meeting her."[4]

Lebel said Duchamp mentioned several smaller versions of *Dulcinea* that "have not been found."[5] This is odd, as during this period Duchamp tended to keep or give to friends studies for important works. When asked whether *Dulcinea* related to an unhappy love affair, he insisted: "No, not at all! 'Dulcinea' is a woman I met on the Avenue de Neuilly, whom I saw from time to time going to lunch, but to whom I never spoke. It wasn't even a matter of being able to speak to her. She walked her dog, and she lived in the neighborhood, that's all."[6] Duchamp would similarly claim he never spoke to a soul in Munich the following summer—an obvious hyperbole. Not speaking of something evokes esotericism. Perhaps Duchamp's quest was not for another person, but for connection with his female energy. This interpretation frames *Dulcinea* as a combination portrait and self-portrait, a painterly foray into esoteric territory from which his early masterpiece, *The Bride Stripped Bare by Her Bachelors, Even* (1915–1923, figure 0.2), would emerge.

"Relation to a woman through a mere glance" is one of six ways of performing "esoteric sacrifice" listed in the *Tantrāloka*—"Light on Tantras," Abhinavagupta's eleventh-century treatise on Shakta Shaivism. (The complete list reads: "in worldly activities, in relation to a woman [through a mere glance], in the couple's union, as well as in body, breath, and thought.")[7] The Sanskrit word *darśana* means "sight," "vision," or "appearance." In the Hindu tradition, darshan implies a mutual interaction between the viewer and the perceived object or being. Might *Dulcinea*, Duchamp's "repetition" of a person "nude, dressed, and in the shape of a bouquet," have recorded his relation with a woman through the act of looking? If so, the actual experience would have evolved not from reading a treatise, but from working with a teacher—specifically a female teacher, according to Abhinavagupta, whose commentator, Jayaratha, adds: "She alone has the capacity of bearing and nourishing the embryo and of making the emission fruitful"[8]—a remark that may help to account for the apparent pregnancy of the central figure in *Dulcinea*.

Duchamp's friend and first biographer, Robert Lebel, hinted at the identity of this female guru in his novel *La double vue, suivi de L'inventeur du temps gratuit* ("Double View, followed by The Inventor of Free Time")—a roman à clef published in 1964.[9] *La double vue*, which won the 1965 *Prix du fantastique* but has never been published in English, is set in the interconnected esoteric circles of pre-World War I Paris. Its accompanying story, "The Inventor of Free Time," is set on the Lower East Side of New York during the early 1940s and has been published in English several times.[10] Lebel had already published this story, which everybody knew was about Duchamp, in André Breton's journal *Le surréalisme, même* in spring 1957. It was published again in 1964, this time appended to *La double vue*, a juxtaposition that positions the novel as a first-person account of the early years of the story's eccentric Inventor.

Reproduced on the cover of the first trade edition of *La double vue, suivi de L'inventeur du temps gratuit* was a horizontal etching by Alberto Giacometti showing a double depiction of the heroine of *La double vue*—one bust-length, the other a close-up of her face with an emphasis on the eyes (figure 2.2).[11] Duchamp contributed an ingenious multiple: *The Clock in Profile* (1964, figure 2.3)—a *pliage*, or pop-up, that was issued along with one or more etchings by Giacometti with the deluxe edition. Two photographs of *The Clock in Profile* were published in the regular edition, "*hors-texte*." One—which shows the *pliage* flat, resembling spectacles—is inserted between the novel and the story. The other—positioned more or less in the middle of "The Inventor of Free Time"—shows the *pliage* slid closed on its runners. In this popped-up form it resembles a freestanding clock with no hands, and holes where the numbers would be.

In 1966 the editor of *The White Box (À l'infinitif)* referred readers to Duchamp's *pliage* for *La double vue, suivi de L'inventeur du temps gratuit*, writing in a note: "A clock seen in profile so that time disappears, but which accepts the idea of time other than linear time. [M.D., 1965.] M. D. suggests reading J. W. Dunne's *Experiment in Time* and *Serialism*. See Robert Lebel's *L'inventeur du temps gratuit*, Le Soleil Noir, Paris 1964, for which M.D. made a 'pliage' of a clock seen in profile."[12] The books referred to are John William Dunne's *An Experiment with Time* (1927) and *The Serial Universe* (1934). Dunne (1875–1949) was a British aircraft designer whose experiments with precognition were sparked by a dream of seeing the correct time on his watch before waking up and looking at it. His explorations of transitional

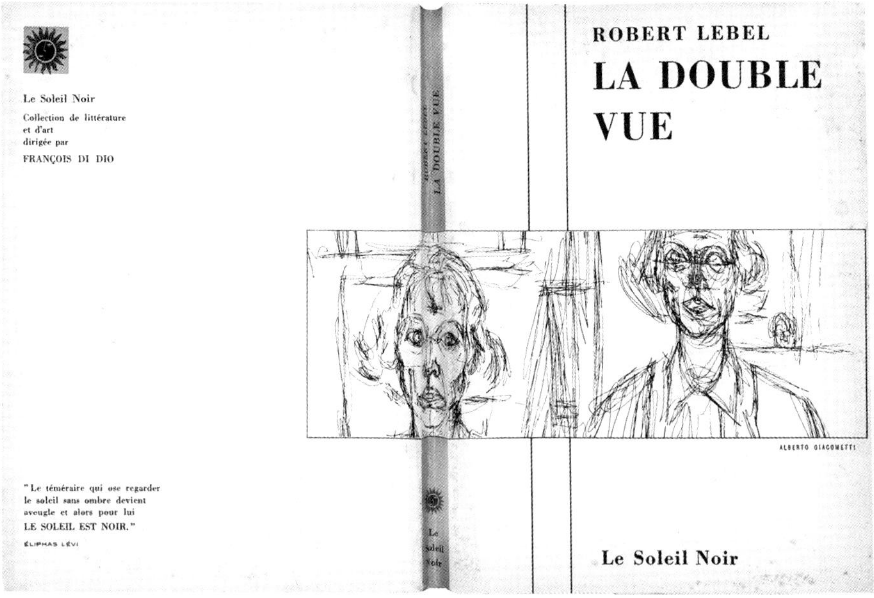

FIGURE 2.2

Robert Lebel, *La double vue suivi de L'inventeur du temps gratuit*, 1964
Cover drawing by Alberto Giacometti

states of consciousness led him to understand the experience of linear time as an illusion. Dunne's second book, *The Serial Universe*, elaborates on "serialism"—time as an "infinite regress," or series of dimensions, with each moment part of an omnipresent past and future.

Dunne's concept of time as multidimensional would have resonated with Duchamp's own understanding of time and the malleability of consciousness as explored in paintings like *Yvonne and Magdeleine Torn in Tatters* (1911, figure 1.2). More directly relevant is his early note, published in *The Green Box* in 1934: "The Clock in profile. And the Inspector of Space,"[13] which the 1964 *Clock in Profile* clearly references. The sole pretext for the 1966 *White Box* comment about Dunne is a brief reference to a "dial seen in

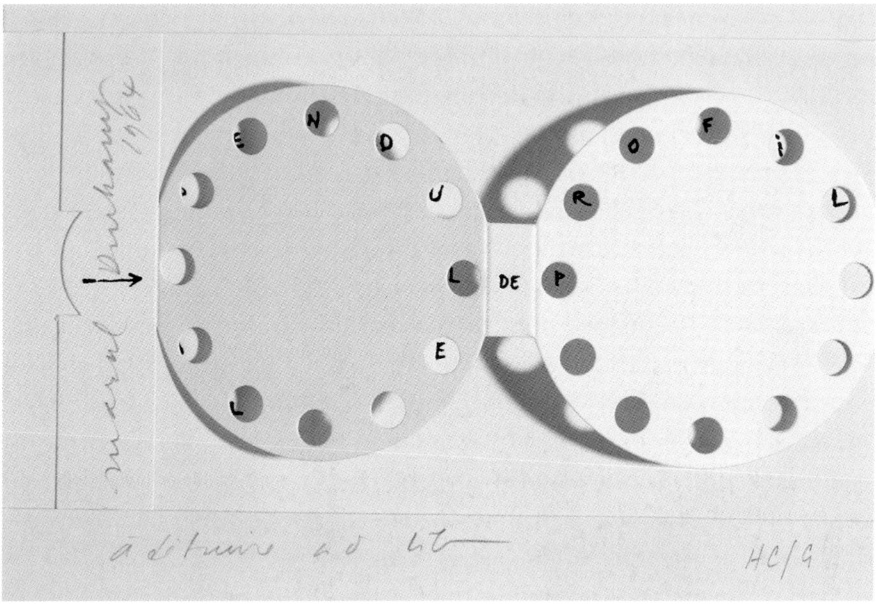

FIGURE 2.3

Marcel Duchamp
La pendule de profil / The Clock in Profile, 1964
Cardboard *pliage* on cardboard, 28 × 22 cm
Issued with the deluxe edition of Robert Lebel, *La double vue, suivi de L'inventeur du temps gratuit*
The Israel Museum, Jerusalem, Israel. Vera & Arturo Schwarz Collection of Dada and Surrealist Art / Bridgeman Images

profile." Duchamp scholar Linda Dalrymple Henderson believes Duchamp referred readers to Dunne in 1966 because "he must have recognized that a reference to Dunne could give his notes new currency."[14] More likely, Duchamp mentioned Dunne to promote Robert Lebel's publication of *La double vue, suivi de L'inventeur du temps gratuit* (1964) describing in veiled fashion Duchamp's own researches into multidimensional time, for which he had made a "dial" that can be seen in profile.

How did Lebel come to write *La double vue*? Years later, he provided a clue: "In 1959 I received from a Parisian publishing house a commission for a book that would have given Duchamp and me complete latitude to illustrate and write it separately, without consulting each other. But when Duchamp, complying immediately, dispatched as illustrations from Cadaqués three hermetically sealed boxes containing *With My Tongue in My Cheek* [figure 10.1], *Torture-morte*, and *Sculpture-morte*, the commission was summarily cancelled."[15] Lebel says nothing about the fate of his own contribution to the joint publication project and he did not specify who cancelled it, though he implies it was the publisher. Lebel's son, the artist and author Jean-Jacques Lebel, says the publisher in question was Arnold Fawcus of Trianon Press, the Parisian publisher of Lebel's 1959 Duchamp monograph.[16]

It seems unlikely that a publisher adventurous enough to publish Lebel and Duchamp's elaborate monograph would have gotten cold feet about a creative project after receiving Duchamp's illustrations. On the other hand, Fawcus was notoriously difficult, and it may be that the reliefs were not all that publishable. It may also be that Duchamp sent his own contribution before he had seen Lebel's (as they had agreed), and when he finally saw what Lebel had written, Duchamp was the one who got cold feet. In this scenario, the book was not published as a collaboration in 1959 at least in part because Duchamp was not comfortable with the manuscript—either because he didn't like it, or because it revealed more about what the elusive Duchamp was up to than the artist wanted known. So Lebel published his novel five years later, along with a previously published short story, as *La double vue, suivi de L'inventeur du temps gratuit*. The dual format may have been intended to deflect biographical attention from the novel to its accompanying story, whose Duchampian protagonist dismisses the narrator with the comments: "it is compulsory that ... we work hard to put others off the scent. ... Freedom is never separate from a certain silence. No doubt I have already said too much."[17] The ploy worked: *La double vue* has never been published in English, and to this day there has been no public discussion of either the many parallels between its protagonist and the young Marcel Duchamp, or whether there may have been a real-life prototype for the heroine in Lebel's novel.

••

Lebel's Inventor of Free Time is a lively French artist-philosopher-yogin whose bed is occupied by a series of young women; the setting is an "extraordinarily cluttered warehouse" in New York during the early 1940s. The unconventional opinions of this thinly disguised Duchamp character fascinate the narrator, and the story is dominated by his pronouncements: "'Everything announces a passage to go through, a rupture to realize. Between this world and the other, there's no legendary transition, no discursive communication. No one offers us the key to some different nirvana because it seems as if, where we're going, ecstasy has no reason to exist. ... No ceremonial, no incantations, no rites, but reaching the point of lucidity where the notion of time becomes a fruit one can peel,' and with his fingers he made these little, nimble movements."[18]

Both story and novel vacillate between ironic farce and mystery, profundity and humor. But while the story has been widely recognized as a caricature of Duchamp, *La double vue* has not been treated in the same way, despite the fact that its narrative would seem to describe a formative moment in the early career of the eccentric fiftyish artist-philosopher of the story. *La double vue* may, in fact, be the result of Lebel's attempt to create a "comedy of consciousness" entertainingly anticipated in "The Inventor of Free Time." It is hard to judge the degree of reality indexed by *La double vue*, but its value as an allegory of Duchamp's lived experience seems clear. Among other things, certain passages offer valuable perspective on his early struggles with art-making. The artist's journey in *La double vue* is one of learning to see clearly, both in art and in life. Woven throughout are passages that read like excerpts from a Duchamp interview, shedding light on his philosophy and on the changes his work underwent during the years 1910–1913.

The plot of *La double vue*, told in the first person, involves an alienated young painter who attempts to refashion his artistic identity:

> Several collectors, long unapproachable, began to become interested in me, but as soon as I found myself in their presence I was seized with panic. They invited me, received me with a solicitude nuanced by that mercantile complicity unique to today's patrons of the arts. But it gave me little pleasure to find my pictures among others, firmly bound to the walls like prisoners in the chariots of the victor, reduced to ornaments for a sinister interior. ...
>
> My weapons were insufficient in the struggle against vulgarity. The atrocious ambiguity of this fraternization with the enemy overwhelmed me, and I resolved to depart the field of battle.[19]

After isolating himself in an industrial area of Paris, and painting only at night, the painter is distracted and then obsessed by midnight chanting that seems to be coming from a derelict piano factory. His investigation takes him to a charismatic "*gardienne*" of the piano factory, a woman who, he will later learn, spent her early adult life in India: "It was said that after a career as a tutor in the East with one of the last governors of French India, she had become a disciple of Sri Aurobindo and received Vedantic and tantric initiations. Repatriated, she married a retired noncommissioned officer—an obtuse person, but fanatically devoted."[20] After surreptitious investigation, the artist discovers behind an old wooden door (an allusion to the door in *Given*) a hidden underground chamber where the *gardienne* and her small group of followers lead nightly inspirational gatherings of underclass people. She in turn follows him to his studio and confronts him, criticizing both his painting and his motives. In response, he begins attacking his paintings until she forcibly stops him and invites him to begin attending her gatherings.

With some difficulty, the painter becomes the ninth member of the *gardienne*'s inner circle of adepts (corresponding to the nine bachelors of *The Large Glass*). They represent a variety of professions, and their interests, running the gamut of Western occult disciplines, paint a vivid picture of the esoteric milieu of early-twentieth-century Paris:

> The adepts differed from one another not only by their appearance, comportment, language, and social class, but also by their ideological positions, which were revealed as contradictory in the first debate I was allowed to witness. The doctor, the most dogmatic of them all, leaned heavily on the Upanishads and, accessorily, on Pythagoras. The lawyer asserted, not without some reservations, that he was Swedenborgian; the writer declared himself a Cathar; the professor practiced alchemy; the geographer claimed to be an anarchist, the wrestler split hairs with the inspector on questions of Rosicrucian discipline; the composer was absorbed in an account of cyclic theories whose origin he traced back to the Egyptians.

Skeptical of her followers' abilities to comprehend Asian mind practices, the *gardienne* allows them to pursue their own esoteric inclinations, while insisting on core perennial teachings. She listens, "unresponsive to these divergences, but quick to seize upon and emphasize any chance agreement as soon as it appeared."[21]

Our hero's cult is the art of painting, which his experiences with the *gardienne* will lead him to completely transform. As her only follower not aligned with a specific Western esoteric tradition, he is alternately irritated and amused by the adepts' endless verbal wrangling. Finally, the *gardienne* invites the young artist to be initiated and taught by her. Lying alongside her in the dark, he is led through their "hypostatic" (nonbodily) encounters to experience a transcendent Self, beyond male or female. A potential Indian source for the *gardienne*'s Western initiation ritual is the Kaula practice of *vedhadiksha*, "initiation of piercing,"[22] in which the guru penetrates the disciple's body with her or his own energy.

> I soared after her without hesitation toward unknown regions that she pointed out to me, murmuring, "Look." I was free from any physical anxiety in the aura of this blossoming body, which revealed itself fully. ... We were like two hereditary enemies finally making peace after centuries of inexpiable massacres ... freed both from the inevitability of mechanical coupling and the mental gangrenes that derive from it. ... Escaped from my emotional prison, I could finally rejoin the gardienne on the impersonal plane where she welcomed me with a smile, inciting in me an endless orgasm of ecstasy without object. ... It was as though my existence split into two distinct registers: I had double sight, with one focus fathoming the inexpressible, while through the other the real never disappeared from my field of vision.[23]

This passage points to Duchamp and his work in several ways. The allusions to *L.H.O.O.Q.* ("LOOK") and *The Large Glass* ("blossoming")[24] are obvious. In French, the last section reads: "*Comme si mon existence s'étant scindé en deux registres distincts, je disposais d'une double vue dont un des foyers me faisait pénétrer dans l'inexprimable, tandis que, par l'autre foyer, le réel ne disparaissait jamais de mon champ.*" The French "*foyer*" means not only "focus," but more commonly, "hearth" or "fire"—a key Duchampian theme. Also note the close pun at the end: "de ... champ" / Duchamp. (Lebel, like Duchamp, was a great punster.)

The young painter's experience with this powerful woman generates a new form of knowledge and new inspiration for his art. In a review of *La double vue* the critic (and friend of Lebel and Duchamp) Patrick Waldberg summarized the plot at this point: "A patient investigation leads him to discover the existence … of a secret society of a stupefying nature. … The passage into this other universe, with its escape from time and from common laws, is reflected in his manner of painting by suddenly endowing him with a sort of double sight, thanks to which a premonition that had long haunted him is verified: 'That painting essentially aims at the representation of ecstasy'."[25] The painter struggles to incorporate this multidimensional field of vision into his work—an effort that manifested in Duchamp's paintings from 1910 to 1912: "Soon I was furiously taken up with my new problem: how, without trickery, to introduce into my painting this light that signaled itself to me, which I did not believe was either revealed or celestial, but where I had caught a glimpse of another dimension, unexpectedly placed within my reach."[26]

Tipped off by the owner of the piano factory, the police raid the *gardienne*'s gathering of would-be anarchists. She and her immediate followers, including the artist, are thrown into jail. At their trial, witnesses testify in various comic scenes. At the last minute, a powerful anonymous defender emerges—apparently one of the *gardienne*'s secret followers. The case is dismissed, but she is ordered to leave Paris. Finding that he occupies no special place in her affections, the disillusioned artist admits to himself that he is in love with her, and debates what his course of action ought to be. He realizes that both he and his art have been changed forever by his experiences, and he spontaneously decides to follow her.

In his review of *La double vue, suivi de L'inventeur du temps gratuit* Patrick Waldberg remarked on the deserted, quasi-industrial settings of both novel and story. He specifically mentions Duchamp only in connection with "The Inventor of Free Time," writing that its hero "cannot fail to evoke Marcel Duchamp, both in his 'ironism of affirmation' and in his art of withdrawal." Waldberg does not mention Duchamp by name in writing about *La double vue*, but he does make clear that the two accounts are connected, and that Lebel's description of Parisian esoteric activity was not complete fantasy:

> The secret society described by the narrator, like all enterprises of this kind, whose temptation remains more frequent than is believed, presents itself in an aspect where the pathetic disputes with the grotesque. Such grandiose derision matters

not in light of what is sought and sometimes obtained: to increase the degree of intensity. What counts here is the tear in the world of dispersion and of the squandering of moments. The "gardienne" achieves this by the conjunction of a candid will and the practice of a discarnate but ritual eroticism, without any concern for dogmatic finality.[27]

With his reference to secret societies and their temptations, Waldberg would have known what he was talking about. As we shall see, during the late 1930s Patrick Waldberg and his wife Isabelle were members of Georges Bataille's secret society, Acéphale, where the ritual eroticism was not always discarnate (see chapter 8). In writing that what matters is "the tear in in the world of dispersion [i.e., the material world]," Waldberg may have had in mind paintings such as *Yvonne and Magdeleine Torn in Tatters* (figure 1.2) and *Tu m'* (figure 4.6), as well as Duchamp's personal practice, which—if the testimony of Gabrielle Buffet-Picabia can be believed—involved what might accurately be described as discarnate eroticism (see chapter 3).

••

From the parallels between the plot of *La double vue* and the career of the young Marcel Duchamp, it seems clear that Robert Lebel intended his novella to account for the dramatic changes that occurred in Duchamp's art between 1910 and 1912. There are simply too many similarities between Lebel's roman à clef and Duchamp's career for *La double vue* to have been either Lebel's semiautobiographical account, as some have claimed,[28] or a complete fiction. What might be the facts hidden behind the fictional veil?

Marcel Duchamp no doubt shared a great deal of personal information with his biographer, who was also a close friend. But not everything he told Lebel would have been appropriate for the 1959 catalogue raisonné. As an advocate for free expression, however, neither would Duchamp have repressed this material completely. I suggest that it surfaced in Lebel's fictionalized narratives, "The Inventor of Free Time" and *La double vue*. The story would appear to be an exaggerated and partly fabricated narrative of Lebel's personal experience of Duchamp, while the novella would have been based on Duchamp's own, no doubt vague, account. Lebel probably did some research of his own, and it is sometimes hard to know whether he is disguising the facts, filling in the blanks, or both. Nevertheless, corresponding to the pattern of Duchamp's growing desire to incorporate erotic energy and out-of-time experience into his art, *La double vue* provides convincing hints that early in his career Marcel Duchamp adapted Western esoteric forms of Asian erotic practices that he proceeded to use as resources for his art practice.

History suggests that Lebel's heroine was modeled on Mirra Alfassa (1878–1973), a Parisian artist who studied tantra yoga with Max and Alma Théon (see chapter 1), traveled to India in 1914, and become famous as The Mother, the spiritual collaborator of Sri Aurobindo (1872–1950). This Parisian artist turned spiritual leader embodies many of the esoteric erotic qualities Duchamp would synthesize in his own views. Alfassa was the daughter of a Turkish-Jewish father and an Egyptian-Jewish mother; her family had migrated to France from Egypt in 1877, the year before she was born. In 1893, at the age of 15, she became a student at the Académie Julian, which Duchamp's friend Kupka attended briefly in spring 1894 before transferring to the École des Beaux-Arts later in the year. That same year Alfassa too joined the École des Beaux-Arts, where she acquired the nickname "The Sphinx"—a subject treated by Kupka in his series *Path of Silence* (1900–1903). She married a student of Gustave Moreau in 1897, and was very much part of the art world of the time.[29]

Around 1903 Alfassa became interested in the Cosmic Philosophy of Algeria-based Max Théon and his wife Alma, discussed in chapter 1. She met the Théons when they visited France in the fall of 1905, and began editing their *Revue Cosmique*, which was published in Paris. Alfassa and her husband spent three months with the Théons in Tlemcen, Algeria, from mid-July to mid-October 1906, returning for another three months in 1907. Théon's tantric practice would appear to have been grounded in the Indian Kaula tantric tradition, a goddess-focused practice in which, as mentioned in chapter 1, the highest form of initiation is performed by a yogini who appears to the adept while in meditative absorption, or by a woman initiate who acts as a master for him.[30] Alfassa would have been initiated by the Théons and likely continued their practice of initiation by mental penetration with her own followers, male and female. This may be what is depicted in Duchamp's paintings of nudes engaged in mysterious, ritualistic activities (see figures 1.8–1.10).

In 1908, the same year Duchamp moved to Neuilly, Alfassa divorced her husband and moved to 49 rue de Lévis in the nearby 17th *arrondissement*. By 1910 she was leading regular evening meetings that included political and philosophical discussions, along with group meditations in a darkened room. Continuing the Théons' perennialist practice of melding traditions (to which she was predisposed anyway), Alfassa had her followers read translations of the *Upanishads*, the *Bhagavad Gita*, *Dhammapada* (teachings of the Buddha), the *Yoga Sutras* of Patanjali, and the *Narada Bhakti Sutra* (on the nature of divine love).[31] From this reading list, it would appear that Alfassa emphasized Hindu and Buddhist perspectives.

A regular participant in Alfassa's study group was the well-known Buddhist explorer and writer Alexandra David-Néel (1868–1969), who later told a journalist: "We spent marvelous evenings together with friends, believing in a great future. At times we went to the Bois de Boulogne gardens, and watched the grasshopper-like early aeroplanes take off." They may have been watching the aviator Henri Farman, originally a painter trained, like Alfassa, at the École des Beaux-Arts. David-Néel continues: "I remember her elegance, her accomplishments, her intellect endowed with mystical tendencies. In spite of her great love and sweetness, in spite even of her inherent ease of making herself forgotten after achieving some noble deed, she couldn't manage to hide very well the tremendous force she bore within herself."[32]

Alfassa's own description of her meetings evokes the auras featured in Duchamp's paintings from 1910, especially the "halo" around the hand in *Portrait of Dr. Dumouchel* that Duchamp told the Arensbergs was *not* expressly motivated by Dumouchel's hand: "'During our reunions a kind of vibration of light would come out of my fingers. It was visible to the naked eye. But it was like electricity. And that was a concentrated vital force.' ... Then she touched her body, her hands, and said, 'You know, even now all this feels so vibrant and alive that it's difficult to sense the limit—as though it extended beyond the body in all directions. The limit doesn't exist anymore.'"[33]

Alfassa's gatherings were probably nothing like Lebel's account of the *gardienne*'s underground meetings of would-be revolutionaries that led to her arrest along with her close followers. In 1910, however, Alfassa wrote about an incident that had taken place in January 1907, "shortly after the bloody repression of the revolutionary movement in Russia. Some friends and I were meeting in a small philosophical study group when the presence of a mysterious visitor ... was announced."[34] The stranger—a noble figure who appeared to have suffered some deep trauma—told them he was a doctor who had come from Kiev, where "a small group of men who call themselves students" met regularly at his home. These young revolutionaries had been happy to find in Alfassa's writings "a synthetic teaching not limited to theory, but calling for action."

During the preceding year, he said, they had fought violently, "hoping to conquer by terror. Any means seemed good in our intense, ardent desire to achieve the Cause of Justice, Freedom, and Love." As a result, this man and his friends had been thrown into prison. But violence, he had come to realize, is not the solution: "We need to develop our intelligence in order better to understand the underlying laws of nature, to act in an orderly way, and to coordinate our efforts. ... We need to educate those around us, get them used to reflecting, to thinking for themselves. ... I have come to ask your help in adapting your ideas to our present situation and with them to draw up a plan of action." Alfassa agreed: "Violence is never a good way for a cause such as yours. ... How can you hope to conquer justice with injustice, harmony with hatred?" She advised her visitor and his friends to go underground: "This desperate, open conflict, while not without a certain grandeur, is also crazy and useless recklessness. Surrender for a time, retreat into the shadows to prepare yourselves in silence. Reassemble your forces and yourselves; increase your number so that, when you have the advantage, you can conquer with the aid of organizing intelligence—that all-powerful lever which, unlike violence, can never be defeated."

Alfassa was urging a strategy of passive resistance: "Do not lend weapons to your opponents. Be impeccable in your behavior toward them; give them the example of courageous patience, rectitude, and justice. Then your triumph will be near at hand, for right will be on your side, integral right, in the means as well as the goal." But even in Paris, Alfassa's Russian visitor had to hide like a bandit: "They take us for dangerous anarchists and spy on us almost as much as in our own country." She invited him to return, but he never did: "Too closely watched, under suspicion, tracked down after he had changed his lodgings many times, this gentle, just man had to return to his own country, a terrible country where perhaps a tragic end awaited him."

Alfassa's 1910 account of this 1907 incident was published in 1946, and Lebel may have adapted her dramatic story for his novel's somewhat awkward conclusion. There are other possible sources: Lebel would have known that Aurobindo had been an instigator of guerrilla warfare against the English in Calcutta, and had served time in prison. It should also be noted that the misadventures of the *gardienne* and her group resemble events surrounding Georges Bataille's philosophical-political groups from the late 1930s, Contre-Attaque and Acéphale.[35] Nevertheless, Alfassa's 1910 account does suggest her as a resource for Duchamp's artistic strategy of going underground, as well as his pacifism—an attitude very different from those of his two brothers and his friend Apollinaire, all of whom enlisted to fight in the First World War.

In May 1911 Alfassa agreed to marry a lawyer named Paul Richard in order, she said later, to try to "convert" him. She made it clear that their relationship would be "on an occult [i.e., nonphysical] plane."[36] An "obtuse person, but fanatically devoted" (to quote *La double vue*), Richard, on a 1910 business trip to the French colony of Pondicherry, India, sought out Aurobindo Ghose—Indian freedom fighter, poet, scholar, and yogin whose subversive activities had led to his arrest by the British. During his revolutionary years Aurobindo had been based in Bengal, where the primary medium for revolutionary activity was a network of secret societies linking revolution with *Shakta*, goddess-focused Hindu tantra. *Shakti* is female energy present in both women and men, the agent not only of creation but of all change, thus an ideal inspiration for freedom fighters.[37] Upon his acquittal and release, Aurobindo renounced political life, moved to Pondicherry, and pursued a spiritual path, becoming one of modern India's great spiritual leaders.

After Paul Richard returned to Paris, he shared what he had learned with Alfassa, and they began studying Aurobindo's writings. Upon their recommendation, Alexandra David-Néel visited Pondicherry as well, writing her husband in November 1911: "I spent two wonderful hours reviewing the ancient philosophical ideas of India with a man of rare intelligence. He belongs to that uncommon category that I so much admire, the reasonable mystics. I am truly grateful to the friends who advised me to visit this man."[38] In the spring of 1914 Alfassa and her husband traveled to Pondicherry and became disciples of Sri Aurobindo. Richard left Pondicherry around 1920, and later divorced Alfassa. In 1926 Aurobindo declared her the manifestation of Shakti, and his own counterpart: "Mother and I are one but in two bodies."[39] Aurobindo credited the development of his Integral Yoga, which combines Indian method with non-Darwinian evolutionary thought, to his spiritual collaboration with Mira Alfassa. His motto, "All life is yoga,"[40] parallels the development of Duchamp's thinking about life as art—a concept that may well have originated with Alfassa, who believed that good artists are those who are "unified—in the sense that they live their art."[41]

••

Some fifteen years earlier, during the period Duchamp would have known Mirra Alfassa, the primary source of her inspiration was Swami Vivekananda, a key figure in the introduction of Westernized Vedanta to the United States and Europe. As mentioned above, the practice Alfassa was originally taught by Max and Alma Théon appears to have been grounded in Indian Kaula tantra, a precursor to the chakra systems of Kundalini yoga. Kaula practice shares a number of features with Robert Lebel's descriptions of his Duchamp-character's tantric initiation, including ritual sexual union via the subtle "energy" body aimed not at satisfaction of desire (*kama*), but rather designed "to probe into one's own heart and ascertain the steadiness of one's own mind."[42] But it would be Vivekananda's *Raja Yoga: Conquering the Internal Nature*, first published in English in 1896 and in French in 1910, that finally helped Alfassa "realize in only a few months what would have otherwise taken years."[43]

Through his lectures and influential publications Vivekananda taught what he believed to be the "classical" yoga of Patanjali. In fact, Vivekananda's *raja* or mental yoga was shaped by a number of factors, including Western-influenced Neo-Vedanta and a period of study with the Shakta tantric saint Ramakrishna (1836–1886).[44] One of the pithier aphorisms of Ramakrishna, who had been initiated by a female guru, Bhairavi Brahmani, was: God is in the vagina!—a sentiment that begs comparison with the focus of Duchamp's *Given* (figure 0.1).[45]

Ramakrishna's disciple Vivekananda introduced the concept of Kundalini tantra to the West.[46] In his public lectures and writings, Vivekananda codified descriptions of this practice, couching it in in scientific metaphors Westerners could understand: "If this coiled-up energy be roused and made active, and then consciously made to travel up the *sushumna* canal [along the spinal column] as it acts upon center after center, a tremendous reaction will set in ... immensely more intense than the reaction of sense perception. It is super-sensuous perception, and the mind in that state is called super-conscious. And when it reaches the metropolis of all sensations, the brain, the whole brain, as it were, reacts, and every perceiving molecule in the body ... reacts, and the result is the full blaze of illumination, the perception of the Self."[47]

In some forms of Kundalini yoga, prana (vital breath) is guided down through the feminine and masculine respiratory channels of the subtle energy body to the root chakra ("wheel" or energy center) at the base of the spine, into the space where Kundalini lies coiled. There the opposite energies unify, and Kundalini Shakti awakens and rises up the central channel, energizing the five body chakras in the course of her progress. When Kundalini Shakti reaches the crown chakra, the result is perception of absolute reality—what Vivekananda describes as "the full blaze of illumination." After a period of trance, Kundalini descends through the chakras to her home base in the root chakra.

This process of Self-revelation is, according to Vivekananda, "only a question of transformation": "The same force which is working outside, as electricity or magnetism, will become changed into inner force. ... The Yogis say that that part of the human energy which is expressed as sex energy, in sexual functions, sexual thought, and so on, when checked and controlled, easily becomes changed into *Ojas* [life energy]. As this lowest center [at the base of the spine] is the one which guides all these functions, therefore the Yogi pays particular attention to that center. He tries to take up all this sexual energy and convert it into [life energy]."[48] This chakra at the base of the spine is "triangular in form." The yogi or yogini is instructed during breathing practice to "think of the triangle, concentrate the mind on that center."[49]

The cover and frontispiece of Vivekananda's *Râja-Yoga* show a flaming, upward-pointing triangle from which a vertical form snakes upward through the chakras, culminating in a halo of radiant light surrounding a "thousand"-petaled lotus representing the crown chakra (figure 2.4). Dominating the cover of the deluxe edition of Robert Lebel's *La double vue* is a luminous upward-pointing triangle (figure 2.5). Duchamp, who created as an insert/illustration for the book *The Clock in Profile* (figure 2.3), no doubt designed the deluxe edition cover as well.

In a letter from 1939, Duchamp's friend Katherine Dreier reminisced: "Dee [her nickname for Duchamp], do you recall that you told me that you had such a marvelous sensation at the base of your spine which you enjoyed?"[50] It is hard to imagine what Duchamp might have been describing, if not a Western form of tantric yoga. Scholar of Kashmiri Shaivism Lakshman Jee writes that as a result of focused breathing practice, in the root chakra at the base of the spine one can "briefly experience a crawling sensation. It is like the experience when a man and a woman are having intercourse and sexual climax is just about to take place. … After the momentary experience of this crawling sensation it rises again in one flash. And when it rises you become filled with absolutely blissful existence … simultaneously with the experience of ecstasy you also realize the reality of Self. … When you are established in the process … then you experience that ecstasy in action. When you eat you are in that bliss. When you talk you are in that bliss. When you walk you are in that bliss. Whatever you do you remain in that Universal state. This is the state of *jivanmukti*, liberated life." This ongoing state, according to Jee, is experienced only by great yogins.[51]

Perhaps Duchamp mentioned his "marvelous sensation" to Dreier in Argentina, where in 1918–1919 they both had taken refuge from the war. Duchamp stayed longer, and after his return to Paris had his hair shaved in a "tonsure" of a star shooting over the crown of his head (figure 2.6). The significance of Duchamp's shooting-star tonsure has never been fully explained. Even the date of *Tonsure*—1919 and/or 1921—is contested.[52] Either way, it seems relevant to Duchamp's shooting-star tonsure that in a February 1912 text for one of her lectures, Mirra Alfassa wrote: "A thought must … come from the inner depths to our surface self like a meteor from inaccessible spaces."[53] Just a month or two earlier, on the last night of December

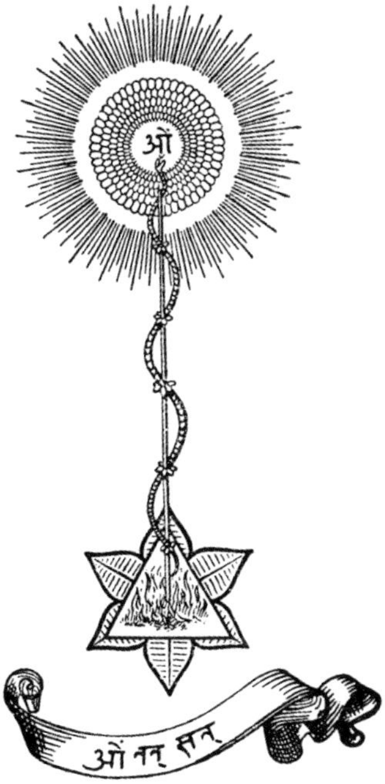

FIGURE 2.4

Frontispiece, Vivekananda, *Râja Yoga (ou Conquête de la nature intérieure)*. Paris: Publications théosophiques, 1910

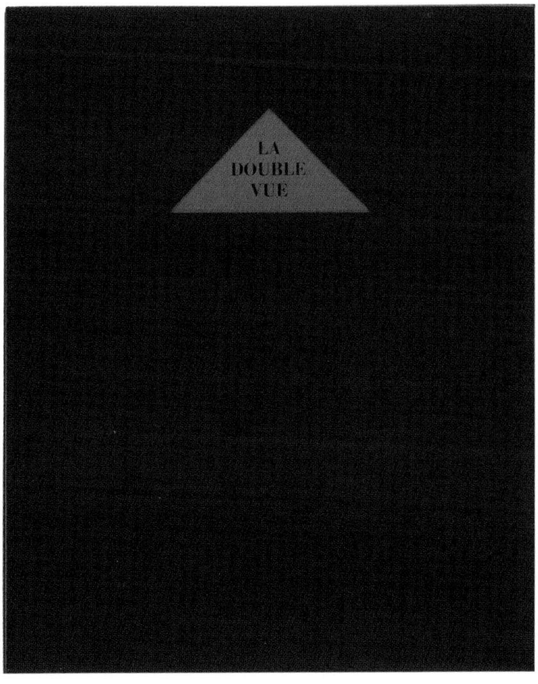

FIGURE 2.5

Robert Lebel ©, cover of *La double vue, suivi de L'inventeur du temps gratuit*. Paris: Soleil noir, deluxe edition, 1964

Art Institute of Chicago, Ryerson & Burnham Libraries (Special 769.9494 G428L) / Bridgeman Images

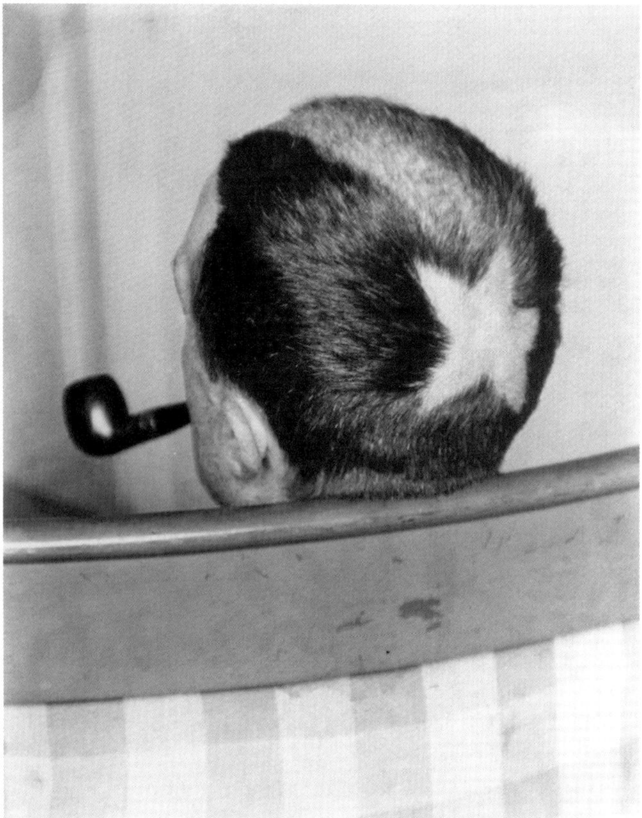

FIGURE 2.6
Man Ray
Marcel Duchamp (tonsure par Zayas), 1921

1911, Alfassa had seen a shooting star. She recalled later: "The moment the star was passing, at that very moment there sprang up from consciousness: 'To realize the divine union, for my body.' ... And before the end of [1912] it was done. ... 'To realize union with the inner Divine.' ... But it is not necessary to have a shooting star in order to realize swiftly! What is necessary is that the whole will of the being should be concentrated on one point."[54] Alfassa's "divine union" of 1911–1912 resembles Vivekananda's Kundalini energy moving up through the chakras to unite with pure consciousness in the brain, where it generates direct perception of absolute reality. This can happen at once, or in stages. Either way, a shooting star is as good a metaphor as any for the brilliant light this experience is said to generate, and a shooting-star tonsure as good a way as any to commemorate the experience.

"Soon I was furiously taken up with my new problem," Lebel's hero recalls: "how ... to introduce into my painting this light that signaled itself to me, which I did not believe was either revealed or celestial, but where I had caught a glimpse of another dimension, unexpectedly placed within my reach." *Clock in Profile* illustrates the passage into "this other universe, with its escape from time and from common laws." With no hands, and holes where numbers should be, *Clock in Profile* is a lawless clock, an esoteric clock that will never tell the time. The passage into this timeless universe emerged in Duchamp's painting, according to Patrick Waldberg, "by suddenly endowing him with a sort of double sight, thanks to which a premonition that had long haunted him is verified: 'painting essentially aims at the representation of ecstasy'." Light envelops and radiates from the morphing *Dulcinea*, which may have been the painting Apollinaire had in mind when he wrote in 1912 of Duchamp's "flame-shaped colors, ... and the effect of teeming movement, tenderly or emphatically expressed."[55]

Lebel's statement that Dulcinea was "a woman whom Duchamp had seen passing by" resembles one of Mirra Alfassa's memories: "I once had—when I was simply walking in the street—a kind of revelation, because a woman was walking in front of me, and she really knew how to walk."[56] A note in Duchamp's *Green Box* describes the "desire-gears" of the bride as "only the string that binds the bouquet."[57] Perhaps *Dulcinea* should be interpreted as a painting not of a *person*, but of *passage* to a state where male and female energies are united in a "bouquet" of interconnected, endless creation—a bouquet of roses, perhaps, and a premonition of Duchamp's female alter ego, Rrose Sélavy. To further explore this realm, and its implications for his art, Duchamp would eventually leave Paris for the erotically supercharged artistic atmosphere of Munich—not coincidentally, ground zero for the spiritual in art.

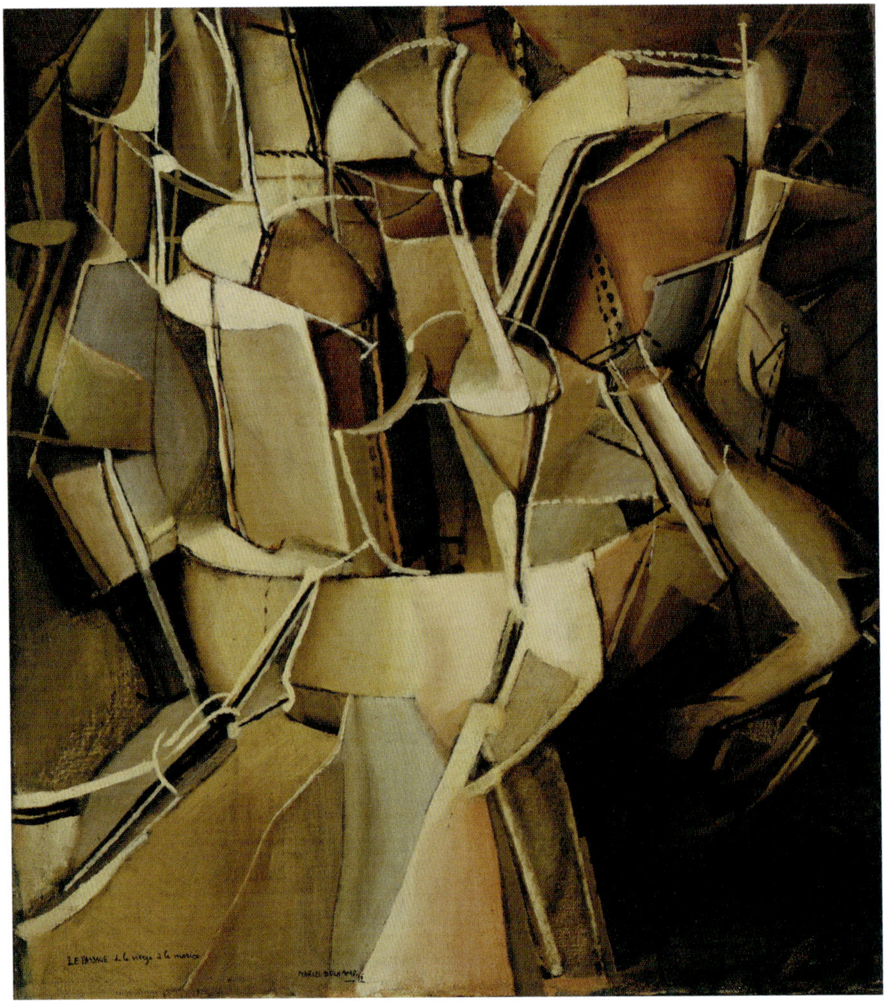

FIGURE 3.1

Marcel Duchamp
Le Passage de la Vierge à la Mariée / The Passage from Virgin to Bride, Munich, July–August 1912
Oil on canvas, 59.4 × 54 cm
The Museum of Modern Art, New York, NY, Purchase / Digital Image © The Museum of Modern Art / Licensed by SCALA / Art Resource, NY

3 MUNICH

Art is an outlet toward regions which are not ruled by space and time. To live is to believe, that's my belief.

—Marcel Duchamp[1]

On April 7, 1910, Max Bergmann, a young painter from Munich visiting Paris, reported in his diary that Marcel Duchamp had taken him "to the Parc Monceau, where we went to the Japanese Museum. Both very interesting."[2] The Parc Monceau had been created in 1779 as an Anglo-Chinese, or "English," garden containing Chinese and other architectural follies. It is a smaller version of Munich's English Garden, famous for its eighteenth-century Chinese Tower surrounded by a festive beer garden. Somewhat modified since Duchamp and Bergmann's visit, Parc Monceau still features a small Egyptian pyramid, a Roman colonnade, a Chinese stone lantern, and a rock grotto with a waterfall and pool that resembles the waterfall and pool in Duchamp's *Given: 1. The Waterfall, 2. The Illuminating Gas* (figure 0.1).

The "Japanese Museum" would be the Musée Cernuschi, just east of the park. It was founded in the last quarter of the nineteenth century by Henri Cernuschi, who in the early 1870s brought back from East Asia Chinese, Japanese, and Korean Buddhist sutras and works of art. Its focal point is the monumental Japanese bronze *Buddha of Meguro* that still dominates a museum whose Asian art collection is second in Paris only to that of the Musée Guimet. Bergmann does not mention the Musée Guimet, a museum Duchamp would likely have visited with his friend the Romanian sculptor

Constantin Brancusi. Brancusi's enthusiasm both for that museum and for Asian art is well known. In 1909, for example, the artist Cecilia Cuţescu-Storck wrote to her husband of repeatedly visiting with Brancusi the Musée Guimet to view "the sculptures of the masters of India, Tibet, China, and Turkistan." She particularly enjoyed "Brancusi's interesting and unexpected comments on certain statuettes of the Buddha."[3]

The earliest documented contact between Duchamp and Brancusi was in the fall of 1912,[4] but they certainly would have known each other before then. Brancusi became part of the École des Beaux-Arts circle soon after his 1904 arrival in Paris from Romania, and by the end of the decade both he and Duchamp were exhibiting their work at various Salons, including the Salon d'Automne and Salon des Indépendants. A letter Duchamp sent to the American critic Walter Pach before leaving for New York in spring 1915 suggests just how important Brancusi had become to him by then. Although he confessed he hadn't "met a single artist I know," Duchamp wrote: "I absolutely must go and see Brancusi."[5]

Brancusi's art is at once sexually explicit and ambiguous. A melding of male and female is clearly evident in his 1915 sculpture *Princess X* (figure 3.2).[6] It can be no coincidence that the closest Duchamp came to revealing publicly a personal familiarity with tantra was when he cited Brancusi in a conversation about androgyny—the union of male and female: "We may also call this perspective Tantric (as Brancusi would say)."[7] His comment hints that together Duchamp and Brancusi explored tantra, including Tibetan Buddhist tantric art, then as now on prominent display at the Musée Guimet, Paris.

Thanks in part to the Guimet, during the first decade of the twentieth century there was at least one Tibetan in Paris. He arrived in 1907 with Jacques Bacot, explorer, collector, and translator of a life of the Tibetan yogi Milarepa, which would become Brancusi's favorite book.[8] Bacot led two expeditions to Tibet from which he brought back objects and, from his first journey in 1907, a Tibetan named Adjourp Gumbo.[9] In 1908 the Musée Guimet exhibited a large number of these objects, and Bacot gave a public lecture (published the following year) about his "pilgrimage" to Tibet, which he described as a mountainous, religious country, a "land of prayer" much like Brancusi's beloved Romania. In May 1909, Bacot departed for

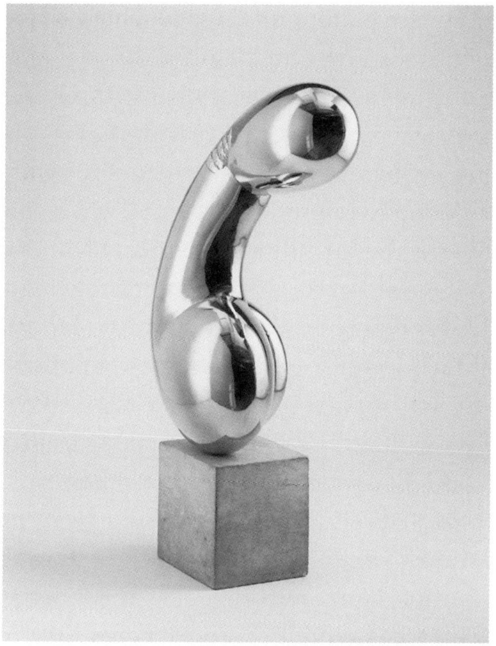

FIGURE 3.2

Constantin Brancusi
Princess X, 1915–1916
Polished bronze and limestone block, 16.7 × 40.5 × 22.2 cm
Philadelphia Museum of Art, Philadelphia, PA, The Louise and Walter Arensberg Collection, 1950 / Bridgeman Images

Tibet a second time, returning in March 1910. The following year he made another presentation at the Musée Guimet, this time on Tibetan art.[10] On this occasion the museum exhibited over 300 of Bacot's Tibetan paintings, sculptures, and other objects, the greater part of which he gave to the museum in 1912. Exploring Tibetan Buddhist tantra with Brancusi would have included visiting the Musée Guimet and attending and/or reading Bacot's lectures (perhaps the source of Brancusi's "interesting comments").

Another friend during these crucial early years was Francis Picabia, a wealthy, adventurous French painter of Spanish-Cuban descent. There is some confusion about exactly when Picabia and Duchamp met. Picabia's first wife, the musician Gabrielle Buffet-Picabia, wrote in 1949: "It was in 1910, on the occasion of an exhibition at the Hedelberg Gallery, that Picabia's friend Dumont introduced us to Marcel Duchamp, then a very young man, but one whose ideas far surpassed the works he had so far accomplished, which were still subject to Cézannian and cubist influence.

Though very much detached from the conventions of his epoch, he had not yet found his mode of expression, and this gave him a kind of disgust with work and an ineptitude for life. Under an appearance of almost romantic timidity, he possessed an exacting dialectical mind, in love with philosophical speculations and absolute conclusions." Eight years later, she again specified that Picabia first met Duchamp in late 1910–early 1911, when "he was still very young and very dominated by the influence of his two brothers."[11] Buffet-Picabia's description of Duchamp's work fits this timing, and Frederick Kiesler confirmed her account in a note for his projected biography of Duchamp, who told Kiesler he had "met … Picabia through schoolmate Dumont in 1910."[12]

In an interview with Pierre Cabanne, however, Duchamp recalled meeting Picabia in October 1911, when they both had work in the Salon d'Automne.[13] Moreover, Gabrielle's reference to the "Hedelberg Gallery" would seem to refer to a gallery on rue Tronchet whose director, Hedelbert, hosted an exhibition of work by members of the Société Normande de Peinture Moderne organized by art critic Pierre Dumont in November–December 1911.[14] Both Picabia and Duchamp had work in this show. It may be that the Picabias were first introduced to Duchamp in late 1910, but their close friendship did not develop until the following year. "Picabia had an amazing spirit," Duchamp added to Cabanne. "I saw a lot of Picabia, until his death." He was emotionally closer, however, to Gabrielle, whose "whole life," according to their friend and colleague Jean Arp, was "devoted to spiritual adventure."[15]

Gabrielle recalled periodic retreats on Marcel's part during this time: "Sometimes he 'took a trip' to his room and vanished for two weeks from the circle of his friends: this was a time of escape into himself, in the course of which the 'sad young man in a train' was transmuted into a captivating, impressive incarnation of Lucifer."[16] Lucifer—"light-bearer"—was originally the name not of the devil but of the state from which that rebellious archangel fell,[17] and to which, according to Buffet-Picabia, Duchamp returned, descending, like *Nude Descending a Staircase* (figure 1.16), in the form of a light-bearer, like the nude in *Given* (figure 0.1). Incarnation in this sense is not so much descent of a deity in human form as the transmutation of a human into a deity. Buffet-Picabia tells us that during Duchamp's two-week disappearances, which she calls his "trips," Duchamp achieved a dramatic change of state in which the *Sad Young Man on a Train* was "transmuted" into a luminous, beatific being. (Other women would make similar observations, as we shall see.)

Duchamp painted *Sad Young Man on a Train* (figure 1.3) in December 1911, just before he began working on *Nude Descending a Staircase*, of which there are several versions, the first also from December 1911. These energetic depictions emerged from Duchamp's previously discussed "method of demultiplication"—the unification of male and female energies that was his "main preoccupation during the first part of 1912."[18]

The train as a metaphor for passage—transformation through space and time—reappeared regularly in Duchamp's art, from the colored lights he claimed he saw from a train and memorialized in *Pharmacy* (1914, figure 3.3) to the electric train bearing the names of exhibiting artists that circled the window of D'Arcy Gallery for Duchamp's 1960 exhibition, *The Surrealist Intrusion in the Enchanters' Domain*.[19] His co-organizer for that exhibition, André Breton, expanded on Duchamp's train metaphor in an essay for the catalogue to their 1936 *Exposition Surréaliste d'Objets*: "we begin to hurry on the platform for the passage of the train that does not stop, which is neither a passenger train nor a freight train. In the windows, beings-objects (or objects-beings?) characterized by the fact that they are prey to a continuous transformation and express the perpetuity of the struggle between the aggregating and disaggregating powers that dispute true reality and life."[20]

By late June 1912, Duchamp was in a train on his way to Munich. The reason he gave publicly for leaving Paris was both personal and professional. The previous March, on the day of the press preview for the annual, unjuried Salon des Indépendants, Duchamp's two artist-brothers asked him on behalf of the hanging committee, which also included their friends, the cubist painters Léger, Gleizes, and Metzinger, to withdraw his *Nude Descending a Staircase, No. 2* (figure 1.16). Cubist nudes, it seems, weren't supposed to move, much less walk down the stairs. Of course, there was more to it than that. A certain cheekiness, a trace of Duchampian humor in *Nude Descending a Staircase*, may have gotten on the nerves of the "serious" artists on the hanging committee.

A more pointed interpretation was provided by artist and author Marcel Jean, who applied his own "psychoanalytical interpretation of the dream of

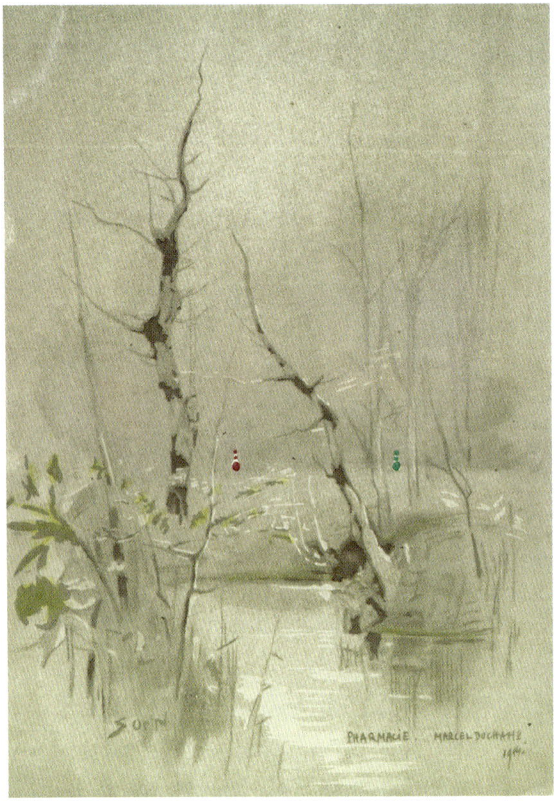

FIGURE 3.3

Marcel Duchamp
Pharmacie / Pharmacy from *View*, volume 5, number 1, 1945
Relief halftone with gouache additions, composition: 21.9 × 15.6 cm, sheet: 31 × 24.3 cm
The Museum of Modern Art, New York, NY. Publisher: View, Inc., New York. Printer: unknown. Edition: 100. Gift of Bernard Reis. / Art Resource, NY

walking down a staircase as symbolizing the act of love" to propose that "the picture suggests a lewd intention, a desecration of the most hidden human impulses." It seems not to have occurred to him that Duchamp may have been depicting an inner journey, something between cubist visual representation and metaphor. Duchamp had painted the words "nu descendant un escalier" along the left bottom edge of the work. "Even the artist's own friends," writes Jean, "—although unable to explain objectively the reason for their disquiet—began to worry about the possible scandal if the picture was hung at the Salon des Indépendants." If Duchamp would just remove the title, they said, the painting could stay.[21] In response, Duchamp withdrew his painting from the show.

••

It is not completely clear why Duchamp chose Munich. He said he knew a cow painter there. That would be Max Bergmann, whom Duchamp had shown around Paris in the spring of 1910 and who was indeed a painter of cows among other things, including horses, mountain landscapes, and especially nudes. As we have seen, it was in Munich that T. S. Eliot experienced his first artistic breakthrough after relocating there from Paris precisely one year before Duchamp did the same. Whatever his personal motivation, Duchamp's professional motivation was clear: after the debacle with *Nude Descending a Staircase* he was fed up with the Paris art scene and wanted to go someplace where there was art, but he wasn't part of the scene. In this way Munich, a major international art capital, was ideal. It had great museums and innovative artists like Wassily Kandinsky (1866–1944), author of *On the Spiritual in Art*, which had just been published.[22]

Duchamp also no doubt knew (perhaps from Bergmann) that his name had been mentioned in Kandinsky and Franz Marc's *Blaue Reiter Almanach*, published in May 1912. In an article entitled "Signs of Renewal in Painting," art writer Roger Allard listed Marcel Duchamp along with other French cubists as part of a "new spiritual movement." Allard introduced a concept that surely would have caught Duchamp's attention: "Two creative people are necessary to enjoy a work of art: the first is the artist who creates it, the great stimulator and inventor, and the second is the viewer whose mind has to return to nature. The further the two of them advance to reach the same goal, the more creative they both are."[23] Allard's formulation, especially his emphasis on the return of the mind of the viewer to nature, can be traced back to dualistic Samkhya-Yoga philosophy as propounded by the great synthesizer of Indian yoga traditions, Patanjali (48 BCE to 49 CE). In Pantanjali's *Yoga Sutras*—a collection of aphorisms with commentary compiled during the first centuries of the Common Era—Nature performs her "dance" only in interaction with individual consciousness. According to David Gordon White, "It is precisely when [matter] comes into contact or proximity with a Person (also called a "Viewer" or "Spectator")—that Nature (also called "What is Seen") is set into motion, evolving and devolving into the various substrates of the phenomenal world, putting on a spectacle for the Spectator to see."[24]

Patanjali's *Yoga Sutras* was popularized in Europe and the Americas in the late nineteenth century due to the efforts of Vivekananda. By the early twentieth century, Patanjali was widely read in European esoteric circles, thanks in part to the publication program of the Theosophical Society. As we have seen, the *Yoga Sutras* was part of Mirra Alfassa's reading regimen, and it became T. S. Eliot's "guide to life" during the period following his visits to Paris and Munich in 1910–1911.

Duchamp's theory of the importance of the spectator in the creative act correlates with Samkhya-Yoga philosophical perspective. Whether Patanjali was his source, or Allard's reformulation, or something else, as early as 1915 Duchamp told an American interviewer: "Rembrandt could never have expressed all the thoughts found in his work. ... This may prove that people give more to pictures than they take from them."[25] Duchamp's conception of art as mutual engagement would resurface more famously over forty years later, when he asserted that the creative act "is not performed by the artist alone; the spectator brings the work in contact with the external world by deciphering and interpreting its inner qualification and thus adds his contribution."[26] In Duchamp's terminology, the artist is the "medium" for absolute reality manifesting as phenomenal reality in the mind of the spectator.

Kandinsky and Marc's *Blaue Reiter Almanach* featured a radically diverse mix of illustrations, many of them drawn from the collection of Munich's State Museum for Ethnology. That museum's brilliant curator, Lucian Scherman, was actively cultivating friendships with artists in his efforts to increase attendance. A Sanskrit specialist, Scherman had traveled in 1910–1911 to India, Ceylon, Assam, and Burma collecting Buddhist sculptures and other devotional objects, as well as items of everyday use. In Darjeeling he rounded out the collection with purchases from Tibet and Nepal. In May–June 1912 Scherman mounted a huge exhibition of this material at the so-called Old Bavarian Academy, not far from the Munich train station. At the same time, the museum had its collection of East Asian art on public view in an attractive gallery arcade along the north side of Munich's Hofgarten.[27]

In the informative centenary anthology *Marcel Duchamp in Munich 1912*, Duchamp scholar Herbert Molderings begins his lead essay with an implicit link to Asia: "In the summer of 1912, roughly at the same time as a group of young artists, tired of civilization, turned their backs on Europe and set out in search of new sources of artistic inspiration in the Orient … Marcel Duchamp spent altogether nearly three months in Munich, one of the leading economic and cultural centers of Europe." Although he does not come right out and say so, Molderings implies that while more adventurous artists sought fresh inspiration by immersing themselves in non-Western cultures (he mentions Matisse in Morocco, Slevogt in Egypt, Klee and others in Tunisia), Duchamp was content to conduct his explorations within the familiar confines of European culture.[28]

European culture, however, was never all that homogeneous: there had been global interminglings of art, science, and philosophy between East and West for millennia.[29] Asian art was on view in Paris at the Louvre and was the focus at the Musée Guimet, where in 1889 Eugène Guimet had installed his collection of religious art from Asia. In 1907, quantities of manuscripts, paintings, and other Buddhist art had been brought back by Aurel Stein from the great Dunhuang Caves in China to the British Museum, followed in 1908 by a French expedition under Paul Pelliot. Even before Bacot's exhibitions at the Musée Guimet in 1908 and 1911, and Scherman's 1912 Munich exhibition, South and Southeast Asian, East Asian, and Himalayan culture was widely available in Europe.

Duchamp arrived in Munich on June 21, 1912 and stayed through most of September. We know from the sparse comments he sent to family and friends that he was a regular visitor to Munich's Alte Pinakothek. There is no documentary evidence that he visited other museums, or the huge Bavarian Trade Fair on view in Munich's Exhibition Park from May 18 to October 13, 1912. But given the length of his stay and his wide-ranging interests, it is unlikely that Duchamp limited his explorations of Munich to its beer halls and Old Masters. He was an artist; artists look at things. Just how much there was for Duchamp to see in Munich that summer has been explored elsewhere, although Scherman's Museum for Ethnology has been almost completely ignored.[30] The museum did not move into its current building on Maximilianstrasse until 1926. Until then that building, known as the Old National Museum, was home to the renowned Deutsches Museum, the world's largest museum of technology and science. Then, as now, the Deutsches Museum featured an impressive collection of airplanes.

There is evidence of a visit by Duchamp to the Deutsches Museum in the form of a wash drawing inscribed "Aéroplane—Münich 1912" (figure 3.4). Duchamp may have visited, if only to compare it with the Conservatoire National des Arts et Métiers, Paris, which has impressive technology collections of its own, including the airplane in which Louis Blériot crossed the English Channel in 1909.[31] Made of stretched canvas (like a painting), Blériot's plane is hung from the ceiling near the model for Bartholdi's *Liberty Enlightening the World*—the Statue of Liberty, which was originally conceived as a lighthouse.[32] To a young artist contemplating the renunciation of painting, the evocative objects in these museums offered other models.

Technology that fulfilled humankind's age-old dream of flying, the airplane had more resonance in 1912 than it does now. We know from Alexandra David-Néel that Mirra Alfassa and her group liked to go to the Bois de Boulogne to watch "the grasshopper-like early aeroplanes take off."[33] In October 1912 Duchamp and Brancusi would go with Fernand Léger to see an airplane show at Paris's Grand Palais. Léger later reported that Duchamp suddenly turned and said: "Painting's finished. Who could do better than this propeller?"[34]

The airplane held personal meaning for Duchamp as well. In the spring of 1912 he went with his brothers to watch Francis Picabia's wife Gabrielle fly. Picabia had arranged for the aviator Henri Farman (mentioned above in connection with Mirra Alfassa) to take Gabrielle up in one of his planes. It must have been a rickety affair, for she described it as "a funny machine":

> There was a small bicycle seat behind [the pilot]. I was to sit there, and was warned not to touch anything. ... From time to time Farman turned round to see if his passenger was still alive or not. There was a dreadful noise, so I made great signs to tell him that all was well and I was really delighted. And then we came down, which was something else. Naturally I must have thanked Farman and then I was cornered by the Duchamps, and Villon simply said that a mother shouldn't expose herself to danger. There were discussions about the Machine, which at that time was considered as anti-artistic and an enemy of the mind.[35]

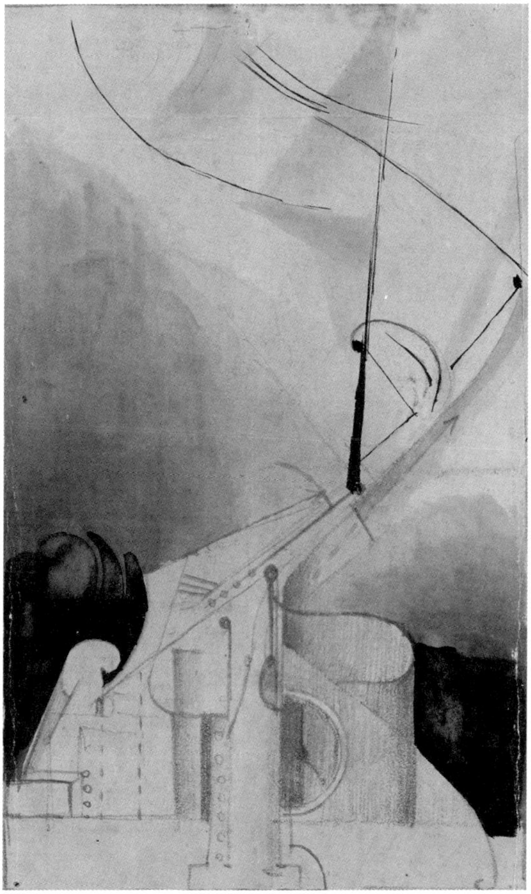

FIGURE 3.4
Marcel Duchamp
Aéroplane / Airplane, 1912
Ink and pencil on paper, 22.9 × 12.7 cm
The Menil Collection, Houston

Picabia and Duchamp had a different view of the Machine. For them, machines provided a visual language with which to portray the workings of the mind. According to Buffet-Picabia, "The multiple possibilities which this unexplored field offered to the imagination seem to have shown Duchamp his true mission. Or perhaps he created for his own personal use an imaginary mechanical world, which became the place, the climate, the substance of his works."[36]

Not surprisingly, Duchamp fell passionately in love with his friend's spiritually adventurous wife. Gabrielle Buffet-Picabia was intelligent and obviously fearless. For Duchamp, as we shall see, fearlessness was an attractive feature. On the eve of his departure for Munich, Marcel called Gabrielle to tell her he loved her and wanted to write her a letter. She said she received "two very beautiful letters" from him. They ended up spending the night at a railway station in the Jura Mountains, where Gabrielle was to catch the train to Paris on her way home from her mother's house in Étival. Marcel took the train all the way from Munich just to be with her for a few hours. Gabrielle later told Calvin Tomkins she believed she had "initiated" him that night: "Even now I find it really astonishing and very moving, very young, too. It was a kind of madness, idiocy, to travel from Munich to the Jura to pass a few hours of the night with me. It was utterly inhumane to sit next to a being whom you sense desires you so much and not even to have been touched. … Above all, I thought, I must be very careful with everything I say to him because he understands things in quite an alarming way, in an absolute way."[37]

In her "Memories of Pre-Dada," Gabrielle described Duchamp's "trips" mentioned earlier—two-week retreats in the course of which the young Duchamp transformed himself into an "incarnation of Lucifer."[38] One wonders how Gabrielle knew about Duchamp's incarnations as Lucifer. Did Duchamp tell her and, if so, how much? What did their night in the train station, side by side, without touching, have to do with it? Tomkins reports that Buffet-Picabia believed she had "initiated" Duchamp, and he added a comment of his own: "she used the French verb *dénaisé*, which usually implies sexual initiation, but in this case she must have meant it metaphorically."[39] Not necessarily: Duchamp told Arturo Schwarz that there is "an expression beyond sex which can be transferred into a fourth dimension."[40] In Kaula tantra, the highest form of initiation is by a woman who has been initiated and is willing to act as master.[41] What if Duchamp's *dénaisé* with Buffet-Picabia was not only sexual, but also fourth-dimensional—beyond sex, "absolute"—as in the Kaula tantric "initiation of piercing," or mental penetration, mentioned above in connection with Mirra Alfassa?

The episode recalls Mirra Alfassa's teacher Max Théon's description of *Pathétisme*: the "infusion of the psychic active being into the psychic passive being," where the "sensitive" plays a central role. "If entrusted to an individual who by his nature and his own knowledge is able to develop her sensitivity," she "is able to enter all degrees of trance according to her capabilities and sensitivity."[42] Buffet-Picabia's account raises the possibility that Duchamp may have honed his "pathetic" skills in Munich, and finally felt ready to try them out on her. In light of all this, what seems in doubt is not the sexual aspect of the encounter, but whether Buffet-Picabia would have been the first to "initiate" Duchamp in a mental practice already depicted in *Once More to This Star* (1911, figure 1.1).

One wonders whether Duchamp told Buffet-Picabia about his live-work situation in Munich, where he had rented a room in a second-floor flat. Much of what we now know about his living arrangement there is thanks to the indefatigable research of Munich artist Rudolf Herz, who shared what he learned in a book, *Marcel Duchamp: Le Mystère de Munich*, and a "temporary memorial"—an "apartment-sculpture" in the form of a full-scale concrete model of the interior of the flat, turned ninety degrees like Duchamp's *Fountain* and plunked down on the lawn of the Alte Pinakothek in June 2012, one hundred years after Duchamp's stay in Munich (figure 3.5). It provided a kind of mental experience of Duchamp's lodging, which, Herz writes, was "at the same time studio and living space … only ten square meters in size, and … furnished with a bed, a wardrobe, and a table with a chair. The easel and the painting materials also had to find a place. … He could only reach his room by walking through the living room and bedroom of the couple letting it."[43]

Who were these people with whom Duchamp was obviously on close, if not intimate, terms for three months? His landlord, August Gress, the same age as Duchamp, was an engineer who worked for a Munich manufacturer of locomotives and engines. Theresa Gress was a dressmaker who worked at home. They had been married for only two months and moved into the flat the month before Duchamp arrived in Munich. Like Duchamp, Theresa already had a daughter conceived outside the marriage; a son would be born the year after Duchamp left. Herz describes August Gress as an engineer who made mechanical drawings in the course of planning his work, and he makes a convincing case for his usefulness to Duchamp as a model for how someone might be a creator without considering himself an artist: "Gress was neither artist nor craftsman nor scientist. He was an engineer who made drawings."[44]

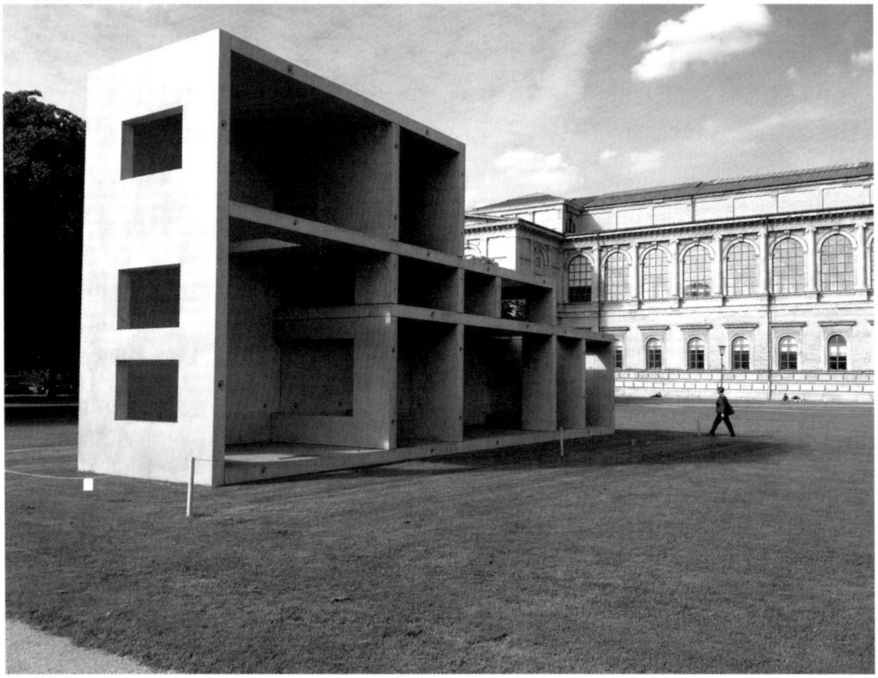

FIGURE 3.5

Rudolf Herz
Marcel Duchamp—Le mystère de Munich
"Apartment-sculpture" (full-scale concrete model of the interior of Duchamp's Munich flat)
22 June–30 September 2012, Alte Pinakothek, Munich

Duchamp's interest in diagrammatic drawings had already surfaced in the dotted line and rotational arrow of *Coffee Mill*, painted in December 1911, six months before he went to Munich (figure 1.18). Regarding *Chocolate Grinder*, created after Munich in early 1913 (figure 3.6), Duchamp told an interviewer: "Of course, the mechanical side of [the chocolate grinder] influenced me. At least, it was the point of departure for a new technique. I couldn't go into haphazard drawing or the splashing of the paint. I wanted to go back to a completely dry drawing, to a dry conception of art. The mechanical drawing, for me, was the best form of that dry form of art. Accuracy, precision—nothing more."[45] This description of "a dry conception of art," along with the blueprint-like preliminary drawings for *The Large*

Glass that Duchamp would make in Paris in 1913–1914 (figure 3.7), suggest inspiration, possibly even tutelage, from his Munich landlord.

Already dissatisfied with painting as an art medium, twenty-five-year-old Marcel nevertheless produced two important paintings and four large drawings in Munich. All of these, with the possible exception of *Aéroplane*

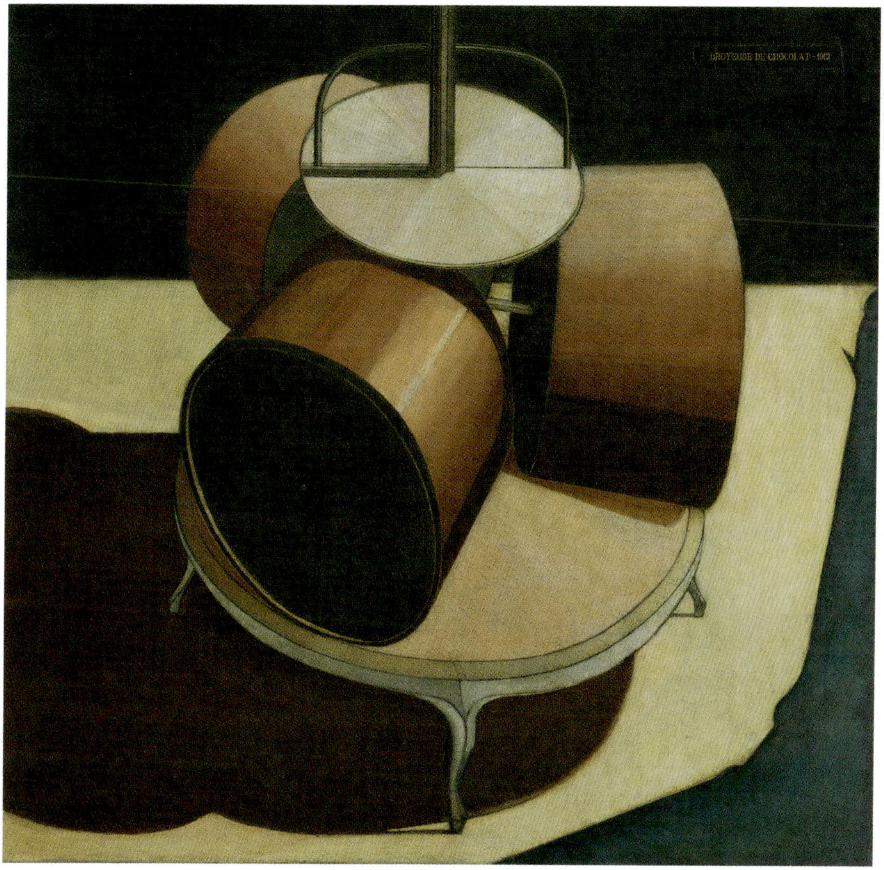

FIGURE 3.6

Marcel Duchamp
Broyeuse de chocolat, No. 1 / Chocolate Grinder, 1913
Oil on canvas, 61.9 × 64.5 cm
Philadelphia Museum of Art, Philadelphia, PA, The Louise and Walter Arensberg Collection, 1950 / Bridgeman Images

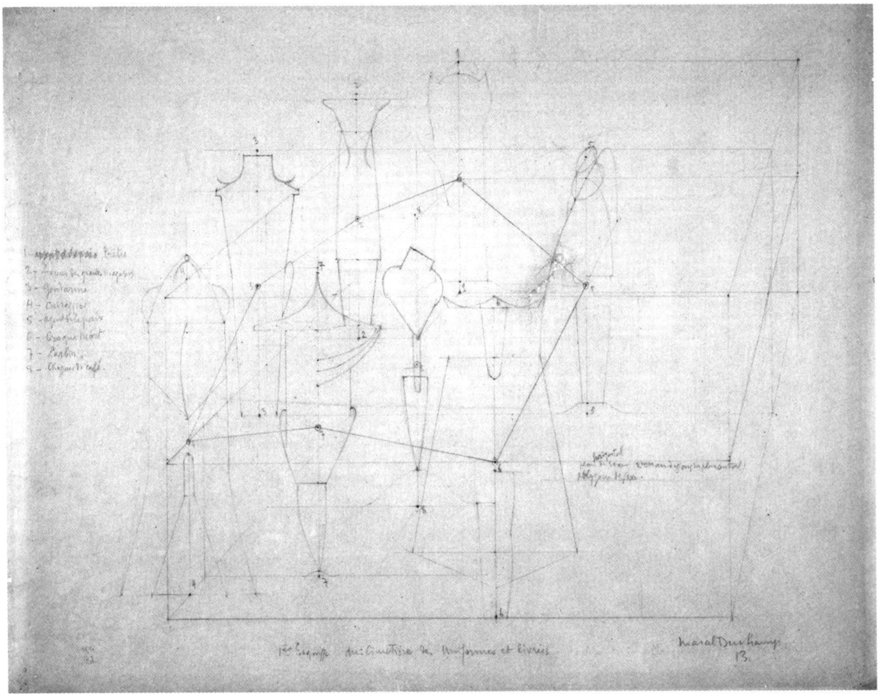

FIGURE 3.7

Marcel Duchamp
Cimetière des uniformes et livrées / Cemetery of Uniforms and Liveries (No. 1), 1913
Pencil on tracing paper, 32.5 × 41.6 cm
Philadelphia Museum of Art, Philadelphia, PA, The Louise and Walter Arensberg Collection, 1950 / Bridgeman Images

discussed above, were in one way or another studies for *The Large Glass* (figure 0.2). Two drawings, *Virgin (No. 1)* and *Virgin (No. 2)* (figures 3.8, 3.9), incorporate what appear to be parts of a sewing machine and thread, connecting them with Gress's dressmaker wife, who worked at home, along with Duchamp.[46] Another connection is Duchamp's *Cemetery of Uniforms and Liveries (No. 1)* (1913, figure 3.7), whose Malic Moulds, Herz proposes, were based on tailor's dummies.[47] Herz credits Teresa Gress with Duchamp's incorporation of thread into *Chocolate Grinder (No. 2)* (1914, figure 3.10) and the "fallen" threads of *3 Standard Stoppages* (1913–1914, figure 3.11): "Pieces of thread would always fall to the floor when the dressmaker was working," he writes.[48]

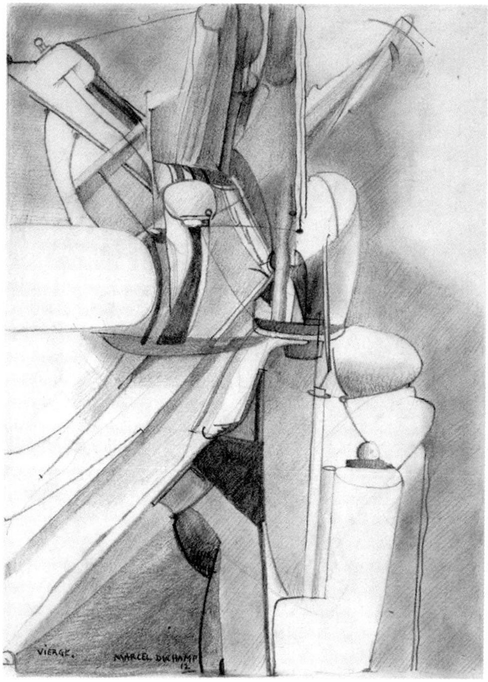

FIGURE 3.8

Marcel Duchamp
Vierge, No. 1 / Virgin (No. 1), 1912
Graphite on paper, 42.9 × 32.5 cm
Philadelphia Museum of Art, Philadelphia, PA, A. E. Gallatin Collection, 1952 / Bridgeman Images

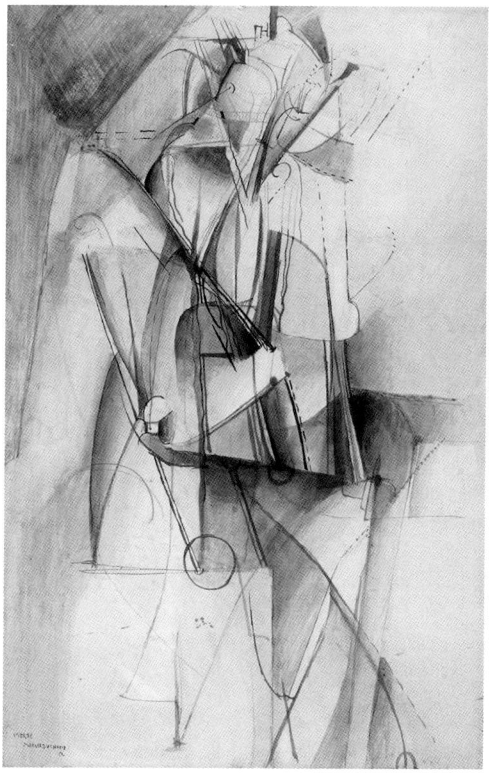

FIGURE 3.9

Marcel Duchamp
Vierge, No. 2 / Virgin (No. 2), 1912
Pen and ink with wash and pencil and watercolor on paper, 40.3 × 26 cm
Philadelphia Museum of Art, Philadelphia, PA, The Louise and Walter Arensberg Collection, 1950 / Bridgeman Images

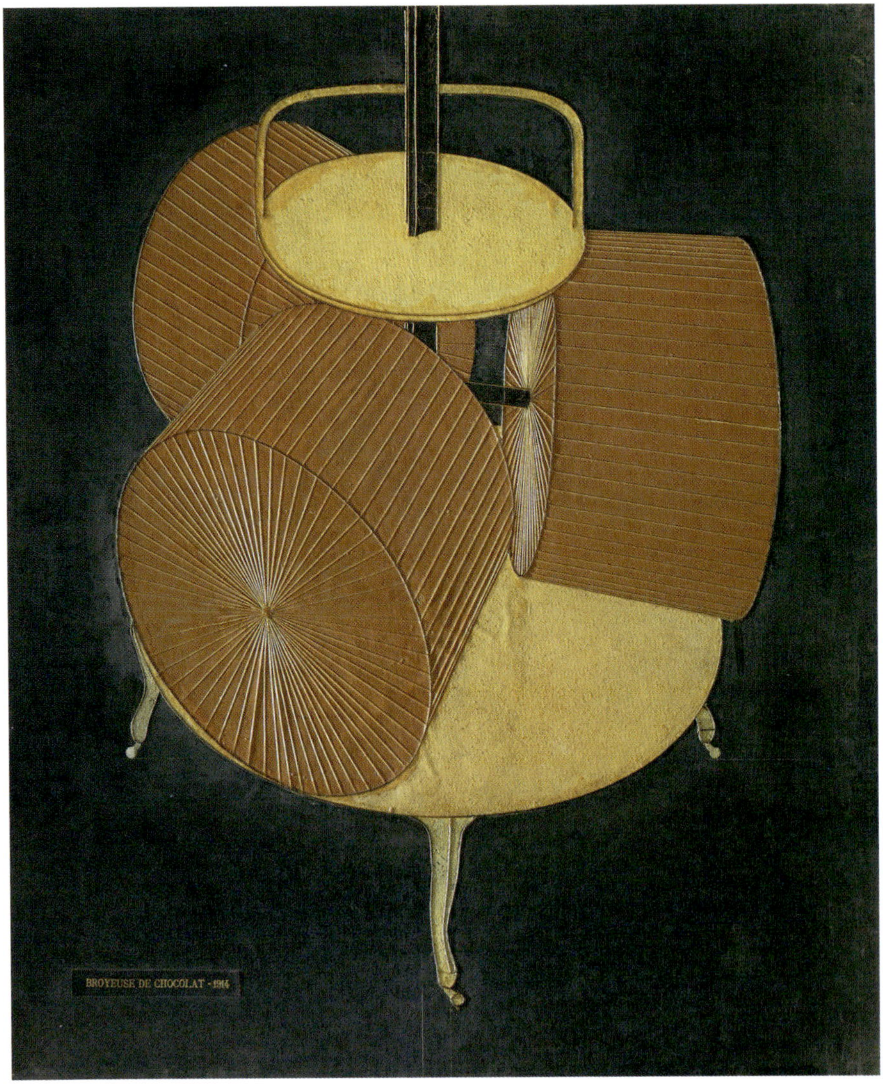

FIGURE 3.10

Marcel Duchamp
Broyeuse de chocolat, No. 2 / Chocolate Grinder (No. 2), 1914
Oil, graphite, and thread on canvas, 65.4 × 54.3 cm
Philadelphia Museum of Art, Philadelphia, PA, The Louise and Walter Arensberg Collection, 1950 / Bridgeman Images

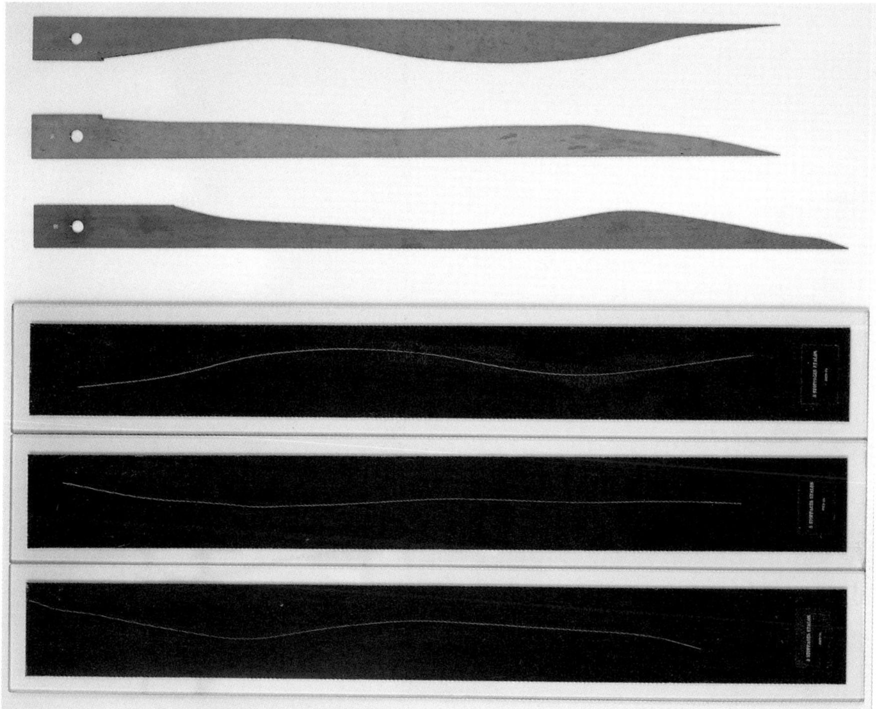

FIGURE 3.11

Marcel Duchamp

3 Stoppages étalon / 3 Standard Stoppages, Paris 1913–1914

Wood box 28.2 × 129.2 × 22.7 cm, with three threads 100 cm, glued to three painted canvas strips 13.3 × 120 cm, each mounted on a glass panel 18.4 × 125.4 × 0.6 cm, three wood slats 6.2 × 109.2 × 0.2 cm, shaped along one edge to match the curves of the threads

The Museum of Modern Art, New York, NY, Katherine S. Dreier Bequest.

The word "malic" comes from the Latin *malus*, "apple tree," evoking the Garden of Eden, the Fall, and sexual desire. *Pendu femelle*, "suspended female thing," in the upper, Bride's portion of the *Glass* directly above the Malic Moulds, could be an apple—source of malic acid: the energy/desire that fills and fuels the Malic Moulds. In the Philadelphia Museum's Arensberg Collection there is a painting by John Covert—Walter Arensberg's cousin and Duchamp's frequent chess partner—depicting an apple sliced in half to show its seeds (figure 3.12). Its title, *Hydro Cell*, implies that the

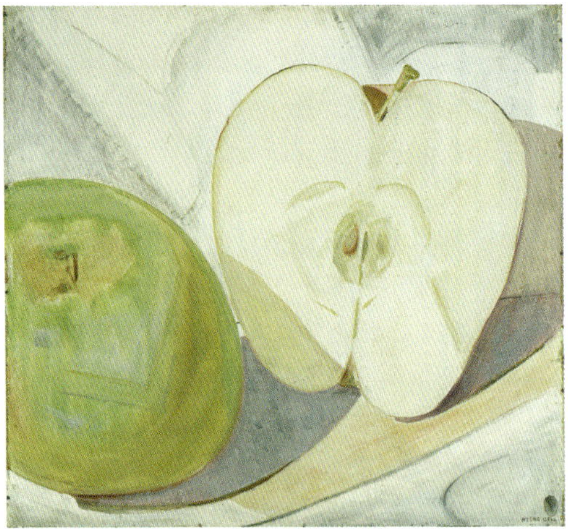

FIGURE 3.12
John R. Covert
Hydro Cell, 1918
Oil on cardboard, 61.6 × 67.3 cm
Philadelphia Museum of Art, Philadelphia, PA, The Louise and Walter Arensberg Collection, 1950 / Bridgeman Images

apple is a source of water-derived energy. Malic acid from an apple could in fact fuel a lead-acid battery, but the reference to water suggests a more multilayered meaning linking it with Duchamp's falling water preceding illumination in *Given: 1. The Waterfall, 2. The Illuminating Gas* (1946–1966, figure 0.1). Painted in 1918, while Duchamp was working on *The Large Glass*, *Hydro Cell* is "signed" in the lower right corner with a thumbprint in the same way Rrose Sélavy would "sign" the last frame of *Anémic cinéma* (1926).

Herz imagines "erotically charged situations" between the artist-lodger and the seamstress-wife—situations that, given Duchamp's romantic history, seem likely, if not inevitable. Duchamp's fourth Munich drawing (figure 3.13) is inscribed "mechanical modesty" (*pudeur mécanique*) and "July 1912 / First study for: The Bride Stripped Bare by Her Bachelors." Its spiky, highly energized forms suggest two aggressive, aroused male figures on either side of a flailing third figure. The drawing hardly resembles the mechanical-organic forms of *The Large Glass*, for which it was supposedly a "first study," evoking instead an erotic competition easily imagined as having been generated by Duchamp's Munich living situation. According to art historian Lawrence D. Steefel, Jr., Duchamp's Munich artworks were "projected fantasies of aggression and obsession, which he prefers to direct towards art rather than towards persons. He achieves an obvious catharsis from his art, yet he insists

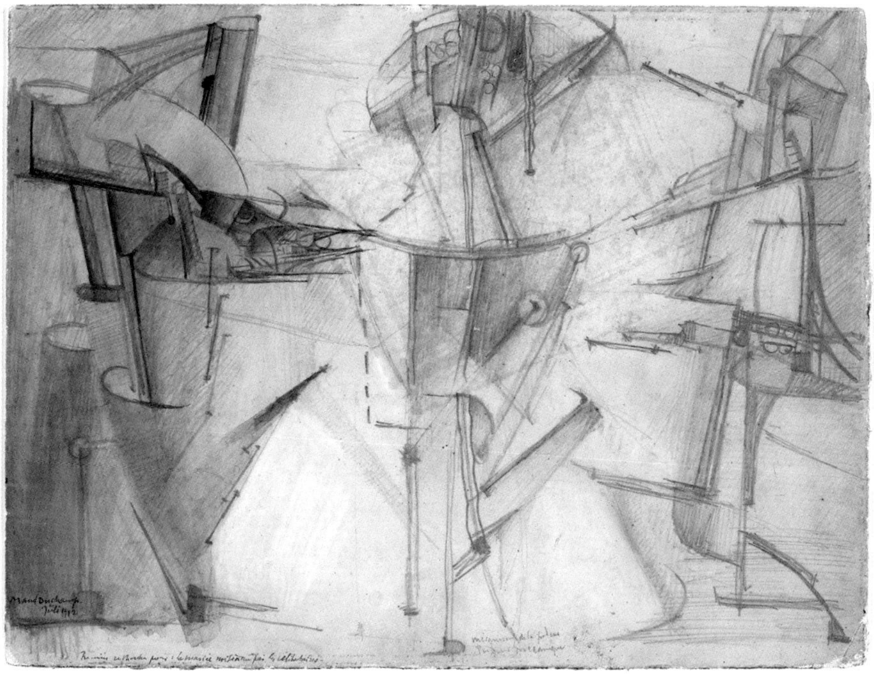

FIGURE 3.13

Marcel Duchamp
Première recherche pour: La Mariée mise à nu par les célibataires (Mécanisme de la pudeur/ Pudeur mécanique) / First Study for: The Bride Stripped Bare by Her Bachelors (Mechanism of Modesty / Mechanical Modesty), 1912
Crayon, graphite, ink on cardboard, 24 × 32 cm
Musée National d'Art Moderne, Centre Georges Pompidou, Paris, France

that it is more than mere self-expression undisciplined and untransmuted into a sublimated and ultimately different form."[49]

Duchamp's statement to Steefel is reminiscent of his quote from T. S. Eliot's 1919 essay "Tradition and the Individual Talent" in "The Creative Act": "The more perfect the artist, the more completely separate in him will be the man who suffers and the mind which creates; the more perfectly will the mind digest and transmute the passions which are its material."[50] As discussed earlier, Eliot was familiar with dhyana yoga—a form of meditation described in the *Bhagavad Gita* and the *Yoga Sutras of Patanjali*. One of Eliot's more memorable formulations in "Tradition and the Individual Talent" strikes a quietist if not overtly mystical note: "The bad poet is usually unconscious where he ought to be conscious, and conscious where he ought to be unconscious. … Poetry is not a turning loose of emotion, but an escape from emotion; it is not the expression of personality, but an escape from personality." Eliot's passage parallels one of Duchamp's comments regarding *Coffee Mill* (figure 1.18): "It was a sort of escape hatch. You know, I've always felt this need to escape myself."[51]

Directly preceding the sentence quoted by Duchamp is Eliot's scientific metaphor for the creative mind as catalyst—effecting change while remaining unaffected: "When [oxygen and sulphur dioxide] are mixed in the presence of a filament of platinum, they form sulphurous acid. … The platinum itself is apparently unaffected; has remained inert, neutral, and unchanged. The mind of the poet is the shred of platinum. It may partly or exclusively operate upon the experience of the man himself; but, the more perfect the artist, the more completely separate in him will be the man who suffers and the mind which creates; the more perfectly will the mind digest and transmute the passions which are its material."[52] Both Eliot and Duchamp compared the mind of the poet/artist with a laboratory or engineer's workshop where obsession and suffering are transmuted to manifest in a form that can be considered dispassionately.

Achievement of this mental state requires as much discipline and practice as any other artistic skill. Such practice may have been one of the goals of Duchamp's train trip to the Jura Mountains to spend an erotic but chaste night with a woman he deeply loved. His fourth Munich drawing thus makes sense as the "first study for the Bride Stripped Bare by Her Bachelors"—the project to which Duchamp would apply himself from late 1912 to 1923. *The Bride Stripped Bare by Her Bachelors, Even* (figure 0.2) is basically a technical work, complete with confusing operating instructions, where Duchamp diagramed for his own benefit an energetic engineering of the mind—in the words of Robert Lebel, "wheels of love-passion assimilated into a productive circuit."[53] Duchamp's motivation was not so much frustrated desire (which is how this work is usually interpreted) as a determination to analyze how desire functions, and how it can be directed to productive ends.

What Duchamp tended to stress when he spoke about Munich was his decision to abandon painting as the primary medium for his art. Toward the beginning of his visit he had been inspired by the seductive, quasi-religious paintings of Lucas Cranach (figure 3.14) and the evocative allegories of Arnold Böcklin. The two paintings he produced in Munich—*The Passage from Virgin to Bride*, painted in July–August 1912; and *Bride*, painted later in August (figures 3.1, 3.15)—are among his best. Yet when Duchamp described being "defrocked" in Munich, it was with specific reference to his identity—you might even say his "livery"—as a painter: "I was truly defrocked, in the religious sense of the word. But not deliberately. [Painting] disgusted me."[54] What could have produced such disgust?

There *is* something—a nightmare Duchamp had in August 1912 which he mentioned to his biographer Robert Lebel and which, according to Lebel, he had never forgotten: "Upon returning from a beer hall where ... he had

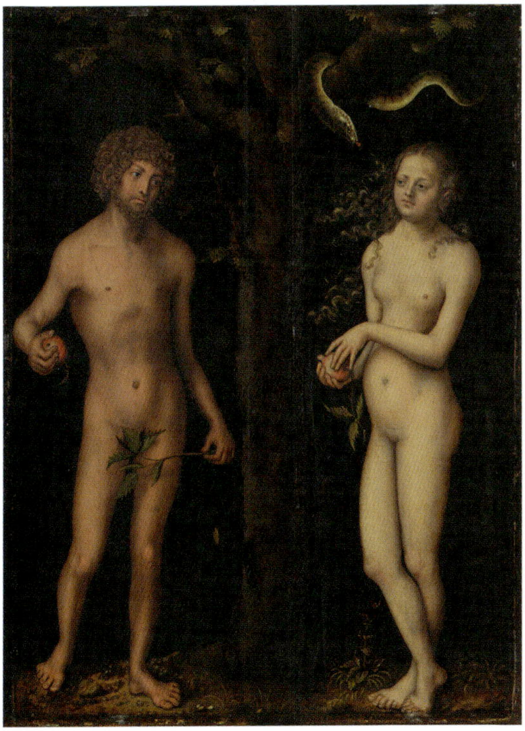

FIGURE 3.14

Lucas Cranach the Elder
The Fall of Man (Adam and Eve), c. 1510–1516
Oil on panel, 47.2 × 35.3 cm.
Alte Pinakothek, Bayerische Staatsgemaeldesammlungen, Munich, Germany, inv. no. 720
Photo: bpk Bildagentur / Alte Pinakothek, Bayerische Staatsgemaeldesammlungen / Art Resource, NY

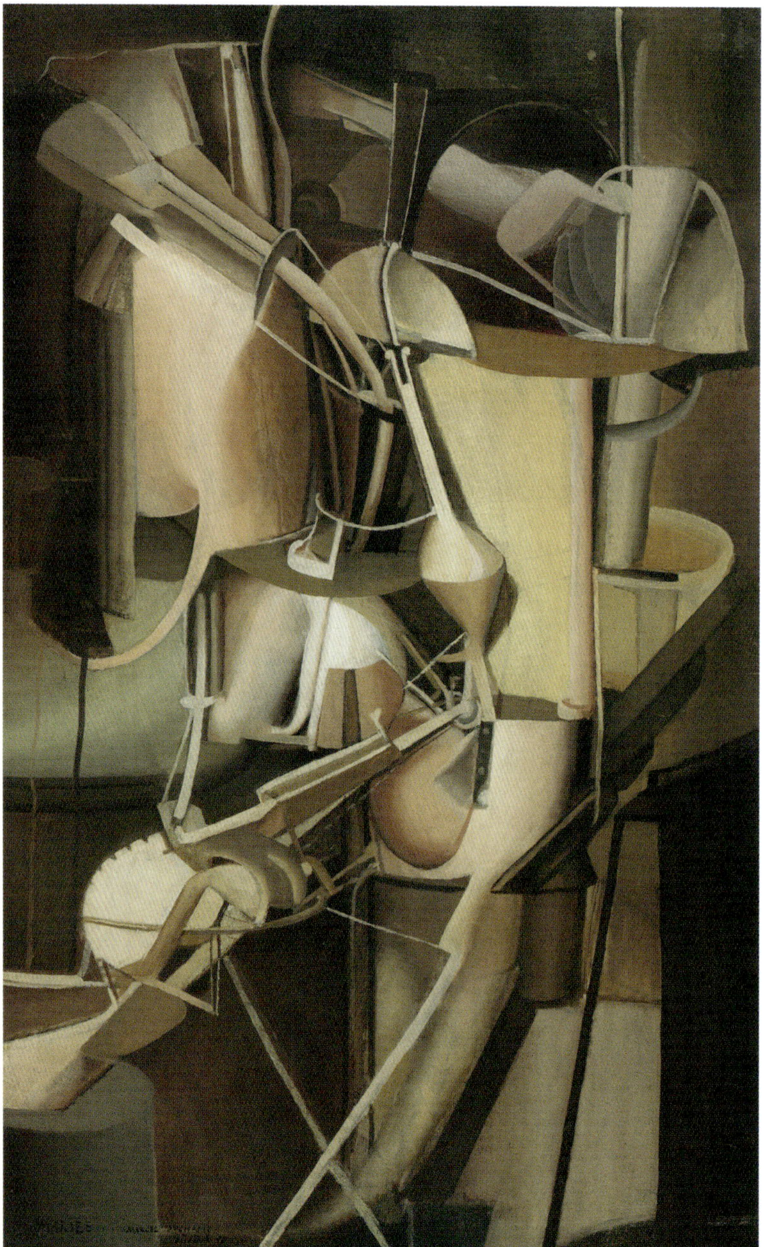

FIGURE 3.15

Marcel Duchamp
Mariée / Bride, 1912
Oil on canvas, 89.5 × 55.6 cm
Philadelphia Museum of Art, Philadelphia, PA, The Louise and Walter Arensberg Collection, 1950 / Bridgeman Images

drunk too much, to his hotel [*sic*] room where he was finishing the Bride, he dreamed that she had become an enormous beetle-like insect which tortured him atrociously with its elytra." Lebel applied a Freudian interpretation to Duchamp's nightmare, linking it with incestuous desire.[55] But there is a likelier link between beetles and armored protection, symbolized by the very elytra, or wing coverings, with which Duchamp's nightmare-beetle tortured him so "atrociously."

Beetles are distinguished by the hard, chitinous casings that cover and protect the fragile, transparent wings with which they fly. Interpreted literally, Duchamp's dream may have demonstrated his unconscious rationale for a move from opaque paint on gessoed canvas to translucent pigment and reflective silver on transparent glass. On the other hand, if we take a Jungian approach and consider what part of Duchamp his painting-transformed-into-beetle represented, the message of his nightmare becomes more significant. His dust-up with the Indépendants had been hard on the sensitive Duchamp. He recounted the episode to Pierre Cabanne decades later: "In the most advanced group of the period, certain people had extraordinary qualms, a sort of fear! ... Cubism had lasted two or three years, and they already had an absolutely clear, dogmatic line on it, foreseeing everything that might happen. ... That cooled me off so much that, as a reaction against such behavior coming from artists whom I had believed to be free, I got a job. I became a librarian at the Sainte-Geneviève Library in Paris."[56] Munich did more than allow Duchamp to regroup, mentally and emotionally. "My stay in Munich," he wrote some fifty years later, "was the scene of my complete liberation." He claimed his most memorable experiences were silent, though not necessarily solitary: "I never spoke to a soul, but I had a great time."[57]

Whatever his experience there, Munich helped Duchamp realize that for him painting had become a protective trap, an abusive straitjacket that was tormenting him by preventing him from flying, from becoming the kind of artist he wanted to be. He was like the hidebound cubists of the Independents' hanging committee whose judgment on *Nude Descending a Staircase* revealed "a sort of fear." Who wanted to live like that? Not Duchamp. He returned to Paris in early October 1912, and several months later began studying at the École Nationale des Chartes. No longer a painter, Marcel Duchamp was transforming himself into an artist of life.

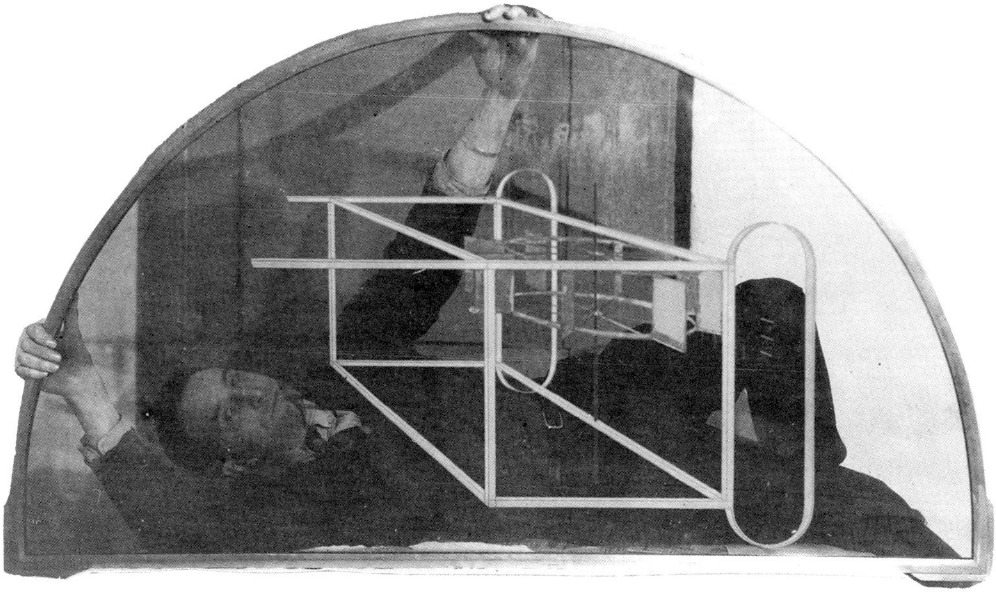

FIGURE 4.1

Man Ray
Duchamp with Glider, 1917
Gelatin silver print (arched) 8.6 × 15.4 cm
The J. Paul Getty Museum, Los Angeles, CA. © Man Ray 2015 Trust / Artists Rights Society (ARS), New York / ADAGP, Paris

4 THE HEADLIGHT-CHILD

Any object of three dimensions that we see dispassionately is a projection of something four-dimensional that we do not know.

—Marcel Duchamp[1]

The art of life as practiced by Marcel Duchamp, I have argued, was based on identification of the artistic impulse with the erotic impulse, and a vivid awareness of absolute reality hidden within everyday reality. From the correlations that have emerged, Duchamp would seem to have grounded this awareness on a form of Western tantric yoga in which sexual union, experienced as the union of consciousness and creative energy, generated the laser-like perception that Duchamp dubbed the "headlight-child." His primary focus in this process would have been his own consciousness, and the implications for his artistic practice. At what point did Duchamp realize that how he experienced life could be framed as "a work of art itself"? "I never set out to do this when I was twenty or fifteen," he said of his enterprise, "but I realize, after many years, that this was fundamentally what I was aiming to do."[2] It would appear that Duchamp's understanding began to coalesce during the years 1912–1915, after he returned from Munich but before he left for the United States. One of the catalysts was the Polish-bred, Italian-born, French poet, playwright, novelist, and art critic Guillaume Apollinaire.

While Duchamp was in Munich, Apollinaire had written to ask for a photograph to use in a book of essays, *The Cubist Painters*. The two men had first met at the home of Francis and Gabrielle Picabia in 1911,[3] and were on friendly terms by June 1912, when the four of them attended Raymond Roussel's avant-garde play *Impressions d'Afrique*.[4] The relationship deepened during a week-long stay at Gabrielle's mother's farmhouse in the village of Étival, in the Jura Mountains. The trip began with a frightening drive on perilous roads during a stormy night, with Picabia at the wheel. Their return journey to Paris a week later was calmer, but Duchamp remained mostly silent.[5] One reason may have been his feelings for Gabrielle, with whom he had spent the night in a train station in these same mountains, and now a week at Étival. Gabrielle never said what transpired between them, but she did write about the intense relationship between her husband, Duchamp, and Apollinaire:

> Better than by any rational method, they ... pursued the disintegration of the concept of art, substituting a personal dynamism, individual forces of suggestion and projection, for the codified values of formal Beauty. These games of exploration in an inaccessible dimension and in unexplored regions of being ... seem to have contained all the germs of what later became Dada, and even of later growths. Thus they arrived at certain postulates which soon developed into the arcana of the new plasticity and poetics: such as the calligrammes and conversation poems of Apollinaire, or the "ready-mades" of Marcel Duchamp.[6]

Having experienced an "initiation" with Duchamp only a few months earlier, Buffet-Picabia may well have participated in these "games of exploration in an inaccessible dimension." Together they translated their techniques for accessing invisible reality into a new artistic language that she termed "arcana": knowledge that is mysterious except to the initiated.

Another reason Duchamp was so silent during their drive back to Paris may have been that he was busily conceiving plans for a work of art capable of expressing what he had experienced in the preceding months. Entitled simply "1912," his text (which he would publish in 1934 in *The Green Box*) is organized around the technological metaphor of the "headlight-child":

> The machine with 5 hearts, the pure child, of nickel and platinum, must dominate the Jura-Paris road.
>
> On the one hand, the chief of the 5 nudes will be ahead of the 4 other nudes towards this Jura-Paris road. On the other hand, the headlight-child will be the instrument conquering this Jura-Paris road.

> This head-light child could, graphically, be a comet, which would have its tail in front. ...
>
> The Jura-Paris road, having to be infinite only humanly, will lose none of its character of infinity in finding a termination at one end in the chief of the 5 nudes, at the other in the headlight child. ...
>
> In the beginning (in the chief of the 5 nudes) it will be very finite in width, thickness, etc., in order little by little, to become without topographical form in coming close to this ideal straight line which finds its opening toward the infinite in the headlight-child.[7]

Duchamp's language in this passage is as coded as any tantric text. Interpreted in the context of Kundalini energy, his technological metaphors point to a perception of what Gabrielle Buffet-Picabia labeled "unexplored regions of being." The "machine" would be the body; the "5 hearts" the five chakras, or energy centers; the "pure child, of nickel and platinum," fiery Kundalini energy rising through the chakras to merge with consciousness at the crown chakra. Energized consciousness gives birth to the "headlight-child," represented by a comet with its tail in front (the erotic implications are obvious).[8]

Erotic/creative energy ascends and then descends the Jura-Paris road, which loses none of its "character of infinity" at its two terminal points: "the chief of the 5 nudes" at the root chakra; and the crown chakra, where it "finds its opening toward the infinite" and emerges as the headlight-child. Duchamp's image of the headlight-child as a comet with its tail in front—no doubt inspired by the headlights of Picabia's car—would in turn inspire his star tonsure seven years later (figure 2.6).

In the eleventh-century *Tantraloka*, Indian philosopher and Kaula practitioner Abhinavagupta wrote: "When knowledge and known unite the knower appears"—a new being, characterized as a child.[9] In Kundalini yoga, the child is made of light. *The Yoga Sutras of Patanjali* describes a radiant light at the crown of the head during the culminating phase of practice: "As the radiance of light inside a house in concentrated in the keyhole, ... so the luminosity of *Sattva* [purity] is concentrated in this opening."[10] Finally, in *Kashmir Shaivism*, Jagadish Chandra Chatterji wrote: "this process of Universal manifestation is ... the same as, or similar to, the psychical process in our daily lives. ... Technically the process is called one of 'Shining out'."[11]

Maintaining this radically new form of being in the course of ordinary life is a goal of tantric yoga.[12]

There is clearly a connection between the headlight-child and Lucifer—Gabrielle Buffet-Picabia's term for Duchamp during his "retreats." These philosophies and the bodily practices associated with them may well have informed the syncretic practice Duchamp developed in the course of his research and his experimentations with Buffet-Picabia, Apollinaire, and Picabia. As for Apollinaire, the visual tracings of Duchamp's headlight-child are echoed by the soundings of a car horn in a verse from his long poem "Les Collines" ("The Hills") from *Calligrammes* (1913–1916):

> The chauffeur grips the steering wheel
> And every time along the road
> He sounds his horn around a curve
> There appears as far as the eye can see
> A still virgin universe[13]

Apollinaire's image of a virgin universe penetrated by the headlights of a moving car corresponds to Buffet-Picabia's inaccessible dimension, and Duchamp's virgin transformed into bride (figure 3.1).

During that same month, October 1912, Apollinaire was busy editing the second proof of *Cubist Painters*. He concluded his short essay on Marcel Duchamp with a prediction that, in hindsight, was about *The Large Glass*—still an embryo in Duchamp's mind, but no doubt a topic of discussion between poet and artist: "It will perhaps fall to an artist as disengaged from aesthetic considerations and as concerned with energy as Marcel Duchamp to reconcile Art and the People."[14] Asked about this statement, Duchamp refused to endorse Apollinaire's claim: "Nothing could have given him the basis for writing such a sentence. Let's say that he sometimes guessed what I was going to do, but 'to reconcile Art and the People,' what a joke!"[15] In the very same interview, however, Duchamp indirectly sanctioned Apollinaire's statement by insisting that art be allowed to play a social role: "Since Courbet, it's been believed that painting is addressed to the retina; that was everyone's error. ... Before, painting had other functions: it could be religious, philosophical, moral. ... It has to change; it hasn't always been like this."[16]

Art *has* changed, in ways Duchamp may have foreseen but Apollinaire probably did not. What Apollinaire may have had in mind is only partially clarified by his preceding text:

> An art that would aim to extract from nature not intellectual generalizations but collective colors and forms, the perception of which has not yet been transformed into abstract ideas, is quite conceivable. ... It is possible that to be emotionally moving these unknown, profound, suddenly grandiose aspects of nature may not need to be aestheticized, and this explains the flame-shaped colors, the N-shaped compositions, and the effect of teeming movement, tenderly or emphatically expressed. These conceptions are not determined by an aesthetic, but by the energy of just a small number of lines (forms or colors).[17]

On his manuscript, Apollinaire noted after "flame-shaped colors": "*de Picabia*." He added the note "*de Marcel Duchamp*" at the end of the passage.[18] Indeed, in his essay on Picabia, Apollinaire used terms similar to those in his essay on Duchamp: "Color is now itself the form and the light of what is being represented. [Picabia] thus moved to an art where ... color is itself the ideal dimension. Consequently it includes all other dimensions. ... In this art, color is saturated with energy and spreads out beyond the edges into surrounding space. Reality here is the material."[19] But Apollinaire did not mention the potential of Picabia's art to play a social role, as he did with Duchamp.

The examples Apollinaire goes on to provide suggest that he and Duchamp had talked in specific terms about the need for art to reclaim its religious, philosophical, and moral function: Cimabue's *Madonna*, which was "paraded through the streets" of Florence on its way to be installed in the Rucellai Chapel; the airplane in which Blériot flew the Channel, which was paraded through Paris before being installed in the deconsecrated chapel at Arts et Métiers in 1909. Blériot's airplane carried, according to Apollinaire, "the weight of humanity, of thousands of years of endeavor, of necessary art." The endeavor in question was Leonardo's: to fly, to be free. Art that serves as a vehicle for consciousness is a mental flying machine.

Apollinaire's characterization of Duchamp's compositions as "N-shaped" would have conveyed more to his contemporary readers than it does today. There are a couple of possibilities aside from simple visual analysis, which, with the exception of *The King and Queen Surrounded by Swift Nudes* (1912; figure 1.17), is not particularly supported by Duchamp's paintings from this period. The first assumes that Apollinaire's "N" refers to higher dimensions of reality, "n-dimensional" being shorthand for the continuum of forms within and beyond three-dimensional perception.[20] Artistic applications for the concept of a fourth spatial dimension had originated within cubist circles; Apollinaire wrote about this in his introduction to *The Cubist Painters*. In contrast to Greek art, which "took man as its measure of perfection," Apollinaire wrote, "the art of the new painters takes the infinite universe as its ideal." The key word here is "infinite": the fourth dimension "represents the vastness of space stretching eternally in all directions at any given moment. It is space itself, the dimensions of infinity." But, Apollinaire cautions, "this utopian turn of phrase is now really only of historical interest."[21] By the end of 1912, the fourth dimension was outdated terminology for the fullness of reality, at least as far as Apollinaire was concerned.

Another interpretation, which complements rather than contradicts the more mathematical interpretation above, takes "N-shaped compositions" as a metaphysical reference to absolute reality, with "N" representing *néant*, "nothingness." Understood in this way, Apollinaire was describing the "form" of Duchamp's compositions as consisting of nothingness, or void—energetically empty paintings. The generative nature of nothingness is central to a number of South and East Asian traditions. In addition to higher dimensions of reality, Duchamp may have been thinking about how to elicit the experience of nothingness in his viewers. Both interpretations accord with Buffet-Picabia's "games of exploration" in an inaccessible dimension and in unexplored regions of "being": games that contained "all the germs of what later became Dada, and even of later growths."

••

One of the characteristics of Dada would be a Tao-inflected focus on nothingness. Duchamp told Pierre Cabanne that in 1911–1912 Picabia "went to smoke opium almost every night," and he told Calvin Tomkins that while he was in Munich, Apollinaire "spent most of his evenings with the Picabias, drinking, talking, smoking opium." Though Duchamp claimed never to have smoked opium himself, he did say that Picabia's hedonistic lifestyle "opened up new horizons for me. And, because I was ready to welcome everything, I learned a lot from it."[22] Parisian opium dens were frequented and usually run by Chinese, who supplied the opium as well as preparing it for non-Chinese smokers. Duchamp said he resisted smoking opium with Picabia, but, "ready to welcome everything," he could well have accompanied Picabia to an opium den and gathered insider information on the practice of Taoist internal alchemy, or nei-tan—the tantra-like process of transforming erotic energy into life energy.[23]

Apollinaire published two articles on Chinese art on view in Paris in 1911, which he dubbed "a year of Chinese art."[24] A rich source of information about Chinese philosophy would have been the Bibliothèque Sainte-Geneviève, an encyclopedic library near the Sorbonne for scholars, students, and the general public. Duchamp was already exploring its collections in 1910, and his researches continued until his departure for New York in June 1915.[25] There is no record of the books consulted by Duchamp,[26] and we know he read authors apparently not in the library's collection at the time, such as the nineteenth-century individualist philosopher Max Stirner (Johann Kaspar Schmidt, 1806–1856). Picabia, who introduced Duchamp to Stirner's writings,[27] helped him find work at the library through an uncle who worked there. In November 1912 Duchamp began studying at the national school of paleography, the École Nationale des Chartes. He began an internship at the Sainte-Geneviève Library in May 1913, held a two-month appointment in November–December of that year (replacing someone on leave), and continued as a volunteer through May 1915, just before his departure for New York.[28]

This two-and-a-half-year, in-house relationship with the library and its staff enabled Duchamp to conduct extensive research on the broad topic of "perspective," by which he seems to have meant scientific and philosophical theories that could help him understand his experiences and devise ways to translate them into art. An early note later published in *À l'infinitif* (*The White Box*, 1966) reads: "Perspective. / See Catalogue of the Library Ste Geneviève the entire topic Perspective: / Niceron (Father J., Fr.) Thaumaturgus opticus."[29] *Thaumaturgus opticus* (1646) is a Latin version of the Minim friar, painter, and mathematician Jean François Niceron's *La perspective curieuse ou magie artificielle des effets merveilleux de l'optique, la catoptique, la dioptique* of 1638 ("curious perspective or artificial magic of the marvelous effects of perspective, reflection, refraction").[30] Niceron's work is a good example of the conflation of magic, art, and science that characterized the seventeenth century and persisted into the early twentieth century.[31] His books were intended to be of practical use to painters and others interested in "magical" effects. Catoptrics deals with the visual effects of reflection and mirrors; dioptics with lenses and the refraction of light. Both would have been useful to Duchamp as he developed his plans for *The Large Glass*. Another important source was Hermann von Helmholtz's *Optique physiologique*, which analyzes how vision functions and emphasizes the importance of touching to seeing.[32]

Duchamp's *aide-mémoire* reads not "*sous* la rubrique Perspective"—*under* the heading Perspective—but "*toute* la rubrique Perspective"—"the *entire* topic Perspective"—wording which indicates that his explorations ranged beyond optical perspective. Duchamp told Arturo Schwarz that during this time he reread the Greek philosophers, finding Pyrrho of Elis, who was influenced by Buddhism and abandoned painting for philosophy, to be "closest to his own views."[33] Greek and Chinese philosophy were juxtaposed in another text in the library's collection: M. Abel Rémusat's *Mémoire sur la vie et les opinions de Lao-Tseu, ... qui a professé les opinions communément attribuées à Pythagor, à Platon et à leurs disciples* ("Dissertation on the life and opinions of Lao Tzu, ... who professed opinions commonly ascribed to Pythagoras, Plato and their followers").[34] Other texts on Taoism included Stanislas Julien's *Le Livre de la voie et de la vertu par le philosophe Lao-Tseu*, still one of the best translations of Lao Tzu's *Tao Te Ching*; and the more humorous and irreverent writings of another defining figure, Chuang Tzu, available in volume two of Léon Wieger's two-volume *Taoïsme*, published in 1911 and 1913.[35]

Alexandra David-Néel, introduced previously as a follower of Mirra Alfassa and thus someone Duchamp could have known, was the author of another book on Chuang Tzu: *Les théories individualistes dans la philosophie chinoise, Yang-tchou* ("Individualistic theories in Chinese philosophy, Chuang Tzu"), published in 1909. David-Néel cites Max Stirner approvingly, including, in one of the epigraphs to her introduction, Stirner's *Rien n'est, pour Moi, au-dessus de Moi* ("For Me, Nothing is higher than Me"), as well as in connection with Chuang Tzu's "amorality."[36] David-Néel does not suggest that Chuang Tzu was a source for Stirner's thinking, but she cannot resist pointing out the parallels: "Taking into account the difference of expression, I have found a deep similarity between the old Chinese thinker and the modern German philosopher. I could not help signaling it in various passages."[37]

Like T. S. Eliot—who, following his sojourns in Paris and Munich, began an intense course of study of Sanskrit and Asian philosophy at Harvard—Duchamp enrolled at the École Nationale des Chartes, nominally to become a librarian.[38] The École Nationale des Chartes was where one went to study paleography (ancient writing systems) and philology (the structure of and relationships between languages). That Duchamp studied Sanskrit during this time is implied by his comment to Pierre Cabanne: "The word 'art'," he said, "interests me very much. If it comes from Sanskrit, as I've heard, it signifies 'making'."[39] He was probably referring to the ancient Indo-European root *ar*, which means to join or fit, and is the root of the Sanskrit word *ara*, which signifies, among other things, the spoke or radius of a wheel.

Newly available around this time were publications on Hindu philosophy and nondual Kashmir Shaivism by the Cambridge-educated Jagadish Chandra Chatterji, whose *La Vision des sages de l'Inde* was already in the Library's collection. Chatterji's treatise *Pratyabhijñā hṛidaya, being a summary of doctrines of the Advaita Shaiva philosophy of Kashmir* (1911), and the 1912 edition of his *Hindu Realism* appeared just before Duchamp began studying at the École des Chartes.[40] Chatterji's *Pratyabhijñā hṛidaya* ("Heart of Recognition") by Kshemaraja, disciple of the great tantric guru Abhinavagupta, would have been an excellent focus for Duchamp's studies in philology. "This work by Kshemaraja," Chatterji wrote in his preface, "is intended to be an easy introduction to, and a summary of the doctrines of, the [nondual Shaiva] System."[41] The treatise itself is in Sanskrit, but comprises only 20 short sutras. Sutra 16 bears directly on what Duchamp would later characterize as his art of life: "When the bliss of *cit* [unity of consciousness] is attained, one is stable in the consciousness of identity with *cit*, even while the body, etc., are being experienced. This state is called *jīvanmukti* (liberation even while one is alive)."[42]

One of the things Duchamp would have observed in his various studies was the price paid in diminution of human wholeness and agency for Western culture's insistence on compliance with convention. The young Duchamp's resentment over rules and restrictions on individual agency in both art and life was surely one reason he cited Max Stirner in response to a questionnaire he was asked to complete when *3 Standard Stoppages* (1913–1914, figure 3.11) entered the collection of the Museum of Modern Art in 1953.[43] Stirner's conviction that language and rationality are limiting human constructs restricting individual creativity made him a pariah in the philosophical community, but it would have been completely in line with the thinking of Duchamp, Apollinaire, and Picabia. Stirner wrote *The Ego and Its Own* (self-published 1845) in a purposefully convoluted style. Translated directly from the German, for example, his title, *Der Einzige und sein Eigentum*, reads something like "The Unique [Self] and Its Own-ness."

Stirner argued that the concept of self is impossible to comprehend, because the so-called "self" is a "creative nothing." In recognizing the self as nothing, one can be said to "own the world" because, as Stirner asserted in the last line of *The Ego and Its Own*, "all things are nothing to me." He further proposed that social institutions—including the State, the right to own private property, the very notion of society—are mere illusions, or "ghosts," in the mind. With regard to society, Stirner believed that "individuals are its reality."[44] He advocated replacing systems of belief with awareness that there is no soul, along with a detached life of nondogmatic, open-minded engagement with the world as it is. Uniqueness is essentially creative potential: "I am not nothing in the sense of emptiness, but I am the creative nothing, the nothing out of which I myself as creator create everything."[45] Understanding the self in this way means that we are all creators: artists both of the world and of our own lives.

Stirner's stance was anarchistic, but not nihilistic. His work inspired the title of the London literary magazine *The Egoist*, founded in 1914 by Dora Marsden as a successor to her feminist *The New Freewoman*. *The Egoist* claimed to recognize no taboos, and declared its "cause to be NO-MAN'S."[46] Stirner's writings had their greatest impact not in the field of philosophy but on artists and writers like Edward Carpenter, a widely published English poet and socialist who, beginning in the early 1900s, pursued a course of research into Asian philosophy and erotic practice that included travel to India and Ceylon. "The Art of Life is to know that Life is Art, that it is Expression," Carpenter wrote in 1898.[47] Carpenter's writings would have been known to the sybarite and Anglophile Apollinaire, and to Duchamp as well: Marcelle Senard's *Edward Carpenter et sa Philosophie* came into the collection of the Bibliothèque Sainte-Geneviève while Duchamp was working there.[48]

Alexandra David-Néel cited Stirner's thinking as Taoist, but his view of the "I" more closely resembled Indian perspectives on the Self. In the *Brihadaranyaka Upanishad*, one of the earliest and most influential of the *Upanishads*, the teacher Yajnavalkya tells his wife Maitreyi: "not for the sake of the universe the universe is dear, but for the sake of the self is dear the universe. ... By seeing, hearing, minding, knowing the self, all this (universe) is comprehended."[49] Central to Advaita Vedanta is the idea that individual consciousness is continuous with and indistinguishable from absolute reality, which cannot be perceived with the senses and thus cannot be described. If you perceive the self, you perceive the Self—the Absolute. Kashmir Shaivism, on the other hand, takes the physical world to be real—a "vibration" of the Absolute. In his *Kashmir Shaivism*, published in 1914, Jagadish Chandra Chatterji described *Sad-Vidyā*, a state of equilibrium that "takes the form, 'I am This' in which both the 'I' and the 'This' are realized with equal clearness."[50] The implications for Duchamp's readymades are obvious, as we shall see.

Stirner's thinking is usually discussed in terms of its Hegelian roots. Like Hegel, Stirner would have been familiar with non-Western perspectives on reality. He attended Hegel's lectures on Religion and on the History of Philosophy in 1827, the same year Hegel published a critique of Wilhelm von Humboldt's lectures on the *Bhagavad Gita*.[51] David Gordon White notes that Hegel discussed the final chapter of Patanjali's *Yoga Sutra* in his 1829–1830 lectures on the History of Philosophy, "singling out its final chapter, on 'abstraction or spiritual isolation' (Samadhi), as 'philosophy proper'." But Hegel, according to White, "never took the next step of incorporating Indian philosophy into his grand scheme of the history of philosophy. ... Eastern philosophy could never have passed his litmus test for philosophy, which was the passage from abstraction to conceptualization."[52] Along similar lines, Hegel erroneously reified the nothingness of Buddhism.[53]

Stirner, on the other hand, treated experience of the Absolute not as an idea or concept, but as a *state* of (Self-) consciousness. While never mentioning Asian philosophy, Stirner managed to avoid Hegel's errors. As for Duchamp, he surely knew that Stirner's "creative nothing" was not unique, even within the European culture of his day: the first European philosopher to acknowledge Asian perspectives as central to his system was Hegel's rival Arthur Schopenhauer, whose enthusiasm for Buddhism first surfaced in *On Will and Nature* (1836).[54]

Duchamp attributed his discovery of Stirner to Picabia. Their mutual investigation of Taoism is confirmed both by internal evidence in their work and by external evidence in the form of testimony from artist-colleagues in the international Dada movement they helped to inspire.[55] The most obvious indication is the yin-yang symbol (*Yīnyáng*, "dark-bright," opposite forces giving rise to one another) that Picabia incorporated into his large painting *Comic Wedlock* in June or July 1914 (figure 4.2). From its title, the theme of *Comic Wedlock* can be connected with Duchamp's preparatory thinking for *The Bride Stripped Bare by Her Bachelors, Even*, which he began planning in 1912 and would begin fabricating in the United States in 1915.

According to Picabia, "the subjective expression is the title, the painting is the object"—an object that "furnishes to a certain point the very means of comprehending the potentiality—the very heart of man."[56] The titles of Picabia's paintings from this time, such as *Udnie*, a scrambling and contraction of "Uni-dimensionnel," suggest an experiential mental realm. He entitled another painting *Edtaonisl*, derived from *Étoile danseuse*, or "Star Dancer"—note the "tao" in *Edtaonisl*.[57] Picabia's integration of the yin-yang form into *Comic Wedlock* indicates familiarity with the principles of Taoism and, in light of the reference to wedlock in his title, with internal alchemy as well.

The three "wheels" of Duchamp's *Chocolate Grinder* (1913–1914, figures 3.6, 3.10), part of the lower, Bachelor portion of *The Large Glass*, may similarly have been inspired by Taoist metaphor. The three energy centers or *tan-tien* of Taoist internal alchemy are located in the abdomen, at the heart, and in the brain. Like the chakras, or "wheels," of tantric yoga, which vary in number depending on the tradition, Taoism's three energy centers have no physical counterparts in the body. Essence (*ching*), a blend of yin and yang reproductive energy, has its home in the lower tan-tien. Vital energy (*ch'i*) resides at the heart, while the ultimate energy, spirit (*shen*), has its home in the center of the head. In internal alchemy, the body is imaged

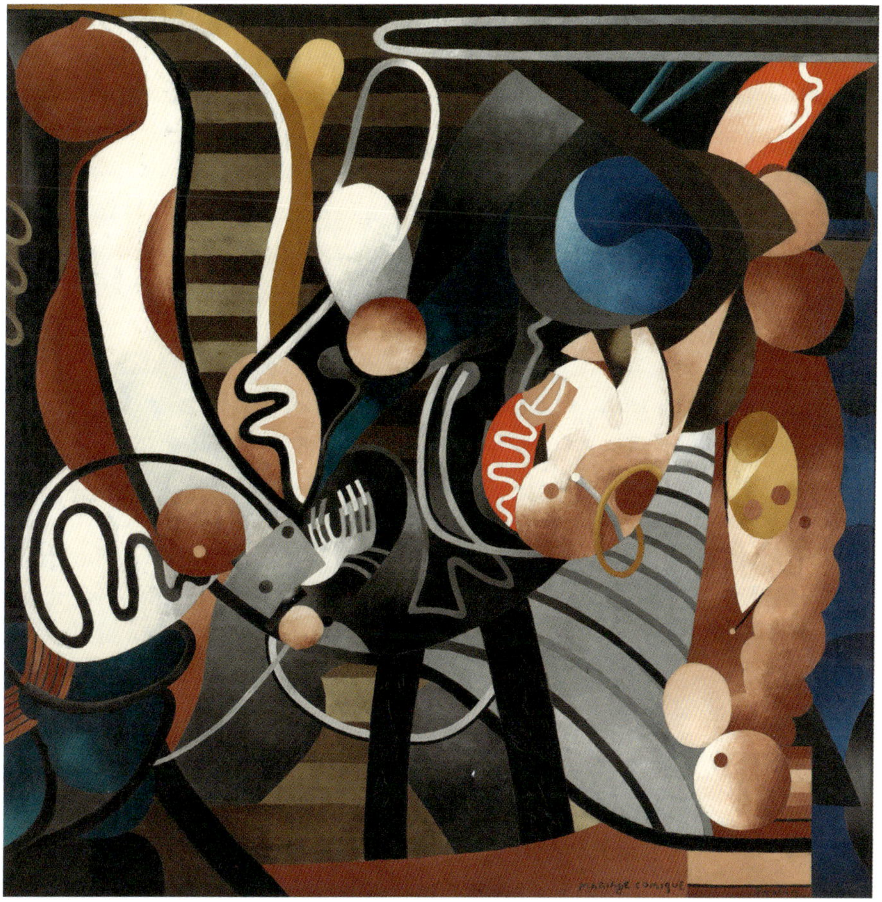

FIGURE 4.2

Francis Picabia

Mariage comique / Comic Wedlock, c. June–July 1914

Oil on canvas, 196.5 × 200 cm

The Museum of Modern Art, New York, NY, Eugene and Agnes E. Meyer Collection, given by their family.

as a laboratory or workshop where energy is cultivated, refined, and transformed in pursuit of physical, emotional, and mental health, culminating in union with the Tao. The three wheels of *Chocolate Grinder* similarly refine the erotic energy cultivated within the Malic Moulds.

Another important motif in the lower portion of *The Large Glass* is the waterwheel, whose turning instigates the action continued by the chocolate grinder. Duchamp began working on *Glissière contenant un moulin à eau (en métaux voisins)* ("Glider Containing a Water Mill [in Neighboring Metals]," see figure 4.1) in 1913. He described it as "worked out on a half-circular glass pane, my first painting on glass. ... The wheel which you see inside is supposed to be activated by a waterfall, which I did not care to represent."[58] In Taoist body energetics, the "waterwheel," located at the perineum, drives "essence" (ching, sexual energy) to flow inward and upward through the three energy centers. In 1917 Duchamp had Man Ray photograph him lying on a table holding the *Glider* in front of him so that the waterwheel hovers above his crotch in a way that emphasizes the anatomical parallel (figure 4.1). Kundalini, the tantric yoga counterpart of the waterwheel, is likewise based at the perineum and moves upward through the chakras. Refocusing orgasm from the genitals to the brain is an aspect of both processes.

Glider Containing a Water Mill hangs from two hinges, like a door. In a note from this time, Duchamp mused: "perhaps make a hinge picture ... develop the principle of hinge in the displacements: first in the plane, second in space."[59] His interest in the "principle of hinge" would persist, as evidenced by the door he installed in his studio at 11 rue Larrey (1927), which serviced three adjacent spaces at once. The Taoist classic *Chuang Tzu*, which was published in French in 1913, the same year Duchamp began working on *Glider*, contains potential inspiration for his hinge principle:

> Everything has its "that," everything has its "this." ... "this" and "that" give birth to each other. ... Therefore the sage ... recognizes a "this," but a "this" which is also a "that," a "that" which is also "this." ... So, in fact, does he still have a "this" and "that"? Or does he in fact no longer have a "this" and "that"? A state in which "this" and "that" no longer find their opposites is called the hinge of the [Tao]. When the hinge is fitted into the socket, it can respond endlessly. ... So I say, the best thing to use is clarity.[60]

It may be too much to suggest that Chuang Tzu's reference to "clarity," which signifies internal alchemy, aka the "great clarity,"[61] explains Duchamp's choice of glass as the support for both *Glider* and *The Large Glass*. There were plenty of other factors. But I do want to point out that the hinge structure—a moveable rod within a tubelike support—is identical to Duchamp's explanation of the link between sex and the fourth dimension: "I noticed that when I hold a knife, a small knife, I get a feeling from all sides at once. And this is as close as it can be to a fourth-dimensional feeling. Of course from there I went on to the physical act of love, which is also a feeling all around, either as a woman or as a man."[62]

Chuang Tzu said: "When the hinge is fitted into the socket, it can respond endlessly." There is a comparable technological metaphor for the source of the phenomenal world in chapter 5 of the *Tao Te Ching*: "What is between the heavens and the earth resembles a bellows that is empty yet never exhausted; put into motion, it yields more and more."[63] Lao Tzu's bellows involves not just the action of a hinge, but also constant coming and going, like breath.

The poetry of the *Tao Te Ching* is notoriously difficult to translate. In 1966 Duchamp told an interviewer: "When you try to analyze a painting using words, you can only manage a very questionable approximation, worse than questionable, because, after all, painting and art in general, especially visual art, is a language in itself, a visual language instead of a spoken language. So it's already like a Chinese poem that has been translated into English—it doesn't mean anything anymore."[64] Tao called Tao is not Tao.[65] Art "translated" is meaningless. Experience trumps exegesis. Intensely interested in not only how the mind works, but also how *art* works, Duchamp questioned presuppositions about art, the artist, and the creative act. This line of inquiry led him to explore the potential of art for revelation: the realization of reality.

••

Talking about his 1912–1915 period of research at the Sainte-Geneviève Library, Duchamp told Cabanne: "Perspective was very important. ... For me, perspective became absolutely scientific." That "absolutely scientific" was at least partly tongue-in-cheek—after talking briefly about "technical problems," Duchamp went on to clarify: "What we were interested in at the time was the fourth dimension. ... Simply, I thought of the idea of a projection, of an invisible fourth dimension, something you couldn't see with your eyes. Since I found that one could make a cast shadow from a three-dimensional thing ... I thought that, by simple intellectual analogy, the fourth dimension could project an object of three dimensions, or, to put it another way, any three-dimensional object, which we see dispassionately, is a projection of something four-dimensional, something we're not familiar with."[66] The key phrase is "which we see dispassionately." We let go of any preconception about or attraction to an object, including aesthetic attraction, and allow its continuity with our Self to emerge from the fourth dimension.

Such pursuit of "indifference" yielded the perspective that led Duchamp to develop his concept of the readymade in 1914: "Instead of choosing something which you like, or something which you dislike, you choose something that has no visual interest for the artist. In other words, to arrive at a state of indifference towards this object; at that moment it becomes a readymade."[67] But visual, "retinal" (to use a Duchamp term) indifference is not necessarily mental indifference. "They look trivial," he said of the readymades, "but they're not. On the contrary, they represent a much higher degree of intellectuality."[68]

Duchamp's choice of words implies that making a readymade involves a fair amount of mental work—an expanded notion of consciousness that encompasses matter as well as mind. "Matter is Mind in an opaque state," Edward Carpenter wrote in 1898.[69] Philosopher Galen Strawson suggests what achieving such a perspective might entail: "The powerfully open state of mind required by true materialism is hard to achieve as a natural attitude to the world. It involves a profound reseating of one's intuitive theoretical understanding of nature."[70] Duchamp's goal with the readymades was just such a profound reseating of his attitude and perceptions. He found the hardest part to be eliminating attraction, and especially aversion: "It's easy to choose something you like," he said. To find a readymade, on the other hand, "It's necessary to choose something tasteless, bland. This is difficult, of course."[71] A good deal of mental energy is required to cultivate this kind of relationship with things-in-the-world, a relationship that obviates judgment, aesthetic or otherwise.

Sometime in 1913—the year after his return from Munich—Duchamp attached a bicycle wheel to a stool. He kept it by the chair in his studio, so he could easily set it spinning. According to Duchamp, the *Bicycle Wheel* (figure 4.3) was originally created not as an art object, but as an object of contemplation: "The Bicycle Wheel is my first Readymade, so much so that at first it wasn't even called a Readymade. ... It had more to do with the idea of chance. In a way, it was simply letting things go by themselves and having a sort of created atmosphere in a studio, an apartment where you live. Probably, to help your ideas come out of your head. To see that wheel turning was very soothing, very comforting, a sort of opening of avenues on other things than material life of every day."[72] The way Duchamp described *Bicycle Wheel* has prompted interpretations of it as a white noise machine for the eyes, but it was more than that. It was a device not for shutting out "material life," but for the "opening of avenues on other things": it was a meditation machine.

Tosi Lee has made a case for the connection between Duchamp's choice of a wheel for his first readymade and the Buddhist Wheel of the Dharma. In the Buddha's first sermon the wheel stands, among other things, for the newly enlightened Buddha's determination to begin his missionary task of turning the wheel of truth in this world. In early Buddhist art, the Wheel of the Dharma is represented by a wheel placed on top of a throne or pillar. The enthronement of Duchamp's wheel on a pillar-like studio stool tacitly compares his recent personal "liberation" with the Buddha's Enlightenment and, according to Lee, "signifies the commencement of Duchamp's new path in art as well as his 'teachings.'"[73]

In Indian and Southeast Asian sculpture, the Wheel of the Dharma is often shown flanked or supported by lions, as on the East Gate of the Great Stupa at Sanchi. Replicas of this large gate dominated the courtyards of both the Ethnographic Museum in Berlin, where Duchamp stopped on his return from Munich, and the Musée Guimet in Paris.[74] On the left pillar of the gate the wheel is flanked at top and bottom by lions; on the central pilasters, it is supported by lions on stool-like columns (figure 4.4). An undated note by Duchamp connects this Wheel of the Dharma with *Bicycle Wheel* via his typical wordplay: "between the lions / lines / Riding between the lines / lions / Reading between the lines / Riding between the lions—"[75]

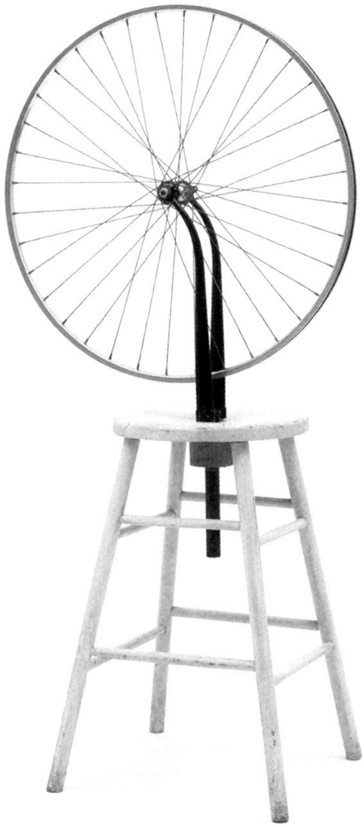

FIGURE 4.3

Marcel Duchamp
Roue de bicyclette / Bicycle Wheel, New York, 1951 (third version, after lost original of 1913)
Metal wheel mounted on painted wood stool, 129.5 × 63.5 × 41.9 cm
The Museum of Modern Art, New York, NY, The Sidney and Harriet Janis Collection

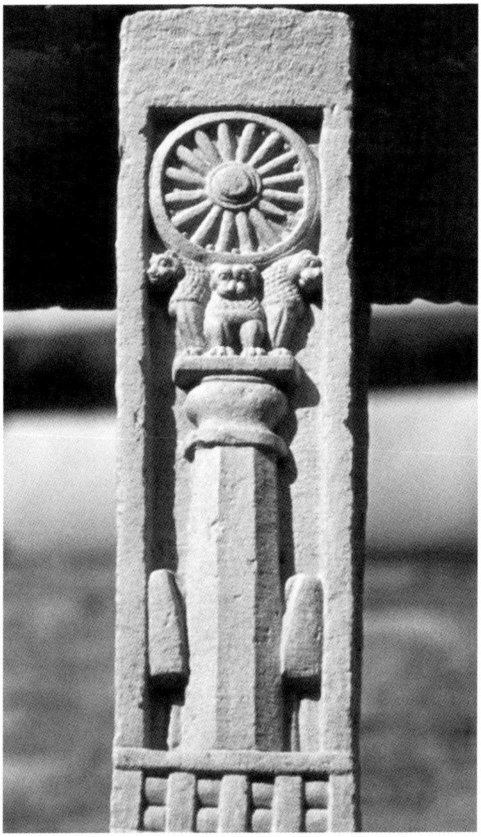

FIGURE 4.4
Indian School
East Gate of the Great Stupa at Sanchi, first century BCE/CE (detail), photo, c. 2012
Sandstone
Indian School / Madhya Pradesh, India / Dinodia / Bridgeman Images

Duchamp turns the usual pair of reading/writing into reading/riding: reading between the lines of the turning bicycle wheel, riding between the lions of enlightenment.

In the course of his wide-ranging research during this time Duchamp concluded that an artist is not somebody who creates, but somebody who chooses to engage the world in a creative way; that is to say, an interactive way. It is this engagement that constitutes "The Creative Act," to cite the title of his 1957 essay. "I don't believe in the creative function of the artist," he told Pierre Cabanne.[76] In a conversation with Georges Charbonnier, Duchamp asked rhetorically: "Why 'make'? To 'make' what? To make something ... is always to choose." He pointed out that somebody else makes everything artists use to "make," like paint and brushes. So, to use something "completely made" isn't a big deal: "Choice is the main thing, in painting ... and in everything"; "The idea of choice interested me in a metaphysical way, at this point [1914]. That was the beginning, and that day I bought a bottlerack and I brought it home. And it was the first readymade. ... I have a replica of this readymade that gives me the same satisfaction. This isn't the whole idea, exactly, of the work of art, you understand. This is [just] the idea that something has been chosen and is, so to speak, sacred because chosen. Is this clear enough as a 'definition'?"[77]

For Duchamp, the readymade seems to have served as a sort of ritual object for reexperiencing a moment of deep engagement. Charbonnier tried to confirm his understanding of what Duchamp had told him by rephrasing: "as soon as I decide there is a readymade, the important thing is my decision, much more than the object." "Exactly," was Duchamp's automatic response. Then he went on to explain how what had for him been a form of engagement with the art of life was mistaken for a merely aesthetic statement: "And this is the great misunderstanding, because everyone can decide, as everyone decides at every moment of his life, and chooses every moment of his life. And that choice is in fact quite tricky." Suddenly Charbonnier gets it, or thinks he does: "Basically, everybody is surrounded by the readymade!" "Exactly," Duchamp repeats. Charbonnier starts back in with "There isn't anything that ..." but Duchamp interrupts him with an "important point" about why the choice of a readymade is so tricky: "—precisely to avoid choosing what recalls a past, or even a future, aesthetic": "It is easy to choose something you like. This 'pleasure' is based on your traditions, your instinctive taste. It's necessary to choose something tasteless, bland. This is difficult, of course. Even if you find a bottle rack that's pretty to look at, it's basically insipid. Clearly. It's devoid of taste, and therefore filled the role that I wanted. I wanted my choice not to be influenced, in any case, by what I wanted to demolish. That was it, the difficulty of the problem."[78]

The French word for "taste" is *goût*. Duchamp's *Bottlerack* (figure 4.5) was not only an *égoutter*, a "de-dropper"; it was also an *égoûter*, a "de-taster"—suggesting the process of stripping oneself bare of preconceptions. Duchamp shifts gears a couple of times in his discussion with Charbonnier: from the concept of the readymade, to the concept of life-as-a-work-of-art,

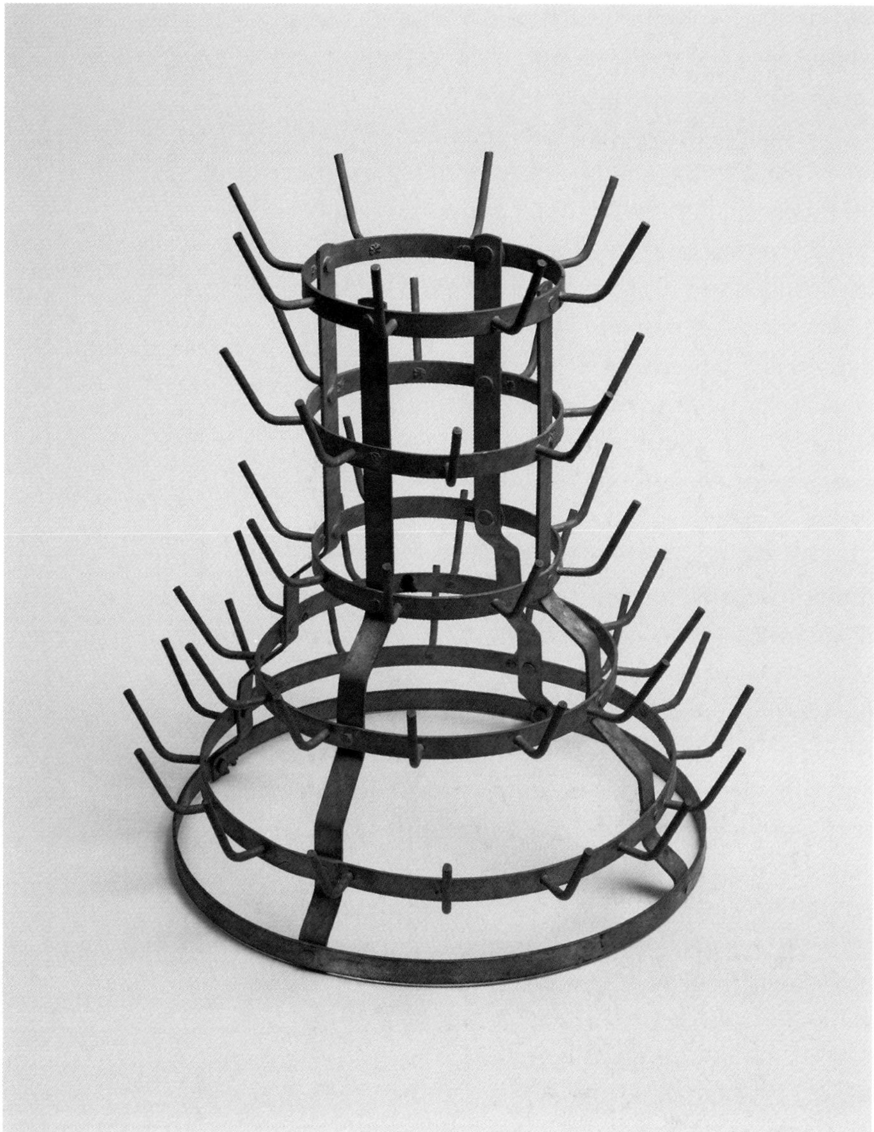

FIGURE 4.5

Marcel Duchamp
Porte-bouteilles / Bottlerack (replica of 1914 original), 1961
Galvanized iron, 49.8 × 41 cm
Philadelphia Museum of Art, Philadelphia, PA, Gift of Jacqueline, Paul, and Peter Matisse in memory of their mother, Alexina Duchamp, 1998 / Bridgeman Images

and back again to the readymade. He warns that the readymade "isn't the whole idea ... of the work of art." It was a first step, a crucial stage in the creation of more developed works.

Duchamp clearly tried hard to "witness" in this nonjudgmental way, to create in himself a mental state of complete openness to engagement—what Buddhism calls "mind of don't-know." His readymades were private experiments carried out for his own purposes, which helps to explain why they have tended not to survive their original "rendezvous" with him—like the corkscrew, which we know only through its painted shadow in *Tu m'* (1918, figure 4.6). "The ready-mades may be unique as a concept," Duchamp's dealers Harriet and Sidney Janis wrote, "but they are not necessarily intended to be unique as examples. ... The act of replacing the object itself grants to the product of mass production the same validity as nature grants to any star in the skies or grain of sand upon the earth."[79]

The readymades help to explain Duchamp's lack of taste in art: he truly didn't have any, or tried not to. Robert Barnes, an artist who helped Duchamp with *Given*, asserted: "Maybe one of the best and the worst things Marcel offered people was a lack of discrimination. He didn't discriminate. In doing so, he made the world easier, but by opening up, eliminating, abolishing decision-making tactics in deciding what is art, I think he created a terrible disaster."[80] Surely Barnes knew this was precisely Duchamp's intent: not just to modify but to demolish restrictions around art-making. And although Barnes did not seem to think much of the result, he does admit that Duchamp made the world easier. How? By demonstrating that an artist is somebody who chooses to engage the world in a creative way: "Everyone can decide, as everyone decides at every moment of his life, and chooses every moment of his life."

Duchamp's brand of indifference helps to clarify the apparent conundrum of Apollinaire's statement about him: "It will perhaps fall to an artist as disengaged from aesthetic considerations and as concerned with energy as Marcel Duchamp to reconcile Art and the People." It was precisely this *dis*engagement from the aesthetic, defined as "what is pleasurable to the senses" (retinal art), that made possible Duchamp's focus on energy, his connection with the world—his continuum of forms within and beyond three-dimensional perception. Duchamp's continuum finds a potential

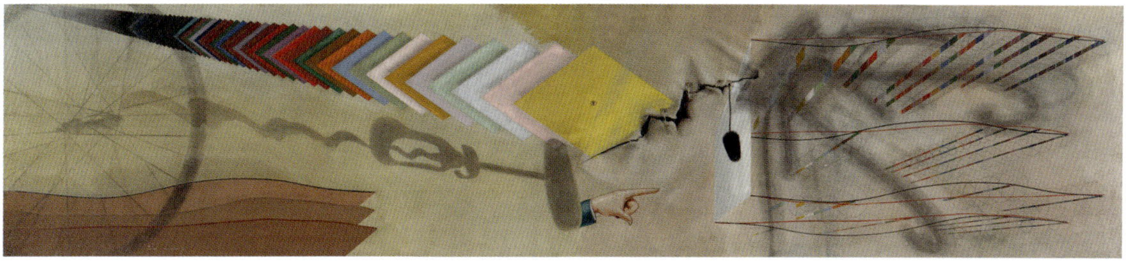

FIGURE 4.6
Marcel Duchamp
Tu m', 1918
Oil on canvas with bottlebrush, safety pins, and bolt, 69.8 × 303 cm
Yale University Art Gallery, Gift of the Estate of Katherine S. Dreier, 1953.6.4

source in the 1912 edition of Chatterji's *Hindu Realism*: "This medium of union must be a non-discrete Reality or a Continuum which is in touch with all discrete things."[81]

Choice is responding rather than simply reacting to chance events, and it takes practice. By 1914 Duchamp's increasingly syncretic art-life practice had begun to generate artworks that were experimental on the part of the artist and insistently experiential on the part of the viewer. *3 Standard Stoppages* (1913–1914, figure 3.11) was a mock experiment in which Duchamp claimed to utilize the scientific method of observation and measurement to test his hypothesis that chance could be mobilized to generate an artistically useful unit of measure. He proceeded to use the resulting forms in a number of subsequent works, beginning with *Network of Stoppages* (figure 4.7) and culminating in *Tu m'* (figure 4.6).

Robert Lebel's 1959 catalogue raisonné of Duchamp's work, created with the close collaboration of the artist, describes this conceptual experiment along with its physical result:

> "A straight horizontal thread one meter in length falls from a height of one meter on to a horizontal plane while twisting *at will* and gives a new form to the unit of length." (Note in the *Green Box*)
>
> The result: 3 threads, less than a meter in length, fixed on strips of canvas pasted on glass. These 3 Standard Stoppages are accompanied by their wooden yardsticks, shaped according to the outlines of the threads.[82]

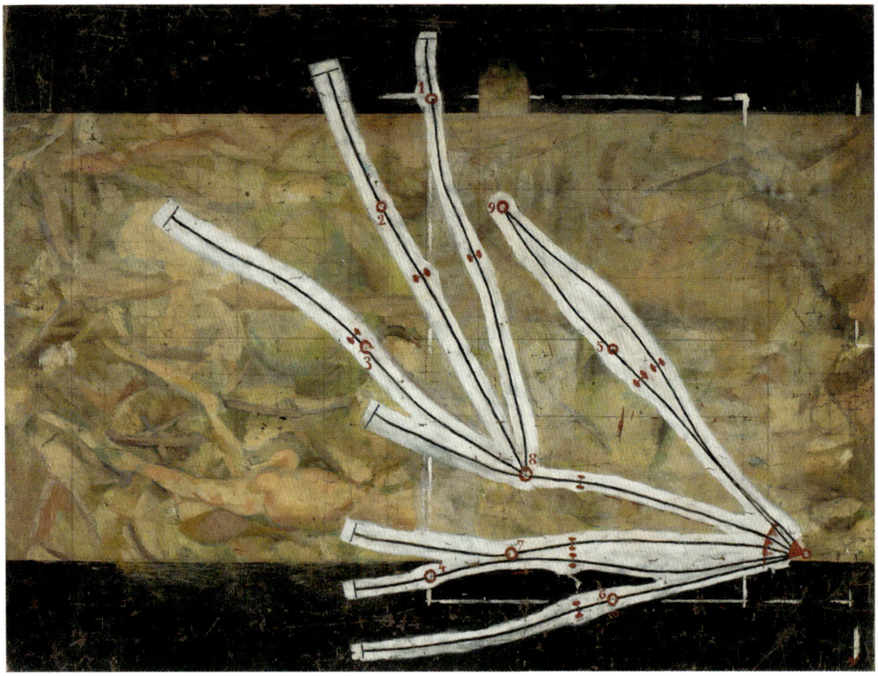

FIGURE 4.7

Marcel Duchamp

Réseaux des stoppages / Network of Stoppages, Paris, 1914

Oil and pencil on canvas, 148.9 × 197.7 cm

The Museum of Modern Art, New York, NY, Abby Aldrich Rockefeller Fund and gift of Mrs. William Sisler. © Association Marcel Duchamp / ADAGP, Paris / Artists Rights Society (ARS), New York 2019

When he talked about *3 Standard Stoppages*, Duchamp liked to imply that the uncontrolled distortions of the falling threads had been precisely preserved: "This experiment was made in 1913 to imprison and preserve forms obtained through chance, through my chance. At the same time, the unit of length: one meter was changed from a straight line to a curved line without actually losing its identity [as] the meter, and yet casting a pataphysical doubt on the concept of a straight line as being the shortest route from one point to another."[83] "Pataphysical doubt" references Alfred Jarry (1873–1907), playwright of the absurd, novelist, and creator of 'pataphysics, the "science of the particular," intended to "explain the universe supplementary to this one."[84] Other hints that the situation may have been more metaphysical than scientific are Duchamp's specification "*my* chance," along with his assertion that each thread twisted "*at will*." Whose will? (The French reads: "en se déformant *à son gré*.")

In fact, the "results" of Duchamp's experiment with the effect of gravity on the standard scientific unit of measure appear to have been an undisguised sham. He may have dropped a few threads, but the ones we see today in the Museum of Modern Art were almost certainly not fixed as they landed, but carefully arranged. As with his contemporaneous *Chocolate Grinder (No. 2)* (1914, figure 3.10), Duchamp sewed the ends of the threads through the canvas and glued them down. He later cut the canvases up and backed them with glass so that the glued-down ends of the strings are hidden in plain sight—for those willing to look.[85] Duchamp hinted at the ruse, telling curator Katherine Kuh that for him making *Stoppages* "was a great experience. The idea of letting a piece of thread fall on a canvas was accidental, but from this accident came a carefully planned work. ... Many of my highly organized works were initially suggested by just such chance encounters."[86] One way *3 Standard Stoppages* is "about" chance is the fact that the idea for it emerged from a chance encounter, perhaps in his Munich landlady's sewing room (as noted in chapter 3). One of the questions *3 Standard Stoppages* poses is your willingness as a viewer to take Duchamp's supposedly scientific explanation at face value, ignoring the evidence of your own eyes and mind.

3 Standard Stoppages thus has a hidden meaning—close in sound to "hidden mending," the French meaning of *stoppage*. Mending what? Duchamp said the piece was intended to cast "a pataphysical doubt" on the concept of a straight line as the shortest route from one point to another. Euclid's definition of a straight line as the shortest distance between two points had been questioned by the nineteenth-century German mathematician Bernhard Riemann, who pointed out that on the plane surface of a sphere the shortest line between two points is a curve.[87] Kandinsky put his own spin on Riemann's challenge to Euclid in the *Blaue Reiter Almanach*, published in the spring of 1912 in Munich, where it was surely read by Duchamp that same summer: "Man cannot move in a straight line physically (look at the paths in fields and meadows!), much less spiritually. And on spiritual paths, especially, the straight line is often the longest because it is false, and the apparently false path is often the right one."[88]

With the scientific method, experimental results—three, in the case of Duchamp's dropped strings—are used to refine a hypothesis and make it more predictable, predictability being the hallmark of scientific truth. This is the opposite of metaphysical systems like that of the *I Ching*, where it is precisely the *unpredictability* of the pattern of dropped yarrow sticks that points to—in Duchamp's words—the "unique and indeterminate" reality "beyond the rational." Duchamp emphasized that *Stoppages*' three strings "should be seen horizontally instead of vertically."[89] In this position, their wavy lines form the Chinese character for the number three—an important number to Duchamp because, as he said, "one is unity, two is double, duality, and three is the rest."[90] His formulation is almost identical to a well-known line from the *Tao Te Ching*: 道生一, 一生二, 二生三, 三生萬物 ("Tao creates one. One creates two. Two creates three. Three creates all things").[91]

The Chinese 三 signifies not just three; it also stands for Heaven, "unity"; Earth, "duality"; and "the rest": everything in-between, including humanity. Duchamp several times indicated his interest in the ideographic character of the Chinese language, telling Arturo Schwarz, for example, that he wanted "to transfer the significance of language from words into signs, into visual expressions of words, similar to the ideograms of the Chinese language" in order to create "a sort of invented language, which would not be intended to communicate physical things, material things."[92] With *3 Standard Stoppages*, Duchamp transformed three "diminished" meters into an ideogram for "the rest"—infinite, unmeasurable reality.

Network of Stoppages (figure 4.7), a "network" of black lines on which small red circles mark connections to the Nine Malic Moulds of *The Large Glass*, would be the only painting Duchamp included in the exhibition *First Papers of Surrealism* (1942, better known for *Mile of String*, figure 6.1). In 1945, architect Frederick Kiesler would reproduce *Network of Stoppages* above a photograph of *Mile of String* on the last page of his Duchamp-themed triptych in the Marcel Duchamp issue of *View* magazine. Kiesler reproduced *Network* vertically, foregrounding the fact that it is painted over a version of Duchamp's depiction of the Fall: *Young Man and Girl in Spring* (1911, figure 4.8). *Network*'s middle layer is a working diagram for *The Large Glass*. *Young*

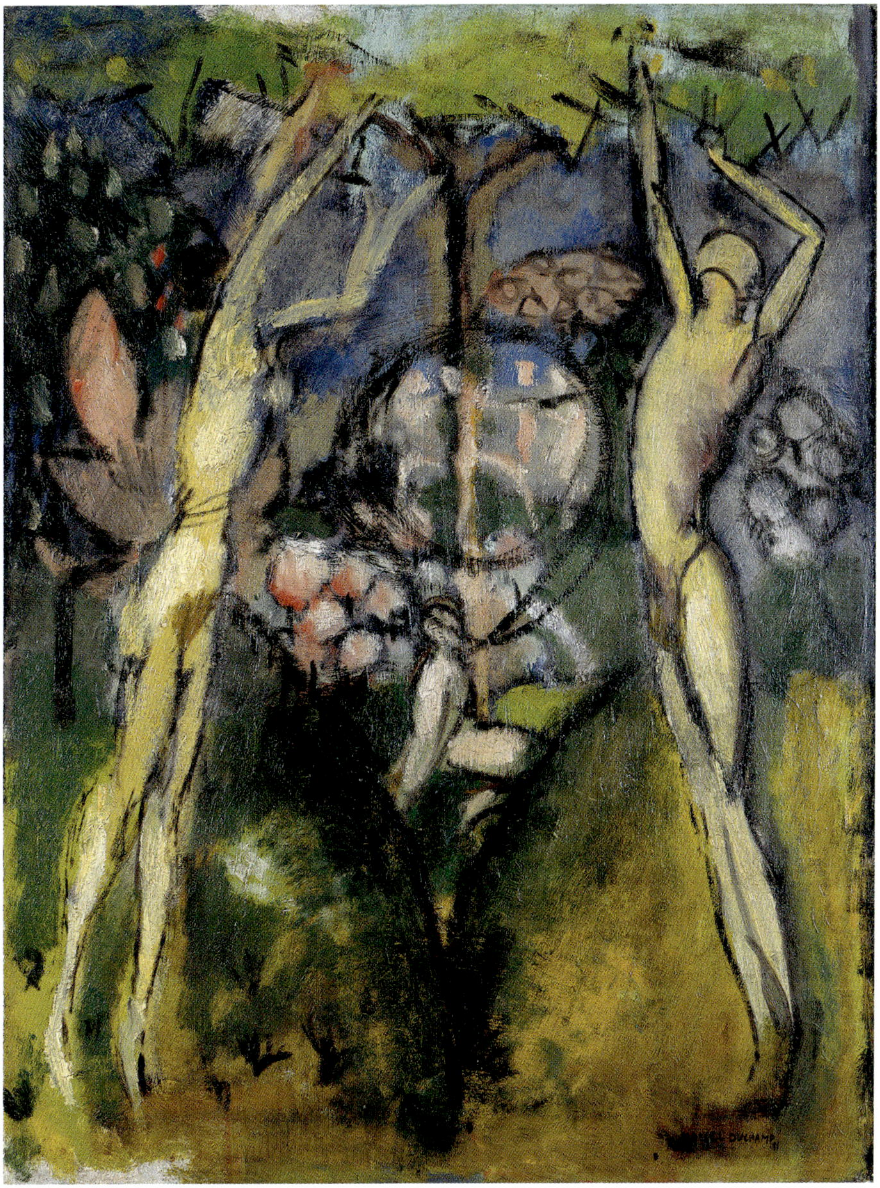

FIGURE 4.8

Marcel Duchamp
Le Printemps / Young Man and Girl in Spring, 1911
Oil on canvas, 65.7 × 50.2 cm
The Israel Museum, Jerusalem, Israel, The Vera and Arturo Schwarz Collection of Dada and Surrealist Art in the Israel Museum / Bridgeman Images

Man and Girl in Spring thus constitutes the still-visible bottom layer of Duchamp's own idiosyncratic triptych, *Network of Stoppages*.

Stoppage in French means hidden mending, but it can also mean (as in English) a halting of motion or of electric current, or physical blockage of a narrow passage, like the *nadis* or "tubes" through which the energies of the subtle body flow, or the Capillary Tubes of *The Large Glass* mapped by *Network of Stoppages*. The "stoppages" are indicated by little red marks that suggest clamps, closing off the connections, and thus the flow of energy from the Malic Moulds through the Capillary Tubes. Only one connection—for Malic Mould number 6, at the bottom right of the Cemetery of Uniforms and Liveries in *The Large Glass*—has advanced past the last stoppage. For Duchamp's 1965 etching *The Large Glass Completed*, this character was identified as "Flunky (liveried servant)."[93] One implication for *The Large Glass* is that the artist at this point in his life, 1912–1914, cast himself in the role of servant, flunky—Apollinaire's elusive but dedicated reconciler of Art and the People.

One of the few things Duchamp would bring from Paris to New York in June 1915 was *Network of Stoppages*, which would serve as both *aide-mémoire* and template for *The Large Glass*, and which Lebel described as "damaged"—perhaps because it had been rolled and unrolled so many times.[94] In New York, the work for which Duchamp was best known was a painting—*Nude Descending a Staircase, No. 2* (figure 1.16)—which had been a sensation at the 1913 Armory Show. By then, Duchamp had already "defrocked" himself as a painter. One of the first works he created after his move to New York was definitively *not* a painting. *THE* (figure 5.1), subtitled "Eye Test, Not a 'Nude Descending a Staircase'" when it was published,[95] was, in its wry Duchampian way, a study for his transparent, translucent, reflective *Large Glass*—the ultimate Eye Test.

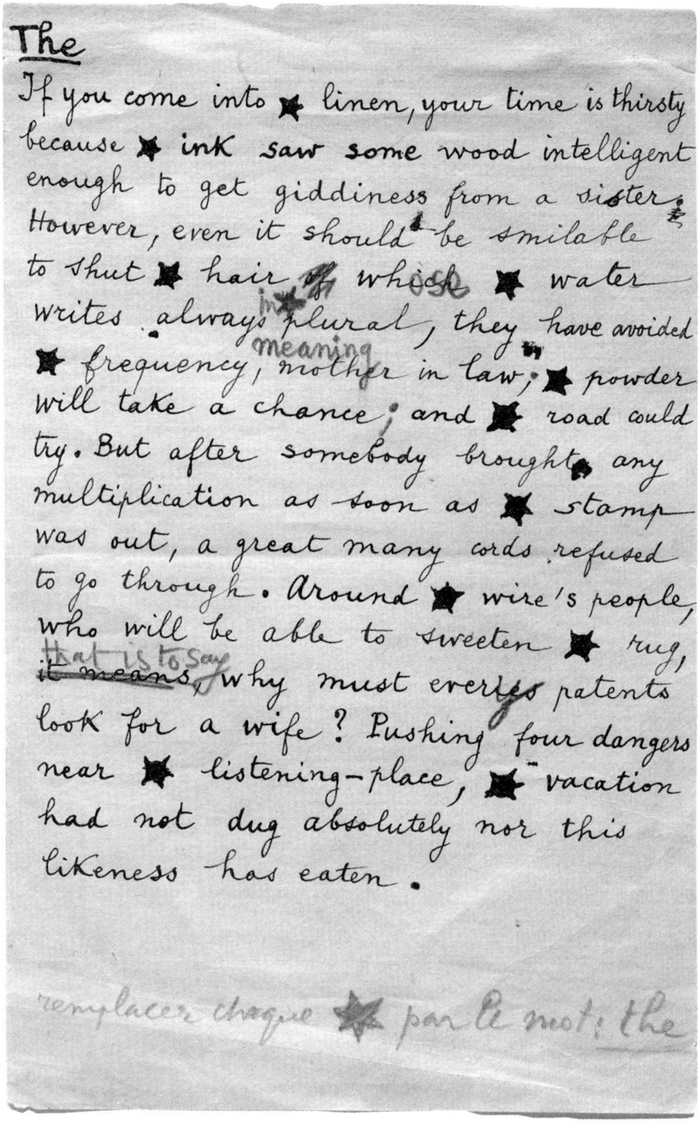
The

If you come into ✱ linen, your time is thirsty
because ✱ ink saw some wood intelligent
enough to get giddiness from a sister.
However, even it should be smilable
to shut ✱ hair of whose ✱ water
writes always plural, they have avoided
✱ frequency, mother in law; ✱ powder
will take a chance; and ✱ road could
try. But after somebody brought any
multiplication as soon as ✱ stamp
was out, a great many cords refused
to go through. Around ✱ wire's people,
who will be able to sweeten ✱ rug,
~~it means~~ that is to say, why must every patents
look for a wife? Pushing four dangers
near ✱ listening-place, ✱ vacation
had not dug absolutely nor this
likeness has eaten.

remplacer chaque ✱ par le mot: the

FIGURE 5.1

Marcel Duchamp
The, 1915, from *The Box of 1914*
Ink and graphite on paper, sheet 22.2 × 14.3 cm
Philadelphia Museum of Art, Philadelphia, PA, The Louise and Walter Arensberg Collection, 1950, 1950-134-79(20)

5 DUCHAMP IN NEW YORK I: VICTOR

*** water writes always in * plural.**

–Marcel Duchamp, 1915[1]

On August 3, 1914, Germany declared war on France. Duchamp's brothers were called to serve, as was Picabia. Apollinaire, an Italian citizen, applied for French citizenship so that he could volunteer. This must have seemed like madness to Duchamp, who had done his obligatory year of military service and had no intention of going to war. He was called before the draft board, but a bout of rheumatic fever in his youth had left him with a damaged heart; he was free, though subjected to disapprobation from relatives, friends, and strangers alike. (It is hard to imagine a worse soldier; Picabia, who eventually went AWOL, was not much better.)

Duchamp was befriended during this time by the American art writer Walter Pach. In late April 1915 he wrote Pach regarding his impending plans: "I do not go to New York I leave Paris. It is altogether different. … New York was my only choice, because I knew you there." San Francisco Bay Area Asian art dealer Frederick Torrey had bought *Nude Descending a Staircase, No. 2* (figure 1.16) from the Armory Show just two years earlier, and New York collector John Quinn had acquired through Pach's efforts two paintings, including *The Chess Game* (figure 1.12). But Duchamp had no more intention of trying to support himself as a painter in New York than he had in Paris. He told Pach he did not want to be "a society painter," and asked how easy it would be to find a job as a librarian, or some other job that would keep him "very busy."[2]

Duchamp arrived in New York in June 1915. Francis and Gabrielle Picabia, who had visited the city earlier in connection with the 1913 Armory Show, preceded him by two weeks. Pach arranged for Duchamp to stay in a duplex on West 67th Street vacated for the summer by Walter and Louise Arensberg. Lou Arensberg was a musician, like Gabrielle. Walter, who had majored in English and philosophy at Harvard, was interested in arcana, cryptography, and the French symbolist poets, including Laforgue. The Arensbergs became Duchamp's steadfast patrons and friends, eventually forming the largest and most important collection of his work. (In 1921, they moved to California for health reasons; Duchamp stayed in touch, visiting them there a number of times.)

Partly to earn money, partly to improve his English, Duchamp taught French, giving several private lessons a day to friends and friends of friends. A few months after his arrival, he created a language exercise, substituting stars for the English definite article "the" in a text of his own devising that he entitled *THE*, in honor of the missing article (figure 5.1). Duchamp accomplished several things with this little text. First, he made all modified definite nouns indefinite—in the spirit of Max Stirner, setting them free from their fixed identities. More importantly, Duchamp's star notation celebrated the marriage in English of French's masculine *le* and feminine *la*, signifying the outcome of an internal erotic process in which male and female energies merge to generate the brilliant headlight-child—the enlightened product of their union.

Stars figured prominently in Duchamp's personal symbolism: from the title of *Once More to This Star* (figure 1.1), to the comet imagery of the headlight-child, to his star tonsure, still in the future. But even with the substitutions taken into account, *THE*'s text makes no more rational sense than Duchamp's hyper-hyphenated *Rendez-vous du dimanche 6 février 1916* (a set of four postcards sent to the Arensbergs), or the spiral "puns" he would inscribe on the disks for *Anémic cinéma* (1926, figure 6.3A). Duchamp later told Arturo Schwarz, regarding *THE*: "I would very often see a meaning and immediately ... would cross out the verb and change it, until, ... the text finally read without any echo of the physical world. ... That was the main point of it."[3] So at the same time Duchamp marked the merging of masculine and feminine with a star, he also dismantled any sense of rationality or materiality by changing verbs.

THE was published in 1916 in Louise Norton's feminist magazine *Rogue*. Beneath its title is the line: "*Eye Test, Not a 'Nude Descending a Staircase'.*"[4] A homophone for "I test," "Eye Test" signifies the personal nature of Duchamp's exercise while connecting it with the Oculist Witnesses of *The Large Glass* (figure 0.2). This relationship between *THE* and *The Large Glass* suggests that both evolved from a process of intensified perception connected with a self-engineered "marriage" of male and female. The reference in the *Rogue* subtitle to *Nude Descending a Staircase* foregrounds the fact that the Marcel Duchamp who was the author of this piece was not the Marcel Duchamp Americans thought they knew: the verb had changed.

••

A significant resource for artists internationally from about 1915 onward was Taoism, with statements by Dada artists themselves providing the strongest evidence. A reaction to the horrors of World War I, Dada evaded definition as an artistic movement by proclaiming itself to be "no thing": "DADA MEANS NOTHING," read the first heading of Tristan Tzara's *Dada Manifesto 1918*. The following year, Raoul Hausmann similarly characterized Dada as "nothing, *i.e.*, everything," and Francis Picabia, in his own "Dada Manifesto" of 1920, wrote: "It's doing something so that the public can say: 'We understand nothing, nothing, nothing,'" signing his manifesto "Francis Picabia / who knows nothing, nothing, nothing." In 1921 Marcel Duchamp told a reporter: "Dada is nothing. For instance the Dadaists say that everything is nothing; nothing is good, nothing is interesting, nothing is important." And in 1922 Tzara asserted: "Dada applies itself to everything, and yet it is nothing. It is the point where the yes and the no and all the opposites meet, not solemnly in the castles of human philosophies, but very simply at street corners, like dogs."[5]

Where did this antirational ideal of "nothing" come from? Duchamp's contemporaries cited Taoism. Tzara claimed: "Chouang-Dsi [Chuang Tzu] was just as Dada as we are. You are mistaken if you take Dada for a modern school, or even for a reaction against the schools of today."[6] Hans Arp similarly stressed the Taoist taproot of Dada: "Dada objects are made of found or manufactured elements, simple or incongruous. The Chinese several millenniums ago, Duchamp and Picabia in the United States, and Schwitters and myself during World War I, were the first to invent and spread these games of wisdom and acumen that were meant to cure human beings of the sheer madness of genius and to lead them back more modestly to their proper place in nature."[7]

The dynamic concept of reality in the *Tao Te Ching*, along with the anti-authoritarianism and ironic humor of *Chuang Tzu*, allowed Dada to develop a shared framework for deconstructing traditional Western perspectives on the nature of knowledge in ways that were at once deeply serious and emphatically humorous. Like Arp, who specified "Duchamp and Picabia *in the United States*," Richard Huelsenbeck emphasized the American context in his introduction to the 1920 *Dada Almanach*: "One cannot understand Dada; one must experience it. ... Dada is the neutral point between content and form, male and female, matter and spirit. ... Dada is the American aspect of Buddhism; it blusters because it knows how to be quiet; it agitates because it is at peace." Huelsenbeck cited Buddhism, but his language was Taoist. This may suggest a certain lack of clarity—perhaps not surprising from artists interested in Asian philosophies primarily as resources for their own work—but it should not be confused with a naïve orientalism. The Dadaists knew what they were up to. Poet Walter Mehring observed in "Unveilings," also published in Huelsenbeck's *Dada Almanach*: "The East Asian Society protests at the way Dada is wrecking Asiatic culture"[8]—i.e., Western versions of Asiatic culture, in which everything is named and classified.

Buddhism adopted key Taoist concepts like "sitting in oblivion" after it reached China in the late Han Dynasty. One result was Ch'an (Japanese: Zen) Buddhism. Taoism returned the favor, generating hybrid practices[9] that might be labeled TABU—a contraction of the first two letters of the words TAo and BUddha. "TABU" was, in fact, what Marcel Duchamp's brother-in-law Jean Crotti called the version of Dada that he and Suzanne Duchamp practiced during the early 1920s. Significantly, Crotti dated his "second birth" to 1915, the year he befriended Duchamp in New York.[10]

Taoism developed in China during the so-called Warring States Period of widespread warfare and social upheaval as a strategy to help people live in a chaotic world.[11] Taoism's sexually charged view of the cosmos as a continuously self-balancing system, its emphasis on perception and perspective, and—perhaps most important—its assumption of the self-transforming power of the individual and rejection of social conventions and definitions, resonated with Western artists at the time of the First World War.[12] There is yet another aspect of Taoism that would have appealed to these artists: the Taoist view of creativity.

In their philosophical analysis of the *Tao Te Ching*, Roger Ames and David Hall point out that in the Judeo-Christian worldview, with its omnipotent "maker," "all subsequent acts of 'creativity' are in fact secondary and derivative exercises of power." In contrast, "real creativity ... can make sense only in a [Taoist] processual world that admits of ontological parity among its constitutive events and of the spontaneous emergence of novelty. ... Creativity is always reflexive and is exercised over and with respect to 'self.' And since self in a processive world is always communal, creativity is contextual, transactional, and multidimensional."[13] Their analysis reads like a recipe for Dada artworks, which, according to Arp, tend to be "made of found or manufactured elements, simple or incongruous." It also challenges the art-historical impulse to establish precise authorship for Dada objects and events.

Because the concepts of Taoism are so abstract, the language of Taoism is the language of metaphor. Nature is a primary source of metaphorical meaning, but so is technology, which is fundamentally the harnessing and channeling of natural forces (linking Taoism to Duchamp's fascination with mechanical objects). The wheel, for example, becomes a metaphor for the fecundity of nothingness in chapter 11 of the *Tao Te Ching*:

> The thirty spokes converge at one hub,
> But the utility of the cart is a function of the nothingness inside the hub. ...
> Thus, it might be something that provides the value,
> But it is nothing that provides the utility.[14]

"Cart" might be any vehicle; substitute "art," and we have: "Thirty spokes converge at one hub, but the utility of the art is a function of the nothingness inside." The image suggests not only Duchamp's 1913 *Bicycle Wheel* (figure

4.3), but also his concept of the art "gap": "What art is in reality is this missing link, not the links which exist. It's not what you see that is art, art is the gap."[15]

••

Duchamp and Picabia were joined in New York by other French artists fleeing the war, including Jean Crotti and the writer Henri-Pierre Roché. In Paris, Picabia had been struggling in his painting to give sensual form to mental experience. Upon his arrival in New York, he immersed himself in the goings-on surrounding the American apostle of modernism, Alfred Stieglitz, and his Gallery 291. The July–August 1915 issue of the large-format journal *291*, a successor to Stieglitz's *Camera Work*, featured six powerful Picabia portrait-drawings of Gallery 291 associates for which machines and technology provided the metaphors and American advertising the model.

Picabia's "portrait" of Stieglitz (figure 5.2) appeared on the cover. Surely his inscription—"Here, here is Stieglitz, faith, and love"—was intended as an affectionate riff on the Apostle Paul's assurance to the Corinthians: "So abide faith, hope, and love." In America, Stieglitz—the champion of modernism—represented hope. This idealistic sentiment is reinforced by Picabia's icon for Stieglitz, which is made up of two mechanical elements: a camera with its bellows detached, preventing recording of exterior images on the photographic plate; and a similarly disengaged brake and gearshift—controls for starting and stopping.[16] Only the lens at the top of the camera is in active mode, stretched heavenward, as if anticipating Stieglitz's future cloud-portrait "equivalents," and focused on the word "IDEAL."

The detached bellows has elicited a wide range of interpretations, from implications regarding Stieglitz's sexual potency to Picabia's supposed opinion of the success of Gallery 291.[17] From a Taoist perspective, however, the bellows suggests something quite different. A bellows is the expandable part of a camera, but it is also a device for generating a strong current of air. In the fifth chapter of the *Tao Te Ching*, quoted above, the bellows is a technological metaphor for the source of spontaneous and inexhaustible phenomena: "What is between the heavens and the earth resembles a bellows that is empty yet never exhausted; put into motion, it yields more and more."[18] In Taoism, the earth is conceived as yin—female/receptive/dark—and the heavens as yang—male/aggressive/light. They are

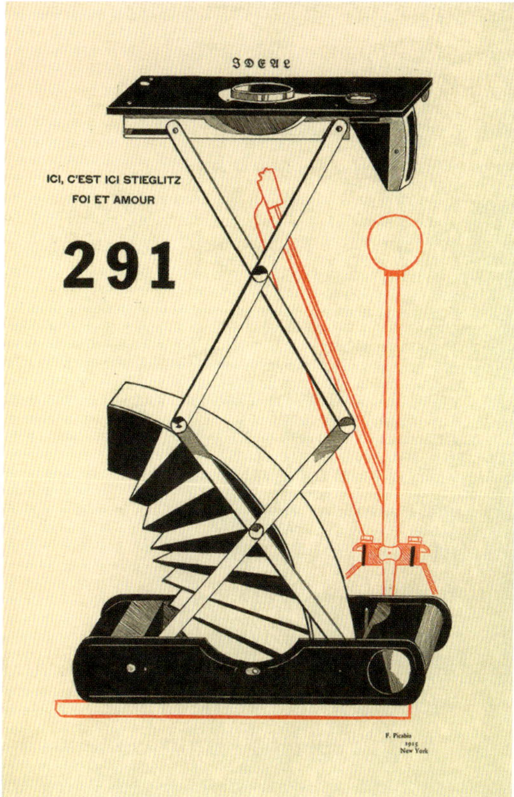

FIGURE 5.2
Francis Picabia
Ici, C'est Ici Stieglitz Foi et Amour / Here, Here Is Stieglitz, cover for *291*, no. 5–6, July–August 1915
Print, 211.6 × 185.7 cm
The Metropolitan Museum of Art, New York, NY, Alfred Stieglitz Collection, 1949, 49.55.330(11)

opposites whose union generates constantly morphing phenomena. What Picabia's detached bellows implies is that Stieglitz is a catalyst for change, but his "camera work" cannot be portrayed only in terms of the mechanically recordable visible world. Stieglitz called this his "'anti-photographic' search—the vision of both the inner and the outer eye"[19]—a double view of reality conveyed in the famous first chapter of the *Tao Te Ching*:

> Nameless is the source of heaven and earth; named, it is the mother of all things.
>
> This is why when one is steadily free of the passions, one sees spiritual essence; immersed in the sensual, one sees bounded form.
>
> These two things have a single origin and are called by different names. One calls them both profound. They are profound, doubly deep. This is the portal to all things.[20]

Picabia's brake and gearshift may refer to what is required in order to achieve this complete vision of reality: disengaged brake and gearshift as a modern metaphor for being "steadily free of the passions."

Jay Bochner has written insightfully about how often the word "ideal" appears in Picabia's work, "in exactly the same position on the page as here": hovering at the top.[21] Picabia's "IDEAL" is printed in German gothic type—perhaps a reference to Stieglitz's German background and education, or his interest in German idealist philosophy. It is also helpful to look at what Stieglitz himself had to say about his cloud-portraits from the 1920s: "Are the sky and water not one, if one truly sees them? Are they not, after all, to be seen as interchangeable? In fact, I feel that all experiences in life are one, if truly seen. ... How is it possible to conceive of black without white? Why reject either the one or the other, since both exist? I feel the duality of world forces forever at work. But it is when conflict hovers about a point—a focal point—and light is in the ascendancy, that I am moved."[22]

Stieglitz's yin-yang "focal point" found an earlier manifestation as a point of light in his photograph of Duchamp's *Fountain* (figure 5.3), the exemplar of how Dada artworks served as "contextual, transactional, and multidimensional" objects of public art practice. An upended urinal signed with a pseudonym and anonymously submitted to New York's Society of Independent Artists in 1917, *Fountain* was created not as an art object but as the focus of a collaborative process designed to question presuppositions about art, the artist, and the creative act. A photograph of *Fountain* taken at 291 by Alfred Stieglitz appeared in the 1917 issue of Duchamp's journal *The Blind Man*, along with an apologia signed by Louise Norton entitled "Buddha of the Bathroom." Like Norton, Stieglitz emphasized the Asian cultural reference behind *Fountain*, writing to Georgia O'Keeffe: "I have made a photograph—suggesting a Buddha form—& there is a large Hartley as a background.—The 'Art of China' brought up-to-date." Later that day he told her: "The *Urinal* photograph is really quite a wonder— ... It has an oriental look about it—a cross between a Buddha & a veiled woman."[23]

It was apparently the young American artist and actress Beatrice Wood, coeditor of *The Blind Man* along with Duchamp and Roché, who made the first contact with Stieglitz. She later wrote that Stieglitz and Duchamp had a long discussion about how to photograph the piece, and that Stieglitz

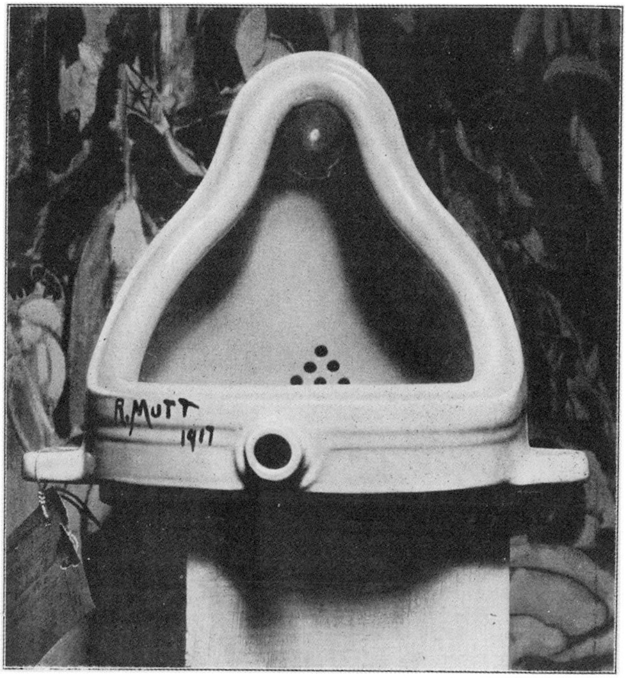

FIGURE 5.3

Alfred Stieglitz

Fountain by R. Mutt. *The Blind Man* (No. 2), May 1917

Periodical with paper covers, published by Beatrice Wood, in collaboration with Marcel Duchamp and Henri-Pierre Roché (edited by Marcel Duchamp with editorial participation by Man Ray). Sheet (each) 27.9 × 20.3 cm

Philadelphia Museum of Art, Philadelphia, PA, The Louise and Walter Arensberg Collection, 1950, 1950-134-1053

"took great pains with the lighting."[24] English poet and artist Mina Loy and German artist and poet Elsa Hildegard Baroness von Freytag-Loringhoven were also probably in on Duchamp's scheme.

The urinal was signed "R. Mutt," purportedly after Mott Ironworks, a plumbing supply company. Said with a French accent, Mutt is "moot"—encounter or meeting—evoking Tzara's dogs, or mutts, meeting at street corners, and the two dogs sticking their noses under each other's tails by way of "greeting" on the cover of Duchamp's little journal *Rongwrong* (1917, figure 5.4).[25] In a letter to an art critic, Duchamp's artist-friend Charles

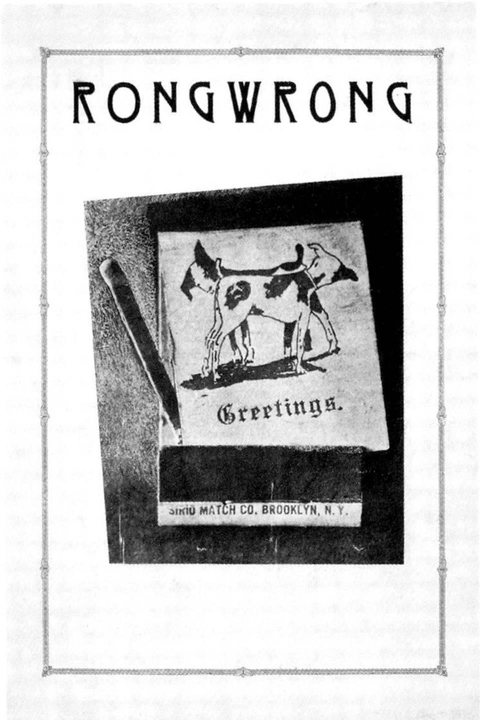

FIGURE 5.4

Marcel Duchamp
Rongwrong (No.1), July 1917
Letterpress with photomechanical metal relief image, 28.1 × 20.3 cm
Philadelphia Museum of Art, Philadelphia, PA, The Louise and Walter Arensberg Collection, 1950 / Bridgeman Images

Demuth spelled Mutt "Mutte," which suggests the French pronunciation. Art historian William A. Camfield speculated that "the 'e' Demuth added to Mutt may have been intended to suggest a female identity."[26] This is a likely scenario, given the involvement of Duchamp's female friends Beatrice Wood, Louise Norton, Mina Loy, and Elsa von Freytag-Loringhoven—who that same year (1917) created *God*, an upside-down plumbing trap affixed to a wooden miter box, with the Philadelphia painter Morton Schamberg.[27]

Mutt[e] also suggests "mute"—silent, and/or shorthand for "mutable" (the same word in both French and English), meaning changeable, perhaps alluding to the flexible sexual identity of *Fountain*'s creator(s). In a letter to his sister Suzanne, Duchamp claimed that "a female friend" had submitted the urinal to the Independents' exhibition: "The Independents opened here with enormous success. A female friend of mine, using a male pseudonym, Richard Mutt, submitted a porcelain urinal as a sculpture. It wasn't at all indecent. No reason to refuse it. The committee decided to refuse to exhibit this thing. I handed in my resignation and it'll be a juicy piece of gossip in New York."[28] Suzanne probably knew perfectly well that her brother was the mastermind behind this feminine caper. In retrospect, what seems likely is that the ambisexual authorship of *Fountain* reflected how Duchamp understood his artist-self, as both/neither male and female—another example of *Chuang Tzu*'s hinge principle (described in chapter 4), where "'this' and 'that' give birth to each other."[29]

When, like his brothers, Duchamp finally adopted an artistic pseudonym for himself, he chose a feminine name: Rose Sélavy, which in French sounds like *éros c'est la vie*, "eros is life."[30] He would then complicate Rose's name by adding an "r"—Rrose Sélavy. Her name first appeared this way in 1921, inscribed on Picabia's collaborative painting *Cacodylatic Eye*,[31] adjacent to two little photographs of Duchamp's shaved and tonsured head. Duchamp told Pierre Cabanne: "I don't remember how I signed it—it was photographed, so someone knows. I think I put '*Pi qu'habilla Rrose Sélavy*.' The word '*arrose*' ['water'] demands two Rs, so I was attracted to the second R—'*Pi qu'habilla* Rrose Sélavy.' All of this was word play."[32] Now faded to near invisibility, Duchamp's inscription in fact read: "*en 6 qu'habilla Rrose Sélavy*." *En 6 qu'* sounds like *ainsi que*, "in the same way as." *Pi qu'habilla* (as Duchamp remembered it) is an obvious play on Picabia's name. *Arroser la vie* can be translated "to water/nourish life," or "to flow through life." Duchamp's inscription, accompanied by photographs of his own tonsured head, thus advised: "This, Picabia, is how you nourish/flow through life"—gnomic personal advice to a close friend who was experiencing more life difficulties than usual at the time. Picabia's mistress Germaine Everling reinforced Duchamp's advice with her own "esoteric" message: "I hope always to awaken!"[33]

Taoism emphasizes the vital role of yin, the female aspect of existence. Chapter 6 of the *Tao Te Ching* expands upon the portal or gateway metaphor in chapter 1, and the generative, self-replenishing bellows energy of chapter 5:

> The Valley Spirit never dies.
> It is named the Mysterious Female
> And the Doorway of the Mysterious Female
> Is the root [of] Heaven and Earth.
> It is the thread forever woven;
> Those who use it can accomplish all things.[34]

"In this chapter and pervasively in the text," Ames and Hall write, "the image of the dark, moist, and accommodatingly vacant interior of the vagina is used as an analogy for [the fecundity of emptiness]."[35] The *Tao Te Ching* presents this powerful female aspect as something to be cultivated. In chapter 28, we read:

> Know the male
> Yet safeguard the female
> And be a river gorge to the world.
> As a river gorge to the world,
> You will not lose your real potency,
> And not losing your real potency,
> You return to the state of the newborn babe.[36]

The return of the mind to its original, preconditioned state—the mind of a "newborn babe"—is the goal of Taoist practice in general and Taoist internal alchemical practice in particular. Lydie Fischer Sarazin-Levassor, who was briefly married to Duchamp in 1927, quoted his advice to her: "Find yourself, the pure self, like a child newborn. ... An equilibrium is maintained, as in chess. You have to try to see everything as if for the first time, all the time."[37] A Taoist metaphor for this mental equilibrium is a pearl of light in the upper energy field in the center of the head—the "core of spirit" in Taoist meditation practice. In a process similar to the spiritual "child" generated in Kaula practice, the "pearl" develops into an "immortal embryo" through the union of the adept's inner yin [female] and yang [male] forces.[38] This bright "focal point," to use Stieglitz's term, is clearly visible, thanks to his careful lighting, in the "head" of the Buddha into which Duchamp and Stieglitz transformed the urinal.

Another notable feature of this photograph of *Fountain* is the moist darkness of the hole where the genitals would be, a feature that emphasizes its womblike aspect. As photographed by Stieglitz the urinal can also be perceived as a vulva, with the point of light at the top as clitoris and the hole at the bottom as vagina.[39] These perspectives on *Fountain* as yoni (the female reproductive system) are supported by Duchamp's tendency to hang *Fountain* from the top of a doorway or passage, like (and occasionally with) mistletoe—a pointer to *The Large Glass*'s *Le Pendu femelle* ("female hanging thing") as the female equivalent of male reproductive organs.

As a piece of bathroom plumbing, *Fountain* bears a clear relationship with Duchamp's note to himself in *Box of 1914*—"arrhe is to art as shitte is to shit."[40] Duchamp published another note in *Box of 1914* that seems equally relevant: "One only has: for female the urinal and one lives by it."[41] What in the world might it mean? William Camfield observed that *Fountain* "transforms an object for use by males into a female, uterine-like shape which receives injections of a male fluid."[42] As in Taoism, in Hindu tantra water is associated with the Divine Feminine, and represents both purification and life.[43] During the first stage of tantric ritual, water sprinkled into the sacrificial fire is transformed into its gaseous state.[44] In tantric ritual practice, emission of semen into the yoni is understood as an offering that parallels this "fall" of water into the fire, generating what Duchamp called the illuminating or enlightening gas ("gas," from the Greek *khaos*: "empty space").

Duchamp's note to himself may also have served as an *aide-mémoire*. Details vary depending on the practice, but in both Indo-Tibetan tantra and Taoist internal alchemy a method for achieving ultimate orgasm in the male is, if necessary, to divert semen into the bladder by pressing on the perineum while moving sexual energy up the spinal column to the brain. By renouncing short-term sexual release, partners are able to experience bliss pervading their entire bodies, culminating in radiant clarity of mind. A Taoist text describes a related process called "duo-cultivation": "[When the Numinous Father and the Holy Mother] are at work, their spirits are in union, but not their bodies. Their *qi*-energies are in coition, but not their forms. ... They keep still without moving until they feel moved by each other, and only then become interconnected."[45] Needless to say, this is an intentional practice that in Taoism is linked with longevity. In tantra, it is linked with immortality—not eternity in time, but liberating recognition of the boundlessness and timelessness of Self. In 1918, Stieglitz Circle guru

Ananda Coomaraswamy connected it with the art of life: "More than all else ... do I cherish at heart that love which makes me to live a limitless life *in this world*."[46] That something like duo-cultivation was Duchamp's erotic practice at this time is implied in Pierre Roché's roman à clef, *Victor*. Roché, who was a lover of Beatrice Wood and was himself in love with Louise Arensberg, wrote: "Pierre [Roché] in spite of himself becomes a specialist in lying chastely with women. ... [Louise] says, '[Marcel] has a lot like that. He tried it with me, like some sort of Eros, the same as with all the other women. But that's not my nature'."[47]

In another roman à clef, *Insel* by Mina Loy, the title character is described in a way that is strikingly reminiscent of Gabrielle Buffet-Picabia's account of Duchamp's dramatic changes of state into the luminous being, Lucifer. *Insel* is presumed to be an account of Loy's friendship with the painter Richard Oelze, but the novel contains so many thinly veiled allusions to Duchamp that he must be considered a primary subject, as he was of Robert Lebel's contemporaneous story, "The Inventor of Free Time," also written in New York in the early 1940s.[48] Loy's description and analysis—which helpfully expands upon Buffet-Picabia's "Lucifer" observation—is reminiscent of a famous scene in the *Bhagavad Gita* in which the archer Arjuna perceives his charioteer, Krishna, in his Absolute manifestation as blazing fire.[49] "He deliberately set himself on fire," Loy wrote; "he did not consistently appear to the naked eye, as a bonfire ... But as if his astounding vibratory flux required a more delicate instrument than the eye for registration. Some infrared or there invisible ray he gave off, was immediately transferred on one's neural current to some dark room in the brain for instantaneous development in all its brilliancy. ... a moment exposed the 'man-of-light'."[50]

••

Although Duchamp assured his sister that the urinal wasn't indecent, it was a urinal, after all, and thus evocative of a private act made socially public—like an art exhibition, to Duchamp's way of thinking. This comparison may in fact have been in his mind when he submitted a urinal for public exhibition. As always with Duchamp, the title of *Fountain* is important to its interpretation. Although some urinals feature constantly running water, this one does not. So what, or who, plays the role of fountain? In keeping with his concept of the experiential nature of art, Duchamp's title implies that "fountain" should be understood not so much as a description of the work as a visualized action—*arroser*, or "watering"—on the part of the maker, which for Duchamp also implied the viewer. As a urinal, *Fountain* would seem to assume a male viewer—which is interesting, given its quasi-female authorship. But since it never made it into the exhibition to which it was submitted, the original urinal never had viewers in the usual public sense. Essentially an interactive process, it was probably never intended to. The mind doesn't have genitals, so the "real" *Fountain* can as easily be "used" by women as by men. In more ways than one, *Fountain* demands to be experienced mentally.

Sometimes characterized as a cynical gesture of "pissing on" the establishment, *Fountain* seems in retrospect more like Duchamp's affectionate, humorous, tough-minded koan, issued as a challenge to the American art community. As a work of art, *Fountain* was—and to some degree still is—regarded as a joke, and that is not wrong. But a joke can make a serious point. This one made several: about the supposed openness of the American Society of Independent Artists, about the "work" of art, about authorship and exhibition, about friendship, about desire, about what it means to be an artist, what it means to be human, how to live. Chuang Tzu described the life of a sage as "a smooth flow."[51] "Rrose Sélavy" suggests not only *éros c'est la vie*, "eros is life," but also *arroser la vie*, "to water/nourish life," or "to flow through life." Loving, nourishing, flowing: it's a very Taoist way to live.

Tu m'—the title of Marcel Duchamp's "last painting" of 1918 (figure 4.6)—reveals the ground from which he operated. Duchamp described *Tu m'* as "a sort of résumé of things I had made earlier, since the title made no sense. You can add whatever verb you want, as long as it begins with a vowel, after "*Tu m'*."[52] Thanks to this missing verb between its subject—*Tu*, "you"—and object—*m'*, "me," *Tu m'*s title encourages viewer participation. The most literal translation of *Tu m'* would be "you-me." As Duchamp pointed out, however, the apostrophe promises a verb that begins with a vowel. *Tu* is the intimate form of "you," so the most natural extrapolation of *Tu m'* would be *Tu m'es*: "You are me." This is, in fact, what *Tu m'* sounds like if you say it out loud. (Consonant endings are normally silent in French.)

Duchamp's title for his résumé of things made earlier—a title that, like the work, "made no [intellectual] sense"—emphasizes connection, continuum, nonduality. It is no coincidence that *Tu m'* was commissioned by Duchamp's patron, Katherine Dreier, a Theosophist who believed in a third, "spiritual" eye, capable of seeing through ordinary reality.[53] She would have understood Duchamp's liberating perspective, or at least her version of it.

The *trompe-l'œil* tear or rent at the center of *Tu m'* serves as a metaphorical three-dimensional rupture in the two-dimensional surface reality of the painting. The interior of this painted passage is dark; its "edges" are held together by three real safety pins. Both the darkness and the safety pins would seem to allude to the difficulty (if not danger) hinted at in Duchamp's *Green Box* note: "Warning / Given (in the dark), if given = 1st the waterfall / 2nd the illuminating gas." Advance preparation would probably be a good idea. And indeed, extending helpfully from the fake rent in *Tu m'* is a real bottlebrush—an item that brings to mind *Bottlerack* (figure 4.5), Duchamp's first readymade from four years earlier. *Bottlerack* is a type of drainer, the French word for which is *égouttoir*, from *égout*, "falling of water." So, the bottlebrush alludes to the cleansing, purifying water that would be part of the title for *Given: 1. The Waterfall, 2. The Illuminating Gas*.

The bottle brush in *Tu m'* is linked not only with Duchamp's earlier *Bottlerack*, but also with a later composite photograph of a bottle emitting a cloud of glowing gas into a starry sky that was the focus of his cover for the March 1945 issue of *View* magazine (figure 5.5). According to a witness to the creation of this cover design, a ray of light "was to have shot from page left across the planetarium illusion of the background, under the smoke."[54] The ray of light could not be photographed effectively, apparently, but the effort leaves little doubt that what emerges from this bottle *égouttée* is illuminating gas, connecting it with its predecessor, *Fountain*, and its successor, *Given*.

Duchamp described *Tu m'* to artist and author Marcel Jean as "a dictionary of the principal ideas preceding 1918: readymades, standard-stoppages, rent, bottle-brush, cast shadows, perspective."[55] He lists the "rent"—the *trompe-l'œil* slash at the center of *Tu m'*—as part of this dictionary of principal ideas. The hole at the bottom of *Fountain* from the previous year (figure 5.3) is one precedent, but there are even earlier examples. A

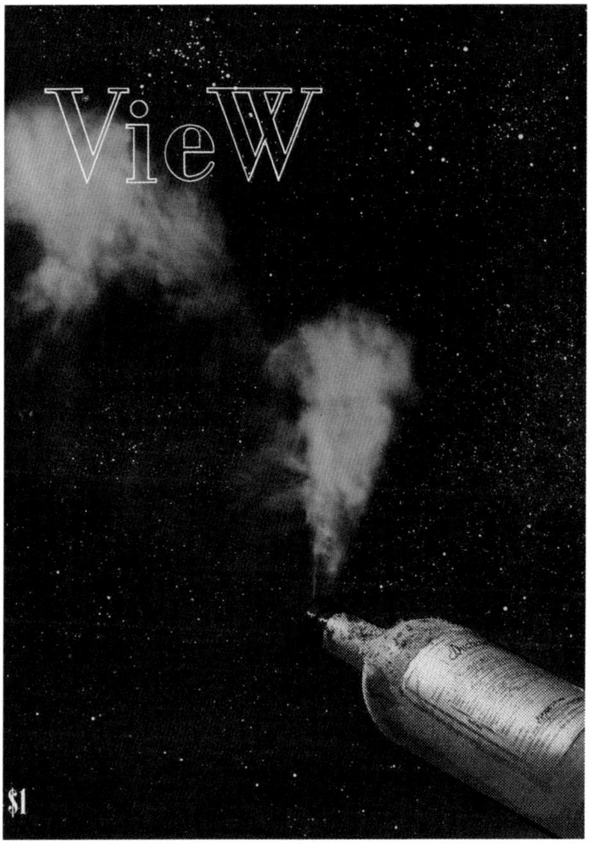

FIGURE 5.5

Marcel Duchamp
Cover, *View* (series V, no. 1), March 1945
Color lithograph, 30.5 × 23 cm
Philadelphia Museum of Art, Philadelphia, PA, The Louise and Walter Arensberg Collection, 1950 / Bridgeman Images

note in Duchamp's *Box of 1914* reads: "Linear perspective is a good means to represent in different ways equalities; that is, the equivalent, the similar (homothetic), and the equal become mingled, in perspective symmetry."[56] Rarely (if ever) mentioned in descriptions of this note is the fact that beneath the inscription is a circular hole (figure 5.6). "Homothetic" has to do with the relationship of microcosm to macrocosm. Duchamp's connecting,

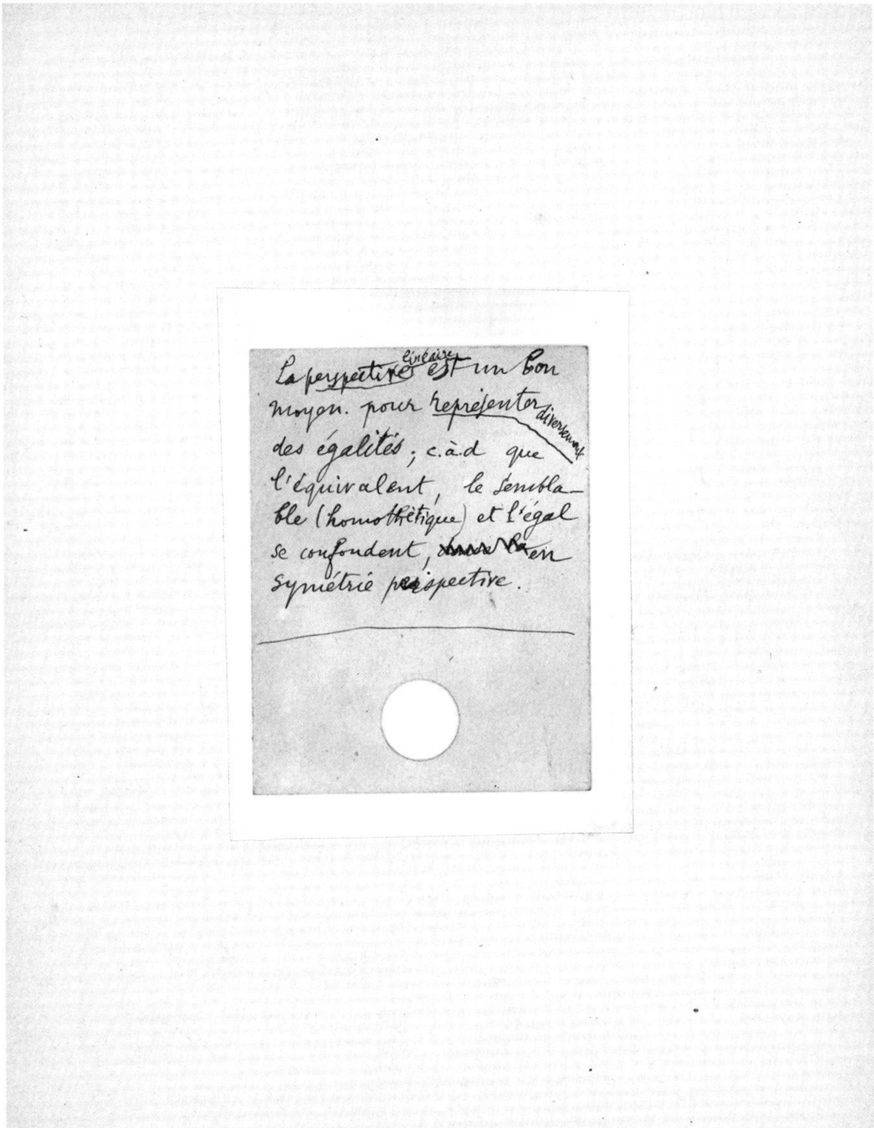

FIGURE 5.6

Marcel Duchamp

"Linear Perspective," note with hole from *The Box of 1914*, 1913–1914 (sixteen photographic facsimiles of manuscript notes and a drawing [*Avoir l'apprenti dans le soleil*] in a black cardboard box with a label, "Société Anonyme ... Lumière ...")

Art Institute of Chicago, Through prior Gift of Albert Kunstadter Family Foundation (1989.387) / Bridgeman Images.

"linear" perspective through a rent or hole allows the equal to mingle—as when *le* and *la* become *the*, transformed into a star.

••

In April 1918 the United States entered World War I. Within months, Duchamp set sail for Buenos Aires, Argentina—presumably to get as far away as possible from any country at war. With him was his companion Yvonne Crotti, former wife of Jean Crotti, and joining them in Buenos Aires was Duchamp's new friend and patron, Katherine Dreier. In October, Duchamp began working on a study for a detail of *The Large Glass*, which he inscribed: *À regarder (l'autre côté du verre) d'un œil, de près, pendant presque une heure / To Be Looked At (from the Other Side of the Glass) with One Eye, Close To, for Almost an Hour* (figure 5.7). Duchamp referred to this "*Small Glass*" as a "voyage sculpture."[57] The French word *voyage* means what it does in English: "travel, journey, sojourn." Travel can provide perspective. The French *voyage* is closely related to *voyant*, "seer," and forms the basis for "clairvoyant": clear-sighted.[58] This connection between traveling and seeing lay behind Duchamp's characterization of *The Small Glass* as a "voyage sculpture": a sculpture for seeing, as well as traveling, into unknown realms.

The instruction Duchamp inscribed on *The Small Glass* reinforces this interpretation. Literally translated, it reads: "To look at (the other side of glass) with one eye, close to, for almost an hour." The literal translation implies not only viewer participation, but also that what is to be looked at for such a long time is not the work itself, but the world on the other side of the glass. This is reinforced by the fact that Duchamp hung his glass voyage sculpture on Dreier's balcony overlooking Buenos Aires and photographed the nighttime city through it.[59] Although the focal point of *To Be Looked At* is not a hole or rent, but a circular convex lens, it clearly belongs to a Duchampian lineage of works offering passage to another dimension that includes *Linear Perspective, Fountain, Tu m'*, and *Given* (figures 5.6, 5.3, 4.6, 0.1; there are others, as we shall see).

At normal viewing distance, everything appears upside down through Duchamp's magnifying lens (see figure 5.8). "Close up," on the other hand, it all becomes a homogeneous blur—the way the world looks to a newborn, or to someone born blind whose sight has been suddenly restored:

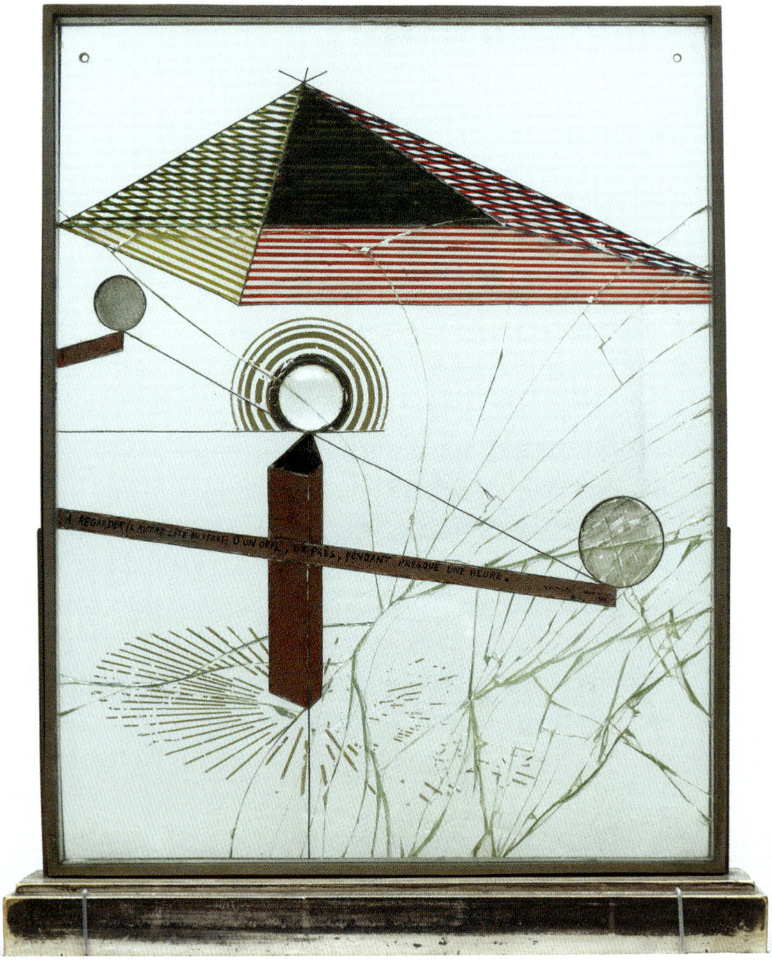

FIGURE 5.7

Marcel Duchamp

À regarder (l'autre côté du verre) d'un œil, de près, pendant presque une heure / To Be Looked At (from the Other Side of the Glass) with One Eye, Close To, for Almost an Hour, Buenos Aires, 1918

Oil, silver leaf, lead wire, and magnifying lens on glass (cracked), mounted between panes of glass in a standing metal frame 51 × 41.2 × 3.7 cm; on painted wood base 4.8 × 45.3 × 11.4 cm; overall 55.8 cm high

The Museum of Modern Art, New York, NY, Katherine S. Dreier Bequest

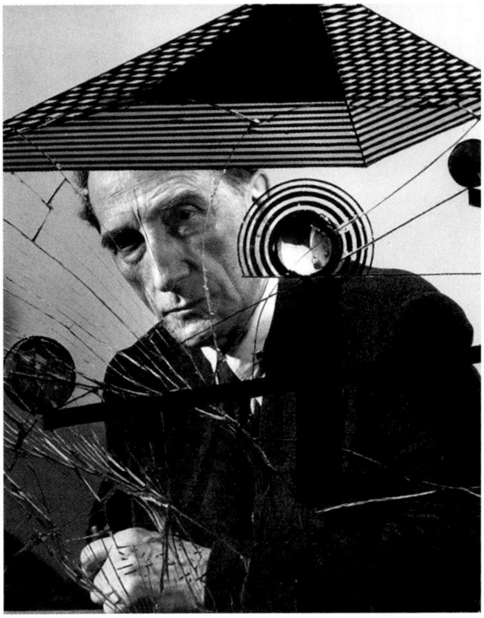

FIGURE 5.8
Allan Grant
Artist Marcel Duchamp sitting behind example of Dada art, 1953
Photo by Allan Grant/The LIFE Picture Collection/Getty Images

"the equal become mingled, in perspective symmetry." It has been argued that Duchamp's intent was to annul vision,[60] but I want to suggest that *To Be Looked At* offers a re-vision of Western Renaissance perspective. As Sarazin-Levassor quoted Duchamp, "You have to try to see everything as if for the first time, all the time."[61] *To Be Looked At* is thus a kind of time machine, a device for taking viewers back to the way the world first appeared to them—as an interwoven, constantly moving tapestry of colors. In this higher-dimensional vision, objects lose their separate identities—you might say their separate selves—and merge into a Self that seems continuous. What the outcome of contemplating such a world for almost an hour might be, I shall leave to you to discover for yourself. (*To Be Looked At* is in the collection of the Museum of Modern Art, New York.)

The convex lens is positioned on *The Small Glass* between two translucent circles, like a third eye. Hovering above it is a striated, multicolored pyramid, which may refer to Leonardo's well-known pyramid of vision. It may also be relevant that in Taoist internal alchemy, it is said that the shape of the upper elixir field at the top of the head is a pyramid. This "home of spirit" (*shen*) is a reservoir of light centered directly behind the *yin tang* point, the third eye. The colors on the sides of Duchamp's pyramid (red, green, and yellow, overlapping as black) appear to have been inspired by the colored thread models for teaching descriptive geometry created by mathematician Théodore Olivier and given to Paris's Musée des Arts et Métiers in 1849.[62]

Duchamp may also have been influenced by a passage in Kandinsky's *On the Spiritual in Art*, where, in a discussion of ways to "exploit" the picture plane by transforming it into a higher-dimensional space, Kandinsky suggested two strategies, both of which play out in the pyramid of *To Be Looked At*: "The very thinness or thickness of a line, the positioning of the form upon the surface, and the superimposition of one form upon another provide sufficient examples of the linear extension of space. Similar possibilities are offered by the correct use of color, which can recede or advance, strive forward or backward, and turn the picture into a being hovering in mid-air."[63] In another link to Munich, *To Be Looked At* is painted on glass, a folk technique popular in Bavaria that Kandinsky and his friends were experimenting with around the time Duchamp was in residence there. Of course there are other things about glass that would have attracted Duchamp, like its combination of transparency and reflectivity, depending on lighting conditions. But he may not have ventured to create a painting on glass as readily without the example of Kandinsky.

For his 1965 etching *The Large Glass Completed*, Duchamp labeled a small circular form toward the right of *The Large Glass* above the Oculist Witnesses a "Mandala."[64] There is an obvious relationship between the Mandala of *The Large Glass* and the convex lens of Duchamp's *Small Glass*. His biographer Robert Lebel commented on this connection: "Above the stake [in *The Small Glass*] Duchamp glued a magnifying glass surrounded by concentric circles and intended for the Peeping Tom (the indispensable oculist witness), who waits 'while looking with one eye for almost an hour,' for the interminable 'disrobing' to make the 'Bride Stripped Bare' appear at last. In *The Large Glass* the magnifying glass might be schematically indicated by the small circle whose center is a dot, perhaps the equivalent of a keyhole."[65] A mandala is a microcosmic reproduction of the universe.

In tantra, the dot at the center of a mandala—the point around which it is created—is called *bindu* ("drop," figure 5.9). In Buddhist tantra, bindu is at once sexual fluid, the seed of the perceived world, and aspiration to enlightenment: "the natural state of the mind as empty, creative."[66] To focus on the bindu is to perceive reality in all of its plenitude: in Lebel's words, "to make the 'Bride Stripped Bare' ... the equivalent of a keyhole"—a prescient reference to the peepholes in the door hiding *Given*.

In tantric symbolism, a circle (or downward-pointing triangle) with a dot at the center (sometimes a spiral) also refers to the female generative organ. In tantric depictions of deities, the third "eye of love and creation"[67] is often depicted as vertical, to emphasize its identification with the vulva (see figures 10.13, 10.14). In a tantric sense, both the "mandala" of *The Large Glass* and the magnifying lens of *The Small Glass* do not just represent but *are* the opening to the vagina, the "eye of love and creation," a third eye that allows seeing-through ordinary looking. Embedded in the French word *oculiste* is "*au cul-iste*"[68]—Lebel's peeping Tom.

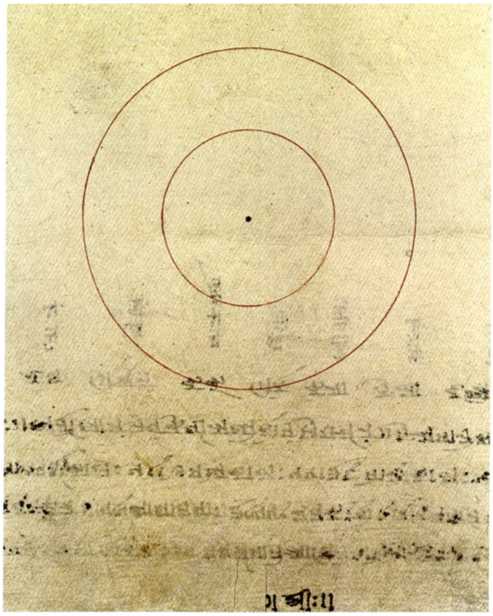

FIGURE 5.9

Rajasthan, 18th century
Bindu: "The expanding universe"
Ink on paper
From the Ajit Mookerjee collection, as published in Mookerjee, *Yoga Art* (London: Thames and Hudson, 1975), plate 1

Reinforcing this interpretation, Duchamp's friend Francis Picabia would publish his own provocative hole in Paul Éluard's review *Proverbe* (1920, figure 5.10). Picabia's title, *Young Girl*, appears above a circular hole on the review's front page. Visible through the hole is a star, while encircling it like a halo are the words "Bracelet of Life." Kundalini in Sanskrit is the feminine form of *kuṇḍalin*—circular, coiled—from *kuṇḍala*: bracelet or ring. With his "Bracelet of Life" Picabia would seem to be offering a

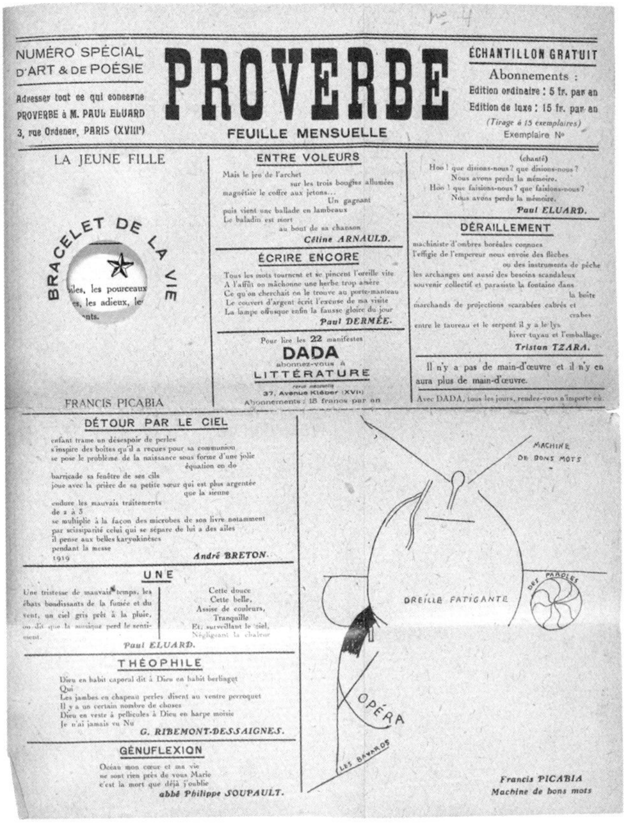

NUMÉRO SPÉCIAL D'ART & DE POÉSIE

Adresser tout ce qui concerne PROVERBE à M. PAUL ELUARD 3, rue Ordener, PARIS (XVIIIe)

PROVERBE

FEUILLE MENSUELLE

ÉCHANTILLON GRATUIT

Abonnements :
Edition ordinaire : 5 fr. par an
Edition de luxe : 15 fr. par an
(Tirage à 15 exemplaires)
Exemplaire N°

LA JEUNE FILLE

BRACELET DE LA VIE

...iles, les pourceaux
...s, les adieux, le...
...nts.

FRANCIS PICABIA

ENTRE VOLEURS

Mais le jeu de l'archet
sur les trois bougies allumées
magnétise le coffre aux jetons...
Un gagnant
puis vient une ballade en lambeaux
Le baladin est mort
au bout de sa chanson

Céline ARNAULD.

ÉCRIRE ENCORE

Tous les mots tournent et se pincent l'oreille vite
A l'affût on mâchonne une herbe trop amère
Ce qu'on cherchait on le trouve au porte-manteau
Le couvert d'argent écrit l'excuse de ma visite
La lampe offusque enfin la fausse gloire du jour

Paul DERMÉE.

Pour lire les 22 manifestes
DADA
abonnez-vous à
LITTÉRATURE
revue mensuelle
37, Avenue Kléber (XVIe)
Abonnements : 18 francs par an

(chanté)
Hoo ! que disions-nous ? que disions-nous ?
Nous avons perdu la mémoire.
Hoo ! que faisions-nous ? que faisions-nous ?
Nous avons perdu la mémoire.

Paul ELUARD.

DÉRAILLEMENT

machiniste d'ombres boréales connues
l'effigie de l'empereur nous envoie des flèches
ou des instruments de pêche
les archanges ont aussi des besoins scandaleux
souvenir collectif et parasiste la fontaine dans
la boite
marchands de projections scarabées cabrés et
crabes
entre le taureau et le serpent il y a le lys
hiver tuyau et l'emballage.

Tristan TZARA.

Il n'y a pas de main-d'œuvre et il n'y en aura plus de main-d'œuvre.

Avec DADA, tous les jours, rendez-vous n'importe où.

DÉTOUR PAR LE CIEL

enfant trame un désespoir de perles
s'inspire des boîtes qu'il a reçues pour sa communion
se pose le problème de la naissance sous forme d'une jolie
équation en do
barricade sa fenêtre de ses cils
joue avec la prière de sa petite sœur qui est plus argentée
que la sienne
endure les mauvais traitements
de 2 à 3
se multiplie à la façon des microbes de son livre notamment
par scissiparité celui qui se sépare de lui a des ailes
il pense aux belles karyokinèses
pendant la messe
1919

André BRETON.

UNE

Une tristesse de mauvais temps, les ébats bondissants de la fumée et du vent, un ciel gris prêt à la pluie, on dit que la musique perd le sentiment.

Cette douce
Cette belle,
Assise de couleurs,
Tranquille
Et, surveillant le ciel,
Négligeant la chaleur

Paul ELUARD.

THÉOPHILE

Dieu en habit caporal dit à Dieu en habit berlinget
Qui
Les jambes en chapeau perles disent au ventre perroquet
Il y a un certain nombre de choses
Dieu en veste à pellicules à Dieu en harpe moisie
Je n'ai jamais vu Nu

G. RIBEMONT-DESSAIGNES.

GÉNUFLEXION

Océan mon cœur et ma vie
ne sont rien près de vous Marie
c'est la mort que déjà j'oublie

abbé Philippe SOUPAULT.

MACHINE DE BONS MOTS
OREILLE FATIGANTE
DES PAROLES
OPÉRA
LES BAVARDS

Francis PICABIA
Machine de bons mots

FIGURE 5.10

Francis Picabia
Young Girl, "Bracelet of Life," as published in *Proverbe*, special number (4), Paris (1920)
21.3 × 13.5 cm
Princeton University Library, Princeton Blue Mountain Project

"passage from virgin to bride" (to quote Duchamp); a "gateway of the mysterious female" (to quote Lao Tzu), which we are invited to visually penetrate.

••

Three months after returning to Paris from Argentina in July 1919, Duchamp drew a moustache and beard on a reproduction of Leonardo da Vinci's *Mona Lisa*, bestowing on her a male alter ego corresponding to his own future female alter ego, Rose/Rrose Sélavy (figure 5.11; Rose's signature would appear for the first time the following year, on *Fresh Widow*). Beneath the image Duchamp inscribed the caption *L.H.O.O.Q.* Read as a single English word, the letters instruct us to "LOOK."[69] Pronounced individually in French, L.H.O.O.Q. declares: *elle a chaud au cul*—"she has a hot ass" or, as Duchamp told an interviewer: "A loose translation of them would be 'there is fire down below'."[70]

With his odd English "translation" of L.H.O.O.Q.—"there is fire down below"—Duchamp may have had in mind the flaming triangle in the root chakra discussed above in connection with Vivekananda's *Râja Yoga* (1910; figure 2.4). According to practitioner and scholar of Kaula tantra Arthur Avalon (pseudonym for Sir John Woodroffe) in his widely read book *The Serpent Power*, published in September 1918,[71] the root chakra "is in the region midway between the genitals and the anus"—i.e., the perineum. "By this ... is not meant that the Chakra proper is in the region of the gross body described, but that it is *the subtle centre* of that gross region, such centre existing in the spinal column which forms its axis."[72]

Avalon's books had a big impact in Europe, elevating Shakta tantra to the status of a complex philosophy.[73] While it conveyed a relatively sanitized version of tantra, *The Serpent Fire* nevertheless influenced the development of Western tantra yoga. Avalon had previously published an account of the flaming triangle at the root chakra in his 1913 *Tantra of the Great Liberation*: "A red fiery triangle surrounds *svayambhū-linga* [primordial phallus], and within the triangle is the red energy of Kandarpa-*vāyu* [pleasurable desire], or air, of *Kāma* ['desire'], ... for here is the seat of creative desire."[74] In *Serpent Power* he specifically refers to "the Force, 'the Serpent Fire,' which the Hindus call Kundalinī, in the lowest centre, the Mūlādharā."[75] Key to the process of transforming desire-energy into bliss are mantras formed of letters

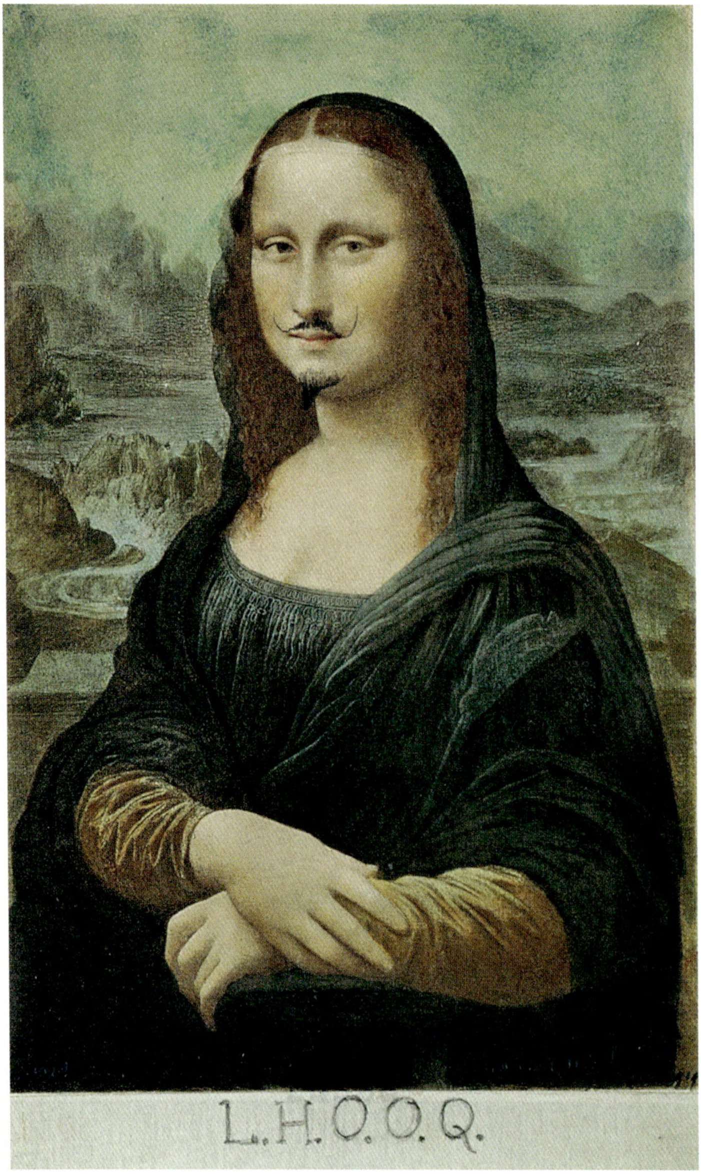

FIGURE 5.11

Marcel Duchamp
L.H.O.O.Q., 1919
Pencil on a reproduction, 19.7 × 12.4 cm
Private Collection / Bridgeman Images

that, "when spoken are ... the manifested aspect in gross speech of the subtle energy of the Shadrabrahman [transcendental sound] as Kundalī. ... The whole human body is in fact a Mantra, and is composed of Mantras."[76] Duchamp's *L.H.O.O.Q.*, which can be read either as letter sounds or as a word, seems to have served as the mantra that allowed Mona Lisa to manifest as not just a woman "disguised as a man," but as what Duchamp would call a "real man"[77]—Shiva-*Ardhanarishvara* ("Lord whose half is woman") representing the equilibrium of male essence and female creative energy.

L.H.O.O.Q. thus might be understood as linking Mona Lisa's mysterious smile with the union of inner masculine and feminine, a situation said to generate a state of perpetual ecstasy. Duchamp created *L.H.O.O.Q.* in October 1919, a year after Avalon's *Serpent Power* was published. Around that same time, Picabia inscribed "LHOOQ" in large letters down the center of a painting (figure 5.12) that would be shown during a staged art display

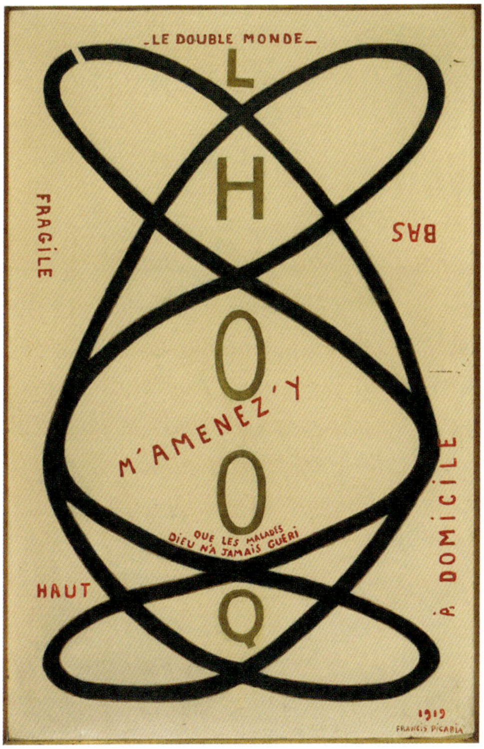

FIGURE 5.12

Francis Picabia
Le double monde / The Double World, 1919
Oil on cardboard, 132 × 85 cm
Musée National d'Art Moderne, Centre Georges Pompidou, Paris, France

interspersed between poetry readings and other performances at the first public Dada event in Paris on January 23, 1920. Dada specialist Michel Sanouillet described Picabia's large "sketch" as "a perfect insult to the audience's taste": "A simple tangle of black lines in enamel house paint against a light background, covered with whimsical inscriptions: 'Top' (at the bottom), 'Bottom' (on top), 'Fragile,' 'At home,' 'M'amenez-y' (pun on 'Amnesia'), etc., and embellished with a series of five enormous red letters arranged from top to bottom: L.H.O.O.Q."[78] In fact, "LHOOQ" is inscribed in gold paint; the other inscriptions are in red, beginning with "*Le double monde*"—"The Double World"—at the very top, directly above the "L" of LHOOQ. *The Double World*, which is what the painting is usually called, evokes the saying "There is another world, but it is in this one" attributed to poet Paul Éluard, who would publish Picabia's circular hole in his journal *Proverbe* later that same year (figure 5.10).[79] *Le double monde* evokes *La double vue*: the title of Robert Lebel's novel discussed in chapter 2. Both "double world" and "double view" suggest union of immanence and transcendence, an ongoing perception that is a goal of tantric practice.

Two of the inscriptions mentioned by Sanouillet—*bas* meaning "low" or "inferior" at the top right, and *haut* meaning "high" or "superior" at the bottom left—signal a world upside down, along the same lines as the upended view through the lens of Duchamp's *Small Glass* from the previous year. The value reversal implied by a world upside down was something of a Dada trope. For example, the frontispiece (*Tabu Dada: poèmes et dessins 1916–1921*) for Duchamp's brother-in-law Jean Crotti's autobiographical *Courants d'air sur le chemin de ma vie* (1941) features a circle containing an upside-down head, as though seen through the lens of Duchamp's *Small Glass*. Sanouillet also mentions the inscriptions "at home" (*à domicile*), along the lower right edge of the painting, and "fragile" along the upper left edge, which resonate with an inscription at bottom center: *que les malades / dieu n'a jamais guéri*. This last is hard to interpret, but it probably means something like "yet the sick, God has never healed." These inscriptions may relate to Picabia's "nervous condition," which his collaborator at the time, Georges Ribemont-Dessaignes, said "did not allow him to appear on stage,"[80] or in fact appear at all, at the Dada event where *The Double World* was first shown.

The "tangle of black lines" surrounding Picabia's inscriptions appears to define a figure in sitting meditation—specifically, the interlacing lines around the five body chakras of Kundalini yoga in the frontispiece to Avalon's *The Serpent Power* (figure 5.13). "It is said that the letters of the alphabet are distributed throughout the bodily centres [i.e., the chakras]," Avalon wrote.[81] If in Picabia's painting the five letters, LHOOQ, are distributed

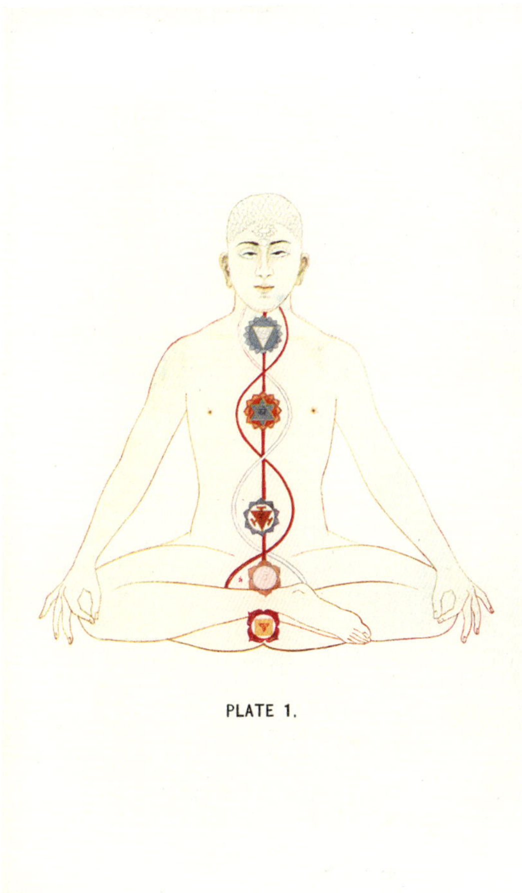

FIGURE 5.13

Frontispiece to Arthur Avalon [Sir John George Woodroffe], *The Serpent Power: Being the Ṣaṭ-chakra-nirūpaṇa and Pādukāpanchaka: Two Works on Tantrik Yoga* (London: Luzac, 1919)

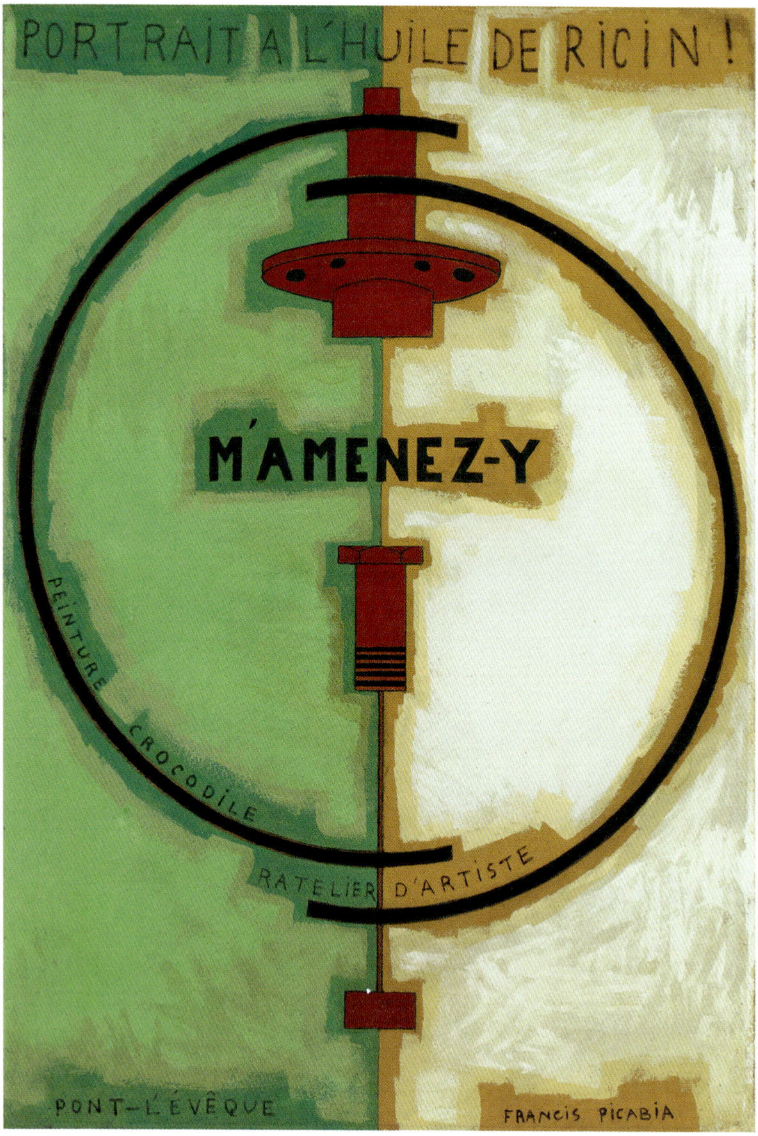

FIGURE 5.14

Francis Picabia
M'Amenez-y / *Take Me There*, 1919–1920
Oil on cardboard, 129.2 × 89.8 cm
The Museum of Modern Art / Helena Rubinstein Fund. © 2019 Artists Rights Society (ARS), New York / ADAGP, Paris

along the five body chakras, then his "Double World" hovers directly above the crown chakra, while "Q"—"*cul*," or "ass"—is the root chakra where Kundalini, "Serpent Fire," Duchamp's "fire down below," lies waiting to be awakened.

Just below the center of *The Double World* and running at an upward angle between the two "O"s is inscribed: *m'amenez-y*. Lebel says that this originated with Duchamp;[82] Sanouillet agrees, calling *m'amenez-y* a pun on "amnesia" (*amnésie*). During the same period—late 1919 to early 1920—Picabia entitled a painting of impending connection *M'Amenez-y* (figure 5.14). Translated literally, *m'amenez-y* means "take me there." Take me where? To "the double world," another dimension, a place where everything connects. A sharp break in the connecting line at the upper left of *The Double World*, combined with the inscription "yet the sick, God has never healed," suggests that Picabia never did achieve a reliable connection—an interpretation supported by Duchamp's 1921 inscription on *L'œil cacodylate* mentioned above. The mantra LHOOQ would have been their access code to this world, for which the password was LOOK.

All of this is extremely esoteric—that was the point. When, in spring 1921, Jean Crotti asked Duchamp, then back in New York, to send something for display at the Dada Salon in Paris, Duchamp could easily have sent *L.H.O.O.Q.* Instead, he responded with just two words: "PODE BAL": "balls to you."[83] Public display of Duchamp's esoteric Mona Lisa—not simply a "disguised female," but a fully realized male—would have been inappropriate in the exoteric context of the Dada Salon.[84] But Duchamp, whose work was Dada even before that word had been coined, was poised to enter a new phase: devising ways to make his esoteric art more exoteric—available, if not to all, at least to those willing to "look."

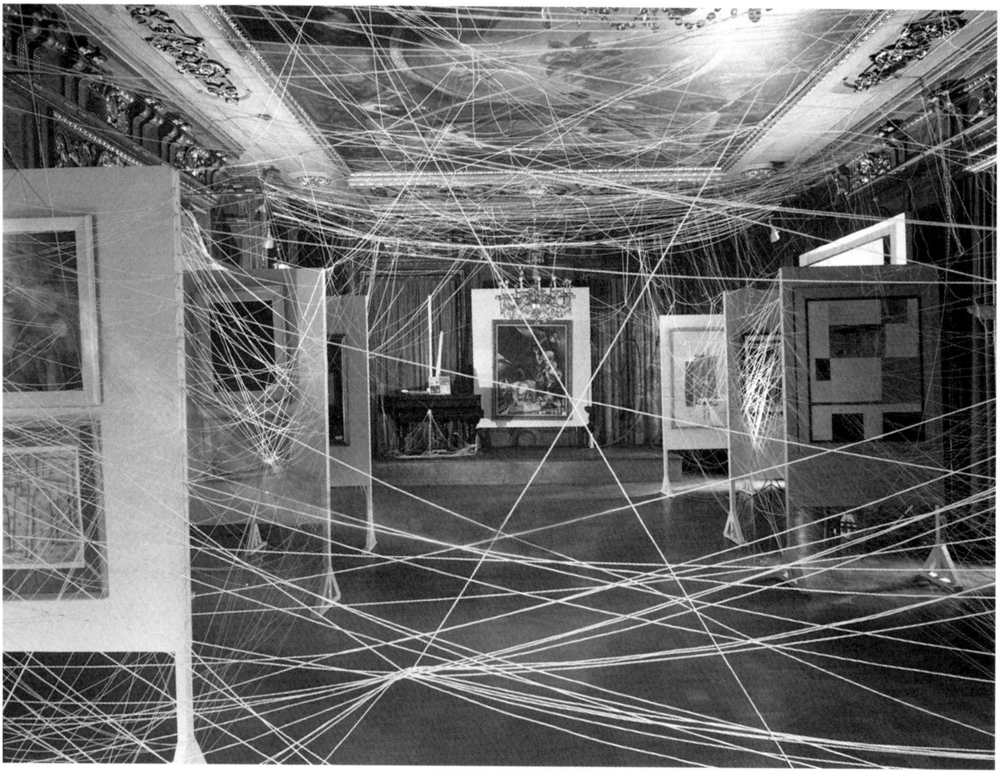

FIGURE 6.1

John Schiff
Installation View of Exhibition "First Papers of Surrealism" showing Marcel Duchamp's *String Installation*, 1942
Gelatin silver print, image/sheet/mount: 19.4 × 25.4 cm
Philadelphia Museum of Art, Philadelphia, PA, Gift of Jacqueline, Paul and Peter Matisse in memory of their mother Alexina Duchamp, 13-1972-9(303)

6 DUCHAMP IN NEW YORK II: HIS TWINE

For Marcel Duchamp, the question of art and life, as well as any other question likely to divide us at the present time, does not arise.

—André Breton, 1922[1]

World War II would prompt Duchamp's return to New York more than two decades after he first left in 1918, opening new chapters in both his life and his art. In the meantime he based himself primarily in Paris, while traveling a good deal and devoting himself increasingly to chess. He did not cease his artistic work, but he refocused it from the internal, esoteric concerns of *The Large Glass* (figure 0.2) to more exoteric techniques intended to enhance viewer engagement (figure 6.1). In retrospect, *The Large Glass*, with its combination of transparency and reflectivity, was already a move in this direction.

In 1923 Duchamp "abandoned" his nine-foot-tall painting on two sheets of glass, unfinished.[2] He had begun fabricating it in New York in 1915. Including plans, notes, and preliminary works, he had been working on it for over ten years. Its official title, *La Mariée mise à nu par ses célibataires, même*, is usually translated: "The Bride Stripped Bare by Her Bachelors, Even." Only as an adverb, however, does *même* mean "even." As an adjective, *même* means "same, self." An alternate translation—*The Bride Stripped Bare by Her Bachelors, Herself*—emphasizes the tantric aspects of this pivotal work, understood in this context to depict, in biomechanical terms, an internal process aimed at merging male and female elements within the self. A vernacular sculptural expression may aid understanding of this concept (see figure 6.2). Awareness of tantric practice enriches perception of *The Large Glass* as combination window and mirror, portrait and self-portrait—a more complex version of *Dulcinea* (figure 2.1) from twelve years earlier.

In 1965 Duchamp created an etching that he entitled *The Large Glass Completed*.[3] It could be argued that *The Large Glass* was actually completed in 1927, when it was broken during return shipment to Katherine Dreier from the Brooklyn Museum, where it had been the focal point of the 1926–1927 *International Exhibition of Modern Art* organized by Dreier and Duchamp's Société Anonyme. The breakage forged a link between this

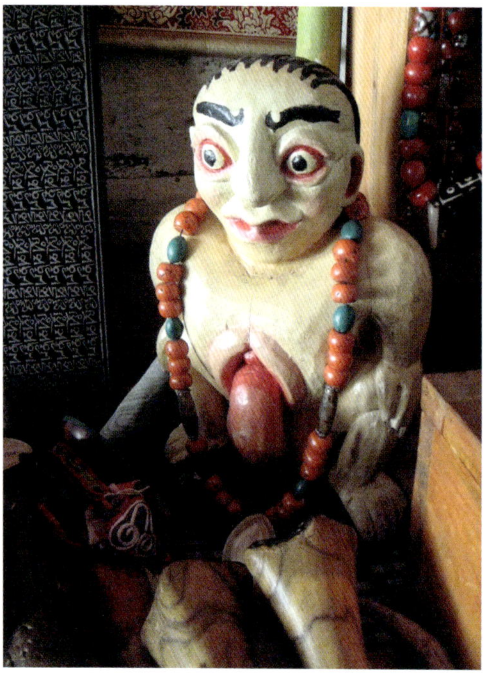

FIGURE 6.2
Sculpture in a gift shop, Paro Taktsang, upper Paro Valley, Bhutan, 2010

work and *Yvonne and Magdeleine Torn in Tatters* (1911, figure 1.2)—a painting that depicts breakage created by time. As it happened, the damage to Duchamp's *Glass* was not discovered until the shipping crate was finally opened in 1931; Duchamp returned from Paris to mend it in the summer of 1936.

Duchamp's artistic partner during the 1920s was the American photographer Man Ray, with whom he created innovative kinetic works like *Rotary Glass Plates (Precision Optics)* (1920) and *Anémic cinéma* (1926, figure 6.3), a film of rotating disks that alternate between spiraling word strings and eccentric circles that appear to move sensuously in and out. The disks of *Anémic cinéma* resemble yantras: two-dimensional tantric

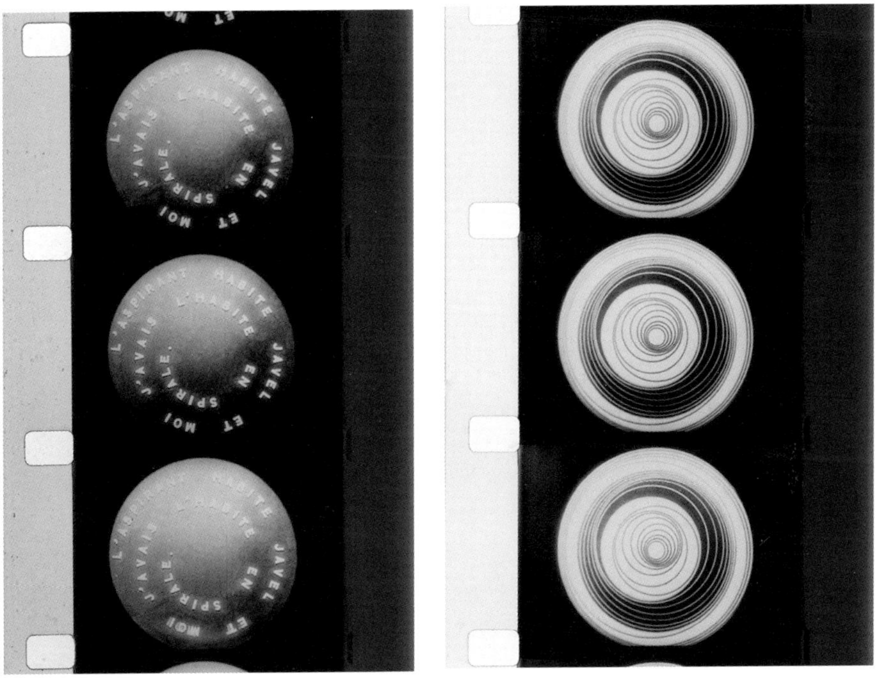

FIGURE 6.3

Marcel Duchamp with technical assistance from Man Ray and Marc Allegret
Anémic cinéma, 1926
35mm black and white silent film
Musée National d'Art Moderne (c) CNAC/MNAM/Dist. RMN-Grand Palais / Art Resource, NY

designs representing three-dimensional objects of meditation (figure 6.4). The Sanskrit root *yan-* means "hold or support," while the suffix *-tra* is a mechanism that turns the verbal root into a noun. Yantras are mechanisms for holding attention, not unlike Duchamp's rotating disks. "Mantra" is a related word based on the root *man-* "to think." In Duchampian terms, a mantra is a mind machine.

Duchamp's spiraling eccentric circles appear to expand and contract, producing a friction or vibration in the mind of the viewer that suggests sexual intercourse. It also suggests the Kashmiri Shaivism practice of retraction and expansion of energy, designed to open the heart to Kundalini.[4] At the same time, the spiraling mantras evoke the Shakta *upaya*, or method, of viewing mantras not as collections of letters, but as pulsating consciousness that has the power to draw awareness back to its source in Pure Consciousness.[5] "The solution of this artistic problem finally came," Duchamp said of his related *Rotoreliefs* (figure 6.6), "with the *Disks* in which

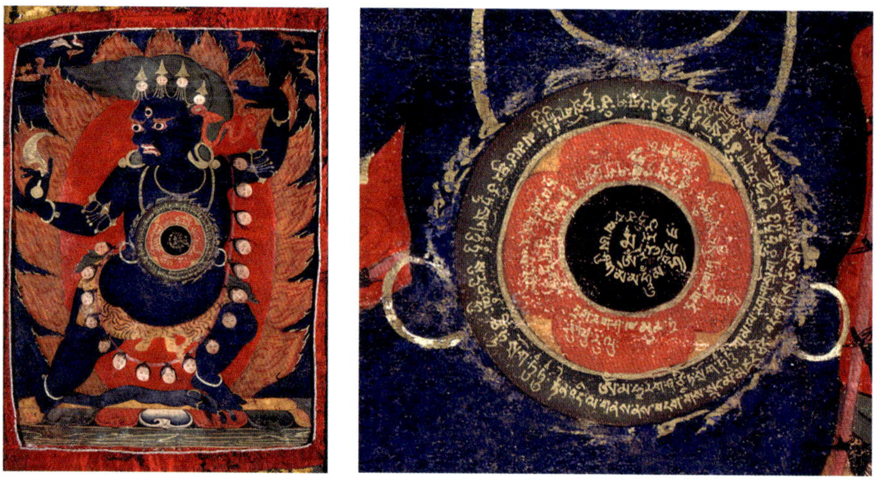

FIGURE 6.4

Yantra, Tibet, 15th–16th century
Pigments on cloth, 29.21 × 22.23 cm
Rubin Museum of Art, New York, NY, C2002.33.1 (HAR 65172)

true three-dimensionality was achieved, not with a complicated machine and a complicated technique, but in the eyes of the onlooker, by a psycho-physiological process."[6]

Note that Duchamp's "onlooker" is singular: Duchamp privileged solitary contemplation, even while trying to make his art more engaging. He refused to allow his *Rotary Demisphere* (figure 6.5) to be shown at the first Surrealist exhibition in Paris in 1925,[7] presumably for the same reason he had refused to show *L.H.O.O.Q.* at the Dada Salon four years earlier: because he had no interest in exhibiting publicly an esoteric object. (*Rotary Demisphere* was commissioned by the Asian art collector Jacques Doucet.) Earlier that year Duchamp's parents had died within days of each other, which seems to have somewhat derailed him. His ill-conceived first marriage to the amiable Lydie Sarazin-Levassor in June 1927 may have been inspired in part by a wish to posthumously please his father; it lasted seven months. By January he was once more ensconced in his solitary studio at 11 rue Larrey, with its door that could be both open and closed at the same time—something Duchamp's heart seemed capable of as well.

In 1934 Duchamp published *The Green Box* in an edition of 320. Subtitled *La Mariée mise à nu par ses célibataires, même*, it contained reproductions of notes and artworks relating to *The Large Glass*. Supposedly a guide to that work, *The Green Box* is no less esoteric; like a tantra, it was intended for the already initiated. The following year, Duchamp produced a work he hoped would have broader appeal: *Rotoreliefs (Optical Disks)* (figure 6.6), a "playtoy" that he attempted to sell at a fair for new inventions, the Concours Lépine. He apparently did not have many takers, but he was not discouraged.[8] That same year, 1935, Duchamp began producing facsimiles for an elaborate, portable, personal retrospective of his work: *Boîte-en-valise* ("Box in a Valise," 1935–1941, figure 6.7). *Boîte* was developed during wartime; Duchamp once referred to it as "ready-made help."[9] As a first aid kit for the mind, *Boîte* may have been inspired by portable Japanese Esoteric Buddhist altars on view at the Musée Guimet as part of a large display of Japanese Esoteric Buddhist art, described and analyzed in regularly updated "little guides" to the collection. (The first edition appeared in 1897.)

In Munich, where Duchamp spent the summer of 1912, there is a striking Japanese portable altar at the former Staatliches Museum für Völkerkunde

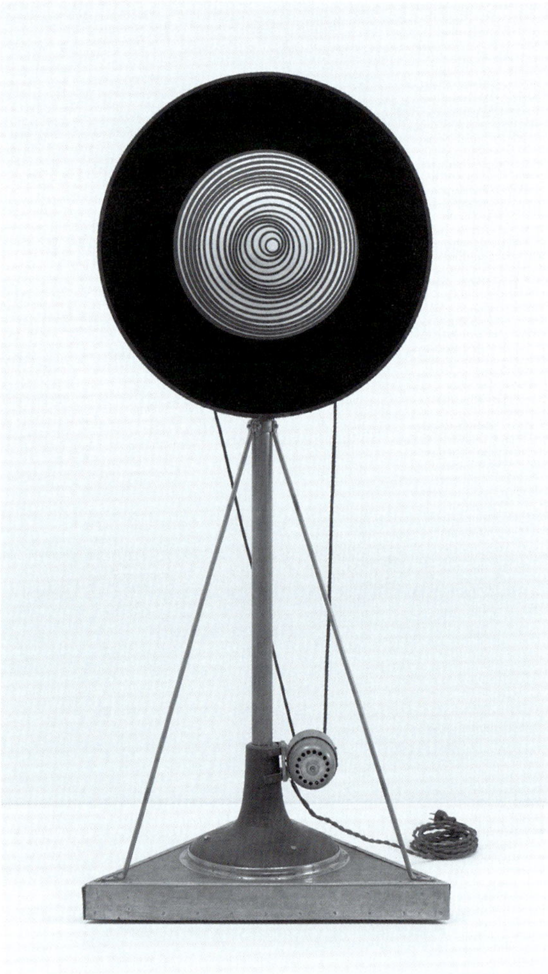

FIGURE 6.5

Marcel Duchamp
Rotary Demisphere (Precision Optics), Paris, 1925
Painted papier-mâché demisphere fitted on velvet-covered disk, copper collar with Plexiglas dome, motor, pulley, and metal stand, 148.6 × 64.2 × 60.9 cm
The Museum of Modern Art, New York, NY, Gift of Mrs. William Sisler and Edward James Fund.

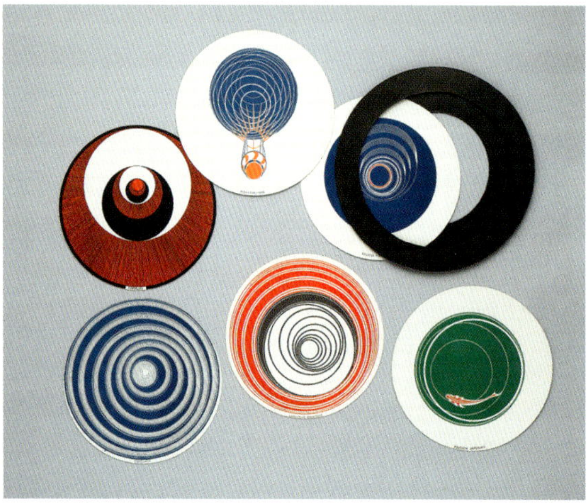

FIGURE 6.6

Marcel Duchamp
Rotoreliefs (Optical Disks), 1935, published by Enrico Donati 1953
Series of six offset lithographs, diameter, each 20 cm
The Museum of Modern Art, New York, NY, Gift of Rose Fried

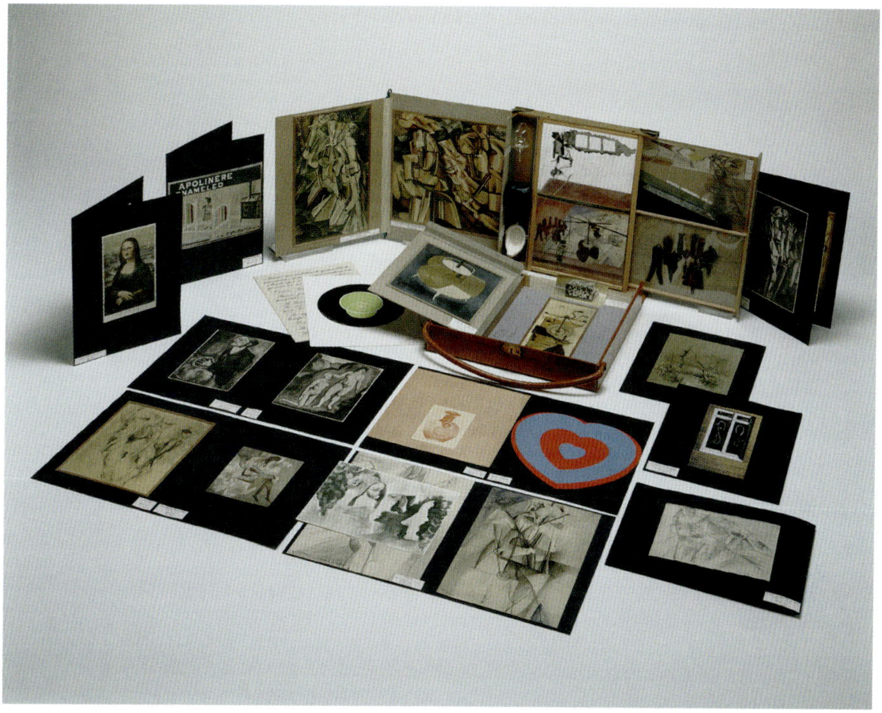

FIGURE 6.7

Marcel Duchamp
Contents of *de ou par Marcel Duchamp ou Rrose Sélavy (Boîte-en-Valise) / From or by Marcel Duchamp or Rrose Sélavy (Box in a Valise)*, 1935–1941
Mixed media, dimensions vary
Philadelphia Museum of Art, Philadelphia, PA, The Louise and Walter Arensberg Collection, 1950 / Bridgeman Images

(figure 6.8). The resemblance between the haloes in the Munich *Amida Triad* and Duchamp's *Oculist Witnesses* (figure 6.9) is worth noting. In Mahayana Buddhism, particularly the tantric Vajrayana tradition, Amitabha is one of the five "self-born" celestial buddhas. Amida is the Japanese name for this Buddha of Consciousness. The Sanskrit *Amitabha* means "Infinite Light," and some depictions show a strong beam of light emerging from the place at the center of his brow, called the *urna*. This attribute suggests a link with Duchamp's "Headlight-Child," conceived immediately after his return from Munich in 1912.[10]

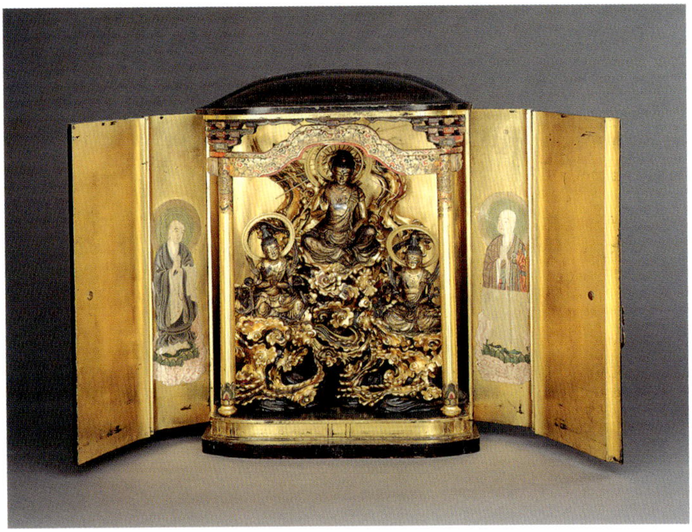

FIGURE 6.8
Altar with Amida Triad (Amida raigo zu), Japan, c. 1800
Wood, lacquer, gilt, paint, copper, and brass fittings, height 72 cm
Museum Five Continents (formerly Staatliches Museum für Völkerkunde), Munich

Amitabha is associated with the attribute of magnetism, the element of red fire, the quality of pure perception or discernment, and a deep awareness of the emptiness of phenomena—all qualities associated with Duchamp, as we have seen. On Amitabha's right is the manifestation of his Wisdom in the form of Bodhisattva Mahasthamaprapta, who brings to humankind knowledge of the need for liberation. On his left is the manifestation of his Compassion: the Bodhisattva Avalokiteshvara, whose Sanskrit name means "the one who observes, or witnesses, the cries of the world"—a potential link with the Oculist Witnesses of *The Large Glass*.[11]

••

Duchamp returned to New York in June 1942 after tortuous journeys through France, smuggling out materials for *Boîte-en-valise* disguised as a cheese broker. Other artist-refugees preceded him, including Mina Loy in 1936, Yves Tanguy, Kay Sage, Dalí, Matta, and Kurt Seligman in 1939; Man Ray (who settled in Southern California) in 1940; and in 1941, André Breton, Marc Chagall, Max Ernst, Jacques Lipchitz, André Masson, and the filmmaker René Clair. Breton, who had officially launched his brand of Surrealism with his first manifesto in 1924, maintained his role as leader, but he was uncomfortable in the United States and never did learn English. For Duchamp—who refused to affiliate with Breton's Surrealists, just as he had refused to affiliate with the Dadaists—New York was a second home: he liked America, he liked Americans, and Americans liked him. His friend

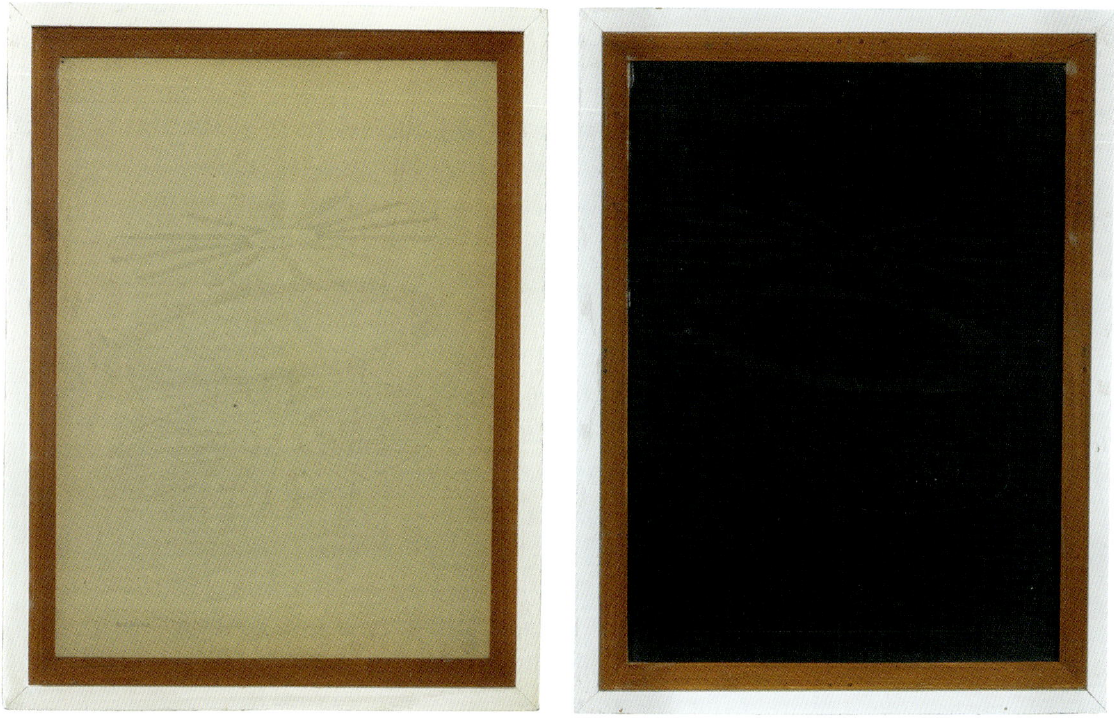

FIGURE 6.9

Marcel Duchamp
Témoins Oculistes / Oculist Witnesses, 1920
Stylus on carbon paper (study for *The Large Glass*; sheet used to transfer Duchamp's design to a silvered section of the glass surface)
Sheet: 50 × 37.5 cm
Philadelphia Museum of Art, Philadelphia, PA, The Louise and Walter Arensberg Collection

and first biographer Robert Lebel later described two Duchamps: "The nonchalant and witty Duchamp, who was a renowned figure in America, and the distant, inscrutable Duchamp, who in France remained a property of the 'happy few,' were not one and the same person. The nearest to the real Duchamp would have been a combination of both."[12] In New York, as in Paris, Duchamp continued practicing the art of life by helping fellow artists like Breton, while keeping mostly to himself.

The most significant life event for Duchamp during this time was meeting Maria Martins, a surrealist sculptor and mother of three married to the Brazilian ambassador to Washington.[13] Duchamp and Martins (*née* Maria de Lourdes Alves) met in New York in 1943 at a show of her sculptures, which reveal the influence of Giacometti, Ernst, Arp, and Lipchitz, from whom she learned bronze casting. Surely part of Martins's appeal for Duchamp were her themes—renditions of morphing Brazilian water, fire, and mother-goddesses—and the unabashedly sexual nature of her work (figures 6.10, 6.11). Duchamp, who was fifty-five when they met, found this intelligent, exotic, forty-eight-year-old earth-mother irresistible. He had always been attracted to intellectual, talented, independent women, and Martins was all three. A successful sculptor with an international career, the wife of a diplomat and a dedicated mother, Martins had it all before that concept existed. Even after her romantic relationship with Duchamp ended, her intellectual involvement with him continued. She published books on China and India (including a discussion of the *Bhagavad Gita*), and a biography of Nietzsche.[14]

Perhaps due partly to the separations and privations of war and its aftermath, partly to his age, once Duchamp was drawn into Martins's orbit, he blossomed emotionally. He developed an immediate and uncharacteristically passionate attachment to her, upending his life for almost a decade and embarking on the most ambitious artwork of his career—the mysterious, complicated diorama *Given*, on which he would work for over twenty years (1946–1966; figure 0.1). The relationship with Martins seems to have mellowed the commitment-averse Duchamp. In 1950 his longtime companion, the American artist Mary Reynolds, died, with Duchamp at her side. The following year, he began a relationship with Alexina "Teeny" Matisse (*née* Sattler), former wife of art dealer Pierre Matisse. An American,

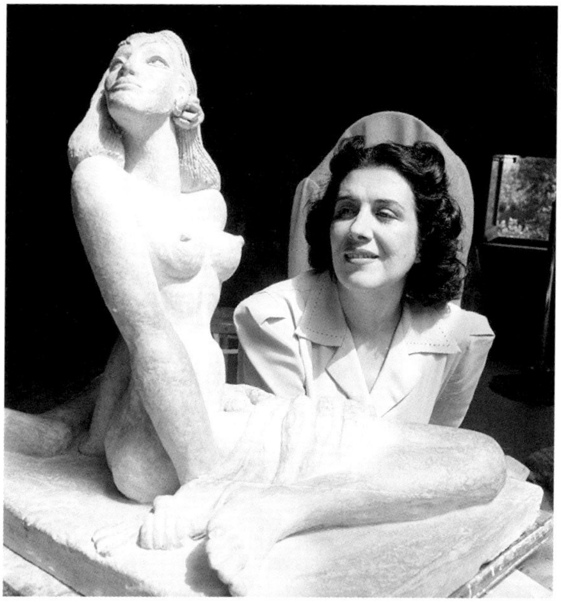

FIGURE 6.10

Herbert Gehr
Maria Martins and Sculpture
Brazilian sculptor Maria Martins (1894–1973) with one of her sculptures, Washington DC, 1941
Photo by Herbert Gehr/The LIFE Images Collection/Getty Images

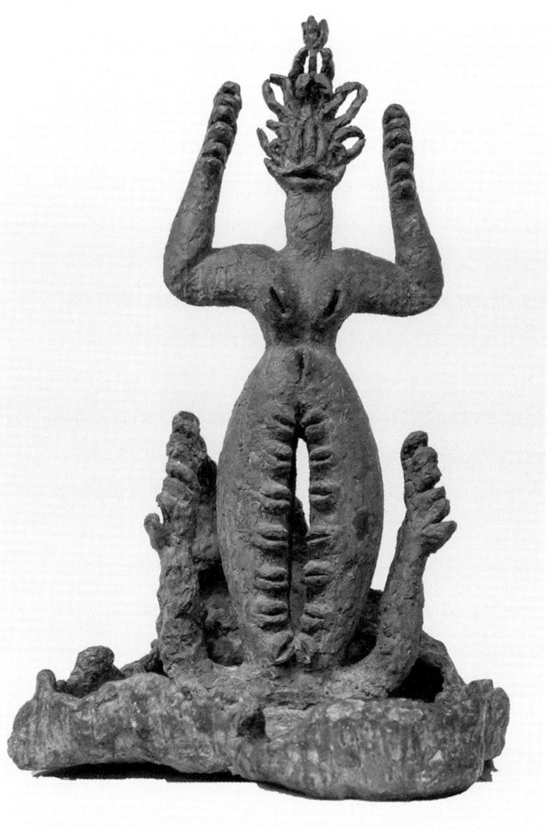

FIGURE 6.11

Maria Martins
Boiuna, 1942
Bronze, 72.4 × 68.6 × 47 cm
Collection of OAS AMA / Art Museum of the Americas, Gift of Nelson Rockefeller

like Reynolds, Teeny had studied sculpture with Duchamp's friend Brancusi in the early 1920s, and she shared Duchamp's passion for chess. They married in 1954, and would remain happily married until his death in 1968.

The major professional event for Duchamp during his second extended stay in New York was *First Papers of Surrealism*, an exhibition he organized with André Breton that opened on October 14, 1942 at the Whitelaw Reid Mansion in midtown Manhattan. Breton hung the works, and Duchamp installed *Mile of String* (figure 6.1), crisscrossing the mansion's grand display spaces. The string installation was described in the catalogue as "his twine Marcel Duchamp"; Lebel, in his Duchamp catalogue raisonné, would list it simply as "String at the Surrealist Exhibition."[15]

Duchamp's string correlates with the Sanskrit words *sutra* and *tantra*, both of which come from verbs connected with sewing. Sutra means thread or string, in the sense of continuum ("suture" is one derivative). Tantra refers to threads woven into a fabric or web, as in *Mile of String*. Both tie things together: in Sanskrit literature, a sutra is a set of rules or aphorisms; a tantra is a Hindu or Buddhist ritual text. Duchamp would have been aware of these meanings thanks to his studies at the École Nationale des Chartes. A more esoteric source is J. C. Chatterji's *Kashmir Shaivism* (1914), where it is explained that "*Ākāsha* ["space"] is nothing but the Dishah or '*directions*' i.e. *lines* of what may be called *forces* spreading out or radiating everywhere. ... These lines interweave themselves into that universally enveloping fabric which is Space."[16]

Aside from *Mile of String*, the only work Duchamp included in *First Papers of Surrealism* was his early painting *Network of Stoppages* (1914, figure 4.7), which he had first brought with him to New York in 1915. "Marcel Duchamp ... contributes a hitherto unshown canvas," critic Henry McBride wrote in the *New York Sun*. "It nestles behind a particularly thick wad of cobwebs."[17] Back in 1914, Duchamp had integrated an earlier visual language into *Network of Stoppages* by painting it on top of a copy of his *Young Man and Girl in Spring* (1911, figure 4.8), which can still faintly be seen between the lines of *Network of Stoppages*. He surrounded *Network*'s lines with a white aura, like that with which he had surrounded his nudes of 1910. Duchamp later described these auras as "a sign of my subconscious preoccupations toward a metarealism."[18] His ongoing preoccupation would be newly relevant in the context of *First Papers of Surrealism*. R. A. Parker could have been writing about *Network of Stoppages* in his catalogue essay, "Explorers of the Pluriverse": "the external world provides no more than the symbols and alphabet of communication, and the 'field' into which [these artists] may project their visions."[19] With his *Mile of String*, Duchamp endowed an updated aura of metarealism on the exhibition as a whole.

Duchamp reproduced *Network* in the catalogue over the caption, *Cimetière des Uniformes et Livrées* ("Cemetery of Uniforms and Liveries"), thus emphasizing its connection with *The Large Glass*. It may be that the painting gave Duchamp the idea for the installation. *Stoppage* in French means hidden mending, but as we have seen, it can also mean, as in English, a halting of motion or of electric current, or physical blockage of a narrow passage, like the Capillary Tubes of *The Large Glass* mapped in *Network of Stoppages*. Both meanings apply to *Mile of String*. Duchamp's "twine" (note the pun on "twin" and the suggestion of "intertwine") partially hid the works on view, *blocking* both movement and lines of sight. At the same time, Duchamp's twine allowed visitors to experience the dramatic space of the Whitelaw Reid Mansion as multidimensional. He interwove *Mile of String* to make "empty" space visible, just as he had used the uniforms and liveries of the Malic Moulds to clothe the four-dimensional erotic energy of the Bachelors.[20]

Reproduced on the same page of the catalogue as *Network of Stoppages* is Duchamp's "compensation portrait"—a photograph of a careworn woman taken by Ben Shahn while working for the Farm Security Administration (figure 6.12).[21] While her face does superficially resemble Duchamp's, it is difficult, intellectually and emotionally, to reconcile this tragic image with its caption, "Marcel Duchamp." Duchamp's choice of image is usually considered ironic, if not cynical. But there is a Shinto saying, "The heart of the person before you is a mirror; see there your own form." Similarly, in Kashmir Shaivism the world is a mirror where practitioners "continually discover their own face in the world and find their own meaning in life reflected back to them."[22] In the context of war and its losses and the connections of "his twine," Robert Lebel's nonchalant and witty American Duchamp may have seen in this anonymous woman's visage not only someone who *looked* like him, but someone who *was* him.

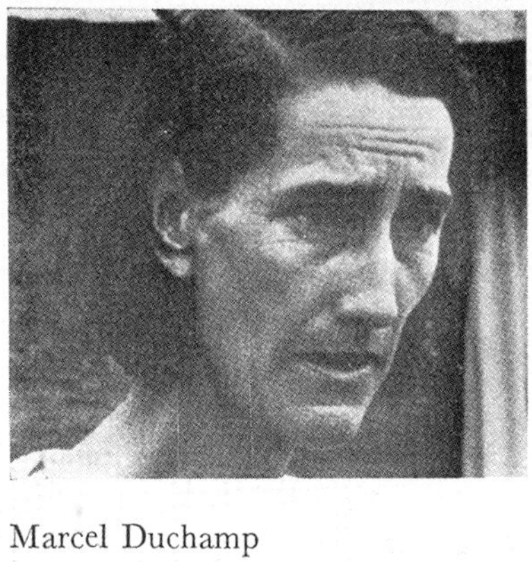

FIGURE 6.12

Marcel Duchamp (Compensation Portrait)

From the catalogue to the exhibition *First Papers of Surrealism*, 1942, 26.5 × 18.3 cm

Philadelphia Museum of Art, Pennsylvania, PA, Gift of Jacqueline, Paul, and Peter Matisse in memory of their mother, Alexina Duchamp, 1998 / Bridgeman Images

In the March 1943 issue of André Breton's periodical *VVV*, Duchamp reproduced upside-down a photograph, "*Ficelles* ['Strings'] *of Marcel Duchamp*," as a "*souvenir* ['memento'] of the surrealist exhibition 1942." This upside-down image of *Mile of String* was related to Duchamp's *Juggler of Gravity*, which never made it into his *Large Glass*, but whose rendition would be overseen by Matta for the postwar Paris Surrealist exhibition of 1947 (figure 9.5). Robert Lebel similarly emphasized the disequilibrium Duchamp's "inextricable tangle of string" induced as it "forced the spectators into contortions inappropriate to their equilibrium and their dignity," adding that fire "consumed over half a mile of string during the installation."[23] Harriet and Sidney Janis explained that *Mile of String* "symbolized literally the difficulties to be circumvented by the uninitiate in order to see, to perceive and understand, the exhibits." Duchamp himself downplayed the occult aspect in an interview with Harriet Janis a few years later: "It was nothing. You can always see through a window, through a curtain ... if you want to, same thing there."[24] Nevertheless, Duchamp's string implied a labyrinth, thus emphasizing the connections and complexities of perception.

As with *Fountain* twenty-five years earlier, Duchamp turned the work of installing the string into a playful, collaborative effort in which a number of artist-friends participated. He invited Sidney and Harriet Janis's son and his friends to play ball at the opening. If anyone asked, the children were to respond: "Mr. Duchamp told us we could play here."[25] Duchamp himself did not attend. On October 15, 1942, he reported to Katherine Dreier: "The opening of the Surrealist show took place last night and seems to be quite a success. I was not there; (this is one of my p[ractices] habits)—but reports indicate that the children played with great gusto."[26] Duchamp's substitution of the benign word "habit" for the more ritualistic "practice" disguises his Taoist determination to avoid social obligation. The musician John Cage, a fellow guest with Duchamp at Peggy Guggenheim's New York apartment during this time, remarked: "One of [Duchamp's] goals was to go underground—which is an Eastern goal—to be a white animal, in the winter, when it's snowing, and so to climb up in the tree, knowing your footsteps are covered by new snow—so nobody knows where you are!"[27]

Earlier in 1942 André Breton had cofounded with Max Ernst and the American sculptor David Hare the avant-garde review *VVV*. Addressing "poetry, plastic arts, anthropology, sociology, psychology," the letters *VVV* referenced three levels of Victory encompassing three Views: the "View around us," the "View inside us," and the "resolution" of these two Views toward "the continual, systematic enlargement of the field of consciousness towards a total view, VVV."[28] The first number appeared in June 1942, just as Duchamp was arriving in New York. By the second, double issue of March 1943, he was on the masthead as editorial advisor along with Breton and Ernst, and had also designed the front and back covers (figures 6.13, 6.14). The front cover of *VVV Almanac for 1943* features what appears to be a nineteenth-century print of Cronus as a scythe-wielding horseman astride the world, partially blotting out the sun. His armor is decorated with the stars and stripes of the American flag. The "VVV" of the title is printed across this image in green ink.

The back cover is a die-cut profile of a female torso into which chicken wire has been inserted. Through this chicken-wire screen part of a photograph is visible showing a woman with her hands together, raised over her head, as in supplication or prayer.[29] When readers open the back cover they are invited to "join hands on both sides of wire-screen, fingertips touching each other and slide gently along screen towards you." As sensitive finger pads encounter each other through the interstices of the hard wire, the effect is uncannily sensuous: you feel yourself feeling. The playful Duchamp

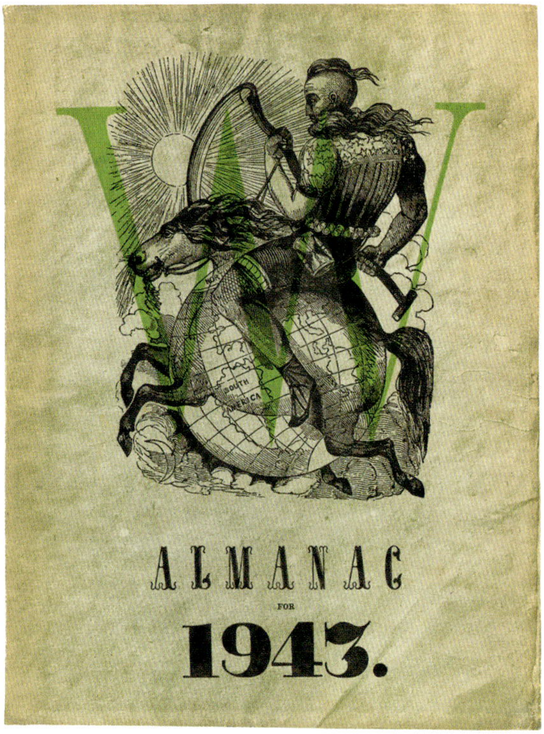

FIGURE 6.13

Marcel Duchamp
Front cover, *VVV Almanac for 1943*, March 1943
Paperbound periodical, 27.9 × 21.4 cm
Philadelphia Museum of Art, Philadelphia, PA, Gift of Jacqueline, Paul, and Peter Matisse in memory of their mother, Alexina Duchamp, 1998 (1998-4-41)

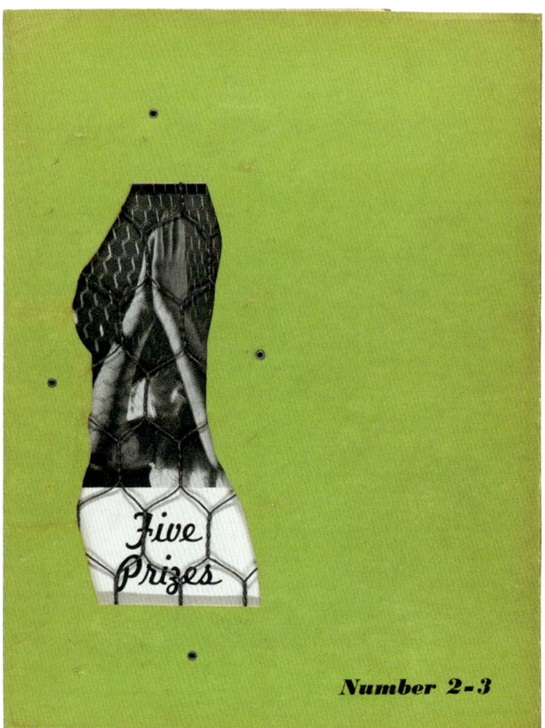

FIGURE 6.14

Marcel Duchamp
Back cover, *VVV Almanac for 1943*, March 1943
Paperbound periodical with chicken-wire insert, 27.9 × 21.4 cm
Philadelphia Museum of Art, Philadelphia, PA, Gift of Carl Zigrosser, 1975

framed this erotic exercise as a "Twin-Touch-Test," and offered "five prizes" for the best descriptions of this essentially indescribable experience. The color of the back cover is the same spring green as the "VVV" printed over the horseman on the front cover, connecting that image of war and death with a proffered experience of "twin-touch"—erotic connection.

"We say ······ ······ ······ " *VVV*'s title page declares. *V* in Morse code is ··· - , so the trio of dots and dashes communicates "VVV" only by extrapolation. Three dots in Morse code is S; three dashes stand for O. This Morse code series thus reads: "SOSOSO"—a combination of distress call (SOS) and statement of fact (SO) that might be understood to convey a progression of the three "Views" (VVV) from exterior, to interior, to resolution in a comprehensive vision of reality. The front and back covers for this double number of 1943 reinforce the sequence: awareness of world war, hinged to enjoyment of sensuous experience that, once comprehended, could win a prize!

••

Two other people Marcel Duchamp already knew had settled in New York for the duration of the war. Author and art expert Robert Lebel would write the first monograph and catalogue raisonné of the artist, published in 1959.[30] The Swiss-German sculptor Isabelle Waldberg would prove a fertile collaborator for Duchamp, serving as an important source for *Given* (figure 0.1). After the war he would bequeath to her his beloved Paris studio at 11 rue Larrey, where she lived for most of the rest of her life.[31]

Robert Lebel, almost fourteen years younger than Duchamp, was first attracted to Surrealism by André Breton's *Manifeste du surréalisme* (1924).[32] He became friends with Breton and knew about Duchamp, whom he finally met at Alfred Stieglitz's gallery in 1936. "I was struck by his radiance," Lebel said of this first meeting, "and his capacity for contempt. Each time somebody mentioned ... the name of a celebrated artist, he would murmur sadly, 'poor man ...'."[33] (This disdain for "celebrated" artists may have been partly for the benefit of Stieglitz's wife, artist Georgia O'Keeffe, who was also present.) In his unpublished autobiography, Lebel wrote that subsequently he and Duchamp "ran into each other every once in a while, and his clarity of mind, his composure, his frugality, his supreme manner of mastering any circumstance filled me with wonder beyond words."[34]

Lebel, his wife Nina, and their son Jean-Jacques (born 1936) were already on their way to New York when war broke out in September 1939. Once Duchamp arrived, almost three years later, Lebel began pursuing a closer relationship with the artist he so admired. This was not easy. "We used to see Breton daily," Lebel wrote, "but Duchamp could never be depended upon for regular discussions. He came and went as he pleased."[35] Nevertheless a strong friendship did develop, based partly on their mutual love of language play. According to Jean-Jacques Lebel, "the main, immediate link between my father and Marcel, out of which their friendship grew, was their love of *calembours*, or puns. My father was a *calembour* maniac! ... This philosophical, linguistic, and humoristic connection developed later into *Le Da Costa Encyclopédique* and into all of my father's future readings between the lines of Marcel's works and writings."[36]

A more nuanced understanding of the relationship between Lebel and Duchamp can be intuited from a short story Lebel wrote in 1943–1944, when he was seeing Duchamp nearly every day.[37] André Breton would publish "The Inventor of Free Time" (*L'Inventeur du temps gratuit*) in the second number of *Le Surréalisme, même* (Spring 1957).[38] As we saw in chapter 2, Lebel would later publish it along with a short novel as *La double vue, suivi de L'inventeur du temps gratuit* (1964), which won the 1965 *Prix du Fantastique*. It would be republished in 1993 with a preface by Alain Fleischer and an afterword by Patrick Waldberg, who described "The Inventor of Free Time" as a "brilliant and curious text ... true speculation, in Alfred Jarry's sense. Long kept secret by its author, it was finally published in André Breton's review. One recognizes without difficulty in the inventor in question if not Marcel Duchamp in person, at least one of his brothers in spirit."[39]

Breton's title *Le Surréalisme, même* was an obvious allusion to *La Mariée mise à nu par ses célibataires, même*. The cover of the first number featured a provocative image of Duchamp's *Female Fig Leaf* (1950), which Duchamp had photographed using his own careful lighting, retouching the photograph so the sculpture would look like the shadowy image of a vulva (figure 6.15).[40] Breton had been pestering Lebel to let him publish in his new journal excerpts from Lebel's forthcoming monograph on Duchamp. Lebel told Breton that both the artist and the publisher felt this would be premature. He proposed instead "another text entitled 'L'Inventeur du

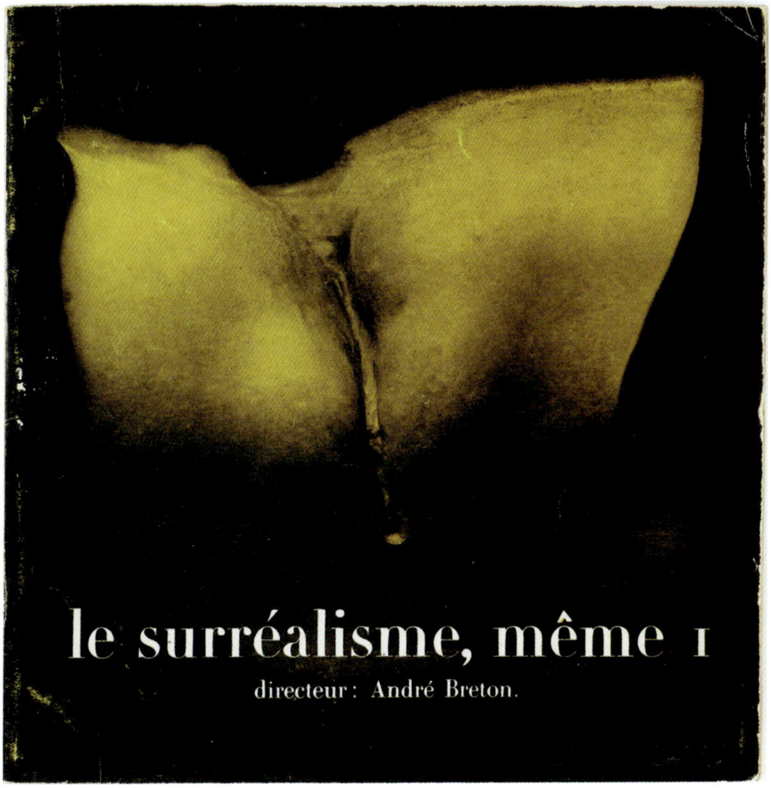

FIGURE 6.15

Marcel Duchamp
Cover design for Le Surréalisme, même, no. 1, October 1956
Paperbound periodical, 19.5 × 19.5 cm
Philadelphia Museum of Art, Philadelphia, PA, Gift of Jacqueline, Paul and Peter Matisse in memory of their mother, Alexina Duchamp / Bridgeman Images

temps gratuit'." "Besides," Lebel added, "the shade of Duchamp is not absent from it."[41] His cautious statement underlines Patrick Waldberg's assertion that "The Inventor of Free Time" had been "long kept secret by its author."[42]

The subject of Lebel's story is a lively artist-philosopher-yogin whose bed is occupied by a series of young women. While searching for an apartment to rent in a commercial district of Lower Manhattan, the narrator happens upon a door bearing an inscription in French: "*A. Loride, Inventeur du Temps Gratuit*." Curious, he enters:

> In the center of a vast, extraordinarily cluttered warehouse, a completely nude man ... going through physical culture movements [*mouvements de culture physique*]. He turned around and I noted that he must be over fifty, although his body was still fairly trim. He was hairless, and his appearance of meticulous cleanliness was surprising, in such a setting. However, I was struck above all by his lack of embarrassment. ... At first I could find only this rather foolish thing to say: "Are you French?" adding after a silence, "I've come about your invention."
>
> With a gesture, he permitted me to sit down but, except for a bed on which a very young woman was lying, no seat could be seen and I leaned against a packing case, politely. ... "I see people by appointment only," he replied abruptly. "Leave your name and address (he pointed to a wall covered with notes and numbers), "I will call you in," and, turning his back on me, he returned to his gymnastics.[43]

"Loride's" *mouvements de culture physique* was no doubt a reference to hatha yoga, which, according to Arthur Avalon's 1913 *Tantra of the Great Liberation*, is "concerned with certain physical processes preparatory or auxiliary to the control of the mind, by which alone union may be directly attained."[44] From 1917 through the 1930s, hatha yoga was marketed to New York's moneyed and artistic classes by the American businessman/guru Pierre Bernard and his band of American yoginis. From 1939 through 1946—during the time Lebel was living in New York—Pierre Bernard's nephew Theos Bernard ran a hatha yoga school out of New York's Pierre Hotel.[45]

Three weeks later the narrator receives a brief note of invitation. Loride's subsequent soliloquy alludes to the machine metaphors in *The Large Glass* and to the mundane materiality of Duchamp's readymades: "All these machines," he informs the narrator, "impose on my inquiry its concrete form, while their eminently nominal character keeps me from giving in, as physicians do, and as, unfortunately, so many alchemists have done, to deadly concern for results."[46] Loride is referring to the alchemical ingestion of deadly mercury in pursuit of immortality. The reference to "concern for results" suggests the teaching in the *Bhagavad Gita* (mentioned in connection with Mina Loy in chapter 5) that actions are best undertaken without attachment to outcomes. The Inventor of Free Time has chosen to focus not on "immortality"—artistic fame—but rather on concrete, everyday production.

Loride goes over to one of his machines and "with his foot, set a pedal in motion. Some slender wooden wands begin to shoot out of an exhaust pipe. 'Excuse me,' he said, 'I have a rush order to meet'."

> "Would those be your time tablets?" I cried, "I'd have imagined them in crystalline form ..." "The symbol matters little," he said, continuing to pedal. "It so happens that, without its having anything to do with me, I have at my disposal this machine that saws up dowels for which the hardware merchants in the neighborhood, my clients, have shown themselves greedy. A surrealist sculptor, so I am told, acquires them in large bundles."

The "surrealist sculptor" was Lebel's lover Isabelle Waldberg, who at the time this story was written was using flexible birch dowels to make her sculptures (figure 6.16).[47]

Time, it turns out, is a matter of perception: "'Everything announces a passage to go through, a rupture to realize'," Loride declares. "'No ceremonial, no incantations, no rites, but reaching the point of lucidity where the

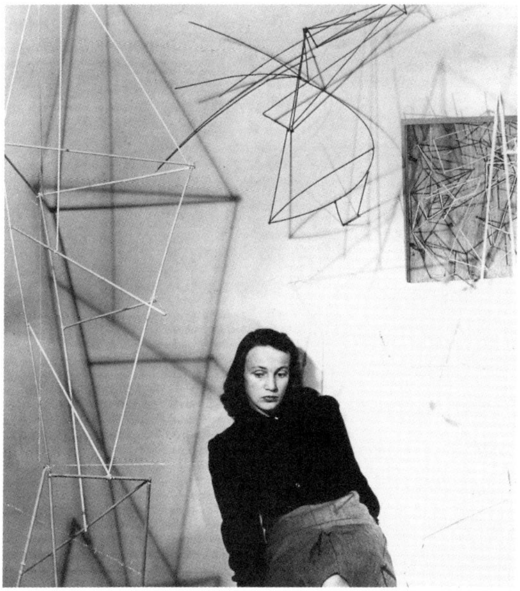

FIGURE 6.16

Isabelle Waldberg in Her New York Studio, 1944
Photo: Archives Michel Waldberg

notion of time becomes a fruit one can peel,' and with his fingers he made these little, nimble movements."[48] The story concludes with a passage that suggests Loride is a member of a group that, while not strictly secret, avoids public attention. The parallel with Duchamp's esoteric attitude is striking:

> "For us ... it is compulsory that this squandering of time not be public, and we work hard to put others off the scent. We will be neither magi nor heroes, neither judges nor prophets, but apply ourselves to playing any role with a false seriousness that is capable of deceiving." ...
>
> At that moment a young woman entered, not the one I had seen before. She seemed satisfied to nod and go seat herself on the bed without saying a word. I was about to continue the discussion when I perceived that the thoughts of my interlocutor had obviously taken another course.
>
> "May I ask you not to return?" he asked after some minutes of silence. "Spare me the disgrace of resuming these oral demonstrations that always only reflect our own prevarications. ..." And pushing me amicably toward the door, he concluded, "Freedom is never separate from a certain disinclination to speak. Doubtless I have already said too much."[49]

Loride's method for rupturing reality, freeing himself from time and space, is clearly erotic in nature, paralleling Duchamp's contemporaneous cover for *VVV* where sensual experience offers liberation from the horseman Cronus, or Time. The last line, "doubtless I have already said too much," is something Lebel may actually have heard from the future subject of *La double vue, suivi de L'inventeur du temps gratuit*.

••

Isabelle Waldberg, born Margaretha Isabella Maria Farner in the canton of Zurich in German Switzerland in 1911, came from a long line of blacksmiths.[50] As the younger son, her father could not inherit the family forge and so turned to farming. Isabelle loved spending time at her uncle's forge, and it is tempting to attribute her future career as a sculptor to her family history. In 1932 she moved to Zurich, where she studied sculpture and immersed herself in the city's art scene. In 1936 Margaretha Farner relocated to Paris, where a year later she met Patrick Waldberg at Café Dôme. They quickly became romantically involved. Patrick convinced her to change her name to Isabelle (he was still married to his first wife, Margareta, perhaps accounting for the change) and to enroll in Marcel Mauss's course in ethnography at the École Pratique des Hautes Études, which Isabelle attended from mid-November 1938 to January 1939. The couple took classes with ethnologist Paul Rivet, who had recently founded the Musée de l'Homme, and together they paid regular visits to museums, including the Musée de l'Homme and the Musée Guimet.

Poet and critic Patrick Waldberg was an American, born in California, who had spent most of his life in France. Late in 1939 Patrick volunteered to serve in the French infantry; in August 1940 he was awarded the Croix de Guerre and demobilized. As an American citizen, Patrick preceded Isabelle to the United States, where he lived for a while in New York. He then traveled with Georges Duthuit, an art historian and fellow member of Georges Bataille's Collège de Sociologie, throughout California and the West, exploring Native American culture. In the summer of 1941, Patrick Waldberg obtained a divorce from his first wife in Reno, Nevada.

Isabelle finally was able to come to New York with their young son, Michel (born March 1940), in July 1942—one month after the arrival of Duchamp. Patrick, Isabelle, and Michel moved into an apartment at 18 East 57th Street, one floor above Robert Lebel and his family. Isabelle and Patrick married in September 1942, just before he departed for London, where he had been assigned by the American Office of War Information (sponsor of Voice of America, where Patrick found employment for artist-friends, including Breton). He subsequently moved between London, North Africa, and Paris while Isabelle remained in New York, seeing him only briefly on the rare occasions when he could get leave. Meanwhile, Isabelle developed an erotic and companionate relationship with Robert Lebel that would endure until Lebel's death in 1986.

Isabelle Waldberg quickly immersed herself in New York's artistic and intellectual life. In a hardware store, she discovered flexible birch dowels that she could bend and fasten together with string along the lines of Giacometti's spare *The Palace at 4 a.m.* (1932), which had deeply impressed her when she saw it in his Paris studio in 1936. She was encouraged to pursue her new "dematerialized" sculpture by André Breton and by Robert Lebel, who early in 1944 published a book of erotic poetry, *Masque à lame*, which he illustrated with photographs of Isabelle's constructions.[51] The title

Masque à lame is usually translated into English somewhat awkwardly as "Plank Mask." Jean-Jacques Lebel has forwarded the plausible theory that the title is a pun on *masque à l'âme*—"mask for the soul"[52]—in other words, the body.

"I loved my life in New York," Isabelle Waldberg recalled in 1963. "In Paris I had studied ethnology at the Sorbonne and I became friends with André Breton and Marcel Duchamp. Marcel seemed kind to everyone, but he didn't really like people that much. Of course, he had very good friends, but he only liked a few people. He didn't talk much; he wasn't like the other surrealists."[53] There is every reason to believe that Isabelle Waldberg was one of the young women who occupied the bed of the charismatic Inventor of Free Time. Although it is hard to know how close she had been to Duchamp in Paris, in New York she was clearly one of Marcel's few "very good friends." "He liked young women," she wrote. "Marcel came to my studio often, and sometimes we would have dinner. ... He had one simple room on West Fourteenth Street. When I returned to Paris after four years, Marcel let me take over his small seventh-floor studio in rue Larrey."[54]

Their professional collaboration was as strong as their personal relationship. Waldberg helped Duchamp with both of the bookstore windows he created for André Breton in 1945, beginning with a display in April for Breton's autobiographical book-length essay *Arcane 17* (figure 6.17), written as the Allied troops were liberating occupied Europe.[55] Breton's title alludes to card seventeen of the Tarot—the Star—which shows a naked woman kneeling by a pool, one foot in the water, the other on land. A large star shines over her head as she pours water into the pool and onto the earth from two urns. This "Star" card of the Major Arcana signifies light and renewal. The theme of Breton's *Arcane 17* is the utopian quest for light, which, he declares at the end, "can only be known by way of three paths: poetry, liberty, and love."

Duchamp was no utopianist, but the themes of love and freedom, and the imagery of the Star, with its naked woman pouring water, were naturals for him. Isabelle Waldberg contributed a starfish-shaped inkwell incorporating the themes of star, water, and authorship. It held a white quill pen, referencing a quote at the end of *Arcane 17*: "The angel of Liberty, born from a white feather shed by Lucifer during his fall, penetrates

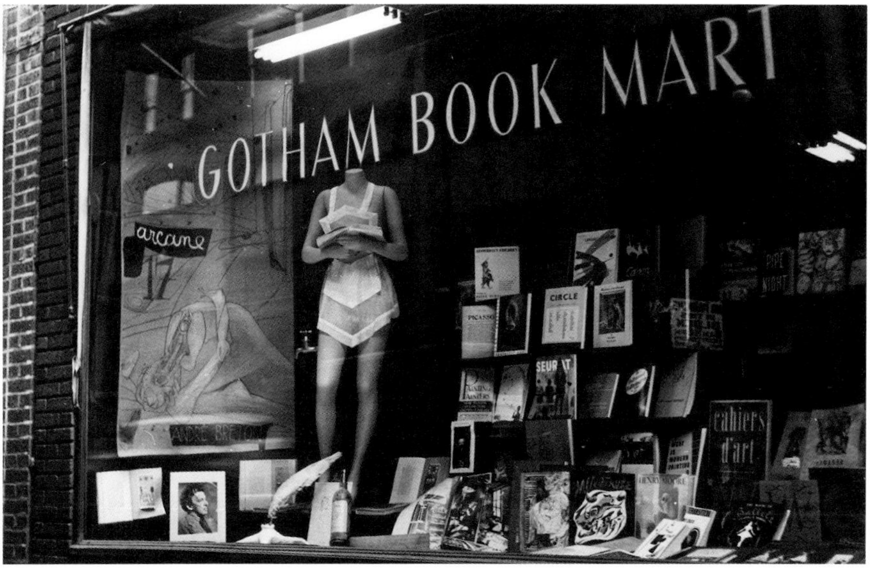

FIGURE 6.17

Elisa Breton
Window of Gotham Book Mart arranged by Marcel Duchamp for the release of *Arcane 17* by André Breton, New York, 1945
Bibliothèque Kandinsky, Musée National d'Art Moderne, Centre Georges Pompidou, Paris, France, inv. no. BRET3.1–6

the darkness."[56] The quill may also have been a pacifist reference to the white feathers handed out by women to noncombatant men like Duchamp during the previous world war. Inserted into the starfish, its phallic reference seems clear.

The window display also featured a large poster by Matta, who had illustrated Breton's book with four Tarot card designs. Accounts have it that the window was censored and had to be relocated due to a breast in Matta's poster. The poster does show a breast, attached to the bottom half of a love-making couple, but this is hardly its most remarkable feature. That would be the "head" of the male lover, which is depicted as a vulva gushing sexual fluid into the head of the woman, while a stylized but explicit cross-section of a cervix and uterus hovers above.[57] The interior space of the uterus replicates the square shape of Duchamp's Draft Pistons in *The Large Glass*.

Matta's poster for *Arcane 17* was in fact a shockingly explicit rendition of tantric mental practice. It is telling that, like so many things associated with Duchamp, to my knowledge no one has remarked on it publicly.

Duchamp's own work for the window alluded to the role of the feminine as a source of falling water. *Lazy Hardware* was a headless manikin holding in her arms an open book, her body veiled only by a translucent white apron. A faucet was attached to her right thigh. The title is from one of Duchamp's notes, which reads: "Among our articles of lazy hardware we recommend a faucet which stops dripping when nobody is listening to it."[58] Theoretically at least, to "turn on" *Lazy Hardware*, all that was necessary was to pay attention. On one level, this is a statement of the importance of mental focus to eroticism; on another, it is a classic example of Duchampian art theory, which incorporated Buddhist and yogic theories of attention.

Breton's book had been inspired by hope for an end to war. In keeping with the themes of compassion and hope, Duchamp's iconography references Tara, a manifestation of the Bodhisattva of Compassion whose name means "star" in Sanskrit. A Mother Goddess (thus the apron) and Tibetan tantric Buddhist meditation deity who bestows the wisdom of compassion, Tara is said to have been born of a tear shed by Bodhisattva Avalokiteshvara on seeing the suffering of humanity. In Hindu mythology, Tara was the pole star and mother of the planet Mercury, a god with whom Duchamp identified, as in *Monte Carlo Bond* (1924).[59] Duchamp's Tara holds an open book in front of her breasts, and is missing her head—she is *acéphale*, "headless," an attribute that connects her with Isabelle Waldberg, as we shall see. True wisdom, Duchamp implies, is born not of the head, but of the heart.

The following November Duchamp created another window display, this time for an expanded edition of André Breton's *Le Surréalisme et la Peinture* (figure 6.18). He was assisted once again by Isabelle Waldberg, along with the Italian-American surrealist painter and sculptor Enrico Donati. Isabelle commented on this second installation in a letter to her husband written on November 10, 1945: "Yesterday morning, the window at Brentano's [for] *Surréalisme et la peinture* was done," she writes. "Marcel naturally did everything—designed and executed everything. Here's a

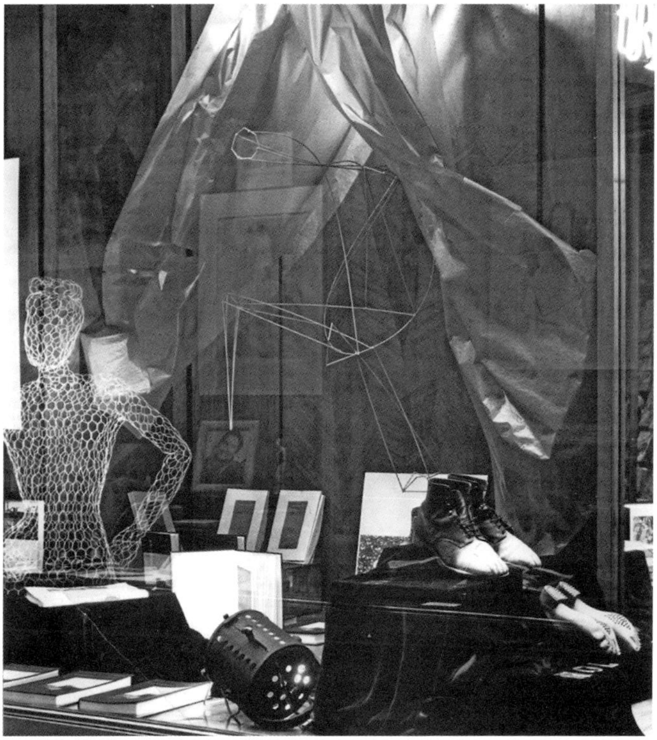

FIGURE 6.18

Lilly Joss
Window installation for André Breton's *Le Surréalisme et la Peinture*, Brentano's bookstore, New York, 1945

drawing of it." Isabelle annotated her little sketch to highlight some of the objects: "chicken wire mannequin bought ready-made," "boots with toes painted by Donati." (At Duchamp's suggestion, Breton had used Magritte's painting of this subject for the cover of his book.) At the top of the drawing is a vulva shape reminiscent of the shape made by the woman's arms on the back cover of *VVV*, which also featured chicken wire (figure 6.14). Isabelle described this vulva shape as having been made from "old paper from M.'s studio in the process of falling [*en chute*]." Nestled within is "an object by me underneath the tent."[60] This "object" was one of Isabelle's dowel sculptures made of birch rods fastened together with string.

Just as *Lazy Hardware* was a focus of the window display Duchamp designed in April 1945, this sculpture, *Always There Beautiful Aqueduct* (1943, figure 6.19), was a focus of this window designed soon after the end of the war. Waldberg's now-lost sculpture was a figure whose head was an upward-pointing triangle and whose crotch featured a downward-pointing triangle. In Indo-Tibetan symbolism—something Isabelle would have known from her visits to the Musée Guimet—an upward-pointing triangle designates male energy and a downward-pointig triangle designates female energy. One of the figure's legs is raised, and she holds aloft an "empty" circular form. This was the last work reproduced in Robert Lebel's book *Masque à lame*, facing his final lines:

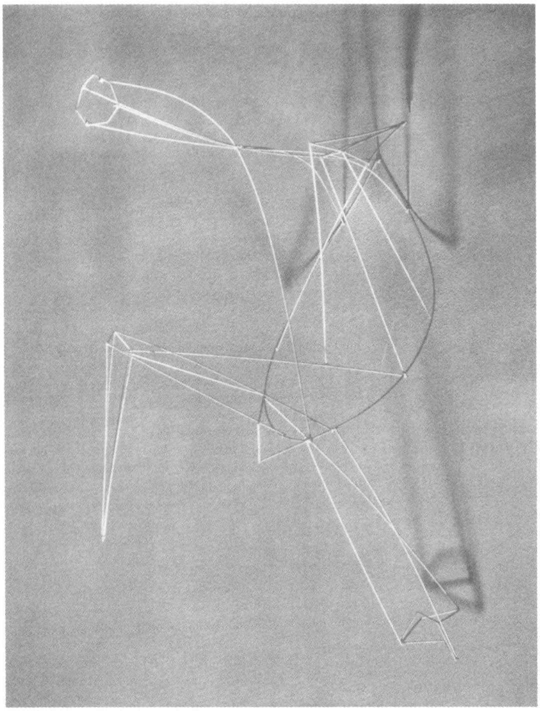

FIGURE 6.19

Isabelle Waldberg
Toujours là bel aqueduc / Always There Beautiful Aqueduct, 1943
As reproduced in *Masque à lame* (New York: Liberal Press/Éditions Hémisphères, "1943" [1944])

Toujours là bel aqueduct
J'aurais voulu recommencer ma vie

J'attendrai le temps qu'il faudra
Je ne suis pas venu ici pour me lamenter

("Always there beautiful aqueduct / I would have liked to begin my life again / I shall wait as long as it takes / I am not here to lament.") Like Duchamp's headless mannequin with the dripping faucet, *Always There Beautiful Aqueduct* proffers the female body as a source of mysteriously available, life-affirming fluid. Reversed, its pose is identical to the pose of Duchamp's figure in *Given*, right down to the absence of a head (figure 0.1).[61]

In 1946, the year following Duchamp's window displays and the year he began working on *Given*, Isabelle Waldberg created an even more startling precedent for that important work. *Luminaire* (figure 6.20) is a plaster sculpture that appears to have been cast from a female pudendum, perhaps as a "how-to" demonstration for Duchamp. Duchamp's *Female Fig Leaf* (1950), as reproduced on the cover of *Le Surréalisme, même* in 1956 (figure 6.15), strongly resembles it. But there is one important difference: *Luminaire*'s focal point, the vulva, is a hole, like the *trompe-l'œil* tear in *Tu m'* (figure 4.6), like the hole at the center of the figure in *Given* (figure 0.1). Waldberg's title—*Luminaire* ("Light")—evokes the lamp held up by Duchamp's figure. All of this implies that the "empty" form held up by "Beautiful Aqueduct" is a light, and the portal to that light is her own moist organ of procreation.

Now apparently lost,[62] *Luminaire* makes little sense except in the context of *Given*. As we shall see, the year Isabelle Waldberg made *Luminaire*, 1946, was a year in which she was working closely with Marcel Duchamp on *Le Da Costa Encyclopédique*. In January 1947 Duchamp would return to New York and his lover Maria Martins, who is usually considered the motivating inspiration for *Given*. In terms of Duchamp's intense emotional infatuation with Martins, that is not wrong. But in terms of direct artistic inspiration, Isabelle Waldberg would appear to have been the more important source.

When he left for New York, Duchamp invited Isabelle to move into his Paris studio. Twenty years later, shortly after finishing *Given*, he wrote a pithy paean to her: *Isabelle sculpte, ausculte, s'occulte et exulte*—more or less, "Isabelle sculpts, sounds, occults, and exults."[63] Unquestionably more

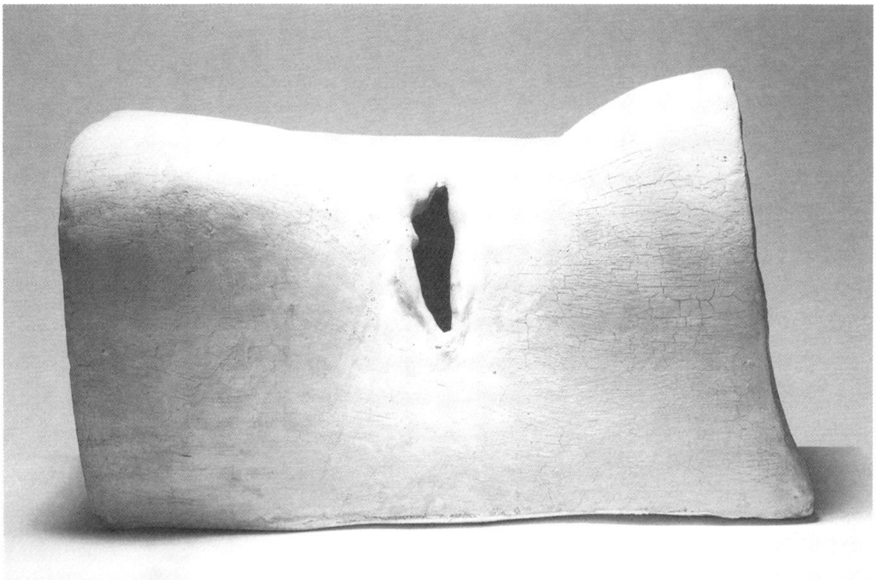

FIGURE 6.20
Isabelle Waldberg
Luminaire, 1946
Plaster, 38 x 25 x 21 cm
Original apparently lost; image from Michel Waldberg, *Isabelle Waldberg* (Paris: Éditions de la Différence, 1992), 82

poetic in the original French, Duchamp's tribute reveals not only his affection, but also his deep respect for Isabelle Waldberg's talent, perception, discretion, and spirit.

What might have inspired Isabelle to create such a startlingly bold conception of female power as *Luminaire*? The obvious answer would seem to be that Duchamp, who was in the early planning stages for *Given*, asked his sculptor friend to show him how to make a plaster cast from the body of Maria Martins.[64] Isabelle complied by making a cast from her own body, and *Luminaire* is the result of that lesson. She did not give it to Duchamp, however. According to Jean-Jacques Lebel, this very intimate self-portrait was "a corner piece which hung in my father's study for as long as I can remember and, given their very intimate and collaborative relationship, it is probable that this was a gift."[65]

There is another possibility, not necessarily in conflict with the motive described above. In 1946, the year *Luminaire* was created, Isabelle Waldberg, Robert Lebel, and Marcel Duchamp were working together on *Le Da Costa Encyclopédique*, a project that involved—indeed, had been inspired by—the iconoclastic French intellectual Georges Bataille. Seven years earlier Isabelle had been Bataille's acolyte during the final phase of his secret society, Acéphale. Just as Robert Lebel, in *La double vue, suivi de L'inventeur du temps gratuit*, translated Duchamp's experience with tantra yoga into surreal fantasy, so Bataille's friend Michel Fardoulis-Lagrange would attempt to convey Patrick and Isabelle Waldberg's experiences with Georges Bataille in his hallucinatory novel *G. B. ou un ami présomptueux*. This book reveals Isabelle Waldberg to have been her own inspiration, in life as in art. *Luminaire* was both a celebration of her experience, and a prototype for Marcel Duchamp's *Given: 1. The Waterfall, 2. The Illuminating Gas*.

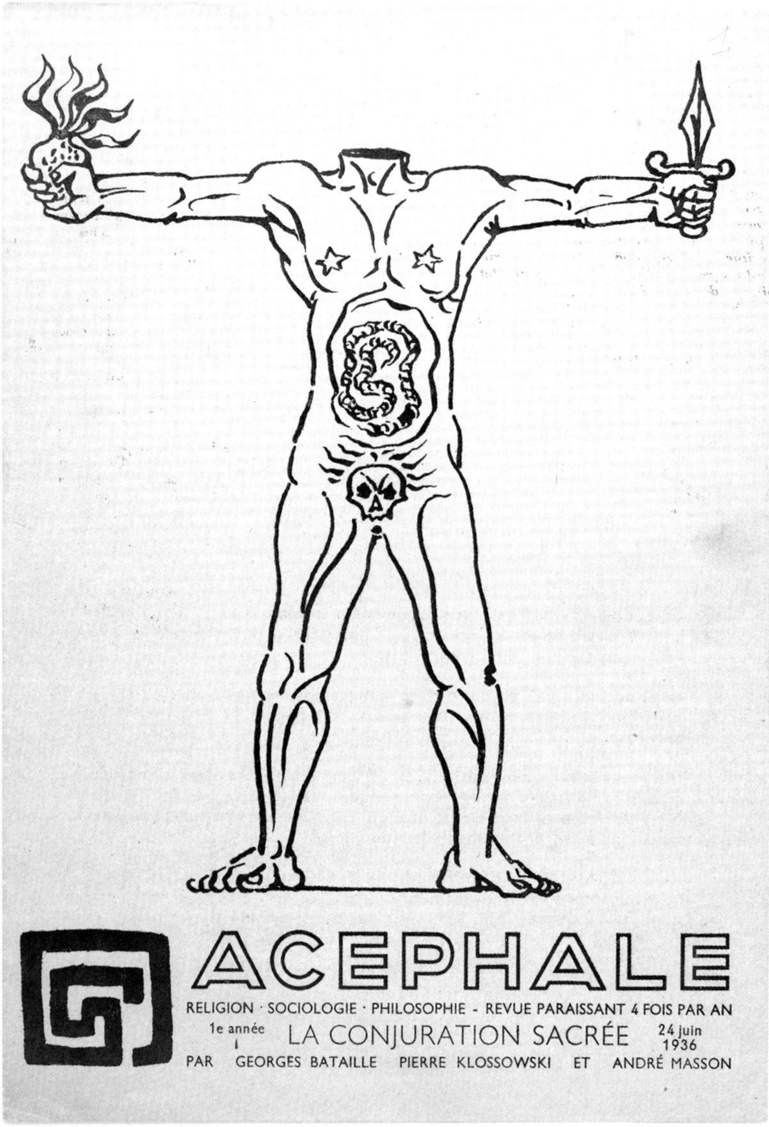

FIGURE 7.1

André Masson

La Conjuration sacrée / The Sacred Conspiracy, cover of *Acéphale*, no. 1, June 24, 1936

25 × 18 cm

Bibliothèque Kandinsky, Musée National d'Art Moderne, Centre Georges Pompidou, Paris, France, inv. no. P381

7 ACÉPHALE

To discover the unity of dread and bliss, these two faces of the same divinity (indeed, they reveal themselves as a single face that presents itself differently according to the way in which we see it): that is the essential meaning and theme ...

—Rainer Maria Rilke, 1923[1]

Isabelle and Patrick Waldberg formally separated in 1953 and, while remaining on good terms, they eventually divorced in 1965. During the late 1930s, however, the Waldbergs shared a history that is essential to understanding Isabelle Waldberg's unique place in the development of Duchamp's work. Their correspondence was published by their son Michel Waldberg under the title *Un amour acéphale*.[2] This title, which translates as "Headless Love," explicitly refers to Acéphale—the secret society formed in 1936 by Georges Bataille, with whom the Waldbergs were intimately involved. *Un amour acéphale* is not only a fascinating record of French intellectual and artistic life in exile; it also contains rare evidence of esoteric erotic activity on the part of two of Duchamp's collaborators.

Isabelle Waldberg was a free spirit who derived an income from the sale of her erotic drawings and small sculptures. Patrick's activity was more politically subversive. He had met Georges Bataille in the early 1930s in the context of Boris Souvarine's *Cercle communiste démocratique*. Expelled from France for his political activism in 1936, Patrick returned to his birthplace in southern California and was in the process of reestablishing himself there when, early in 1937, he received by mail the first issue of Bataille's journal *Acéphale*, subtitled *La Conjuration sacrée* or "Sacred Conspiracy."

Enclosed was a letter from Bataille urging him to return to France. According to Patrick, "In this letter he announced to me the formation of a secret society comprising a ceremony of initiation, of rites, and the acceptance of a change of mode of life destined to separate out the adepts without being externally visible to a world now regarded as secular. This was the sign, the trigger … for playing out the direction of a life. Though I had already taken measures for a definite settlement in the United States, the mad project of Bataille, because he was so insane, instantly overthrew mine and, ceasing my affairs, I re-embarked for France."[3] His account of that moment conveys the sheer charisma of this man, whom Patrick would faithfully serve and support until Bataille's death in 1962.

Georges Bataille receives what may seem an inordinate amount of attention in this book about Marcel Duchamp. There are reasons for this. Duchamp and Bataille not only knew each other, but worked together on several projects. As we shall see in chapter 8, Bataille would appear to have been an important underground influence on the Surrealist Exhibition of 1938, for which Duchamp served as "Generator-Arbitrator." Most importantly, while Duchamp was secretive about his sources, Bataille wrote openly about the parallels between his meditation techniques and Asian traditions and practices. He thus offers a solid case study on which to base speculations about the Asian philosophical perspectives and tantra yoga practices that served as resources for Marcel Duchamp's art and life.

Born in 1897, Georges Bataille was a major figure in French twentieth-century philosophy and literature. Some of his obsessions—which included eroticism, but also preoccupations with filth, excrement, violence, and death—met with disapproval from French existentialists like Sartre and mainstream surrealists like André Breton, whose "Surrealism" was modeled on alchemy and involved reconciliation of opposites in pursuit of a transcendent ideal. For Bataille, art was not the pursuit of an ideal, but pursuit of the *sur*real, as the inventor of the term, Guillaume Apollinaire, had first used this neologism in 1917 in the preface to his play *Les Mamelles de Tirésias* (which Bataille checked out from the Bibliothèque Nationale on February 2, 1925).[4] In a variation on the French translation of Nietzsche's *Übermensch* as *le surhomme*, Apollinaire incorporated the French preposition *sur* in his *drame surréaliste* to indicate a drama of heightened reality as an ongoing experiential process of destruction and creation: "A complete universe with its creator."[5]

Bataille's goal was not to transcend reality, but to merge and morph with it in a process of rapturous psychosomatic experience. Specifically, the terrifying reality of death was to be realized and embraced to the point of ecstasy. The result was an exhilarating awareness of *absence* at the center of existence. In his essay "The Absence of Myth," published in the catalogue to the Breton/Duchamp-organized exhibition *Le Surréalisme en 1947*, Bataille wrote: "The *absence of God* is no longer a closure: it is the opening up to the infinite."[6] For Bataille, such radical opening to infinitely heterogeneous, ever-shifting reality demanded nothing less than complete dismantling of the conditioned rational mind. The practitioner had to become *acéphale*—headless.

Like Duchamp, Bataille was an outlier. His translator and biographer Stuart Kendall describes his corpus as "an assault on the concept of autonomy, whether of individuals, objects, images or texts"[7]—a characterization that also applies to Duchamp's *œuvre*. He had other things in common with Duchamp, including attendance at the École Nationale des Chartes, where Duchamp had studied in 1912–1913, and from which Bataille graduated in February 1922. They shared on-again, off-again sources of income as librarians, as well as tendencies toward asceticism and licentiousness that were only apparently contradictory.[8] Bataille emulated Duchamp's friend Apollinaire by publishing pornographic novels. Best known is *Histoire de l'œil* (*History of the Eye*), published in 1928 under the pseudonym Lord Auch—Lord "To the Shithouse," "*auch*" being a contraction of "*aux chiottes*," to the latrines.

Bataille lacked Duchamp's penetrating humor, but otherwise Duchamp was temperamentally and philosophically closer to Bataille than to André Breton, who, according to Robert Lebel, "remained a vulnerable person, often buffeted by crises, exile, disappointments, and insults." Duchamp, Lebel added, "felt free from any 'thesis' or allegiance. He thought his existence in the world was completely his own and that he owed nothing to anyone but himself."[9] Duchamp's stance as Lebel describes it is close to Max Stirner's, but also close to that of Bataille, who, like Duchamp, had read Stirner's *The Ego and Its Own*.[10] Finally, both Duchamp and Bataille were fans of Nietzsche, who had read Eugène Burnouf's translations of Indian Buddhist texts and been influenced by Asian perspectives, including Taoism.[11] Bataille's edited collection of excerpts from Nietzsche—*Memorandum*, published by Gallimard in 1945—was the only volume of Nietzsche's writings in Duchamp's "library" at the time of his death.[12]

In 1963 Bataille was memorialized in a special issue of *Critique* (a journal he had founded in 1946) with articles by colleagues like Raymond Queneau and Michel Leiris, as well as younger intellectuals including Roland Barthes and Michel Foucault—who would introduce his multivolume *Œuvres complètes* of Bataille with the words: "We know it today: Bataille is one of the most important writers of his century."[13] Barthes's article in *Critique* is entitled "The Metaphor of the Eye," from the title of Bataille's novel. He focused on the linguistic aspects of Bataille's writing, and this is the context within which Bataille has largely been considered—as "a key figure in the history of what we call theory. He was a direct interlocutor for the French existentialists, for psychoanalyst Jacques Lacan, for the Surrealists, and a powerful influence on Michel Foucault, Julia Kristeva, Jacques Derrida."[14] More recently, however, another Bataille has emerged: the atheistic but intensely mystical Georges Bataille first described by Jean Bruno, Bataille's colleague at the Bibliothèque Nationale. In an article in this same issue of *Critique* entitled "Techniques of Illumination in Georges Bataille," Bruno detailed Bataille's progress from "Access to Silence" to "A Yoga Stripped of Moral and Metaphysical Excrescences."[15]

The source of Bataille's philosophy and practice was personal experience—a horrific childhood with a suicidal mother and a blind, syphilitic father whom Georges and his mother abandoned to a solitary death during World War I. (Bataille was conscripted but released early after being diagnosed with tuberculosis.) The suffering, degradation, and death of his father, who may have physically abused the young Bataille, became a complex lifelong project of atonement. Bataille entitled one of his books, written between September 1939 (the month World War II began) and October 1943, *Le Coupable*—"Guilty."[16] In a chapter entitled "The Point of Ecstasy," he describes ecstasy as "The lost movement of a blind man, arms raised, eyes wide open, fixedly regarding the sun and himself, within, becoming light."[17]

In *Inner Experience*, published in 1943, Bataille described an early transformation of anguish caused by "a separation that was a little cruel" into rapture. About this moment in 1933, he recalled: "I was sick, in bed—I remember a beautiful afternoon sun—I suddenly glimpsed the identity of my pain—that a departure had just caused—with an ecstasy, a sudden rapture."[18] Only in retrospect did he understand that he had instinctively discovered Buddhism's second truth: to overcome suffering, it is necessary to perceive the "identity" or origin of suffering in the human tendency to cling to what is impermanent, bound to change. But Bataille would go beyond the Buddha's recognition that suffering is caused not simply by desire, but by clinging—resistance to change. Bataille's ultimate source of "rapture" would be to *embrace* change, and to be absorbed by it.

In a section of *Inner Experience* entitled "Torture" (*Supplice*), Bataille describes another spontaneous event—a "glimpse," a premonition, of the path he would eventually travel:

> Fifteen years ago (perhaps a little more), I returned from I don't know where, late at night. The rue de Rennes was deserted. Coming from Saint-Germain, I crossed the rue du Four (the post office side). I held in my hand an open umbrella and I believe it wasn't raining. (But I hadn't been drinking; I say it, I'm sure.) I had this umbrella open without needing it (if not for what I will speak about later). I was very young then, chaotic and full of empty drunkenness: a round of indecent, dizzying ideas, but already full of anxieties, rigor, and crucifying, running their course. ... In this shipwreck of reason, anguish, solitary degradation, baseness, worthlessness came due: a little later the festivity started again.

Bataille was observing his mind spinning intoxicating ideas that were tangled and restrained by guilty emotions. Then the tension mysteriously broke. The absurdity of the situation revealed itself, and Bataille experienced an exhilarating foretaste of death:

> a collision with the "impossible," burst in my head. A space constellated with laughter opened its dark abyss before me. Crossing the rue du Four, I became in this unknown "nothingness," suddenly ... I rushed into a kind of rapture. I laughed divinely: the umbrella came down on my head covering me (I covered myself expressly with this black shroud). I laughed as perhaps no one had ever laughed, the final depth of each thing opened, laid bare, as if I were dead.

> I don't know if I stopped, in the middle of the street, masking my delirium under an umbrella. Perhaps I jumped (no doubt it's illusory): I was convulsively illuminated, I laughed, I imagine, while running.

Bataille's mental adventure, dramatic as it was, changed nothing: "Doubt fills me with anguish without respite." "What does illumination mean?" He asks himself. He quotes his hero, Nietzsche: "'I teach the art of turning anguish into delight.'"[19]

In *Guilty*, Bataille described the preliminary yoga meditation practice he was eventually taught by an anonymous friend:

> It is good to maintain a relaxed but steady and "flowing" body position. Personal opportunities exist, but first we might trust effective methods: deep breathing, concentrating attention on the breath, as on the intuited secret of all life. To the flow of images, and to relieve the flight of ideas from the fact of endless associations, we can suggest the help of obsessive words and phrases [i.e., mantras], equivalent to the immobile bed of a river. ... For several days, life enters an empty darkness. A marvelous relaxation results. Unlimited power is revealed to the mind, the universe is available to desire, but trouble comes quick.[20]

Through focused breathing meditation Bataille eventually achieved freedom of mind and a sensation of ecstatic love that encompassed the entire universe. But "trouble comes quick." Bataille does not say what kind of trouble. It may be internal: "The mind moves in a strange world where anguish and ecstasy take shape," he wrote in the Foreword to *Inner Experience*.[21] The "trouble" may also be external, having to do with something Bataille points out earlier in the chapter: "These principles oppose morality, which is necessarily leveling."[22]

Bataille's description is followed by a brief mention of how he first learned to practice meditative yoga: "In the first movement, the traditional precepts are irrefutable; they are marvelous. I got them from one of my friends, who got them from an oriental source."[23] Who was this friend kind enough to school Bataille in the basics of yogic breathing practice? Bataille never said precisely who taught him the meditation practice described above. His biographer Michel Surya guessed it was Bataille's colleague at the Bibliothèque Nationale, Jean Bruno, "although this is not certain."[24] No one has come up with a better idea, and Surya's speculation has become more or less accepted as fact. Bataille, on the other hand, was very specific about having received the "traditional precepts ... from one of my friends, who got them from an oriental source." This "oriental source" would not have been textual, since Bataille (who was at least as well read as Bruno) made it clear that "the written tradition is hardly more than an introduction to the oral one."[25] Bataille thus placed himself squarely within a European lineage of Asian oral teachings, but precisely who his guru was remained undocumented.

Bataille's ultimate goal was to escape cognition and take refuge in the fecund realm of "empty darkness"—nothingness, the only place where life is finally illuminated. Bataille wanted to experience death without actually dying. Sex was as close as he could come before the end of 1938, when he learned tantra yoga and adapted it to his own needs: "*religious eroticism*, the identity of horror and the religious. ... Only an interminable detour allows us to reach that instant where the contraries seem visibly conjoined, where the religious horror disclosed in sacrifice becomes linked to the abyss of eroticism."[26] It was probably the same friend who taught Bataille yogic breathing practice who would initiate him into the practice of tantra yoga. Soon thereafter, Bataille began integrating into his meditations intense visualizations of self-sacrifice based on the Tibetan rite of *chöd*.

In the chöd ritual, vividly described by Alexandra David-Néel in her 1929 book *Mystiques et magiciens du Thibet*, the practitioner experiences his body being torn apart and offered as a sacrifice to all beings. In light of the title of Bataille's secret society—Acéphale, "Headless"—it is significant that a key element of the chöd rite is decapitation:

> The celebrant ... imagines that a feminine deity, which esoterically personifies his own will, springs from the top of his head and stands before him, sword in hand. With one stroke she cuts off the head of the *naljorpa* ["one who has attained perfect serenity"]. Then, while troops of ghouls crowd round for the feast, the goddess severs his limbs, skins him and rips open his belly. The bowels fall out, the blood flows like a river, and the hideous guests bite here and there, masticate noisily, while the celebrant excites and urges them with the liturgic words of unreserved surrender: "For ages, in the course of renewed births I have borrowed from countless living beings—at the cost of their welfare and life. ... Today I pay my debt, offering for destruction this body which I have held so dear.

> I give my flesh to the hungry, my blood to the thirsty, my skin to clothe those who are naked, my bones as fuel to those who suffer from cold. I give my happiness to the unhappy ones. I give my breath to bring back the dying to life. …"
>
> [The practitioner] must realize that the very idea of sacrifice is but an illusion, an offshoot of blind, groundless pride. In fact, he *has nothing* to give away, because he *is nothing*.[27]

I quote this passage at length because Bataille is too often reductively portrayed as "the metaphysician of evil … interested in sex, death, degradation, and the power and potential of the obscene."[28] The reality behind the stereotype is more complex. Chöd derives from the Bodhisattva tradition and stories of previous lives of the Buddha.[29] As David-Néel's account demonstrates, the offering of one's own body can be the highest form of compassion and the ultimate generosity. The body becomes what is "*Given*," to cite the title of Duchamp's last work (figure 0.1)—a sacrifice whose focus is nothingness.

Bataille concluded his own last work, *Tears of Eros*, with a series of photographs documenting the public execution of a naked murderer through the Chinese torture "of the *Hundred Pieces*, reserved for the gravest of crimes." The images are horrifically violent, at once fascinating and sickening. The natural response is to try and imagine the suffering of the victim. This is difficult, because his face expresses not agony, but ecstasy. (Bataille speculated that this was an effect of opium, administered "to prolong the torture"; others have concluded that the victim was in fact quite dead at this point.) It is not hard to understand why Bataille, with his twin obsessions with death and sexual ecstasy, had been haunted by these photographs since they were first shown to him by his psychoanalyst in the mid-1920s. "This photograph had a decisive role in my life," Bataille wrote. He then shifts directly to a discussion of yoga: "Much later, in 1938, a friend initiated me into the practice of yoga. It was on this occasion that I discerned, in the violence of this image, an infinite capacity for reversal. Through this violence … I was so stunned that I reached the point of ecstasy. … What I suddenly saw, and what imprisoned me in anguish—but which at the same time delivered me from it—was the identity of these perfect contraries, divine ecstasy and its opposite, extreme horror."[30]

Alexandra David-Néel had stressed that the practitioner of chöd "must realize that the very idea of sacrifice is but an illusion. … In fact, he *has nothing* to give away, because he *is nothing*." Chöd is a Mahāyāna Buddhist *Prajñāpāramitā* ("Perfection of Wisdom") practice. This "perfected" way of seeing the nature of reality is associated with the doctrine of emptiness or nothingness, a concept personified in Hinduism by the goddess Kali, the "Great Mother"—Bataille's "abyss of eroticism." Physical erotic activity (along with alcohol, Bataille's previous preferred method of escape from psychological suffering) could not compare with yoga's mental "detour" to "that instant" in which Bataille blissfully experienced the contraries of ecstasy and suffering conjoined.

••

I would argue that both Duchamp and Bataille owed a large part of whatever integration they achieved to yogic mind practices, but there were important differences. Judging by evidence in his work, Duchamp's earliest instruction appears to have occurred around 1910–1911. Robert Lebel's roman à clef *La double vue* implies that the young Duchamp absorbed a type of Westernized tantric yoga as taught by Mirra Alfassa, who learned it from Max and Alma Théon. Despite extensive explorations of other systems, Duchamp's practice appears to have remained grounded in Kundalini-type body energetics involving unification and transformation of sexual energies. (As his stepson Paul Matisse recalled, "Marcel conducted his own research and, when he reached the stage where the opposites were able to live together, he held himself there.")[31] Whatever personal and/or professional crises may have occasioned them, Duchamp's explorations and experimentations were fundamentally pragmatic, in the service of his art, which Duchamp reframed as an art of life.

In contrast, one might characterize Bataille's art as an art of death—or, better, the art of turning death into art. He was driven by personal demons and had undergone psychotherapy, which Duchamp scorned. Bataille grew up in a nonreligious household, but converted to Catholicism in 1914 at the age of seventeen and remained a devout Catholic for nine years. He considered entering the priesthood and attended a Catholic seminary briefly but quit, apparently partly in order to pursue an occupation that would allow him to support his mother. He renounced Christianity in the early 1920s, but continued to practice "Simple Contemplation"—an experiential method described in Saint Ignatius of Loyola's *Spiritual Exercises* (1522–1524). He had read Romain Rolland's biographies of Ramakrishna (1929) and Vivekananda (1930), and owned the 1930 edition of Vivekananda's *Raja Yoga*, which he "heavily annotated."[32] His first experiments with meditation were based on these and other textual sources, which seem not to have been particularly effective. "The written tradition is hardly more than an introduction to the oral one," Bataille later admitted.

Bataille's interest in erotic and sacrificial practices led him to Nietzsche and to comparative history, including the cult of Dionysus and the belief system of the Aztecs. He was also fascinated by tantric practices. In an article from 1930 in his journal *Documents*, Bataille discussed lurid accounts of sacrifices to Kali—wife of Shiva in Hinduism; representing ultimate reality in Shakta Hindu and tantric sects. He referred to the writings of "the painter S. Dali,"[33] suggesting that he was in contact with artists in connection with his research, which was both more wide-ranging and more thorough than Duchamp's, and had different results. Bataille's sociophilosophical concept of "sovereignty," for example, emerged primarily from Nietzsche (Sade used the word as well),[34] but would also have been influenced by Mircea Eliade, who wrote: "In India as elsewhere, sovereignty is related to the sacred. The Buddha is the *cakravartin* par excellence, the cosmocrat. … The disciple is assimilated to the sovereign because he rises above the play of cosmic forces; he is autonomous, wholly free. Spiritual freedom—and this is true not only of India—has always been expressed by sovereignty."[35] According to Bataille scholar Stuart Kendall, "inner experience means sovereign experience, not subjective experience; it means experiencing the world not in relation to God, but from the position of God."[36] Bataille's Sovereign was aligned with Duchamp's Roché-bestowed honorific, "Victor." Victory and sovereignty occur when small-*s* self becomes universal Self: *cakravartin*, ruler of the cosmos.

On the other hand, Bataille claimed that Eliade's detailed description of *maithuna*—ritual sexual union—left him "with a feeling of aversion. I keep my passions separate, without mixing them."[37] Bataille almost certainly tried physical tantric techniques only to reject them—not for moral but for ethical reasons. As he explained in a note to *Inner Experience*:

"Tantric *yoga* uses sexual pleasure, not in order to ruin oneself in it but to detach oneself from the object, the woman, whom they use, before the end: they avoid the last moment of pleasure ... entering into possession of interiority, acquiring the mastery of inner movements, detached from the objects of our life. ... Not being easily offended by licentiousness, I find it vile to 'abuse' a woman and pleasure for other ends than themselves, vile certainly to 'exploit' experience, to make it into an affected exercise, as in a competition."[38] Tantra yoga was a mental experience that Bataille apparently kept separate from his physical sexual relations.

We know from Jean Bruno that Bataille experimented with Kundalini yoga, researched tantric rituals, and was planning a book on tantra when he died. "If one knows how to direct it, a powerful sexuality is capable of precipitating inner experience," Bruno wrote.

> Although interested in Tantrism (regarding which he had rediscovered some principles and planned a work), Bataille does not seem to have utilized it. From his first meditations, he perceived that they were capable of neutralizing desire without suppressing feeling. Later he noted that when illumination had been attained, sexual life diminished its intensity, but did not disappear. As the completion of this experience gives more freedom and leads to a surpassing of asceticism, one understands the urgency of developing more efficient accelerated techniques to shorten the initial period.[39]

In other words, once Bataille had mastered tantra yoga's self-administered psychosomatic erotic techniques, he found that he could reduce time spent in preliminary meditational stages.

Bruno repeated Bataille's claim that he did not practice "Tantrism," by which Bruno seems to have meant tantric practice with a sexual partner. Much of tantric practice in India is reportedly the kind of "right-handed" tantra that Bataille practiced: without a partner but in the imagination. It would have been unlike Bataille, however, not to experiment with so-called "left-handed" tantric practices, including ritualistic group sexual activity and the consumption of "forbidden" substances, such as alcohol and sexual fluids.[40] Like Bataille, Bruno may have been obfuscating; or perhaps he was simply being discreet. Whatever the stages of Bataille's development, his preferred meditation practice seems to have been a personal form of tantra yoga that was both mental and solitary. At any rate, this is what is emphasized by Bruno, as well as by Bataille himself.

Bruno informs us that Bataille's "first meditation on peace," probably engendered by the yogic breathing practices Bataille referred to as "traditional precepts," took place at the end of May 1938.[41] On November 7 of that same year Bataille's soul mate Colette Peignot, known as "Laure," died of tuberculosis. Bataille himself contracted tuberculosis during World War I, and never fully recovered. His suffering over Laure's death, and the prospect of his own, must have been profound. Patrick and Isabelle Waldberg moved in with him, and toward the end of 1938 Bataille received what he described as "initiation" into the practice of tantra yoga by "a friend"—most likely the same friend who had taught him preliminary breathing practices in May.

By February 1939, Bruno writes, "on the brink of completing his meditation in a state of excessive tension, [Bataille] felt that he had to avoid brutally interrupting it under penalty of a shock. He relaxed then, and his state suddenly changed, became effusive, ascended, as if caught up in an immense force." He felt in "the obscure but very powerful grip of an element external to himself, and to which he was bound in contemplation."[42] Bataille described this experience as one of connection: "'to go the furthest possible' has no meaning once one has recognized the primacy of a 'continuum.' By *continuum*, I mean the continuous surroundings of the human group, opposed to a rudimentary representation of indivisible and decidedly separated *individuals*." He added a note: "The separation of beings, the abyss separating *you* from *me*, usually has a primary meaning. ... If it is true that in one case, that in a given time the passage from *you* to *me* has a continuous character, the apparent discontinuity of beings is no longer a fundamental quality."[43] For Bataille, who so valued communication and community, this experience of continuum must have been exhilarating indeed.

His description notably echoes the title of Duchamp's "résumé of things made earlier," the painting *Tu m'*—"You Are Me" (1918, figure 4.6). This title—which, like the work itself, "made no sense"—emphasizes connection and continuum.[44] One of the things *Tu m'* portrays is a passage to the mental state Bataille memorialized with the name of his secret society, Acéphale, in which their mutual friend Isabelle Waldberg played a pivotal role.

••

In order to understand these interconnections, we need to know more about the morphing rituals of Acéphale, conceived by Georges Bataille in April 1936 in response to the intensifying threat of war.[45] Previously he had been involved in groups whose aims were more purely sociopolitical.[46] In reaction to the looming threat of another world war, however, Bataille created Acéphale to serve as a platform for developing personal and communal energies. The preliminary program, written in April 1936, was socioreligious in nature.[47] But Bataille's goals were far from utopian, and what he was offering had nothing to do with passive resistance.

Bataille connected violence with virility, and it played a prominent role in his fiction, as well as his essays.[48] Violence would manifest in Acéphale with Bataille's insistence on the importance of sacrifice, and in his elaborate commemorations of the beheading of Louis XVI in the Place de la Concorde. That event related directly to the central point of Acéphale's preliminary program: "To realize the universal fulfillment of personal being in the irony of the world of animals, and by the revelation of a headless universe as a game, not as a state or obligation."[49] This two-pronged goal boiled down to experiential realization of interdependence, along with recognition of the random nature of the universe. Both are opposed to hierarchy—whether of king, state, or morality.

Acéphale's insignia was André Masson's drawing of a headless man (figure 7.1)—described by one Acéphale member as an "image depicting a man without a head; an image of reality, of life and of the Universe; reality intolerable to contemplation and inaccessible to intellectual speculation, but the only object of the all-consuming love of those who desire existence as a whole."[50] An obvious riff on Leonardo's *Vitruvian Man*, Masson's *Acéphale* was a new kind of Universal Man—an image of the Universe as universal *being*, without a head and thus without purpose or aim. His labyrinthine gut refers to Nietzsche's labyrinth of the soul. The death's head in place of his sex signifies, from Bataille's prospectus for Acéphale: "the universal fulfillment of personal being in the irony of the world of animals," where sex and death are inextricably linked.[51]

As an organization, Acéphale was a three-legged stool consisting of a journal, *Acéphale*, which Bataille published in five numbers between June 1936 and June 1939;[52] a discussion group, the Collège de Sociologie, led by Bataille, Roger Caillois, and Michel Leiris;[53] and an esoteric coterie whose membership overlapped only slightly with the two exoteric aspects. This secret society would be composed of "participants"—initiates who took part in discussions and in preliminary rituals in the forest—and "adepts" who additionally took part in rituals whose details remained murky even following Bataille's death in 1962.[54] Acéphale "conceived itself as a secret society," Stuart Kendall aptly wrote, "in the strict sense that it was a society of *secrets*, a group founded on mysteries about which *one could not speak*."[55]

Original members of the secret society listed by Bataille in his "Constitution of the Interior Journal" in February 1937 were physicist Georges ("Zino") Ambrosino, Georges Bataille, Germanophile architect Jacques Chavy, mathematician René Chenon, historian Henri Dubief, Pierre Dugan (aka Pierre Andler), Henri Dussat, Imre Kelemen, and Pierre Klossowski, elder brother of the painter Balthus. Members came and (mostly) went, so it is difficult to devise a definitive list. Other early members appear to have included Jean Atlan, Alain Girard, and Jean Dautry.[56] Bataille's partner Laure (Colette Peignot) was to be proposed as a member at a group meeting in December 1937. Whether or not Laure was ever a formal participant, evidence suggests she was an important presence at the "interior gatherings" (*réunions intérieures*) in 1938, until tuberculosis took her life early in November of that year.

Acéphale met every month on the new moon in the forest of Marly, at the foot of an oak that had been struck by lightning. Initiates were given a map, along with Bataille's instructions, to be carefully read "several times," and memorized. Bataille's "Instructions for the 'Encounter' (*Rencontre*) in the Forest" included buying a return ticket from Gare Saint-Lazare to Saint-Nom-la-Bretèche and finding a seat on the train without speaking to anyone. At Saint-Nom, initiates were to leave the train and march single-file toward the left. They were then to follow, in groups of two or three, whoever would be waiting for them, still maintaining silence. They were to march on the path to the forest single file, a few meters apart, to the meeting site, then stop and wait to be led individually to their places. They were to remain motionless and silent until the end of the ceremony, led by Bataille and/or Ambrosino, conducted inside a star-shaped mandala traced on the ground next to the blasted tree. When the session was over, participants were to return as they came. "Without seeming sinister or morose," they were still not to talk at any time. Once back in Paris, they were to depart the station individually. Afterward, all conversation about the meeting, under any pretext, was forbidden.

Bataille also provided information about the physical limits of the gathering place, along with some interpretive information: "It is possible to recognize in this [blasted] tree the mute presence of that which has taken the name Acéphale, expressed in arms without a head. This is the will to seek and to meet a presence that fills our life with reason for being, and which gives these proceedings a sense of opposition to those of others. This ENCOUNTER, which is *attempted* in the forest, will take place in reality insofar as death shines through there. To go beyond this presence is to want to throw open the garment with which our death is covered."[57] Bataille wanted to create a situation in which participants could experience the presence of their own deaths. This goal was not metaphorical or spiritual, but was meant to take place "in reality." Attainment was not guaranteed: the encounter with death by Acéphale members would be "attempted" in the forest. The French word for death is feminine—*la mort*. Bataille's wording, along with his reference to going beyond a mere encounter with death to erotically unveiling her, suggests that there would be further stages.

By autumn 1937 the meetings of the secret society had apparently borne fruit. In advance of the meeting of October 1, 1937 Bataille wrote his members: "We have said from the first ENCOUNTER that what we attempted in the forest would take place insofar as death would appear there: however we can say today that this took place. We are going to *recognize* tonight what we have already *met*. And we do not want to go further into the world where we have discovered a presence." Acéphale members had encountered death, but Bataille apparently did not intend to go further in that direction, meaning that nobody was going to actually die.

Members must have wondered, however, about the potential for human sacrifice in the elaborate scheme Bataille was slowly rolling out. "What took place there was a birth," he went on, "with all the word implies of shattering weakness, but at the same time the hope of power. There was also birth in our own life: that is what we experienced before this presence. Tonight, in the night, we are still looking for this birth, and our birth, in the same way as the first time it was revealed. ... This is the will to seek and to meet a presence that fills our life with *raison d'être*, giving these proceedings a meaning in opposition to the approaches of others."[58] Participants had "met" their deaths. The next steps (to be taken "in opposition to the approaches of others") would be toward the generation and birth of a new self, without fear of death, ready for war.

In a section of *The Gay Science* entitled "The Madman," Nietzsche asked how humankind could possibly atone for its guilt for the murder of God: "What was holiest and mightiest of all that the world has yet owned has bled to death under our knives: who will wipe this blood off us? What water is there for us to clean ourselves? What festivals of atonement, what sacred games shall we have to invent? Is not the greatness of this deed too great for us? Must we ourselves not become gods simply to appear worthy of it?"[59] It is impossible to overestimate Bataille's ambition for Acéphale, which was nothing less than the development of new rituals of cleansing, atonement, and transformation in preparation for impending war in which, as he was all too aware, many would die.

Bataille had spent the previous decade researching comparative religious practices. He was unapologetic about the cherry-picked nature of his rituals, but he dismissed any substantive connection with the religions of either Europe or Asia. His research and his own experience had made it clear that what was required was not only intellectual acceptance of Nietzsche's death of God, but also experiential delight in the fact that there is no "deeper reality," no "*beyond*." Bataille's "joy" had no object beyond generating in his followers—and, not incidentally, in himself—the will to live and to act in the face of impending catastrophe. Born into a headless universe, they would become their own gods.

By the end of 1937 Acéphale was ready to begin moving toward its final goal. Bataille published the results of his research and experimentation in "The Practice of Joy Before Death"—the last essay in the last issue of *Acéphale* (June 1939):

> While it is appropriate to use the word *mysticism* when speaking of "joy before death" and its practice, this implies no more than an affective resemblance between this practice and those of the religions of Asia or Europe. There is no reason to link any presuppositions concerning an alleged deeper reality with a joy that has no object other than immediate life. "Joy before death" belongs only to the person for whom there is no *beyond*; it is the only intellectually honest route in the search for ecstasy.[60]

This practice is perhaps most clearly described in an informational communication Bataille sent in October 1939 after the war had broken out, just before he formally dissolved Acéphale:

> In its origins, joy before death is a formula of mystical meditation. It is a joy before the certainty of death and the foundation of a religious existence separate from Christianity. A man can take the representation of his own death (not the representation of God) as an object of meditation and of ecstasy.
>
> The desired outcome of such a practice can only be death suffered with joy as the fulfillment of a life, but not a search for death that would mean the condemnation of life. Death is not a sovereign good. What can be loved is life, but life is what is lost in death and it is this possibility of getting lost that can be loved to ecstasy.[61]

Bataille's initial goal seems to have been development of a Nietzschean religion that would be effective in a godless universe. The sacrificial aspect dominated the early gatherings, but as the meetings developed the focus shifted to sexual activity and a worship of the vulva that also could have been inspired by Nietzsche, who wrote in the last section of his preface to *The Gay Science* (1887): "'Is it true that God is present everywhere?' a little girl asked her mother; 'I think that's indecent'—a hint for philosophers! ... Perhaps truth is a woman who has reasons for not letting us see her reasons? Perhaps her name is—to speak Greek—*Baubo?*"[62] Baubo was a Greek goddess whose images present the vulva as an object of devotion.

Worship of the vulva as described by Nietzsche remained foundational for Bataille, but the little girl's question is reminiscent of Ramakrishna's "God is in the vagina!"[63] Scholar of comparative religion Hugh B. Urban has emphasized that "Tantric sexual rites do seem to confirm Bataille's key insight that blood sacrifice, violence, and sexual transgression all share a common link: they each involve a kind of 'organized explosion,' or controlled violation of normal social and moral laws which gives birth to a radical sense of freedom, power and liberating ecstasy."[64] By its final year, Bataille's version of Indian tantric practice would dominate the proceedings of Acéphale.

In *Inner Experience* Bataille described at length the "various means of the Hindus," including Advaita Vedanta, "in which Nietzsche saw precursors." He also discussed "the Tantrics," who "have recourse to sexual pleasure: they don't sink into it; it serves as a springboard." He made special note of the Indian "principle of equilibrium" in which ascetic practices balance the strategic deployment of intoxicants and eroticism.[65] Alexandra David-Néel wrote extensively about tantric practices in Tibet and India, including a passage that may have served Bataille as a "springboard": "The Hindu Shaktas hold nocturnal meetings called *chakra* (a circle). During these meetings, both men and women form a circle, each man seated by the side of a woman. The elements of the cult are *panchatatva* (the five elements) which they designate as the five M's, because the Sanskrit name of each of them begins with this letter. They are: *madya*, wine; *mansa*, meat; *matsya*, fish; *mudra*, dried grain; *maithuna*, sexual union. ... The wine which has to be drunk at the *chakra* is real wine and the women with whom one must be united is any woman, *except* one's legitimate wife."[66]

The increasing complexity of the secret meetings called for additional rules. Bataille drew up six new rules for a session on December 28, 1937 having to do with the proposing and integration of new members, how many "adepts" and "participants" were required for a forum, and the differences between main and secondary meetings, where discussion took place.[67] Patrick Waldberg, who would become Bataille's most trusted confidant in the group, was proposed as a "participant" at an organizational meeting of March 8, 1938. (He also served as secretary of the College of Sociology.) Isabelle Waldberg's name appeared as "Isabelle Farner" among others to be "added to the list" in an Acéphale document for the secondary meeting (*réunion sessionnelle*) of July 25, 1938.[68]

By March 1938 Bataille had moved into a house on the outskirts of Saint-Germain-en-Laye; his partner Laure joined him there in July. Patrick

Waldberg later described this house, including its underground passage, in some detail: "It was a peasant dwelling … traditionally said to have been connected to the château by a passage that had long since been obstructed, … those who knew Bataille's house in St. Germain—and there were not many—remained astonished by the atmosphere that emanated from these rooms, and the singular rhythm of the spiritual breath that Bataille had imprinted there."[69] Bataille's Saint-Germain house was within walking distance from the forest of Marly, where the meetings of Acéphale took place. It was probably in March 1938 that the inner meetings following the gatherings at the tree relocated from the ruins of Montjoie in the forest of Marly to Bataille's "peasant dwelling" in Saint-Germain, with its underground passage.

Bataille's consistent instruction was never to speak of what transpired in the secret meetings of Acéphale—"Thereafter, any conversation on the subject of 'encounter' is excluded, under any pretext whatsoever," he wrote in his preliminary program. "What each of us will have to express can be done only as a text intended for the interior journal."[70] Acéphale members more or less obeyed, with the exception of Patrick Waldberg, who in 1977 described his initiation experience in an essay, "Acéphalogramme," which was not published until 1995, ten years after his death. His account includes the lighting of a torch, the burning of sulfur, and the cutting of a "notch" (*entaille*) into Patrick's forearm with a ceremonial dagger like the weapon wielded by Masson's headless man. (It must have been very sharp—the scar was still visible almost forty years later, but Patrick claimed he had not felt "the slightest pain.") This initiation ceremony was followed by a period of group meditation.

Patrick's account of his initiation ends here, except for a mention that after the ceremony the group returned not to the station at Saint-Nom-la-Bretèche, but "this time in the direction of Sainte-Germain-en-Laye," where Bataille and Laure were living.[71] He added another important fact: the monthly meetings on the night of the new moon at the foot of the lightening-struck tree had generated a "communal unity" that led to the "establishment of new rules of life." Members' time began to be divided into "periods of tension and periods of license. During the first, silence and a certain asceticism were recommended [by Bataille] to members of the community. ... The periods of license, on the other hand, allowed all the excesses, including those involved in promiscuity."[72]

Patrick Waldberg was accepted as an adept on September 19, 1938, and the initiation ceremony he described probably took place later that month. A statement of August 30, entitled "The Image of Death," may have been his qualifying thesis. "The image of Death is linked to Passion," Patrick wrote: "It cannot arise with any force unless total existence is in play. Death ... finds itself, terrible and magnificent, when two lovers at the most intense moment of their union mutually give themselves to death. Each of the lovers has broken the habitual bonds that united them with the world; even the bonds that united each to the Other have disappeared. Each finds himself alone; and only at that moment does the image of Death have meaning."[73]

Bataille's lover Laure died of tuberculosis on November 7, 1938, at the house in Saint-Germain-en-Laye where she and Bataille had moved the previous spring—really died, not just the rehearsal their group had been practicing. During this time of crisis Patrick and Isabelle Waldberg moved into the Saint-Germain-en-Laye house with Bataille, who received his second lesson in tantra yoga soon thereafter. Both experiences changed his approach to Acéphale and its rituals. Up to this point, Bataille had adapted and applied a range of initiatory and sacrificial practices drawn primarily from Dionysian rites to evoke both in himself and in his Acéphale adepts the experience of "getting lost" in death. Some of these would have been erotic in nature, and may have included the participation of prostitutes recruited by Bataille and Laure in Saint-Germain-en-Laye.

The life Bataille and Laure had lived together involved not only heavy drinking and promiscuity, but rigorous travel as well. Their lifestyle may have hastened Laure's demise, causing Bataille's instinct for guilt to flare, threatening his own life. After the Waldbergs moved in with him, Patrick observed that Bataille's "rules of frugality and austerity during the periods of tension were quite strictly observed."[74] It was around this time that Bataille received inner teachings in tantric yoga, adding visualization practices to the yogic breathing practice he had learned the previous May. Naturally, Bataille's *yidam* (his personal deity and object of meditation) was Death, specifically, the image of death by torture he had been given by his psychiatrist more than ten years earlier. This final stage of Bataille's training enabled the breakthrough he wrote about in *Guilty*: "It was on this occasion that I discerned ... an infinite capacity for reversal. ... I was so stunned that I reached the point of ecstasy."[75] Acéphale's second phase was about to begin.

Sometime in the first part of 1939 Bataille wrote down for Isabelle Waldberg his techniques for the Practice of Joy Before Death. In a nod to Apollinaire, he entitled this exercise *L'étoile Alcool. Texte de méditation* ("The Star Spirit. Meditation Text"). *Alcools* ("*Spirits*," 1913), was the title of Apollinaire's first major published collection of poetry. Bataille's recitation included the following lines: "The depth of space is joy in the face of death. ... The sun, ardor, alcohol, blinding *light* turning closed and bursting eyes to undo breath. All the depth of the sky like an orgy of icy *light*, losing itself, fleeing ..."[76] Isabelle Waldberg would entitle her 1946 sculpture of a vulva opening to "the depth of space" *Luminaire* ("Light," figure 6.20).

Through his practice of tantra yoga, Bataille had finally realized death transformed by the power of Eros into ecstasy. With war more of a certainty every day, he wanted to make his experience available to other Acéphale adepts. In early 1939 he sent Patrick Waldberg a note: "What happened seems to me suddenly to impose on us the extreme harshness, the extreme rigor of which we have hitherto spoken. Please reflect on this, and consider also any evasion in your reflection. ... I propose, for the whole organization, to envisage solutions that are the most radical, in every sense. Half-measures and false pretenses have become impossible, stifling. We need our faces raw, whether naked or masked, and no more ripplings of uncertainty." Partly because Bataille's note is not precisely dated, it is impossible to know whether, in referring to "what happened," Bataille meant his own personal experience, or an international political event. One possibility: on March 15, 1939, Germany invaded Czechoslovakia. This unmistakable step toward war may have served Bataille as a pretext for an equally radical response by Acéphale. He urged Patrick to embrace "the mystical experience demanded by the erotic experience," which alone is capable of overcoming prejudices. "At the point where we are, it is out of the question not to do everything possible to burn like fire."[77]

Bataille is suggesting that some new form of physical sexual practice is in the offing for his little band of adepts. He may have addressed this proposal to Patrick because he wanted Isabelle to replace Laure as the main female focus in this enterprise. Bataille's tantric inspiration is betrayed by his characterization of the erotic experience as an *ascetic* practice built upon a rigorous period of preparation followed by a mystical release—what Patrick later described as periods of tension leading up to periods of license. On May 31, 1939, Bataille wrote Acéphale members that their previous pact revealed only a "larval and sickly existence." He called for an end to "half measures," reminding his followers "that what exists between us is *inflexible* and will prevail; it is something that could become a drama and which can in no way end in comedy. ... I take it upon myself to observe the rules of closed [*fermés*] days not only within the agreed limits, but also on all asexual days and, if necessary, even every day. I will add nothing to this letter. I will not refer to anything. But each among us ought to know that, the next time he meets me, he will find himself in the presence of a changed man."[78]

Acéphale was on its way to some kind of culmination. How did it all play out? Bataille never put in writing what went on at the tumultuous penultimate inner meeting. Thanks to Patrick Waldberg, we know that by the end Acéphale membership had dwindled dramatically: "At the last meeting in the heart of the forest we were only four [incuding Patrick, Isabelle, and Ambrosino]. Bataille solemnly asked the three others to put him to death so that sacrifice, founding a myth, would assure the survival of the community. This favor was refused him. Several months later real war raged, sweeping away what remained of hope."[79] Bataille later admitted the folly of attempting to develop an esoteric religion for the modern era: "I then thought myself drawn to found a religion, at least in a paradoxical form," he wrote in a "Notice" to a later edition of *Guilty*. "It was a monstrous mistake."[80]

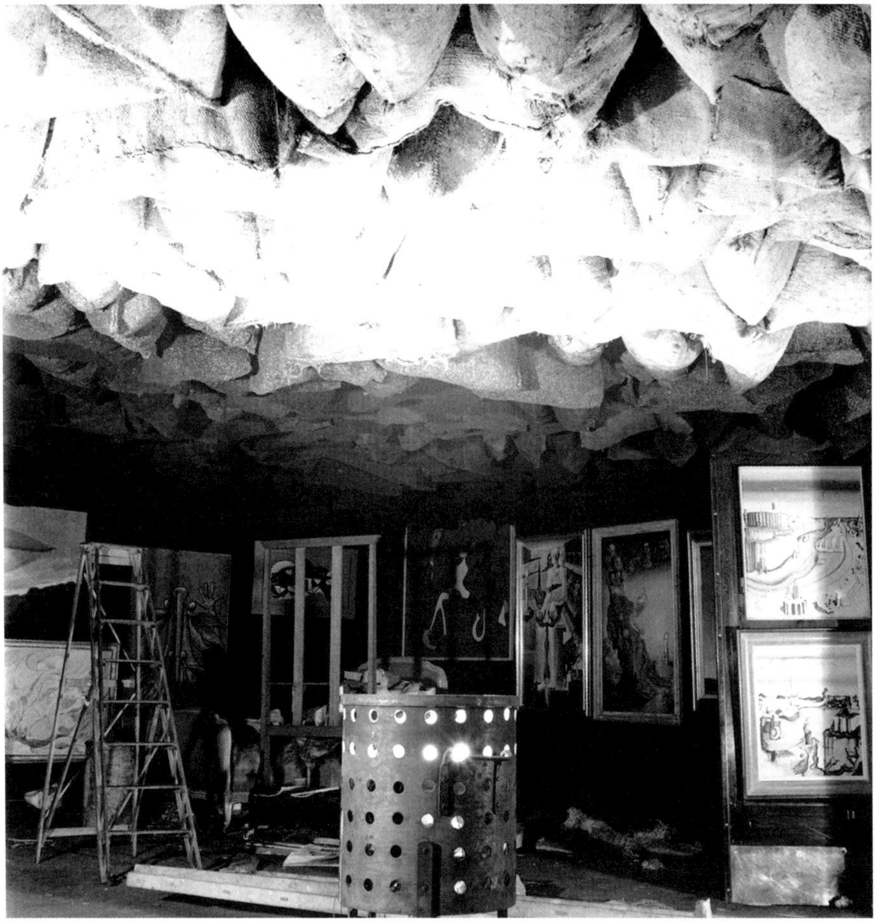

FIGURE 8.1

Marcel Duchamp

Exposition Internationale du Surréalisme, Paris, Galérie des Beaux-Arts, January–February 1938

Interior of the main room during installation; concept by Marcel Duchamp, including *1,200 Coal Sacks*

8 SUMPTUOUS SUBTERRANEAN CEREMONY

ÉROTISME—Cérémonie fastueuse dans un souterrain.

***—Dictionnaire abrégé du surréalisme*, 1938**[1]

Precisely what went on during the secret, "inner" meetings of Acéphale remains a source of conjecture. Isabelle Waldberg's husband Patrick wrote in 1977 that during Acéphale's last year, Bataille "instituted oriental practices, to which he brought the corrective of his own method of illumination."[2] He referred readers to Jean Bruno's essay on the Asian techniques adapted by Bataille to achieve his unique version of enlightenment.[3] But Bruno wrote only about Bataille's textual sources and the stages of his spiritual development, saying nothing about the specific practices he introduced into Acéphale.

Mostly overlooked has been a fictionalized account by the French author Michel Fardoulis-Lagrange, whose novel *G. B. ou un ami présomptueux* (*G. B. or a Presumptuous Friend*) appeared in 1969, seven years after Bataille's death. It was almost certainly based on information obtained from core Acéphale members Patrick and Isabelle Waldberg, and possibly from Bataille himself. Fardoulis-Lagrange took refuge with Bataille in Vézelay from April through June 1943 before being incarcerated as a communist propagandist. (He was freed by the Resistance in 1944.) Patrick Waldberg's personal experiences with Bataille and Acéphale would appear to have informed and perhaps even inspired *G. B.*, while Isabelle Waldberg's illustrations are critical to understanding the novel's hallucinatory text.[4]

Like Robert Lebel's *La double vue, suivi de L'inventeur du temps gratuit* five years earlier, *G. B.* was published by François Di Dio, director of Éditions Le Soleil Noir. Di Dio's partner both in business and in life was the scholar of Indian culture Nicole Ménant, who coedited and translated the first book on tantric art published in France—Ajit Mookerjee's *Tantra Asana* (1971). Beginning in the early 1960s, Di Dio began publishing the same text in three simultaneous limited and numbered editions. For both *La double vue* and *G. B.*, there was a collectors' edition, issued with original works of art and published in fewer than 100 copies; the "Club du Soleil Noir" edition, comprising 150–300 copies that included a single multiple artwork; and finally, there was what we would now call the trade edition, published in pocket format with a cover illustration.[5]

The cover for *G. B.* (figure 8.2) features a horizontal design identical to that of Robert Lebel's *La double vue, suivi de L'inventeur du temps gratuit*

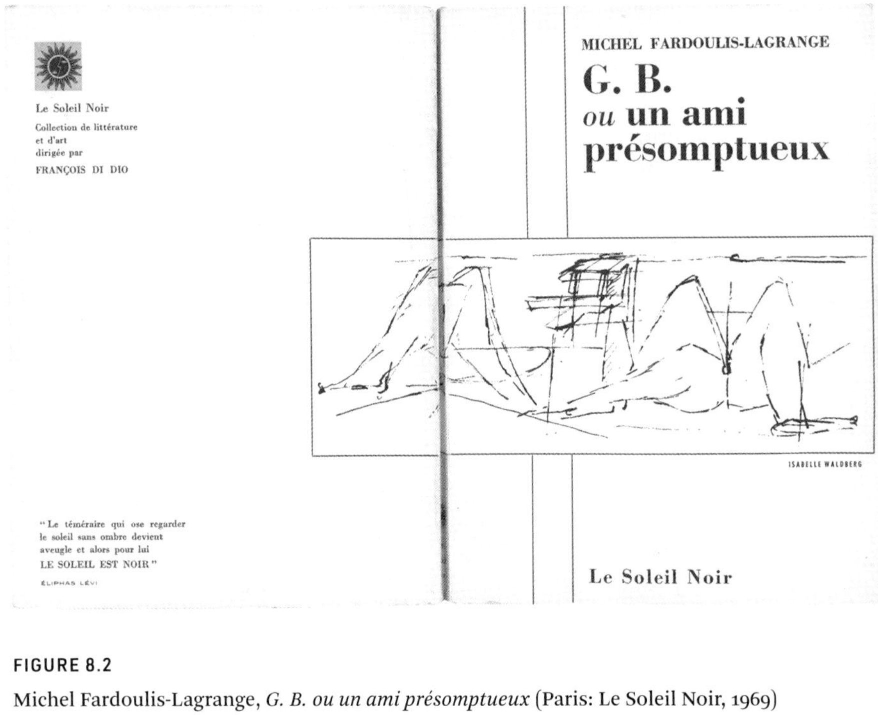

FIGURE 8.2

Michel Fardoulis-Lagrange, *G. B. ou un ami présomptueux* (Paris: Le Soleil Noir, 1969)
Cover illustration by Isabelle Waldberg

(figure 2.2). The images on the covers of both books are repeated, or doubled, with the left-hand figure wrapping around the spine of the book. But in place of *La double vue*'s images of a woman's head by Isabelle Waldberg's friend Giacometti, the cover of *G. B.* features a sketchy drawing by Waldberg herself featuring two naked, recumbent women with legs spread, a blocky object between them. Significantly, the women's heads are not visible: they are *acéphale*.

Why are there *two* women, and what is the blocky object? It may be that Waldberg wanted to create a cover with another "double view," connecting her book with that of her long-time lover Robert Lebel. If so, then this is the same woman in two different moments, as on the cover of *La double vue*. Or perhaps the two women refer to two female participants in Acéphale's secret meetings. As for the object between them, it appears to be a stove, which in this context would seem to represent "fire down below."

The multiples issued with the deluxe edition of *G. B.* were even more graphic than the cover drawing. Engraved with a steel-tipped stylus on aluminum sheets cut and glued onto opaque black Plexiglas, the images depict a woman's spread legs and vulva, now the riveting focus of attention (figure 8.3). In a text for the inside cover flap of the trade edition, Robert Lebel teasingly described "the plastic contribution of Isabelle Waldberg, who was the only female affiliate of Acéphale and who sets at the threshold of this book-trap a sort of household deity of Silence, prolonged by graphic screens that weave their trembling and nocturnal gestures in unison with the text."[6] Lebel stressed the "allusive" nature of *G. B.*, which—everybody knew—referred to Georges Bataille:

> Some personages, rare beyond measure, had such a strong taste for secrecy that it is difficult even to pronounce their names, still less to make them the title of a book. … Prosper Mérimée published his *H. B.* after the death of Stendhal; … Jean Paulhan, … entitled his study of Félix Fénéon *F. F. or the Critic*. Who deserves better than Georges Bataille the right to access this gallery of anonymous portraits? But Michel Fardoulis-Lagrange, while still more allusive than the aforementioned authors, nevertheless managed to make his model physically recognizable and to restore the climate of conspiracy he imposed around him.[7]

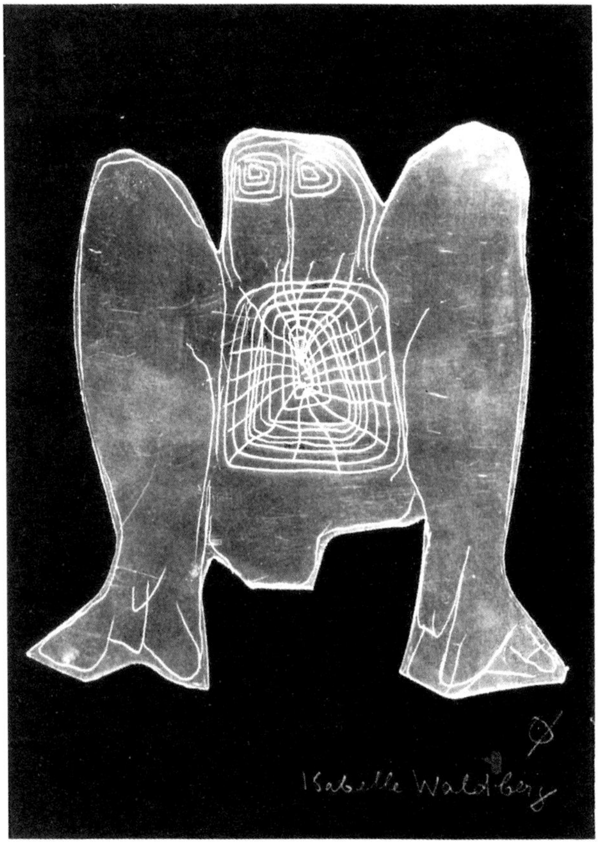

FIGURE 8.3

Isabelle Waldberg
Special edition artwork for Michel Fardoulis-Lagrange, *G. B. ou un ami présomptueux*, 1969
Drypoint drawing on aluminum, mounted on black Plexiglas, 18.8 × 13.7 cm
Private collection

In noting that certain "personages" have such "a strong taste for secrecy that it is difficult even to pronounce their names, still less to make them the title of a book," Lebel may also have had in mind Marcel Duchamp. Biographical information too personal to be published in Lebel's 1959 catalogue raisonné, *Sur Marcel Duchamp*, seems to have found more creative expression in *La double vue, suivi de L'inventeur du temps gratuit*, published just five years earlier.[8]

"Indisputable" is how *Étant donné Marcel Duchamp* editor Paul B. Franklin characterized the relationship between Isabelle Waldberg's illustrations for *G. B.* and Marcel Duchamp's *Given* (figure 0.1).[9] *G. B.* was published in 1969, *after* the completion of *Given* (1946–1966), and it may be that Franklin intended to suggest that the relationship consisted of Duchamp's influence on Waldberg. But comparison with Waldberg's 1946 sculpture *Luminaire* (figure 6.20) suggests that the influence was mutual, and may even have gone the other way. What could have inspired Waldberg to create such works?

The poetic euphemisms in which Michel Fardoulis-Lagrange couches the prose of *G. B.* make the actions of Georges Bataille and the goings-on of his secret society hard to pin down. This was probably intentional. "Tantric texts," according to historian of religion Mircea Eliade, "are often composed in an "intentional language, a secret, dark, ambiguous language" incomprehensible to the uninitiated reader.[10] This "twilight language," as it is also called, encompasses visual, verbal, and nonverbal communication meant to ensure that the uninitiated cannot easily gain access to what is essentially experiential knowledge.

The text of *G. B.* suggests that September 1938, when Patrick Waldberg was initiated as an Acéphale adept, marked a shift in the rituals of the secret society. In his 1977 account cited in chapter 7, Patrick wrote that after his initiation ceremony in the forest the group headed not back to the train station, but to Bataille's house in Saint-Germain. Patrick's account ends there, but Fardoulis-Lagrange's *G. B.* describes how, after the initiation ceremony in the forest, the adepts encountered in a hidden room an "idol" seated next to Bataille, "legs crossed, surrounded by pillows." The "obscure activities, imprinted with obscenity" in which the couple subsequently engaged did not dispel the adepts' discomfort with this strange spectacle, or with the "threat of death that hovered in the apartment." The "idol" would have been Laure, in the role of Kali, goddess of death: "A stale smell was circulating, as if her feverish flesh had become clammy, its humors requiring incessant sponging. Perhaps it was perversion hiding in the smells that penetrated the nostrils, like the odor of female genitals. And the moist climate continued assailing intimacies, rotting them. … The lascivious poses of the idol seemed to repel without effort the dark forces behind [Bataille's] shoulders."[11] Eventually the idol yielded "to the forces she repressed," but not before indulging in the "luxury to suspend, as she did, the effects to come, and to mate for some time with her mind."[12] If Fardoulis-Lagrange's account is accurate, during at least one "inner meeting" of Acéphale, Bataille and Laure engaged in ritualistic tantric sex.

Laure's anguished but uncompromising lifestyle had inspired Bataille from the time they began their affair in 1934. Her psyche, like his, had been warped by a horrific childhood that, in her case, included sexual abuse by the family priest, and the loss of her father and three uncles during World War I. Like Bataille, she suffered all her life from tuberculosis, which nearly killed her at age 13. Also like him, she attempted to assuage her despair through drinking and debauchery. They frequented brothels together, both in Paris and in Saint-Germain-en-Laye. Laure spent much of the money she inherited from her father in support of political journals including, no doubt, *Acéphale*. She believed in transgressing societal norms no matter what the cost. (Her writings would be published posthumously by Bataille and Michel Leiris, against the wishes of her brother Charles Peignot.)

In *G. B.* Fardoulis-Lagrange describes a woman sick with tuberculosis (her "feverish flesh" had become "clammy"). The event would have taken place shortly before Laure died, and one might ask whether she was up to the role. Knowing what we do about Bataille and Laure, however, there is a good chance she would have wanted to die the way she had lived: outrageously. Aside from whatever group promiscuity may have occurred, the only other person who participated actively in this erotic rite would seem to have been Bataille himself. It is important to note how the action shifts from a physical encounter between Bataille and Laure to a form of mental eroticism in which Laure seized control of her own dying body by way of her mind.

The role of Kali would be Laure's last—she died less than two months after the events described here. Patrick Waldberg and Fardoulis-Lagrange agree that following Laure's death Bataille escalated his emphasis on sacrifice and established distinct periods of self-sacrifice in the form of asceticism, self-mutilation, and trial by fire.[13] In terms of Acéphale's ritual practices, Bataille seems to have been feeling his way along. Rumors of human sacrifice and cannibalism circulated. Regarding these practices,

Bataille later wrote: "I approve of neither exploitation nor murder (and for cannibals, it goes without saying ...)."[14] Just as "murder" would not include self-sacrifice, so "exploitation" would not describe consensual sexual acts. Although there is no evidence that any human was sacrificed, willingly or otherwise, there *is* evidence that ritualistic "sacrifice" in the form of erotic activity was a feature of what Isabelle Waldberg characterized as Bataille's *rituel intime*.[15]

The climax and denouement of Acéphale—described in the last twenty pages of *G. B.*—seem to have featured, in addition to voyeurism, the "cannibal" consumption of sexual fluids. Contemporary accounts of ritual sexual practices in India described the offering of bodily fluids as a devotional act of sacrifice, with the female as both recipient and source. "The sexual act is a sacrifice that must be performed with the same rigor and precision as any other ritual," Mircea Eliade wrote in an account published in 1936 that Bataille read. "The identification of woman with the elements of the sacrifice is clear: She has pelvis as altar, [pubic] hair for grass, skin to press for soma [Vedic ritual drink]." Eliade went on to stress that—in contrast with ancient Vedic practice, which focused on the sacrificial element—in tantric practice the sexual act "becomes a means of meditation and a technique for achieving oneness with divinity."[16]

In 1930 Alexandra David-Néel had written about a Tibetan practice in which the guru designates a follower to procreate a child "with the object of making of him an initiate and the successor of his father or of his father's *guru*." A woman is chosen who is regarded as one of the "incarnate fairies." After living in seclusion and undergoing austerities for a period of time, the couple unites in a sacramental act that takes place "in the midst of a *kyilkhor* (magic circle)." According to David-Néel, "Other methods have been imagined aiming at the same end, though involving coarse—and from our point of view utterly repulsive—practices, which symbolise the relation of father to son established between the parents' master and the child that is to be born. Tradition says that this realistic rite was performed by Marpa for his married disciple, Ngog Chösdor. ... Marpa received his sperm in a goblet made of a human skull, and after mixing with it various ingredients supposed to possess magical properties, the potion was drunk by the disciple and his wife."[17] The practice described by David-Néel is particularly interesting in light of the fact that Michel Waldberg, son of Isabelle and Patrick, was born on March 5, 1940, nine months after the penultimate meeting of the secret society.

More common in India and Nepal are tantric practices of veneration of the vulva and consumption of sexual emissions. In another account, David-Néel describes a communal ritual that, based on both visual and verbal evidence contained in *G. B.*, Bataille attempted to integrate into his penultimate Acéphale meetings in the spring of 1939: "Certain 'left-handed' practices vaguely recall our Black Masses from another time. A spread-out naked woman represents the Goddess and receives the adoration of the worshipers; her sex is considered a *yantra*. In its proper sense, the term *yantra* means a machine, an instrument used to do something. In the figurative sense in Tantrism, it is a diagram, a symbolic drawing on which attention must be fixed during meditation."[18] This comparison with the Black Mass (a ritualistic perversion of the traditional Catholic Latin Mass) would have appealed to Bataille, who had incorporated similar blasphemous elements into his *Story of the Eye* and other writings.

By the end of *G. B.* the theme of sex and death morphs into that of conception and birth. The female sexual organ as source of enlightenment featured prominently in the art of both Marcel Duchamp and Isabelle Waldberg, who in spring 1939 appears to have replaced Laure as the female focus of Bataille's rituals. From *G. B.*:

> The members encircled the victim—the idol that contained in herself the coveted substance, but they were afraid of their inclinations. ... The victim was adorned with riches in order to face the failed act of the sacrificer whose raised arm would not bring itself down upon her. ... Then, by an imperceptible swaying, attraction began to circulate between the male element and the female element. It was in vain that precautions were taken to ensure that the sacrificial act was carried out according to the rules of slowness (since the victim blossomed only in proportion to the slowness of the execution). His hands began to work more feverishly, as though involved in a birth, or the anointing of a second creation.[19]

At this point the novel's action reaches fever pitch, and it is well-nigh impossible to follow what is going on, either with the victim or in the minds of the participants. They fear the bottomless vagina, whose "devouring nature was associated with that of fire"—accounting for the stove on the cover of *G. B.* But the fire also bestows on the proceedings a sacred quality, "the victim having prostituted herself to appease anger and suppress unclean reflexes." Only by suppressing lascivious desire "could the spiritual quintessence that regenerated the fire be obtained."[20] "Spiritual quintessence" seems to be a metaphor for *soma*, a Vedic Sanskrit word that literally means "distill, extract, sprinkle." In much the same way, Duchamp used *la chute d'eau*, the "fall of water" that mysteriously regenerates the illuminating, enlightening gas in the title for *Given*.

Finally, the adepts begin circling our heroine, revealing "a collective nervousness, as if other, unknown desires were being fulfilled." This instinctive behavior introduces another ritual. The victim hoists herself onto a platform, out of reach of the participants: "It was she who took responsibility for the outcome by taking refuge, placing herself above everything. So many moves in order to exhibit herself, to excite desire; then to remove herself, to make it ascetic. She took refuge at the focal point to escape the aggression, which was then reflected and melted into its illuminating object. … And from the reality that nothing came to meet her, she became mistress of herself."[21] Two things should be noted. First is the reference to a "focal point," paralleling Mirra Alfassa's insistence that "the whole will of the being should be concentrated on one point to realize union with the inner Divine."[22] The second is that the yoni is characterized here as an "illuminating object"—the connection with *Luminaire* (figure 6.20) seems clear.

Isabelle, like Laure before her, experiences psychosomatic union as she prepares to give birth to a new Self: "The gaze of the victim, fixed somewhere else, had its own turgescence that was preparing to turn, penetrate, and fertilize her. In front of her appeared simultaneously the grace of this image, its youth before tearing [*déchirement*]. It was difficult thus to conceive her maternity, yet she was already embracing the unformed, to mold and give birth to it. She was placed at the point of turning with an order of such power that the supernatural receded."[23] *Déchirement* would seem to be another reference to Duchamp, who compared passage through time with being torn, as in *Yvonne et Magdeleine déchiquetées* (1911, figure 1.2), and his (torn) *Self-Portrait in Profile* (1958).[24]

Fardoulis-Lagrange goes on, but what he describes above could only have come from Isabelle Waldberg, whose illustrations for his book convey the generational power of self-directed erotic energy. It is obvious from the lengthy denouement of *G. B.* that the responses of Bataille's adepts to these events were considerably more mixed than Isabelle's. Surely, the motive for her participation in the creation of *G. B. ou un ami présomptueux* was, at least in part, to set the story straight from her own perspective.

After the explosive spring 1939 meeting Acéphale kept going, though in dramatically truncated form. The same June 1939 issue of *Acéphale* in which Bataille published "The Practice of Joy Before Death" was dedicated to Nietzsche's madness—a state into which Nietzsche had descended fifty years earlier. On July 1, 1939, Ambrosino, who had gone off abruptly for military training, wrote Patrick to confirm that he would continue to participate (along with Patrick, Isabelle, and Chavy) by reading Nietzsche's *Gay Science.* "Each week we will exchange a letter—you three and me," he wrote. "This letter will focus on the reading we have done." He suggests that Isabelle "be in charge of" translations of Nietzsche's correspondence into French.[25]

On September 3, 1939, England declared war on Germany and World War II officially began. On October 20 Bataille sent several letters, including a letter to his inner circle informing them that they should henceforth consider themselves free of all ties to him. He added that he did not intend to hide out: "I do not experience weariness or bitterness: if one of you is still waiting for something from me (that wouldn't be wrong, because *I abandon nothing*), he will see that I am neither dead nor resentful." Bataille's obsession with abandonment came through even more strongly in another letter sent on October 20, this time to the larger group: "Waldberg was able to say nothing when I confronted him with the fact that some of you had *abandoned* me. What hurts me in this abandonment is that it was brutal and deaf. I do not regret abandonment itself."[26] In the end, Isabelle and Patrick Waldberg would be among the very few Acéphale members still loyal to Bataille.[27]

••

G. B. ou un ami présomptueux is stuffed with allusions to the sprawling writings of Georges Bataille, and to insider knowledge of Acéphale. Without some knowledge of both, it is difficult to follow the narrative, and without Isabelle Waldberg's explicit illustrations, it is virtually impossible. If not through Breton, Marcel Duchamp would have known Georges Bataille through Isabelle, who said she knew both Duchamp and Breton in Paris before the war.[28] Bataille and Breton were competitors, but they had shared interests, including psychology, ethnology, and myth. After a very public break at the end of the 1920s, they were reconciled in 1935 in connection with the revolutionary group Contre-Attaque, which unraveled the following year.[29] Breton had a "keen interest" in Acéphale,[30] which Bataille began organizing immediately after the acrimonious breakup of Contre-Attaque. His interest would only have intensified as Bataille developed Acéphale's secret society, which met every month on the new moon in the Forest of Marly to engage in mysterious nighttime rituals.

Guy Wildenstein had invited the Surrealists to show at his Galerie des Beaux-Arts from January 17 through February 24, 1938.[31] Art historian Elena Filopovic has suggested that Breton and his co-organizer, poet Paul Éluard, selected Duchamp as "Generator-Arbitrator" for *L'Exposition Internationale du Surréalisme* in order to "create an exhibition that would position itself against the very bastion of bourgeois good taste" represented by the Galerie des Beaux-Arts.[32] If this was indeed their aim, they could have done no better than to enroll that opponent of good taste, Marcel Duchamp. And Duchamp could have done no better than to introduce Bataillean elements, perhaps with the support of Salvador Dalí, whose *Rainy Taxi* would be an important component,[33] and Bataille's close artistic collaborator André Masson, who participated in the exhibition and had his work featured in Breton's journal *Minotaure* that same year.[34] Whatever the case, the 1938 Surrealist exhibition was markedly different from anything either Breton or Duchamp had done before. Wildenstein, who had financed and served on the editorial board for Bataille's journal *Documents* (1929–1930) only to acrimoniously pull his funding, could not have been surprised at what ensued. Yet Wildenstein was publisher of record for the exhibition's accompanying *Dictionnaire abrégé du surréalisme*. No editor is listed, but Duchamp would have designed it, and very likely played an editorial role as well.

The *Dictionnaire*'s brief entry for *ÉROTISME*—"sumptuous subterranean ceremony"[35]—surely was intended as a teasing reference to Bataille's contemporaneous secret society, Acéphale. In the July 1937 issue of his journal *Acéphale*, Bataille had announced that the subject of the next issue would be "*L'Érotisme*." That issue never appeared; instead, Bataille devoted his energies to taking Acéphale literally underground. According to Isabelle Waldberg, during the late fall of 1937, when *L'Exposition Internationale du Surréalisme* and the *Dictionnaire abrégé* would have been in preparation, Acéphale's secret rituals in the Forest of Marly began taking place in "a sort of very deep gallery" amid ruins in the forest.[36]

In another entry in *Dictionnaire abrégé*, "umbrella" (*parapluie*) is defined as "blue bird become black"—a pithy little poem that can be interpreted both as an experiential description of opening an umbrella, and as a metaphor for death.[37] "Blue bird" may be an ironic reference to *The Blue Bird*, Maurice Maeterlinck's mystical play about the secret of happiness (1908, adapted often for stage and film). "Blue bird become black" would also appear to be related to the title of a violent, erotic novella Bataille had recently finished: *Le Bleu du Ciel* ("Blue of Sky," 1935, published in English as *Blue of Noon*). Finally, "blue bird become black" recalls a Nietzschean enigma—"night is also a sun"—which would be quoted by Bataille in his essay for *Surréalisme en 1947*—the catalogue to the 1947 *Exposition Internationale du Surréalisme*.[38] As a definition, it is nonsensical outside the context of Bataille's umbrella enlightenment (described in chapter 7), during which "the umbrella came down on my head covering me (I covered myself expressly with this black shroud)."[39]

Unlike other entries in the *Dictionnaire*, neither "Érotisme" nor "Parapluie" is attributed. Bataille was an acknowledged contributor to *Surréalisme en 1947*, and it seems within the realm of possibility that he contributed, either directly or indirectly, to the *Dictionnaire abrégé*. If so, his poetic definition of umbrella was just the kind of linguistic brilliance that would have appealed to Duchamp. The concept of shield become shroud is already implicit in the word *parapluie* ("rain-shield"), which derives from the Latin *parāre*, "to defend, shield, shroud."

Breton had asked Duchamp to darken the main gallery of the Galerie des Beaux-Arts by covering its skylights. The *1,200 Coal Sacks* that were installed beneath this glass ceiling (figure 8.1) were Duchamp's idea, according to Pierre Roché, who said Duchamp originally planned to cover the ceiling "with hundreds of bulging open umbrellas with their domes turned downwards, but it proved difficult to find so many second-hand umbrellas on such short notice."[40] If the umbrellas were indeed Duchamp's idea, they were no doubt intended to evoke an erotic atmosphere. Five years later, Duchamp would install a ceiling of open umbrellas above his design for Brentano's window promoting Denis de Rougemont's book *La Part du diable* (1942; window installation, January 1943). De Rougemont reported that Duchamp "arrives and proposes a ceiling made of open umbrellas hanging by their handles. Mysteriously, [Duchamp] adds that 'all the women will understand'."[41] Duchamp may have been referring to the resemblance between open umbrellas and women's breasts. He may also have had in mind cervical caps, barriers that cover a woman's cervix to protect it from sperm, just as umbrellas protect the body from falling water.

"The open umbrellas are like the wings of giant bats," De Rougemont added. This simile probably came from Duchamp, who on the opening invitation to the 1938 exhibition had promised a "Sky of fruit bats" (*Ciel de roussettes*).[42] His paper-filled coal sacks, which apparently moved slightly with shifting air currents, would have created an overtly Bataillean atmosphere of dirt and decay, while their gentle movements may indeed have evoked the "sky of fruit bats" mentioned on the invitation. Bats on the ceiling suggest the roof of a cave, and thus an underground environment.

Austrian artist Wolfgang Paalen blanketed the floor of this darkened central exhibition space with moss and dead leaves punctuated by *Water and Brushwood*—a small pond surrounded by ferns and pampas grass.[43] At the center of the room a brazier glowed, and visitors were given flashlights with which to view the works. The smell of roasting coffee beans permeated the gallery—a *sub rosa* reference to *Coffee Mill* (1911, figure 1.18). Duchamp hung two-dimensional objects not only on the walls, but also on revolving doors brought in for the occasion. Beds were installed in the room's four corners; at the opening, dancer Hélène Vanel performed "The Unconsummated Act" on one of them.[44] Critics described the room as "'oppressive,' even 'sinisterly erotic'; one felt the need to flee the 'choking' claustrophobic atmosphere."[45] To those in surrealist circles, however, this central gallery would have offered a simulacrum of the dead-of-night forest meetings engaged in by the members of Acéphale. The late hour of the opening—10 p.m.—reinforced the concept. By then, Duchamp was on a train to London to help Peggy Guggenheim set up her new gallery.

Among the more puzzling details of Fardoulis-Lagrange's novel are repeated actions involving a glass ceiling and revolving doors—details that, given the correspondences between Acéphale and the 1938 *Exposition Internationale du Surréalisme*, would seem to refer to Duchamp's "grotto" installation incorporating the gallery's glass ceiling, which he covered with coal sacks, and the freestanding revolving doors on which he displayed artworks. In an adjacent room "a pair of pantaloons" hung from the ceiling above another revolving door.[46] These cross-references between *G. B.* and Duchamp's 1938 Paris installation reinforce the connections between Duchamp and Bataille during a year that was pivotal for the development of Bataille's practice of tantra yoga.

The dominant critical view of the 1938 *Exposition Internationale du Surréalisme* has been that it marked the withdrawal of surrealism from political engagement.[47] This view is misleading in its narrow interpretation of "engagement" to mean organized, targeted group activity. What occurred within surrealism during the course of the 1930s in response to the rise of fascism was a shift from external political involvement to a focus on individual empowerment and subversive resistance to the accepted order. Georges Bataille conceived Acéphale as a heterogeneous collection of individuals empowered to respond to the threat of war by practicing the experience of death. With his Acéphale seminars, publications, and private group rituals, Bataille aimed to foster personal realization, thus engendering in Acéphale members the will not only to live, but to live *fearlessly*, and to *act* in the face of impending catastrophe. Surrealist artists and writers were following the path Duchamp had discovered years earlier—a path toward personal freedom and self-realization.

Different as they were, for both Breton and Bataille this involved exploration of alternative traditions and belief systems. For example, in the catalogue to the *Exposition Surréaliste d'Objets*, which opened in May 1936, one month after the founding of Acéphale, Breton expressed a distinctly Vedic view of reality (quoted above, in chapter 3): "we begin to hurry on the platform for the passage of the train that does not stop, which is neither a passenger train nor a freight train. In the windows, beings-objects (or objects-beings?) characterized by the fact that they are prey to a continuous transformation and express the perpetuity of the struggle between the aggregating and disaggregating powers that dispute true reality and life."[48] And in a postwar assessment of the "mental climate" surrounding the 1938 *Exposition Internationale du Surréalisme*, Breton characterized his changed perspective as, not "Art," but the need to make "very accessible the terrain of agitation extending to the borders of the poetic and the real." Bataille's version: "The war put an end to my 'activity' and my life became all the less separated from the object of its search."[49] Both artists, it seems, had become converts to their own versions of Marcel Duchamp's Art of Life.

••

On September 8, 1943, Patrick Waldberg wrote Isabelle in New York, informing her that he had received by mail a copy of Georges Bataille's *Inner Experience*. He didn't think much of it: "It is not without a very lively repulsion that one arrives at the end of this laborious pseudo-Nietzschean onanism, especially if, like you and me, we knew the thing in its beginnings. The book consists of mystico-philosophical description of an 'experience' destined to realize the void through destruction of the self. ... The little beast has come a long way since our stay in Saint-Germain!"[50] In retrospect, Patrick seems to have regarded their group experience with something like repulsion.

Eleven days later he wrote again, asking her: "How were we able to remain for so long in the mystical trap of Bataille? The more I think about it, the more I see in it a terrible fool's bargain." He talks about their fellow secret society members and then asks again, almost compulsively, "How, I ask you, did we for so long accept Bataille's management? 'Everyone carries with him his little pinnacle!' Such is the title of one of the chapters of his last book. And this book was already in him even before we knew him."[51] Patrick would not seem to have read Bataille's book very closely—the chapter to which he refers is actually entitled "I want to carry My Person to the Pinnacle"—an attitude Bataille criticizes.[52]

Patrick went on to reference the "second phase" of Acéphale: "It must also be recognized that Bataille's choice for the second phase of the enterprise, which eliminated part of the effective force, was judicious. ... We started with too many people. ... Also, we started with too many words and too many objects." He goes on to criticize at length Bataille's entire Acéphale program—publications as well as meetings—and to praise Breton. (A heavily redacted version of his letter would be published in the fourth and last issue of Breton's journal *VVV* in 1944.) He then returns to the crux of the matter as far as the two of them were concerned:

> I have not yet spoken of this "mystical" experience dear to Bataille; what he calls "torture." I see nothing other than the very negation of what we wanted to create. It is an escape from life—escape, renunciation, hypocrisy, and swindling. Bataille takes good care to disguise the "naked women and whiskey" aspect, and his funerary eroticism finds there an advantage; similarly his fear of risk, his megalomania. …
>
> Without a doubt, we must disqualify the whole part of our activity in Saint-Germain whose theme was "Joy in the Face of Death." More than anywhere else, we seriously failed there in decency, humor, and dignity. We must have the courage to admit it. And there I alone was the cause: Zino, Chenon, Chavy were not in the game. You yourself, you do not have the same responsibilities.

Having unloaded his animus against Bataille's obsessive project, Patrick finally adopts a softer tone: "Bataille himself is out of the question: I have nothing with which to reproach Bataille, who was as transparent as possible in his ruses and his proceedings as well as his spontaneous gestures (rare as they were). The truth is that Bataille has not changed, and thus he has not betrayed. We, we betrayed him from the beginning in refusing to see him for what he was."[53]

Patrick Waldberg clearly believed that he and Isabelle had allowed themselves to be swept up and carried away by Bataille's obsessions and sheer craziness. Even before it ended, Acéphale acquired a legendary occult status. Isabelle Waldberg played a central role—a role she never talked about, but one which would shape her art and transform her into a role model for Marcel Duchamp's legendary occult work, *Given*.

By 1942 Bataille's worsening tuberculosis made it necessary for him to leave his position at the Bibliothèque Nationale, and his deteriorating finances led him to resettle in Vézelay. "Disappeared body and all [*disparu corps et bien*]," was how Patrick characterized the situation to Isabelle in 1943.[54] Bataille had warned his secret society that the final phase of Acéphale might end in drama; he may have anticipated, even hoped, that the drama would be a Nietzschean tragedy. With his scheme for Acéphale, Bataille was, in his own tragic way, an idealist. This is how Patrick Waldberg would eventually come to think of him: "Never, perhaps, had such formidable seriousness been associated with childishness just as enormous—with the aim of bringing to life a certain degree of incandescence and of obtaining those 'privileged moments' to which we aspire from childhood. … Failure was unavoidable. But for some, including myself, the expression 'to change life' had ceased to be a hollow formula. As for the 'transformation of the world,' it has become increasingly clear that this concept remains forever powerless due to the profound nature of the human being."[55]

Georges Bataille could not transform the world or change life, but he did change lives, including his own. As Patrick Waldberg noted, what got lost in the process was irony-leavening humor. Only after the war was Bataille persuaded to deploy this vital component through his participation in another group project with Patrick and Isabelle Waldberg, Robert Lebel, and the humor-loving Marcel Duchamp. *Le Da Costa Encyclopédique* (1947) and its successor *Le Mémento Universel Da Costa* (1948–1949) were, in their own way, a continuation of *Acéphale* as publication, as well as secret society. This time, however, the even more secretive Marcel Duchamp would play a leading role.

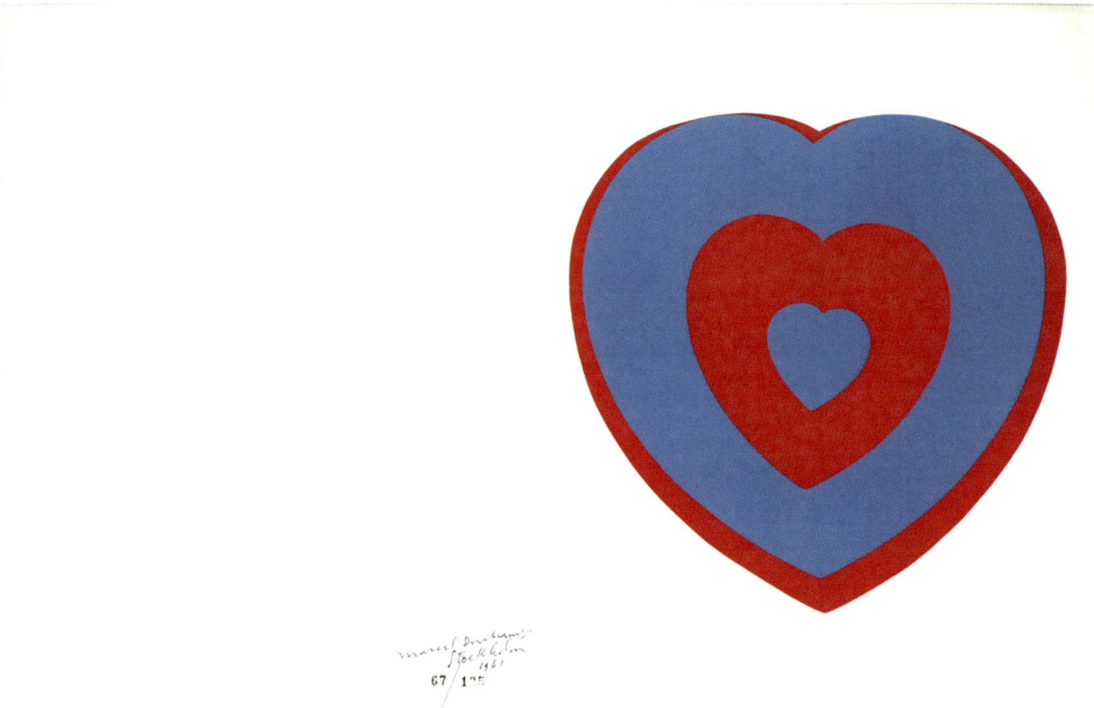

FIGURE 9.1

Marcel Duchamp
Coeurs volants / Fluttering Hearts, based on the cover of *Cahiers d'Art* number 1–2, 1936
Screenprint, 1961 (edition 67/125), sheet: 31.75 × 50.8 cm
Albright-Knox Art Gallery, Buffalo, New York, NY, Gift of Cordier & Ekstrom Gallery, NY, 1968 (P1968:16)

9 DUCHAMP AND THE CLAN DA COSTA

Nothing seems conceivable or tolerable without humor.

–Robert Lebel, 1944[1]

Marcel Duchamp's art of life was nourished by Buddha-like equanimity,[2] tantra-empowered creativity, and Taoist-infused humor. During the second half of the 1940s he engaged with André Breton, Robert Lebel, Isabelle Waldberg, and Georges Bataille in deploying these tactics to negotiate postwar cultural battlefields. The ambitious and chaotic sixth Surrealist exhibition would be one outcome. Another—originally intended to accompany that exhibition in 1947, but taking on a life of its own—was the wickedly humorous *Da Costa Encyclopédique*. In contrast to the deadly seriousness of Acéphale, the *famille Da Costa* was fueled by the subversive power of humor. Duchamp's catalytic role in the "family" or "clan" Da Costa is supported by his 1945 comment: "You tell me that we have never seen a human group live in anarchy as I advocate it. Yet I know a group where it works very well is the family ... The family is the model of a society completely anarchic."[3]

In *Acéphale* Bataille had proposed a "community of heart,"[4] and it may have been he who suggested the name. Uriel Da Costa (1585–1640) was a Jewish philosopher and skeptic who questioned the Catholic and Rabbinic institutions of his time, and died a suicide. Da Costa's cynically humorous and heart-wrenching autobiography, *Exemplar humanae vita* (1640), was translated into French by Bataille's close friend Pierre Kaan and published in 1926 as *Une vie humaine*, along with Kaan's account of Da Costa's life and work. Another Da Costa may be relevant as well. Da Costa syndrome—a wartime neurotic condition characterized by heart palpitations, chest pain, a rapid pulse, and fatigue[5]—was named after Dr. Jacob Mendes da Costa, an American surgeon who first diagnosed it during the American Civil War. As a form of war trauma, Da Costa syndrome would have been known to Patrick Waldberg, who worked for the United States Office of War Information, an American propaganda agency. Duchamp may have been familiar with Da Costa syndrome through Waldberg, as well as another possible source: In 1930, Thomas Eakins's widow donated an oil *Sketch for "Portrait of Dr. Jacob Mendez da Costa"* (about 1893) to the Philadelphia Museum of Art, later home to the Arensberg Collection. As we have seen, Duchamp escaped serving in World War I thanks to his rheumatic heart. More than once, he characterized conventional relations between the sexes as warfare. *Fluttering Hearts* (figure 9.1), created in 1936 during the period leading up to World War II, may have been partly inspired by Da Costa syndrome.

World War II was a tragic and confusing time for French artists and intellectuals. Many who remained in Paris at the beginning of the war participated in the French Resistance—among them Duchamp's companion Mary Reynolds and Gabrielle Buffet-Picabia's daughter Jeannine. The staff of Musée de l'Homme formed an organized cell, and the underground magazine *Résistance* was printed in the museum's basement. They were betrayed in early 1941; most of the men were shot, and the women sent to concentration camps.[6] The situation for those who fled the war was not as dire, but it was dismal nevertheless. This was a time characterized by recrimination and concern for friends and family. Duchamp later referred to himself as "a deserter," adding: "I left France during the war, in 1942, when I would have had to have been part of the Resistance. I don't have what is called a strong patriotic sense; I'd rather not even talk about it."[7]

French artists and writers who made it to New York did what they could with the art means at hand. Their efforts included the 1942 exhibition *First Papers of Surrealism*, organized to benefit the Coordinating Council of French Relief Societies, and *VVV*—André Breton's journal of "poetry, plastic arts, anthropology, sociology, and psychology." The last issue, published in February 1944, concluded with critiques of Acéphale, Bataille's prewar effort to steel the cultural community for war. Acéphale participant Patrick Waldberg published an edited version of the letter he had written to Isabelle Waldberg in September 1943.[8] Entitled "Towards a New Myth? Premonitions and Challenges," Waldberg's letter was followed by a response from Robert Lebel. Inserted between the two is a photograph of Patrick's wife and Lebel's lover, Isabelle Waldberg, amidst her ephemeral sculptures (figure 6.16).

The month before this issue of *VVV* appeared, Patrick, then in London, sent Isabelle a letter conveying his hope that after the war she would join him in a group effort to replace Bataille's failed godless religion with a unifying new myth:

> The question is whether certain rules of life shared by a greater or lesser number of individuals, and certain acts performed in common in certain circumstances, would not be capable ... of taking on meaning and power, and of hastening the death of traditional forms and the development of new constructions. What rules? What actions? Which individuals? That remains to be defined. The very fact that Acéphale existed, whatever its defects, remains a token of hope, and the interest shown by André [Breton] seems to me significant. I am very interested also in the reaction of Robert—negative in its expression, but implying a happy willingness to participate.[9]

Patrick was referring to Robert Lebel's response to his letter, both about to be published in *VVV*. Lebel had defended Bataille by reminding Patrick that Bataille had been quite open to the possibility of failure. He was indeed negative: "To try and create a new myth," Lebel wrote, "is rather like establishing the 'myth of those without myths,' or the 'clan of those without a clan,' since the individuals it is proposed to bring together are precisely those who have found that none of the public forms of collective activity measure up to their standards." Lebel then went on to propose a clan fueled not by ritual, but by the collective power of humor: "Nothing seems conceivable or tolerable without humor." Their next concerted action, he wrote, ought to systematically exploit the resources of skepticism and humor.[10] Thus the birth of the clan Da Costa, the "clan of those without a clan." In the end, Patrick would remain missing in action. *Le Da Costa Encyclopédique*, which appeared in fall 1947, would be produced by Isabelle

Waldberg, Robert Lebel, and Marcel Duchamp in collaboration with others, including Bataille and Breton.

Paris was liberated in August 1944, and its exiles began returning the following year. In early 1945 Patrick, already back in Paris, sent Isabelle, still in New York, a positive report regarding Bataille: "Yesterday, Bataille came to see me, laughing, happy, and kind. ... He seems to be in great shape."[11] Despite his unsettling experience with Acéphale, Patrick was not ready to surrender his faith in group efficacy. This perspective, which he shared both with Bataille and with André Breton, would be the germ of the post-war *Exposition Internationale du Surréalisme*, held July 7 to September 30, 1947; and *Le Da Costa Encyclopédique*, originally planned to coincide with the exhibition, but which due to problems with the printer did not appear until later that fall. Duchamp would be deeply involved with both.

Robert Lebel returned to Paris in the summer of 1945, Isabelle Waldberg in November of that year, Duchamp and Breton in May 1946. Duchamp was engaged in an intense affair with sculptor Maria Martins and was not eager to return, but he needed to get his visa renewed. In October, Breton and Duchamp began planning the sixth international surrealist exhibition, scheduled to take place at the new Galerie Maeght the following summer. For Breton, this last big international exhibition was a way to try and reestablish his Surrealist brand after the war. Duchamp, always the individualist, had no commitment to Surrealism as a movement, but he was loyal to his friend Breton and enjoyed opportunities to exercise his creativity. There would be considerable overlap between those who wrote for the exhibition catalogue—as usual, designed by Duchamp—and those who wrote anonymously for *Da Costa*, also designed by Duchamp. *Da Costa*'s core authors comprised former members of Acéphale including Bataille, who had plenty of other projects and seemed more than happy to let others take the lead.

Marcel Duchamp had first become seriously engaged with exhibition design in New York in 1917 for the Society of Independent Artists, and again in 1920 for Katherine Dreier's Société Anonyme.[12] He was drawn back to it in 1937 by Breton, for whom he designed a door in the shape of an embracing couple for Gradiva, Breton's Paris gallery of surrealist and ethnographic art (figure 9.2). The surrealists associated Gradiva with a novel by the German

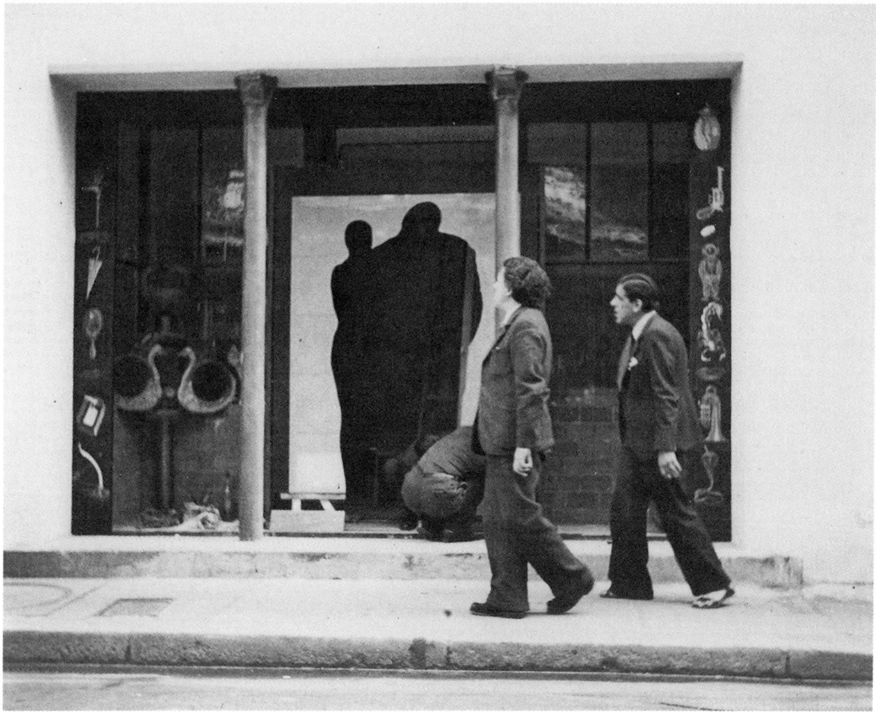

FIGURE 9.2
Andre Breton and Oscar Dominguez discovering the trompe l'oeil entrance to the Gradiva Gallery, just as it is being installed by Marcel Duchamp, 1937
Photograph
Private collection / Photo © Christie's Images / Bridgeman

writer Wilhelm Jensen: *Gradiva: Ein pompejanisches Phantasiestück* (*Gradiva: A Pompeian Fantasy*, 1903), inspired by an ancient relief sculpture of a "woman who walks." The novel's main character (analyzed by Freud in *Der Wahn und die Träume in W. Jensens Gradiva* [*Delusions and Dreams in Jensen's 'Gradiva'*], 1907) learns from the woman he loves that his attraction to art is based on erotic desire—a Duchampian perspective, as we have seen.

A linguistic slip transforms Gradiva to "gravida"—a pregnant woman. Duchamp's door for Gradiva implied opening oneself to mental insemination—a view that foreshadowed his 1949 assertion that "the 'victim' of an aesthetic echo is in a position comparable to that of a man in love, or of a believer, who dismisses automatically his demanding ego and, helpless, submits to a pleasurable and mysterious constraint."[13] The fused lovers of Duchamp's *Door* may also have been his answer to André Gide's question in *La porte étroite* (*Strait is the Gate*, 1909), a book cited by Duchamp to Gabrielle Buffet-Picabia in 1912: can lovers enter paradise side by side, or must they enter one by one?[14] *Door for Gradiva* was a work on the threshold, both literally and symbolically. When the Gradiva gallery closed after eighteen months, Duchamp made sure his door was destroyed.[15]

He followed this foray with a succession of major exhibition installations. In 1938 he installed *1,200 Coal Sacks* (stuffed with paper), covering the skylit ceiling of the central gallery of Georges Wildenstein's Galerie Beaux-Arts, Paris (figure 8.1). A brazier glowed at the center of the room, which was otherwise dark; visitors were given flashlights with which to view the works on display. Four years later, Duchamp installed *Mile of String*, connecting and energizing the display spaces of New York's Reid Mansion (figure 6.1).[16] On January 12, 1947, pursuant to Patrick Waldberg's letter published in *VVV* three years earlier, Breton announced that a sixth surrealist exhibition would explore the possibilities of a "New Myth."[17] Duchamp left Paris for New York the very next day,[18] but he convinced Breton to engage architect-designer Frederick Kiesler to implement their ideas for the sixth International Exhibition of Surrealism.[19]

Duchamp later said that Breton had asked him the previous October to begin thinking about another surrealist exhibition that would "occult" surrealism. He proposed a few ideas: "the rain, superstitions, the labyrinth, without going into any details of presentation, for I was returning to the USA and I asked Kiesler to go to Paris as architect of the expo." During the five months of implementation, however, "Breton introduced all his own intentions, especially into the labyrinth, which he worked out with his friends on the ground." Duchamp, who said he had "never had any interest in the occult sciences," learned to his dismay "the extent to which it was important for Breton to steer surrealism in that direction."[20]

Best known today for his *Endless House* (1947–1960), Frederick Kiesler claimed to have discovered architecture when, at the age of three, he crept under the "voluminous peasant skirts of his Ukrainian nanny and struck a match."[21] This reference to "fire down below" illuminates Kiesler's belief that architecture should not only feel like but also function as a womb—a creative, nourishing environment where art, broadly conceived, and human consciousness endlessly renew one another. In his "Second Manifesto of Correalism," Kiesler asserted: "The environment becomes equally as important as the [art] object, if not more so, because the object breathes into the surrounding and also inhales the realities of the environment."[22] With this shared interest in continuum, it is not hard to understand why Duchamp would entrust the implementation of his ideas to Kiesler, whose theory of "Correalism"—the "science of reciprocal relationships"[23]—attempted to provide an experientially unifying through-line for the disparate elements and ideas of the 1947 *Exposition Internationale du Surréalisme*.

Breton's January 12 letter of invitation described what he envisioned as an Acéphale-like process of increasingly intense ritualistic experiences: "The general structure of the exhibition will respond to the primordial concern to retrace successive steps of an INITIATION, in which passage from one piece to another implies graduation."[24] Visitors were to have begun on the ground floor of Galerie Maeght with a (never-realized) retrospective entitled "Surrealists Despite Themselves." This mini-exhibition would have featured works by past artists like Bosch and Arcimboldo, along with works by contemporaries like Masson, Magritte, and Dalí who, "for one reason or another," had "stopped gravitating in [Surrealism's] orbit."

Next, viewers were to ascend a flight of 21 stairs, their edges painted to resemble the spines of books meant to correspond to 21 of the major arcana of the tarot, and bearing the names of authors ranging from Rousseau, to Meister Eckhart, to Sade, to Apollinaire.[25] Nestled in the curve of this stairway an operating lighthouse showed the way to the womblike environment of Kiesler's "Hall of Superstitions," where visitors were supposed to abandon rational thinking and engage other strategies for overcoming fear. "Feeding-source of Fear," Kiesler noted on a sketch for Max Ernst's *Black Lake*—a black circular form painted on the floor.[26]

Nearby was Duchamp's *Le rayon vert*, a circular hole cut into Kiesler's dark green fabric through which was visible a photograph of the sea, its tilted horizon illuminated by a green light (figure 9.3). The concept was Duchamp's, but *Le rayon vert*—essentially a light box—was designed and installed by Kiesler.[27] Given propitious atmospheric conditions, every sunset over a flat horizon like that of the sea offers the possibility of seeing a final flicker of emerald light popularly known as the green flash (*le rayon vert* in French). I have seen a few and so presumably had Duchamp, during his many ocean crossings, perhaps especially during his long north-south voyage from New York to Argentina in 1918. A green flash is a prismatic

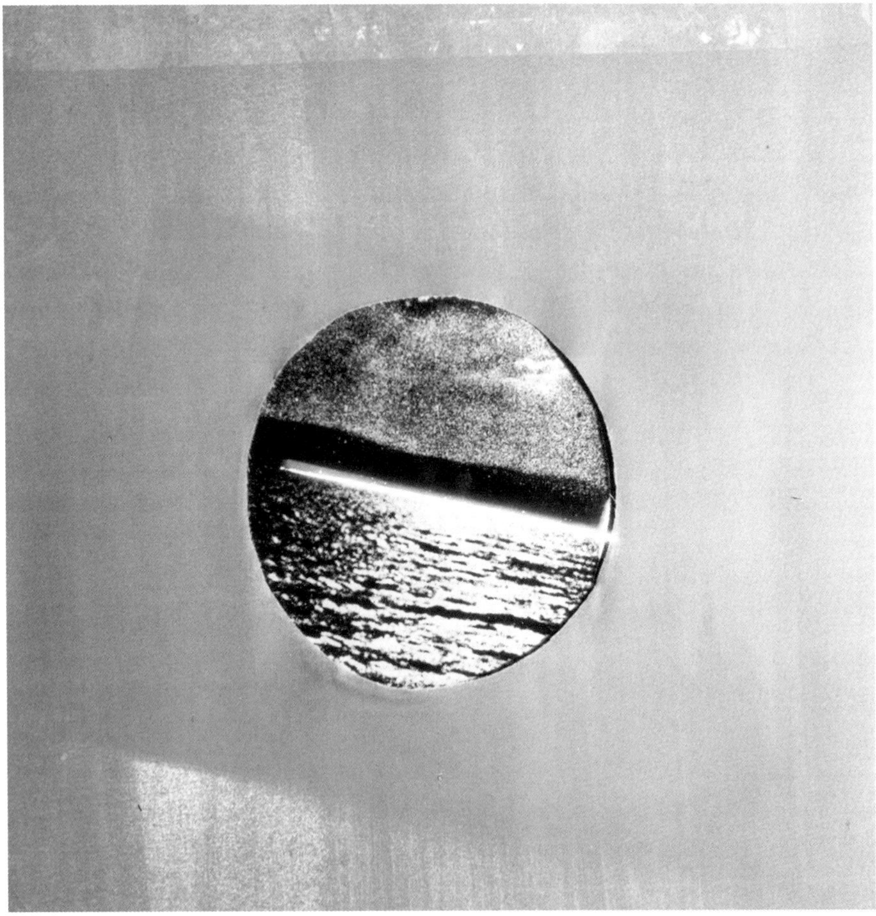

FIGURE 9.3

Marcel Duchamp
Le rayon vert / The Green Flash, 1947
Exposition Internationale du Surréalisme, 1947, Galerie Maeght, Paris
akg-images © Association Marcel Duchamp / ADAGP, Paris / Artists Rights Society (ARS), New York 2019

optical effect; why place a perceptual phenomenon in a Hall of Superstitions? Due to its rarity, and the element of chance associated with seeing it, the green flash is a traditional metaphor for enlightenment. Green is also associated with the life force: Eros. Many works by Duchamp (e.g., *The Green Box*) attest to the importance of green in his creative life. *Le rayon vert* seems to have been intended to make the "superstitious" aspect of green comprehensible—even if only subliminally—to viewers of the *Exposition Internationale du Surréalisme*. It is surely no coincidence that Paris's museum of Asian art, the Musée Guimet, was originally characterized by the anticlerical city council as the "Musée des Superstitions."[28]

Le rayon vert was originally planned to have the green light shine through a hole cut into the side of a suitcase, suggesting that Duchamp considered it to be another voyage/*clairvoyage* sculpture, like his earlier *To Be Looked At* (1918, figure 5.7).[29] Kiesler's drawings show the suitcase perched on a flimsy tripod—a concept not particularly suited to his curvilinear, womblike exhibition space.[30] Another drawing shows a rectangular hole and a level horizon, but Duchamp specified in a note that he wanted "a 'port hole' effect."[31] In the final work the round "port hole" in the fabric wall, combined with the photograph's tumultuously tilting horizon line, communicated loss of balance, linking *Le rayon vert* with the tilted tabletop of Duchamp's *Juggler of Gravity* further on in the exhibition (figure 9.5).

"A porthole allows Marcel Duchamp's green flash to pass," noted the exhibition checklist.[32] This is reminiscent of what Duchamp said about *Coffee Mill* (1911, figure 1.18): "It was a sort of escape hatch. You know, I've always felt this need to escape myself."[33] *Rayon vert*'s circular hole corresponds with the circular "mandala" of *The Large Glass*, while its tilted horizon line recalls the world-upside-down visible through the circular lens of *To Be Looked At*. It also harks back to the hole in Duchamp's note on "Linear Perspective" in the *Box of 1914* (figure 5.6), as well as Picabia's *Young Girl*—the circular opening to a star published in the journal *Proverbe* in 1920 (figure 5.10). In short, *Le rayon vert*'s role in the Hall of Superstitions seems to have been that of a potential "escape hatch" from Ernst's nearby *Black Lake* of fear.

This connection between death, fear, eroticism, and enlightenment was characteristic of Georges Bataille's thinking as well. Bataille's essay for the catalogue to the 1947 *Exposition Internationale du Surréalisme* emphasized absence or emptiness as an opening to infinity. In a passage that could have served as a caption for *Le rayon vert*, Bataille quoted Nietzsche's *Thus Spoke Zarathustra*: "The *absence of God* is no longer a closure: it is the opening up to the infinite. ... 'Night is also a sun,' and the absence of myth is also a myth."[34] As so often with Duchamp, however, *Le rayon vert* is less about absence than about *passage*. Implied passage from one condition to another, from rational consciousness to experiential awareness, connects *Le rayon vert* not only with other Duchamp "passages" mentioned above, but also with the *trompe-l'œil* "tear" at the center of *Tu m'*, and the fecund emptiness that serves as the focal point of *Given* (figures 4.6, 0.1).

To make their way to the Labyrinth from the Hall of Superstitions, visitors had to pass through Duchamp's Rain Room, where a pipe running along the ceiling emitted a "fall of water" onto Maria Martins's massive bronze, *The Path, The Shadow, Too Long, Too Narrow*. After baptizing visitors, the water drained into trays filled with earth and grass seeds that were seemingly intended to sprout. Directly beyond, displayed atop a billiard table, was Martins's sculpture *The Impossible* (*O Impossível*, 1944–1946, figure 10.5)—two surrealistically abstracted figures intensely engaged with one another. An airy, ephemeral bentwood sculpture by Isabelle Waldberg hung from the ceiling just beyond Martins's bronzes. To those in the know, this work and its title—*La Nue*, or *Premier du fil* ("*The Nude/Cloud*" or "*First Thread*")—would have evoked both Duchamp's *Large Glass* and his *Mile of String*.

Like *Le rayon vert*, the Rain Room was conceived as a passage. The initial project description in the catalogue reads: "The following room will oblige the visitor to bypass several curtains of multicolored rain to arrive, without disturbing Billiard players, into a room divided into octagons." Next comes a long description of the Labyrinth, which begins: "Each of the twelve octagonal cells ... will be consecrated to a being, a category of beings, or object SUSCEPTIBLE TO BEING ENDOWED WITH MYTHICAL LIFE, and to which an 'altar' modelled on those of pagan cults will have been raised. ..."[35] The capitalized words foregrounded Duchamp's concept of the importance of the spectator to the creation of art, while the quotation marks around "altar" suggest a conflict between the seriousness of Breton's interest in the occult and Duchamp's tongue-in-cheek attitude.

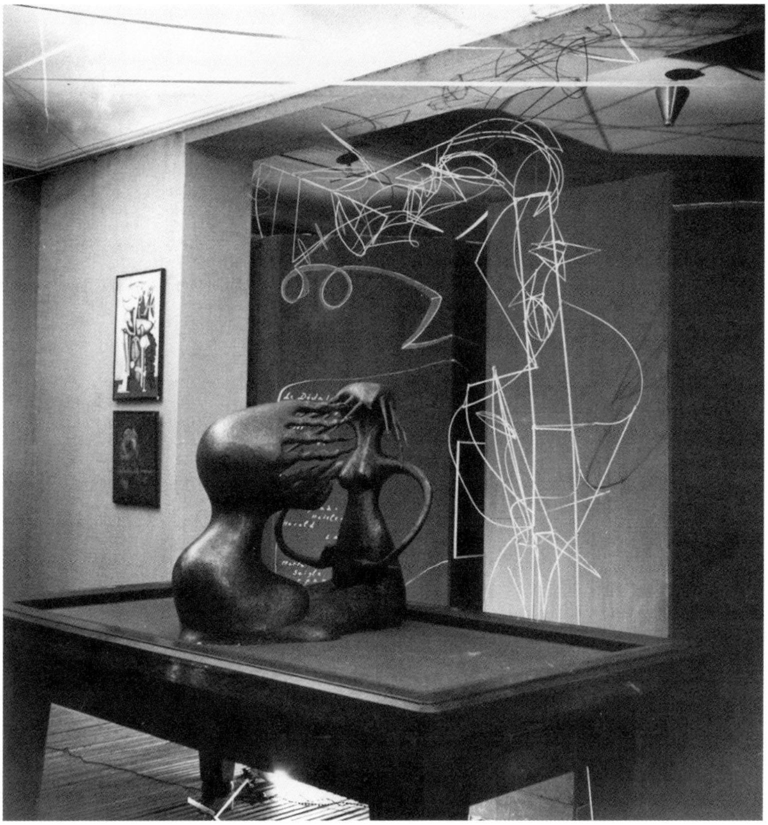

FIGURE 9.4

Willy Maywald
Marcel Duchamp's Rain Room at the *Exposition International du Surréalisme*, Galerie Maeght, Paris, 1947
Foreground, on billiard table: Maria Martins, *The Impossible*, bronze; behind: Isabelle Waldberg, *La Nue, Premier du fil*, birch dowels (now lost)

Duchamp's contribution to the Labyrinth was *Juggler of Gravity*, a never-realized refugee from his *Large Glass* fabricated by Matta and surrounded by "offerings" from other artists (figure 9.5). The off-kilter *Green Flash* in the Hall of Superstitions and the implied billiard balls on the green table in the Rain Room were experientially connected to the Labyrinth's *Juggler of Gravity*, where a white cue ball threatened to tumble off a precariously tilting tabletop. The culmination of Breton's series of "initiations" was a

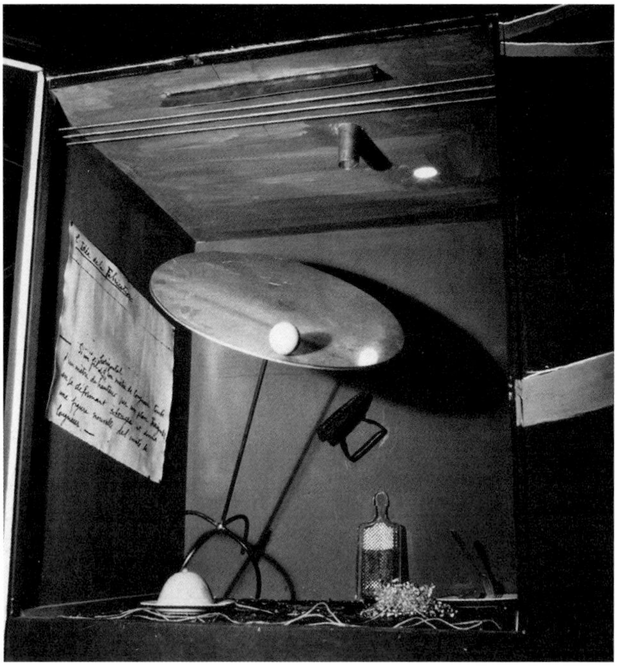

FIGURE 9.5

Roberto Matta
L'idée de la fabrication, "altar" to Duchamp's *Juggler of Gravity*, 1947
Exposition internationale du Surréalisme, Galerie Maeght, Paris
akg-images © 2019 Artists Rights Society (ARS), New York / ADAGP, Paris

thirteenth altar not mentioned in the catalogue. *L'Athanor* was created by Maurice Baskine,[36] a minor surrealist esteemed by Breton, who that same year asked him to illustrate a deluxe edition of *Arcane 17*. An athanor is an alchemical oven. Baskine's *L'Athanor* was apparently a homage to the art of alchemy that may have functioned somewhat like the glowing brazier that was a focal point of Duchamp's installation for the 1938 international surrealist exhibition (figure 8.1). As we shall see, the following year Duchamp would appropriate Baskine's identity for the *Mémento Universel Da Costa*.

Surrounding each of the altars, including Duchamp's, were relics and sacrificial offerings from other artists. Duchamp had little to do with the actual fabrication of *The Juggler of Gravity*—or, for that matter, with the fabrication of any his works in the 1947 *Exposition Internationale du Surréalisme*—which helps to explain the uncharacteristically haphazard nature of his contributions. In this case, Duchamp went beyond his previous practice of disappearing before the opening of exhibitions he had conceived to disappear well before the 1947 installation had even begun, essentially ceding artistic control to his close associates Kiesler and Matta. Clearly, his attention was elsewhere.

Several erstwhile Acéphale members contributed essays to the catalogue *Surréalisme en 1947*, which was designed by Duchamp. Ever the contrarian, Georges Bataille entitled his essay "The Absence of Myth." He began it with a more-surrealist-than-thou affirmation of what, in his experience, lay beyond myth: "The mind that determines this moment in time necessarily withers and, stretched to the limit, desires this withering. Myth and the possibility of myth unravel: only an immense void remains, beloved and miserable."[37] Breton responded—or rather, refused to respond—in his introductory essay: "This is not the place for us to pronounce upon the thorny question of whether the absence of myth is still a myth, and whether we must see in it the myth of today."[38] The skeptical Duchamp clearly sided with Bataille. As designer of the catalogue, he seems to have affectionately teased his randy friend by reproducing on the page opposite Bataille's essay paintings of a brothel by the Haitian artist and Voodoo priest Hector Hippolyte, along with a painting by Henry Miller (*Totem and Taboo*, 1943).

When he was asked by Cabanne about the 1947 exhibition, the only aspect Duchamp described in any detail was the Rain Room: "I had asked that they make some rain. It poured down on banks of artificial grass, and on a billiard table."[39] He did not mention the sculptures by Martins and Waldberg, but surely they were integral to his theme: the evocative reverberations between falling water, green grass, green billiard table with its holes, Martins's erotic sculpture, Waldberg's floaty piece (whose shape appears to echo the outlines of the Bride and the Milky Way in *The Large Glass*), and the work Duchamp was then intensely engaged with in New York—*Given: 1. The Waterfall, 2. The Illuminating Gas.*

••

By the time *L'Exposition Internationale du Surréalisme* opened in July 1947, Isabelle Waldberg, Robert Lebel, and Marcel Duchamp had been working for more than six months on *Le Da Costa Encyclopédique* with the collaboration of Bataille, Breton, and others—including Patrick Waldberg, who apparently provided the name and then more or less disappeared. (Isabelle kept him updated by mail while trying, unsuccessfully, to pry entries out of him.) This satirical postwar publication, which did not appear until after the close of the surrealist exhibition in fall 1947, had quite a few authors, most of whom had been involved in one way or another with Bataille's prewar group Acéphale. But the articles were all anonymous—with *Da Costa*, anonymity served as "headlessness" of another kind, whether with respect to organization or authorship.

About Duchamp and the *Da Costa* publications, Robert Lebel later wrote: "While [Duchamp] was engaged in engineering the Surrealist Exhibition of 1947, we were, along with André Breton, Patrick Waldberg, Jean Ferry, Georges Bataille, and Charles Duits, the instigators of the *Da Costa Encyclopédique*, a voluntary dissident, marginal, and very confidential enterprise devoted to anonymity and virulent humor. It was too much perhaps to ask of the participants who, mostly, soon scattered, Duchamp remaining the only one to support this ephemeral publication through its third and last fascicule."[40] Curiously, Lebel does not mention Isabelle Waldberg, who managed the project. By the end, it appears to have been Duchamp, along with Isabelle and Lebel and with the distracted participation of Bataille, who kept things going.

It was not uncommon for either Duchamp or Bataille to sign their work with pseudonyms. The anonymous character of *Da Costa* harks back to enterprises Duchamp had been involved in earlier. *Da Costa*'s humor and its esotericism paralleled his post-World War I publications as described by Gabrielle Buffet-Picabia: "The magazines *The Blind Man* and *Wrong-Rong* … which appeared under the aegis of M. Duchamp, were intended as nothing more than somewhat subversive amusements. They appeared in only a single issue each—deluxe issues, one might call them—for their circulation was restricted to close friends and contributors."[41] *Da Costa* distribution was similarly limited to insiders—the reviewer for *Paru* noted peevishly: "the recently published fascicule has been carefully suppressed by the publisher and booksellers. To obtain it, one must insist vigorously."[42]

Le Da Costa Encyclopédique and two subsequent *Mémentos Universel Da Costa* have been exhaustively documented by Pierre-Henri Kleiber, who emphasized that "the experience of *Da Costa* is inseparable from war—the upheavals it introduces into individual existence, the demoralization it entails, the unexpected contacts it promotes, the demands it imposes on those who have long questioned the fate of civilization." Kleiber credits Patrick Waldberg with the "operational origin" of *Da Costa* and notes that Patrick's letter to Isabelle of March 19, 1943, a version of which was published in *VVV* early the following year, was an "extraordinary convergence of intentions between what Bataille had attempted with the strange and radical experience of Acéphale, and the preoccupations of the Surrealist group in New York, at least those of Breton."[43]

Lebel's contribution was equally important, however. In his *VVV* response to Waldberg, Lebel focused on the inappropriateness of "sacred sentiment," which in modern individuals "gets identified with a sense of their own importance." (He may have had in mind Breton, or Bataille, or both.) Lebel ended by contrasting the superficiality of traditional rituals and values with the unifying—and very American—efficacy of humor: "To communion in bombast, we must oppose communion in what the Americans call 'debunking'—the deflation of all that is bloated, even in ourselves. Between those who tolerate the healthy test of humor, and those who take refuge in their miasma, the most significant of demarcation lines will immediately form." Development of a revolutionary language grounded in humor would be the mission of the clan Da Costa. Lebel insisted that humor, "as long as one chooses systematically to exploit its resources, has all the elements of any other effective concerted action." Humor was a resource for the creation of "a new language, whose access would be possible only through allusions, or the ellipses of metaphor and pun. Such language," he added, "might form the solid tie that we have hitherto vainly sought among a certain species of men."[44] Like Acéphale, Da Costa would be occult, but unlike Acéphale it would not be bound by occult ritual. *Le Da Costa Encyclopédique* was esoteric only in the sense that its authors were anonymous.

Despite his constant travels, Isabelle Waldberg did her best to keep Patrick in the loop. Her first reference to "Da Costa" appears in a letter of February 18, 1946 concerning Patrick's impending return to Paris: "Your return to the clan Da Costa [*famille Da Costa*] pleases me very much, since you seem to consider this name as a way of warding off the jinx of Paris—notably exaggerated seriousness." She wrote him again three days later: "I have the greatest sympathy for the clan Da Costa ... and what most distresses me in

Paris is that the members (of this clan) are rare."[45] Duchamp and Breton had not yet returned to Paris, so by "clan Da Costa" Isabelle was probably referring to herself, Lebel, Bataille, and any other former Acéphale members who shared their belief in the importance of humor. Whatever the significance of its name (both Alastair Brotchie and Kleiber have theories),[46] *Le Da Costa Encyclopédique* was not meant to be taken seriously.

Artistic manipulations of the encyclopedia or dictionary format include Duchamp's aforementioned interest in mining the Larousse encyclopedia; the reading out loud of random dictionary definitions during the "Dada excursions and visits" in 1920 Paris;[47] Bataille's "Critical Dictionary," which played an increasingly subversive role in his journal *Documents* (1929–1930);[48] and the *Dictionnaire abrégé du surréalisme*, published in connection with the 1938 surrealist exhibition discussed in chapter 8. *Le Da Costa Encyclopédique* was similarly intended to accompany the catalogue *Le Surréalisme en 1947*, which featured random quotes from authors like Fourier and Pascal that, while typical of the 1938 *Dictionnaire abrégé*, were not appropriate for the anonymous *Da Costa*. Finally, the catalogue for Duchamp and Breton's *Exposition inteRnatiOnale du Surréalisme 1959–1960* (the capitalizations in the title signaled the exhibition's dedication to EROS) would feature a *Lexique succinct de l'érotisme* that was the opposite of succinct.[49]

Bataille's influence within the clan Da Costa is confirmed by their *Encyclopédique*'s readymade illustrations sourced from the Fonderie Deberny et Peignot. "Peignot" was Georges Peignot, father of Bataille's beloved companion Colette (Laure) Peignot, who had died in 1938. After Laure's father and his brothers died in World War I, the family firm, G. Peignot & Fils, merged with that of her uncle, owner of the Fonderies Deberny. "No doubt the game of acquaintances," writes Kleiber, "explains the use of [Deberny et Peignot] catalogues by the designers of *Da Costa*."[50] Laure had worked with Boris Souvarine as editor and designer of *La Critique sociale* (1931–1934), the context in which Bataille had come to know her.[51] Among other things, *Le Da Costa Encyclopédique* was a *sub rosa* tribute to Laure.

Duchamp served as both designer and typographer for *Le Da Costa Encyclopédique*, which was modeled on *Le Petit Larousse illustré*—a favored source for him.[52] *Da Costa* was presented as one "fascicule" of an ongoing publication. Every one of its entries begins with the letter "e" except for the first, which begins mid-entry on page "207" (actually page 1) with a broken word: "*-festations inexplicables. ...*" Duchamp's authorship of this first entry becomes clear by the last entry of the final fascicule of *Le Mémento Universel Da Costa*, which begins with a broken header ("*-TOIR.*"), begins and ends almost every line with a broken word, concluding with "*dis-je, pr-*" ("I say, pr-"). This final entry is signed "M. D." followed by: "(*à suivre*)"—"to be continued."[53] It never was, of course, so "(*à suivre*)" was probably a temporal riff referring to the texts of three more postcards in Duchamp's 1916 series of four sent to Arensberg entitled *Rendez-vous du dimanche 6 février*, of which the text published in the final issue of *Da Costa* is the first.

Like Larousse, the entries in *Le Da Costa Encyclopédique* were anonymous, a policy that would change only nominally with the advent of *Le Mémento Universel Da Costa*. The shift was described in an anonymous entry in the 1964 *Encyclopédie des farces et attrapes et des mystifications* (*Encyclopedia of Jokes, Hoaxes, and Mystifications*) that could only have been written by a *Da Costa* insider—most likely Robert Lebel: "No collaborator's name appeared on this fascicule [*Le Da Costa Encyclopédique*]. ... *Da Costa* distinguished itself above all by its insolence, and by its immoderate use of sarcasm. ... The defection of most of the first collaborators led to the abandonment of the rule of anonymity, which hardly facilitated the recruitment of new authors. Several names or pseudonyms therefore figure in Fascicule I of *Mémento Da Costa*, but as the number of contributors considerably diminished again in the course of further dissensions, the names mentioned in Fascicule II are almost all fictitious."[54] *Da Costa* thus remained essentially anonymous, which means that the initials and names appearing in *Mémento Universel Da Costa* should be taken with several grains of salt.

Even after the shift from encyclopedia to "memento" format with the names of the supposed authors revealed, the two issues of *Mémento Universel Da Costa* are smaller and shorter than the preceding *Da Costa Encyclopédique*. Why this thinning of the ranks? The puzzling conclusion to Lebel's *Encyclopédie des farces* entry contains a clue: "... the time is still not right to reveal details of this enterprise, or to evoke the very particular violence of which it was the expression."[55] If "very particular violence" refers to World War II, why not say so? Lebel's tantalizing hint more likely refers to the antisocial, erotic mayhem of Georges Bataille, which would only be revealed five years later in *G. B.*[56]

According to the *Encyclopédie des farces*, many *Da Costa* readers "were offended by several corrosive texts, notably the 'License to Live,' both sides of which were reproduced in facsimile." "License to Live" was more than just a sarcastic protest against governmental regulation and oppression; it was a wicked sendup of the covertly repressive nature of "humanistic" modern society. An addendum to the entry on "Emancipation," whose authorship is unclear,[57] "License to Live" was reproduced as a service to readers who wanted to "prepare themselves for the preliminary tests and checks" about to take place throughout France as a "hallmark of a humanism at once generous and clear-sighted, the precious heritage of twenty centuries of Christian civilization."[58] The author of this license supposedly about to be issued in 1947 by the "République Française" was Duchamp, who in one of his notes published in *The Green Box* had vowed to "Establish a society in which the individual has to pay for the air he breathes ... in case of non-payment simple asphyxiation if necessary (cut off the air)."[59] "License to Live" suggested that moment was about to arrive.

On December 20, 1946, Isabelle Waldberg wrote her husband: "André Breton has submitted his texts, as has Bataille. Both are quite short, especially Bataille's, but rather beautiful."[60] Bataille sent two entries for *Le Da Costa Encyclopédique*,[61] "*Érotisme*," and "*Extase*":

> ECSTASY. Sensibility in a pure state, deprived of any intelligible element, reduced to the condition of a sewer in which rapidly flowing waters converge (but the sewer is a bottomless chasm); sentiment of evasion and of infinite hilarity in which absurdity runs riot and abandons itself, with its contrary, to instantaneous exchanges which go astray in space. Joy that is insupportable, useless, impossible—and joyless.[62]

Those familiar with Bataille's prose will easily recognize in this passage his telltale elisions of purity and filth, flow and bottomlessness, merging and space, absurdity and ecstasy and, most of all, joyless joy.[63] Several tantalizing references should be noted. One is the potential link between Bataille's bottomless chasm and the *Tao Te Ching*'s "river gorge to the world." Another is the parallel with Duchamp's *Fountain*—an upended plumbing fixture submitted to an art exhibition—which reduced any "intelligible element … to the condition of a sewer." Perhaps most intriguing is the potential connection with Isabelle Waldberg's *Always There Beautiful Aqueduct* (1943, figure 6.19), which similarly references flowing water. These *sub rosa* parallels and connections suggest that the clan Da Costa was more than just a group of humor-loving friends; it was an ongoing, multilevel conversation among like-minded subversives.

Kleiber points out that Bataille had announced in the July 1937 issue of *Acéphale* that the next issue would be devoted to "*L'Érotisme*."[64] This issue never appeared in its entirety, although the subsequent (and last) issue of *Acéphale* did conclude with Bataille's "Practice of Joy Before Death." A summary of Bataille's thoughts on "Erotism" finally appeared eight years later in *Le Da Costa Encyclopédique*:

> **EROTISM.—Whoever has not chosen obscenity, recognized in obscenity the presence and the shock of poetry, and, more intimately, the elusive brightness of a star, is not worthy to die and their death will extend upon earth the industrious anxiety of priests.**[65]

Duchamp would appear to have been the creator of a chart that accompanied Bataille's entry for "Erotism." It is as brilliant in its way as "License to Live," and even more offensive (figure 9.6). Labelled "*Érotisme*," the chart reproduces twenty-seven hand gestures keyed to obscene or esoteric meanings, including *Cunnilinger*, *Déflorer*, *Occulter*, and *Yonir*—a made-up French verb based on the Sanskrit *yoni*, referring to the female reproductive system, from vulva to womb.[66] Isabelle Waldberg's 1946 sculpture *Luminaire* and Marcel Duchamp's 1956 cover for *Le Surréalisme, même* (figures 6.20, 6.15) are yonis, as is the focal point of *Given* (figure 0.1).

The collaboration between Duchamp and Bataille seems to have continued, but identifying Bataille's contributions to the two issues of *Mémento Universel Da Costa* is not easy. His name does not appear among the contributors, and Kleiber does not list him as an author. There is, however, one entry in the first fascicule of *Mémento* that is a strong candidate: the entry for "EVE. Biblically, the first woman." The *Da Costa* entry for "Adam," Eve's male counterpart, appeared in the second fascicule. "Eve" and

"Adam" are both signed "M. B." According to the note on collaborators on the inside front covers, "M. B." refers to Maurice Baskine—the same Maurice Baskine who created the alchemical *L'Athanor* as the centerpiece of the Labyrinth of Initiations at the 1947 *Exposition Internationale du Surréalisme.* Kleiber does not question Baskine's authorship,[67] but surely *Da Costa* insiders would have known that "M. B." was a front. Aside from the purported entries in *Da Costa*, Baskine published nothing of note. Given the erudition and wit that characterize "Eve" and "Adam," the suggestion that these entries in *Mémento Universel Da Costa* are by Maurice Baskine is so surprising as to be unbelievable.[68] Their style and content point to a partnership between M[arcel] and B[ataille] that was more complex than their parallel contributions to the topic of "Erotism" in *Le Da Costa Encyclopédique.*

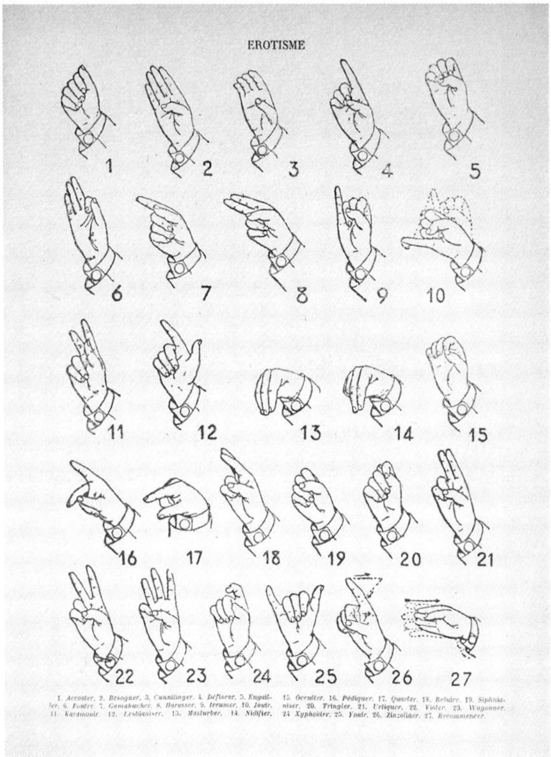

FIGURE 9.6

Erotisme, from *Le Da Costa encyclopédique*, fascicule VII, volume II, 1947 (*Yonir* is number 25) (Key: 1. Accoster, 2. Besogner, 3. Cunnilinger, 4. Déflorer, 5. Engailler, 6. Foutre, 7. Gamahucher, 8. Harasser, 9. Irrumer, 10. Jouir, 11. Karamonir, 12. Lesbianiser, 13. Masturber, 14. Nidifier, 15. Occulter, 16. Pédiquer, 17. Quarter, 18. Reluire, 19. Siphnianiser, 20. Tringler, 21. Urtiquer, 22. Violer, 23. Wagonner, 24. Xyphoïder, 25. Yonir, 26. Zinzoliner, 27. Recommencer)

Adam and Eve—more specifically, the episode of the Fall—was a concern of Duchamp's throughout his life (e.g., *Young Man and Girl in Spring*, 1911, figure 4.8). This may have had to do with reading Pascal in his youth,[69] but more generally with the Fall as introducing dualism into the world—specifically the "knowledge" of good and evil leading to judgment and shame. For his part, Bataille would have been interested in the Fall as the cause of separation from and abandonment by God. There is a noticeable shift in tone from the scholarly, myth-obsessed "Eve," which is more characteristic of Bataille's writing, to the terse, scientific-philological-mathematical "Adam," which reads more like Duchamp. Still, it is impossible to be definitive—both had studied philology at the École des Chartes, and any interest in tantra they may have shared comes through clearly in the entries and accompanying chart for "Erotism" and diagram for "Adam" (figures 9.6, 9.7).

"Eve" begins with a pseudo-kabalistic creation myth and ends in a Dionysian vision that is almost impossible to follow: "Eve, divine spirit of *Iève* ['organizer' of the world from chaos], and her daughters, had to find in themselves all the necessary artifices to tempt, excite, and, finally, to seduce the Serpent, their bad boy [*leur mal et leur mâle*]. For a long time this was their only means of attracting a husband. It was not until the twentieth century that, finally, conscious of their rights and wresting them from the ophidian [reptilian] vanity of Man, life and strength were returned to *Iève*, the spiritual part of the human couple—Woman, resuscitated in all the brilliance of her divine glory. *Io Evohé*."[70] *Io Evohé!* was the cry emitted by ecstatic dancers during the ancient Dionysian mystery rites—a research interest of Bataille's.[71] Only in the twentieth century, according to the *Da Costa* entry, did Woman finally free herself from the need to subjugate herself to satisfy Man.

"Eve" recapitulates the trajectory of Bataille's Acéphale with, as the central protagonist, its only female member, *Da Costa* editor Isabelle Waldberg. The epitome of sexually liberated Woman, Isabelle no doubt served as go-between for Bataille and Duchamp, who had been in New York since winter 1947. But the pun on *mal* (bad) and *mâle* (male) is unlike Bataille, who was more comfortable writing *about* humor than he was trying to write humorously.[72] More likely, this little insertion, which harks back to the Nine Malic Moulds in *The Large Glass*, was Duchamp's.

The much shorter "Adam" (figure 9.7) reads, in its entirety:

> According to the Bible, the world was created in six days. On the sixth day, the first man appeared. According to Da Costa (*Origines cosmiques du Genre Humain*, Amsterdam 1644), the Bible could be deciphered with the aid of Platonic geometry and the French phonetic Cabala.
>
> It would thus be appropriate to consider that ADAM = a dame = who had a wife.
>
> Adam was androgynous until the sixth day and possessed within himself the two sexes. The human being is polarized into three active parts: mind, heart, sex. Man has negative mind, neutral heart, positive sex.
>
> Woman has positive mind, neutral heart, negative sex.
>
> The mystery of Adam before and after his division can thus be schematized in the following fashion: [see figure 9.7].
>
> So it was not a rib [*côte*] that was removed from Adam by the creation of Eve.
>
> It was a side [*côté*, "aspect"].
>
> A geometrically symbolic side.[73]

"Adam" humorously parodies alchemically infused, Fourier-influenced postwar Surrealists like Breton,[74] but the "mystery of Adam" harks back to Duchamp's own, much earlier *Young Man and Girl in Spring*.

Da Costa's interpretation of the Genesis account to mean creation of the human as an androgynous being wrenched apart, spiritually as well as physically, into two polarized beings yearning for reunion, is a classic example of perennial philosophy. Precursors can be found in Taoism, Buddhism, tantra, the Greek mysteries, alchemical theory, and *Mysterium Magnum*, Jacob Boehme's account of the Fall (1623).[75] Unique to Duchamp, however, is *Da Costa*'s "scientific" male-female reverse polarization of mind and sex. As opposed to the original being's single heart with positive/negative sex and brain, Adam and Eve "after" the Fall have oppositely charged sexes and brains. Their separate hearts, however, are represented by a neutral, "geometrically symbolic side"—an infinity sign. Adam and Eve's polarized minds and genitals attract each other, but true union can be attained only at the heart.

The infinity sign, like the star, was something of a Duchamp leitmotiv. Examples include *Brawl at Austerlitz* (figure 9.8), where infinity signs mark transparent windows; and Man Ray's portrait of Duchamp (1923, frontispiece), with two infinity signs in the upper left corner coupled in such a way that their halves form hearts. These infinity signs are for the most part

ADA

ADAM. D'après la Bible, le monde fut créé en six jours. Au sixième jour parut le premier homme, Adam. Selon Da Costa (*Origines cosmiques du Genre Humain*, Amsterdam 1644), la Bible pourrait se déchiffrer à l'aide de la géométrie platonicienne et de la Cabale phonétique française.

Il y aurait alors lieu de considérer que ADAM = a dam = qui a dame.

Adam au sixième jour était androgyne et possédait en lui les deux sexes. L'être humain est polarisé dans ses trois parties agissantes : cerveau, cœur, sexe. L'homme a le cerveau négatif, le cœur neutre, le sexe positif.

La femme a le cerveau positif, le cœur neutre, le sexe négatif.

Le mystère d'Adam avant et après son dédoublement peut donc se schématiser de la façon suivante :

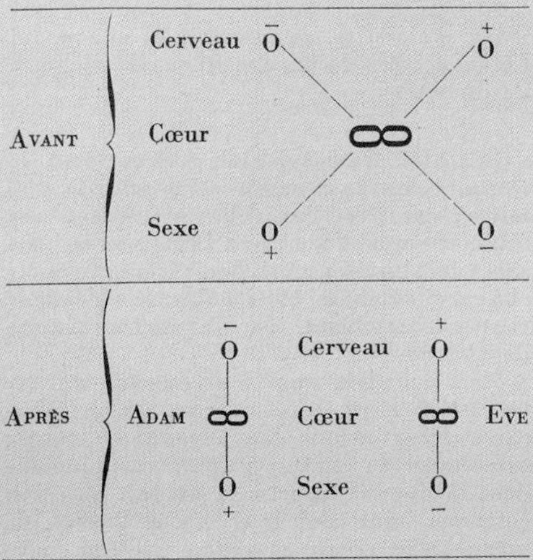

Ce ne fut donc pas une côte qui fut enlevée à Adam par la création d'Ève.

Ce fut un côté.

Un côté géométriquement symbolique.

M. B.

Cf. l'article Ève dans le précédent fascicule.

CRITIQUE. Cette opération de censure prélude généralement à ce qu'on nomme une proposition constructive. Il s'agit en somme

FIGURE 9.7

Adam, from *Le Mémento Universal Da Costa*, fascicule II, 1949

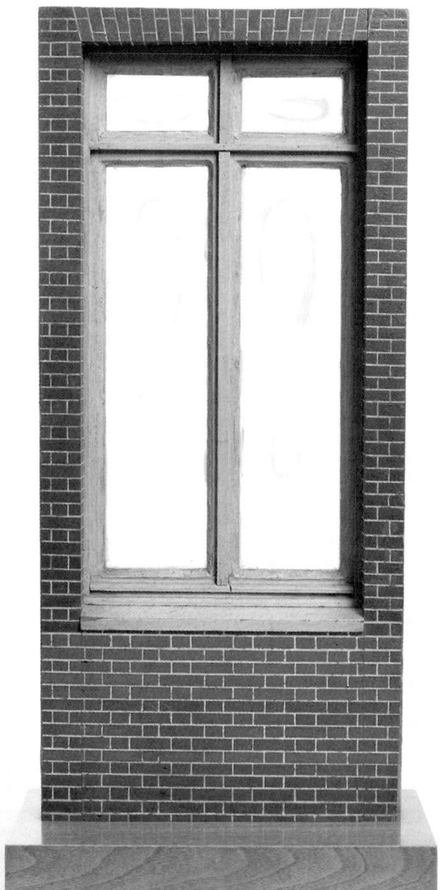

FIGURE 9.8

Marcel Duchamp
La Bagarre d'Austerlitz / The Brawl at Austerlitz, 1921
Oil, glass, wood, 62.8 × 28.7 × 6.3 cm
Staatsgalerie, Stuttgart, Germany, inv. P 360

vertical. An example of a horizontal infinity sign, like the ones in *Da Costa*, appeared in Vivekananda's *Râja Yoga* (1910). On the same page where the root chakra is described as triangular, Vivekananda inserts "∞" to suggest a cross section of the spinal column along which Kundalini ascends.[76]

The humorous, tongue-in-cheek nature of "Eve" and "Adam" is clear enough; the two *Da Costa* entries make fun of a gamut of religious and occult beliefs. About one thing, though, they are serious: the potential of mental and erotic attraction to generate a new being: "Woman, resuscitated in all the brilliance of her divine glory"—a line from "Eve" that may have been intended to describe Isabelle Waldberg, and that could serve as a caption for *Given* (figure 0.1).

••

The Waldbergs, Lebel, and Duchamp began planning *Le Da Costa Encyclopédique* in 1946; it finally appeared in the fall of 1947. The first fascicule of *Le Mémento Universel Da Costa* was probably published in November 1948—one full year later—with the second fascicule following in April 1949.[77] We know from Lebel that *Le Mémento* was primarily Duchamp's endeavor.[78] He would have had to direct it largely from New York, with Isabelle Waldberg and Robert Lebel overseeing production in Paris. Then *Da Costa* disappeared, belying the full-page advertisement in the last issue announcing a Duchamp-style "contest":

GREAT "DA COSTA" CONTEST
WHAT WILL BE
THE NEXT INCARNATION OF EVIL?

> ... In the course of [just a] few years, we have been enjoined to detest in turn, and sometimes even simultaneously, the Germans, the Italians, the Japanese, the English, the Jews, the Americans or the Russians: what matters now IS TO DISCOVER WHO TO DETEST NEXT. Our civilization has hitherto been an incomparable devourer of viciousness. If we continue along this path much longer, we risk finding ourselves suddenly with nothing to hate. ...
>
> It is therefore necessary and urgent to deal with this possible vacancy as soon as possible. ... Let us safeguard both our good old days and the future of our children. Readers, we count on you! ...
>
> **What are the new incarnations of evil for which you can envision immediate utilization?**

a) In a situation where the Democrats exterminate the Communists,
b) In a situation where the Communists exterminate the Democrats.
... The most significant responses will be published in a forthcoming fascicule.

BE FOREWARNED, HELP US PREPARE TODAY
FOR THE HATREDS OF TOMORROW

There would be no more fascicules. The tongue-in-cheek contest format was classic Duchamp (recall his "Twin-Touch-Test" in *VVV*), but the overt political content and aggressive tone are characteristic of Bataille. This artistic and philosophical distance between Duchamp's light touch and Bataille's heavy hand seems ultimately to have led to the undoing of *Da Costa*. On October 6, 1949, Duchamp wrote Maria Martins: "What is lacking now, at least in France, is that celebrated sense of humor that has been quite simply trampled upon and cast to the wayside for several years to come by political fanaticism. And the Surrealists are a sad lot, they who stand up in defense of humor, with 'theory'."[79] Duchamp could work with just about anybody, even Breton, but he met his match in Bataille. Considering their different perspectives, the on-and-off collaboration between these two "Da Costas" lasted a surprisingly long time. What they shared, aside from their mutual interest in tantra—very evident in the *Da Costa* entry for Adam in the last fascicule—was citizenship in that post-World War II community of heart, the clan Da Costa.

On September 6, 1948, while the *Da Costa* fascicules containing "Eve" and "Adam" would still have been in preparation, Duchamp wrote Maria Martins, then in Paris, from Endicott, New York, where he had gone for a chess tournament. He had played well and was "delighted" with himself: "These 8 green days [*jours au vert*] have done me an enormous good." Duchamp's terminology is telling: as we know from *Le rayon vert*, for him green represented not just the life force, but escape to freedom: "I had lots of free time between the hours of play and I thought a lot about us—that life is simple when one doesn't think only of one's own inner self [*son moi intérieur*]—So I made an excursion into your self [*ton moi*] and found what I thought would be there, through exterior contact alone—I found some 'things' that have no name in even the most poetic language—We have to live with these 'things' and these 'things' only—The rest, physical survival, must be reduced to its minimum—"[80]

As opposed to purely meditative practices involving one's own spiritual energies, the sexual practices of the Kaula lineages emphasized engagement with an "external Shakti." This dual practice entailed maintaining a state of spiritual illumination in sexual union, a state in which the two become absorbed in consciousness of the Self and are united on all levels. The resulting "subtle emission" can be either "rested" or "risen." In the rested form, the focus is absorbed within one's own self in an act of transcendence. Kaula practice focuses on the "sacred place" of one's lover and emphasizes the risen form, associated with immanence (perceivable through the senses and the mind).[81] I suggest that Duchamp's mental excursion in search of "some 'things'" within the inner self of his lover was grounded in a tantra-influenced search for wholeness—the infinite "life and strength" of "the spiritual part of the human couple."

All this helps to explain what Gabrielle Buffet-Picabia described as her "initiation" experience with Duchamp in that mountain train station during the pivotal year of 1912 (see chapter 3). In the Kaula practice of "penetration," the minds of guru and disciple "become perfectly fused. Both acquire the transmental state, and by their arrival at the transmental, at that moment, [the disciple] is initiated."[82] Duchamp would not have needed physical contact with Gabrielle for him to merge his erotic energy with hers, to take his excursion in search of those perennial "things" that have no name—any more than he needed physical contact to find them in Maria, half a world away.

"I return tomorrow," he added in his letter to Maria, "and I am going to find my dry skin under its steel rods—you alone can understand this sentence." Duchamp was referring to *Given: 1. The Waterfall, 2. The Illuminating Gas*, then under construction. His final artistic message to the world may have been conceived during his passionate relationship with Maria Martins, but it received the breath of life from Rrose Sélavy. The fact that *Given* was conceived by Marcel Duchamp means that this occult artistic expression of the source of enlightenment was not intended to be taken completely seriously. Ramakrishna's pronouncement: "God is in the vagina!"—is bound to be an incongruous, even funny, thought to most Westerners. As the clan da Costa knew, nothing is conceivable without humor.

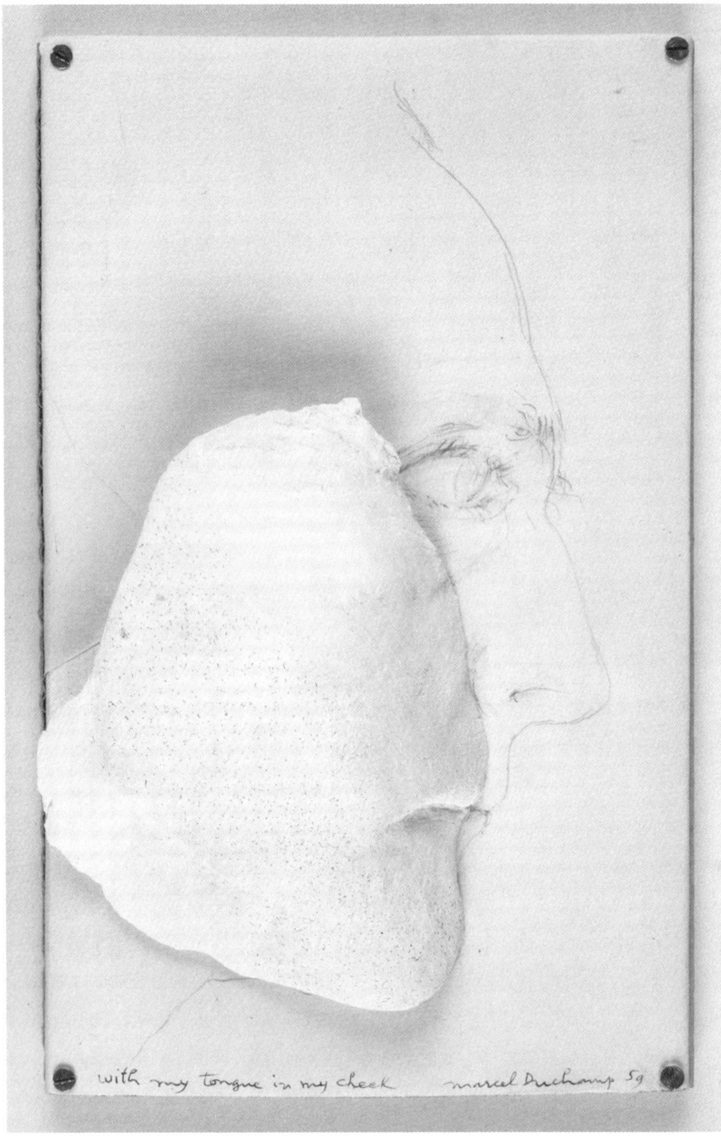

FIGURE 10.1

Marcel Duchamp
With My Tongue in My Cheek, 1959
Plaster, pencil on wood-mounted paper, 25 × 15 × 5.1 cm
Musée National d'Art Moderne, Centre Georges Pompidou, Paris, France, AM1993-123
Photo: © CNAC/MNAM/Dist. RMN-Grand Palais / Art Resource, NY

10 WHAT IS GIVEN?

Everything announces a passage to go through, a rupture to realize.

—Robert Lebel, "The Inventor of Free Time"[1]

The 1940s were a decade of change for Marcel Duchamp: he lived through another catastrophic world war and returned to New York once again, this time more or less for good. He fell profoundly in love—an experience that prompted his last major work, *Given: 1. The Waterfall, 2. The Illuminating Gas* (figure 0.1). It would take him twenty years to develop this large, complex installation, and even then it did not go on view until after his death in 1968.[2] *Given* made blindingly explicit what Duchamp's earlier magnum opus, *The Large Glass* (figure 0.2), abstractly implied. Both are about connection and transformation: the power of erotic energy to connect, transformed into the creative power of art to illuminate. Even with the perspective granted by time, however, *Given* remains a stubbornly esoteric work of art. In order to begin to understand it, we need to return to a discussion of tantra.

Tantra evokes "continuum."[3] *Tan* in Sanskrit signifies "to stretch out" or "weave," as in a pattern. In India, the word "tantra" has been used since Vedic times to signify anything from a mechanical aid for weaving, such as a loom, to a system of philosophy, to a remedy for life's ailments.[4] In 1922 Duchamp wrote his Dada colleague Tristan Tzara to propose that they produce a multiple consisting of four cast letters, "D, A, D, A," strung together and sold with what Duchamp described as "A fairly short prospectus ... [where] we would enumerate the virtues of Dada. So that ordinary people from every land will buy it, we'd price it at a dollar, or the equivalent in other currencies. The act of buying this insignia will consecrate the buyer as Dada. ... [It] would protect against certain maladies, against life's multiple anxieties, something like those Little Pink Pills for everything. ... You get my idea: nothing "literary," "artistic"; just straight medicine, universal panacea, fetish—in the sense that if you have a toothache you can go to your dentist and ask him if he is Dada."[5] From his dentist example, Duchamp's "Dada" would seem to be not just an avant-garde art movement, but also an attitude that could provide relief from life's "multiple anxieties."

His interest in the potentially connecting, pain-relieving power of art helps to explain *Mile of String* (figure 6.1)—a continuum whose lines "interweave themselves into that universally enveloping fabric which is Space."[6] The function of Duchamp's string was arguably to connect and guide, as in a labyrinth, one of Duchamp's metaphors in "The Creative Act." Recalling that tantra means "loom" would also help to explain the woven plaid fabric in *Couple of Laundresses' Aprons* (figure 10.2), a quirky collaborative effort created for the *Boîte Alerte* that Duchamp and Canadian artist Mimi Parent compiled for the deluxe edition of the catalogue to the 1959 *Exposition inteRnatiOnale du Surréalisme*, organized by Breton and Duchamp.

"I'm sending you two little aprons destined to protect the hands from the excessive heat of the pots and casseroles on the fire," Duchamp wrote Breton during planning for the 1959 exhibition. "One is male, the other female."[7] *Laundresses' Aprons* consists of two red plaid potholders: one "male," with a red-tipped penis popping out from a fly at the center; the other "female," with a flap at the "crotch" that lifts to reveal a patch of fur. In Indian *maithuna* (ritual sexual union), the male practitioner theoretically seeks out a "forbidden" partner such as a low-caste laundress (*dhobi*). Sexual intercourse with a laundress is considered transgressive because of her association with soiled garments and dirt.[8] Dirt was a recurrent theme in Duchamp's art, from *Dust Breeding* (1920) to his installation in the 1961 exhibition *Surrealist Intrusion in the Enchanter's Domain* at D'Arcy Galleries in New York entitled *Coin sale* ("Dirty Corner").[9]

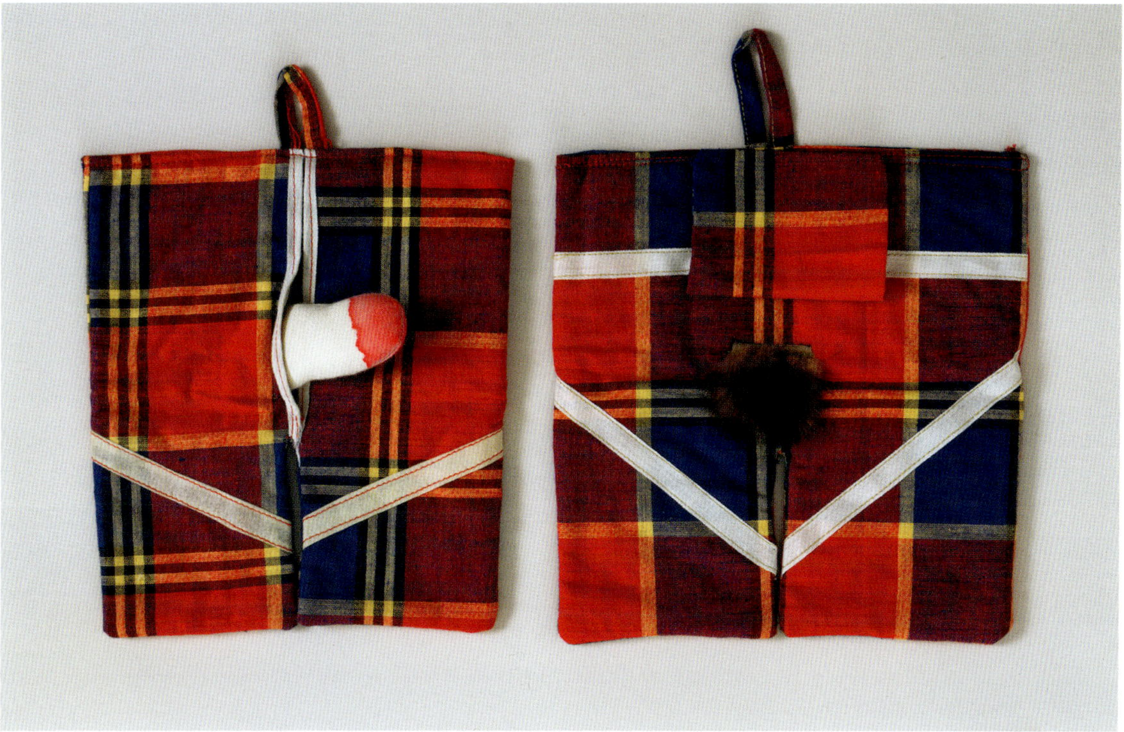

FIGURE 10.2

Marcel Duchamp

Couple of Laundresses' Aprons, 1959

Two multiples of cloth and fur, overall (male, irreg.): 22.8 × 17.7 × 3.2 cm; overall (female, irreg.): 24.8 × 19.8 × 2.3 cm

Publisher: Galerie Daniel Cordier, Paris. Fabricator: Mimi Parent, Paris. Edition: 20.

The Museum of Modern Art, New York, Gift of Arthur A. Goldberg

According to Genesis 3:7, Adam and Eve made themselves aprons to hide their nakedness. The identification of Duchamp's potholders as *laundresses*' aprons "alerts" us to their tantric shamelessness, while the gendered identities indicate that their holding action is erotic union. Signifying the energizing, cleansing power of water and the transformative power of fire, Duchamp's immodest potholders are perhaps the clearest evidence of his tantric interests. They alert us to the dimension of reality accessed in *Given*, and to the importance of humor in Duchamp's work—a role foregrounded by his contemporaneous *With My Tongue in My Cheek* (1959, figure 10.1). *With My Tongue in My Cheek* indicates that Duchamp intended his work in general, and perhaps *Given* in particular, as something not to be taken too seriously. Still, it should not be regarded simply as a joke. A "tongue-in-cheek" statement typically has a double meaning, or contains some sort of innuendo, even when its context (such as in a museum) suggests that it is meant to be contemplated.

In another work from 1959—*Cols alités* (figure 10.3)—the composition of *The Large Glass* is superimposed over a hilly landscape with an electrical pole in the lower right foreground. According to Robert Lebel, who owned this drawing, a note on the reverse reads: *Cols alités: Projet pour le Modèle 1959 de La Mariée mise à nu par ses célibataires, même.*[10] This "1959 model" of *The Large Glass* obviously refers to *Given*, on which Duchamp was then working. *Cols alités* is usually translated as "Bedridden Mountains."[11] *Alités* can be translated as "bedridden," but also "bedded." Although the drawing does show mountains, "mountain" is not a very good translation for *col*, which literally means "neck," as in a bottle. *Col* can also mean cervix, mountain pass, or passage. A more comprehensible translation for *Cols alités* would be *Bedded Passes*.

In Taoist energy practices, "Mysterious Pass" is code for an experiential mental opening that allows practitioners to access the "grand mystery" of Tao.[12] All *cols*, or passages, are essentially Tao, but the mountain landscape, where heaven's male *yang* mingles with earth's female *yin*, is the most dramatic manifestation of this generative relationship. With its mountain background, Duchamp's *Cols* would seem to relate most clearly to the concept of mountain pass, but also to other passages in his work—such as the "Mandala" in *The Large Glass*, or the circular lens in *To Be Looked At* (figure 5.7), or *Le rayon vert* in the sixth surrealist exhibition (figure 9.3).

Lebel said something else that helps explain why in *Cols alités* the water wheel and chocolate grinder of *The Large Glass* might be juxtaposed with mountains and a prominent electrical pole. He wrote that 1913, when Duchamp created the first version of *Chocolate Grinder* (figure 3.6), he had become engaged in "a dry, transparent, linear kind of art that he took up as a demonstration of his total materialism, leavened by a formidable humor, schematizing with the precision of a geometrician-land-surveyor the

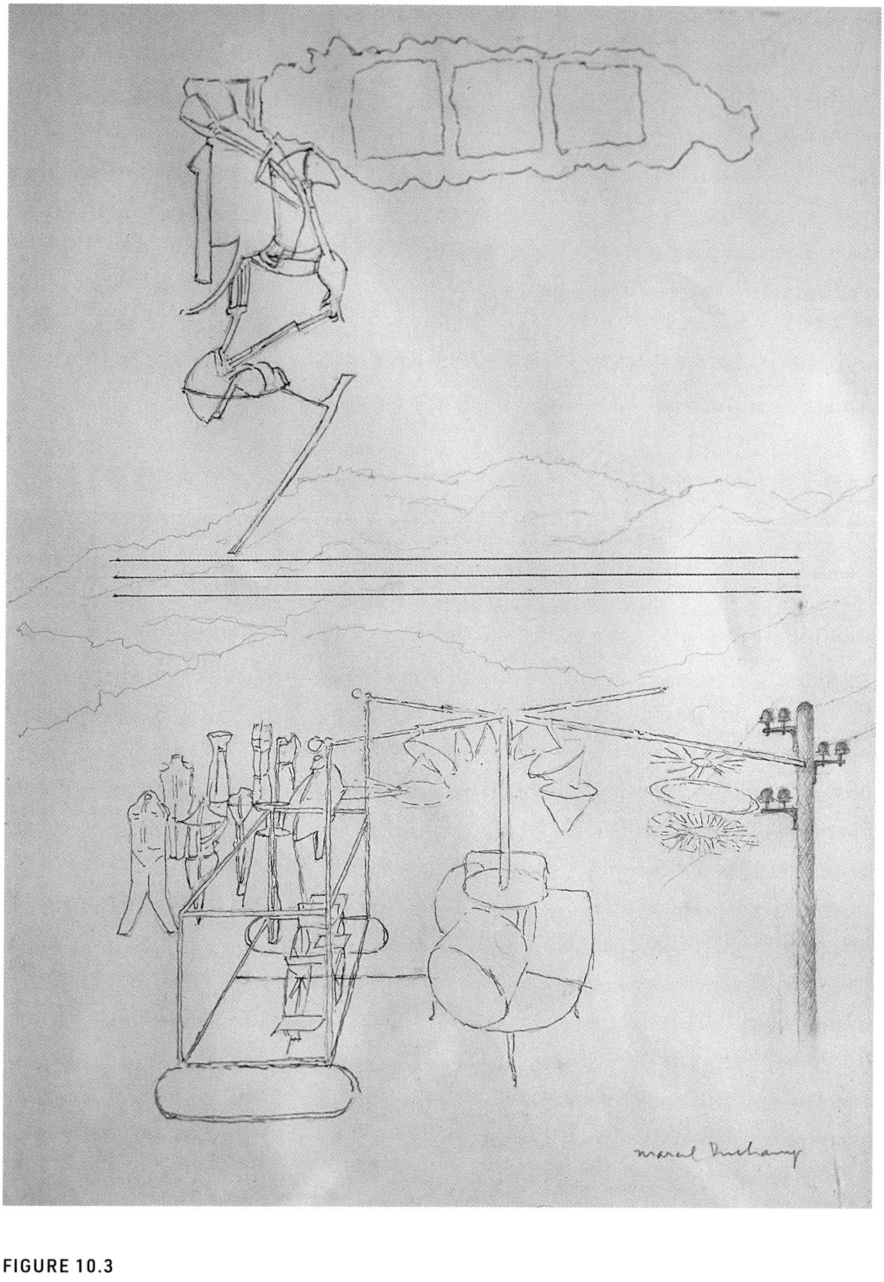

FIGURE 10.3

Marcel Duchamp
Cols alités / Bedded Passes, 1959
Pen, ink, and pencil on paper, 32 × 24.5 cm
Private collection / Bridgeman Images

wheels of love-passion assimilated into a productive circuit."[13] Since Descartes, the body has been compared with a machine; since the nineteenth century, it has been known that the activity of the brain and nervous system involves electrical connections. So it is not a leap to interpret Duchamp's water wheel and chocolate grinder as part of a circuit. Materialism, not mysticism; ironic humor rather than reverence; precision, not expression: this is the Duchamp we think we know. But what is this about erotic desire assimilated into a *productive* circuit? Isn't *The Large Glass* supposed to be about *frustrated* desire? It may be time for another look.

In an electrical circuit, current flows through wires that connect individual components, enabling a variety of transformative operations. What drives all this is the interaction of positive and negatively charged matter. In Duchamp's erotic parallel, "the spark that comes from that bipolar action gives birth to something—like electricity."[14] The comparison of electrical energy with erotic energy was ubiquitous around the turn of the twentieth century. In 1896, for example, Vivekananda wrote: "The same force which is working outside, as electricity or magnetism, will become changed into inner force."[15] In her 1903 book *The Lover's World*, American feminist obstetrician, writer, and publisher Alice Bunker Stockham, who had personally researched tantric practices in India during the early 1890s, compared erotic energy with the kinetic energy of a waterfall that can either dissipate or be harnessed to generate light: "The rushing flood ... is poured deep down upon the great wheels that put in motion the whirring dynamos. ... Through this subtle, unseen agent, whose power is only known by its results, ... it becomes a searchlight for remote corners and deep caverns."[16] Falling water from mountain passes driving wheels whose rotational movement generates light would become Duchamp's metaphor as well: "First the Waterfall, second the Illuminating Gas," he reminded himself in a note from 1912.[17]

Hidden in the formal title of *The Large Glass* is Duchamp's first name: *MARiée mise à nu par ses CÉLlibataires, même*; "MAR" is associated with the Bride, "CÉL" with the Bachelors. As previously explained, *La Mariée mise à nu par ses célibataires, même*, can be translated as "The Bride Stripped Bare by Her Bachelors, *Herself*," with both the Bride and Her Bachelors understood as aspects of Marcel. From this perspective, the erotic theme of *The Large Glass* is not frustrated desire, but desire processed and transformed.

Duchamp was fond of referring to his *Large Glass* as "Delay in Glass." This phrase shows up in his notes for the work as a "kind of subtitle,"[18] and surfaces again in his later comments about it. The Bride is stripped bare, uncovered by her "*célibataires*"—the French word for "bachelors." But *célibataires* also means, as in English, "celibates." In tantra, celibacy is not refusal of sexual relations, but *brahmacaryam*, "moving in the *brahman*": keeping the mind focused on the Absolute. This goal, "enstasy"—inner illumination—is achieved by learning to control breath, seminal fluid, and mind.[19] The order is according to presumed degree of difficulty, but the aim is simultaneity. From Abhinvagupta's *Tantrāloka*:

> He who ... is committed to restraint, who is at ease regarding the *brahmacarya* and who, even while involved in sexual union, is perfectly mindful, his body utterly tranquil, ... who is fully enlightened as well, who indeed is composed of consciousness, is autonomous at all times, who comes in contact with the particular object in order to acquire the supernatural power of experiencing his own consciousness and not because of an attitude of greed. ... He whose conduct shows an attentiveness to his own self ... always retains his seed during the observance [of ritual intercourse]. He, whose mind, at the moment of emitting semen, ... has spontaneously settled in respect to all the fluctuations of thought, all at once there arises in his mind the consciousness of bliss. The resulting form is perfectly described as 'pertaining to *brahman*'."[20]

In this practice, celibacy becomes a kind of delay. The goal of Duchamp's *célibataires* is not the deflowering of the Bride, but unveiling her—and their—inherent luminosity.

The "garment of the bride" is represented in *The Large Glass* by three horizontal green glass strips (clearly visible as three lines in *Cols alités*) that mark the separation between the domain of the Bride and that of the Bachelors.[21] Hovering above the Oculist Witnesses in the lower right portion is a circular form that Duchamp labeled "Mandala."[22] This mandala offers passage to the fourth dimension—reality in all of its luminous plenitude—available in the upper portion of the *Glass*. In its own peculiarly transparent/reflective, illusive/elusive way, *The Large Glass* thus can be understood as a vehicle for enlightenment that models achievement of both hypostatic union and the ongoing mental radiance associated with perception of the continuous nature of reality. The instigation and mechanics of this process are depicted in the lower part of the *Glass* containing the "bachelor apparatus," while the conclusion and blissful "blossoming" are portrayed in the "Bride's Domain," above. Far from creating a "fantasized" world, Lebel wrote, *The Large Glass* was intended "to penetrate further into the real through a ruthless 'laying bare' of its structures, its rules, its inner parts, its repression and its repressed."[23] For Duchamp, the goal of art and the goal of life had become the same: a relentless analysis of reality, with art as a means of dissection.

The primary proof for this interpretation of *The Large Glass* is *Given*, whose three-dimensional nude figure is, according to Duchamp, "the Bride in the Large Glass, finally unclothed and realized in *trompe l'œil* fashion."[24] Like *The Large Glass*, *Given* can be understood as a vehicle for enlightenment, its hyperrealism a polar attempt to convey Duchamp's view of "existence split into two distinct registers," with one focus on manifest and the other on unmanifest reality—the "inexpressible."[25] Both *The Bride Stripped Bare by Her Bachelors, Even* and *Given: 1. The Waterfall, 2. The Illuminating Gas* are about the transformation of one kind of energy into another: erotic energy into enlightenment.

In a 1961 symposium at the Philadelphia Museum College of Art, Duchamp addressed the age-old artistic problem of how to render light: "I am convinced that, like Alice in Wonderland, [the young artist of tomorrow] will be led to pass through the looking glass of the retina, to reach a more profound expression. ... We can foresee that just as the invention of new musical instruments changes the whole sensibility of an era, the phenomenon of light can, due to current scientific progress, among other things, become the new tool for the new artist." He concluded with another reference to *Alice in Wonderland*: "The great artist of tomorrow will go underground."[26] Duchamp may have had John Cage in mind with that reference to music, but "going underground" suggests both working in secret and going within. In retrospect, it seems obvious that, along with the hypothetical artist of the future, Marcel Duchamp was describing his own adventurous self, and not only in terms of the new tool of light.

Early-twentieth-century Parisian guru Mirra Alfassa recalled: "I remember an artist with whom I had talked of the possibility of immortality, who had asked me what the new world would be like. I told him that, for example, things would be self-luminous and there wouldn't be any more of this kind of reflected light which comes here, on the earth, from the sun."[27] In *Portrait of Chess Players* (1911, figure 1.15), we saw Duchamp grappling with the problem of rendering light from a source neither external nor mystical but integral to a reality imbued with the qualities of awakened mind. At that early moment he was struggling with how to depict this self-lit, "enlightened" quality by way of oil on canvas. Some fifty years later, in *Given*, he integrated light directly—a "new tool for the new artist." The lamp held up by Duchamp's nude figure was modeled on Bec Auer gas lamps, dating to his youth, that burned with a green flame. The year after he finished *Given*, Duchamp referred to their distinctive light in the comment to Pierre Cabanne quoted in chapter 1:

DUCHAMP: "Portrait of Chess Players" ... was painted by gaslight. It was a tempting experiment. You know, that gaslight from the old Auer jet is green; I wanted to see what the changing of colors would do ...

CABANNE: It's one of the rare times when you were preoccupied with problems of light.

DUCHAMP: Yes, but it isn't even really the light. It's the light that enlightened me.[28]

••

For fifteen years after it went on view, reproduction of the interior of *Given*, and of the instruction manual Duchamp had developed for its installation, was forbidden. Except for those willing to undergo darshan—willing to *look*, one at a time, through the peepholes—no one saw what lay behind the battered wooden door. One of those who made the pilgrimage was the painter and art historian Robert Motherwell. "This extraordinary achievement," Motherwell wrote in his 1971 introduction to Pierre Cabanne's *Dialogues with Marcel Duchamp*, "exemplifies another aspect of the artist's character. I mean a theatricality and a brutality of effect wholly remote from the intellectualism and refinement of the early work." *Given* clearly took Motherwell by surprise, revealing another side of an artist whose demeanor, Motherwell reports, quoting Cabanne, was characterized by a "serenity from which he never departed."[29] For the art world, the shocker was not only *Given*'s sexual explicitness, but also its startling hyperrealism—its "theatricality," which seemed so unlike the reticent, intellectual Duchamp people thought they knew.

It is not as though there were no clues. In the early 1950s Duchamp began giving friends small sculptures that, though abstract, suggest casts of intimate body parts. (They were in fact by-products of the molding process for the vellum skin of the figure in *Given*.)[30] And in 1966 Maria Martins startled the artist Richard Hamilton by sending to a Duchamp retrospective Hamilton was organizing a small but powerful relief of a female torso in an explicit pose (figure 10.4). An inscription on the back reads: "This lady is owned by Maria Martins / with all my affection / Marcel Duchamp 1948–1949," followed by the instruction: "to light: from the right and at the height of the upper part with a diffuse light to avoid casting strong shadows."[31] Hamilton was no more startled than the creator of the piece. When he spotted it in the show, Duchamp asked: "Where did you get that?"[32] The little relief Martins sent Hamilton was a small version of *Given*, which Duchamp finished that same year. Nevertheless, Duchamp did not reveal *Given*'s existence, either to Hamilton or to Arturo Schwarz, just then completing his massive catalogue raisonné. (Duchamp told Schwarz only that Martins's little relief was "the Bride in the Large Glass, finally unclothed and realized in *trompe l'œil* fashion.")[33]

Surrealist sculptor Maria Martins appears to have been the impetus for the creation of *Given*, and it is generally accepted that Duchamp made his first plaster casts for the nude figure directly from her body. In April 1946, just before his departure for Paris, Duchamp gave Martins a work entitled *Paysage fautif* (*Wayward Landscape*), consisting of ejaculate on black satin that he mounted on the inside lid of her gift copy of *Boîte-en-valise*.[34] At the same time, he inscribed her copy of *The Green Box* with a special dedication: "For Maria, finally arrived." That same year, the year he began working on *Given*, Duchamp wrote Martins from his New York studio: "If you want to unite with [*faire corps*] this freedom and enter into my freedom there is space there for two, and a still greater freedom will be born because yours will protect and increase mine and, I hope, vice versa."[35]

More than a proposal to share studio space, Duchamp's invitation recalls Max Théon's "duality of being." It has overtones as well of Edward Carpenter's "soul-union, a strange and intoxicating exchange of life, and

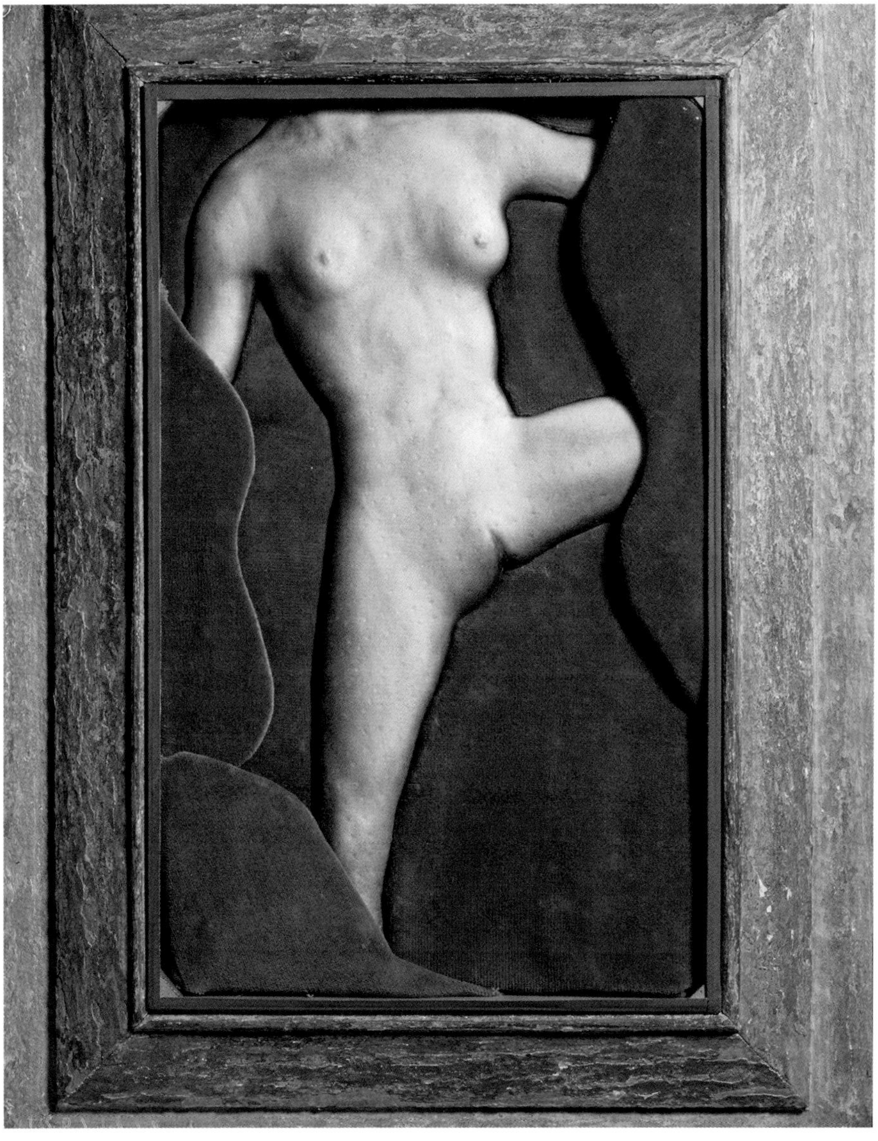

FIGURE 10.4

Marcel Duchamp
Étant donnés 1. la chute d'eau et 2. le gaz d'éclairage, 1948–1949
Leather, plaster, velvet, 50 × 31 cm
Moderna Museet, Stockholm, Sweden

transmutation of elements," in which—Carpenter here quotes Alice Bunker Stockham—"'the whole being of each is submerged in the other, and an exquisite exaltation experienced ... visions of transcendent life are seen, and consciousness of new powers experienced'."[36] Around the turn of the twentieth century, both the English sexual revolutionary and the American obstetrician and social reformer had framed tantric sexual practice as a liberating form of contraception. *Wayward Landscape* suggests that Duchamp may have used a similar rationale in proposing not just solidarity but a more erotic *faire corps* to the married Maria Martins. Her contemporaneous sculpture *The Impossible* (*O Impossível*, 1944–1946, figure 10.5), which

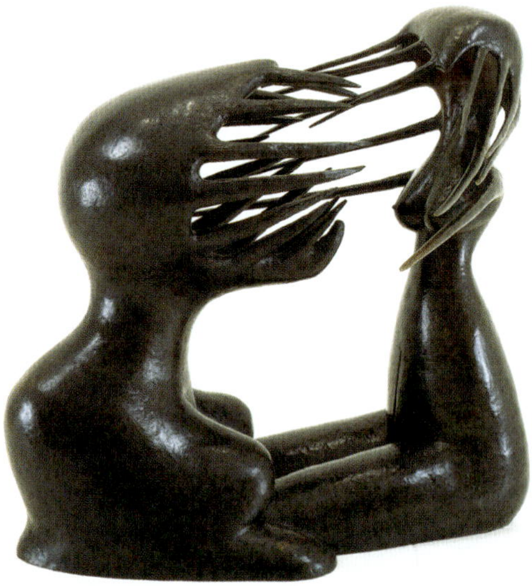

FIGURE 10.5

Maria Martins
The Impossible, III, 1946
Bronze, 80 × 82.5 × 53.3 cm
The Museum of Modern Art, New York, NY, Purchase

she worked on somewhat obsessively, producing a number of versions both in plaster and bronze, would seem to express her attitude toward Duchamp's proposed merger of minds.[37]

The Impossible shows two surrealistically abstracted figures intensely engaged with one another. The flamelike head of the male exerts an aggressively attracting force on the more tentative tendrils of the female. Their genitals, however, remain unengaged—his penis lies passively between her kneeling thighs; her vulva is a simple vertical slit in her lower belly (figure 10.6). The title, *The Impossible*, suggests that Martins did not feel quite up to Duchamp's ongoing requirements. Yet his dedication in her copy of *The*

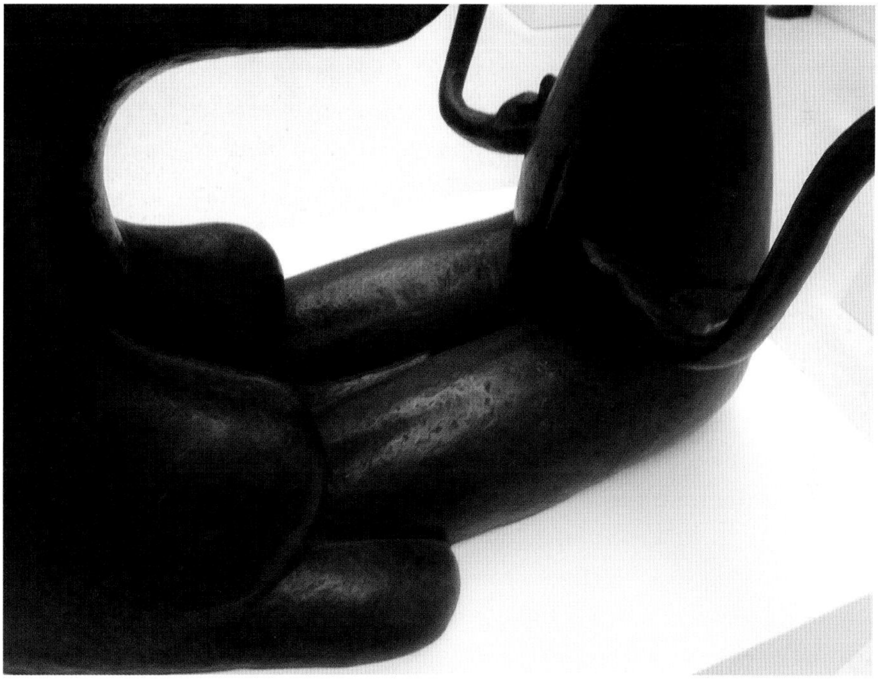

FIGURE 10.6

Maria Martins
The Impossible (detail), 1945
Museu de Arte Moderna, Rio de Janeiro

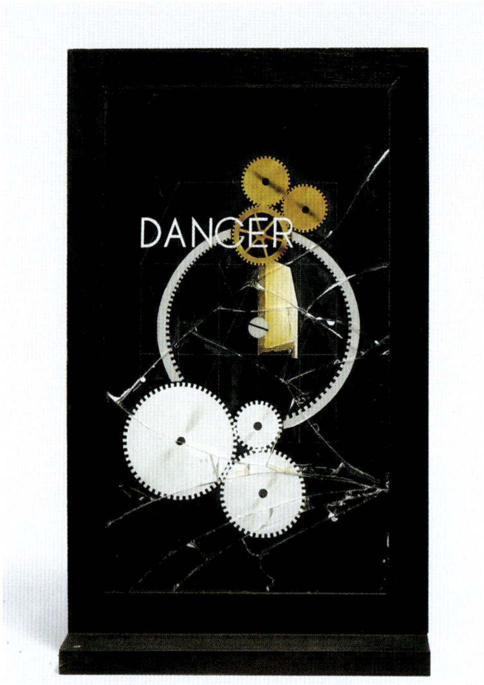

FIGURE 10.7

Man Ray
The Impossible ("Danger/Dancer"), 1917–1920
Airbrush painting on glass in a wooden frame (broken in 1968), 60.8 × 35.2 × 2 cm
Musée National d'Art Moderne, Centre Georges Pompidou, Paris, France, Gift of Mrs. Aube Breton-Elléouët and Oona Elléouët, 2003, AM2003-581

Green Box: "For Maria, finally arrived," seems to indicate that she gamely did her best.

Works created by two of Duchamp's closest friends suggest that *The Impossible* may relate to the challenging mental nature of the union depicted, and need not be interpreted literally. Much earlier, Man Ray had created a painting on glass obviously inspired by Duchamp's *Large Glass* that he entitled *The Impossible* (figure 10.7). Man Ray's *Impossible* combines an image of interlocked gears, alluding to mutual engagement, with letters that can be read alternately as "dancer" and "danger"—words reminiscent of the danger associated with performing tantric practices without full awareness. His title, which is inscribed directly on the piece, *à la* Duchamp, may have motivated Martins to apply the same ambiguous title to her own work. Or perhaps Duchamp suggested both titles. (Georges Bataille would similarly entitle his last collection of stories *L'Impossible*.)[38]

Like Martins's *The Impossible*, Beatrice Wood's 1917 painting *Sleepless Night* (figure 10.8) appears to portray mental intercourse. Artist Darren Waterston, who knew Beatrice Wood well, once asked her what it was like to be Duchamp's lover. She told him she and Duchamp shared an erotic life which did not include sexual intercourse, but in which the intellectual and the erotic were fused into "a complete erotic experience."[39] *Sleepless Night* suggests what this practice would have been like. In her energetic shorthand style, Wood portrayed a semi-recumbent woman riveted by the gaze of a standing male—a gaze that manifests as a dotted red line running from his head to her heart. A solid red line runs up through his body, and the hair of both figures is flaming red as well, presaging the flaming heads

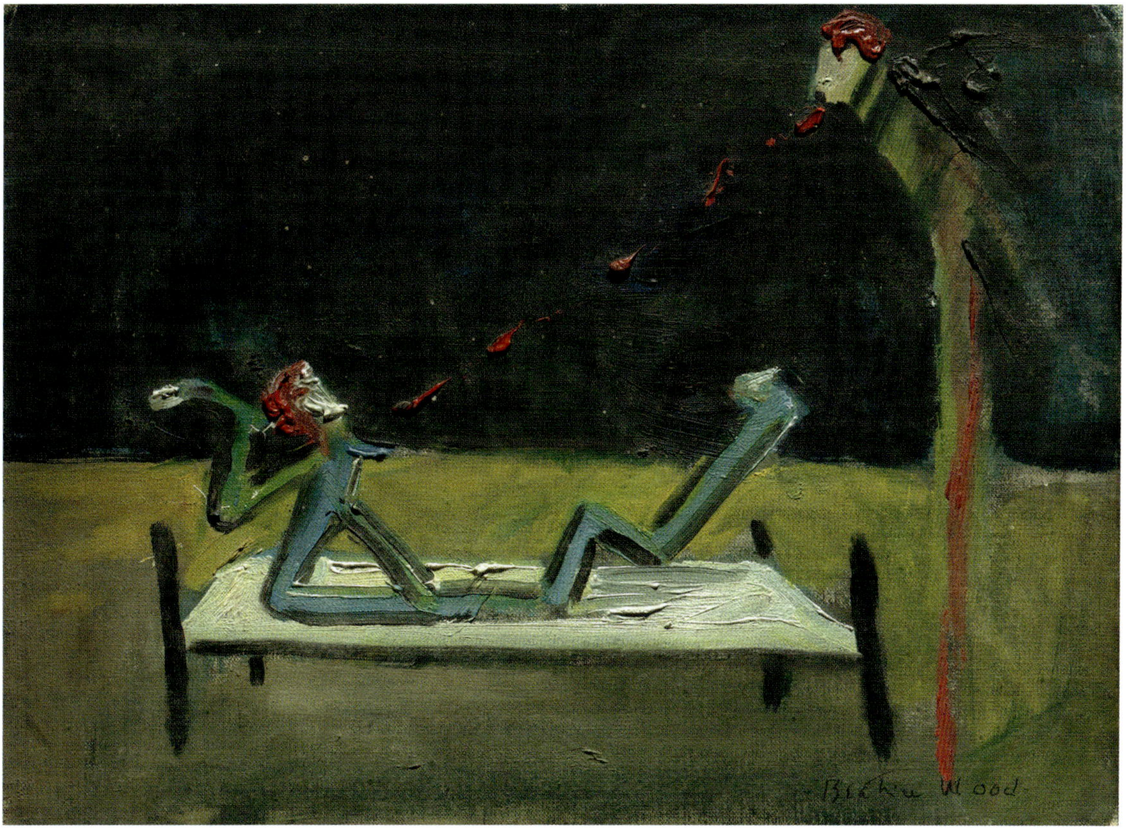

FIGURE 10.8

Beatrice Wood
Nuit Blanche / Sleepless Night, 1917
Oil on canvas board, 25.4 × 35.6 cm
Philadelphia Museum of Art, Philadelphia, PA, Gift of the artist, 1978, 1978-98-1

of Martins's figures. Wood gave this painting to the Philadelphia Museum of Art, where it complements the museum's extensive Duchamp holdings.

A similar scene is described in the posthumously published novel *Insel* by Duchamp's lifelong friend Mina Loy: "Shafts from his eyes became so penetrating I could feel myself dissolve to a transparent target, they pierced me, and, travelling to the further side, stared through my back on their return to his irises. ... Then he deliberately set himself on fire."[40] Like Wood, Loy first became intimately engaged with Duchamp after his arrival in New York in 1915: a period when, as Pierre Roché related in his roman à clef *Victor*, Duchamp's erotic practices included "lying chastely with women ... like some sort of Eros."[41] Another of Duchamp's lovers from this period, Baroness Elsa von Freytag-Loringhoven, created a now-lost portrait of Duchamp as a light bulb dripping with icicles. Both Duchamp's dazzling intensity and what Freytag-Loringhoven experienced as his coldness are conveyed by her comment about this work: "Something of his dynamic warmth—electrically—would be dissipated through contact."[42]

Isabelle Waldberg created works with more obvious visual links to *Given*, as we have seen. *Toujours là bel aqueduc* ("Always There Beautiful Aqueduct," 1943, figure 6.19) was part of the November 1945 window installation at Brentano's New York bookshop that Duchamp designed for the launch of André Breton's *Le Surréalisme et la peinture* (figure 6.18). Reversed, the pose of Waldberg's abstracted figure is identical to that of the figure in *Given*, conceived by Duchamp shortly thereafter. In the Brentano's installation, Waldberg's sculpture was placed beneath a paper veil *en chute*—in the process of falling. As photographed, this veil obscures the figure's head, just as the brick wall hides the head of Duchamp's figure in *Given*—both are *acéphale*, signaling their experiential nature. Other links between works by Waldberg and the figure in *Given* are *Luminaire* (1946, figure 6.20) and the drypoint drawings on aluminum created for the luxury edition of Michel Fardoulis-Lagrange's *G. B. ou un ami présomptueux* (1968–1969, figure 8.3).[43] "Beautiful aqueduct" parallels Duchamp's waterfall, while the wood from which the figure is constructed correlates with his conception of the *Bride* as an "arbor-type."[44] This element of *The Large Glass* may relate to *yakshi*: female earth spirits and symbols of fertility in the Hindu, Buddhist, and Jain traditions often portrayed, as at Sanchi (figure 10.9), grasping the branch of a tree in a posture of giving birth, allowing the pull of gravity to assist in the delivery of life.

••

What is *Given*? Its official title—*Étant donnés: 1° la chute d'eau 2° le gaz d'éclairage*—was lifted verbatim from a 1912 note for *The Large Glass*, which Duchamp began fabricating in New York in 1915 and abandoned in 1923. He published the note in 1934 as part of a collection of facsimile notes and

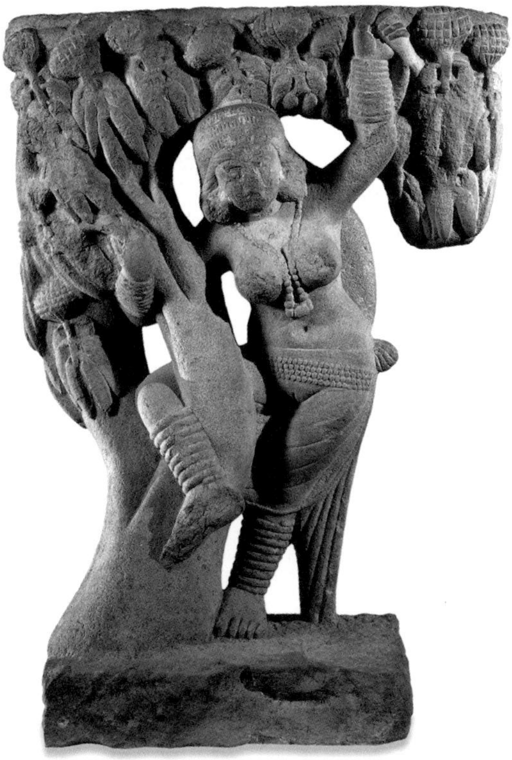

FIGURE 10.9
Shalabhanjika Yakṣī (female tree spirit), bracket from a stupa gateway, stupa 1 at Sanchi
Central India, 1st century BCE/CE
Sandstone, 64.5 × 47 × 28 cm
British Museum, London, Great Britain, Donated by Mrs. Tucker, AC 1842,1210.1

reproductions entitled *La Mariée mise à nu par ses célibataires, même*. This is the collection usually referred to as *The Green Box*, from the color of its container. *Given*'s title would seem to signal that the work is an outcome of a conversation with himself that Duchamp began with *The Large Glass*. The note "*Étant donnés: 1° la chute d'eau 2° le gaz d'éclairage*" actually appears twice in *The Green Box*, in slightly different forms and accompanied by different text. The first, under the heading *Préface*, reads as above. With the other, it is difficult to figure out Duchamp's edits, but he seems to have intended it to read: "Warning / Given (in the dark), if given = 1st the waterfall / 2nd the illuminating gas."[45] This version implies both the hidden nature and the uncertainty, even danger, associated with the activity to which *Given*'s title refers.

Twenty years before Duchamp published *The Green Box*, he had published in his *Box of 1914* a related note, with ellipses: "Given that. ... ; if I assume I am suffering a lot. ..."[46] Combined and slightly edited, the notes from the *Box of 1914* and *The Green Box* read: "Given that if I assume I am suffering a lot: 1st the waterfall, 2nd the illuminating gas." One thing *Given*'s waterfall and lamp would seem to offer is a solution to the universal "given" of suffering—an unmistakable echo of the first of the Buddha's four "truths," which go something like (1) Life is suffering (2) because we want things and fear losing them. (3) It is possible to stop suffering (4) by cultivating attitudes and behaviors consistent with the changing, interrelated nature of all things.

Just as in 1938 Bataille upped the ante on this ancient solution to the problem of suffering by applying tantra yoga to vigorously embrace change and loss, including death, so Duchamp had previously managed to co-opt suffering through a rebus-like, four-dimensional, attitudinal twist. "There is no solution because there is no problem," his friends recall him asserting.[47] Apropos *Unhappy Readymade* (1919), a geometry textbook Duchamp instructed his sister to expose to wind and rain, he told Harriet and Sidney Janis: "The treatise seriously got the facts of life," continuing: "What is the solution? There is no solution because there is no problem. Problem is the invention of man—it is nonsensical."[48] A problem is something to solve; things that cannot be solved are not problems, they are things to apprehend and integrate. It's all a matter of perspective. How does someone attain this equanimous attitude toward life? By training the mind to respond creatively to life's chance events rather than simply reacting on the basis of prior conditioning.

Duchamp's godson, the artist Gordon Matta-Clark, reminded himself of Duchamp's motto and the four truths of Buddhism in an undated note: "There are no solutions because there are no—problems. There are no solutions because there is nothing but change. There are only problems because of human resistance. Passing through resistance-surprise is passing through ... seeing what you have always expected. ... Surprise is a state of consciousness. ... If you look long enough you will be surprised."[49] Like Duchamp, Matta-Clark emphasized both looking and the process of passage.

Passing through resistance to change generates an intentional state of happy surprise, complete openness to what-is. Matta-Clark seems to be observing that surprise can be an engineered state of mind, a mind-of-don't-know in which conditioned framing devices, both social and psychological, have been dismantled. He created unexpected penetrations of ordinary surface existence with his radical building cuttings that let in the light, both literally and metaphorically. And in an unmistakable reference to *Given*, he nicknamed one of his building cuttings, the circular *Conical Intersect* (1975, figure 10.10), "Quel Con"—loosely translated: "What [a] cunt."

So, what about Duchamp's "cunt"? The hairless, slashlike vulva in *Given* has been the subject of much speculation, with interpretations ranging from rape victim, to castration wound, to part anus–part vagina, to the result of an awkward process of casting and assemblage.[50] While there may be some truth to that last rationale—Duchamp did, in fact, have a great deal of trouble getting his figure to look the way he wanted, and may not have totally succeeded—I want to propose another way of looking at the situation. The *trompe-l'œil* tear or rent in *Tu m'* (figure 4.6) serves as a metaphorical three-dimensional rupture in the two-dimensional surface reality of the painting. Its doppelgänger is the rupture-like vaginal passage of the three-dimensional nude in *Given*. Both are portals to the fourth dimension.

Given's nude is on her back, presumably to allow an unimpeded view of this focus of attention. In earlier studies the nude is upright, in the pose of an energetic dancer (figure 10.4). As I have suggested elsewhere, her stance is very like that of Nepalese and Tibetan images of *yoginis* and *dakinis*: naked female dancers representing the transformative power of consciousness.[51] There is an unusually large sculptural example in Paris's Musée Guimet whose vulva, like the vulva of the female figure in Maria Martins's sculpture *The Impossible* (figure 10.6) is represented by a vertical slit in her lower belly (figure 10.12).

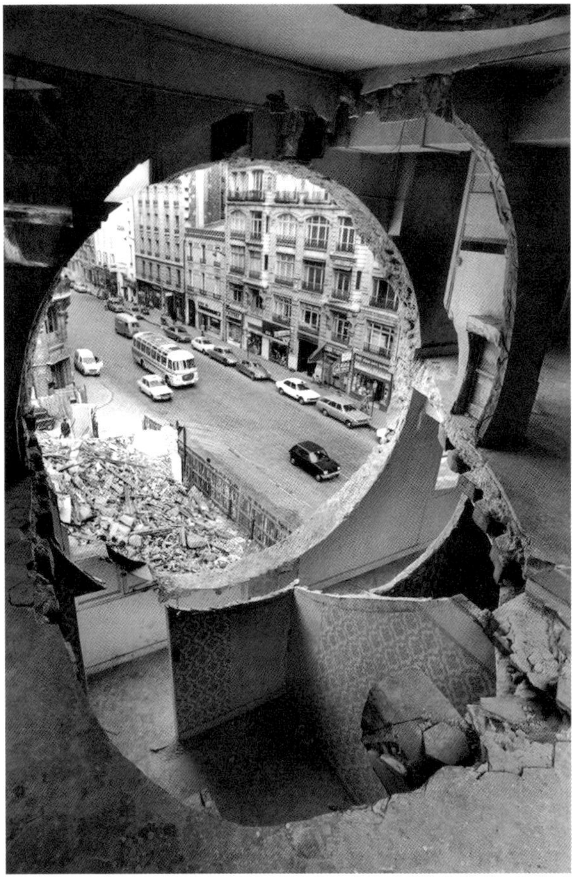

FIGURE 10.10

Gordon Matta-Clark
Conical Intersect ("*Quel con*"), Paris, 1975
Courtesy the Estate of Gordon Matta-Clark and David Zwirner, New York

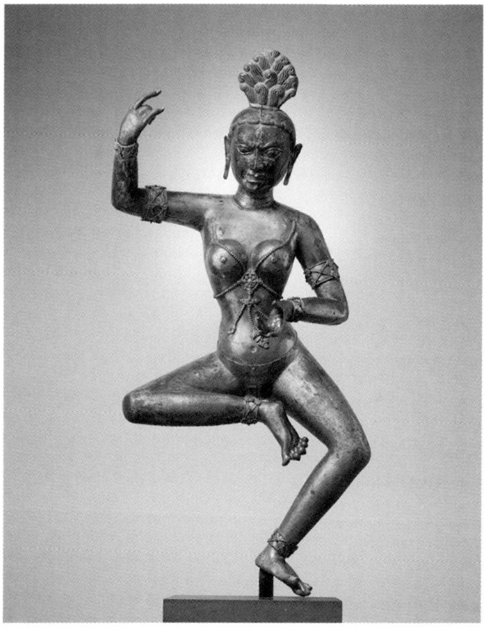

FIGURE 10.11

Dakini in the attitude of dance (Ardhaparyankasana), 19th century Nepal
Copper (metal [lost wax], gilding), traces polychromy, 126 × 62 × 40 cm
Musée des Arts Asiatiques Guimet, Paris, France, inv. no. MA1631

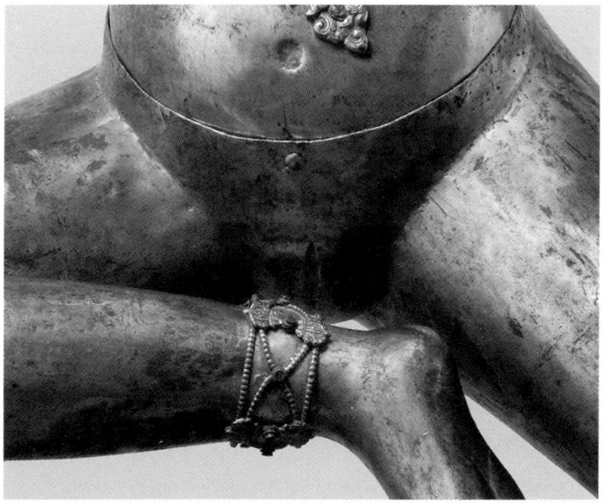

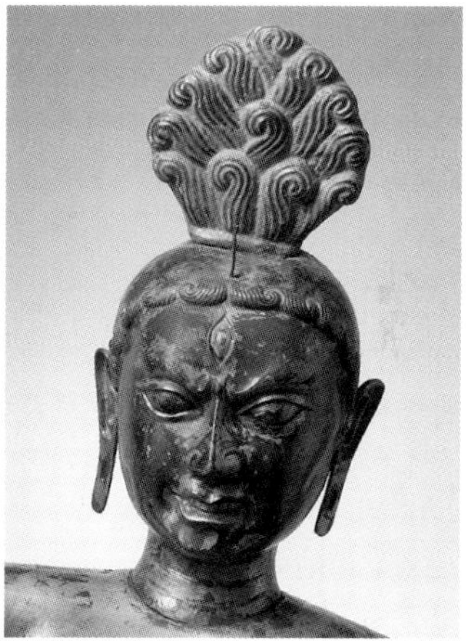

FIGURE 10.12 AND FIGURE 10.13

Dakini in the attitude of dance (Ardhaparyankasana) (details), 19th century Nepal
Copper (metal [lost wax], gilding), traces polychromy, 126 × 62 × 40 cm
Musée des Arts Asiatiques Guimet, Paris, France, inv. no. MA1631

A common image in Indo-Tibetan art, *dakini* is a Sanskrit word. In Tibetan, she is called *khadroma. Kha* means "celestial space," or emptiness; *dro* suggests movement or dance; *ma* signals her feminine gender. Thus, *khadroma* is a female moving, or dancing, within emptiness. The nakedness of this "sky dancer," which extends to her hairless pubis, is a metaphor for reality unveiled. As with Duchamp's figure, one leg of these images is typically raised, while one hand holds aloft an object (usually a bowl made from the upper section of a human skull). Duchamp's figure holds a lamp, but there is a study in which she holds a mirror[52]—symbol for pure consciousness in the Buddhist tradition. Regarding the link between dakini and mirror, Buddhist scholar Judith Simmer-Brown writes: "The *dakini* is a traditional Vajrayana symbol of the profundity of seeing phenomena and the mind as they really are. ... When the guru points out the nature of mind ... he or she points out the secret *dakini*, the feminine principle. ... 'Look into the mirror of your mind, which is *Mahamudra*, the mysterious home of the *dakini*'."[53]

The pudendum of the dancing dakini, though exposed, is not revealed as fully as the vulva of the figure in *Given*. This feature of Duchamp's nude more closely resembles tantric depictions of the open yoni of Vajrayogini in her aspect of emptiness (figure 10.14). Due to its experiential nature, the concept of mental emptiness (*shunyata*) is hard to represent, but the "empty" vaginal passage to creativity and bliss is an effective metaphor. Shockingly explicit to the uninitiated or the unprepared, for the practitioner Vajrayogini in her manifestation of emptiness serves as an object of meditation to help integrate energies liberated in the process of visualization, or inner "looking." Vajrayogini's sexual organ points directly to emptiness: the inner experience of space at the heart of enlightenment.[54]

All of this suggests that Duchamp intended *Given: 1. The Waterfall, 2. The Illuminating Gas* to help viewers conflate the bliss experienced by both sexes within the fecund emptiness of the female vagina with the bliss of seeing things as they really are: empty of inherent self-existence and, simultaneously, the manifestation of continual creation. *Given* is thus a proper object of meditation, an artistic tool for the transformation of consciousness. As with other "passages" that crop up in Duchamp's art, beginning as early as 1911 with *Coffee Mill* (figure 1.18), the vulva in *Given* represents

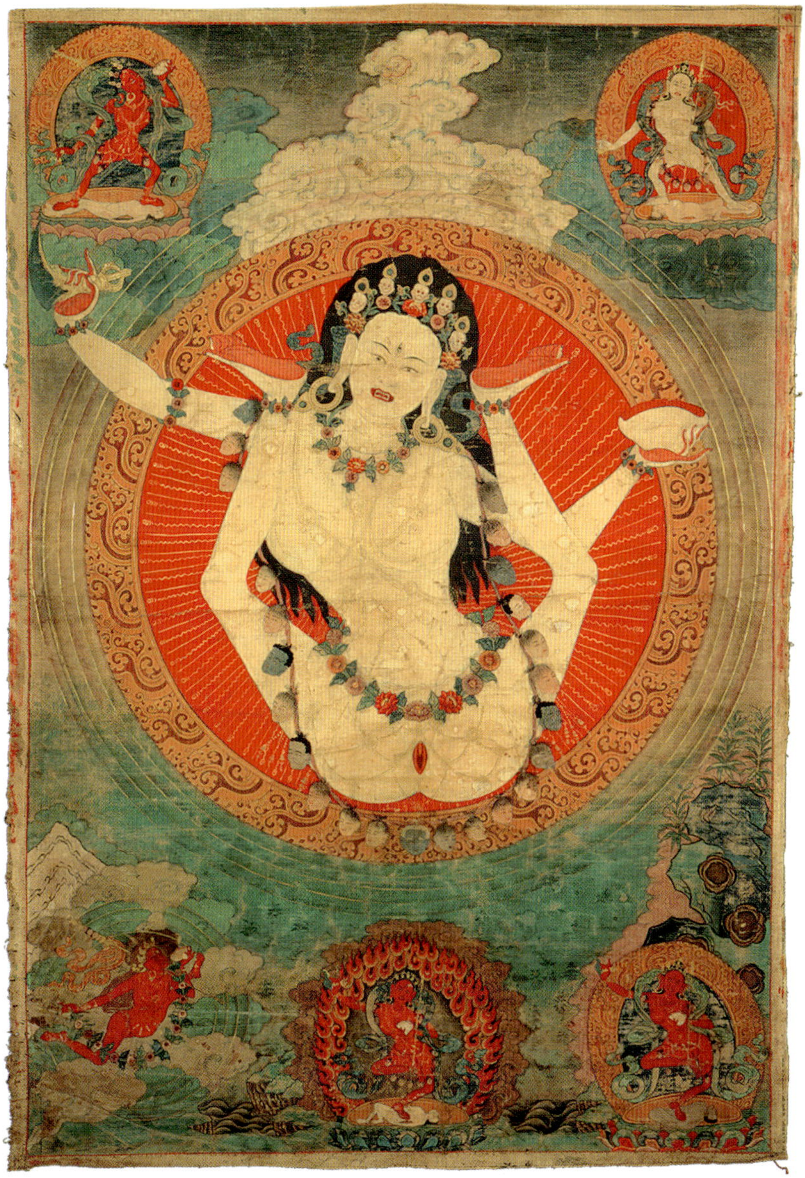

FIGURE 10.14

Tibet, Shangpa Kagyu lineage *Vajrayogini*, 18th century
Ground mineral pigment on cotton
Private collection, photo courtesy of Arnold Lieberman

a penetration of surface reality: a mandala, the labyrinth beyond time and space through which both artist and viewer find their way to a clearing.

••

Around 1915, the year Duchamp began fabricating *The Large Glass*, with its Milky Way and *Pendu femelle*—"suspended female thing"—in the upper, Bride's portion of the *Glass*, a shared interest in the concept of dakini—sky dancer—began manifesting among his closest artist-friends. Confined to hospital with a head wound in 1916, Guillaume Apollinaire made a number of large watercolors, one of which depicts a naked woman with flaming hair spread-eagled across a star-spangled night sky in a pose much like that of Duchamp's figure in *Given* (figure 10.15). Inscribed beneath are the words: "What Fun One Can Have With Astronomical Harmony!!!"

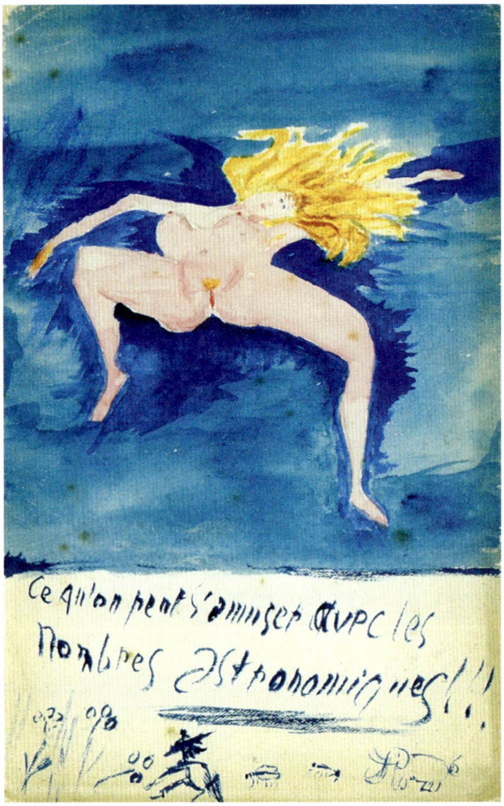

FIGURE 10.15

Guillaume Apollinaire
Ce qu'on peut s'amuser avec les nombres astronomiques!!! / What Fun One Can Have With Astronomical Harmony!!!, c. 1916
Watercolor, 21.5 × 13 cm
Heritage-Images / Art Media / akg-images

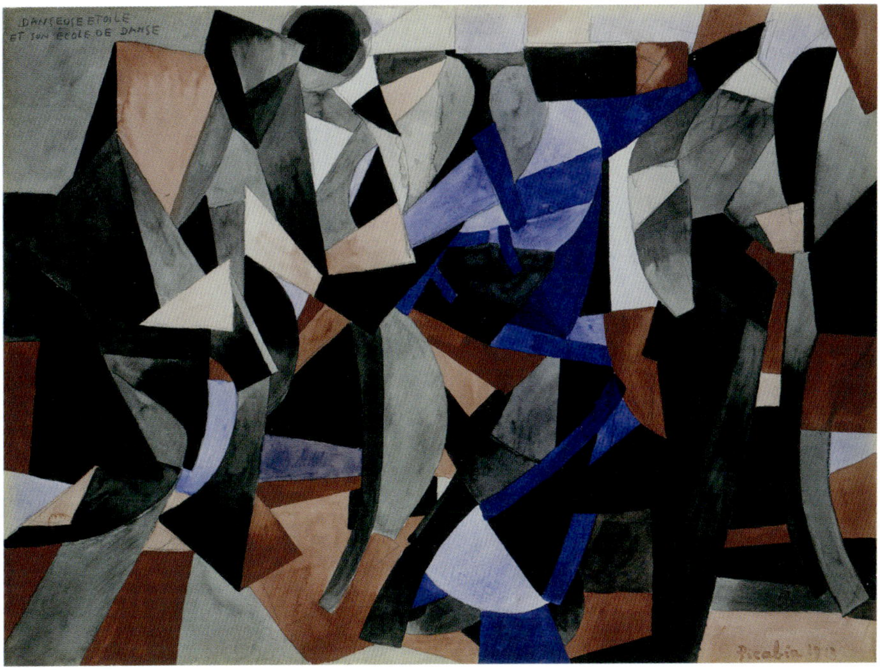

FIGURE 10.16
Francis Picabia
Danseuse étoile et son école de danse / Star Dancer and Her School of Dance, 1913
Watercolor on paper, 55.6 x 76.2 cm
The Metropolitan Museum of Art, New York, NY, Alfred Stieglitz Collection, 1949, 49.70.12

In 1913, Francis Picabia created a large watercolor entitled *Star Dancer and Her School of Dance* (figure 10.16), showing a figure with spread arms and bent leg surrounded by energetic forms. The title of another watercolor from the same year, *Star Dancer on a Transatlantic Steamer*, foregrounds concepts of voyage and transition. (Picabia's immediate inspiration was an exotic dancer he saw aboard ship en route to the Armory Show.) Then there is the title for Picabia's 1913 painting *Edtaonisl*, a scrambling of *Étoile danseuse* that incorporates the word "tao," as mentioned above. Its subtitle, *Ecclesiastic*, signifies a religious or ecstatic state. Picabia used "Edtaonisl" as his signature on another painting, *Catch as Catch Can*, also from 1913, suggesting identification with the star dancer that parallels Duchamp's identification with his Bride.

The star- or sky-dancer theme showed up again in Picabia's film *Intermission* (*Entr'acte*), made with René Clair in 1924. Interspersed with other scenes, including a "fall of water" that sweeps away a chess game between Duchamp and Man Ray, are sequences showing the underside of a dancing ballerina shot from beneath a sheet of glass. The dancer is eventually revealed to be wearing a fake beard and mustache—gender confusion that alludes to the beard and mustache of *L.H.O.O.Q.*, Duchamp's modified version of *Mona Lisa*.

Man Ray's most important painting, *The Rope Dancer Accompanies Herself with Her Shadows* (1916, figure 10.17), shows a dancer in the form of a star

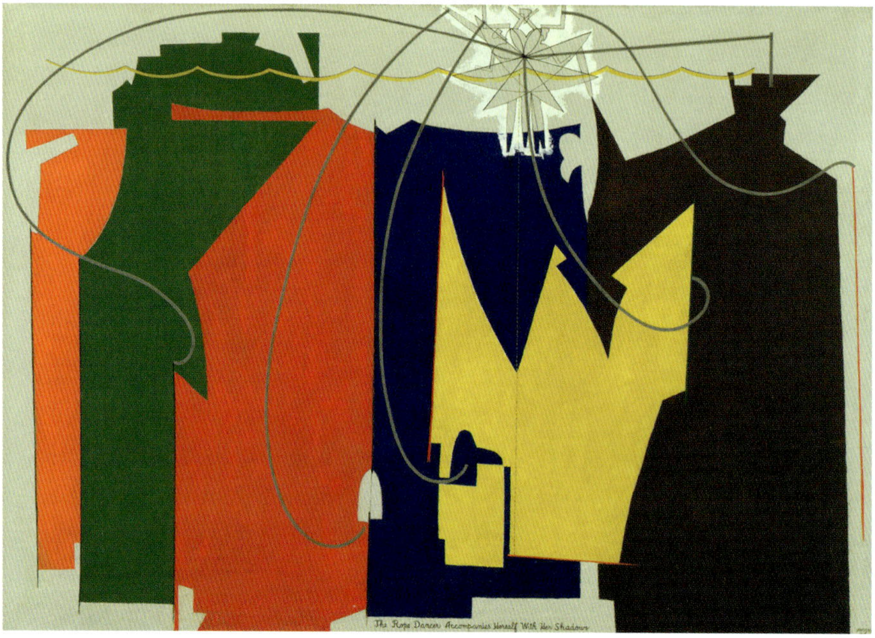

FIGURE 10.17

Man Ray
The Rope Dancer Accompanies Herself with Her Shadows, 1916
Oil on canvas, 132.1 × 185.4 cm
The Museum of Modern Art, New York, NY, Gift of G. David Thompson, 33.195

surrounded by a white aura, like the auras surrounding Duchamp's figures from around 1910. Man Ray's star dancer hovers behind a watery horizon line while playing with ropes or strings (evoking tantra's association with string) connected to large planes of color. A study for *Rope Dancer* entitled *Silhouette* (1916, figure 10.18) shows three dancers with parasol-like skirts flanked by the outline of a woman's crotch on one side and the spiral at the top of a string instrument on the other. Three vibrating strings stretch out horizontally under the dancers' feet, like the three horizontal lines of the Bride's garment above which the arbor-type *Pendu femelle* of *The Large Glass* dances. Man Ray's three large black ovoids—apparently shadows of the dancers' skirts—loom in the background, like the three "Draft Pistons or Nets" in Duchamp's *Glass*.

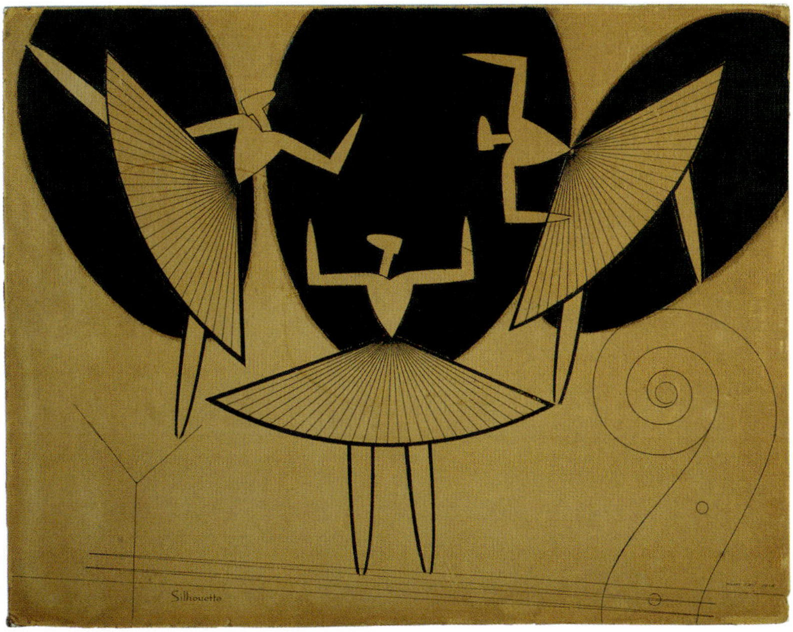

FIGURE 10.18

Man Ray
Silhouette, 1916
India ink, charcoal, and gouache on wood pulp board, 51.6 × 64.1 cm
The Solomon R. Guggenheim Foundation, Peggy Guggenheim Collection, Venice, 1976, 76.2553.68

The work by Man Ray that most strikingly paralleled *Given* was a painting that Duchamp displayed on the ceiling of the inner chamber of the labyrinthine 1959 *Exposition inteRnatiOnale du Surréalisme* at Galerie Daniel Cordier. Entitled *Virgin*, Man Ray's painting provided a between-the-thighs view of a woman's crotch, torso, and lower face. Duchamp installed her on a ceiling, above visitors' heads, transforming her into a naked sky dancer.[55] The original painting is apparently lost, but a watercolor version was featured on the cover of a special July 1966 Duchamp issue of *Art and Artists* timed to coincide with the Duchamp retrospective at the Tate Gallery, London. Man Ray published a color lithograph version in 1973 (figure 10.19).

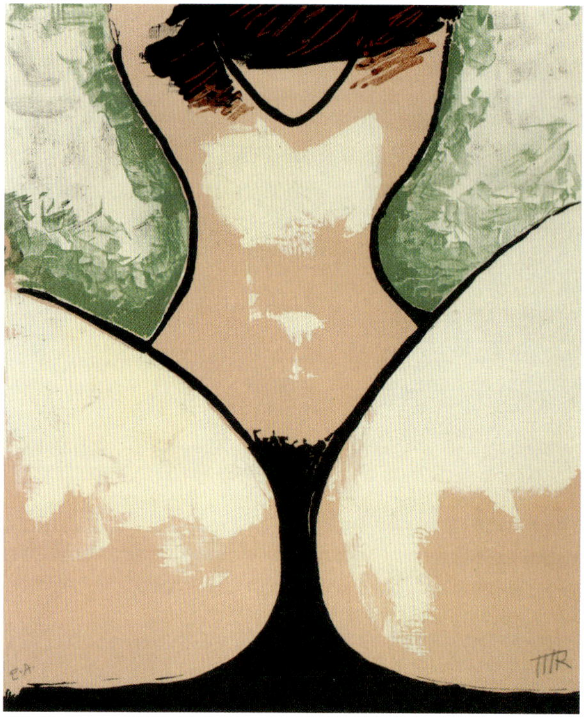

FIGURE 10.19

Man Ray
La Vierge, ca. 1955/1973
Color lithograph on paper, 30.6 × 25.7 cm
Smithsonian American Art Museum, Gift of Juliet Man Ray, 1982.88.2

Virgin is a variation on *The Colored One* (1919–1920, figure 10.20) by that adventurous friend of Duchamp's youth, František Kupka. *The Colored One* shows a female nude on her back, her bent legs stretched upward and apart. A radiant male head gazes down at her, his eyes shooting rays of light toward her genitals. As a white ray penetrates her, rainbow colors, like the colors accompanying Man Ray's *Rope Dancer*, swirl around her body. Kupka's painting echoes Beatrice Wood's depiction of Duchamp's erotic gaze (figure 10.8), as well as Mina Loy's account of "shafts from his eyes" that became so penetrating she could feel herself "dissolve to a transparent target." In Tibetan Buddhism, "rainbow body" is said to be the last stage before attaining the clear light of Nirvana. The composition could also serve as an illustration for Max Théon's "infusion of the psychic active being into the psychic passive being, and the consequent development of the passive sensitive to the highest perfection of which s/he is capable in all states of being."[56]

The evident inspiration from Tantric Buddhism and tantra yoga within the art of Duchamp and his friends over the years finally allows us to understand Isabelle Waldberg's *Always There Beautiful Aqueduct* (figure 6.19) not simply as a *sui generis* artwork that may have played a role in the creation of *Given*, but as part of a conversation among artists and writers in Duchamp's circle who shared his interest in tantra. Waldberg was a regular visitor to the Musée Guimet, where *Dancing Dakini* (figure 10.11) and similar objects were on view. But Isabelle had her own tantric experience to draw upon, and had no need for inspiration from Asian art to create *Luminaire* (figure 6.20), her plaster sculpture that served as precedent for Duchamp's *Female Fig Leaf* (figure 6.15) and the exposed vulva of his figure in *Given*.

With the notable exception of Waldberg, Duchamp's last major work is more explicit than the work of his friends, and thus more challenging. Appreciation of the esoteric *Given: 1. The Waterfall, 2. The Illuminating Gas* requires an attitude few can manage. Duchamp did his best to make this lit-from-within work disarming, even seductive, with an enchanting, *trompe-l'œil* landscape featuring an amusing moving waterfall. He ensured that *Given* would be hard to find, arranging for it to be installed at the end of a darkened gallery, and that it would be seen three-dimensionally, one viewer at a time, placing his diorama behind two peepholes in ancient

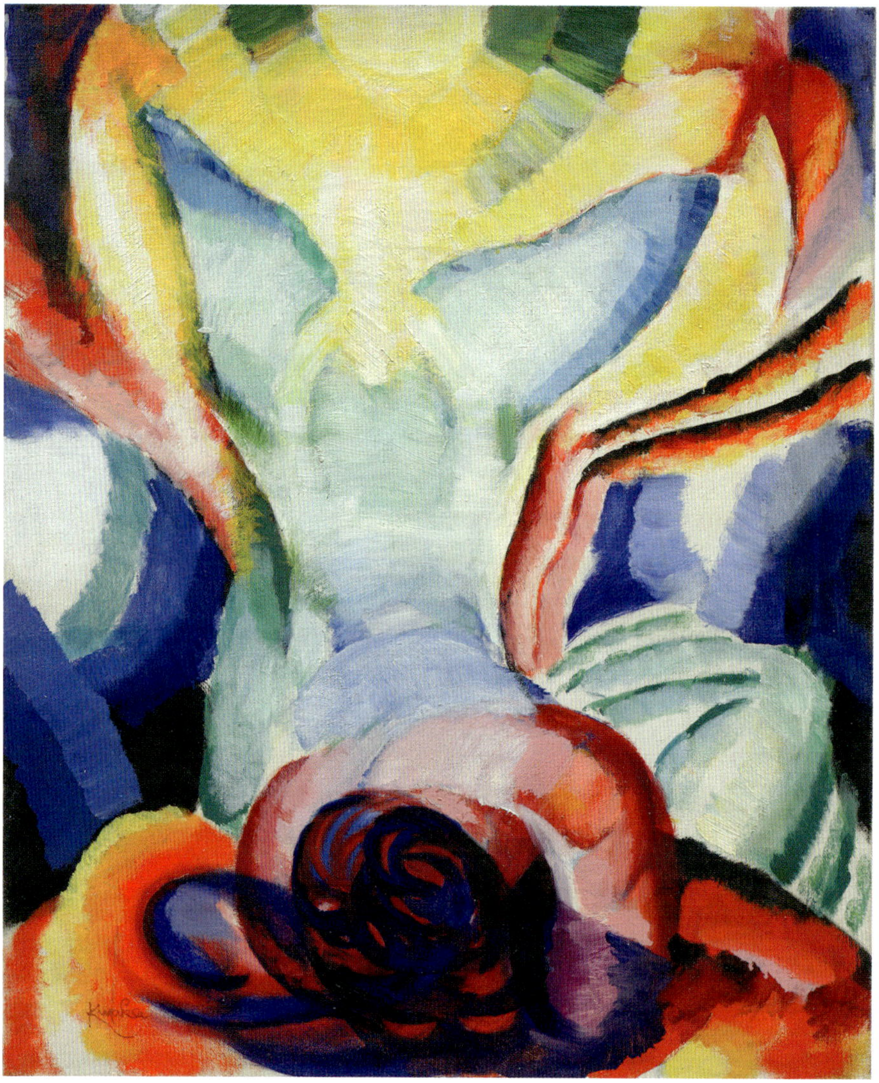

FIGURE 10.20

František Kupka
La colorée / The Colored One, c. 1919–1920
Oil on canvas, 65 × 54 cm
The Solomon R. Guggenheim Museum, New York, NY, Gift, Mrs. Andrew P. Fuller, 1966

wooden doors. The actual experience of *Given* is not only occult, it is also intentional: you have to make an effort to look in order to see it.

Duchamp must have hoped that at least some of his more informed viewers would understand how overdetermined the work is, and rise to the occasion. His intended audience, however, are viewers who allow themselves to be vulnerable. At a 1949 "Western Round Table for Modern Art" in San Francisco, Duchamp declared that "while many people have taste, only a few are equipped with aesthetic receptivity" to be "capable of an aesthetic emotion"—what he interactively termed "an aesthetic echo": "Taste presupposes a domineering onlooker who dictates what he likes and dislikes, and translates it into beautiful and ugly when he is sensuously pleased or displeased. Quite differently, the 'victim' of an aesthetic echo is in a position comparable to that of a man in love, or of a believer, who dismisses automatically his demanding ego and, helpless, submits to a pleasurable and mysterious constraint. While in exercising his taste he adopts a commanding attitude, when touched by the aesthetic revelation the same man, almost in an ecstatic mood, becomes receptive and humble."[57] Duchamp's conflation of art "victim" and lover recalls his *Door for Gradiva* (figure 9.2), while his comparison of the engaged art participant with a man in love or a believer is typical of his tendency to describe aesthetic experience in language normally used for erotic or mystical experience. For Duchamp, the two were identical. His language was carefully chosen to convey by analogy how the mind works, and thus how art works. Art, like mysticism, like erotic love, is simultaneously interactive and a very private experience.

••

Given: 1. The Waterfall, 2. The Illuminating Gas is an impressive, even riveting, work of art, but is it effective? How well does it convey its maker's intention? As we have seen, Robert Motherwell, a more sympathetic and informed viewer than most, considered *Given* theatrical, even brutal. Other commentators have seen in it a scene of violence, which cannot have been Duchamp's intent.[58] He may have had doubts of his own. In April 1957, a little more than halfway through the creation of *Given*, Duchamp confessed at an assembled gathering of the American Federation of Arts: "In the creative act, the artist goes from intention to realization through a chain of totally subjective reactions. His struggle toward the realization is a series of efforts, pains, satisfactions, refusals, decisions, which also cannot and must not be fully self-conscious, at least on the aesthetic plane. The result of this struggle is a difference between the intention and its realization, a difference which the artist is not aware of."[59]

The statement is reminiscent of Duchamp's advice to his brother-in-law Jean Crotti: "[I] counsel you not to judge your work, for you are the last to see it (with true eyes). … Quite simply, do less self-analysis and work with pleasure, without being concerned about opinion, your own or that of others."[60] Duchamp's admonition to his brother-in-law simply to work for the pleasure of working corresponds to the well-known karma yoga teaching from the *Bhagavad Gita* that actions are best undertaken without attachment to outcomes. In the end, Duchamp was able to take his own advice and leave analysis and judgment of *Given* to posterity: "the public that will come fifty years—or a hundred years—after my death."[61] (Duchamp died on October 2, 1968.)

He must have enjoyed teasing Pierre Cabanne, who interviewed him a couple of years before *Given* went public, about the importance of eroticism in his work:

DUCHAMP: Eroticism was a theme, even an "ism," which was the basis of everything I was doing at the time of the "Large Glass." …

CABANNE: Still, in your work, this eroticism has remained disguised for a rather long time.

DUCHAMP: Always disguised, more or less, but not disguised out of shame.

CABANNE: No, hidden.

DUCHAMP: That's it.[62]

Turns out that *was* it. What lies hidden behind *Given*'s door is a metaphorical mental cleansing offered by the waterfall, and an equally metaphorical passage to transformative clarity of mind illuminated by Duchamp's own Statue of Liberty.

It is telling that in a 1959 interview, Duchamp used a Sanskrit prefix to explain his thinking about art making: "An atheist is just as … religious …

as the believer is, and an 'anti-artist' is just as much of an artist as the other artist. 'Anartist' would be much better. ... 'a, n' -artist, meaning, 'no artist at all.' That would be my conception." The Sanskrit prefix "an," meaning "not" or "non-," becomes "a" or "un" in English. An anartist is an unartist. But Duchamp did not say "unartist" or "a-artist," which is how his interviewer wrongly repeated the neologism.[63] The more culturally specific "anartist" parallels the key Buddhist concept of *anatman*, or "nonself," in contrast with Hinduism's Atman, or enduring soul. At the same time, anatman counters the belief in annihilation of the self—which, the Buddha pointed out, presupposes the existence of a separate self to be annihilated. Anatman is no self at all, just as anartist is no artist at all.[64]

Duchamp's art of life allowed him to realize the inherently aesthetic nature of lived experience. On the basis of numerous correlations between his art, his statements, and his writings with elements of Asian practices and philosophies it would appear that, early on, Duchamp learned a Western form of tantric yoga that had its source in Kaula tantric practices of Indian Kashmir Shaivism. In keeping with the perennialist impulses of his era he went on to draw on a range of sources, Western as well as Eastern, to develop an energetic practice fueled by erotic desire, which in turn fueled his creativity. Whatever the specific sources, a strong contender for the "hidden" practice, the erotic "ism" that generated Marcel Duchamp's enigmatic art, appears from the evidence to have been a personal amalgam of mind training and body energetics from Asia, leavened with linguistic humor, designed to precipitate release into a place of creative freedom.

When he was asked toward the end of his life what his greatest achievement was, Duchamp said:

> Using painting, using art, to create a *modus vivendi*, a way of understanding life; that is, for the time being, of trying to make my life into a work of art itself, instead of spending my life creating works of art in the form of paintings or sculptures. I now believe that you can quite readily treat your life, the way you breathe, act, interact with other people, as a picture, a tableau vivant or a film scene. ... These are my conclusions now: I never set out to do this when I was twenty or fifteen, but I realize, after many years, that this was fundamentally what I was aiming to do.[65]

There is a variation on this statement to which he added: "I am my own living Readymade, so to speak."[66] Duchamp's art of life proposes that an artist is somebody who chooses to engage the world in a creative way: "Everyone can decide, as everyone decides at every moment of his life, and chooses every moment of his life."[67] In the process of using art as a way to accommodate himself to life, Marcel Duchamp came to understand that life *is* art—an art whose medium is breath and whose expression is perception of the material world as morphing, vibrating erotic bliss. He attempted to portray his experience in *The Large Glass* as blossoming; in *Given*, as a luminous vision. With the right "givens," art, like love, like life itself, can be a completely transformative experience.

When Duchamp died, the artist Jasper Johns wrote: "The art community feels Duchamp's presence and his absence. He has changed the condition of being here."[68] Marcel Duchamp's goal, both for art and for himself, was to disappear. There is an understanding in Mahayana Buddhism that important texts recording the teachings of the Buddha existed during and for a while after the Buddha's lifetime and then, having liberated everyone within their reach, went "underground," ready to be rediscovered when needed.[69] Maybe this is what Duchamp had in mind when he concluded that 1961 lecture with the news that "the great artist of tomorrow will go underground." Maybe he was talking about himself.

Above his name on the family grave marker in Rouen is an epitaph, his last message to us: "Besides, it's always the other people who die."[70] Marcel Duchamp is still prodding us, humorously, from beyond the grave, to think not about him, but about our relationship to others; about our attitude toward death and, by implication, life; still trying to make us aware of our own perspective. This is how art changes the world: by changing minds. As Apollinaire predicted: "It will perhaps fall to an artist as disengaged from aesthetic considerations and as concerned with energy as Marcel Duchamp to reconcile Art and the People."

APPENDIX
MARCEL DUCHAMP, "THE CREATIVE ACT"

Marcel Duchamp delivered "The Creative Act" as part of a session on the creative act at the convention of the American Federation of Arts in Houston, Texas, in April 1957. The other participants were art historian William Seitz, art and film theorist and perceptual psychologist Rudolf Arnheim, and anthropologist Gregory Bateson. (Duchamp described himself as "mere artist.") "The Creative Act" was first published in essay form in *Art News*, and has been republished often. It confirms that Duchamp viewed art as religion, with "true" artists its shamans, able to go beyond time and space. As artist Bruce Nauman asserted in his 1967 neon window sign: *The True Artist Helps the World by Revealing Mystic Truths*.

THE CREATIVE ACT
BY MARCEL DUCHAMP

Let us consider two important factors, the two poles of the creation of art: the artist on the one hand, and on the other the spectator who later becomes the posterity.

To all appearances, the artist acts like a mediumistic being who, from the labyrinth beyond time and space, seeks his way out to a clearing. If we give the attributes of a medium to the artist, we must then deny him the state of consciousness on the aesthetic plane about what he is doing or why he is doing it. All his decisions in the artistic execution of the work rest with pure intuition and cannot be translated into a self-analysis, spoken or written, or even thought out.

T.S. Eliot, in his essay on "Tradition and Individual Talent," writes: "The more perfect the artist, the more completely separate in him will be the man who suffers and the mind which creates; the more perfectly will the mind digest and transmute the passions which are its material."

Millions of artists create; only a few thousands are discussed or accepted by the spectator and many less again are consecrated by posterity.

In the last analysis, the artist may shout from all the rooftops that he is a genius: he will have to wait for the verdict of the spectator in order that his declarations take a social value and that, finally, posterity includes him in the primers of Art History.

I know that this statement will not meet with the approval of many artists who refuse this mediumistic role and insist on the validity of their awareness in the creative act—yet, art history has consistently decided upon the virtues of a work of art through considerations completely divorced from the rationalized explanations of the artist.

If the artist, as a human being, full of the best intentions toward himself and the whole world, plays no role at all in the judgment of his own work, how can one describe the phenomenon which prompts the spectator to react critically to the work of art? In other words, how does this reaction come about?

This phenomenon is comparable to a transference from the artist to the spectator in the form of an aesthetic osmosis taking place through the inert matter, such as pigment, piano or marble.

But before we go further, I want to clarify our understanding of the word "art"—to be sure, without any attempt at a definition. What I have in mind is that art may be bad, good or indifferent, but, whatever adjective is used, we must call it art, and bad art is still art in the same way that a bad emotion is still an emotion.

Therefore, when I refer to "art coefficient," it will be understood that I refer not only to great art, but I am trying to describe the subjective mechanism which produces art in the raw state—*à l'état brut*—bad, good or indifferent.

In the creative act, the artist goes from intention to realization through a chain of totally subjective reactions. His struggle toward the realization is a series of efforts, pains, satisfactions, refusals, decisions, which also cannot and must not be fully self-conscious, at least on the aesthetic plane.

The result of this struggle is a difference between the intention and its realization, a difference which the artist is not aware of.

Consequently, in the chain of reactions accompanying the creative act, a link is missing. This gap, representing the inability of the artist to express fully his intention, this difference between what he intended to realize and did realize, is the personal "art coefficient" contained in the work.

In other words, the personal "art coefficient" is like an arithmetical relation between the unexpressed but intended and the unintentionally expressed.

To avoid a misunderstanding, we must remember that this "art coefficient" is a personal expression of art *à l'état brut*, that is, still in a raw state, which must be "refined" as pure sugar from molasses by the spectator; the digit of this coefficient has no bearing whatsoever on his verdict. The creative act takes another aspect when the spectator experiences the phenomenon of transmutation: through the change from inert matter into a work of art, an actual transubstantiation has taken place, and the role of the spectator is to determine the weight of the work on the aesthetic scale.

All in all, the creative act is not performed by the artist alone; the spectator brings the work in contact with the external world by deciphering and interpreting its inner qualification and thus adds his contribution to the creative act. This becomes even more obvious when posterity gives a final verdict and sometimes rehabilitates forgotten artists.

NOTES

PREFACE AND ACKNOWLEDGMENTS

1. Denis de Rougemont, *Journal d'une époque 1926–1946* (Paris: Gallimard, 1968), 568–569. Unless otherwise noted, translations from the French are my own.

2. My thanks to John Elderfield for this quote.

3. *Hidden Intercourse: Eros and Sexuality in the History of Western Esotericism*, ed. Wouter J. Hanegraaff and Jeffrey J. Kripal (New York: Fordham University Press, 2011), xii–xiii.

4. My training was in Soto Zen meditation and I have practiced Taoist "sitting in oblivion." I have not seriously undertaken the rigors of Taoist internal alchemy or tantric practices, but while on meditation retreats I have experienced altered states of consciousness involving both seeing and hearing, and once had a spontaneous experience of so-called Kundalini energy.

5. 1953 interview by Dorothy Norman published in *Art in America* 57, no. 4 (July–August 1969), 38.

6. Séverine Gossart provides a summary of explorations of Duchamp's art in the context of eroticism in: "To Each His Own: Marcel Duchamp, Duchampians, and Veil Games," *Marcel Duchamp and Eroticism*, ed. Marc Décimo (Newcastle: Cambridge Scholars Publishing, 2007), 255–265.

7. Pierre Cabanne, *Dialogues with Marcel Duchamp*, trans. Rod Padgett (London: Thames and Hudson, 1971; reprinted Cambridge, MA: Da Capo Press, 1987), 88.

INTRODUCTION

1. J. W. Dunne, *The Serial Universe* (London: Faber and Faber, 1934), 15. Duchamp recommended Dunne's book to readers of *À l'infinitif* (*The White Box*, 1966); see *The Writings of Marcel Duchamp*, ed. Michel Sanouillet and Elmer Peterson (New York: Da Capo Press, 1989), 101.

2. Jindřich Chalupecký, "rien qu'un artiste … ," in *Marcel Duchamp abécédaire*, ed. Jean Clair (Paris: Centre Georges Pompidou, 1977), 27. Jindřich Chalupecký, "Nothing but an Artist … ," in *Duchamp: Passim*, ed. Anthony Hill (London: G+B Arts, 1994), 40.

3. Gabrielle Buffet-Picabia, "Some Memories of Pre-Dada: Picabia and Duchamp (1949)," in *The Dada Painters and Poets: An Anthology*, ed. Robert Motherwell (Cambridge, MA: Harvard University Press, 1981), 261. Roché in Robert Lebel, *Marcel Duchamp*, trans. George Heard Hamilton (New York: Grove Press, 1959), 79. Georges Ribemont-Dessaignes, *Déjà jadis ou du mouvement Dada à l'espace abstrait* (Paris: Julliard, 1958), 33. Regarding Breton: Jean-Jacques Lebel interviewed by Paul Franklin, "Coming of Age with Marcel," *Étant donné Marcel Duchamp*, no. 7 (2006), 19. Robert Lebel quote from *The Artist and His Critic Stripped Bare: The Correspondence of Marcel Duchamp and Robert Lebel*, ed. and trans. Paul B. Franklin (Los Angeles: Getty Research Institute, 2016), 33.

4. Robert Lebel, "Portrait of Marcel Duchamp as a Dropout," *Étant donné Marcel Duchamp*, no. 7 (2006), 73–74 (lecture delivered February 21, 1974 at the Museum of Modern Art). With his reference to psychotropics Lebel may have been referencing Carlos Castaneda, who in his third book, *Journey to Ixtlan*, published in 1972, shifted his emphasis from entheogens to mental practices.

5. *The Artist and His Critic*, 88. This quote is from 1969, soon after Duchamp's death.

6. Harriet and Sidney Janis, "Marcel Duchamp: Anti-Artist," published in *View*, series V, no. 1 (New York, March 1945) reprinted in Motherwell, ed., *The Dada Painters and Poets*, 311.

7. On Kaula, see Lilian Silburn, *Kundalini: Energy of the Depths* (Albany: SUNY Press, 1988); Paul Muller-Ortega, *The Triadic Heart of Śiva* (Albany: SUNY Press, 1989); and John R. Dupuche, *Abhinavagupta, The Kula Ritual as Elaborated in Chapter 29 of the Tantrāloka* (Delhi: Motilal Banarsidass, 2003).

8. I use the term "tantra yoga" to denote meditative body energetics originating in India as practiced in the West around the turn of the twentieth century, in order to distinguish it from "neotantra"—Western adaptations of Indian tantric sexual practices that emerged in the 1960s as part of the New Age movement.

9. Sanouillet and Peterson, *Writings of Marcel Duchamp*, 24.

10. Ibid., 31. The heading is from *Petit Larousse illustré* (Paris: Librairie Larousse, 1912).

11. "Application des connaissances à la réalisation d'une conception," *Petit Larousse*, 64.

12. Elizabeth K. Menon, "The Excrement of Power: Alfred Jarry, Ubu Roi, and Dada," in *Paris Dada: The Barbarians Storm the Gates*, ed. Elmer Peterson (Farmington Hills, MI: Gale Group, 2001), 39.

13. Christian K. Wedemeyer, *Making Sense of Tantric Buddhism: History, Semiology, and Transgression in the Indian Traditions* (New York: Columbia University Press, 2013), 122.

14. Gabrielle Buffet-Picabia, "Marcel Duchamp: Fluttering Hearts," trans. Nigel Gearing from an essay originally published in *Cahiers d'Art* 11, nos. 1–2 (1936); in *Duchamp: Passim*, 15–16.

15. See Livia Kohn, *Meditation Works in the Hindu, Buddhist and Daoist Traditions* (Magdalena, NM: Three Pines Press, 2008).

16. Pierre Cabanne, *Dialogues with Marcel Duchamp*, trans. Rod Padgett (London: Thames and Hudson, 1971; reprinted Cambridge, MA: Da Capo Press, 1987), 72.

17. From Henri-Pierre Roché's novel *Victor (Marcel Duchamp)*, published by Centre Georges Pompidou as vol. 4 of four books dedicated to Marcel Duchamp (Paris, 1977), 53–54. *Victor* has also been published in English, in *Three New York Dadas and The Blind Man*, intr. Dawn Ades (London: Atlas Press, 2013).

18. Gianfranco Baruchello and Henry Martin, *Why Duchamp: An Essay on Aesthetic Impact* (New Paltz, NY: McPherson, 1985), 91.

19. Francis Naumann, John Tancock, Philip Tinari, *Duchamp and / or / in China* (Beijing: Ullens Center for Contemporary Art, 2014), 64–65. Exhibition: 26 April–16 June 2013.

20. See Jacquelynn Baas, *Smile of the Buddha: Eastern Philosophy and Western Art from Monet to Today* (Berkeley: University of California Press, 2005).

21. See David Weir, *Brahma in the West: William Blake and the Oriental Renaissance* (Albany: State University of New York Press, 2003), especially 10–12 and 90–104; and Marsha Keith Schuchard, *William Blake's Sexual Path to Spiritual Vision* (Rochester, VT: Inner Traditions, 2008).

22. See Christopher I. Beckwith, *Greek Buddha: Pyrrho's Encounter with Early Buddhism in Central Asia* (Princeton, NJ: Princeton University Press, 2015). Duchamp told Arturo Schwarz that among the Greek philosophers, he found Pyrrho of Elis to be "closest to his own views" (Arturo Schwarz, *The Complete Works of Marcel Duchamp* [New York: Abrams, 1970], 38, note 23).

23. Johannes Bronkhorst, *The Two Traditions of Meditation in Ancient India* (Stuttgart: Franz Steiner Verlag Wiesbaden, 1986), 124.

24. See Livia Kohn, *Sitting in Oblivion: The Heart of Daoist Meditation* (Dunedin, FL: Three Pines Press, 2010).

25. See Stephen Batchelor, *Buddhism without Beliefs* (New York: Riverhead, 1997), 3ff.

26. Eugène Burnouf was the first to translate Sanskrit texts reliably into French, including the *Bhagavata Purana ou histoire poétique de Krichna* (1840–1847), *Introduction à l'histoire du Bouddhisme indien* (1844), and a translation of the Lotus Sutra: *Le lotus de la bonne loi* (1852). His translations were widely read not only in France but in the United States, England, and Germany, where they influenced Schopenhauer and Nietzsche. See Burnouf, *Introduction to the History of Indian Buddhism*, trans. Katia Buffetrille and Donald S. Lopez, Jr. (Chicago: University of Chicago Press, 2010).

27. Duchamp mentioned Redon as an influence more than once; his early painting *Draft on the Japanese Apple Tree* (1911, figure 1.11), may have been modeled on *Buddha in His Youth* (reproduced in Baas, *Smile of the Buddha*, 42).

28. See Baas, *Smile of the Buddha*, 70ff.

29. Thanks to Livia Kohn for information on Taoism; the reader is directed to her publications listed in the bibliography for more information.

30. Roger T. Ames and David L. Hall, *Daodejing "Making This Life Significant": A Philosophical Translation* (New York: Ballantine, 2003): 13, 60, 18; Thomas Cleary, *The Taoist Classics*, vol. 1 (Boston: Shambhala, 1999): 3–4.

31. Early Western translations of *Tao Te Ching* and *Chuang Tzu* include Stanislas Julien, *Le Livre de la voie et de la vertu par le philosophe Lao-Tseu* (Paris: L'Imprimerie Royale, 1842); F. Max Müller, ed., *The Sacred Books of the East*, vols. 39 and 40 (Oxford: Clarendon Press, 1891); and Léon Wieger, *Taoïsme*, 2 vols. (Xian Xian: Imp. de Xian Xian, 1911–1913).

32. See Jacquelynn Baas, "Before Zen: The Nothing of American Dada," in *East-West Interchanges in American Art: A Long and Tumultuous Relationship*, ed. Cynthia Mills, Lee Glazer, and Amelia A. Goerlitz (Washington, DC: Smithsonian Institution Scholarly Press, 2009), 52–65 (https://opensi.si.edu/index.php/smithsonian/catalog/book/25, accessed February 1, 2019).

33. Wendy Doniger, *The Rig Veda* (London: Penguin, 1981), 25.

34. According to Thomas Merton, "We know that Blake knew the *Bhagavad Gita*, because he did a picture of Sir Charles Wilkins translating it" (Thomas Merton, "Nature and Art in William Blake: An Essay in Interpretation" [1939 Master's Thesis, Columbia University], Appendix I in *The Literary Essays of Thomas Merton*, ed. Patrick Hart [New York: New Directions, 1981], 415).

35. See Bronkhorst, *Two Traditions of Meditation*, 124.

36. Richard H. Davis, "Religions of India in Practice," in *Asian Religions in Practice: An Introduction*, ed. Donald S. Lopez, Jr. (Princeton, NJ: Princeton University Press, 1999) 18–19.

37. Joseph Needham, *Science and Civilisation in China*, vol. 5, part 5 (Cambridge: Cambridge University Press, 1983), 257–288; David Gordon White, *The Alchemical Body: Siddha Traditions in Medieval India* (Chicago: University of Chicago Press, 1996), esp. 61 ff. Regarding the development and various expressions of tantra in Asia, see "Appendix I: Indian and Chinese sexual mysticism," in R. H. van Gulik, *Sexual Life in Ancient China* ([1961] Leiden and Boston: Brill, 2003), 339ff.

38. Burnouf included Buddhist tantric texts in his *Introduction à l'histoire du Bouddhisme indien* (1844; see note 26 above). Burnouf's attitude toward tantra was markedly negative compared with his attitude toward more orthodox Hindu and Buddhist texts. In 1896 Louis de La Vallée Poussin edited and published (in Sanskrit) Nagarjuna's Buddhist tantra, *Pancakrama*, based on a manuscript in the Bibliothèque Nationale.

39. S. K. Ramachandra Rao, *Yoga-Tantra-Sampradāya: Yoga and Tantra in India and Tibet*, Part I (Bangalore: Kalpatharu Research Academy, 1999), 3.

40. Gavin Flood, *The Tantric Body* (London, I. B. Tauris, 2006), 12–13.

41. My primary source is Muller-Ortega, *The Triadic Heart of Śiva*, 53.

42. From the *Kularnava Tantra*: "This must not be given to just anyone. It must only be given to a devoted disciple. It will be death to any others" (Hugh Urban, "The Yoga of Sex," in *Hidden Intercourse: Eros and Sexuality in the History of Western Esotericism*, ed. Wouter J. Hanegraaff and Jeffey J. Kripal [New York: Fordham University Press, 2011], 407).

43. See Kurt Leland, *Rainbow Body: A History of the Western Chakra System* (Lake Worth, FL: Ibis Press, 2016).

44. In *The Triadic Heart of Śiva* Muller-Ortega analyses the term *kula* (*kaula*), which basically means "group": "each smaller unit of manifest reality—a universe, a world, a family, an individual person (a body)—can be termed a *kula*, because it is a conglomeration of disparate objects held together by an overarching unity. ... We may posit as a primary translation something like "Embodied Cosmos" (59).

45. The spectator "relishes [the object] from a detached angle, and with the necessary aesthetic or psychic distance. It is only then that the real meaning or beauty of the dramatic theme dawns on him, and he becomes the recipient of the highest aesthetic bliss" (Y. S. Walimbe, *Abhinavagupta on Indian Aesthetics* [Delhi, Ajanta Publications, 1980], 5).

46. See note 21.

47. See Wouter J. Hanegraaff, *Western Esotericism: A Guide for the Perplexed* (London: Bloomsbury, 2013); and Arthur Versluis, *The Secret History of Western Sexual Mysticism* (Rochester, VT: Destiny Books, 2008).

48. From a letter in the collection of the Ransom Humanities Research Center, Austin, quoted by Calvin Tomkins, *Duchamp: A Biography* (New York: Museum of Modern Art, 2014), 385.

49. "*Tantrisme. Corps de doctrines cosmologiques et mystiques d'origine indoue. Dans le yoga tantrique, la prise de conscience de l'énergie sexuelle (Shakti) comme modalité de l'énergie cosmique permit à ascète la réintégration de l'Unité primordiale*" ("Lexique Succinct de L'Érotisme," in *Boîte alerte, missives lascives*, published in conjunction with André Breton and Marcel Duchamp, *L'Exposition inteRnatiOnale du Surréalisme 1959–1960* [Paris: Galerie Daniel Cordier, 1959], 140).

50. See chapter 4.

51. William Barnard, preface to J. C. Chatterji, *Kashmir Shaivism* [1914] (Albany: SUNY Press, 1986), ix–x.

52. J. J. Clarke, *The Tao of the West: Western Transformations of Taoist Thought* (London: Routledge, 2000), 120.

53. Hanegraaff, *Western Esotericism*, 24.

54. See, for example: Arturo Schwarz, "The Alchemist Stripped Bare in the Bachelor, Even," in *Marcel Duchamp*, ed. Anne d'Harnoncourt and Kynaston McShine (New York: Museum of Modern Art, 1973), 80–98; Ulf Linde, "l'Esotérique," in *Marcel Duchamp abécédaire*, 60–85; and John F. Moffitt, *Alchemist of the Avant-Garde: The Case of Marcel Duchamp* (Albany: State University of New York, 2003).

55. Lanier Graham, *Duchamp and Androgyny: Art, Gender, and Metaphysics* (Berkeley: No-Thing Press, 2003), 11.

56. Ibid., 15.

57. *Marcel Duchamp: Work and Life*, ed. Pontus Hulten (Cambridge: MIT Press, 1993), unpaginated, 19 August 1959.

58. Anna C. Chave, *Constantin Brancusi: Shifting the Bases of Art* (New Haven: Yale University Press, 1993), 119–123.

59. The term *philosophia perennis* was first used by Agostino Steuco (1497–1548), who drew on the fifteenth-century Neoplatonic philosophy of Marsilio Ficino and Giovanni Pico della Mirandola. For an in-depth analysis of this complex historical idea, see Wouter J. Hanegraaff, *Esotericism and the Academy: Rejected Knowledge in Western Culture* (New York: Cambridge University Press, 2012), 6 ff. Evidence that early Zoroastrianism, early Brahmanism, Taoism, and the teachings of the Greek philosopher Pyrrho all did in fact draw on early forms of Buddhism is presented in Christopher I. Beckwith, *Greek Buddha* (Princeton, NJ: Princeton University Press, 2015).

60. Aldous Huxley, *The Perennial Philosophy* [1945] (New York: HarperCollins, 2009).

61. See Elizabeth De Michelis, *A History of Modern Yoga: Patanjali and Western Esotericism* (London: Continuum, 2004), especially 9–12.

62. As opposed to Christian theosophy, an esoteric phenomenon that emerged during the late fifteenth century, Theosophy (with a capital "T") developed from the writings of the Russian religious universalist Helena P. Blavatsky (1831–1891), who established Theosophy as a secret society in 1876. Two years later Blavatsky and her compatriot Henry Steel Olcott left New York for India, where they began publishing *The Theosophist*, a journal where non-Western scholars published articles about Asian religions including Hinduism, Buddhism, and Zoroastrianism. For more on Theosophy, see Joscelyn Godwin, *The Theosophical Enlightenment* (Albany: State University of New York, 1994), 277ff. Duchamp was apparently not much interested in Theosophy, but a number of his close friends and acquaintances were, including František Kupka, Walter Arensberg, and Katherine Dreier.

63. Pierre Cabanne, *Entretiens avec Marcel Duchamp* (Paris: Pierre Belfond, 1967), 166.

64. Jacques Matter first used esoteric as an "-ism" in his 1828 *Histoire critique du gnosticisme et de son influence*, which portrayed second-century gnosticism as a syncretism between the teachings of Christ and Chinese, Jewish, and Greek religious-philosophical traditions; see *Dictionary of Gnosis and Western Esotericism*, ed. Wouter J. Hanegraaff (Leiden: Brill, 2006), 337.

65. David Gordon White, *Kiss of the Yogini* (University of Chicago Press, 2003), 157–159; for parallels in ancient Greece, 187.

66. Cynthea J. Bogel, *With a Single Glance: Buddhist Icon and Early Mikkyō Vision* (Seattle: University of Washington Press, 2009), 11. Tosi Lee emphasized Duchamp's role-playing in "Fire Down Below and Watering, That's Life," in *Buddha Mind in Contemporary Art*, ed. Jacquelynn Baas and Mary Jane Jacob (Berkeley: University of California Press, 2004), 123–125.

67. Robert Lebel, "Marcel Duchamp et André Breton," *Étant donné Marcel Duchamp*, no. 7 (2006), 67.

68. Cabanne, *Dialogues*, 88.

69. Jeffrey J. Kripal, *Kali's Child: The Mystical and the Erotic in the Life and Teachings of Ramakrishna* (Chicago: University of Chicago Press, 1995), 23.

70. Silburn, *Kundalini*, 208.

71. Dupuche, *Abhinavagupta*, 260.

72. From a 1956 interview with Lawrence D. Steefel, Jr., *The Position of Duchamp's Glass in the Development of His Art* (New York: Garland, 1977), 312 (end of note 39).

73. Robert E. Buswell, Jr. and Donald S. Lopez, Jr., *The Princeton Dictionary of Buddhism* (Princeton, NJ: Princeton University Press, 2014), 108 ("*bhāga*").

74. Letter to Jean Crotti, August 17, 1952, reprinted in *TABU DADA: Jean Crotti and Suzanne Duchamp, 1915–1922*, ed. William A. Camfield and Jean-Hubert Martin (Kunsthalle Bern, 1983), 8; transcribed in *Affectionately Marcel: The Selected Correspondence of Marcel Duchamp*, ed. Francis M. Naumann and Hector Obalk (Ghent: Ludion Press, 2000), 318–320.

75. From a telegram of June 1, 1921 (*Selected Correspondence*, 98). See also Cabanne, *Dialogues*, 65.

76. Paul Matisse, interviewed by Michel Vapeene, "Les Clefs de la rue Parmentier: entretien avec Paul Matisse et Jacqueline Matisse Monnier," *Étant donné Marcel Duchamp*, no. 4 (2002), 17. Italics are in English in the original.

77. From *The Creative Act*, a talk delivered as part of a session on the creative act at the convention of the American Federation of Arts in Houston, Texas in April 1957; see Appendix.

78. Taiwanese art historian Tosi Lee has written the most extensive analyses of Duchamp and Asian philosophies, particularly Buddhism. For specific mentions of tantra, see Schwarz, *The Complete Works*, 97; and Octavio Paz, *Marcel Duchamp: Appearance Stripped Bare*, trans. Rachel Phillips and Donald Gardner (New York: Viking, 1978), 64 ff. The open-minded Schwarz tends to emphasize the importance of Western alchemy, while Paz's approach is distinctly Jungian.

79. Lebel, *Marcel Duchamp*, 69.

CHAPTER 1

1. My biographical information is primarily from Calvin Tomkins, *Duchamp: A Biography* (New York: Henry Holt, 1996).

2. George Hagman, "The Beauty of Indifference: The Art of Marcel Duchamp," in *The Artist's Mind: A Psychoanalytic Perspective on Creativity, Modern Art and Modern Artists* (London: Routledge, 2010), 72ff.

3. Tomkins, *Duchamp*, 19. Lucie's favorites (according to Marcel) were her two youngest children, who did *not* become artists.

4. Pierre Cabanne, *Dialogues with Marcel Duchamp*, trans. Rod Padgett (London: Thames and Hudson, 1971; reprinted Cambridge, MA: Da Capo Press, 1979), 20. Lucie Duchamp created designs for an entire dinner service in the style of Strasbourg, but never realized her project. For more on Lucie Duchamp and her artistic family, see *Marcel Duchamp: Work and Life*, ed. Pontus Hulten (Cambridge: MIT Press, 1993), unpaginated, 29 January 1925.

5. Lydie Fischer Sarazin-Levassor, *A Marriage in Check: The Heart of the Bride Stripped Bare by Her Bachelors, Even*, trans. Paul Edwards (Dijon: Les presses du réel, 2007), 144.

6. Cf. Jean Clair, "V: Villon, mariage, hasard, et pendaison," in *Marcel Duchamp abécédaire, approches critiques* (Paris: Centre Georges Pompidou), 1977, 201–202.

7. Tomkins, *Duchamp*, 32.

8. Linda Dalrymple Henderson, "Mysticism, Romanticism, and the Fourth Dimension," in *The Spiritual in Art: Abstract Painting 1890–1985*, ed. Maurice Tuchman (Los Angeles and New York: Los Angeles County Museum of Art and Abbeville Press, 1986), 219. See also Linda Dalrymple Henderson, *The Fourth Dimension and Non-Euclidean Geometry in Modern Art* ([1983] revised edition, Cambridge, MA: MIT Press, 2013).

9. The "Conflict Thesis" between science and spirituality has been discredited by historians of science since the 1980s; see Wouter J. Hanegraaff, *Esotericism and the Academy: Rejected Knowledge in Western Culture* (Cambridge: Cambridge University Press, 2012), 196.

10. See the catalogue to the recent exhibition *Kupka: Pionnier de abstraction* (Paris: Grand Palais, Galeries nationales, 2018).

11. French art historian Jean Clair has published extensively on Duchamp and Western occultism and other topics, but he does not discuss Asian philosophical resources, which Tosi Lee was the first to analyze (see Bibliography).

12. "Marcel poked fun at me and at the idea of having to 'furnish' the mind as if it were a room in a hotel, his ideal being on the contrary to keep his mind empty, open, ... he was forever trying to discover what his truth was, hence his apparent contradictions, which were just part of what must have been a personal system of evaluation of his own thought mechanisms" (Sarazin-Levassor, *A Marriage in Check*, 84, 86).

13. Arturo Schwarz, *The Complete Works of Marcel Duchamp* ([1969, 1970] revised and expanded edition, New York: Delano Greenidge, 2000), 527, no. 178.

14. Letter of July 22, 1951, in *Affectionately Marcel: The Selected Correspondence of Marcel Duchamp*, ed. Francis M. Naumann and Hector Obalk (Ghent: Ludion Press, 2000), 303.

15. Linda Dalrymple Henderson, *Duchamp in Context: Science and Technology in the Large Glass and Related Works* (Princeton, NJ: Princeton University Press, 1998), 3.

16. Ibid., 22.

17. P. Camille Revel, *Le Hasard, sa loi ses conséquences dans les sciences et en philosophie, suivi d'un essai ur La Métempsycose* (Paris: Bibliothèque Chacornac / H. Durville, 1909), cited by Henderson, *Duchamp in Context*, 22, 246 n. 57.

18. Henderson, *Duchamp in Context*, figure 28A, from Albert de Rochas, *L'Extériorisation de la sensibilité* [1895] (Paris, 1909), plate 2. The little flames shown emerging from fingertips in the drawing do not much resemble the glowing emanations that surround Duchamp's figures. More convincing are the photographic images of energetic auras reproduced by Cécile Debray in *Marcel Duchamp: la peinture, même* (Paris: Centre Georges Pompidou, 2014), 115–118.

19. Swami Vivekananda, *Raja Yoga: Conquering the Internal Nature* [1896] (San Diego: The Book Tree, 2010), 31. Electrical engineer Nikola Tesla was a friend and student of Vivekananda; see Philip Goldberg, *American Veda* (New York: Three Rivers Press, 1910), 72.

20. Christian Chanel, "Théon, Max," in *Dictionary of Gnosis and Western Esotericism*, ed. Wouter J. Hanegraaff (Leiden: Brill, 2006), 1112–1113. Regarding Théon, see also Joscelyn Godwin, *The Theosophical Enlightenment* (Albany: SUNY Press, 1994), 351, 378; and Joscelyn Godwin, Christian Chanel, and John P. Deveny, *The Hermetic Brotherhood of Luxor* (York Beach, ME: Samuel Weiser, 1995), 6–21, 214–215.

21. From the subhead to the journal.

22. Chanel, "Théon," 1112; the source is Mirra Alfassa, aka The Mother: *The Mother's Agenda*, ed. Satprem, vol. 1 (Paris: Institut de Recherches Évolutives, 1982), 144, http://www.mirrabliss.com/uploads/1/7/7/9/17790039/agenda.pdf (accessed September 22, 2017).

23. For a summary of Kaula, see https://saivatantra.com/the-kulamarga/ (accessed September 20, 2017).

24. Regarding Avalon, see Kathleen Taylor, *Sir John Woodroffe, Tantra and Bengal* (London: Routledge, 2001). Avalon was the first to publish a complete Indian tantra in a European language: *The Great Liberation Mahanirvana Tantra* (1913). Cambridge-educated Jagadish Chandra Chatterji also published a number of books on Kashmir Shaivism around this time, including *The Pratyabhijñā hṛidaya, being a summary of doctrines of the Advaita Shaiva philosophy of Kashmir* (Archæological & Research Department, Jammu & Kashmir State, 1911); *The Shiva sūtra vimarshinī: being the sūtras of Vasu Gupta, with the commentary called Vimarshinī by Kshemarāja* (Srinagar, Kashmir, Archeological and Research Department, 1911); and *Kashmir Shaivism* (Srinagar: Research Department Jammu, 1912/14). The French Theosophical Society published Chatterji's more popular *La philosophie ésotérique de l'Inde* (1899, 1903, 1909, etc.) and *La Vision des sages de l'Inde* (1900, 1904). In 1928 Chatterji would be hired by the American Pierre Bernard to direct his International School for Vedic and Allied Research; see Robert Love, *The Great Oom* (New York: Viking, 2010), 218, 231–232.

25. The advertisement continues: "Tantriks sojourning on coast must first register for examination with attendant" (Love, *The Great Oom*, 29).

26. Jeffrey J. Kripal, *Kali's Child: The Mystical and the Erotic in the Life and Teachings of Ramakrishna* (Chicago: University of Chicago Press, 1995), 23.

27. Godwin et al., *Hermetic Brotherhood*, 13–14, 214.

28. Max Théon, "Comment il faut considérer le magnétisme," in *Journal du Magnétisme et de la Psychologie* (February 5, 1899), 61–62. My thanks to Maureen Davis at University of California Berkeley Interlibrary Loan for locating a copy of this article.

29. Lilian Silburn, *Kundalini: The Energy of the Depths*, trans. Jacques Gontier (Albany: SUNY Press, 1988), 158.

30. J. C. Chatterji, *Kashmir Shaivism* [1914] (Albany: SUNY Press, 1986), 43–44. The concept calls to mind the jackets and waistcoats Duchamp produced for his friends in New York in 1956–1961 (the buttons bear their names); see Schwarz, *The Complete Works*, 808–809.

31. Silburn, *Kundalini*, 157–158.

32. Schwarz, *The Complete Works*, 879–880. This was one of a series of nine etchings on the theme of "The Lovers" made by Duchamp for publication in Schwarz's *The Large Glass and Related Works*, vol. 2 (Milan, 1968); Duchamp added the white nimbus in the second state of the etching.

33. S. K. Ramachandra Rao, *Yoga-Tantra-Sampradāya: Yoga and Tantra in India and Tibet*, Part I (Bangalore: Kalpatharu Research Academy, 1999), 274.

34. *Ephemerides*, 21 April 1911. Max Bergmann wrote in his diary on April 16, 1910: "I went to the Salon de la Société Nationale des Beaux Arts in order to meet Duchamp, who was there with his affair, a married woman who lives vis-à-vis of his flat. She is very interesting, only she is extremely short and has a slight limp, what a shame" (Rudolf Herz, *Marcel Duchamp: Le Mystère de Munich* [Munich: Moser, 2012], 63). A daughter, recognized by Serre's husband, was born in February 1911. Named Yvonne, she would become a painter and marry a chess player. She met her actual father only many years later, in 1966, when Duchamp's then-wife Teeny suggested they visit her studio (*Ephemerides*, 23 June 1966).

35. *Marcel Duchamp,* ed. Anne d'Harnoncourt and Kynaston McShine (New York: Museum of Modern Art, 1973), 249. The statement is from Duchamp's notes for a slide lecture he gave in Saint Louis in November 1964.

36. From "The Creative Act"; see Appendix.

37. See Schwarz, *The Complete Works*, 544, for an account of Duchamp's title for this work.

38. Rao, *Yoga-Tantra-Sampradāya*, 275.

39. Chapter 6, verse 34: http://vedabase.net/bg/6/34/en (accessed June 16, 2017).

40. Marcel Jean, *The History of Surrealist Painting*, trans. Simon Watson Taylor (New York: Grove Press, 1959), 32, note 1; Henderson, *Duchamp in Context*, 236, note 4.

41. Cloisonnism was a symbolist painting style in which colored forms are separated by dark contours. Futurism, which emphasized dynamic movement, emerged in Italy in 1909, around the same time as cubism in France; futurism and cubism influenced one another.

42. Jean-Jacques Lebel interviewed by Paul Franklin, "Coming of Age with Marcel," *Étant donné Marcel Duchamp*, no. 7 (2006), 21.

43. Henderson, *Duchamp in Context*, 11ff.

44. *Nude with Green Hair* was retitled *Nu sur nu—"Nude on Nude"*—in 1960 when, according to Arturo Schwarz, Duchamp "noticed that the figure in the foreground is painted over the buttocks of a larger, horizontal nude"; see Schwarz, *The Complete Works*, 542, no. 212.

45. Caroline Cros, *Marcel Duchamp*, trans. Vivian Rehberg (London: Reaktion, 2006), 13.

46. Cabanne, *Dialogues*, 27. The English translation of Duchamp's last line—"c'est la lumière qui m'éclairait" (Pierre Cabanne, *Entretiens avec Marcel Duchamp* [Paris: Belfond, 1967], 41)—is given in the English edition as "it's light that illuminated me." *Cassell's French Dictionary* gives the meaning of the reflexive verb *s'éclairer* as "to become enlightened." According to Duchamp, "that gaslight from the old Auer jet is green." As we shall see, green is the color of fertility, life, and enlightenment. It shows up often in the work of Duchamp, who would incorporate the Auer jet's light into his last major work, *Given* (1946–1966).

47. D'Harnoncourt and McShine, *Marcel Duchamp*, 254, 256.

48. Ibid., 260.

49. Alfred Jarry and Pierre Bonnard, *Alphabet du Père Ubu* from *Almanach du Père Ubu illustré* (Paris: Vollard, 1901). Artist William Anastasi has published extensively on Jarry and Duchamp; see, for example, "Alfred Jarry and l'Accident of Duchamp" in the online Duchamp journal *Tout-Fait*: http://www.toutfait.com/issues/issue_1/Articles/Glass.html (accessed June 8, 2017). See also Henderson, *Duchamp in Context*, chapter 4; and Andrew Hugill, *'Pataphysics: A Useless Guide* (Cambridge, MA: MIT Press, 2012), 157–165.

50. Cabanne, *Dialogues*, 31.

51. Ibid.; French: Cabanne, *Entretiens*, 51. I have modified the translation by changing "loophole" to "escape hatch" (*une sorte d'échappatoire* in the original French). For more on *Coffee Mill*, see Jacquelynn Baas, *Smile of the Buddha: Eastern Philosophy and Western Art from Monet to Today* (Berkeley: University of California Press, 2005), 83, 85.

52. Robert Lebel, *Marcel Duchamp*, trans. George Heard Hamilton (New York: Grove Press, 1959), 74.

53. Jean Vinchon, *La Magie du dessin: Du griffonage automatique au dessin thérapeutique* (Paris: Desclée de Brouwer, 1959).

54. Ibid., 126.

55. Lebel, *Marcel Duchamp*, 74–75.

56. Reproduced in Schwarz, *The Complete Works*, 560. In 1913 Duchamp gave *Once More to This Star* to Frederick Torrey, a San Francisco dealer in Asian antiquities who had purchased *Nude Descending a Staircase, No. 2* from the Armory Show that year.

57. Thanks to Tosi Lee for pointing out the genderless "nude" of the title. American journalist Nixola Greeley-Smith wrote in the *The Evening World* (April 4, 1916): "M. Duchant [*sic*] told me last week that "The Nude Descending a Stairway" is not a woman. Neither is it a man" (Rudolf E. Kuenzli, *New York Dada* [New York: Willis Locker & Owens, 1986], 135).

58. Cabanne, *Dialogues*, 30.

59. Ibid., 29–30.

60. T. S. Eliot, lecture delivered in 1932, published in *The Varieties of Metaphysical Poetry*, ed. Ronald Schuchard (New York: Harcourt Brace, 1993), 282.

61. Robert Crawford, *Young Eliot: From St. Louis to The Waste Land* (New York: Farrar, Straus and Giroux, 2015), 122. For more on Eliot and Asian Philosophy, see P. S. Sri, *T. S. Eliot, Vedanta and Buddhism* (Vancouver: University of British Columbia Press, 1985) and Cleo McNelly Kearns, *T. S. Eliot and Indic Traditions* (Cambridge: Cambridge University Press, 1987). For a different view of the Duchamp/Eliot connection, see Marjorie Perloff, "Duchamp's Eliot," in *T. S. Eliot*

and the Concept of Tradition, ed. Giovanni Cianci and Jason Harding (Cambridge: Cambridge University Press, 2007), 177–184.

62. As mentioned above, Duchamp had two close friends who were medical students: Raymond Dumouchel and Ferdinand Tribout. Eliot's friend was Jean Verdenal, a fellow lodger who died in World War I and to whom Eliot dedicated his first volume of poetry, *Prufrock and other Observations* (1917). See Crawford, *Young Eliot*, *passim*.

63. Ibid., 148. This connection also fascinated Duchamp's friend Apollinaire.

64. "Ironically," Crawford writes, "the highly sexed Munich milieu may have heightened and crystalised J. Alfred Prufrock's memorable sexual anxieties" (ibid., 161–162).

65. Ibid., 168ff. In another parallel with Duchamp, Eliot also studied the algebra of logic (179–180).

66. Burnouf's *Introduction à l'histoire du Bouddhisme indien* (1844) included a section on the tantras. See *Introduction to the History of Indian Buddhism*, trans. Katia Buffetrille and Donald S. Lopez Jr. (Chicago: University of Chicago Press, 2010), 470–504.

67. Cabanne, *Dialogues*, 16; *Entretiens*, 71.

68. Crawford, *Young Eliot*, 108–110.

69. T. S. Eliot, "Dante," in *Selected Essays* (London: Faber and Faber, 1958), 258.

70. Schwarz, *The Complete Works*, 554–555.

71. T. S. Eliot, *Four Quartets* (New York: Harcourt Brace, 1943), 44. "The Dry Salvages" was written during the German air raids on Great Britain in 1940–1941, toward the end of Eliot's poetic career.

72. Sri, *T. S. Eliot, Vedanta and Buddhism*, 105. Eliot would conclude the last of his *Four Quartets*, "Little Gidding" of 1942, with a vision at once tantric and Duchampian: "Through the unknown, unremembered gate ... At the source of the longest river / The voice of the hidden waterfall ... When the tongues of flame are in-folded / Into the crowned knot of fire / And the fire and the rose are one" (Eliot, *Four Quartets*, 59).

73. T. S. Eliot, *After Strange Gods: A Primer of Modern Heresy* (London: Faber and Faber, 1933), 40–41.

74. Dore Ashton, "An Interview with Marcel Duchamp," *Studio International* 171, no. 878 (June 1966), 245.

75. "*LE POÈTE A FEU CONTINU. A vendre gros et détail. Livraison rapide à domicile. S'adresser à T. S. Eliot qui transmettre*," Pierre-Henri Kleiber, *L'Encyclopédie "Da Costa" (1947–1949)* (Lausanne: Éditions L'Âge d'Homme, 2014), integral facsimile, page 16.

76. See Appendix. The quote is from T. S. Eliot's "Tradition and the Individual Talent" (1919), published in *The Sacred Wood and Major Early Essays* [1920] (Mineola, NY: Dover, 1998), 31.

77. From "Discussion" of Eric Cameron's "*Given*," in *The Definitively Unfinished Marcel Duchamp*, ed. Thierry De Duve (Cambridge, MA: MIT Press, 1991), 31.

CHAPTER 2

1. Robert Lebel, *La double vue, suivi de L'inventeur du temps gratuit* (Paris: Le Soleil Noir, 1964), 78.

2. Pierre Cabanne, *Dialogues with Marcel Duchamp*, trans. Rod Padgett (London: Thames and Hudson, 1971; reprinted Cambridge, MA: Da Capo Press, 1987), 28.

3. Ecke Bonk, *Marcel Duchamp: The Box in a Valise*, trans. David Britt (New York: Rizzoli, 1989), 226.

4. Robert Lebel, *Marcel Duchamp*, trans. George Heard Hamilton (New York: Grove Press, 1959), 160, 6.

5. Ibid., 161.

6. Cabanne, *Dialogues*, 33.

7. Lilian Silburn, *Kundalini: The Energy of the Depths* (Albany: State University of New York, 1988), 178.

8. Ibid., 189–190: "Although both [man and woman] are equally possessed of the awareness of the quiescent and emergent states, the [female] energy alone and not the [male] owner, is capable of developing creation … so to her alone should the *guru* impart the whole of the secret doctrine; and through her, by the practice of union … it is imparted to man."

9. *La double vue, suivi de L'inventeur du temps gratuit* was issued in 1,461 copies, of which 111 were numbered and presented in a black casing stamped with a gold triangle with an etching by Alberto Giacometti and a "*pliage*," *La pendule de profile*, by Marcel Duchamp. The deluxe "Club du Soleil Noir" series was issued in an edition of 150 with an etched portrait of Robert Lebel by Ferró [Erró]. The trade edition comprised 1,200 paperback copies stamped 151 through 1,350 with a reproduction of an etching by Giocometti on the cover, the Ferró portrait on the inside front flap, and two photographs of Duchamp's *La pendule de profile* "hors texte." The book was republished by Deyolle in 1993 with a preface by Alain Fleischer and an afterword by Patrick Waldberg.

10. Translated by J. H. Matthews and published in *The Custom-House of Desire: A Half-Century of Surrealist Stories* (Berkeley: University of California Press, 1975), 150–160. Translated by Sarah Skinner Kilborne with Julia Koteliansky and published in the online journal *Tout-Fait*, http://toutfait.com/the-inventor-of-gratuitous-time/ (May 1, 2000, updated July 13, 2016, accessed November 18, 2016). Both Matthews and Kilborne translate the title, *L'inventeur du temps gratuit*, as "The Inventor of Gratuitous Time." I prefer the connection with *Given* implied by "free" time ("gratuitous," from the Latin *grātuīt-us*: free, spontaneous voluntary). See chapter 6 for more on New York in the 1940s.

11. The model was Giacometti's wife Annette.

12. *The Writings of Marcel Duchamp*, ed. Michel Sanouillet and Elmer Peterson (New York: Da Capo Press, 1989), 101. *The White Box* was edited by Cleve Gray and published in New York by Cordier & Ekstrom Gallery in 1966.

13. Ibid., 31.

14. Linda Henderson, "Paradigm Shifts and Shifting Identities in the Career of Marcel Duchamp," in *aka Marcel Duchamp: Meditations on the Identities of an Artist*, ed. Anne Collins Goodyear and James W. McManus (Washington, DC: Smithsonian Institution Scholarly Press, 2014), 90.

15. Robert Lebel, "Duchamp au musée," in *Marcel Duchamp* (Paris: Belfond, 1985), 191.

16. *Étant donné Marcel Duchamp*, no. 7 (2006), 21, where Jean-Jacques Lebel tells interviewer Paul Franklin that "the manuscript probably exists in my father's archives, but that remains to be seen." Robert Lebel's archives are not available to researchers.

17. Lebel, *La double vue*, 136–137.

18. Ibid., 135. The passage is reminiscent of a quote from Mirra Alfassa: "All the explanations I sought were always of a material nature; it seemed so obvious to me: no need for mysteries or things of that sort—you must explain things in material terms" (Satprem, *The Mind of the Cells*, trans. Luc Venet [Mt. Vernon, WA: Institute for Evolutionary Research, 1992], 13).

19. Lebel, *La double vue*, 12–13. According to Duchamp's art patron friend Katherine Dreier, "Many a museum or dealer has been unable to secure [a Duchamp] because he would not sell to them—since they were only collectors and had no love for true art" (*Étant donné Marcel Duchamp*, no. 9 [2009], 68).

20. Lebel, *La double vue*, 56.

21. Ibid., 57–58.

22. See Silburn, *Kundalini*, 87ff; and John R. Dupuche, *Abhinavagupta: the Kula ritual, as elaborated in chapter 29 of the Tantrāloka* (Delhi: Motilal Banarsidass Publishers, 2003), 337–342.

23. Lebel, *La double vue*, 74–78.

24. In a note from *The Green Box* Duchamp describes the upper portion of *The Large Glass* as "the blossoming of this virgin who has reached the goal of her desires" (Sanouillet and Peterson, eds., *Writings*, 42).

25. Patrick Waldberg, "Robert Lebel, ou les complicités ambiguës," *Preuves*, no. 181 (March 1966), 81.

26. Lebel, *La double vue*, 81. Cf. the electrical lighting in *Given*.

27. Waldberg, "Robert Lebel," 81–82.

28. Arturo Schwarz called *La double vue* an "imaginary autobiographical novel" (Arturo Schwarz, *The Complete Works of Marcel Duchamp* [1969, 1970; revised and expanded edition, New York: Delano Greenidge, 2000], 845); Paul Franklin describes it as a "semiautobiographical text" (Paul B. Franklin, *The Artist and His Critic Stripped Bare: The Correspondence of Marcel Duchamp and Robert Lebel* [Los Angeles: Getty Research Institute, 2016], 56, note 13).

29. To see what Alfassa's own art from this period was like, and to get a sampling of her later philosophy of art, see "Occult Paintings by Mother Mirra Alfassa," http://www.youtube.com/watch?v=Tc5pXLnG6rI&list=TLrgmg_sNV73Y (accessed May 26, 2017). My biographical information on Mirra Alfassa comes primarily from the first four volumes of Sujata Nahar, *Mother's Chronicles* (Paris: Institut de Recherches Évolutives, 1985–1995), along with Georges van Vrekhem's *The Mother: The Story of Her Life* (India: HarperCollins, 2000). There is a great deal of material available online, including: *Wikipedia* (http://en.wikipedia.org/wiki/Mirra_Alfassa); *Collected Works of The Mother* (http://www.sriaurobindoashram.org/ashram/mother/writings.php); and *Mother's Agenda* (http://www.auroville.org/contents/527), all accessed May 26, 2017.

30. Silburn, *Kundalini*, 158.

31. Prema Nandakumar, *The Mother* (New Delhi: National Book Trust, 1977), 10.

32. From an interview with Alexandra David-Néel by Prithwindra Mukherjee, *The Sunday Standard*, June 15, 1969; quoted in Nandakumar, *The Mother*, 9–10.

33. Nahar, *Mother's Chronicles, book three, Mirra the Occultist* (1989), 246.

34. This and the quotes below from Mirra Alfassa, *Paroles d'autrefois* (Pondicherry: Sri Aurobindo Ashram [1946] 1983), 16–22. English version: *Words of Long Ago*, vol. 2, *Collected Works of The Mother* (Pondicherry: Sri Aurobindo Ashram, [1978] 2004), 13–19.

35. For more on Contre-Attaque, see Michel Surya, *Georges Bataille: An Intellectual Biography*, trans. Krzysztof Fijalkowski and Michael Richardson (London: Verso, 2002), 226–227. Regarding Acéphale, see Georges Duthuit's letter to André Breton, *VVV*, no. 4 (February 1944), 45–49.

36. Nahar, *Mother's Chronicles, book three*, 292.

37. Hugh B. Urban, *Tantra: Sex, Secrecy, Politics, and Power in the Study of Religion* (Berkeley: University of California Press, 2003), 91ff. According to Urban, shakti is "the power that creates, sustains, and destroys the universe—but it is also the power that flows through the social and political world as well" ("The Yoga of Sex," in *Hidden Intercourse: Eros and Sexuality in the History of Western Esotericism*, ed. Wouter J. Hanegraaff and Jeffey J. Kripal [New York: Fordham University Press, 2011], 406).

38. https://overmanfoundation.wordpress.com/2012/10/08/alexandra-david-neels-reminiscences-of-sri-aurobindo/ (accessed January 18, 2019).

39. Urban, *Tantra*, 101.

40. See Ann Gleig and Charles I. Flores, "Remembering Sri Aurobindo and the Mother: The Forgotten Lineage of Integral Yoga," in *Gurus of Modern Yoga*, ed. Mark Singleton and Ellen Goldberg (New York: Oxford University Press, 2014), 38–59.

41. Sujata Nahar, *Mother's Chronicles, book two, Mirra the Artist* (Paris: Institut de Recherches Évolutives, 1986), 85.

42. Silburn, *Kundalini*, 181; cf. parallels between Kaula and features of *The Large Glass* such as the generation of soma (144) with Duchamp's chocolate grinder; and the spangles as products of "churning" by a "whirling force" that "produces sparkles perceptible to the yogin when Kundalini rises, with a throb of pure knowledge" (43).

43. http://mother-agenda.narod.ru/Agenda_1/1954-08-25.htm (accessed June 29, 2017).

44. See Elizabeth De Michelis, *A History of Modern Yoga: Patanjali and Western Esotericism* (London: Continuum, 2004), 91–126; David Gordon White, *Yoga in Practice* (Princeton, NJ: Princeton University Press, 2012), 20–21; David Gordon White, *The Yoga Sutra of Patanjali: A Biography* (Princeton, NJ: Princeton University Press, 2014), 116–158.

45. "'I saw with my own eyes God dwelling in the vagina! I saw God in the intercourse of a dog and a bitch.' This vision is preceded by the bold-print phrase: '*Listen! I'm telling you something very secret!*'" (Jeffrey J. Kripal, *Kali's Child: The Mystical and the Erotic in the Life and Teachings of Ramakrishna* [Chicago: University of Chicago Press, 1995], 349, note 71). In modern Western art, this tantric view of sexuality can be traced back to the eighteenth century when, during a period of "intense psychoerotic experimentation" in the 1790s, William Blake sketched a naked woman with genitals in the form of a chapel containing an erect penis. Her head is crowned with a star not unlike Duchamp's star tonsure discussed at the end of this chapter. See Marsha Keith Schuchard, *William Blake's Sexual Path to Spiritual Vision* (Rochester, VT: Inner Traditions, 2008), 38–39.

46. The other important influence was Arthur Avalon [Sir John George Woodroffe], *The Serpent Power: Being the Ṣaṭ-chakra-nirūpaṇa and Pādukāpanchaka: two works on tantric yoga* ([London: Luzac, 1919] New York: Dover, 1974), see 11. Avalon published the first scholarly expositions of tantric texts. Depending on how you count, *The Serpent Power* was his fifth book on tantra. It was preceded by *Tantra of the Great Liberation (Mahānirvāna Tantra)* and *Hymns to the Goddess* (both 1913), the two-volume *Principles of Tantra* (1914–1916), and *Shakti and Shâkta* (1918). See chapter 5 for Avalon as a resource for Picabia and Duchamp.

47. Not individual self, but universal Self with a capital S. Sri Vivekananda, *Raja Yoga: Conquering the Internal Nature* [1896] (San Diego: The Book Tree, 2010), 53–54.

48. Vivekananda, *Raja Yoga*, 61, 54.

49. Ibid., 48, 58.

50. Letter of October 20, 1936, quoted in Tosi Lee, *Watering, That's My Life: The Symbolism and Self-Imaging of Marcel Duchamp*, unpublished doctoral thesis, University of Illinois at Urbana-Champaign, 1993, 143 (the letter is at Yale).

51. Swami Lakshman Jee, *Kashmir Shaivism: The Secret Supreme* (Albany, NY: SUNY for Universal Shaiva Trust, 1988), 121–122.

52. Schwarz, *The Complete Works*, argues that 1919 is a likely date (672–673), but there is documentary evidence that Duchamp reprised his star tonsure in August–September 1921 (James W. McManus, "Not Seen and/or Less Seen: Hiding in Front of the Camera," in *Inventing Marcel Duchamp: The Dynamics of Portraiture* [Cambridge, MA: MIT Press, 2009], 79, n. 100). James Housefield believes all the photographs of *Tonsure* record the results, over time, of the same 1921 event ("Starry Messenger: Astronomy, Fashion, and Identity in Marcel Duchamp's Comet Haircut," in *aka Marcel Duchamp: Meditations on the Identities of an Artist* [Smithsonian Institution Scholarly Press, 2014], 45ff). But a visual comparison between the tonsure Schwarz reproduces and the one in McManus, page 159, show enough differences to suggest that there were two tonsures, one in 1919 and another in 1921.

53. Alfassa, *Words of Long Ago*, 89.

54. A point like the one at the center of Duchamp's "Mandala" in *The Large Glass*; see chapter 5. Van Vrekhem, *The Mother*, 77–78; *The Mother, Questions and Answers 1956*, *Collected Works of The Mother*, vol. 8 (Pondicherry: Sri Aurobindo Ashram [1977] 2004), 210–211.

55. Guillaume Apollinaire, *Les peintres cubistes* [1912], ed. and annotated by L. C. Breunig and J.-Cl. Chevalier (Paris: Hermann, 1965), 92. See chapter 4.

56. Nahar, *Mother's Chronicles, book two*, 79.

57. Sanouillet and Peterson, ed., *Writings*, 42.

CHAPTER 3

1. From a 1956 interview with James Johnson Sweeney quoted by Calvin Tomkins, *Duchamp: A Biography* (New York: Henry Holt, 1996), 394.

2. Rudolf Herz, *Marcel Duchamp: Le Mystère de Munich* (Munich: Moser, 2012), 62.

3. Cecilia Cuțescu-Storck, unpublished 1961 ms. quoted in Barbu Brezianu, "Pages inédites de la correspondance de Brancusi," *Revue Roumaine d'Histoire de l'Art* 1, no. 2 (1964), 398, note 18; from Margit Rowell, "Brancusi: Timelessness in a Modern Mode," in Friedrich Teja Bach, Margit Rowell, and Ann Temkin, *Constantin Brancusi, 1876–1957* (Philadelphia Museum of Art with MIT Press, 1995), 42.

4. Centre Pompidou, *Brancusi and Duchamp: Regards historiques* (Paris: Centre Georges Pompidou, 2000), 90.

5. Letter of March 12, 1915, published in *Affectionately Marcel: The Selected Correspondence of Marcel Duchamp*, ed. Francis M. Naumann and Hector Obalk (Ghent: Ludion Press, 2000), 32. (Picabia had already left for New York.)

6. On Brancusi and tantra, see Anna C. Chave, *Constantin Brancusi: Shifting the Bases of Art* (New Haven: Yale University Press, 1993), 119–123. See also Jacquelynn Baas, *Smile of the Buddha* (Berkeley: University of California Press, 2005), 70–77.

7. See Introduction and Lanier Graham, "Duchamp and Androgyny: The Concept and its Context," *Tout-Fait* 2, no. 4 (January 2002), http://www.toutfait.com/issues/volume2/issue_4/articles/graham/graham1.html (accessed May 30, 2017); and Graham, *Duchamp and Androgyny: Art, Gender, and Metaphysics* (Berkeley: No-Thing Press, 2003), 15.

8. *Le Poète Tibétain Milarépa: Ses Crimes—Ses Épreuves—Ses Nirvana*, trans. Jacques Bacot (Paris: Bossard, 1925).

9. Gilles Bégin, *Les Peintures du Bouddhisme Tibétain* (Paris: Musée National des Arts Asiatiques-Guimet, 1996), 16.

10. Jacques Bacot, "Pèlerinage du Dokerla (Tibet Sud-Oriental)," *Annales du Musée Guimet, Bibliothèque de Vulgarisation, Tome 32: Conférences Faites au Musée Guimet* (Paris: Leroux, 1909), 195–218; Jacques Bacot, "L'art tibétain," *Annales du Musée Guimet, Bibliothèque de Vulgarisation, Tome 36: Conférences Faites au Musée Guimet* (Paris: Hachette, 1912), 191–220.

11. Gabrielle Buffet-Picabia "Some Memories of Pre-Dada: Picabia and Duchamp (1949)," in *The Dada Painters and Poets: An Anthology*, ed. Robert Motherwell (Cambridge, MA: Harvard University Press, 1981), 256; Gabrielle Buffet-Picabia, *Rencontres* (Paris: Belfond, 1977), 45.

12. www.toutfait.com/issues/volume2/issue_5/collections/kiesler/popup_p6.html (accessed May 30, 2017).

13. Cabanne, *Dialogues with Marcel Duchamp*, trans. Rod Padgett (Cambridge, MA: Da Capo Press, 1987), 32.

14. Pierre Arnauld, *Francis Picabia: La peinture sans aura* (Paris: Gallimard, 2002), 76–77.

15. Cabanne, *Dialogues*, 32. Jean Arp, "Gabrielle Buffet-Picabia," in Buffet-Picabia, *Rencontres*, 25.

16. Buffet-Picabia, "Memories of Pre-Dada," 256.

17. *Lucifer* was the title of a Theosophist journal published by Helena Blavatsky; the first issue appeared in London in September 1887. *Lucifer the Lightbearer* was the title of an

individualist-anarchist journal published in the United States around the turn of the twentieth century. According to its publisher, Moses Harman, the name was chosen because "Lucifer, the ancient name of the Morning Star, now called Venus, seems to us unsurpassed as a cognomen for a journal whose mission is to bring light to the dwellers in darkness" (http://en.wikipedia.org/wiki/Lucifer_the_Lightbearer; accessed May 30, 2017).

18. *Marcel Duchamp*, ed. Anne d'Harnoncourt and Kynaston McShine (New York: Museum of Modern Art, 1973), 256.

19. See his letters to André Breton about this exhibition published in Naumann and Obalk, eds., *Affectionately Marcel*, esp. 370, where the train is mentioned.

20. Catalogue to *Exposition Surréaliste d'Objets* (Paris: Charles Ratton, 1936), unpaginated. In 1954 Duchamp's acolyte Richard Hamilton created a series of paintings on the theme *Trainsition*.

21. Marcel Jean, *The History of Surrealist Painting*, trans. Simon Watson Taylor (New York, Grove Press, 1959), 34. The nuances of Duchamp's inscribed titles are explored by Didier Semin in "Le paradigme du dessin d'humour: La légende du *Nu descendant un escalier*," in *Marcel Duchamp: la peinture, même* (Paris: Centre Georges Pompidou, 2014), 156–159.

22. The first edition appeared in January 1912, the second in April. Kandinsky is often described, inaccurately, as a Theosophist. His version of Theosophy (such as it was) was that of Rudolf Steiner (1861–1925), who was based in Munich at the time. The third of Steiner's four mystery dramas was performed in Munich on August 24, 1912, during Duchamp's period of residence there. Steiner was in the process of resigning his position as head of the German and Austrian branches of the Theosophical Society to found his own Anthroposophial Society, established February 2, 1913. The rift had to do with the Theosophical Society's adoption of Asian religious terminology; Steiner preferred Christian tropes, as did Kandinsky.

23. Roger Allard, "Signs of Renewal in Painting," in *The Blaue Reiter Almanac*, trans. Henning Falkenstein (Boston: MFA Publications, 2005), 111 and 106.

24. David Gordon White, *The Yoga Sutra of Patanjali: A Biography* (Princeton, NJ: Princeton University Press, 2014), 27.

25. "A Complete Reversal of Art Opinions by Marcel Duchamp, Iconoclast," *Arts and Decoration* 5, no. 11 (September 1915), 427.

26. See Appendix.

27. Thanks to Drs. Anka Krämer, Rachel King, and especially Wolfgang Stein of the Staatliches Museum für Völkerkunde München (now Museum Fünf Kontinente) for their kind assistance in the course of my research into the history of the museum.

28. Herbert Molderings, in *Marcel Duchamp in Munich 1912*, ed. Helmut Friedel et al. (Munich: Schirmer/Mosel, 2012), 11. One factor in the choice of North Africa by Matisse et al. may have been the availability of mind-altering, thus art-altering, substances there.

29. See Thomas McEvilley, *The Shape of Ancient Thought: Comparative Studies in Greek and Indian Philosophies* (New York: Allworth Press, 2002); Roger-Pol Droit, *The Cult of Nothingness: The Philosophers and the Buddha* (Chapel Hill: University of North Carolina Press, 2003); Christopher I. Beckwith, *Greek Buddha: Pyrrho's Encounter with Early Buddhism in Central Asia* (Princeton, NJ: Princeton University Press, 2015); and my introduction to *Smile of the Buddha*, 1–11.

30. See *Marcel Duchamp in Munich 1912*, and Herz, *Le Mystère de Munich*. Regarding Duchamp and the Museum of Ethnology, see Tosi Lee, "Fire Down Below and Watering, That's Life: A Buddhist Reader's Response to Marcel Duchamp," in *Buddha Mind in Contemporary Art*, ed. Jacquelynn Baas and Mary Jane Jacob (Berkeley: University of California Press, 2005), 123–139.

31. Regarding Duchamp's interest in these museums, see Linda Dalrymple Henderson, *Duchamp in Context: Science and Technology in the Large Glass and Related Works* (Princeton, NJ: Princeton University Press, 1998), 17–18.

32. The artist's widow bequeathed the original plaster to the museum in 1907. In the 1860s Bartholdi had approached the Khedive of Egypt with a plan to build a lighthouse in the form of a robed woman holding aloft a torch at the northern entrance to the Suez Canal in Port Said. That was the idea behind the Statue of Liberty too, but her light proved too feeble (https://en.wikipedia.org/wiki/Statue_of_Liberty, accessed January 18, 2019).

33. From an interview with Alexandra David-Néel by Prithwindra Mukherjee, *The Sunday Standard*, June 15, 1969.

34. This is Duchamp and Brancusi's first documented meeting, mentioned earlier. Dora Vallier, "La vie fait l'œuvre de Fernand Léger," *Cahiers d'Art* 29, no. 2 (1954), 140. Léger implied that Duchamp was speaking to Brancusi, who was a sculptor, but surely he was also addressing Léger, a painter. Léger eventually took on his challenge: *Propellers*, 1918, was bought by Duchamp's friend Katherine Dreier and is now in the Museum of Modern Art.

35. *Marcel Duchamp: Work and Life*, ed. Pontus Hulten (Cambridge: MIT Press, 1993), unpaginated, August 19, 1912.

36. Buffet-Picabia, "Some Memories of Pre-Dada," 257. Cf. the similar statement by Robert Lebel in my introduction.

37. Tomkins, *Duchamp: A Biography*, 111–112.

38. See note 11 of this chapter.

39. Tomkins, *Duchamp: A Biography*, 112. Buffet-Picabia made this statement to Matta's wife Malitte in an interview published in *Paris-New York* (Paris: Centre Georges Pompidou, 1977), 54–62.

40. Arturo Schwarz, *The Complete Works of Marcel Duchamp* (1969, 1970; revised and expanded paperback edition, New York: Delano Greenidge, 2000), 35, note 9.

41. Lilian Silburn, *Kundalini: The Energy of the Depths*, trans. Jacques Gontier (Albany: State University of New York, 1988), 158.

42. Max Théon, "Comment il faut considérer le magnétisme," *Journal du Magnétisme et de la Psychologie* (5 February 1899), 61–62.

43. Herz, *Le Mystère de Munich*, 98. There was also, handily enough, an art supply store on the ground floor.

44. Ibid., 158.

45. From a 1955 interview with James Johnson Sweeney published in *Wisdom: Conversations with the Elder Wise Men of Our Day*, ed. James Nelson (New York: Norton, 1958), 92.

46. For more on the links between these drawings and sewing machines, see W. Bowdoin Davis, Jr., *Duchamp: Domestic Patterns, Covers, and Threads* (New York: Midmarch Arts Press, 1997), 102 ff.

47. Herz, *Le Mystère de Munich*, 163.

48. Ibid.

49. Lawrence D. Steefel, Jr., "The Art of Marcel Duchamp," *Art Journal* 22, no. 2 (Winter 1962–1963), 74; quoted in Herz, *Le Mystère de Munich*, 318, note 131.

50. See Appendix.

51. T. S. Eliot, "Tradition and the Individual Talent," in *The Sacred Wood and Major Early Essays* [1920] (Mineola, NY: Dover, 1998), 33. Cabanne, *Dialogues*, 31.

52. Eliot, *The Sacred Wood*, 30–31.

53. Robert Lebel, *Marcel Duchamp* (Paris: Belfond, 1985), 185.

54. Cabanne, *Dialogues*, 67; French: Pierre Cabanne, *Entretiens avec Marcel Duchamp* (Paris: Pierre Belfond, 1967), 124.

55. Robert Lebel, *Marcel Duchamp*, trans. George Heard Hamilton (New York: Grove Press, 1959), 73, note 1.

56. Cabanne, *Dialogues*, 17. In November 1912, after his return from Munich, where he had stayed for almost three months, Duchamp would begin taking courses at the École des Chartes. A year later he got a job, albeit a temporary one, at the Sainte-Geneviève Library (see chapter 4).

57. First quote from Duchamp's unpublished notes for a 1964 lecture: Calvin Tompkins, *Duchamp: A Biography* (New York: Henry Holt, 1996), 99; second quote from a 1968 interview with John Russell: Herbert Molderings, "The Discovery of the Mind's Eye: Marcel Duchamp in Munich 1912," in *Marcel Duchamp in Munich 1912*, 12.

CHAPTER 4

1. *Tout objet de trois dimensions, que nous voyons froidement, est une projection d'une chose à quatre dimensions que nous ne connaissons pas.* Pierre Cabanne, *Entretiens avec Marcel Duchamp* (Paris: Belfond, 1967), 68.

2. From a 1966 interview for Belgian television by Jean Antoine, trans. Sue Rose, *Art Newspaper*, no. 27, April 1993, http://ec2-79-125-124-178.eu-west-1.compute.amazonaws.com/articles/An-interview-with-Marcel-Duchamp/29278 (accessed May 14, 2018).

3. Marcel Jean, *The History of Surrealist Painting*, trans. Simon Watson Taylor (New York, Grove Press, 1959), 29.

4. Calvin Tomkins, *Duchamp: A Biography* (New York: Henry Holt, 1996), 90–91.

5. Ibid., 109, 112.

6. Gabrielle Buffet-Picabia, "Some Memories of Pre-Dada" [1949], in *The Dada Painters and Poets: An Anthology*, ed. Robert Motherwell (Cambridge, MA: Harvard University Press, 1981), 257.

7. *The Writings of Marcel Duchamp*, ed. Michel Sanouillet and Elmer Peterson (Cambridge, MA: Da Capo Press, 1989), 26–27. French: *Marcel Duchamp: Duchamp du signe suivi de Notes*,

ed. Michel Sanouillet and Paul Matisse with the collaboration of Anne Sanouillet and Paul B. Franklin (Paris: Flammarion, 2008), 63–64.

8. Cf. *Tableau Dada* (1920), Picabia's monkey "with its tail in front"—i.e., pulling his tail between his legs—illustration in *Cannibale*, no. 1 (April 25, 1920); reproduced in William A. Camfield et al., *Francis Picabia: Catalogue Raisonné*, vol. 2 (Brussels: Mercatorfonds, 2016), 290–291.

9. Lilian Silburn, *Kundalini: Energy of the Depths* (Albany: State University of New York Press, 1988), 199.

10. Edwin F. Bryant, *The Yoga sūtras of Patañjali* (New York: North Point Press, 2009), 362.

11. J. C. Chatterji, *Kashmir Shaivism* [1914] (Albany: State University of New York Press, 1986), 13–14.

12. Silburn, *Kundalini*, 138; and Sanjukta Gupta and Richard Gombrich, "Kings, Power, and the Goddess," *South Asia Research* 6, no. 2 (1986), 129.

13. Guillaume Apollinaire, *Calligrammes: Poems of Peace and War (1913–1916)* (Berkeley: University of California Press, 1980), 44.

14. Guillaume Apollinaire, *The Cubist Painters* [1913], trans. Peter Read (Berkeley: University of California Press, 2004), 75. I have modified Read's translation slightly; see *Guillaume Apollinaire: Les peintres cubistes*, ed. L.C. Breunig and J.-Cl. Chevalier (Paris: Hermann, 1965), 90–92.

15. Pierre Cabanne, *Dialogues with Marcel Duchamp*, trans. Rod Padgett (Cambridge, MA: Da Capo Press, 1987), 37–38. When questioned by Cabanne about Apollinaire's assertion in *The Cubist Painters* that he was "the only painter of the modern school who concerns himself today [autumn 1912] with the nude," Duchamp responded: "You know, he wrote whatever came into his head." He admitted, however: "I like what he did very much."

16. Cabanne, *Dialogues*, 43.

17. *Apollinaire: Les peintres cubistes*, 92.

18. Ibid., 116, note 4.

19. Apollinaire, *The Cubist Painters*, 69.

20. Regarding *n*-dimensional geometry, see Linda Dalrymple Henderson, *The Fourth Dimension and Non-Euclidean Geometry in Modern Art* (revised edition, Cambridge, MA: MIT Press, 2013), 105ff.

21. Apollinaire, *The Cubist Painters*, 16–17.

22. Cabanne, *Dialogues*, 32; Tomkins, *Duchamp: A Biography*, 108.

23. Cabanne, *Dialogues*, 32. Among other things, opium is helpful in achieving the control needed to prevent ejaculation during the practice of nei-tan.

24. *Apollinaire on Art: Essays and Reviews 1902–1918*, ed. Leroy C. Breunig (Boston: MFA Publications, 2001), 127–129, 164–166.

25. Yves Peyré, "Le séjour de Marcel Duchamp à la Bibliothèque Sainte-Geneviève," in *Marcel Duchamp: la peinture, même* (Paris: Centre Georges Pompidou, 2014), 220–225. See also Yves Peyré and Evelyne Toussaint, *Duchamp à la Bibliothèque Sainte-Geneviève* (Paris: Éditions du Regard, 2014), 14ff.

26. Peyré and Toussaint, *Duchamp à la Bibliothèque*, 102. The library's online catalogue does helpfully provide the year of acquisition.

27. http://www.toutfait.com/issues/volume2/issue_5/collections/kiesler/popup_p6.html (accessed September 5, 2018).

28. Peyré and Toussaint, *Duchamp à la Bibliothèque*, 16–17.

29. Sanouillet and Matisse, *Duchamp du signe*, 124.

30. Paris: Pierre Billaine, 1638. The full subtitle reads: "L'Optique, par la vision directe; La Catoptrique, par réflexion des miroirs plats, cylindriques & coniques; La Dioptrique, par la refraction des crystaux."

31. See Wouter J. Hanegraaff, *Esotericism and the Academy: Rejected Knowledge in Western Culture* (Cambridge: Cambridge University Press, 2012), 166–177; and Lawrence Lipking, *What Galileo Saw: Imagining the Scientific Revolution* (Ithaca: Cornell University Press, 2014).

32. Paris: Masson, 1877. Cf. Duchamp's *Prière de toucher* (*Please Touch*), cover for the exhibition catalogue for *Le Surréalisme en 1947* (Paris: Maeght); see Arturo Schwarz, *The Complete Works of Marcel Duchamp* (New York: Abrams, 1970), 786–788.

33. Schwarz, *The Complete Works*, 38, note 23. Regarding Pyrrho and Buddhism, see Christopher I. Beckwith, *Greek Buddha: Pyrrho's Encounter with Early Buddhism in Central Asia* (Princeton, NJ: Princeton University Press, 2015).

34. Paris: Imprimerie Royale, 1823. Rémusat was also the author of an earlier book of Chinese philosophy in the library's collection: *Le livre des récompenses et des peines / traduit du chinois, avec des notes et des éclaircissemens* (Paris: Renouard, 1816).

35. Stanislas Julien, *Le Livre de la voie et de la vertu par le philosophe Lao-tseu* (Paris: L'Imprimerie Royale, 1842). Léon Wieger, *Taoïsm. tome II. Les Pères du système taoïste: Lao-tzeu, Lie-tzeu, Tchoang-tzeu* (Xian Xian: Imp. de Xian Xian), 1913.

36. Alexandra David-Néel, *Les théories individualistes dans la philosophie chinoise, Yang-tchou* (Paris: V. Giard & E. Brière, 1909), 1, 10, http://hdl.handle.net/2027/coo.31924022995439 (accessed June 6, 2017). Another of David-Néel's epigraphs is from the *Bhagavad Gita*.

37. David-Néel, *Yang-tchou*, 14.

38. Cabanne, *Dialogues*, 17.

39. Ibid., 16.

40. Jagadish Chandra Chatterji, *La Vision des sages de l'Inde, ou le Sentier de la perfection* (second edition, Paris: Publications Théosophiques, 1904); *The Pratyabhijñā hṛidaya, being a summary of doctrines of the Advaita Shaiva philosophy of Kashmir* (Archæological & Research Department, Jammu & Kashmir State, 1911); *Hindu Realism* (Gurgaon: Shubhi Publications, 1908–).

41. Chatterji, *Pratyabhijñā hṛidaya*, unpaginated.

42. *The Doctrine of Recognition: A Translation of Pratyabhijñāhr̥dayam* [by] *Kshemaraja, with an introduction and notes by Jaideva Singh*, foreword by Paul Muller-Ortega (Albany: State University of New York Press, 1990), 79.

43. See Francis M. Naumann, "Aesthetic Anarchy," in *Duchamp, Man Ray, Picabia*, ed. Jennifer Mundy (London: Tate Publishing, 2008), 59–62.

44. My information on Stirner and all quotes are from David Leopold's edition of Max Stirner, *The Ego and Its Own* (Cambridge: Cambridge University Press, 1995); this quote, xiiiff.

45. Ibid., 7.

46. Mary Ann Caws, *Manifesto: A Century of Isms* (Lincoln: University of Nebraska Press, 2001), 341. See also John F. Welsh, "Egoism and the Political Thought of Dora Marsden," in *Max Stirner's Dialectical Egoism: A New Interpretation* (Lanham, MD: Lexington, 2010), 191–225. One of *The Egoist*'s supporters was Duchamp's friend, the Irish-American collector John Quinn.

47. *Angels' Wings: A Series of Essays on Art and its Relation to Life* (London: S. Sonnenschein; New York: Macmillan, 1898), 219. On Carpenter's travels in India, see *A Visit to a Gnani or Wise Man of the East* (London: Allen, 1911).

48. M. Senard, *Edward Carpenter et sa Philosophie* (Paris: Librairie de L'Art Indépendant, 1914) was the abridged French version of *The Art of Creation: Essays on the Self and Its Powers* (London: George Allen [1904, revised 1907], 1912).

49. *Bṛhadāraṇyaka-Upaniṣad: text in Sanskrit and translation with notes in English from the commentaries of Śaṅkarācārya and the gloss of Ānandagiri by E. Roer; with a preface by Manilal N. Dvivedi* [1856] (Delhi: Bharatiya Kala Prakashan, 2000), 238.

50. *Kashmir Shaivism* (Srinagar: Research Department Jammu, [1914] 1962), 73. Cf. the title of Duchamp's *Tu m'* (1918, figure 4.6).

51. Humboldt actually read Sanskrit, unlike Hegel.

52. David Gordon White, *The Yoga Sutra of Patanjali: A Biography* (Princeton, NJ: Princeton University Press, 2014), 90.

53. Timothy Morton, "Hegel on Buddhism," in *Romantic Circles* (February 2007), http://www.rc.umd.edu/praxis/buddhism/morton/morton.html (accessed June 8, 2017).

54. See Urs App, "The Tibet of the Philosophers: Kant, Hegel, and Schopenhauer," in *Images of Tibet in the 19th and 20th Centuries*, vol. 1, ed. Monica Esposito (Paris: École française d'Extrême-Orient, 2008), 54.

55. Richard Sheppard discusses Taoism and international Dada in chapter 10 of *Modernism—Dada—Postmodernism* (Evanston, IL: Northwestern University Press, 2000), but his lack of knowledge of Asian philosophies limits his perspective.

56. From *291*, no. 12 (February 1916), as quoted in Marcel Jean, *History of Surrealist Painting*, 30.

57. Regarding Picabia's titles, see Roger I. Rothman, "Between Music and the Machine," *Tout-Fait* 2, no. 4 (2002), note 14, https://www.academia.edu/1557705/Between_Music_and_the_Machine_Francis_Picabia_and_the_End_of_Abstraction (accessed June 8, 2017).

58. *Marcel Duchamp*, ed. Anne d'Harnoncourt and Kynaston McShine (New York: Museum of Modern Art, 1973), 276.

59. Sanouillet and Matisse, *Duchamp du signe*, 2008, 64.

60. Léon Wieger's *Taoïsme* was published in two volumes: the first, containing a bibliography and index, in 1911, and the second—*Les Pères du Système Taoïste*, which includes a translation of and commentary on Chuang Tzu—in 1913, when Duchamp was working at the Bibliothèque Sainte-Geneviève. (Both are in the collection.) The English is from Burton Watson, *Zhuangzi: Basic Writings* (New York: Columbia University Press, 2003), 35.

61. Thanks to Livia Kohn for pointing out this connection.

62. Calvin Tomkins, *Marcel Duchamp: The Afternoon Interviews* (Brooklyn: Badlands, 2013), 92–93.

63. Julien, *Le Livre de la voie*, 18.

64. http://ec2-79-125-124-178.eu-west-1.compute.amazonaws.com/articles/An-interview-with-Marcel-Duchamp/29278 (accessed May 14, 2018). Duchamp's last sentence suggests that he knew Ezra Pound's *Instigations of Ezra Pound, Together with an Essay on the Chinese Written Character by Ernest Fenollosa* (New York: Boni and Liveright, 1920).

65. *Lao-Tzu: Tao Te Ching*, trans. Stephen Addiss and Stanley Lombardo (Indianapolis/Cambridge: Hackett, 1993), chapter 1 (unpaginated).

66. Cabanne, *Dialogues*, 38, 40.

67. *Marcel Duchamp: Work and Life*, ed. Pontus Hulten (Cambridge: MIT Press, 1993), unpaginated, June 21, 1967.

68. Francis Roberts, "I Propose to Strain the Laws of Physics," *Art News* 67, no. 8 (December 1968), 62.

69. Carpenter, *Angels' Wings*, 216.

70. Galen Strawson, *Real Materialism and Other Essays* (New York: Oxford University Press, 2008), 36–37.

71. Georges Charbonnier, *Entretiens avec Marcel Duchamp* (Marseille: André Dimanche, 1994), 65.

72. Arturo Schwarz, *The Complete Works of Marcel Duchamp* [1969, 1970] (revised and expanded edition, New York: Delano Greenidge, 2000), 588.

73. Tosi Lee, *Watering, That's My Life: The Symbolism and Self-Imaging of Marcel Duchamp* (Doctoral thesis, University of Illinois at Urbana-Champaign, 1993), 61.

74. The Sanchi Stupa was much-published around the turn of the twentieth century. Albert Grünwedel documented and wrote about it in the several editions of his *Buddhist Art in India* (1893 in German, 1901 in English), and Alfred Foucher's 1910 lecture at the Musée Guimet, "The Eastern Gate of the Sançi Stupa," was published with numerous illustrations in his *Beginnings of Buddhist Art*. The English edition was published in 1914, so the French edition presumably appeared in 1911–1913.

75. Duchamp's note is in English; Sanouillet and Matisse, *Duchamp du signe*, 2008, 391, note 261.

76. Cabanne, *Dialogues*, 16.

77. Charbonnier, *Entretiens*, 61–62.

78. Ibid., 65–66.

79. Harriet and Sidney Janis, "Marcel Duchamp: Anti-Artist," *View*, series 5, no. 1 (March 1945), 24; reprinted in Robert Motherwell, *The Dada Painters and Poets: An Anthology* (Cambridge, MA: Harvard University Press, 1981), 311.

80. Thomas Girst, "A Very Normal Guy: An Interview with Robert Barnes on Marcel Duchamp and *Étant donnés*," in *The Indefinite Duchamp* (Ostfildern: Hatje Cantz, 2013), 247.

81. J. C. Chatterji, *Hindu Realism* (from the 1975 reprint [Delhi: Swastika]), 48–49.

82. Robert Lebel, *Marcel Duchamp* (New York: Grove Press, 1959), 165, no. 105; the italics are Duchamp/Lebel's. An almost identical Note had been published in *Box of 1914* under the heading, "Idea of Making," and again in *The Green Box* (as Lebel notes).

83. From Duchamp's lecture, "A Propos of Myself," quoted in D'Harnoncourt and McShine, eds., *Marcel Duchamp*, 273–274.

84. Alfred Jarry, *Exploits and Opinions of Doctor Faustroll, Pataphysician: A Neo-Scientific Novel* [1911], trans. Simon Watson Taylor (Boston, MA: Exact Change, 1996), 21.

85. These technical details were published in 1999 in Rhonda Roland Shearer and Stephen Jay Gould's "Hidden in Plain Sight: Duchamp's *3 Standard Stoppages*" in the online Duchamp journal *Tout-Fait*, http://www.toutfait.com/issues/issue_1/News/stoppages.html (accessed June 11, 2017). Duchamp scholar Herbert Molderings gives his take on the situation in *Duchamp and the Aesthetics of Chance: Art as Experiment*, trans. John Brogden (New York: Columbia University Press, 2010), 33ff.

86. From an interview published in Katherine Kuh, *The Artist's Voice: Talks with Seventeen Artists* (New York: Harper & Row, 1962), 92. Duchamp's works from this period were all in fact "carefully planned," *The Large Glass* being the most notable example.

87. Duchamp mentioned Riemann in a 1953 text written when *3 Standard Stoppages* entered the collection of the Museum of Modern Art: "... a joke about the meter—a humorous application of Riemann's post-Euclidean geometry, which was devoid of straight lines." See Herbert Molderings, "*Tu m'*: La peinture face à l'espace amorphe," in *Marcel Duchamp: la peinture, même* (Paris: Centre Georges Pompidou, 2014), 267; and Linda Dalrymple Henderson, *Duchamp in Context: Science and Technology in the Large Glass and Related Works* (Princeton, NJ: Princeton University Press, 1998), 61–63.

88. Wassily Kandinsky, "On the Question of Form," in *The Blaue Reiter Almanac*, trans. Henning Falkenstein (Boston, MA: MFA Publications, 2005), 157.

89. D'Harnoncourt and McShine, eds., *Marcel Duchamp*, 273.

90. Cabanne, *Dialogues*, 47.

91. *Tao Te Ching*, chapter 42. The most likely source for Duchamp at this time was *Le Tao a produit un; un a produit deux; deux a produit trois, trois a produit tous les êtres* (Stanislas Julien, *Le Livre de la voie et de la vertu par le philosophe Lao-Tseu* [Paris: L'Imprimerie Royale, 1842], 158). This English translation: Wong Yoo-Chong, "42—The Supreme Ultimate," in *OmniVerse*, http://omniverse.us/poetry-and-translation-wong-yoo-chong/ (accessed May 15, 2018).

92. Schwarz, *The Complete Works*, 30.

93. See the diagram based on *The Large Glass Completed* reproduced in d'Harnoncourt and McShine, eds., *Marcel Duchamp*, 64.

94. Robert Lebel, *Sur Marcel Duchamp* (Paris: Trianon Press, 1959), 166, no. 115. This note does not appear in the Engish edition.

95. *Rogue* 3, no. 1 (New York, October 1916), 2.

CHAPTER 5

1. Excerpt from *THE / "Eye Test, Not a 'Nude Descending a Staircase'"* published in *Rogue* 3, no. 1 (New York, October 1916), 2.

2. Calvin Tomkins, *Duchamp: A Biography* (New York: Henry Holt, 1996), 141–142.

3. Arturo Schwarz, *The Complete Works of Marcel Duchamp* (1969, 1970; revised and expanded edition, New York: Delano Greenidge, 2000), 642.

4. *Rogue* (October 1916), 2. *THE* was found in the Arensbergs' copy of Duchamp's *Box of 1914* when the collection was accessioned by the Philadelphia Museum of Art in 1950 (Schwarz, *The Complete Works*, 638, no. 334).

5. For the Tzara quotes, see Robert Motherwell et al., *The Dada Painters and Poets: An Anthology* (Cambridge, MA: Harvard University Press, 1981), 77, 251. Raoul Hausmann, "Was ist dada?" [text collage], *Der Dada*, no. 2, ed. Hausmann (Berlin 1919); reprinted Hausmann, *Am Anfang war Dada*, 1972, 8; trans. and quoted by Dorothée Brill, *Shock and the Senseless in Dada and Fluxus* (Hanover: Dartmouth College Press, 2010), 72. Francis Picabia, "Dada Manifesto," trans. Margaret I. Lippard from *391*, no. 12 (Paris, March 1920), published in Lucy R. Lippard, ed., *Dadas on Art: Tzara, Arp, Duchamp and Others* (Englewood Cliffs, NJ: Prentice-Hall, 1971), 166. For the Duchamp quote, see Margery Rex, "'Dada' Will Get You if You Don't Watch Out: It Is on the Way Here," *New York Evening Journal*, January 29, 1921; quoted by Rudolf E. Kuenzli, ed., *New York Dada* (New York: Willis Locker & Owens, 1986), 140.

6. Motherwell, *Dada Painters and Poets*, 250.

7. Jean (Hans) Arp, "Dadaland" (1948), in *Collected French Writings: Poems, Essays, Memories*, ed. Marcel Jean, trans. Joachim Neugroschel (London: Calder & Boyars, 1974), 235. For Arp and Schwitters, the source was probably the China specialist Alfred Salmony, who was born in Cologne and served as curator of the museum of East Asian Art there before emigrating in 1933 to Paris and then the US. When he was in his late twenties, Salmony was personally involved with artists in the Dada movement that emerged in British-occupied Cologne (Gustave Ecke, "In Memorium: Alfred Salmony," *Ars Orientalis* 4 [1961], 453).

8. Richard Huelsenbeck, *The Dada Almanac* [Berlin, 1920], ed. and trans. Malcolm Green (London: Atlas, 1993), 9–10, 75. For the relationship between Taoism and Buddhism, see Christopher I. Beckwith, *Greek Buddha: Pyrrho's Encounter with Early Buddhism in Central Asia* (Princeton, NJ: Princeton University Press, 2015), chapter 3: "Jade Yoga and Heavenly Dharma," 110ff.

9. See Livia Kohn, *Sitting in Oblivion: The Heart of Daoist Meditation* (Dunedin, FL: Three Pines Press, 2010). *The Secret of the Golden Flower* is a good example, being more Ch'an Buddhist than Taoist and, according to translator Richard Wilhelm, even demonstrating "a strong admixture of Nestorian ideals (London: Kegan Paul, Trench, Trubner, 1931), 11.

10. *TABU DADA: Jean Crotti & Suzanne Duchamp, 1915–1922*, ed. William A. Camfield and Jean-Hubert Martin (Kunsthalle Bern, 1983), 82 and "Chronology," 129. A similar interpretation of TABU, minus the Taoism, is offered by Martin, who points out that inverting the syllables of TABU yields BUTA, a pun on "Buddha." See "TABU: Artistic Movement or Religion?" in *TABU DADA*, 88.

11. 475–221 BCE; see Livia Kohn, *Daoism and Chinese Culture* (Madgalena, NM: Three Pines Press, 2001), 11–12.

12. For a period discussion of Taoism's radical antiauthoritarianism, see Charles F. Horne, *The Sacred books and early literature of the East*, vol. 12, Medieval China (New York: Parke, Austin, and Lipscomb, 1917), 2.

13. Roger T. Ames and David L. Hall, *Daodejing "Making This Life Significant": A Philosophical Translation* (New York: Ballantine, 2003), 17.

14. Ibid., 91.

15. Schwarz, *The Complete Works*, 258. In a note (262, note 15), Schwarz quotes Lao Tzu along with Jung.

16. See Jay Bochner, *An American Lens* (Cambridge, MA: MIT Press, 2005), 144.

17. Pepe Karmel cogently observed that the bellows appears to have collapsed because it has torn loose from the lens, which is unnaturally extended in its pursuit of the "ideal." See Karmel, "Francis Picabia, 1915: The Sex of a New Machine," in *Alfred Stieglitz and His New York Galleries*, ed. Sarah Greenough (Washington, DC: National Gallery of Art, 2000), 216–217.

18. Stanislas Julien, *Le Livre de la voie et de la vertu par le philosophe Lao-tseu* (Paris: L'Imprimerie Royale, 1842), 18.

19. Dorothy Norman, *Alfred Stieglitz: Introduction to an American Seer* (New York: Duell, Sloan and Pearce, 1960), 20.

20. Julien, *Le Livre de la voie*, 2.

21. Bochner, *An American Lens*, 145.

22. Norman, *Alfred Stieglitz*, 36.

23. Letter of April 19, 1917, in *My Faraway One: Selected Letters of Georgia O'Keeffe and Alfred Stieglitz*, vol. I, 1915–1933, ed. Sarah Greenough (New Haven: Yale University Press, 2011), 135.

24. Beatrice Wood, *I Shock Myself: The Autobiography of Beatrice Wood* (San Francisco: Chronicle Books, 1985), 30. See also William A. Camfield, "Marcel Duchamp's *Fountain*: Its History and Aesthetics in the Context of 1917," in *Marcel Duchamp: Artist of the Century*, ed. Rudolf E. Kuenzli and Francis M. Naumann (Cambridge, MA: MIT Press, 1990), 74. That Wood made the first contact is suggested by her diary entry for April 13, 1917: "See Stieglitz about 'Fountain'" (William A. Camfield, *Marcel Duchamp: Fountain* [Houston: Menil Collection, 1989], 33).

25. The title *Rongwrong* may have a Taoist origin: Li Rong was a seventh-century Chinese Taoist monk who wrote a set of commentaries on the *Tao Te Ching* and also played an important role in public Taoist-Buddhist debates at a time when Taoism and Buddhism were strongly influencing one other. According to the remaining (biased) Buddhist accounts, Li Rong's opponents invariably managed to render him "utterly speechless and stunned by the power of [their] superior argument." In public debate at least, the Taoist Li Rong was always wrong. Livia Kohn, *Daoist Mystical Philosophy: The Scripture of Western Ascension* (Magdalena, NM: Three Pines Press, 2007), 189.

26. Camfield in Kuenzli and Naumann, *Marcel Duchamp*, 72 and 90, note 28.

27. For more on *God*, see Jacquelynn Baas, "Before Zen: The Nothing of American Dada," in *East-West Interchanges in American Art: A Long and Tumultuous Relationship*, ed. Cynthia Mills, Lee Glazer, and Amelia A. Goerlitz (Washington, DC: Smithsonian Institution Scholarly Press, 2009), 56–57.

28. Letter of April 11, 1917, published in *Affectionately Marcel: The Selected Correspondence of Marcel Duchamp*, ed. Francis M. Naumann and Hector Obalk (Ghent: Ludion Press, 2000), 47.

29. The concept of "this and that" as experiential manifestations of an undifferentiated universe linked by a hingelike "Middle" form (Madhyama) is also a feature of Kashmir Shaivism; see Jagadish Chandra Chatterji, *Kashmir Shaivism* (Srinagar: Research Department Jammu, 1914), 4.

30. Rose's name first appeared on *Fresh Widow* in 1920.

31. In spring 1921 Picabia came down with ophthalmic shingles, requiring treatment with sodium cacodylate. He drew a large eye at the bottom of a canvas that he entitled *L'Oeil cacodylate* ("The Cacodylatic Eye") and invited his friends to add their sentiments and signatures.

32. Pierre Cabanne, *Dialogues with Marcel Duchamp*, trans. Rod Padgett (London: Thames and Hudson, 1971; reprinted Cambridge, MA: Da Capo Press, 1987), 65.

33. "*J'espère toujours me réveiller!*" Paula K. Kamenish, *Mamas of Dada: Women of the European Avant-Garde* (Columbia: University of South Carolina Press, 2015), 53.

34. Joseph Needham, *Science and Civilisation in China*, vol. 2 (Cambridge: Cambridge University Press, 1956), 58 (slightly edited).

35. Ames and Hall, *Daodejing*, 86.

36. Ibid., 120.

37. Lydie Fischer Sarazin-Levassor, *A Marriage in Check: The Heart of the Bride Stripped Bare by Her Bachelors, Even*, trans. Paul Edwards (Dijon: Les presses du réel, 2007), 48.

38. See Livia Kohn, *The Taoist Experience* (Binghamton: State University of New York Press, 1993), 229.

39. My thanks to Joel Isaacson for this observation, which is reinforced by a photograph of *Fountain* in which the point of light appears not in the "head," but in the "vagina" of *Fountain* (exhibited courtesy of Francis M. Naumann in the fall 2018 exhibition *Brancusi and Duchamp* at Kasmin Gallery).

40. See Introduction.

41. *On n'a que: pour femelle la pissotière et on en vit. Duchamp du signe suivi de Notes*, ed. Michel Sanouillet and Paul Matisse (Paris: Flammarion, 2008), 60.

42. Camfield, *Marcel Duchamp: Fountain*, 50.

43. See Deepak Simkhada and Michael Reading, "Return to the Womb: Feminine Creative Imagery of *Arghaya* in a Tantric Ritual," in *International Journal of Dharma Studies*, 3:12 (2015), https://internationaljournaldharmastudies.springeropen.com/articles/10.1186/s40613-015-0022-4 (accessed December 13, 2017).

44. See, for example, Arthur Avalon [Sir John George Woodroffe], *Tantra of the Great Liberation (Mahānirvāna Tantra)* (Madras: Ganesh, 1913), 196.

45. *Internal Alchemy: Self, Society, and the Quest for Immortality*, ed. Livia Kohn and Robin R. Wang (Magdalena, NM: Three Pines Press, 2009), 130. See also R. H. van Gulik, *Sexual Life in Ancient China* ([1961] Leiden and Boston: Brill, 2003), especially 193ff.

46. Ananda Coomaraswamy, *The Dance of Śiva* (New York: Sunwise Turn, 1918), 7. Beatrice Wood was particularly close to Coomaraswamy, Keeper of Indian Art at the Boston Museum of Fine Arts and part of the Stieglitz Circle in New York.

47. Henri-Pierre Roché, *Victor (Marcel Duchamp)*, published by Centre Georges Pompidou as vol. 4 of four books dedicated to Marcel Duchamp (Paris, 1977), this passage, 95. *Victor* has recently been published in English in *Three New York Dadas and The Blind Man*, introd. Dawn Ades (London: Atlas Press, 2013), this passage, 114–115.

48. Evidence that *Insel* was inspired at least in part by Duchamp includes a reference to his Paris studio, 11 rue Larrey, where from 1927 to 1946 he occupied an attic room on the seventh floor: "The very name of the street he lived in had the sound of a ghostly exhaustion. His attic was on the seventh story" (Mina Loy, *Insel*, ed. Elizabeth Arnold [Brooklyn: Melville House, 2014], 108). Another clue is a reference to *Comb* (Schwarz, *The Complete Works*, 643, no. 339), Duchamp's readymade from January 1916, soon after Loy came to know him: "evidently the bone of some prehistoric fish. A white comb shrill with the accumulated phosphorus of the ages" (89).

49. Verses 28–30, http://www.asitis.com/11/ (accessed September 6, 2018). Loy knew the *Bhagavad Gita* through her first husband, a follower of Vivekandanda; see Carolyn Burke, *Becoming Modern: The Life of Mina Loy* (New York: Farrar, Straus and Giroux, 1996), 132.

50. Loy, *Insel*, 76–77.

51. *Chuang Tzu*, chapter 15; see Livia Kohn, *Chuang-tzu: The Tao of Perfect Happiness* (Woodstock, VT: Skylight Paths, 2011), 137.

52. Cabanne, *Dialogues*, 60.

53. Dreier laid out her views in an essay, "Intrinsic Significance in Modern Art," in *Three Lectures on Modern Art* (New York: Philosophical Library, 1949), 1–30. *Tu m'*s long horizontal shape is due to the fact that it was designed for a space above Dreier's bookshelf.

54. Schwarz, *The Complete Works*, 779.

55. Marcel Jean, *The History of Surrealist Painting*, trans. Simon Watson Taylor (New York, Grove Press, 1959), 59.

56. Sanouillet and Matisse, *Duchamp du signe*, 61.

57. Duchamp's "sculptures de voyage" also included *Sculpture for Traveling*—"some rubber objects" created in New York in 1918; Cabanne, *Dialogues*, 59; *Entretiens*, 107.

58. Arthur Rimbaud characterized his poetic aspiration as that of "voyant": "I want to be a poet," Rimbaud wrote a former professor in 1871, "and I'm working to make myself a Seer: you will not understand at all, and I hardly know how to explain it to you" (Arthur Rimbaud, *Œuvres complètes*, ed. Antoine Adam [Paris: Gallimard, 1972], 249).

59. Reproduced in Schwarz, *The Complete Works*, 663.

60. Hans Belting, *Looking Through Duchamp's Door* (Cologne: Walther König, 2009), 36–37.

61. Sarazin-Levassor, *A Marriage in Check*, 48.

62. See *Musée des Arts et Métiers*, special issue of *Connaissance des Arts* (Paris: Société Française de Promotion Artistique, 2000), 26–27.

63. *Kandinsky: Complete Writings on Art*, ed. Kenneth C. Linsay and Peter Vergo (Cambridge, MA: Da Capo Press, 1994), 194–195.

64. See the diagram of *The Large Glass Completed* reproduced in *Marcel Duchamp*, ed. Anne d'Harnoncourt and Kynaston McShine (New York: Museum of Modern Art, 1973), 64.

65. Robert Lebel, *Marcel Duchamp*, trans. George Heard Hamilton (New York: Grove Press, 1959), 44.

66. Robert E. Buswell, Jr. and Donald S. Lopez, Jr., *The Princeton Dictionary of Buddhism* (Princeton, NJ: Princeton University Press, 2014), 120.

67. Pupul Jayakar, *The Earth Mother: Legends, Goddesses, and Ritual Arts of India* (New York: Harper & Row, 1990), 125.

68. Ulf Linde, "MARiée CELibataire," in *Marcel Duchamp Ready-Mades, etc.* (Paris: Le Terrain Vague, 1964), 58.

69. This "reading" of "L.H.O.O.Q." as "LOOK" may explain why, in his lecture notes from the early 1960s, Duchamp said: "I inscribed at the bottom four [*sic*] letters" (d'Harnoncourt and McShine, eds., *Marcel Duchamp*, 289).

70. From a 1961 interview with Herbert Crehan transcribed by Robert Cowan, quoted in Schwarz, *The Complete Works*, 670.

71. Kathleen Taylor, *Sir John Woodroffe, Tantra and Bengal* (London: Routledge, 2001), 134. The printed publication date is 1919.

72. Arthur Avalon, *The Serpent Power: Being the Ṣaṭ-chakra-nirūpaṇa and Pādukāpanchaka: two works on tantric yoga* (London: Luzac, [1918] 1919), 135.

73. Taylor, *Sir John Woodroffe*, 135. "Avalon," whose main collaborator and translator was the Bengali Atal Behari Ghosh, published *Principles of Tantra*, part I (1913) and II (1915), and over twenty Sanskrit tantric texts.

74. Avalon, *Tantra of the Great Liberation*, lviii. This nondualist tantra describes the four types of *avadhūta*—mystics who are beyond duality and common concerns, and act without consideration for standard social etiquette. Duchamp would have identified with the type who lives outwardly like ordinary people and is thus difficult to recognize (352).

75. Avalon, *The Serpent Power*, 38.

76. Ibid., 182.

77. From a 1961 interview with Herbert Crehan, quoted in Schwarz, *The Complete Works*, 670. When Crehan steered the conversation to Leonardo's reputed homosexuality, Duchamp commented: "The curious thing about that moustache and goatee is that when you look at it the Mona Lisa becomes a man. It is not a woman disguised as a man; it is a real man, and that was my discovery, without realizing it at the time."

78. Michel Sanouillet, *Dada in Paris*, rev. Anne Sanouillet, trans. Sharmila Ganguly (Cambridge, MA: MIT Press, 2009), 104.

79. *Il y a un autre monde mais il est dans celui-ci*. The statement was apparently verbal, as I have found no published source. It is also attributed to William Butler Yeats with, again, no specific source.

80. Sanouillet *Dada in Paris*, 546, note 61.

81. Avalon, *The Serpent Power*, 103.

82. Lebel, *Marcel Duchamp*, 45, note 1.

83. Telegram of June 1, 1921, published in Naumann and Obalk, eds., *Affectionately Marcel*, 98; see also Cabanne, *Dialogues*, 65.

84. In contrast, when in 1930 Louis Aragon asked Duchamp to contribute to a very different Paris exhibition, *La Peinture au défi* ("Painting Challenged"), Duchamp sent not only the reproduction of *Mona Lisa* that he had modified in 1919, but also another version, signed "Marcel Duchamp (réplique 1930)." For more on this, see Elena Filipovic, *The Apparently Marginal Activities of Marcel Duchamp* (Cambridge, MA: MIT Press, 2016), 49–53.

CHAPTER 6

1. André Breton, "Marcel Duchamp," *Littérature*, n.s. 5 (October 1922), 10.

2. "When I came to New York in 1915, I started this painting, … it was not finished in 1923 when I finally abandoned it" (*Marcel Duchamp*, ed. Anne d'Harnoncourt and Kynaston McShine [New York: Museum of Modern Art, 1973], 296).

3. Reproduced in Arturo Schwarz, *The Complete Works of Marcel Duchamp* ([1969, 1970], revised and expanded edition, New York: Delano Greenidge, 2000), 863.

4. See Lilian Silburn, *Kundalini: The Energy of the Depths*, trans. Jacques Gontier (Albany: State University of New York, 1988), 50–51.

5. William Barnard, preface to J. C. Chatterji, *Kashmir Shaivism* [1914] (Albany: State University of New York Press, 1986), xii–xiii.

6. Quoted in Hans Richter, *Dada: Art and Anti-Art* (New York: McGraw-Hill, 1965), 99. For more on *Anémic cinéma*, see Jacquelynn Baas, "Meditations on the Medium of Time," in *Measure of Time*, ed. Lucinda Barnes (Berkeley: University of California Berkeley Art Museum and Pacific Film Archive, 2007), 72–76.

7. Adam Jolles, *The Curatorial Avant-Garde: Surrealism and Exhibition Practice in France, 1925–1941* (University Park: Pennsylvania State University Press, 2013), 43.

8. "Playtoy" was the term Duchamp used when writing of this project to Katherine Dreier. About selling the *Rotoreliefs* in the US, he wrote, tongue in cheek: "I can't sell them anymore than $1.25. … If people find it too cheap, too bad, but the cost of making it does not allow me to more profit" (*Affectionately Marcel: The Selected Correspondence of Marcel Duchamp*, ed. Francis M. Naumann and Hector Obalk [Ghent: Ludion Press, 2000], 203, 205).

9. Interview with James Johnson Sweeny, in *Wisdom: Conversations with the Elder Wise Men of Our Day*, ed. James Nelson (New York: W. W. Norton, 1958), 98; regarding the parallel between *Boîte* and Japanese esoteric altars, see Jacquelynn Baas, *Smile of the Buddha* (Berkeley: University of California Press, 2005), 89–90.

10. See chapter 4.

11. For parallels between Duchamp and Avalokiteshvara, see Baas, *Smile of the Buddha*, 90–92. Among other things, there is an intriguing connection between Avalokiteshvara, who "sees" cries, and Duchamp's deaf mother. "One can look at seeing," Duchamp wrote; "one can't hear

hearing" (*The Writings of Marcel Duchamp*, ed. Michel Sanouillet and Elmer Peterson [New York: Da Capo Press, 1989], 23).

12. Robert Lebel, "Marcel Duchamp and André Breton," in d'Harnoncourt and McShine, eds., *Marcel Duchamp*, 138.

13. For Duchamp's relationship with Martins, see Calvin Tomkins, *Duchamp: A Biography* (New York: Henry Holt, 1996), 353ff; Francis M. Naumann, "Marcel & Maria," *Art in America* 89, no. 4 (April 2001), 98–111; and Michael R. Taylor, *Marcel Duchamp Étant donnés* (Philadelphia and New Haven: Philadelphia Museum of Art with Yale University Press, 2009), 26ff. Regarding Martins and her work, see Veronica Stigger et al., *Maria Martins: Metamorfoses* (São Paulo Museum of Modern Art, 2013), https://www.academia.edu/7064318/Cat%C3%A1logo_Maria_Martins_metamorfoses_Catalogue_Maria_Martins_metamorphoses (accessed August 14, 2017).

14. *Asia Maior: o planêta China* (Rio de Janeiro: Civilização Brasileira, 1958); *Asia Maior: Brama, Gandi e Nehru* (Rio de Janeiro: Civilização Brasileira, 1961); *Deuses malditos I: Nietzsche* (Rio de Janeiro: Civilização Brasileira, 1965).

15. Robert Lebel, *Marcel Duchamp*, trans. George Heard Hamilton (New York: Grove Press, 1959), 174, no. 181. Elena Filipovic, in *The Apparently Marginal Activities of Marcel Duchamp* (Cambridge, MA: MIT Press, 2016), 108, writes: "the title for the installation was fixed: *Sixteen Miles of String*." "Sixteen miles" supposedly refers to how much string Duchamp originally bought; I prefer the more accurate and equally common *Mile of String*. That title was apparently fixed by Arturo Schwarz, in *The Complete Works of Marcel Duchamp*, 767, no. 488. See also Lewis Kachur, *Displaying the Marvelous: Marcel Duchamp, Salvador Dali, and Surrealist Exhibition Installation* (Cambridge: MIT Press, 2001), 166–194.

16. Chatterji, *Kashmir Shaivism*, 92. On the Continuum, see chapter 4.

17. Filipovic, *The Apparently Marginal Activities of Marcel Duchamp*, 109.

18. Letter to Louise and Walter Arensberg, July 22, 1951, published in Naumann and Obalk, eds., *Affectionately Marcel*, 303.

19. R. A. Parker, "Explorers of the Pluriverse," in *First Papers of Surrealism* (New York: Coordinating Council of French Relief Societies, 1942), unpaginated.

20. According to Schwarz (*The Complete Works*, 767), the installation was commissioned by designer Elsa Schiaparelli, who "asked Duchamp to prepare an installation that would be as economical as possible, since the exhibition was organized to benefit the French Relief Societies." For more on the Malic Moulds, see chapter 3; for *Network of Stoppages*, see chapter 4.

21. From *First Papers of Surrealism*: "not being able to offer an entirely adequate photographic image of each of the principal exhibitors, we have thought it best here to resort to the general scheme of 'compensation portraits.' (Suggested by Duchamp and Breton.)"

22. Barnard in Chatterji, *Kashmiri Shaivism*, x.

23. Lebel, *Marcel Duchamp*, 55. The string was originally wrapped around the chandeliers. During his interview with Pierre Cabanne, Duchamp said: "Imagine that these strings were really guncotton—they always are when they're attached to a light bulb, and I don't know how, but at a given moment they burned. Since guncotton burns without a flame, it was terrifying. But it worked out all right. It was rather funny" (Pierre Cabanne, *Dialogues with Marcel Duchamp*, trans. Rod Padgett [London: Thames and Hudson, 1971; reprinted Cambridge, MA: Da Capo Press, 1987], 86).

24. Harriet and Sidney Janis, "Marcel Duchamp: Anti-Artist," *View*, series 5, no. 1 (March 1945), 24; reprinted in Robert Motherwell, *The Dada Painters and Poets: An Anthology* (Cambridge, MA: Harvard University Press, 1981), 307. Second quote from a 1953 interview in Kachur, *Displaying the Marvelous*, 183.

25. Kachur, *Displaying the Marvelous*, 182ff.

26. From "Dear Dee, Dear Miss Dreier: The Selected Correspondence of Katherine S. Dreier and Marcel Duchamp," *Étant donné Marcel Duchamp*, no. 9 (2009), 131.

27. *Musicage: Cage Muses on Words, Art, Music*, ed. Joan Retallack (Hanover, NH: Wesleyan University Press, 1996), 156.

28. See Marcel Jean, ed., *The Autobiography of Surrealism* (New York: Viking Press, 1980), 381ff.

29. Architect and exhibition designer Frederick Kiesler partnered with Duchamp in the design of this back cover; Peggy Guggenheim's daughter, Pegeen Vail, posed for the photograph.

30. *Sur Marcel Duchamp* (Paris: Éditions Trianon, 1959); published in English as *Marcel Duchamp*, trans. George Heard Hamilton (New York: Grove Press, 1959).

31. Born in 1911, Isabelle Waldberg died in 1990, outliving both Duchamp and Lebel (born 1901), who died in 1986. The relationships among Duchamp, Lebel, and the Waldbergs is the focus of *Étant donné Marcel Duchamp*, no. 7 (Paris: Association Marcel Duchamp, 2006).

32. For information on Lebel's career, see Paul B. Franklin, "Marcel Duchamp and Robert Lebel: The Art of Friendship, A Friendship in Art," in *The Artist and His Critic Stripped Bare: The Correspondence of Marcel Duchamp and Robert Lebel*, ed. and trans. Paul B. Franklin (Los Angeles: Getty Research Institute, 2016), 22–63.

33. Robert Lebel, "Paris–New York et retour avec Marcel Duchamp, Dada, et le surréalisme," in *Paris–New York* (Paris: Centre Georges Pompidou, 1977), 68.

34. Franklin, *The Artist and His Critic Stripped Bare*, 33.

35. Robert Lebel, "Marcel Duchamp and André Breton," in d'Harnoncourt and McShine, *Marcel Duchamp*, 140.

36. Paul B. Franklin, "Coming of Age with Marcel: An Interview with Jean-Jacques Lebel," *Étant donné Marcel Duchamp*, no. 7 (2006), 15.

37. Robert Lebel, letter to André Gervais, May 21, 1979, quoted in the online journal *Tout-Fait*, http://toutfait.com/the-inventor-of-gratuitous-time/ (published May 1, 2000, updated July 13, 2016; accessed May 16, 2018).

38. *Le Surréalisme, même* was published by book dealer Jean-Jacques Pauvert from October 1956 to spring 1959.

39. *La double vue, suivi de L'inventeur du temps gratuit* (Paris: Deyrolle, 1993), 115. See also Patrick Waldberg, "Marcel Duchamp: l'Unique et ses Propriétés," in *Critique*, no. 149 (October 1959), 854; and Patrick Waldberg, "Robert Lebel, ou les complicités ambiguës," in *Preuves*, no. 181 (March 1966), 82.

40. See Schwarz, *The Complete Works*, 805, no. 548; for *Female Fig Leaf*, see ibid., 797, no. 536.

41. Letter of January 19, 1956, quoted by Patrick Waldberg, "Marcel Duchamp, the Unique One and His Properties," *Étant donné Marcel Duchamp*, no. 7 (2006), 58, note 18. Breton eventually published the first chapter of Lebel's monograph in *Le Surréalisme, même*, no. 3 (Autumn 1957), 21–31. *Sur Marcel Duchamp* would not appear until 1959.

42. But not from its subject: there is an undated typescript of the story in the Archives Marcel Duchamp (Franklin, *The Artist and His Critic*, 59, note 44).

43. J. H. Matthews, trans., "Robert Lebel: The Inventor of Gratuitous Time," in *The Custom-House of Desire: A Half-Century of Surrealist Stories* (Berkeley: University of California Press, 1975), 151.

44. Arthur Avalon [Sir John George Woodroffe], *Tantra of the Great Liberation (Mahānirvāna Tantra)* (Madras: Ganesh, 1913), cxxii.

45. On Pierre Bernard, see Robert Love, *The Great Oom* (New York: Viking, 2010). On Theos Bernard, see Paul G. Hackettt, *Theos Bernard, The White Lama* (New York: Columbia University Press, 2012); and Hackett, "Barbarian Lands: Theos Bernard, Tibet, and the American Religious Life" (Columbia University Ph.D. dissertation, 2008), 726–730.

46. Matthews, *The Custom-House of Desire*, 153.

47. Ibid., 154. In a letter of February 18, 1946, Isabelle, back in Paris after the end of the war, asked her husband Patrick to bring her from New York "sticks, [as] mine have begun to run out and are irreplaceable here." She gives him the location of a hardware store "at or near the corner of 60th Street and 3rd Avenue, next to Nedick, Stool, and Pain Inc. They are called 'Dowels.' Size above the finest. Bring 1,000 pieces, if possible, and order them in advance now and insist. ... (in addition 500 of the finest)" (Patrick and Isabelle Waldberg, *Un amour acéphale: correspondance, 1940–1949*, ed. Michel Waldberg [Paris: Éditions de la Différence, 1992], 432).

48. Matthews, *The Custom-House of Desire*, 159. I have modified Matthews's translation slightly; the original of this passage appears in Lebel, *La double vue, suivi de L'inventeur du temps gratuit* (Paris: Le Soleil Noir, 1964), 135.

49. Matthews, *The Custom-House of Desire*, 159–160; Lebel, *La double vue, suivi de L'inventeur du temps gratuit*, 136–137.

50. The best sources for information about Isabelle Waldberg are Patrick and Isabelle Waldberg, *Un amour acéphale: correspondance, 1940–1949*, ed. Michel Waldberg (Paris: Éditions de la Différence, 1992); Michel Waldberg's monograph on his mother, *Isabelle Waldberg* (Paris: Éditions de la Différence, 1992); and Robert Lebel, "Isabelle Waldberg: à l'entrée ou à la sortie de son palais de la mémoire," *Étant donné Marcel Duchamp*, no. 7 (2006), 86–107. The Isabelle Waldberg Committee maintains a website that is an excellent source of biographical and other information: www.isabellewaldberg.com/en/committee.html (accessed September 7, 2018).

51. Robert Lebel, *Masque à lame* (New York: Liberal Press/Éditions Hémisphères, "1943" [1944]; republished Geneva: Mamco, 2015). The term "dematerialized sculptures" is from Claude Givaudan, *Catalogue sculpteurs* (Geneva, 1966), unpaginated.

52. Franklin, "Coming of Age," *Étant donné Marcel Duchamp*, no. 7 (2006), 17.

53. Isabelle Waldberg, "Peggy Guggenheim, Marcel Duchamp & André Breton," *Étant donné Marcel Duchamp*, no. 7 (2006), 138.

54. Ibid.

55. Published in New York, in French, by Brentano's in 1945. The display was first mounted in Brentano's window on Fifth Avenue but was moved to Gotham Book Mart following objections from the Society for Suppression of Vice. See Schwarz, *The Complete Works*, 781, no. 511.

56. André Breton, *Arcanum 17 with Apertures Grafted to the End*, trans. Zack Rogow (Los Angeles: Sun & Moon Press, 1994), 97. The quote, from Auguste Viatte, refers to Victor Hugo.

57. Only partially visible in Figure 6.17, but there are two examples of Matta's poster in the collection of the Centre Pompidou: https://www.centrepompidou.fr/cpv/ressource .action?param.id=FR_R-9f41d652326bed5b1c35395a7efd8c87&param.idSource=FR_O-fa48aebb46b6368b17ea39d37eab3 (accessed January 25, 2019).

58. Sanouillet and Peterson, eds., *Writings*, 106.

59. Schwarz, *The Complete Works*, 703–704.

60. *Un amour acéphale*, 331, including Isabelle's little sketch. For more on this window, see Thomas Girst, "Duchamp's Window Display for André Breton's *Le Surréalisme et la Peinture* (1945)" (published 2002/01/01, updated 2016/07/08: http://toutfait.com/duchamps-window-display-for-andra-bretons-le-surraalisme-et-la-peinture-1945/ [accessed September 7, 2018]).

61. In *Given* the head is hidden, with only a shock of blond hair (like Isabelle's) visible. The connection between the pose of Waldberg's *Beautiful Aqueduct* and that of the figure in *Given* has to my knowledge been noted only by Michael R. Taylor: see Taylor, *Marcel Duchamp Étant donnés*, 59, note 142.

62. Isabelle Waldberg's granddaughter, Corinne Waldberg, put me in touch with Jean-Jacques Lebel, who on April 3, 2017 sent an email informing me that the current whereabouts of *Luminaire* is unknown. In 1970, the year after Michel Fardoulis-Lagrange published *G. B. ou un ami présomptueux* (see chapter 8), Isabelle would make a much smaller bronze, *Bijou (feuille-clitorus)*, cast from modeling clay; see Michel Waldberg, *Isabelle Waldberg*, 159.

63. Reproduced in *Étant donné Marcel Duchamp*, no. 7 (2006), 102. My copy-editor, Gillian Beaumont, notes that *ausculte* refers to listening to a person's body, as with a stethoscope; the English would be "auscultate."

64. Martins cast her bronzes using the lost-wax method. In the late 1940s Duchamp and Martins would study life-casting with Ettore Salvatore, a sculpture instructor at Columbia University; see Matthew Affron, *The Essential Duchamp* (Philadelphia, PA: Philadelphia Museum of Art, 2018), 122.

65. Personal email, April 3, 2017.

CHAPTER 7

1. Letter to Countess Margot Sizzo-Noris-Crouy, April 12, 1923, in Rainer Maria Rilke, *A Year with Rilke*, trans. and ed. Joanna Macy and Anita Barrows (New York: Harper-Collins, 2009), 88.

2. *Un amour acéphale: correspondance, 1940–1949*, ed. Michel Waldberg (Paris: Éditions de la Différence, 1992).

3. Patrick Waldberg, "Acéphalogramme," *Magazine Littéraire*, no. 331 (April 1995), 157–158.

4. Georges Bataille, *Œuvres complètes*, ed. Michel Foucault, vol. 12 (Paris: Gallimard, 1988), 559.

5. "In other words nature itself and not only the representation of a small fragment of what surrounds us or what once took place" (Michel Décaudin, *Œuvres complètes de Guillaume Apollinaire* [Paris: A. Ballard, J. Lecat, 1965], vol. 1, "L'Enchanteur pourrissant, suivi des les mamelles de Tirésias de Couleurs du Temps," 609–611; English translation from Jacques Guicharnaud, *Modern French Theatre* [New Haven: Yale University Press, 1975], 280).

6. Georges Bataille, *The Absence of Myth: Writings on Surrealism*, trans. and intro. Michael Richardson (London: Verso, 1994), 48.

7. From the Commentary to Georges Bataille, *Louis XXX*, trans. Stuart Kendall (London: Equus Press, 2013), 91.

8. The only extended published comparison between Duchamp and Bataille that I have found is Jacqueline Chénieux, "L'Érotisme chez Marcel Duchamp et Georges Bataille," in *Marcel Duchamp: tradition de la rupture ou rupture de la tradition?*, ed. Jean Clair (Paris: Union Générale, 1979), 193–221. For a good short synopsis of Bataille's life, see the introduction by Stuart Kendall in Georges Bataille, *The Unfinished System of Nonknowledge* (Minneapolis: University of Minnesota Press, 2001), xi–xliv. Kendall is also the author of *Georges Bataille* (London: Reaktion, 2007). The standard biography in English is Michel Surya, *Georges Bataille: An Intellectual Biography*, trans. Krzysztof Fijalkowski and Michael Richardson (London: Verso, 2002).

9. Robert Lebel, "Marcel Duchamp and André Breton," in *Marcel Duchamp*, ed. Anne d'Harnoncourt and Kynaston McShine (New York: Museum of Modern Art, 1973), 140.

10. Bataille checked out Stirner's *L'Unique et sa propriété* from the Bibliothèque Nationale in June 1930 and again in February–March 1937 (Bataille, *Œuvres complètes* XII, 573, 608).

11. See *Nietzsche and Asian Thought*, ed. Graham Parkes (Chicago, University of Chicago Press, 1991).

12. Jean-Jacques Lebel said that in 1961 he spotted Nietzsche's *Also sprach Zarathustra* at Duchamp's bedside alongside Stirner's *L'Unique et sa propriété* (Paul B. Franklin, "Coming of Age with Marcel: An Interview with Jean-Jacques Lebel," *Étant donné Marcel Duchamp*, no. 7 [2006], 14). Nevertheless, the only volume by Nietzsche in Duchamp's possession at the time of his death seems to have been Bataille's collection of Nietzsche's writings, *Mémorandum* (Paris: Gallimard, 1945); see Marc Décimo, *La Bibliothèque de Marcel Duchamp, peut-être* (Dijon: Les presses du réel, 2002), 135.

13. Stuart Kendall, *Georges Bataille* (London: Reaktion, 2007), 8.

14. Marcus Boon, "To Live in a Glass House is a Revolutionary Virtue Par Excellence: Marxism, Buddhism, and the Politics of Nonalignment," in *Nothing: Three Inquiries in Buddhism* (Chicago: University of Chicago Press, 2015), 31.

15. Jean Bruno, "Les techniques d'illumination chez Georges Bataille," *Critique* 19, nos. 195–196 (August–September 1963), 706–720. Also important in this context: Andrew Hussey, *The Inner Scar: The Mysticism of Georges Bataille* (Amsterdam: Rodopi, 2000); Alan Folijambe, *An Intimate Destruction: Tantric Buddhism, Desire, and the Body in Surrealism and Georges Bataille* (unpublished doctoral thesis, University of Manchester, 2008); Hugh B. Urban, "Desire, Blood, and Power: Georges Bataille and the Study of Hindu Tantra in Northeastern India," in *Negative Ecstasies: Georges Bataille and the Study of Religion*, ed. Jeremy Biles and Kent Brintnall (New York: Fordham University Press, 2015), 68–80; and Marcus Boon in *Nothing*, 31–57.

16. Georges Bataille, *Guilty* [French edition 1944], trans. Stuart Kendall (Albany: SUNY, 2011), 151. Bataille had already published *La Pratique de la joie devant la mort* ("The Practice of Joy in the Face of Death") in the final issue of *Acéphale* (June 1939). *Method of Meditation* would appear in 1947; "Post-Scriptum 1953" was published in 1954, in the second edition of *Inner Experience*.

17. Bataille, *Guilty*, 25.

18. Georges Bataille, *Inner Experience: L'Expérience intérieure*, trans. Stuart Kendall (Albany: SUNY Press, 1914), 72.

19. Ibid., 40. The title of Bataille's 1943 *L'Expérience intérieure* echoes Romain Rolland's *Le voyage intérieur* published in 1942, just before Bataille became his neighbor in Vézelay (March 1943). In chapter 2 of *Voyage intérieur* Rolland describes his early "spiritual outbursts, three of those Revelations that filled my veins with the fire that nourishes the heart of the universe" (Romain Rolland, *Journey Within*, trans. Elsie Pell [New York: Philosophical Library, 1947], 11). In *L'Expérience intérieure*, Bataille relates similar revelations. His umbrella enlightenment, in particular, closely parallels Rolland's "revelation in the darkness of the tunnel" (30–31).

20. Bataille, *Guilty*, 31.

21. Bataille, *Inner Experience*, 4.

22. Bataille, *Guilty*, 24–25.

23. Ibid., 25, 31–32.

24. Surya, *Georges Bataille*, 511, note 10.

25. Bataille, *Inner Experience*, 4.

26. Georges Bataille, *The Tears of Eros* [French edition 1961] (San Francisco: City Lights Books, 1989), 206–207.

27. Alexandra David-Néel, *Magic and Mystery in Tibet* (New York: Kendall, 1932), 148–152. On April 1, 1932, Bataille checked out from the Bibliothèque Nationale the original edition of this book (Paris: Plon, 1929), along with two other books by David-Néel: *Voyage d'une parisienne à Lhassa* (Plon, 1927) and *Initiations lamaïques* (Adyar, 1930), which he would check out again in February 1937. On May 7, 1942, Bataille once again checked out *Mystiques et magiciens du Thibet*, returning it on July 16 (*Œuvres complètes* XII, 584, 618). Chöd was discussed by other authors Bataille read, including Mircea Eliade and W. Y. Evans-Wentz. The concept of the body torn apart and sacrificed is also central to the myth of Dionysus, a foundational influence on Bataille.

28. http://www.goodreads.com/author/show/20842.Georges_Bataille (accessed May 17, 2018).

29. In a former life the Buddha is said to have offered his body to feed starving tiger cubs; see Jérôme Edou, *Machig Labdrön and the Foundations of Chöd* (Ithaca, NY: Snow Lion, 1996), 9.

30. Bataille, *Tears of Eros*, 206–207. "This book is not written from within the limited experience of most men," added Bataille, who could be a master of understatement.

31. Paul Matisse, interviewed by Michel Vanpeene, "Les Clefs de la rue Parmentier: entretien avec Paul Matisse et Jacqueline Matisse Monnier," *Étant donné Marcel Duchamp*, no. 4 (2002), 17.

32. Surya, *Georges Bataille*, 553, note 11.

33. Georges Bataille, "*Kâlî*," *Documents* 6 (1930), 368–369; *Œuvres complètes* I (1970), 243–244.

34. My thanks to Stuart Kendall for pointing out the link to Marquis de Sade.

35. Mircea Eliade, *Yoga: Immortality and Freedom* [French edition 1954] (Princeton, NJ: Princeton University Press, 1969), 221. Bataille and Eliade knew each other; beginning in 1948, Eliade wrote for Bataille's journal *Critique*; in his autobiography Eliade reports that Bataille told him he had read Eliade's *Yoga: essai sur les origins de la mystique indienne*, published in 1936.

36. Stuart Kendall, in Bataille, *Unfinished System of Nonknowledge*, xxx.

37. Bataille, *Guilty*, 17. On *maithuna*, see Mircea Eliade, *Yoga: essai sur les origines de la mystique indienne* (Paris: Geuthner, 1936), 232–243.

38. Bataille, *Inner Experience*, 224.

39. Bruno, "Les techniques d'illumination," 718–719.

40. According to Stuart Kendall (personal email, May 11, 2017), "Bataille is explicit about participating in orgies. See *Guilty*, 11, but also 195–196, which is more intimate in its description in terms of participants. More important is Bataille's lack of hierarchy regarding paths to ecstasy. See 'Method of Meditation' in *Inner Experience*, 193–194."

41. Bruno, "Les techniques d'illumination," 709.

42. Ibid., 711–712.

43. Bataille, *Unfinished System of Nonknowledge*, 78, 283, note 2.

44. See chapter 5. Closer in time to Bataille's 1938–1939 experiences was Duchamp's continuum-reifying installation, *Mile of String* in *First Papers of Surrealism* (1942); see chapter 6.

45. A selection of texts relating to *Acéphale* has recently been published in English: *The Sacred Conspiracy: The Internal Papers of the Secret Society of Acéphale and Lectures to the College of Sociology*, ed. Marina Galletti and Alastair Brotchie (London: Atlas Press, 2017).

46. For a good short summary of Bataille's previous involvements, see Patrick Waldberg, "Avec Georges Duthuit" (1973), in Marina Galletti, *Georges Bataille: L'Apprenti Sorcier: Textes, Lettres et Documents (1932–1939)* (Paris: La Différence, 1999), 579–580.

47. Bataille, *Œuvres complètes* II (1970), 273.

48. In a letter of October 1, 1939, to "Saint-Paul" [Robert Folio], Bataille wrote that what emerges from his "principles is the simple virile attitude, without escape [from death] but without the search for opportunities [for death]" (Galletti, *Georges Bataille*, 561).

49. Bataille, *Œuvres complètes* II, 273.

50. Imre Kelemen's "Déclaration à la réunion sessionnelle de décembre 1937," in Galletti, *Georges Bataille*, 426.

51. Bataille, *Œuvres complètes* II, 273.

52. Reprinted with an introduction by Michel Camus: *Acéphale* (Paris: Jean-Michel Place, 1980).

53. The College of Sociology drew on anthropology and sociology to analyze ways that human communities have engaged in collective rituals; see Georges Bataille et al., *The College of Sociology (1937–39)*, ed. Denis Hollier, trans. Betsy Wing (Minneapolis: University of Minnesota Press, 1988).

54. Galletti, *Georges Bataille*, 424–425.

55. Kendall, *Georges Bataille*, 132. This is the reverse of tantric practices in India, where everybody knew *what* went on, but not precisely *who* was participating.

56. Galletti, *Georges Bataille*, 336. Galletti points out that Bataille's list lacked the names of Atlan, Girard, and Dautry, who appear in secret society documents for June 25, 1938.

57. Ibid., 359–361. The instructions, in the archive of Jacques Chavy, were written for a meeting that took place on March 25, 1937.

58. Ibid., 409–410.

59. Friedrich Wilhelm Nietzsche, *The Gay Science*, trans. Walter Kaufmann (New York: Vintage Books, 1974), 181.

60. Georges Bataille, *Visions of Excess: Selected Writings, 1927–1939*, ed. and trans. Allan Stoekl (Minneapolis: University of Minnesota Press, 1985), 236.

61. From a letter of October 1, 1939 to "Saint-Paul" [Robert Folio], in Galletti, *Georges Bataille*, 561.

62. Nietzsche, *The Gay Science*, 38. My thanks to Stuart Kendall for directing me to this reference, and for emphasizing Bataille's foundational inspiration from Nietzsche and Dionysian myth, for which tantra served as both endorsement and enrichment.

63. http://sulochanosho.wordpress.com/2010/02/23/god-is-in-the-vagina/ (accessed May 20, 2017); Jeffrey K. Kripal, *Kali's Child: The Mystical and the Erotic in the Life and Teachings of Ramakrishna* (University of Chicago Press, 1995), 349, note 71.

64. Hugh B. Urban, *The Power of Tantra: Religion, Sexuality, and the Politics of South Asian Studies* (London: I. B. Tauris, 2010), 118–119.

65. Bataille, *Inner Experience*, 24–25.

66. Alexandra David-Neel, *Initiations and Initiates in Tibet*, trans. Fred Rothwell [from *Initiations Lamaïques* published Paris: Adyar, 1930] (London: Rider, 1931; ed. 1970), 35–36. Bataille checked out *Initiations Lamaïques* from the Bibliothèque Nationale in April 1932 and again in February 1937 (Bataille, *Œuvres complètes* XII, 584). For another description of the practice to which David-Néel refers, see John R. Dupuche, *Abhinavagupta, The Kula Ritual as Elaborated in Chapter 29 of the Tantrlokā* (Delhi: Motilal Banarsidass Publishers, 2003), esp. 128.

67. Galletti, *Georges Bataille*, 424–425.

68. Ibid., 433, 440.

69. Waldberg, "Avec Georges Duthuit," in ibid., 577–578.

70. From the preliminary program, in Bataille, *Œuvres complètes* II, 277–278.

71. Waldberg, "Acéphalogramme," 158–159.

72. Ibid., 159.

73. Galletti, *Georges Bataille*, 456–457.

74. Waldberg, "Acéphalogramme," 159.

75. Bataille, *Tears of Eros*, 206–207.

76. Galletti, *Georges Bataille*, 537 (I have italicized the word *light*, which appears twice in this short passage).

77. Ibid., 540–541. "Burn like fire" evokes both Mina Loy's "he deliberately set himself on fire" (see chapter 5) and the stove Isabelle Waldberg would depict in her drawing for the cover of *G. B.* (see chapter 8).

78. Ibid., 544–545. Bataille's reference to a previous "larval" existence was not simply metaphorical: Within the category of "adept" he had set three levels of achievement: *larve* ("larva"), *muet* ("silent"), and *prodigue* ("wasteful"); ibid., 486–487.

79. Waldberg, "Acéphalogramme," 159. It is not clear when this meeting took place. Waldberg referred to war breaking out a few months later; World War II officially began on September 1, 1939, when Germany invaded Poland. Stuart Kendall believes that the last "sacrificial" meeting took place around the time of the October 20, 1939 letter dissolving Acéphale, and the anniversary of Laure's death in early November. He points out that Waldberg wrote his account years after the actual events, and his reference to "real war" may have been to the German invasion of June 1940 (personal email, May 11, 2017).

80. Bataille, *Guilty*, 162.

CHAPTER 8

1. *Dictionnaire abrégé du surréalisme* (Paris: Galerie Beaux-Arts, 1938, republished Rennes: José Corti, 1969), 11.

2. Patrick Waldberg, "Acéphalogramme" [1977], *Magazine Littéraire*, no. 331 (April 1995), 159.

3. Jean Bruno, "Les techniques d'illumination chez Georges Bataille," in *Critique* 19, nos. 195–196 (August–September 1963), 706–720.

4. By the time *G. B.* was published, in 1969, the notion of group enlightenment via alcohol and sex had become, if not part of the cultural mainstream, at least an accepted counterculture practice. But, just as Duchamp scholars have ignored Robert Lebel's *La double vue, suivi de L'inventeur du temps gratuit* (1964), so Bataille scholars have ignored *G. B.* This is partly due to the fact that its prose is hard to interpret, or even follow, and partly because the edition published by José Corti in 1996 omitted Isabelle's illustrations, which are key to its interpretation.

5. *G. B. ou un ami présomptueux* was to have been issued in 2,500 copies, of which 50 were numbered and presented in a transparent yellow Plexiglas casing along with a bronze sculpture by Isabelle Waldberg. These presentation copies, with their sculpted "illustrations," also included an original gouache signed by the artist. The deluxe "Club du Soleil Noir" series was to have been issued in a simple black paper casing in an edition of 150, each with an engraved aluminum cutout mounted on black opaque Plexiglas. The trade edition comprised 2,300 paperback copies with a stamped numeral, 151 through 2,450, and a drawing by Isabel Waldberg reproduced on the cover.

6. Inside front cover flap of the trade edition, Michel Fardoulis-Lagrange, *G. B. ou un ami présomptueux* (Paris: Le Soleil Noir, 1969).

7. Ibid.

8. See chapter 2. The title of Lebel's Duchamp biography—*Sur Marcel Duchamp*—openly references Georges Bataille's *Sur Nietzsche* (1945).

9. *Étant donné Marcel Duchamp*, no. 7 (2006), 103. At the time Isabelle Waldberg's works for *G. B.* were created, *Given* was not yet public, but she would certainly have known about it.

10. Mircea Eliade, *Yoga: Immortality and Freedom* (French edition 1954; Princeton, NJ: Princeton University Press, 1969), 249ff.

11. Fardoulis-Lagrange, *G. B.*, 26–27. Bataille published an essay on Kali in 1930: "Kâlî," *Documents* 6 (1930), 368–369; Georges Bataille, *Oeuvres complètes*, ed. Michel Foucault, vol. 1 (Paris: Gallimard, 1970), 239–240.

12. Fardoulis-Lagrange, *G. B.*, 33.

13. Ibid., 55–56, 66–69; Waldberg, "Acéphalogramme," 159.

14. "Post-Scriptum 1953," in Georges Bataille, *Inner Experience: L'Expérience intérieure*, trans. Stuart Kendall (Albany: SUNY Press, 1914), 206.

15. Isabelle described Acéphale meetings "where … contemplation transformed itself into action. … We made a fire at the foot of a tree […]. Bataille practiced a kind of sacrifice. There are some very curious buildings in this forest, a sort of very deep gallery where Bataille had brought down a horse's skull, but this belonged to his intimate ritual [*rituel intime*]" (Marina Galletti, *Georges Bataille: L'Apprenti Sorcier: Textes, Lettres et Documents (1932–1939)* [Paris: La Différence, 1999], 362).

16. Mircea Eliade, *Yoga: essai sur les origins de la mystique indienne* (Paris: Geuthner, 1936), 232. Eliade's source was the *Brhadaranyaka Upanishad*: "Her vulva is the sacrificial ground; her pubic hair is the sacred grass; her labia majora are the Soma-press; and her labia minora are the fire blazing at the center. A man who engages in sexual intercourse with this knowledge obtains as great a world as a man who performs a Soma sacrifice" (Patrick Olivelle, *The Early Upanishads: Annotated Text and Translation* [New York: Oxford University Press, 1998] 155).

17. Alexandra David-Neel, *Initiations and Initiates in Tibet*, trans. Fred Rothwell [from *Initiations Lamaïques* published Paris: Adyar, 1930] (London: Rider, 1931; ed. 1970), 33–34.

18. Alexandra David-Neel, *L'Inde: Hier-Aujourd'hui-Demain* (Paris: Plon, 1951), 142. Although this book appeared after Bataille's last Acéphale meetings, he clearly knew about this practice. For similar practices, see David Gordon White, *Kiss of the Yogini* (Chicago: University of Chicago Press, 2003) and, with specific application to Bataille: Hugh B. Urban, "Desire, Blood, and Power: Georges Bataille and the Study of Hindu Tantra in Northeastern India," in *Negative Ecstasies: Georges Bataille and the Study of Religion*, ed. Jeremy Biles and Kent Brintnall (New York: Fordham University Press, 2015), 68–80.

19. Fardoulis-Lagrange, *G. B.*, 72. There is a Duchamp reference here: to the "blossoming" of the Bride in *The Large Glass*.

20. Ibid., 76.

21. Ibid., 78.

22. See chapter 2, note 54. There is also an intriguing parallel with Alfred Stieglitz's assertion quoted in chapter 5: "it is when conflict hovers about a point—a focal point—and light is in the ascendancy, that I am moved."

23. Fardoulis-Lagrange, *G. B.*, 79.

24. Arturo Schwarz, *The Complete Works of Marcel Duchamp* ([1969, 1970] revised and expanded edition, New York: Delano Greenidge, 2000), 811–812.

25. Marina Galletti, *Georges Bataille: Apprenti Sorcier: Textes, Lettres et Documents (1932–1939)* (Paris: La Différence, 1999), 547. Duchamp's lover Maria Martins would also write about Nietzsche, publishing a biography in 1965.

26. Ibid., 564–565.

27. Patrick Waldberg discussed their fellow members in a letter to Isabelle of September 19, 1943; see Patrick and Isabelle Waldberg, *Un amour acéphale: correspondance, 1940–1949*, ed. Michel Waldberg (Paris: Éditions de la Différence, 1992), especially 84–85.

28. Isabelle Waldberg, "Peggy Guggenheim, Marcel Duchamp & André Breton," *Étant donné Marcel Duchamp*, no. 7 (2006), 138.

29. See the chapter "Revolutionary offensive or death," in Michel Surya, *Georges Bataille: An Intellectual Biography*, trans. Krzysztof Fijalkowski and Michael Richardson (London: Verso, 2002), 218–227.

30. Pierre-Henri Kleiber, *L'Encyclopédie "Da Costa" (1947–1949): D'Acéphale au Collège de 'Pataphysique* (Lausanne: Éditions L'Âge d'Homme, 2014), 132.

31. Wildenstein was also the publisher of the venerable *Gazette des Beaux-Arts*. The most complete account of this exhibition was provided by one of the participants: Marcel Jean, *The History of Surrealist Painting*, trans. Simon Watson Taylor (New York: Grove, 1959), 280–289. For whatever reason, Jean downplays the involvement of Duchamp, who was the source of much of his information.

32. Elena Filipovic, *The Apparently Marginal Activities of Marcel Duchamp* (Cambridge, MA: MIT Press, 2016), 96. "Générateur-Arbitre" was the title assigned Duchamp in the catalogue; André Breton and Paul Éluard were listed as "Organisateurs." For more information on Duchamp and the 1938 exhibition, see Lewis Kachur, *Displaying the Marvelous: Marcel Duchamp, Salvador Dali, and Surrealist Exhibition Installation* (Cambridge, MA: MIT Press, 2001), 22ff; and Nathalie Stefanov, "1 200 Sacs À Charbon: est-ce-assez? Quelques notes sur la participation de Marcel Duchamp à l'Exposition Internationale du Surréalisme de 1938," *Étant donné Marcel Duchamp*, no. 4 (2002), 146–155.

33. Bataille gave Dalí as a reference in "*Kâlî*," *Documents* 6 (1930), 368–369; *Œuvres complètes* I (1970), 244.

34. Number 11. According to Stuart Kendall, "*Minotaure* had almost been Bataille and Masson's journal when Skira launched it. ... Masson somehow managed to stay friends with everyone" (personal email, May 11, 2017). Masson, who furnished illustrations for Bataille's *Acéphale*, would also design the cover for the subsequent double issue of *Minotaure*, nos. 12–13, which included reproductions of two of Masson's paintings (Jean, *History of Surrealist Painting*, 294).

35. "*Cérémonie fastueuse dans un souterrain*" (*Dictionnaire abrégé*, 11).

36. Galletti, *Georges Bataille*, 362.

37. "*Oiseau bleu devenu noir*" (*Dictionnaire abrégé*, 20).

38. See chapter 9. The Nietzsche quote is from *Thus Spoke Zarathustra*: "Just now my world became perfect, midnight is also noon—Pain is also a joy, a curse is also a blessing, night is also a sun—go away or else you will learn: a wise man is also a fool" (trans. Adrian Del Caro [Cambridge: Cambridge University Press, 2006], 263). My thanks to Stuart Kendall for directing me to Bataille's source. For a translation of Bataille's essay, see Georges Bataille, *The Absence of Myth: Writings on Surrealism*, ed. and trans. Michael Richardson (London: Verso, 1994), 48.

39. Georges Bataille, *Inner Experience: L'Expérience intérieure*, trans. Stuart Kendall (Albany: SUNY Press, 1914), 40.

40. H. P. Roché, "Souvenirs of Marcel Duchamp," in Robert Lebel, *Marcel Duchamp*, trans. George Heard Hamilton (New York: Grove Press, 1959), 84. They would not have been the only umbrellas at the *Exposition Internationale*: Wolfgang Paalen showed his *Nuage articulé* ("Articulated cloud," 1937)—an umbrella covered with natural sponges intended to absorb rather than repel water.

41. Schwarz, *The Complete Works*, 768.

42. Invitation reproduced in Bruce Altshuler, *Salon to Biennial: Exhibitions That Made Art History*, vol. 1: *1863–1959* (London: Phaidon, 2008), 282.

43. See illustration in Jean, *History of Surrealist Painting*, 285. Reproduced on the facing page is Paalen's mannequin dressed in a gown covered with mushrooms; on her head is a bat that appears to be about to take flight.

44. Reproduced in Filipovic, *The Apparently Marginal Activities of Marcel Duchamp*, 104. See illustrations and captions in Altshuler, *Salon to Biennial*, 284–287. There was also a sound component, according to Marcel Jean: "a loud-speaker blared out the German army's parade march" (282). The revolving doors may have been suggested by Man Ray, who in 1926 had published a portfolio of screen prints entitled *Revolving Doors* based on compositions from 1916–1917.

45. Kachur, *Displaying the Marvelous*, 72.

46. See illustrations and captions in Altshuler, *Salon to Biennial*, 284–287. Duchamp discussed the revolving doors with Pierre Cabanne, *Dialogues with Marcel Duchamp*, trans. Rod Padgett (London: Thames and Hudson, 1971; reprinted Cambridge, MA: Da Capo Press, 1987), 81.

47. Elena Filipovic, "Surrealism in 1938: The Exhibition at War," in *Surrealism, Politics and Culture*, ed. Raymond Spiteri and Donald LaCoss (Aldershot: Ashgate, 2003), 179.

48. *Exposition Surréaliste d'Objets* (Paris: Charles Ratton, 1936), unpaginated. Ratton, a dealer in *arts des primitifs*, advertised in the 1937 issues of *Acéphale*. Displayed in this "surrealist" exhibition of objects alongside Duchamp's "ready-made" *Bottlerack* (1914) and "assisted ready-made" *Why Not Sneeze?* (1921) was Hans Bellmer's *Ball Joint* (1936), a glass eye embedded in the "joint" between two baby doll arms in unmistakable homage to Bataille's *L'Histoire de l'œil* (*The Story of the Eye*, 1928).

49. André Breton, "Devant le rideau," in *Le Surréalisme en 1947*, catalogue to the Exposition Internationale du Surréalisme (Paris: Maeght, 1947), 13–14. Bataille, *Inner Experience*, 95.

50. Isabelle and Patrick Waldberg, *Un amour acéphale*, 72–73.

51. Ibid., 84.

52. Bataille, *Inner Experience*, 70.

53. Isabelle and Patrick Waldberg, *Un amour acéphale*, 88.

54. Ibid., 84.

55. Patrick Waldberg, "Acéphalogramme," 159.

CHAPTER 9

1. *VVV*, vol. 4 (February 1944), 44.

2. *Upeksha* (Sanskrit), *Upekka* (Pali) means equanimity, nonattachment, nondiscrimination, letting go. Duchamp was not "indifferent" to the well-being of his fellow humans, only to the demands of the self and its cravings.

3. Denis de Rougemont, *Journal d'une époque 1926–1946* (Paris: Gallimard, 1968), 564–565.

4. Georges Bataille, "Chronique Nietzschéenne (I)," in *Acéphale*, nos. 3–4 (July 1937; Paris: Jean-Michel Place, 1980), 21.

5. https://en.wikipedia.org/wiki/Da_Costa%27s_syndrome (accessed May 21, 2018).

6. Alastair Brotchie, *Encyclopaedia Acephalica* (London: Atlas Press, 1995), 16.

7. Pierre Cabanne, *Dialogues with Marcel Duchamp*, trans. Rod Padgett (Cambridge, MA: Da Capo Press, 1987), 85.

8. Isabelle and Patrick Waldberg, *Un amour acéphale: correspondance, 1940–1949*, ed. Michel Waldberg (Paris: Éditions de la Différence, 1992), 84–89.

9. Lettter of January 12, 1944, in ibid., 143.

10. *VVV*, vol. 4, 41–44.

11. Isabelle and Patrick Waldberg, *Un amour acéphale*, 325.

12. In 1917 Duchamp hung the works edge-to-edge alphabetically by artist name, beginning with "R," the first letter drawn from a hat. His design for the inaugural exhibition of the Société Anonyme (April 1920) featured gray industrial ribbed rubber matting laid over the wooden floors, and paper lace doily edgings around some of the frames. See Kristina Wilson, "One Big Painting," in *The Société Anonyme: Modernism for America*, ed. Jennifer R. Gross (New Haven: Yale University Press, 2006), 77.

13. *West Coast Duchamp*, ed. Bonnie Clearwater (Miami Beach: Grassfield Press, 1991), 110. For Mirra Alfassa, "conceiving (*concevoir*)" was "a higher way of seeing (*voir*)" (*Words of Long Ago*, vol. 2, *Collected Works of The Mother* [Pondicherry: Sri Aurobindo Ashram, (1978) 2004], 89).

14. See Calvin Tomkins, *Duchamp: A Biography* (New York: Henry Holt, 1996), 111.

15. Arturo Schwarz, *The Complete Works of Marcel Duchamp* (New York: Delano Greenidge, 2000), 742. Duchamp re-created it for the exhibition "Doors" at Cordier & Ekstrom Gallery, New York, in 1968.

16. See chapters 8 and 6.

17. André Breton, "Projet Initial," in *Le Surréalisme en 1947*, catalogue to the Exposition Internationale du Surréalisme presented by André Breton and Marcel Duchamp (Paris: Maeght, 1947), 135.

18. On January 10, 1947, Isabelle wrote Patrick Waldberg: "Duchamp leaves next Monday, and as agreed, I'll have the workshop [11 rue Larrey]. It is unfortunate for Da Costa that Duchamp is leaving so soon, but he was so wanting to go" (*Un amour acéphale*, 439).

19. For a description of the exhibition and catalogue, see Marcel Jean, *The History of Surrealist Painting*, trans. Simon Watson Taylor (New York: Grove, 1959), 341–344. For more recent analyses, see Cynthia Goodman, "The Art of Revolutionary Display Techniques," in Lisa Phillips et al., *Frederick Kiesler* (New York: Whitney Museum of American Art, 1989), 71–76; Michael R. Taylor, *Marcel Duchamp: Étant donnés* (Philadelphia Museum of Art with Yale University Press, 2009), 71ff; Herbert Molderings, "*The Green Ray*: Marcel Duchamp's Lost Work of Art," in Stefan Banz et al., *Marcel Duchamp and the Forestay Waterfall* (Cully and Zurich: Kunsthalle Marcel Duchamp with JRP/Ringier, 2010), 240–257; and Eva Kraus and Monika Pessler, *Breton Duchamp Kiesler: Surreal Space 1947* (Vienna: Austrian Frederick and Lillian Kiesler Private Foundation, 2013).

20. Paul B. Franklin, "Accounting for the Occult: A letter from Marcel Duchamp to Jacques van Lennep," *Étant donné Marcel Duchamp*, no. 4 (2002), 157. The "Hall of Superstitions" appears to have been more under the control of Duchamp, via Kiesler.

21. Press release for an exhibition of Kiesler's "Galaxies" at the Howard Wise Gallery, New York, April 12– May 10, 1969; quoted by Beatriz Colomina in "Endless Drawing: Architecture as Self-Analysis," *Frederick Kiesler: Co-Realities*, Drawing Papers 77 (New York: The Drawing Center, 2008), 24.

22. *Art International* 9, no. 2 (March 1965), 16. According to Jeffrey Kripal, "the inner, most holy interior of a Hindu temple is sometimes called a *garbha-griha*, a womb-house" (personal note, July 23, 2018).

23. Frederick Kiesler, "On Correalism and Biotechnique: A Definition and Test of a New Approach to Building Design," *Architectural Record* 86, no. 9 (September 1939), 61.

24. Breton, "Projet Initial," in *Le Surréalisme en 1947*, 135.

25. Ibid., 135–136. The stairs were edited in the process of execution: a photograph in Kraus and Pessler shows a first step with a name not mentioned in Breton's list: "Facteur Cheval"—an outsider architect who created an "ideal palace" documented in André Jean's *Palais Idéal du Facteur Cheval* (Valence: Imprimerie nouvelle, 1939).

26. Reproduced in Goodman, "Art of Revolutionary Display Techniques," 72.

27. See Molderings, "*The Green Ray*," 240–257. Molderings and other recent commentators have linked *Le rayon vert* with Jules Verne's 1882 novel of the same title.

28. Michel Strickmann, *Mantras et Mandarins: Le Bouddhisme Tantrique en Chine* (Paris: Gallimard, 1996), 32.

29. See chapter 5.

30. These drawings are reproduced in Molderings, "*The Green Ray*," 242, 245.

31. Reproduced in ibid., 246.

32. Schwarz, *The Complete Works*, 788 (where *hublot* is translated as "scuttle hole").

33. Pierre Cabanne, *Entretiens avec Marcel Duchamp* (Paris: Pierre Belfond, 1967), 51.

34. Georges Bataille, *The Absence of Myth: Writings on Surrealism*, ed. and trans. Michael Richardson (London: Verso, 1994), 48. Friedrich Nietzsche, *Thus Spoke Zarathustra: A Book for All and None*, trans. Adrian Del Caro (Cambridge: Cambridge University Press, 2006), 263.

35. Breton, "Projet Initial," in *Le Surréalisme en 1947*, 136.

36. Kraus and Pessler, *Breton Duchamp Kiesler*, 12. I have been unable to find a reproduction or description of *L'Athanor*. Another work by Baskine shown at the 1947 surrealist exhibition was the sculpture *Le Mas Goth* (*Gothic Mass*), a lumpy Janus head with "mandrake root," reproduced opposite page 84, *Le Surréalisme en 1947*.

37. Georges Bataille, "L'Absence de mythe," in *Le Surréalisme en 1947*, 65. For a translation of the entire essay, see Bataille, *Absence of Myth*, 48.

38. André Breton, "Devant le rideau," in *Le Surréalisme en 1947*, 19.

39. Cabanne, *Dialogues*, 86. Duchamp's reference to artificial grass suggests that the seeds were replaced with artificial turf.

40. Robert Lebel, *Marcel Duchamp* (Paris: Belfond, 1985), 11–12.

41. Gabrielle Buffet-Picabia, "Some Memories of Pre-Dada: Picabia and Duchamp (1949)," in *The Dada Painters and Poets: An Anthology*, ed. Robert Motherwell (Cambridge, MA: Harvard University Press, 1981), 263.

42. Hector Niel in *Paru*, no. 39 (February 1948), 65.

43. Pierre-Henri Kleiber, *L'Encyclopédie "Da Costa" (1947–1949)* (Lausanne: Éditions L'Âge d'Homme, 2014), 113. See also Pierre-Henri Kleiber, "Le *Da Costa*: histoire d'une obscure aventure encyclopédique," *Étant donné Marcel Duchamp*, no. 7 (2006), 108–137.

44. *VVV*, vol. 4, 41–44; Kleiber, *L'Encyclopédie "Da Costa,"* 125. Georges Duthuit, who had been a member of Acéphale but not a member of the inner group, also contributed a long response, which was published in the same issue, 45–49; reprinted in Kleiber, *L'Encyclopédie "Da Costa,"* 127–132. Not all of the original Da Costa clan members would be able to endure "deflation of all that is bloated, even in ourselves"—André Breton, in particular, objected when Surrealism became a target; see ibid., 142–146.

45. Isabelle and Patrick Waldberg, *Un amour acéphale*, 432–433.

46. See Brotchie, *Encyclopeaedia Acephalica*, 19; Kleiber, *L'Encyclopédie "Da Costa,"* 189ff.

47. The event was organized by André Breton; see Georges Ribemont-Dessaignes, "History of Dada (1931)," in Buffet-Picabia, *The Dada Painters and Poets*, 115–116.

48. Bataille's short essays on subjects such as "Absolute," "Eye," "Factory Chimney," and "Keaton (Buster)," were accompanied by dark, erotic, violent photographs intended to counteract what Bataille viewed as Breton's overly sanitized brand of Surrealism. Bataille's deadpan prose could be ironic, but rarely was it overtly humorous.

49. Hugh Edwards, *Surrealism and Its Affinities: The Mary Reynolds Collection, A Bibliography* (The Art Institute of Chicago, [1956] 1973), 47.

50. Kleiber, *L'Encyclopédie "Da Costa,"* 184–188.

51. Michel Surya, *Georges Bataille: An Intellectual Biography*, trans. Krzysztof Fijalkowski and Michael Richardson (London: Verso, 2002), 164.

52. As witnessed by a note in *The Green Box*: "take a Larousse dictionary and copy all the so called "abstract' words ..." (*The Writings of Marcel Duchamp*, ed. Michel Sanouillet and Elmer Peterson [New York: Da Capo Press, 1989], 31).

53. All three issues of *Da Costa* are reproduced at the beginning of Kleiber, *L'Encyclopédie "Da Costa"*; "-TOIR" is on page 16 of fascicule II.

54. *Encyclopédie des farces et attrapes et des mystifications*, ed. François Caradec and Noël Arnaud (Paris: J. J. Pauvert, 1964), 229–230.

55. Ibid., 230.

56. The *Encyclopédie des farces* was published in 1964—the same year as Lebel's *La double vue*, five years before *G. B.* appeared. See chapter 8.

57. Kleiber, *L'Encyclopédie "Da Costa,"* 285–286.

58. As translated in Brotchie, *Encyclopeaedia Acephalica*, 119–120, 132–133.

59. Robert Lebel, *Marcel Duchamp*, trans. George Heard Hamilton (New York: Grove Press, 1959), 34; Sanouillet and Peterson, eds., *Writings of Marcel Duchamp*, 31.

60. Isabelle and Patrick Waldberg, *Un amour acéphale*, 435.

61. Brotchie, *Encyclopeaedia Acephalica*, 18; Kleiber, *L'Encyclopédie "Da Costa,"* 291–292, 309.

62. *Le Da Costa Encyclopédique*, 238; translation from Brotchie, *Encyclopeaedia Acephalica*, 156.

63. Stuart Kendall considers William Blake to have been the primary source of Bataille's "contraries"; see Stuart Kendall, "Eternal Delight: Bataille, Blake and the 'State' of Grace," paper delivered at a Stanford symposium, May 15, 2009, https://www.academia.edu/32145574/Eternal_Delight_Bataille_Blake_and_the_State_of_Grace (accessed September 17, 2018).

64. Kleiber, *L'Encyclopédie "Da Costa,"* 292. Regarding Bataille's evolving projects on eroticism, see Georges Bataille, *Œuvres Complètes*, vol. 8 (Paris: Gallimard, 1976), 524ff.

65. *Le Da Costa Encyclopédique*, 220; translation from Brotchie, *Encyclopeaedia Acephalica*, 129.

66. *Le Da Costa Encyclopédique*, 231. Brotchie, 146, translates this verb as "yonirise." A better translation might be "yonise." In yogic practice, *yoni mudra* is said to promote a calm state of mind. It looks nothing like Duchamp's illustration, but rather like the Western hand gesture corresponding to the recitation "Here is the church, here is the steeple, open the doors and see all the people."

67. Kleiber, *L'Encyclopédie "Da Costa,"* 314, 323–324.

68. Baskine seems to have played the role of Douanier Rousseau to the Surrealists. He was perhaps best known for having been so frightened when he tried to deliver a lecture at one of their gatherings that he was rendered speechless; http://www.thesurrealists.org/maurice-baskine.html (accessed September 17, 2018).

69. Blaise Pascal (1623–1662) was a mathematician, physicist, religious philosopher, and developer of projective geometry, the first theory of probabilities, the roulette machine, and estimation of atmospheric pressure by weight (that is, by gravity). Like Duchamp, Pascal was from Rouen; and like Duchamp, Pascal wrote his thoughts on random scraps of paper, later published as Pascal's *Pensées* (1669). The following Pascal quote appears twice in the Duchamp-designed catalogue *Le Surréalisme en 1947* (83 and 127): "What vanity is painting, which attracts admiration by resembling things the originals of which we do not admire."

70. *Le Mémento Universel Da Costa*, fascicule I, 5.

71. The penultimate issue of *Acéphale* was devoted to "Dionysos," including an essay by Bataille on "Les Mystères Dionysiaques": *Acéphale*, nos. 3–4 (July 1937), 22–23.

72. See, for example, "Nonknowledge, Laughter, and Tears," in Bataille, *The Unfinished System of Nonknowledge*, ed. Stuart Kendall (Minneapolis: University of Minnesota Press, 2001), 133ff.

73. *Le Mémento Universel Da Costa*, fascicule II, 1. There is no book with the title *Origines cosmiques du Genre Humain* by "Da Costa"—presumably Uriel Da Costa (1585–1640). The reference to "French phonetic Cabala" was a tongue-in-cheek poke at Breton, a fan of the French alchemist and esoteric author Fulcanelli (fl. 1920s), whose Phonetic Cabala—unrelated to the Hebrew Kabbalah—emphasized phonetic similarities between words for expressive purposes.

74. *Da Costa*'s "Adam" shares elements with a long quote in *Surréalisme en 1947* from the utopian philosopher Charles Fourier (1772–1837, page 83) describing magnetic energy and Fourier's theory of Passionate Attraction.

75. See Alex Wayman, "Male, Female, and Androgyne," in *Tantric and Taoist Studies*, vol. 2, ed. Michel Strickmann (Brussels: Institut Belge des Hautes Etudes Chinoises, 1983), 593–631.

76. Sri Vivekananda, *Raja Yoga: Conquering the Internal Nature* [1896] (San Diego: The Book Tree, 2010), 48.

77. Kleiber, *L'Encyclopédie "Da Costa,"* 218–220.

78. Lebel, *Marcel Duchamp* (1985), 12.

79. Taylor, *Marcel Duchamp: Étant donnés*, 415.

80. Ibid., 406. Duchamp's statement recalls André Breton and Paul Éluard's definition of "*Amour*" from the 1938 *Dictionnaire abrégé du surréalisme*: "The perception of the inner object in the external object" (*Dictionnaire abrégé du surreéalisme* [Paris: (Wildenstein, 1938) José Corti, 1969], 3).

81. John R. Dupuche, *Abhinavagupta: the Kula ritual, as elaborated in chapter 29 of the Tantrāloka* (Delhi: Motilal Banarsidass Publishers, 2003), 263.

82. Ibid., 339. For descriptions of tantric initiation by penetration, including penetration by the guru's *śakti*, or energy, of the subtle body of another, see David Gordon White, *The Alchemical Body: Siddha Traditions in Medieval India* (Chicago: University of Chicago Press, 1996), 312–314.

CHAPTER 10

1. Robert Lebel, *La double vue, suivi de L'inventeur du temps gratuit* (Paris: Le Soleil Noir, 1964), 135.

2. The definitive publication on Duchamp's last major work is Michael R. Taylor's *Marcel Duchamp: Étant donnés* (Philadelphia Museum of Art with Yale University Press, 2009).

3. See chapters 4, 6.

4. Hugh B. Urban, *The Power of Tantra* (London: I. B. Tauris, 2010), 5.

5. *Marcel Duchamp: Duchamp du signe suivi de Notes*, ed. Michel Sanouillet and Paul Matisse with the collaboration of Anne Sanouillet and Paul B. Franklin (Paris: Flammarion, 2008), 238.

6. J. C. Chatterji, *Kashmir Shaivism* [1914] (Albany: State University of New York Press, 1986), 92.

7. Arturo Schwarz, *The Complete Works of Marcel Duchamp* (1969, 1970; revised and expanded edition, New York: Delano Greenidge, 2000), 822.

8. See Mircea Eliade, *Yoga: Immortality and Freedom*, trans. Willard R. Trask ([Paris: Librairie Payot, 1954] Princeton, NJ: Princeton University Press [1959], 1969), 261, note 204; and Urban, *The Power of Tantra*, 132.

9. Above a closet containing three white chickens illuminated by green light, American pennies spelled out "*coin sale*"—a French slang reference to female genitals. The French word for "hen" (*poule*) has the same connotation as "bird" in English: a sexually attractive woman. The English noun "coin" means not only money (implied by "sale"), but also corner or wedge, thus linking *coin sale* with Duchamp's *Wedge of Chastity* (1954). The English verb "coin" means to make or create, connecting it with generation, and perhaps a reference to the indivisibility of heads and tails. Green light signifies enlightenment, as we have seen.

10. See Taylor, *Marcel Duchamp*, 131.

11. Arturo Schwarz also points out that *Cols alités* is a pun on *causalité*—"causality" (*The Complete Works*, 819).

12. *Internal Alchemy: Self, Society, and the Quest for Immortality*, ed. Livia Kohn and Robin R. Wang (Magdalena, NM: Three Pines Press, 2009), 46.

13. Robert Lebel, *Marcel Duchamp* (Paris: Belfond, 1985), 185.

14. Calvin Tomkins, *Marcel Duchamp: The Afternoon Interviews* (Brooklyn: Badlands Unlimited, 2013), 31.

15. Vivekananda, *Raja Yoga: Conquering the Internal Nature* [1896] (San Diego: The Book Tree, 2010), 61.

16. Alice B. Stockham, *The Lover's World: A Wheel of Life* (Chicago: Stockham Publishing, 1903), 102–103. Although she is little known today, American doctor, feminist, and birth control advocate Alice Bunker Stockham (1833–1912) was an important Western advocate for more open attitudes toward sexuality and the mystical components of eroticism. Her books provide examples of how Asian esoteric sexual practices were adapted in the West around the turn of the twentieth century. Stockham researched tantra firsthand in India, founded her own publishing company in Chicago, and was the first to publish Edward Carpenter's *A Visit to a Gñáni* (1900). Her own books include *Tokology: A Book for Every Woman* (1886, revised edition 1881, French edition 1911), *Karezza: Ethics of Marriage* (1896, revised edition 1903), and *The Lover's World: A Wheel of Life* (1903). Parallels between her thinking and aspects of Duchamp's are striking.

17. Sanouillet and Matisse, *Duchamp du signe*, 64.

18. *The Writings of Marcel Duchamp*, ed. Michel Sanouillet and Elmer Peterson (Cambridge, MA: Da Capo Press, 1989), 26.

19. Agehananda Bharati, *The Tantric Tradition* (Westport, CT: Greenwood Press, [1965] 1977), 293.

20. John R. Dupuche, *Abhinavagupta, The Kula Ritual as Elaborated in Chapter 29 of the Tantrāloka* (Delhi: Motilal Banarsidass Publishers, 2003), 244–245.

21. Reproduced in *Duchamp du signe* is a diagram published in *The Green Box* where the "juggler of the centers of gravity" is described as having "its 3 points of support on this garment" (102–103). The Juggler of Gravity never made it into *The Large Glass*, but the "Bride's garment" remained a pivotal element; see diagram in *Marcel Duchamp*, ed. Anne d'Harnoncourt and Kynaston McShine (New York: Museum of Modern Art, 1973), 64.

22. Ibid.

23. Lebel, *Marcel Duchamp*, 185.

24. Schwarz, *The Complete Works*, 794.

25. Lebel, *La double vue*, 78.

26. "Where Do We Go From Here?," published French and English (last line is English in both), in *Studio International* 189, no. 973 (January/February 1975), 28. Before passing through the looking-glass Alice went underground, down a rabbit-hole, coming in for a landing on "a heap of sticks and dry leaves" (*The Annotated Alice ... by Lewis Carroll*, introduction and notes by Martin Gardner [New York: Norton, 2000], 14). Might this explain why Duchamp's naked woman lies on a heap of sticks and dry leaves? If so, the hole is *within* her.

27. Sujata Nahar, *Mother's Chronicles, book two, Mirra the Artist* (Paris: Institut de Recherches Évolutives, 1986), 171.

28. Cabanne, *Dialogues*, 27. See chapter 1, note 46.

29. Robert Motherwell, in Pierre Cabanne, *Dialogues with Marcel Duchamp*, trans. Rod Padgett (London: Thames and Hudson, 1971; reprinted Cambridge, MA: Da Capo Press, 1987), 12, 7.

30. See Andrew Lins, "Marcel Duchamp's Electroplated Plasters at the Philadelphia Museum of Art," in Taylor, *Marcel Duchamp*, 231ff.

31. Schwarz, *The Complete Works*, 794.

32. Calvin Tompkins, *Duchamp: A Biography* (New York: Henry Holt, 1996), 437. For more on Duchamp's relationship with Martins, see chapter 6.

33. Schwarz, *The Complete Works*, 794. Schwarz's *Complete Works of Marcel Duchamp* was published in 1969, the same year *Given* finally went on view; he published a revised edition the following year.

34. Schwarz, *The Complete Works*, 784.

35. Taylor, *Marcel Duchamp*, 404.

36. Edward Carpenter, *Love's Coming-of-Age: A Series of Papers on the Relations of the Sexes* [1896, French edition 1914] (New York: Kennerley, 1911), 179.

37. Martins used the lost-wax method of bronze casting, meaning that each of her bronzes is unique. *O Impossível* is discussed in an essay by Raul Antello, "Maria Martins: O Impossível," in *Maria Martins: Metamorfoses* (São Paulo: Museum of Modern Art, 2013), 35ff; English 254ff.

38. Georges Bataille, *L'Impossible: Histoire de rats suivi de Dianus et de L'Orestie* (Paris: Les Éditions de Minuit, 1962).

39. Personal email communication, September 30, 2015.

40. Mina Loy, *Insel*, ed. Elizabeth Arnold (Brooklyn: Melville House, 2014), 72, 76. For more on *Insel*, see chapter 5, note 48.

41. Henri-Pierre Roché, *Victor (Marcel Duchamp)* (Paris: Centre Georges Pompidou, 1977), 95. See chapter 5.

42. Irene Gammel, *Baroness Elsa: Gender, Dada, and Everyday Modernity* (Cambridge, MA: MIT Press, 2002), 176. Duchamp's "hypostatic" erotic practice clearly frustrated the carnal Baroness. Mina Loy would have encountered a similar (though presumably less intense) situation with her first husband, who in the course of their marriage became a celibate follower of Vivekananda; see Carolyn Burke, *Becoming Modern: The Life of Mina Loy* (New York: Farrar, Straus and Giroux, 1996), 132.

43. Paris: Le Soleil Noir, 1969. See chapter 6.

44. From *The Green Box*: "This blossoming should be the refined development of the arbor type" (Sanouillet and Peterson, ed., *Writings*, 43).

45. Sanouillet and Matisse, *Duchamp du signe*, 64. My translation is from the note in the box in the Ryerson Library, Art Institute of Chicago.

46. "*Étant donné que. ... ; si je suppose que je sois souffrant beaucoup. ...*" (*Duchamp du signe*, 60).

47. The statement was quoted often, including by Duchamp's friend Henri-Pierre Roché in his "Souvenirs sur Marcel Duchamp, *La Nouvelle N. R. F.* 1, no. 6 (June 1953), 1136 (William N. Copley's translation of this essay was published in Robert Lebel, *Marcel Duchamp*, trans. George Heard Hamilton [New York: Grove Press, 1959], this quote 85).

48. Harriet and Sidney Janis, "Marcel Duchamp: Anti-Artist," *View*, series 5, no. 1 (March 1945), 24; reprinted in Robert Motherwell, *The Dada Painters and Poets: An Anthology* (Cambridge, MA: Harvard University Press, 1981), 313.

49. Gloria Moure, *Gordon Matta-Clark: Works and Collected Writings* (Barcelona: Poligrafa, 2006), 122.

50. See Francis M. Naumann, "Notre Dame des désirs: Gynomorphism in Marcel Duchamp's *Chat Ouvert*," in *Marcel Duchamp and the Forestay Waterfall*, ed. Stefan Banz (Cully and Zurich: Kunsthalle Marcel Duchamp with JRP/Ringier, 2010), 155–157, especially note 1.

51. *Smile of the Buddha: Eastern Philosophy and Western Art from Monet to Today* (Berkeley: University of California Press, 2005), 92–95; and "Unframing Experience," in *Learning Mind: Experience into Art* (Berkeley: University of California Press, 2009), 221–222.

52. Schwarz, *The Complete Works*, 792.

53. Judith Simmer-Brown, *Dakini's Warm Breath: The Feminine Principle in Tibetan Buddhism* (Boston, MA: Shambhala, 2002), 95–96.

54. Ibid., 52. The vertical, vulva-shaped "third eye" of many tantric deities (see figure 10.13) is another instance of this metaphor; see David Gordon White, *Kiss of the Yogini* (University of Chicago Press, 2003), 101.

55. For more on the exhibition and this work, see Michael R. Taylor, "Eros Triumphant," in *Duchamp Man Ray Picabia*, ed. Jennifer Mundy (London: Tate Publishing, 2008), 172–175.

56. See chapter 1.

57. *West Coast Duchamp*, ed. Bonnie Clearwater (Miami Beach: Grassfield Press, 1991), 110.

58. Most notably the theory that Duchamp was influenced by the 1947 Black Dahlia murder in Los Angeles elaborated by Mark Nelson ("Surrealism and the Black Dahlia Murder," in *Marcel Duchamp and the Forestay Waterfall*, 190–207) and rebutted by Michael R. Taylor (*Marcel Duchamp: Étant donnés*, 194ff). The pose of the nude in *Given* is superficially similar to the mutilated, carefully arranged body of Black Dahlia. The likely murderer, however—surgeon and collector George Hodel—was interested in Tibetan tantric art, and my hunch is that dakini imagery served as a model for both Duchamp and Hodel. Nelson reproduces a photograph taken by Man Ray of Hodel "cradling" a sculpture of *Yamāntaka* ("terminator of death") in sexual embrace with his consort. Hodel and Man Ray would have been familiar with dakini imagery—Man Ray through Duchamp, and Hodel through his art dealer friend Ernst von Harringa, with whom he discussed going on the lam to Tibet. In another parallel,

the murderer cut a vertical slit just above his victim's pubis, like the vertical slit on the lower belly of the large dakini in the Musée Guimet (figure 10.12). Maria Martins's sculpture *The Impossible*, purchased by the Museum of Modern Art in 1946, the year before the Black Dahlia murder (figure 10.6), features a similar slit. All of this suggests that any influence would have to have been Duchamp/Martins on Hodel, presumably via Man Ray, rather than the other way around, with Tibetan iconography an important mutual influence. That Duchamp and Martins knew about the case is suggested by a March 19, 1950 letter to Martins in which Duchamp refers to his figure as "the white orchid" (Taylor, 416–417).

59. See Appendix.

60. Letter to Jean Crotti, August 17, 1952, reprinted in *TABU DADA: Jean Crotti and Suzanne Duchamp, 1915–1922*, ed. William A. Camfield and Jean-Hubert Martin (Kunsthalle Bern, 1983), 8; transcribed in *Affectionately Marcel: The Selected Correspondence of Marcel Duchamp*, ed. Francis M. Naumann and Hector Obalk (Ghent: Ludion Press, 2000), 318–320.

61. Calvin Tompkins, *Duchamp: A Biography* (New York: Henry Holt, 1996), 393.

62. Cabanne, *Dialogues*, 88.

63. From a January 19, 1959 interview with Richard Hamilton broadcast November 13, 1959 by the BBC as part of the series "Art, Anti-Art"; excerpts available at http://www.ubu.com/sound /duchamp.html, accessed May 23, 2018.

64. For a history of Atman versus anatman, see Johannes Bronkhorst, *Greater Magadha* (Leiden/Boston: Brill, 2007), 28ff. As Duchamp pointed out in an interview with Don Bell, published in *Canadian Art* 4, no. 4 (Winter 1987), 59, "Anartist" is evocative of "anarchist." Anarchist Max Stirner's concept of the "un-human," which he deployed to inveigh equally against Christianity and atheistic humanism, may likewise have been inspired by the Sanskrit anatman (see Lawrence Stepelvich, "Beyond Atheism: Max Stirner," in i, issue 1 [March 9, 2011], https://www.unionofegoists.com/wp-content/uploads/2016/04/io1.pdf, accessed May 5, 2018).

65. From a 1966 interview for Belgian television by Jean Antoine, trans. Sue Rose, *Art Newspaper*, no. 27 (April 1993); *Art Newspaper*, web only [March 29, 2013], http://ec2-79-125-124-178.eu-west-1.compute.amazonaws.com/articles/An-interview-with-Marcel-Duchamp/29278 (accessed May 23, 2018).

66. Quoted by Paul B. Franklin, "Marcel Duchamp, ses maîtres et ses pirouettes autour de la peinture," in *Marcel Duchamp: la peinture, même* (Paris: Centre Georges Pompidou, 2014), 37.

67. Georges Charbonnier, *Entretiens avec Marcel Duchamp* (Marseille: André Dimanche, 1994), 65.

68. *Artforum* 7, no. 3 (November 1968), 6; reprinted in *Jasper Johns: Writings, Sketchbook Notes, Interviews*, ed. Kirk Varnedoe (New York: Museum of Modern Art/Abrams, 1996), 22.

69. Especially true of tantric texts; see Christian K. Wedemeyer, *Making Sense of Tantric Buddhism: History, Semiology, and Transgression in the Indian Traditions* (New York: Columbia University Press, 2013), 92.

70. *D'ailleurs, c'est toujours les autres qui meurent.* English translation is Duchamp's; see Bell, *Canadian Art* 4, no. 4, 59. At the end of his life Duchamp apparently carried a slip of paper with this *memento mori* around with him in his breast pocket. See Donald Shambroom, *Duchamp's Last Day* (New York: David Zwirner Books, 2018).

SELECT BIBLIOGRAPHY

Alfassa, Mirra. *The Mother, Questions and Answers 1956, Collected Works of The Mother*, vol. 8. Pondicherry: Sri Aurobindo Ashram, 1977, 2004.

Alfassa, Mirra. *Paroles d'autrefois.* Pondicherry: Sri Aurobindo Ashram, 1946. [English version: *Words of Long Ago*, vol. 2, *Collected Works of The Mother*. Pondicherry: Sri Aurobindo Ashram, 1978, 2004.]

Ames, Roger T., and David L. Hall. *Daodejing "Making This Life Significant": A Philosophical Translation*. New York: Ballantine, 2003.

Apollinaire, Guillaume. *The Cubist Painters*, ed. and trans. Peter Read. Berkeley: University of California Press, 2004.

Apollinaire, Guillaume. *Les peintres cubistes* [1912], ed. L.C. Breunig and J.-Cl. Chevalier. Paris: Hermann, 1965.

App, Urs. *The Birth of Orientalism.* Philadelphia: University of Pennsylvania Press, 2010.

Association pour l'étude de Marcel Duchamp. *Étant donné Marcel Duchamp*, ed. Paul B. Franklin. Nos. 1–10, 1999–2013, Baby, France.

Avalon, Arthur [Sir John George Woodroffe]. *The Great Liberation (Mahānirvāna Tantra).* Madras: Ganesh, 1913.

Avalon, Arthur [Sir John George Woodroffe]. *The Serpent Power: Being the Ṣaṭ-chakra-nirūpaṇa and Pādukāpanchaka: two works on tantric yoga*. London: Luzac, [1918] 1919.

Baas, Jacquelynn. "Before Zen: The Nothing of American Dada." *East-West Interchanges in American Art: A Long and Tumultuous Relationship*, ed. Cynthia Mills, Lee Glazer, Amelia A. Goerlitz. Washington DC: Smithsonian Institution Scholarly Press, 2009.

Baas, Jacquelynn. "Meditations on the Medium of Time." *Measure of Time*, ed. Lucinda Barnes. Berkeley: University of California Berkeley Art Museum and Pacific Film Archive, 2007.

Baas, Jacquelynn. *Smile of the Buddha: Eastern Philosophy and Western Art from Monet to Today.* Berkeley: University of California Press, 2005.

Baas, Jacquelynn. "Unframing Experience." *Learning Mind: Experience into Art*, ed. Mary Jane Jacob and Jacquelynn Baas. Berkeley and Chicago: University of California Press and School of the Art Institute of Chicago, 2009.

Baas, Jacquelynn, and Mary Jane Jacob, eds. *Buddha Mind in Contemporary Art*. Berkeley: University of California Press, 2004.

Banz, Stefan, ed. *Marcel Duchamp and the Forestay Waterfall*. Cully and Zurich: Kunsthalle Marcel Duchamp with JRP/Ringier, 2010.

Bataille, Georges. *Guilty* [1944], trans. and intro. Stuart Kendall. Albany: State University of New York, 2011.

Bataille, Georges. *Inner Experience* [1943], trans. and intro. Stuart Kendall. Albany: State University of New York, 2014.

Bataille, Georges. *The Tears of Eros* [1961], trans. Peter Connor. San Francisco: City Lights, 1989.

Batchelor, Stephen. *The Awakening of the West: The Encounter of Buddhism and Western Culture*. Berkeley, CA: Parallax Press, 1994.

Batchelor, Stephen. *Buddhism Without Beliefs*. New York: Riverhead, 1997.

Beckwith, Christopher I. *Greek Buddha: Pyrrho's Encounter with Early Buddhism in Central Asia.* Princeton, NJ: Princeton University Press, 2015.

Belting, Hans. *Looking Through Duchamp's Door*. Köln: Walther König, 2009.

Bharati, Agehananda. *The Tantric Tradition*. Westport, CT: Greenwood Press, [1965] 1977.

Bonk, Ecke. *Marcel Duchamp, The Box in a Valise, de ou par Marcel Duchamp ou Rrose Selavy, Inventory of an Edition*, trans. David Britt. New York: Rizzoli, 1989.

Brotchie, Alastair. *Encyclopeaedia Acephalica*. London: Atlas Press, 1995.

Burnouf, Eugène. *Introduction to the History of Indian Buddhism*, trans. Katia Buffetrille and Donald S. Lopez Jr. Chicago: University of Chicago Press, 2010.

Buswell, Robert E. Jr., and Donald S. Lopez Jr. *The Princeton Dictionary of Buddhism*. Princeton, NJ: Princeton University Press, 2014.

Cabanne, Pierre. *Dialogues with Marcel Duchamp*, trans. Rod Padgett. London: Thames and Hudson, 1971; reprinted Cambridge, MA: Da Capo Press, 1987.

Cabanne, Pierre. *Entretiens avec Marcel Duchamp*. Paris: Belfond, 1967.

Camfield, William A. *Francis Picabia: His Art, Life and Times.* Princeton, NJ: Princeton University Press, 1979.

Camfield, William A. *Marcel Duchamp Fountain*. Houston: Menil Collection, 1989.

Camfield, William A., and Jean-Hubert Martin, eds. *TABU DADA: Jean Crotti and Suzanne Duchamp, 1915–1922*. Bern: Kunsthalle Bern, 1983.

Carpenter, Edward. *Angels' Wings: Essays on Art and its Relation to Life*. London: S. Sonnenschein; New York: Macmillan, 1898.

Carpenter, Edward. *The Art of Creation: Essays on the Self and Its Powers*. London: George Allen [1904, revised 1907], 1912. Abridged French version in: Senard, M. *Edward Carpenter et sa Philosophie* (Paris: Librairie de L'Art Indépendant, 1914).

Carpenter, Edward. *A Visit to a Gnani or Wise Man of the East*. [Chicago: A. B. Stockham, 1900] London: Allen, 1911.

Centre Georges Pompidou. *Brancusi et Duchamp: Regards historiques*. Paris: Centre Georges Pompidou, 2000.

Centre Georges Pompidou. *Marcel Duchamp abécédaire, approches critiques*. Paris: Centre Georges Pompidou, 1977.

Centre Georges Pompidou. *Marcel Duchamp: la peinture, même*. Paris: Centre Georges Pompidou, 2014.

Charbonnier, Georges. *Entretiens avec Marcel Duchamp.* Marseille: André Dimanche, 1994.

Chatterji, J. C. *Kashmir Shaivism* [1914]. Albany: State University of New York Press, 1986.

Cianci, Giovanni, and Jason Harding, eds. *T. S. Eliot and the Concept of Tradition*. Cambridge: Cambridge University Press, 2007.

Clair, Jean. *Duchamp et la photographie: Essai d'analyse d'un primat technique sur le développement d'un oeuvre*. Paris: Chêne, 1977.

Clair, Jean. *Marcel Duchamp: Catalogue raisonné*. Paris: Centre Georges Pompidou, 1977.

Clair, Jean. *Marcel Duchamp et la fin de l'art*. Paris: Gallimard, 2000.

Clair, Jean. *Marcel Duchamp, ou, Le Grand Fictif: Essai de mythanalyse du "Grand Verre."* Paris: Galilee, 1975.

Clarke, J. J. *Oriental Enlightenment: The Encounter Between Asian and Western Thought*. London: Routledge, 1997.

Clarke, J. J. *The Tao of the West: Western Transformations of Taoist Thought*. London: Routledge, 2000.

Clearwater, Bonnie, ed. *West Coast Duchamp*. Miami Beach: Grassfield Press, 1991.

Cleary, Thomas. *Understanding Reality: A Taoist Alchemical Classic by Chang Po-tuan with a Concise Commentary by Liu I-ming*. Honolulu: University of Hawaii Press, 1987.

David-Néel, Alexandra. *Initiations lamaïques: des théories, des pratiques, des hommes*. Paris: Adyar, 1930.

David-Néel, Alexandra. *Le Modernisme bouddhiste et le bouddhisme du Bouddha*. Paris: F. Alcan, 1911.

David-Néel, Alexandra. *Les théories individualistes dans la philosophie chinoise, Yang-tchou*. Paris: V. Giard & E. Brie, 1909.

David-Néel, Alexandra. *Voyage d'un Parisienne à Lhassa*. Paris: Plon, 1927.

Décimo, Marc. *La Bibliothèque de Marcel Duchamp, peut-être*. Dijon: Les Presses du Réel, 2002.

Décimo, Marc, ed. *Marcel Duchamp and Eroticism*. Newcastle: Cambridge Scholars Publishing, 2007.

De Duve, Thierry, ed. *The Definitively Unfinished Marcel Duchamp*. Cambridge, MA: MIT Press, 1991.

De Michelis, Elizabeth. *A History of Modern Yoga: Patanjali and Western Esotericism*. London: Continuum, 2004.

d'Harnoncourt, Anne, and Kynaston McShine, eds. *Marcel Duchamp*. New York: Museum of Modern Art, 1973.

Diamond, Debra. *Yoga: The Art of Transformation*. Washington, DC: Smithsonian Institution, 2013.

Droit, Roger-Pol. *The Cult of Nothingness: The Philosophers and the Buddha*, trans. David Steight and Pamela Vohnson. Chapel Hill: University of North Carolina Press, 2003.

Duchamp, Marcel. *Affectionately Marcel: The Selected Correspondence of Marcel Duchamp*, ed. Francis M. Naumann and Hector Obalk. Ghent: Ludion Press, 2000.

Duchamp, Marcel. *Marcel Duchamp: Duchamp du signe suivi de Notes*, ed. Michel Sanouillet and Paul Matisse, with the collaboration of Anne Sanouillet and Paul B. Franklin. Paris: Flammarion, 2008.

Duchamp, Marcel. *Salt Seller: The Writings of Marcel Duchamp*, ed. Michel Sanouillet and Elmer Peterson. New York: Oxford University Press, 1973. Republished as *The Writings of Marcel Duchamp*, New York: Da Capo Press, 1989.

Dupuche, John R. *Abhinavagupta, The Kula Ritual as Elaborated in Chapter 29 of the Tantrāloka*. Delhi: Motilal Banarsidass Publishers, 2003.

Eliot, T. S. "Tradition and the Individual Talent." *The Egoist* (London) 6, nos. 4–5 (September-December 1919), 54–55; 72–73. Republished *The Sacred Wood* [1920]. Mineola, NY: Dover, 1998.

Fardoulis-Lagrange, Michel. *G. B. ou un ami présomptueux*. Paris: Le Soleil Noir, 1969.

Filipovic, Elena. *The Apparently Marginal Activities of Marcel Duchamp*. Cambridge, MA: MIT Press, 2016.

Friedel, Helmut, Thomas Girst, Matthias Mühling, and Felicia Rappe, eds. *Marcel Duchamp in Munich 1912*. Munich: Schirmer/Mosel, 2012.

Girst, Thomas. *The Indefinite Duchamp*. Ostfildern: Hatje Cantz, 2013.

Gleig, Ann, and Charles I. Flores. "Remembering Sri Aurobindo and the Mother: The Forgotten Lineage of Integral Yoga." *Gurus of Modern Yoga*, ed. Mark Singleton and Ellen Goldberg. New York: Oxford University Press, 2014.

Godwin, Joscelyn. *The Golden Thread: The Ageless Wisdom of the Western Mystery Traditions*. Wheaton, IL: Theosophical Publishing House, 2007.

Godwin, Joscelyn. *The Theosophical Enlightenment*. Albany: State University of New York, 1994.

Goodyear, Anne Collins, and James W. McManus, eds. *aka Marcel Duchamp: Meditations on the Identities of an Artist.* Washington, DC: Smithsonian Institution Scholarly Press, 2014.

Goodyear, Anne Collins, and James W. McManus, eds. *Inventing Marcel Duchamp: The Dynamics of Portraiture*. Washington, DC: National Portrait Gallery, Smithsonian Institution, 2009.

Graham, Lanier. *Duchamp and Androgyny: Art, Gender, and Metaphysics*. Berkeley: No-Thing Press, 2003.

Hanegraaff, Wouter J., ed. *Dictionary of Gnosis and Western Esotericism*. Leiden: Brill, 2006.

Hanegraaff, Wouter J. *Esotericism and the Academy: Rejected Knowledge in Western Culture*. Cambridge: Cambridge University Press, 2012.

Hanegraaff, Wouter J. *Western Esotericism: A Guide for the Perplexed*. London: Bloomsbury, 2013.

Hanegraaff, Wouter J., and Jeffrey J. Kripal, eds. *Hidden Intercourse: Eros and Sexuality in the History of Western Esotericism*. New York: Fordham University Press, 2011.

Heehs, Peter. *The Lives of Sri Aurobindo*. New York: Columbia University Press, 2008.

Helmholtz, H. *Optique physiologique*. Paris: Victor Masson, 1867.

Henderson, Linda Dalrymple. *Duchamp in Context: Science and Technology in the Large Glass and Related Works*. Princeton, NJ: Princeton University Press, 1998.

Henderson, Linda Dalrymple. *The Fourth Dimension and Non-Euclidean Geometry in Modern Art*. Princeton, NJ: Princeton University Press, 1983. Revised edition, Cambridge, MA: MIT Press, 2013.

Henderson, Linda Dalrymple. "Space, Time, and Space-Time: Changing Identities of the Fourth Dimension in Twentieth-Century Art." *Measure of Time*, ed. Lucinda Barnes. Berkeley: University of California Berkeley Art Museum and Pacific Film Archive, 2006.

Herz, Rudolf. *Marcel Duchamp: Le Mystère de Munich*. Munich: Moser, 2012.

Hill, Anthony. *Duchamp: Passim, A Marcel Duchamp Anthology*. Gordon and Breach Arts International, 1994.

Hoffman, Donald D. *Visual Intelligence: How We Create What We See*. New York: W. W Norton, 1998.

Hopps, Walter, Ulf Linde, and Arturo Schwarz. *Marcel Duchamp: Ready-Mades, etc. (1913–1964)*. Paris: Le terrain Vague, 1964

Huelsenbeck, Richard. *Dada Almanac* [Berlin 1920], ed. and trans. Malcolm Green. London: Atlas, 1993.

Hulten, Pontus, ed. and intro. *Marcel Duchamp: Work and Life*. With texts by Jennifer Gough-Cooper and Jacques Caumont. Cambridge, MA: MIT Press, 1993.

Humphrey, Nicholas. *A History of the Mind*. New York: Simon and Schuster, 1992.

Huntington, John C., and Dina Bangdel. *The Circle of Bliss: Buddhist Meditational Art*. Chicago: Columbus Museum of Art with Serindia Publications, 2003.

Ings, Simon. *A Natural History of Seeing: The Art and Science of Vision*. London: Norton, 2007.

James, William. *The Varieties of Religious Experience; A Study in Human Nature.* New York: Modern Library, 1902.

Jarry, Alfred. *Exploits and Opinions of Doctor Faustroll, Pataphysician: A Neo-Scientific Novel* [1911], trans. Simon Watson Taylor. Boston: Exact Change, 1996.

Jay, Martin. *Downcast Eyes: The Denigration of Vision in Twentieth-Century French Thought*. Berkeley: University of California Press, 1993.

Jay, Martin. "Scopic Regimes of Modernity." *Vision and Visuality*, ed. Hal Foster. New York: New Press, 1988.

Jayakar, Pupul. *The Earth Mother: Legends, Goddesses, and Ritual Arts of India*. New York: Harper & Row, 1990.

Jean, Marcel. *The History of Surrealist Painting*, trans. Simon Watson Taylor. New York: Grove Press, 1959.

Joselit, David. *Infinite Regress: Marcel Duchamp, 1910–1941*. Cambridge, MA: MIT Press, 1998.

Judovitz, Dalia. *Drawing on Art: Duchamp & Company*. Minneapolis: University of Minnesota Press, 2010.

Judovitz, Dalia. *Unpacking Duchamp: Art in Transit*. Berkeley: University of California Press, 1995.

Julien, Stanislas. *Le Livre de la voie et de la vertu par le philosophe Lao-Tseu*. Paris: L'Imprimerie Royale, 1842.

Kachur, Lewis. *Displaying the Marvelous: Marcel Duchamp, Salvador Dalí, and Surrealist Exhibition Installation*. Cambridge, MA: MIT Press, 2001.

Kaufman, Lloyd. *Sight and Mind: An Introduction to Visual Perspective*. New York: Oxford University Press, 1974.

Kearns, Cleo McNelly. *T. S. Eliot and Indic Traditions*. Cambridge: Cambridge University Press, 1987.

Kleiber, Pierre-Henri. *L'Encyclopédie "Da Costa" (1947–1949): D'Acéphale au Collège de Pataphysique.* Lausanne: Editions L'Âge d'Homme, 2014.

Kohn, Livia. *Chuang-tzu: The Tao of Perfect Happiness*. Woodstock, VT: Skylight Paths, 2011.

Kohn, Livia. *Daoism and Chinese Culture*. Madgalena, NM: Three Pines Press, 2001.

Kohn, Livia. *Daoist Mystical Philosophy: the Scripture of Western Ascension*. Magdalena, NM: Three Pines Press, 2007.

Kohn, Livia. *Meditation Works: In the Hindu, Buddhist, and Daoist Traditions.* Magdalena, NM: Three Pines Press, 2008.

Kohn, Livia. *Sitting in Oblivion: The Heart of Daoist Meditation*. Dunedin, FL: Three Pines Press, 2010.

Kohn, Livia. *The Taoist Experience.* Binghamton: State University of New York Press, 1993.

Kohn, Livia. *Zhuangzi: Text and Context*. St. Petersburg, FL: Three Pines Press, 2014.

Kohn, Livia, and Robin R. Wang, eds. *Internal Alchemy: Self, Society, and the Quest for Immortality*. Magdalena, NM: Three Pines Press, 2009.

Kripal, Jeffrey J. *Kali's Child: The Mystical and the Erotic in the Life and Teachings of Ramakrishna*. Chicago: University of Chicago Press, 1995.

Kuenzli, Rudolf E., ed. *New York Dada*. New York: Willis Locker & Owens, 1986.

Kuenzli, Rudolf E., and Francis M. Naumann, eds. *Marcel Duchamp: Artist of the Century*. Cambridge, MA: MIT Press, 1990.

Kuh, Katherine. *The Artist's Voice: Talks with Seventeen Artists*. New York: Harper & Row, 1962.

Lebel, Robert. *La double vue, suivi de L'inventeur du temps gratuit.* Paris: Le Soleil Noir, 1964. (Republished 1993, Deyrolle, with preface by Alain Fleischer and afterword by Patrick Waldberg.)

Lebel, Robert. *Marcel Duchamp.* Paris: Belfond, 1985.

Lebel, Robert. *Marcel Duchamp*, trans. George Heard Hamilton. New York: Grove Press, 1959.

Lebel, Robert. *Sur Marcel Duchamp*. Paris: Trianon Press, 1959.

Lee, Tosi. "Fire Down Below and Watering, That's Life." *Buddha Mind in Contemporary Art*, Jacquelynn Baas and Mary Jane Jacob, eds. Berkeley: University of California Press, 2004.

Lee, Tosi. *Watering, That's My Life: The Symbolism and Self-Imaging of Marcel Duchamp*. Doctoral thesis, University of Illinois at Urbana-Champaign, 1993.

Linde, Ulf. *Marcel Duchamp*. Stockholm: Rabén & Sjögren, 1986.

Little, Stephen. *Taoism and the Arts of China*. Art Institute of Chicago in Association with University of California Press, 2000.

Lopez, Donald S. Jr., ed. *Asian Religions in Practice: An Introduction*. Princeton, NJ: Princeton University Press, 1999.

Lopez, Donald S. Jr. *From Stone to Flesh: A Short History of the Buddha.* Chicago: University of Chicago Press, 2013.

McEvilley, Thomas. *The Shape of Ancient Thought: Comparative Studies in Greek and Indian Philosophies*. New York: Allworth Press, 2002.

Moffitt, John F. *Alchemist of the Avant-Garde: The Case of Marcel Duchamp.* Albany: State University of New York, 2003.

Molderings, Herbert. *Duchamp and the Aesthetics of Chance: Art as Experiment*, trans. John Brogden. New York: Columbia University Press, 2010.

Mookerjee, Ajit. *Tantra asana: une voie de la réalisation du Soi*. Paris: Le Soleil Noir, 1971.

Mookerjee, Ajit. *Yoga Art*. London: Thames and Hudson, 1975.

Motherwell, Robert, ed. *The Dada Painters and Poets: An Anthology*. Cambridge, MA: Harvard University Press, 1981.

Muller-Ortega, Paul. *The Triadic Heart of Śiva.* Albany: State University of New York Press, 1989.

Mundy, Jennifer, ed. *Duchamp, Man Ray, Picabia*. London: Tate Publishing, 2008.

Nahar, Sujata. *Mother's Chronicles*, vols. 1–3. Paris: Institut de Recherches Évolutives, 1985–1989.

Nandakumar, Prema. *The Mother*. New Delhi: National Book Trust, 1977.

Naumann, Francis M., John Tancock, Philip Tinari. *Duchamp and / or / in China*. Beijing: Ullens Center for Contemporary Art, 2014.

Naumann, Francis M., with Beth Venn. *Making Mischief: Dada Invades New York*. New York: Whitney Museum of American Art with Abrams, 1996.

Needham, Joseph. *Science and Civilisation in China*, vol. 5, part 5. Cambridge: Cambridge University Press, 1983.

Peyré, Yves, and Evelyne Toussaint. *Duchamp à la Bibliothèque Sainte-Geneviève*. Paris: Editions du Regard, 2014.

Roché, Henri-Pierre [Victor]. *Three New York Dadas and The Blind Man*, intr. Dawn Ades, trans. Chris Allen. London: Atlas Press, 2013.

Roché, Henri-Pierre. *Victor (Marcel Duchamp).* Paris: Centre Georges Pompidou, 1977.

Sanouillet, Michel. *Dada in Paris*, rev. Anne Sanouillet, trans. Sharmila Ganguly. Cambridge, MA: MIT Press, 2009.

Sarazin-Levassor, Lydie Fischer. *A Marriage in Check: The Heart of the Bride Stripped Bare by Her Bachelor, Even*, trans. Paul Edwards. Dijon: Les presses du réel, 2007.

Schuchard, Marsha Keith. *William Blake's Sexual Path to Spiritual Vision*. Rochester, VT: Inner Traditions, 2008. (Originally published as *Why Mrs. Blake Cried*. London: Century, 2006.)

Schwarz, Arturo. *The Complete Works of Marcel Duchamp* [1969, 1970]. Revised and expanded edition, New York: Delano Greenidge, 2000.

Seigel, Jerrold. *The Private Worlds of Marcel Duchamp*. Berkeley: University of California Press, 1995.

Senard, M. *Edward Carpenter et sa philosophie*. Paris: Librarie de l'Art Indépendent, 1914.

Shattuck, Roger. *Selected Writings of Guillaume Apollinaire*. New York: New Directions, 1971.

Shaw, Miranda. *Buddhist Goddesses of India*. Princeton, NJ: Princeton University Press, 2006.

Silburn, Lilian. *Kundalini: Energy of the Depths*, trans. Jacques Gontier. Albany: State University of New York Press, 1988.

Simmer-Brown, Judith. *Dakini's Warm Breath: The Feminine Principle in Tibetan Buddhism*. Boston: Shambhala, 2002.

Singleton, Mark, and Ellen Goldberg, eds. *Gurus of Modern Yoga*. Oxford: Oxford University Press, 2014.

Steefel, Lawrence D. Jr. "The Art of Marcel Duchamp." *Art Journal* 22, no. 2 (Winter 1962–1963).

Steefel, Lawrence D. Jr. *The Position of Duchamp's Glass in the Development of His Art* [1961 doctoral dissertation, Princeton University]. New York: Garland, 1977.

Stirner, Max. *The Ego and Its Own* [1845], ed. David Leopold. Cambridge: Cambridge University Press, 1995.

Stockham, Alice B. *Karezza: Ethics of Marriage*. New York: R. F. Fenno and Company, 1896; New and rev. ed. New York: R. F. Fenno, 1903.

Stockham, Alice B. *The Lover's World: A Wheel of Life*. Chicago: Stockham Publishing, 1903.

Summers, David. *Real Spaces: World Art History and the Rise of Western Modernism*. London: Phaidon, 2003.

Suquet, Jean. *Le Grand Verre rêve*. Paris: Éditions Aubier, 1991.

Sweeney, James Johnson. *Wisdom: Conversations with the Elder Wise Men of Our Day*, ed. James Nelson. New York: Norton, 1958.

Taylor, Michael R. *Marcel Duchamp: Étant donnés*. Philadelphia and New Haven: Philadelphia Museum of Art with Yale University Press, 2009.

Tomkins, Calvin. *The Bride and the Bachelors: Five Masters of the Avant-Garde*. Expanded edition, New York: Viking, 1965.

Tomkins, Calvin. *Duchamp: A Biography*. New York: Henry Holt, 1996 (republished by the Museum of Modern Art, 2014).

Tomkins, Calvin. *Marcel Duchamp: The Afternoon Interviews*. Brooklyn: Badlands Unlimited, 2013.

Tuchman, Maurice, et al. *The Spiritual in Art: Abstract Painting 1890–1985*. Los Angeles and New York: Los Angeles County Museum of Art and Abbeville Press, 1986.

Urban, Hugh B. *Magia Sexualis: Sex, Magic, and Liberation in Modern Western Esotericism*. Berkeley: University of California Press, 2006.

Urban, Hugh B. *Tantra: Sex, Secrecy, Politics, and Power in the Study of Religion*. Berkeley: University of California Press, 2003.

Van Lysebeth, André. *Tantra: The Cult of the Feminine*. York Beach, ME: Red Wheel/Weiser, 1995.

Van Vrekhem, Georges. *The Mother: The Story of Her Life*. India: HarperCollins, 2000.

Varela, Fancisco J., Evan Thompson, and Eleanor Rosch. *The Embodied Mind: Cognitive Science and Human Experience*. Cambridge, MA: MIT Press, 1991.

Versluis, Arthur. *The Secret History of Western Sexual Mysticism: Sacred Practices and Spiritual Marriage*. Rochester, VT: Inner Traditions, 2008.

Vivekananda, Swami. *Raja Yoga: Conquering the Internal Nature* [1896]. San Diego: The Book Tree, 2010. French: *Râja yoga ou Conquête de la nature intérieure*. Paris: Publications Théosophiques, 1910.

Waldberg, Michel. *Isabelle Waldberg*. Paris: Editions de la Différence, 1992.

Waldberg, Patrick, and Isabelle Waldberg. *Un amour acéphale: correspondance, 1940–1949*, ed. Michel Waldberg. Paris: Editions de la Différence, 1992.

Watson, Burton. *Zhuangzi: Basic Writings*. New York: Columbia University Press, 2003.

Wedemeyer, Christian K. *Making Sense of Tantric Buddhism: History, Semiology, and Transgression in the Indian Traditions.* New York: Columbia University Press, 2013.

White, David Gordon. *The Alchemical Body: Siddha Traditions in Medieval India*. Chicago: University of Chicago Press, 1996.

White, David Gordon. *Kiss of the Yoginī: "Tantric Sex" in its South Asian Contexts*. Chicago: University of Chicago Press, 2003.

White, David Gordon, ed. *Tantra in Practice*. Princeton, NJ: Princeton University Press, 2000.

White, David Gordon, ed. *Yoga in Practice*. Princeton, NJ: Princeton University Press, 2012.

White, David Gordon. *The Yoga Sutra of Patanjali: A Biography*. Princeton, NJ: Princeton University Press, 2014.

Wolfson, Elliot R., ed. *Rending the Veil: Concealment and Secrecy in the History of Religions*. Chappaqua, NY: Seven Bridges Press, 1999.

Wong, Eva. *Holding Yin, Embracing Yang: Three Taoist Classics on Meditation, Breath Regulation, Sexual Yoga, and the Circulation of Internal Energy*. Boston: Shambhala, 2005.

IMAGE CREDITS

Every effort has been made to obtain the permission of and to acknowledge the current owners of illustrated art. Errors or omissions in credit citations or failure to obtain permission if required by copyright law have been either unavoidable or unintentional. The author and publisher welcome any information that would allow them to correct future reprints.

© Association Marcel Duchamp / ADAGP, Paris / Artists Rights Society (ARS), New York 2019: figures 0.1, 0.2, 1.1, 1.2, 1.3, 1.4, 1.5, 1.6, 1.7, 1.8, 1.9, 1.10, 1.11, 1.12, 1.13, 1.15, 1.16, 1.17, 1.18, 2.1, 2.3, 3.1, 3.3, 3.4, 3.6, 3.7, 3.8, 3.9, 3.10, 3.11, 3.13, 3.15, 4.3, 4.5, 4.6, 4.7, 4.8, 5.1, 5.4, 5.5, 5.6, 5.7, 5.11, 6.3A, 6.3b, 6.5, 6.6, 6.7, 6.9, 6.12, 6.13, 6.14, 6.15, 8.1, 9.1, 9.3, 9.8, 10.1, 10.2, 10.2, 10.3, 10.4; cover

© Man Ray 2015 Trust / Artists Rights Society (ARS), New York / ADAGP, Paris: figures 0.3, 2.6, 4.1, 10.7, 10.17, 10.18, 10.19; frontispiece

Photo: Digital Image © The Museum of Modern Art/Licensed by SCALA / Art Resource, NY: figures 1.4, 1.7, 3.1, 3.11, 4.2, 4.3, 4.7, 5.7, 5.14, 6.5, 6.6, 10.2, 10.5, 10.17

Photo: Copyright 1963 © Julian Wasser: figure 1.14

© 2019 Alberto Giacometti Estate / VAGA at Artists Rights Society (ARS), New York: figure 2.2

Photo: Princeton University through Hathi Trust Digital Library: figure 2.4

Photo: Hickey-Robertson: figure 3.4

Photo: Jacquelynn Baas: figures 3.5, 6.2, 10.6

Photo: Georges Meguerditchian: figures 3.13, 5.12

Photo: bpk Bildagentur / Alte Pinakothek, Bayerische Staatsgemaeldesammlungen / Art Resource, NY: figure 3.14

© Succession Brancusi—All rights reserved (ARS) 2019: figure 3.2

© 2019 Artists Rights Society (ARS), New York / VG Bild-Kunst, Bonn: figure 3.5

Photo: © CNAC/MNAM/Dist. RMN-Grand Palais / Art Resource, NY: figures 3.13, 5.12, 6.17, 7.1, 10.1, 10.7

© 2019 Artists Rights Society (ARS), New York / ADAGP, Paris: figures 4.2, 5.2, 5.10, 5.12, 5.14, 10.16

Photo: Yale University Art Gallery: figure 4.6

Photo: The Philadelphia Museum of Art / Art Resource, NY: figures 5.1, 5.3, 6.1, 6.13, 6.14, 10.8

Photo: Image copyright © The Metropolitan Museum of Art. Image source: Art Resource, NY: figures 5.2, 10.16

Photo: Allan Grant/The LIFE Picture Collection/Getty Images: figure 5.8

Princeton University Library, Princeton Blue Mountain Project: figure 5.10

Musée National d'Art Moderne (c) CNAC/MNAM/Dist. RMN-Grand Palais / Art Resource, NY: figures 6.3 A, 6.3B

Photo: © Rubin Museum of Art / Art Resource, NY: figures, 6.4 a, 6.4b

Photo: Marianne Franke, Munich: figure 6.8

Photo by Herbert Gehr/The LIFE Images Collection/Getty Images: figure 6.10

© 2019 Estate of Maria Martins / SPA, Lisbon/ Licensed by VAGA at Artists Rights Society (ARS), New York: figures 6.11, 10.5

© 2019 Artists Rights Society (ARS), New York / ADAGP, Paris: figures 6.16, 6.19, 6.20, 8.2, 8.3

Photo: Lilly Joss: figure 6.18

Photo: Hermann Brammer: figure 6.19

© 2019 Artists Rights Society (ARS), New York / ADAGP, Paris: figure 7.1

akg-images © Association Marcel Duchamp / ADAGP, Paris / Artists Rights Society (ARS), New York 2019: figures 8.1, 9.3

Photo: akg-images / Denise Bellon: figures 8.1, 9.3, 9.5

Photo: Albright-Knox Art Gallery / Art Resource, NY: figure 9.1

Photo © Christie's Images / Bridgeman: figure 9.2

© 2019 Association Willy Maywald / Artists Rights Society (ARS), New York / ADAGP, Paris: figure 9.4

Roberto Matta (Roberto-Sebastian Matta Echaurren)—© 2019 Artists Rights Society (ARS), New York / ADAGP, Paris: figure 9.5

akg-images © 2019 Artists Rights Society (ARS), New York / ADAGP, Paris: figure 9.5

Photo: Nina Zurier: figures 9.6, 9.7

Photo: bpk Bildagentur / Staatsgalerie, Stuttgart / Art Resource, NY: figure 9.8

Photo: Jacques Faujour: figure 10.1

Photo: Cameraphoto Arte, Venice / Art Resource, NY: figure 10.4

Photo: © The Trustees of the British Museum / Art Resource, NY: figure 10.9

Courtesy the Estate of Gordon Matta-Clark and David Zwirner, New York: figure 10.10

© 2019 Estate of Gordon Matta-Clark / Artists Rights Society (ARS), New York: figure 10.10

Photo: Thierry Ollivier: figures 10.11, 10.12, 10.13

Photo: © RMN-Grand Palais / Art Resource, NY: figures 10.11, 10.12, 10.13

Photo: courtesy of Arnold Lieberman: figure 10.14

Heritage-Images / Art Media / akg-images: figure 10.15

Photo: The Solomon R. Guggenheim Foundation / Art Resource, NY: figure 10.20

© 2019 Artist Rights Society (ARS), New York / ADAGP, Paris: figure 10.20

INDEX

Page numbers in boldface indicate illustrations.

PERSONS, PLACES, AND THINGS

WORKS OF MARCEL DUCHAMP